D1594130

MARINE INSURANCE

Its Principles and Practice

McGRAW-HILL INSURANCE SERIES

CHARLES C. CENTER, CONSULTING EDITOR

RICHARD M. HEINS, CONSULTING EDITOR

C. ARTHUR WILLIAMS, JR., CONSULTING EDITOR

CRIST · Corporate Suretyship

FACTORY MUTUAL ENGINEERING DIVISION · Handbook of Industrial Loss Prevention

FAULKNER · Health Insurance

HAMILTON AND BRONSON · Pensions

MACLEAN · Life Insurance

MICHELBACHER · Multiple-line Insurance

MOWBRAY AND BLANCHARD · Insurance

PATTERSON · Essentials of Insurance Law

REED · Adjustment of Property Losses

UNIVERSITY OF WISCONSIN FUND FOR INSURANCE EDUCATION AND RESEARCH (CENTER AND HEINS, EDITORS) · Insurance and Government

WILLIAMS AND HEINS · Risk Management and Insurance

WINTER · Marine Insurance

Ralph H. Blanchard was editor of the series from its inception until his retirement in 1958. Since this time he has maintained editorial responsibility for Faulkner's "Health Insurance" and Mowbray and Blanchard's "Insurance," and Maclean's "Life Insurance."

MARINE INSURANCE

Its Principles and Practice

WILLIAM D. WINTER, LL.B., LL.D., F.I.I.A.

Chairman of the Executive Committee
Atlantic Mutual Insurance Company of New York

THIRD EDITION

McGRAW-HILL BOOK COMPANY, Inc.

NEW YORK TORONTO LONDON

1952

MARINE INSURANCE

Library of Congress Catalog Card Number: 51-12657

10 11 12 13 14 - MP - 9 8 7 6

71119

THE MAPLE PRESS COMPANY, YORK, PA.

TO ALICE

who during a long life has been

my considerate companion, counselor, and critic

Preface to the Third Edition

In the more than twenty years that have passed since this book was last revised, momentous events have taken place. Some of these have left their impress on the marine-insurance business. In this new edition an effort has been made to reflect the changes that have occurred in the practice of marine insurance. The principles do not change.

The text has been completely reviewed. The order of chapters has been changed, and new ones have been added to make a more logical presentation of the subject. A few sections of the previous editions have been omitted referring to questions that have become of little importance or have been considered more adequately in other textbooks. Much new matter has been added to give the reader a better understanding of underwriting problems.

It had been my hope that a book would be prepared dealing solely with marine-insurance loss adjusting. It has not seemed practicable to publish such a volume. I have therefore enlarged the section dealing with marine loss adjusting. In this I have had the cooperation of my associate, F. George Forrow, an expert in this field. To him I owe a deep debt of gratitude. To many other associates, particularly W. Irving Plitt, Walter J. Thompson, Roy Thurnall, and Miss Elizabeth Cullen, I am greatly indebted for their assistance in preparing the revised text.

This new edition is offered in the hope that it may continue to be an accurate source of information on marine insurance. The original method of presenting this information in a nontechnical manner is continued.

WILLIAM D. WINTER

NEW YORK, N. Y.
February, 1952

Preface to the Second Edition

Almost ten years have passed since this book was first presented as a contribution to foreign trade literature. It was well received, evidently satisfying the need for a nontechnical textbook on marine insurance.

Various modifications and extensions of the application of marine insurance principles have occurred in the development of overseas commerce since the close of the World War. It accordingly seemed fitting that the text should be reviewed and revised to conform to these changed conditions.

This new edition is presented in the hope that it will continue to afford an accurate source of nontechnical information on ocean marine insurance to all those who require a general knowledge of this subject.

I wish to express my gratitude to all who from time to time have offered helpful criticism of the first edition, and especially to J. Arthur Bogardus and Charles Edey Fay, who have materially aided me in the preparation of the revised text.

WILLIAM D. WINTER

NEW YORK, N. Y.
February, 1929

Preface to the First Edition

The past four years have witnessed many changes in the commercial life of the United States, not the least of which has been the renaissance of the American Merchant Marine, and with it a marvelous growth in our overseas trade. Shipping, banking, and insurance—the trinity of foreign trade—have taken a new lease of life, and American commercial activities are reaching into fields hitherto untouched by purely American enterprise.

This naturally has caused a demand for knowledge concerning these three subjects. New York University, in the foreign trade courses offered in the Wall Street Division of its School of Commerce, Accounts, and Finance, has met this demand. It has been my privilege during the past year to lecture before the University on the subject of Marine Insurance. The attendance at these lectures has indicated that a real need exists for nontechnical information in regard to this important, but little-known, branch of insurance science.

It therefore seemed fitting that the matter contained in the lectures should be rewritten and published in book form so that it might be available to students, and to shipping men, bankers, merchants, and insurance men who require a general knowledge of marine insurance. It is the purpose of this treatise to present the subject in a thorough yet simple form, so that the principles and practice of this necessary element in our overseas commerce may become more generally known.

I wish to avail myself of this opportunity of expressing my gratitude to many who have taken a helpful interest in the preparation of this work, making special mention of Herbert F. Eggert and Prof. A. Wellington Taylor, for their aid in the revision of the manuscript.

NEW YORK, N. Y.
February, 1919

WILLIAM D. WINTER

Contents

Preface to the Third Edition vii

Preface to the Second Edition viii

Preface to the First Edition ix

1. Historical Background 1

Origin of Marine Insurance Doubtful, 1. *Ancient Commercial Activity,* 1. *Early Forms of Insurance,* 2. *General Average,* 2. *Bottomry Bonds,* 2. *Grecian Commerce and the First Insurance Exchange,* 3. *The Carthaginians, Phoenicians, and Romans,* 4. *Commerce in the Middle Ages,* 5. *The Hanseatic League,* 5. *The First Sea Codes,* 5. *Early Insurance Rules,* 5. *Modern Marine Insurance,* 6. *First Use of Word Insurance,* 6. *The Age of Discovery,* 7. *Rules to Prevent Misuse of Insurance,* 7. *Insurance Well Established in Fifteenth Century,* 8. *The "Guidon de la Mer,"* 8. *Marine Insurance in England,* 9. *The Hansa Merchants and the Steelyard,* 9. *The Lombards in England,* 10. *Lombard Street,* 11. *Departure of Hansa Merchants and Lombards,* 11. *Influence of Foreign Merchants,* 11. *First English Marine-insurance Statute,* 12. *Individual Underwriters,* 13. *Lloyd's Coffee House and Lloyd's News,* 13. *A Meeting Place of Underwriters,* 13. *Insurance Companies Organized,* 14. *The Monopoly,* 15. *Growth of Marine Insurance. Lloyd's,* 15. *Standard Policy Adopted,* 16. *Increase of Individual Underwriters,* 16. *Efforts to Incorporate New Companies,* 16. *Lloyd's Reorganized,* 17. *The Monopoly Repealed,* 18. *New Companies,* 19. *Marine-insurance Law,* 19. *Lord Mansfield,* 20. *The Marine Insurance Act, 1906,* 20. *Early Underwriting in the United States,* 20. *First American Insurance Corporation,* 21. *Corporation Development,* 21. *Competition and Failures among Companies,* 22. *The Clipper Ship and Insurance Frauds,* 22. *Marine Insurance Revives,* 23. *The Civil War,* 23. *Mutual Companies,* 24. *Nonassessment Companies,* 24. *A Capitalistic Scheme,* 24. *Unfortunate Experience,* 25. *Foreign Companies Enter the United States,* 26. *The Marine-insurance Market Broadens,* 26. *Little American Capital Invested in Marine Companies,* 27. *Steady Growth of Marine*

Insurance, 27. *World War I and New American Companies*, 27. *The Postwar Period*, 28. *Business Revives*, 29. *Cooperation*, 29. *World War II*, 30. *History Repeats*, 30. *Government Indifference*, 30. *New Factors*, 31.

2. Physical Geography and Marine Insurance 32

Effect of Natural Conditions on Trade Routes, 32. *Water Routes*, 32. *Natural Law Discovered*, 33. *Ocean Navigation*, 33. *Aids to Navigation*, 34. *Effect of Oceans on Climate*, 34. *Ocean Distances*, 35. *The Physical Forces of Nature*, 35. *Harbors and Their Development*, 42. *Types of Harbors*, 43.

3. Commercial Geography and Marine Insurance. Commercial Documents 47

The Processes of Trade, 47. *Commerce Is the Exchange of Products*, 47. *The Demand for Goods*, 48. *The Opening of New Trade Routes*, 48. *Primitive Barter*, 49. *Types of Trade*, 49. *The Use of Symbols and the Bill of Exchange*, 49. *Marine Insurance Essential to Overseas Trade*, 50. *Contract of Sale*, 50. COMMERCIAL DOCUMENTS, 51. *The Invoice*, 51. *Cost Sales, F.O.B. and F.A.S.*, 51. *Cost and Freight Sales (C. & F.)*, 52. *Cost, Insurance, and Freight Sales (C.I.F.)*, 53. *Sales Contract Determines Relation of Buyer and Seller*, 53. *The Charter Party*, 54. *The Bill of Lading*, 55. *Letters of Indemnity*, 57. *The Manifest*, 58. *The Marine-insurance Policy or Certificate*, 58. *Special Policies of Insurance*, 59. *The Symbols of Ownership*, 59. *The Draft or Bill of Exchange*, 60. *Letters of Credit*, 62. *The Balance of Trade*, 63. *Goods the Basis for Exchange*, 63. *Temporary Problems*, 63.

4. Ships and Shipbuilding 65

A Vessel the Basis of All Marine Insurance, 65. *Mediums Used in Construction of Vessels*, 65. *Modern Construction*, 66. *Wooden Ships. Difficulties in Construction*, 66. *Composite Ships*, 67. *Steel Vessels*, 67. *The Marine Engine*, 68. *Liners and Cargo Vessels*, 69. *Longitudinal Framing*, 70. *Bulk Carriers*, 70. *Special Designs*, 71. *Lake Vessels*, 71. *River and Harbor Craft*, 72. *Types of Marine Engines*, 72. *Why Does a Vessel Float?* 72. *Displacement*, 73. *Displacement Curve*, 73. *When Will a Vessel Float? Buoyancy*, 74. *Freeboard and Load Lines*, 75. *Stability. The Centers of Buoyancy and Gravity*, 78. *Why a Vessel Rights after Rolling*, 78. *The Law of Inertia*, 79. *Shifted Cargoes*, 80. *The Metacenter. Stiff and Tender Vessels*, 80. *The Control of Metacenter Height*, 81. *Loading Problems*, 81. *Stresses and Strains*, 81. *Vessels in Ballast*, 84.

5. Introduction to Marine Insurance 86

Reasonable Care Essential, 87. *Standards*, 87. *Hazards*, 87. *Cargoes*, 88. *Problems*, 89. *Loading Hazards*, 90. *Sea Perils*, 90.

Shipper's Responsibility, 90. *Vessel's Responsibility,* 91. *Transit Interruptions,* 92. *Value or Valuation,* 92. *Average,* 93. *Losses,* 94. *General Average,* 94. *Effect of Insurance,* 96. *Averages. Competition,* 96.

6. Factors in Marine Underwriting 98

The Classification Societies, 98. *What a "Class" Signifies,* 98. *Lloyd's Register,* 99. *Rival Organizations,* 99. *Necessity for Understanding Classification-society Codes,* 100. *The American Record,* 100. *Underwriters' Surveyors,* 102. *Underwriters' Organizations,* 102. *Underwriters' Boards and Loss Agents,* 102. *Salvage Associations,* 103. *Maps, Charts, and Port Books,* 103. *Nationality,* 103. *Owners, Managers, and Masters,* 104. *Structural Characteristics of Ship and Its Physical Condition,* 105. *Other Considerations,* 106. *Measurement of Ships,* 106. *Measurement of Cargo Capacity,* 107. *Cargoes and Shipping Packages,* 107. *The Moral Hazard,* 108.

7. Brokers and Managing Agents 110

THE BROKER, 110. *He Is Not a New Factor,* 111. *He Is Indispensable,* 111. *He Occupies an Anomalous Position,* 111. *He Offers a Service,* 112. *He Is a Trained Expert,* 112. *He Knows the Market,* 113. *Progressive Underwriting,* 113. *Twofold Duty,* 114. *Attitude toward Losses,* 115. *Arranges Settlement of Losses,* 115. *Services in General Average,* 116. *Commissions,* 116. *Does Not Guarantee Payment of Premiums,* 116. *The Broker as an Underwriter,* 117. MANAGING AGENTS, 118. *Local Agents,* 119. BROKERS IN GREAT BRITAIN, 119. *Losses and Return Premiums,* 120. *Current Accounts,* 120.

8. The Contract of Marine Insurance 121

Definition of Marine Insurance, 121. *Not a Perfect Contract of Indemnity,* 121. *Only Fortuitous Losses Covered,* 121. *Negligence Should Not be Covered by Policy,* 122. *Agreed-value Clauses,* 123. *Modern Policy Broad in Its Protection,* 124. *Good Faith,* 125. *Elements of a Contract,* 125. *Corporate and Individual Underwriters,* 125. *An Insurable Interest Necessary,* 126. *The Premium a Valid Consideration,* 126. *The Minds of the Contracting Parties Must Meet,* 127. *A Legal Purpose Necessary,* 127. *Direct and Indirect Placing of Insurance,* 128. *Brokers,* 128. *The Insurance Application,* 128. *Binders and Inquiries,* 129. *Cancellation and Modification of Contracts,* 129. *Usage,* 130. *Mercantile Customs,* 131. *Printed, Written, and Stamped Words,* 131. *The Intention of the Parties,* 131. *Does the Application Control the Policy?* 132. *The Law of the Place,* 133. *Clarity Essential in the Writing of Policies,* 133. *Insurance Interest Must be Actual,* 134. *Extent of the Insurable Interest,* 134. *Persons Who Have Insurable Interests,* 135. *Definition of Marine Insurance,* 137.

9. The Policy—ASSURER AND ASSURED 139

The Policy, 139. *Types of Policies,* 139. *Form of Policy,* 140. *British Form of Policy,* 141. *The Assurer,* 141. *The Assured,* 141. *"For Account of,"* 144. *Attachment of Policy,* 145. *Description of Parties and Property Should Be Definite,* 145. *An Insurable Interest Must Exist,* 146. *"Whom It May Concern,"* 147. *"Whom It May Concern" Is Not All-inclusive,* 147. *The Payee of Loss,* 148. *The Special Policy Transfers the Payment of Loss,* 148. *Loss May Be Made Payable in Foreign Countries,* 149. *Loss Orders,* 149. *Open Policies,* 149. *Book Policies,* 150. *Blanket Policies,* 150.

10. The Policy—DURATION OF RISK AND VALUATION 153

"Lost or Not Lost," 153. *"Lost or Not Lost" a Necessary Condition,* 153. *The Termini,* 154. *The Subject Matter of Insurance,* 155. *Goods Presumed to Be Laden under Deck,* 155. *Some Kinds of Property Should Be Specifically Mentioned,* 156. *The Vessel and Its Master,* 157. *Attachment of the Risk,* 158. *Date of Attachment,* 158. *Time of Attachment,* 159. *Insured until Safely Landed,* 159. *Warehouse-to-warehouse Clause,* 160. *At and From,* 164. *Attachment of Cargo Insurance,* 164. *Risk after Discharge from Vessel,* 165. *Ex-dock Sales,* 165. *Attachment of Hull Risks on Time,* 166. *Attachment of Voyage Risks on Hull,* 166. *Policy May Terminate by Breach of Contract,* 167. *The Doctrine of No Deviation,* 167. *The Valuation,* 170.

11. The Policy—THE PERILS CLAUSE 174

Perils Insured against, 174. *Doctrine of Proximate Cause,* 175. *Loss Not Covered,* 176. *Fraud or Misconduct,* 176. *Perils of the Sea,* 177. *Casting Away,* 179. *Third-party Interests,* 179. *Inchmaree Clause,* 180. *Fire,* 180. *Jettison,* 182. *Barratry,* 183. *Lawless Acts and War Perils,* 184. *Thieves,* 184. *Nondelivery Risks,* 185. *Pirates and Rovers,* 186. *War Perils,* 186. *All Other Perils,* 189. *The Free-of-capture Clause,* 189. *Explosions,* 190. *Strikes, Riots and Civil-commotions Clause,* 190. *Cancellation Clause,* 192. *Risks on Shore,* 192. *Broad Forms,* 193. *Modifying Clauses,* 194.

12. The Policy—MISCELLANEOUS PROVISIONS 195

Sue-and-labor Clause, 195. *The Premium,* 197. *Proof and Payment of Loss,* 199. *Adjustment of Loss,* 200. *Average Clauses. "The Franchise,"* 201. *Double Insurance,* 203. *Underinsurance,* 205. *Insurance on Same Property Covering Different Risks,* 205. *Carrier's Liability,* 206. *Illicit or Prohibited Trade,* 206. *Abandonment,* 207. *Purpose of Abandonment Clause,* 207. *Liability for Expenses,* 208. *Liberty to Deviate in Event of Blockade,* 208. *The Attestation Clause,* 209. *Memorandum Clause,* 209. *Underwriter Retains Premium on Risk Unwittingly Insured after Arrival,* 209. *Résumé,* 210.

13. Basic Conditions 211

All Goods Not Equally Susceptible to Damage, 211. *A Uniform Rate of Premium Desirable,* 211. *The Memorandum Clause,* 212. *General Average Introduced into Marine Policy,* 213. *Excepted Risks,* 213. *Separation of Damaged Goods,* 213. *Insurance Does Not Restore Property,* 214. IMPLIED WARRANTIES, 215. *Legal Conduct,* 215. *Seaworthiness,* 215. *Implied Warranty of Prompt Attachment of Risk,* 220. *Implied Warranty of No Deviation,* 221. *Other Implied Warranties,* 221. *Breach of Warranty May Be Excused,* 221. EXPRESS WARRANTIES, 222. *Warranties and Stipulations,* 222. *Express Warranties Usually Relate to Material Conditions,* 222. REPRESENTATION, MISREPRESENTATION, AND CONCEALMENT, 223. *The Avoidance of Contracts—Fraud,* 224. *What Must Be Disclosed,* 224. *The Effect of a Representation,* 224. *Certain Facts Need Not Be Disclosed,* 225. *What a Representation Implies,* 225. *Fraud,* 226.

14. Cargo Insurance as an Underwriting Problem 227

Basic Form of Policy Necessary, 227. *Cargo, Hull, and Freight Insurance,* 227. *General and Full Cargoes,* 228. *Under- and On-deck Cargoes,* 228. *A General Knowledge of All Commodities Essential,* 228. *Marine Insurance Conforms to Trade Customs,* 229. *Methods of Shipment Controlled by Physical Environment,* 229. *Knowledge of Trade Customs Important,* 230. *Racial Characteristics Affect Marine Insurance,* 230. *Sale of Goods at Port of Refuge,* 231. *Falling Markets,* 232. *Effect of Vessel Types on Cargo Insurance,* 232. *Vessel Speed an Element in Cargo Insurance,* 233. *Structural Design in Its Relation to Cargo,* 233. *Natural Forces as Related to Cargo Insurance,* 234. *Optional Routes,* 234. *Other Elements in Cargo Insurance,* 235. *Average Conditions,* 235. *Duration of Risk,* 239. *Rate of Premium Based on Ordinary Transit,* 240. *Cancellation,* 241. *Cargo Clauses are Numberless,* 241.

15. Specific Cargo Risks 243

Full-cargo Business, 243. CLASSES OF CARGO, 246. *Products of Agriculture,* 246. *Products of Animals,* 250. *Frozen Fruit, Vegetables, and Fish,* 254. *Canned and Bottled Goods. Dairy Products,* 254. *Products of the Forest,* 254. *Products of the Mines,* 255. *Coal and Ore,* 256. *Manufactured Products,* 256. *Machinery,* 257. *Burlap and Bags. Fire Hazard,* 257. OTHER RISKS, 257. *Leakage and Breakage,* 257. *Common Carriers' Insurance,* 258. *Carriers' Liability Policies,* 259. *Common Carriers' Liability,* 259. *Parcel-post and Registered-mail Insurance,* 260. *Securities and Currency,* 261.

16. Hull Insurance 262

Classes of Hull Insurance, 262. *Single-vessel and Fleet Insurance,* 262. *Moral Hazard,* 263. *Valuation,* 265. *Trading Warranties,*

268. *Loading Warranties,* 269. *Purpose of Warranties,* 269. *Average Clauses,* 269. *Thirds off,* 270. *Machinery Claims,* 271. *Collision Liability,* 272. *Club Insurance,* 274. *Protection-and-indemnity Clause,* 274. *Cancellation and Lay-up Return Premiums,* 275. *"And Arrival,"* 277. *Extension into Port,* 277. *General Average,* 278. *Total-loss-only Insurance,* 278. *Disbursements,* 278. *Port-risk Insurance,* 279.

17. Special Hull Forms—LARGE VESSELS 280

Work of the Hull Associations, 280. *Marine-insurance Syndicates,* 281. *Basis of All Policies the Same,* 282. *Rates of Premium,* 282. *The Syndicate Form,* 284. *Warranties,* 285. *Disbursements Warranty,* 285. *Syndicate Disbursements Warranty,* 286. *Breach of Certain Warranties Held Covered,* 289. *Average Clauses,* 289. *Contributory Values,* 289. *Lake Time Clauses,* 290. *Wooden Sailing Vessels,* 292. *Marine Engines,* 293.

18. Special Hull Forms—SMALL CRAFT 295

TYPES OF SMALL CRAFT, 295. *Tugboats,* 295. *Ocean Barges,* 298. *River and Harbor Craft,* 298. *Fishing Vessels,* 299. *Pleasure Craft,* 300. BUILDER'S RISKS, 303. *Special Hazards Insured against,* 303. *Risks after Launching,* 304. *Underwriter Guarantees Integrity of Material,* 304. *Special Clauses and Warranties,* 304. *Return Premiums,* 305. MARINE PROTECTION-AND-INDEMNITY INSURANCE, 306. *Persons,* 307. *Cargo,* 307. *Other Property,* 308. *Government Regulations,* 308. *The Policy,* 308. *Rates,* 309.

19. Freight Insurance 310

Freight Insurance a Difficult Subject, 310. *Meaning of Freight in Marine Insurance,* 310. *Vessels Built to Earn Freight,* 311. *When Is Freight Earned?* 311. *Freight "Pro Rata Itineris Peracti,"* 312. *Prepaid and Guaranteed Freight,* 313. *Prepaid Freight Wrong in Principle,* 313. *Underwriting Problems,* 314. *Charter Parties,* 314. *Bill-of-lading Freight,* 315. *Delivery of Cargo in Specie,* 316. *Collectible Freight or Freight Contingency,* 317. *Various Freight Interests in a Single Venture,* 318. *Freight a Contingent Interest. Dead Freight,* 318. *When Does Insurable Interest Commence?* 319. *Future Freights,* 320. *Anticipated Freight,* 320. *On Board or Not on Board,* 321. *Chartered or as if Chartered,* 321. *Termination of Risk,* 322. *Amount Insured,* 322. *Duty Insurance,* 322. *Premium Due Even if Duty Not Paid,* 323. *Contingent Risks,* 324.

20. War Insurance 325

The Problem, 325. *War Insurance Vital,* 325. *The Past No Certain Guide for the Future,* 326. *A Great War Thought to Be Impossible,* 326. *Perils Judged by International Law,* 327. *The Declaration of London,* 328. *International Law Not Observed,* 331. *Doctrine of Ultimate Destination. Preemption,* 332. *Unforeseen*

Perils, 332. *Neutrality Warranties,* 333. *Free-of-British-capture Clause,* 333. *Trading with the Enemy,* 333. *Licenses,* 334. *Water-borne Clauses,* 334. *Free-of-capture-and-seizure Clause,* 335. *Separate War Policy,* 335. *Perils Clause,* 336. *War and Marine Policies not Coextensive,* 337. *War and Marine Risks Separately Insured,* 338. *Sanctions,* 340. *Frustration Clause,* 341. *New War Devices,* 341. *Aircraft,* 342. *Submarines, Raiders, and Bombers,* 342. *New and Unusual Hazards,* 342. *Warranty of Proper Documents,* 343. *Seizure,* 343. *Cancellation Clauses,* 343. *Government War-risk Bureaus,* 345. *Strikes, Riots, and Civil Commotions,* 346.

21. Reinsurance 347

The Problem, 347. *Destruction of Large Values,* 347. *Reinsurance,* 348. *Distribution of Risks,* 348. *Growth of Reinsurance,* 348. *Necessity for Large Limits,* 349. *Retained Lines,* 350. *Purpose of Reinsurance,* 351. *Reinsurance Not Different in Principle,* 351. *Reinsurance Clause,* 351. *Reinsurer Bound by Acts of Reassured,* 353. *Limitations of Liability,* 353. *Definitions,* 354. TYPES OF REINSURANCE CONTRACTS, 354. *Quota-share Reinsurance,* 354. *Participating Reinsurance,* 355. *Excess-of-line Reinsurance,* 355. *Excess-of-loss Reinsurance,* 358. *Facultative or Special Reinsurance,* 362. OTHER FEATURES OF REINSURANCE, 362. *Reinsurance Syndicates,* 362. *Reinsurance Subject to Original Conditions,* 363. *Reinsurance at Original Rates,* 363. *Partially Terminated Risks,* 364. *Undesirable Risks,* 364. *Arbitrage,* 364. *Unterminated Risks,* 365. *Overdue Vessels and Vessels in Disaster,* 365. *Foreign and Domestic Reinsurance,* 366. *Syndicate Reinsurance,* 366. *Original Assured Indirectly Depends on Reinsurance,* 366.

22. Particular Average—CARGO 367

Losses the Foundation of Marine Insurance, 367. *Conduct of Loss Affairs Important,* 367. *Insurance Funds Must Be Conserved,* 368. *Loss Adjusting a Profession,* 368. *Specialization in Loss Adjusting,* 369. *Kinds of Loss,* 369. *Most Claims Are for Partial Loss,* 370. *Particular Average Refers to a Special Interest,* 370. *Particular Charges,* 371. *Notice of Loss,* 371. *Proximate Cause,* 372. *Losses Not Insured,* 372. *Delay—Loss of Market,* 373. *The Question of Franchise,* 374. *Cause of Loss,* 374. *Comparison of Gross Sound and Damaged Values,* 375. *Comparison of Gross Values Justified,* 375. *Freight and Duty,* 376. *Policy Value Controls,* 378. *Determining Depreciation by Appraisal,* 378. *Salvage Losses,* 378. *Certificate of Damage,* 378. *Special Adjustment,* 379. *Special Cases,* 379. *Particular Average on Profits and Commissions,* 380. *Protest of Master,* 380. *Proofs of Loss,* 381. *Duplicate Documents,* 382. *Other Claim Documents,* 382.

23. Particular Average—HULL AND FREIGHT 383

HULL, 383. *Apportionment of Expenses,* 384. *Temporary Repairs,* 384. *Valuation of Hulls,* 385. *Cause of Damage to Hulls,* 386.

Documents Required, 388. FREIGHT, 389. *Partial Loss of Freight,* 389. *Collectible Freight,* 389. *Substitution of Vessel or Cargo,* 389. *Freight Not Always Involved in Damage to Ship or Cargo,* 390.

24. Total Losses—Collision Liabilities 392

TOTAL LOSSES, 392. *Definition,* 392. *Constructive Total Loss,* 392. *Adjustment May Be Simple,* 392. *Assured Must Endeavor to Preserve Property,* 393. *When Is a Thing Lost?* 393. *When Does a Constructive Total Loss Occur?* 393. *American and British Practices Differ,* 394. *Abandonment,* 395. *Assignment Dates from Time of Loss,* 398. *Total and Constructive Total Loss of Vessel,* 399. *Total Loss of Cargo,* 399. *Total Loss of Freight,* 400. *War Losses,* 400. *Missing Vessels,* 400. *Presumption of Cause of Loss,* 401. *Documents Required,* 402. THIRD-PARTY LIABILITIES, 402. *Collision Clause,* 402. *Sister-ship Clause,* 402. *Both-to-blame Collision Clause,* 402.

25. General Average 405

Definition, 405. *No Reasonable Substitute for General Average,* 406. *The General-average Adjuster,* 407. *Laws of General Average Not Uniform,* 407. *Elements Necessary to Valid General Average,* 408. *The Peril and the Sacrifice,* 408. *The Preservation of Part of the Venture,* 409. *What Is a Voluntary Sacrifice?* 410. *The General-average Adjustment,* 410. *Contributory Values,* 411. *General-average Cases Often Complicated,* 412. *Statement of Both General and Particular Average,* 413. *York-Antwerp Rules,* 413. *Documents Required,* 419. *The Statement,* 419.

26. Subrogation—Salvage 423

SUBROGATION, 423. *Open Items,* 423. *Subrogation,* 423. *Underwriter's Liability,* 424. *Carriers Slow to Respond for Losses,* 425. *Benefit-of-insurance Clauses,* 425. *Loan Receipts,* 425. *Classes of Claims,* 426. *Carriers by Water,* 426. *Hague Rules,* 427. *Carriage of Goods by Sea Act,* 427. *Carriage by Air,* 428. *Rail and Express Carriers,* 428. *Motor Carriers,* 429. *Warehousemen,* 429. SALVAGE, 430. *Marine Salvage,* 430.

27. Profit or Loss—Statistics 433

Freedom from Rating Laws, 434. *Marine Insurance Not an Exact Science,* 434. *Preparation of Statistics,* 435. *Analysis,* 435. *Deductions,* 438. *Statistics Must Be Accurate,* 439. *Competition,* 439.

A Selected List of Reference Books 441

Appendix A: Standard Application Form Used in Placing Special Risks on Cargo 443

Appendix B: Standard Form Used in Requesting Return Premium, Either Because of Cancellation or Reduction of Risk 445

Appendix C: American Institute Cargo Clauses 446

Appendix D: Special Policy of Insurance Issued Under Open Policy 448

Appendix E: American Institute War Cargo Policy 452

Appendix F: Syndicate Hull Form 455

Appendix G: Syndicate Builder's Risk Form 463

Appendix H: Syndicate Disbursements Form 466

Appendix I: Marine Insurance Act, 1906 468

Appendix J: Marine Insurance (Gambling Policies) 501

Appendix K: Statement of Value Used in General Average 503

Appendix L: Average Agreement 504

Appendix M: General Average Guarantee 506

Appendix N: The Harter Act 507

Appendix O: U.S. Carriage of Goods by Sea Act 509

Appendix P: York-Antwerp Rules 1950 521

Index 533

CHAPTER 1

Historical Background

Origin of Marine Insurance Doubtful. Marine insurance is the oldest form of indemnity of which there is any record. It is known to have been practiced for over seven hundred years. When, where, and by whom it was first devised, however, remains one of the unanswered questions of commercial history. Several nations have claimed the honor of having invented this system of indemnity, but the best evidence indicates that the Jews, at the time of their banishment from France in the latter part of the twelfth century, introduced such a scheme of insurance for the protection of their property during its removal from France. Villani, a fourteenth-century historian, is the authority for this theory, stating that the system was devised in Lombardy in 1182. Whether this is correct or not is of little moment—the fact remains that early in the development of commercial intercourse the need arose for some system of distributing marine losses, and the present method of insuring came into use.

Ancient Commercial Activity. In order to obtain a proper perspective of marine insurance, it is important to trace the development of commercial intercourse among the nations of the world. That the seas were used as the highways of trade early in the history of man is evidenced by both sacred and profane history. In the Bible there are many references to ships, especially to the ships of Tarshish in one of which Jonah was fleeing from Joppa to Tarshish when the ship was overtaken by a mighty tempest. The story of Jonah is interesting in this connection in that it cites a perfect example of jettison, one of the perils covered by the present marine-insurance policy. In order to avoid destruction of their vessel, the mariners cast into the sea the wares that were in the ship in order to lighten it. This experience occurred in 862 B.C., about the time that the Rhodians obtained sovereignty of the sea.

Early Forms of Insurance. While there is no evidence that insurance in its present form was practiced prior to the twelfth century, there is abundant historical record of the use, at an early date in commercial history, of general average and, at a somewhat later time, of a system of indemnity known as *bottomry.*

General Average. In early days it was customary for merchants to travel with their wares in order to dispose of them at destination, there to convert the proceeds into other commodities suitable for their home market. In the same ship it was not unusual to find several merchants, each accompanying his cargo. There was no supervision of the loading of vessels, and it is probable that ships were very much overloaded, safe enough in calm weather but in danger of sinking the moment storms arose. In such case *jettison* was the natural remedy and was immediately applied. No merchant would wish his goods sacrificed, but in an emergency there would be little time for debate, and the most accessible goods would be cast overboard. In many cases valuable time was lost in quarreling over whose goods should be jettisoned. To prevent these delays and in the common interest, a system was devised of assessing the value of the jettisoned goods pro rata over the entire value of ship and cargo, including the jettisoned goods. That this system was originated early in the history of overseas commerce is attested by the fact that in the maritime law code promulgated by the Rhodians in 916 B.C., general average is recognized as a maritime custom. That this system of distribution of loss is sound is proved by the fact that the principle of general average, greatly broadened to meet modern conditions, still persists and is part of the law of every maritime nation, while the modern marine-insurance policy affords protection against losses of a general-average nature. The word *average,* as used in marine insurance, means loss or damage, less than a total loss. A *general average* is a partial loss falling generally on all the interests involved in a maritime adventure, while a *particular average* is a partial loss, not due to a general-average sacrifice, falling on one particular interest.

Bottomry Bonds. In the early days of commercial history shipowners and cargo owners were accustomed to borrow money with which to carry on their ventures, pledging their vessels or their cargoes as security for such loans. The document setting forth the terms of the agreement was known as a *bottomry bond* when the vessel was pledged and a *respondentia bond* when the cargo was hypothecated. By the terms of such an agreement the sum named in the bond was loaned, subject to the condition that it should be repaid upon the arrival of the vessel or cargo at a named port. If the vessel was lost, the borrower was discharged from his obligation. The rate of interest which such bonds carried was very high, since the lender practically insured the property. The rate of interest charged, which, like the principal sum, was payable only in the event of safe arrival, included compensation not only for the use of the money loaned but also for the possible loss of the money itself through the failure of the venture. This method of loaning money was really the reverse of our present system of marine insurance. At the present time the underwriter charges a rate of premium on an amount representing the fair value of the vessel or cargo, plus the insurance premium and other expenses, which amount he agrees to pay in the event that vessel or cargo is lost through perils insured against.

Forms of Bottomry Bonds Distinguished. Under the bottomry-bond system, the lender in effect paid for the property at the beginning of the venture, the borrower repaying the amount loaned plus interest (premium) only in the event of safe arrival. This form of bottomry bond, which represented a voluntary pledge of property, must be distinguished from bonds, called by the same name, which the master of a vessel in distress must give when all other means of raising funds to effect repairs in order to save vessel and cargo have failed. The conditions in regard to the repayment of the amount loaned, plus *maritime interest*, as it is called, are the same in this latter form of bond as in its earlier prototype. With the advent of the ocean cable the use of such bonds became less frequent, and since the equipment of vessels with radio they have practically disappeared. Under present mercantile usage, loans on vessels are made by the execution of a bond secured by a mortgage on the hull, which in turn is protected by a policy of insurance payable to the lender or to the lender and the owner as their respective interests may appear.

Grecian Commerce and the First Insurance Exchange. Among the early maritime nations were the Greeks whose commerce, though extensive, was confined largely to the Euxine Sea, especially at Corinth and Athens. A development of interest to the student of marine insurance was an Exchange which the Greeks established at Athens for the placing of bottomry bonds. In a very interesting paper on "Marine Insurance in Old Greece,"[1] Dr. Benjamin W. Wells describes the operation of this exchange and the news system working in connection with it. Bankers and merchants operated swift dispatch boats which brought early news of wars and rumors of wars and of the state of the market, so that vessels could be diverted to safe ports and to favorable markets. The whole scheme seems to have been a forerunner of the modern Lloyd's, London. It also appears that human nature has changed little since the days of the early Greeks, for Dr. Wells cites numerous cases brought into court for the collection of money loaned on bottomry, where it was charged by the lender that the vessel or cargo had been lost under suspicious circumstances. It is quite evident from the arguments made by counsel in these reported cases that insurance by bottomry bond was an established and essential feature of commercial transactions not only in Ancient Greece, but also in the other maritime nations.

The Carthaginians, Phœnicians, and Romans. Early in the development of commerce, the Carthaginians and the Phœnicians exercised a potent influence in the markets of the then known world. These nations later fell a prey to Alexander, who destroyed their cities and removed their commerce to Alexandria. But Alexandria, too, passed away, and, at the dawn of the Christian era, Rome held sway as the mistress of the world. Rome is remembered, however, not for her commercial progress, but rather for her military achievements. In fact, it was the policy of Rome to discourage mercantile endeavor as being harmful to the State. The commerce of the Roman Empire consisted largely in carrying supplies and provisions for her armies of conquest. Nevertheless, Roman bankers were not averse to investing their surplus funds in bottomry bonds, although officially the loaning of money at interest was discouraged. By an edict of the Roman Emperor Justinian, dated A.D. 583, the rate for such loans was fixed at 12 per

[1] *Insurance and Commercial Magazine,* March, 1918.

cent. After the fall of the Roman Empire little information is obtainable for many centuries in regard to the development of commerce.

Commerce in the Middle Ages. With the revival of commerce in the Middle Ages two centers of commercial activity developed, one in the Mediterranean Sea, the other in the Baltic Sea. The Venetians and Genoese were the leaders in the Mediterranean, these two peoples becoming the merchants of the world. They had been driven from their homes in Central Europe to the shores and adjacent islands of Italy, where they were able to defend themselves against their enemies and to establish an overseas commerce that covered the whole of the then known world. The Crusades did much to increase the prosperity of these peoples, as their cities made convenient supply stations on the road to the Holy Land, and they were not slow to take advantage of the situation. The returning Crusaders had acquired a taste for the products of the Eastern nations, and the Italian merchants imported and distributed these goods to the other European peoples.

The Hanseatic League. Commercial activity in the Baltic Sea was also controlled by peoples who had been driven out of Central Europe by the Barbarians but had fled north and established various centers of commerce on the Baltic and North Seas. As a measure of mutual protection these several communities organized the Hanseatic League, which undoubtedly was the most powerful offensive and defensive commercial alliance the world has ever seen.

The First Sea Codes. In the "Laws of Wisby," a sea code compiled probably in the early part of the fourteenth century for the government of the Hanseatic League, reference is made to bottomry. It is, however, in some of the Collections of Ordinances, decreed at general meetings of the League, that regulations are promulgated for the correction of abuses in connection with the issuance of bottomry bonds. These sea codes, the *Recessus Hansæ* and *Recessus Civitatum Hanseaticarum* indicate that at this period the practice of bottomry was still an important part of maritime commerce.

Early Insurance Rules. Frederick Martin in his interesting work on the history of Lloyd's states that one of these early *Recessi,* issued at Lübeck, where most of the meetings of the Hanseatic League were held, devotes a whole chapter to the subject of bottomry. It appears from this record that insurance frauds are as old as the business itself. The sixth chapter of this *Recessus* states that:[1]

> Whereas there occur every day more deceptions as regards Bottomry, and there is not wanting even discovery of wicked crimes, it is ordered that henceforth masters of vessels shall have no power to raise money on Bottomry at the place where the freighters reside, in order that the free parts of the ship may not be burthened with charges resting on those that are engaged. And in case masters wish to raise money on Bottomry on parts belonging to them, it must be with the knowledge of the freighters, at the place where they live, and only to the extent of their interest. Should anybody lend more than this, he who has advanced the money shall only have a claim on the master's property and not on the ship, and the master, if necessary, shall be punished.

In another paragraph of the same chapter an exception is made to the above rule, and permission is granted to masters, should they meet with accidents in foreign countries and have no goods to sell, to pledge the vessel to raise money to effect necessary repairs. The amount to be thus raised, however, is limited to the sum required to make such repairs. In the event of the master raising money in foreign countries in a fraudulent manner, he not only was held answerable with his property but might also incur the penalty of imprisonment and even death.

Modern Marine Insurance. The Hanseatic codes indicate that bottomry was practiced more in the form of loans made of necessity to effect the preservation of the venture than as mere insurance. Marine insurance in its direct form having been introduced among the merchants of the Mediterranean Sea, it is altogether probable that it was adopted at a very early period by the members of the Hanseatic League. The Lombards and the Hansa merchants controlled the commerce of the world. The Lombards operated as far north as Bruges, and the Hansa merchants controlled commerce from Bruges north. The two groups traded with each other, and as will appear, both had their share in the development of commercial England.

First Use of Word Insurance. In an old historical work, the *Chronyk van Vlaendern,* the term *insurance* in the modern meaning of the word appears. The authenticity of this *Chronyk* has been doubted,

[1] Frederick Martin, "History of Lloyd's and of Marine Insurance in Great Britain," p. 5.

but Martin says, "if there is no evidence—that is, no evidence that has come down to us—in its favor, neither is there any against it."[1] The words of this *Chronyk* read in part as follows:[2]

> On the demand of the Inhabitants of Bruges, the Count of Flanders permitted in the year 1310, the establishment in this Town of a Chamber of Assurance, by means of which the Merchants could insure their Goods, exposed to the Risks of the Sea, or elsewhere, in paying a stipulated Percentage.

Bruges was one of the leading ports of the Hanseatic League, where much of the trading between the Hansa merchants and the Lombards took place, and it is not unreasonable to suppose that some such insurance market was there established. It is a matter of record that as many as 150 vessels would arrive at Sluys, the outer harbor of Bruges, on a single tide. Such commercial development at so early a period in maritime history seems incredible.

The Age of Discovery. Commercial development was not confined to the Lombards and to the Hansa merchants. With the perfecting of a practical mariner's compass, other nations rapidly entered the overseas trade. The Age of Discovery was ushered in. Mariners no longer needed to skirt the shores of the continents or dash from headland to headland but could fearlessly launch out into the deep on voyages of discovery and conquest. It was discovered that the world was round and not square and that by sailing west the East was reached. The taste which Europe had had of the products of the East had developed a real and growing demand for these commodities, but the long and hazardous overland haul from India to the eastern shores of the Mediterranean made desirable a quicker and less expensive route. This was soon found by the hardy mariners who braved the terrors of the unknown oceans in their frail vessels and opened up new avenues of commerce. Soon Spain, Portugal, France, Holland, and, last but not least, England entered into the race for commercial prestige and colonial development.

Rules to Prevent Misuse of Insurance. With this rapid growth in overseas commerce it is not surprising that marine insurance grew into

[1] *Ibid.*, p. 6.
[2] *Ibid.*, p. 5.

a definite system of indemnity and that the various Continental nations issued ordinances, or codes, which set forth the usages and customs relating to marine insurance and laws for the government of its practice. The earliest of these codes is the ordinance issued by the Magistrates of Barcelona in 1435. The necessity for law arises because men, uncontrolled, take advantage of their weaker fellows, and this first code relating to marine insurance is no exception to the rule, for it is largely concerned with the prevention of fraud in connection with marine underwriting. Rules are included in this ordinance limiting the amount which may be insured on certain vessels and prohibiting altogether the insurance of vessels owned and freighted by foreigners. The code also provides that those "who write policies shall be bound to see that they are properly drawn" and, differing from modern practice, requires that the policy must be signed by the assured or his representative, "who must declare on oath the particulars of the insurance." Wager policies were prohibited, and in order that the premium might be secured to the underwriter, it was provided that the policy should be of no effect unless the premium was actually paid and acknowledged in the contract. On the other hand, the underwriter was held to a strict compliance with his contract, the time within which proved losses and losses arising from cases of missing vessels must be paid being minutely prescribed.

Insurance Well Established in Fifteenth Century. This first ordinance of Barcelona was followed by others issued in 1436, in 1458, and in 1461. In 1468 the Grand Council of Venice issued a decree fixing the place of trial for actions arising out of marine-insurance disputes, and a somewhat later decree issued in Venice imposed heavy fines on owners who loaded their ships with deckloads that imperiled the safety of the vessel. While these ordinances and similar ones issued in Florence, Bilbao, and other cities are of great interest in tracing the growth of marine-insurance customs and practice, they are also of great importance historically as indicating very clearly that by the fifteenth century marine insurance was well enough established to require stringent rules to govern its practice and to prevent its abuse.

The *Guidon de la Mer*. One of the most interesting of all the early works on marine insurance is the *Guidon de la Mer,* written by an unknown author late in the sixteenth or early in the seventeenth century and apparently published in Rouen, France. This work gives a rather complete outline of the rules and conditions under which marine insurance was practiced at this time. Not only were contracts of insurance required to be in writing, but it was necessary to have such contracts enrolled as public acts before a register. Without such registration the policies were null and void. Elaborate rules were set down for the government of the register, or *greffier*. Among other things, he was required to collect a fixed fee for his services and to keep in his office a collection box for the poor, into which the assured was ordered to drop "six deniers for every thousand of livres assured." Indications appear in the *Guidon* that at the time of its issuance marine insurance was generally practiced in all the Continental countries and in England and that policies made in one country were payable in another at a fixed rate of conversion for foreign currency. A form of policy also appears in the *Guidon* which conforms closely to the earliest English policy dated 1613 and found in the Bodleian Library at Oxford.

Marine Insurance in England. While it is of interest to trace the growth of marine insurance in Continental Europe, the American student is more deeply interested in the rise and growth of insurance in England. Our system conforms more closely to the system common in England, where marine insurance has reached its highest development, than to that of the Continental countries. England, the last of the European countries to obtain prominence as a commercial nation, in time became the commercial leader of the world. Two streams of influence shaped the commercial and incidentally the marine-insurance development of England. The earliest influence was that of the Hanseatic League, which for nearly five centuries controlled to a large extent the foreign commerce of England. The later influence was that of the Lombards, who, driven out of their homes in Italy, settled in various parts of Europe, many of them finding refuge in England.

The Hansa Merchants and the Steelyard. The Hansa merchants found in England a fertile field for the practice of their efficient commercial methods, because the English monarchs in the early history of the country were more interested in fighting their neighbors and in defending themselves from attacks at home and abroad than in the development of the country. Incidentally, these English kings were always in debt, and they found the Hansa merchants accommodating lenders at first, but severe taskmasters at last. These merchants established themselves in London in the Steelyard, a group of buildings in which they lived and stored their merchandise. They lived under the strictest discipline. They neither married nor were permitted to associate with the gentler sex. They were commercial monks, living a narrow but luxurious life, for all that was best of every land came to their hands. Their rules and regulations not only were for the personal government of the members but related also to the commercial and political affairs of the organization. They entered England in the tenth century, 300 years later were the favorites of English royalty, and, for a time, practically controlled the trade of England. But such consideration on the part of England's kings could have but one result. The first signs of the coming commercial superiority of the English people were beginning to show, and the native merchants rose in their wrath to drive out these Teutonic tradesmen. The men of the Steelyard, however, were deeply entrenched in the commercial life of England, and it was only after a bitter struggle that they were finally banished and a wonderful era of commercial progress was ushered in with the coming of Queen Elizabeth to the throne. Disliked as these Hansa traders were by the English merchants, they helped in large measure to lay the foundations of British overseas trade. The members of the Hanseatic League practiced marine insurance and probably introduced it into England.

The Lombards in England. The Lombards, whose impress is deeply marked on the commercial history of England, while engaging to a certain extent in overseas commerce, reached their highest success as money lenders. They, too, having funds with which to finance the wars of England's kings, found great favor with them and received many privileges not accorded to the native citizens. The first great wave of Lombard traders reached the shores of England about the middle of the thirteenth century, and as their power and wealth increased, many of their fellows from Lombardy and other places on the Continent joined them. The men of England, however, were highly incensed against these "usurers." In order to satisfy the demands of the people the kings of England issued many edicts for the control of the Lombard bankers. The kings themselves, nevertheless, continued to borrow from them, regardless of the fact that the rates charged on their loans violated their own decrees. Not only did the Lombards become money lenders to Britain's monarchs, but they also were the fiscal agents of the Pope, selling pardons and collecting and remitting to Rome the revenues of the Church.

Lombard Street. Prospering greatly but nevertheless being persecuted by the public, the Lombards petitioned King Henry IV to grant them a section of the City of London where they might build their homes and conduct their trade in security. The King, probably in return for some financial accommodation, granted their petition, and there was allotted to them a portion of ground, on which the Lombards built their homes and which took the name of Lombard Street. This street has become famous in marine-insurance history, and even to this day there appears in the British marine-insurance policy this clause:

> And it is agreed by us, the insurers, that this writing or policy of assurance shall be of as much force and effect as the surest writing or policy of assurance heretofore made in Lombard Street, or in the Royal Exchange, or elsewhere in London.

Departure of Hansa Merchants and Lombards. Little information is obtainable in regard to the commercial and insurance transactions of the Lombards, but it is certain that with the decline in power of the Hansa merchants in Europe, the Lombards gained a considerable part of their trade, and at the close of the fifteenth century much of the overseas commerce of England was in their control. This is evidenced by an Act of Parliament of 1483 and by subsequent Acts reciting the evil practices of the Italian merchants and designed to curb their activities. With the coming of the day of England's commercial awakening, the Lombards' power began to decline. Gradually the Italian merchants quitted England, some returning to their ancestral homes, others finding new fields of activity in the Continental countries.

Influence of Foreign Merchants. While the Hansa merchants left their greatest impress on the bartering side of trade, the Lombards firmly established in England the banking and insurance branches of commercial activity. Marine insurance, introduced into England by the Hansa merchants, was perfected by the Lombards, and at the time of their passing from England its practice was well established.

First English Marine-insurance Statute. In the forty-third year of the reign of Queen Elizabeth, in December, 1601, 4 years after the last of the Hansa merchants had left England, there was passed by Parliament "An Acte concerninge matters of Assurances amongste merchantes." This Act stands as a landmark in the history of marine insurance, not because the law itself had any great influence on the course of the business, but because it is the first English statute dealing with marine insurance. Its purpose was the establishment of a special court for the trial of marine-insurance cases in order to expedite their adjudication. The court, although organized, was little used, merchants preferring to have their cases tried in the regular courts. The preamble of this statute reads in part as follows:

> Whereas it ever hathe bene the policie of this realme by all good meanes to comforte and encourage the merchante, therebie to advance and increase the general wealthe of the realme, her majesties customes and strengthe of shippinge, which consideracion is nowe the more requisite because trade and traffique is not at this presente soe open as at other tymes it hathe bene; And whereas it has bene tyme out of mynde an usage amongste merchantes, both of this realme and of forraine nacyons, when they make any great adventure (speciallie into remote partes) to give some consideracion of money to other persons (which commonlie are in noe small number) to have from them assurance made of their goodes, merchandizes, ships and things adventured, or some parte thereof, at suche rates and in such sorte as the parties assurers and the parties assured can agree, which course of dealinge is commonlie termed a policie of assurance; by means of whiche policie of assurance it comethe to passe that upon the losse or perishinge of any shippe there followethe not the undoinge of any man, but the losse lightethe rather easilie upon many than heavilie upon fewe, and rather upon them that adventure not than those that doe adventure, whereby all merchante, speciallie the younger sorte, are allured to venture more willinglie and more freely.

In a later part of this Act reference is made to causes "arisinge out of pollicies of assurance, suche as now are or hereafter shall be entered within the office of assurances within the Citie of London," indicating that the Continental system of officially recording policies was followed in England.

Individual Underwriters. At this time underwriting was done by individuals, many of whom were bankers or money lenders who adopted underwriting as an additional method of employing their funds. These men had no general gathering place, but policies were carried around by brokers, who obtained from each underwriter his acceptance of a share of the risk. Each individual noted on the policy the amount of liability which he assumed and signed his name; hence the term *underwriter.*

Lloyd's Coffee House and Lloyd's News. The introduction of the use of coffee and with it the establishment in London of coffee houses, where the beverage was dispensed, had a decided effect on the course of marine insurance in England. Notwithstanding an ordinance of Charles II closing the coffee houses on the ground that they were breeding places for sedition against the government, these gathering places continued to prosper. Some of them became the meeting places of merchants and mariners where, over the fragrant cups of coffee, the latest marine news was discussed. One of these houses was conducted by Edward Lloyd, a man of no mean ability, who, seeing that this marine gossip might be of general interest, began in 1696 the publication of *Lloyd's News.* This small sheet, most of the numbers of which are to be found in the Bodleian Library, represents the germ idea from which has grown the present news service of Lloyd's, London. After the publication of 76 numbers, the government, angered over some item appearing in the *News,* stopped its publication. Thirty years later the paper again appears as *Lloyd's List* and under this name is still published.

A Meeting Place of Underwriters. Gradually Edward Lloyd's coffee house became the meeting place of many of London's underwriters, and here they underwrote their risks. Not only was underwriting carried on in this coffee house, but ships were sold and merchandise was auctioned. Merchants and shippers frequented its rooms, and all kinds of business incidental to shipping was transacted. Advertisements appearing in papers published in the early years of the eighteenth century constantly refer to this coffee house as the place of sale of ships, goods, real estate, and stocks and as the meeting place of the stockholders of associations. Lloyd's coffee house was indeed the mart of many kinds of trade, and the story of its evolution into the modern London Lloyd's is one of the interesting chapters in commercial history.

Insurance Companies Organized. In a day when the English people had run wild in the incorporation of companies for the carrying on of every conceivable activity, at a time when the South Sea Bubble was expanding but had not yet burst, it is not surprising that the field of marine insurance was invaded and that efforts were made to do corporate underwriting. Individual underwriting had by this time, the early part of the eighteenth century, brought fortunes to many. The security for the insurance was, however, individual security, and it appeared that better protection could be given by a corporation with a definite known capital under the control of the government. Not only would this better security be given, but the profits arising from the conduct of the business would be distributed to many persons, owners of the stock of the corporation. The underwriters who congregated at Lloyd's coffee house and others who had private offices earnestly opposed the establishment of a chartered marine-insurance company. Many arguments pro and con were advanced, those petitioning for the incorporation claiming that many individual underwriters failed and could not pay their obligations, a charge not well substantiated. On the other hand, underwriters argued that the business could be better carried on by individuals, since its conduct required personal skill and experience which a corporation could not give. They also showed that underwriting was not practiced on the Continent by corporations and that the existing system had adequately met the needs of England's growing commerce. The House of Commons favored the underwriters, but no action was taken by Parliament until 1720, when a new and always powerful argument was presented on behalf of the petitioners, who on this occasion sought the establishment of two corporations. The finances of England were in an embarrassing condition, owing to the civil list being burdened with heavy debts which Parliament was unwilling to pay. The incorporators therefore skillfully proposed that, in exchange for the granting of the two charters, including a monopoly of corporate underwriting, they would pay into the exchequer for the discharge of debts on the civil list the sum of £600,000.

This proposal struck a responsive chord in the heart of King George I, and a royal message was sent to the faithful Commons strongly recommending the passage of the bill granting the two charters.

The Monopoly. Notwithstanding serious opposition, the bill became a law, and charters were granted on June 24, 1720 to the London Assurance Corporation and the Royal Exchange Assurance Corporation. These two companies thus received the monopoly, as corporations, of insuring ships and their cargoes. The fears of the individual underwriters that their business would be ruined proved groundless. The volume of business obtained by the corporations was small, and in the early years of their operation, the results were unsuccessful. By a saving clause in the bill which provided for the monopoly, the charters were subject to forfeiture if the installments of the £600,000 payment were not forthcoming at the dates provided. The companies failed to make the payments as required, but owing to the influence of their sponsors, Parliament reduced the debt to £150,000, which sum was ultimately received by the government.

Growth of Marine Insurance. Lloyd's. For the next hundred years during which the two corporations made a slow growth, the business of the individual underwriters increased by leaps and bounds. Instead of being a hindrance to these underwriters, it was soon seen that the monopoly was a protection to them in that it prevented the establishment of other competing companies. In 1769 the underwriters who congregated at Lloyd's coffee house formed a definite organization and obtained the control of *Lloyd's List.* One object of the organization was to stamp out the gambling which, under the guise of insurance, was being carried on at the coffee house. Such insurance dealt with every conceivable subject, from the result of a political election to the duration of the life of a prominent citizen who might be sick and dying. The underwriters thus organized under the name of "Lloyd's" moved to the Royal Exchange, the idea of the coffee house still being continued. The control of this particular part of the organization was vested in a headwaiter and his two associates, who cared for the physical needs of the members "at Lloyd's." In 1928 Lloyd's moved to its own home, a monumental building erected a short distance from the Royal Exchange. The bombing of London during World War II destroyed acres of buildings near Lloyd's. Lloyd's miraculously escaped. All through the months of terror Lloyd's underwriters carried on as usual, oftentimes conducting their activities in the cellar of the building.

It is a quaint item of marine-insurance history that in New York during the last century it was customary to have a sideboard in the marine-insurance company offices whereon were placed crackers, cheese, and other viands, some of a liquid nature, for the physical refreshment of those who entered to transact business.

Standard Policy Adopted. From 1769 Lloyd's was the underwriting center of London. Controlled by men of great ability and integrity, resolutions were passed condemning the underwriting of gambling policies. These resolutions were observed by the greater portion of the membership, and Lloyd's gained a reputation for fair dealing which aided not a little in the phenomenal success that came to its members. In 1779, at a meeting of Lloyd's, a uniform printed form of marine-insurance policy was adopted, and all the members agreed to its use. The resolutions passed by Lloyd's embodying this form were submitted to Parliament and approved by that body. Lloyd's form thus became the official British form of marine-insurance policy.

Increase of Individual Underwriters. At the time of the adoption of this form of policy the American Revolution was being fought. Marine insurance was increasing greatly owing to this war, which made overseas commerce extrahazardous and led many to insure who formerly "ran their own risk." This conflict and the wars that followed occupied the attention of Great Britain almost continuously for a period of 50 years. During this time Britain developed into a great nation, and the prosperity which came to the country was not without its effect on the underwriting fraternity. Wealth made, with great hazard but in large volume, attracted many merchants into the underwriting field, some of whom would stake thousands of pounds on a single venture.

Efforts to Incorporate New Companies. The natural consequence of this great prosperity was the desire on the part of many to enter the marine-insurance field as corporate underwriters, but the monopoly created in 1720 proved an effective barrier to such efforts. The two corporations and the underwriters at Lloyd's were now business friends and no longer rivals and jointly resented all efforts made to break the monopoly. Business had naturally gravitated to Lloyd's, as the companies, while engaging to some extent in marine insurance, preferred the fields of fire and life insurance with their surer rewards. The original grant of monopoly in its saving clause permitted the termination of the special privilege if it were found at any time that the monopoly was "hurtful or inconvenient to the public." Relying on this phrase, in 1798 the directors of the Globe Insurance Company, who wished to enter their company in the marine field, petitioned Parliament for a repeal of the monopoly. Opposed by the power of Lloyd's, the petition died in committee. Making new efforts in 1806 and 1807 the Globe Company was again defeated and ceased its efforts. Again in 1809 a powerful group of men petitioned for the repeal of the monopoly, but they, too, were unsuccessful. This time, however, the question was thoroughly discussed before Parliament, able speakers advocating, respectively, both the repeal and the retention of the monopoly. One gains from the debates an accurate view of the state of marine insurance in England at this time and a very clear presentation of the powerful position which Lloyd's had assumed. However, the most potent argument presented by the opposition to the mind of the House of Commons was that the repeal of the monopoly not only would injure Lloyd's but would probably destroy the "system of commercial intelligence" of Lloyd's which was essential not only to marine insurance but to commerce in general. Frederick Martin in his history gives a detailed account of these debates, together with pen pictures of some of the leading figures in the marine-insurance world at that time. During the investigations made at this time by the special committee of Parliament, much evidence was presented showing that insurance frauds were exceedingly common at this period. This was largely caused by the fact that the punishment meted out to such offenders was not commensurate with the gravity of the offenses.

Lloyd's Reorganized. The efforts made to defeat the repeal of the monopoly brought home to the members of Lloyd's various defects in their own organization. As a result, a committee was appointed and a new constitution was drawn up and adopted providing rules for the admission of members, for their government, and for the care of the meeting place of the organization. The rooms were still operated on a modified plan of the old coffee house. The control of the organization was vested in a governing committee of twelve, who were charged, among other things, with the duty of appointing Lloyd's agents. The post of Lloyd's agent in a foreign port had by this time become a position of honor much sought after, and men of the highest standing in their respective communities occupied these positions. The work of these agents did much to stamp out shipping frauds, and the wealth of commercial information gathered from their reports was of immeasurable value, not only to the commercial world, but to the government as well.

The Monopoly Repealed. The insurance monopoly was finally broken on June 24, 1824. The circumstances leading up to the repeal of this Act (the sixth of George I) are interesting and show how slight incidents sometimes have great results. Nathan Rothschild, son of the great German banker, had emigrated to England and there became a commercial and financial power. His brother-in-law, Benjamin Gompertz, a distinguished mathematician, sought the appointment to the vacant post of actuary of a large insurance company but failed because he was a Jew. He appealed to the powerful Nathan, who, infuriated at this slight to his race, vowed that he would create a bigger company than any existing and provide a better position for his relative than the one he sought. Immediately gathering together some of his prominent and influential friends, Rothschild organized the Alliance British & Foreign Fire and Life Assurance Company with a capital of £5,000,000. The shares of the new company under the magic of the Rothschild name were quickly subscribed. The directors then petitioned Parliament for the repeal of the marine-insurance monopoly so that the new company could engage in this branch of insurance. The main argument advanced for the repeal of the old Act was that competition in the marine-insurance field should be free. The opposition argued that there was sufficient competition, there being over one thousand underwriters at Lloyd's, and that the creation of this gigantic company would throttle competition and a new monopoly would be created. Nevertheless, the repeal of the monopoly was approved. However, Nathan Rothschild had one further bridge to cross, as the prospectus of the Alliance Company provided only for fire and life insurance, and one of the members of Lloyd's, who had purchased 15 shares in the new company, commenced suit against the directors to restrain them from entering the marine-insurance field as a breach of the contract entered into between the directors and the subscribers. The court upheld this view, but nothing daunted, Nathan Rothschild immediately organized the Alliance Marine Insurance Company, the active management of which was given to Benjamin Gompertz.

New Companies. The fears of underwriters at Lloyd's that company competition would ruin their business again proved groundless. The public was slow to leave the old paths of marine insurance, and the Alliance Company met with only moderate success. In 1840, finding that the huge capital of £5,000,000 was unnecessary, a reduction to £1,000,000 was made. The subsequent history of marine underwriting in England is one of the organization of many companies and of the failure of most of them. However, now and again, records are found of the establishment of new companies which, carefully organized and managed, prospered and, with the Alliance, still aid in caring for the vast values that enter the British market seeking protection. In 1950 the business was about evenly divided between Lloyd's and the companies.

Marine-insurance Law. No history of marine insurance in England would be complete unless reference were made to the development of the law relating to this branch of commercial activity. The Continental nations were given to the codification of their laws and, as already indicated, adopted many commercial codes. The English legal mind, however, tended rather to draw conclusions from precedents than to bind itself by any definite code of laws. The court for the trial of insurance cases, organized in the reign of Queen Elizabeth, never achieved its objective. Merchants and underwriters preferred the regular courts of law. In these courts, the judges decided cases by considering the Continental codes and the usages of merchants in England respecting the case in point, drawing their conclusions from and basing their judgments on these precedents. Up to the middle of the eighteenth century there appear in the English court records less than one hundred cases relating to insurance. It is not reasonable to assume, in view of the growth of marine insurance, that this is any indication that disputes did not arise in connection with marine-insurance transactions. Rather does it indicate that merchants were not satisfied with the marine-insurance knowledge of English jurists of this time and preferred to settle disputes out of court by arbitration or by some other method of reference before men experienced in the customs of commerce.

Lord Mansfield. In the year 1756 the Earl of Mansfield ascended the bench as Lord Chief Justice of England, and for 32 years thereafter he molded and clarified English law. Of broad knowledge and keen intellect, he took insurance law as he found it, both in the English precedents and in the Continental codes, applied it in the light of commerical customs and usages to the cases presented to him, and developed a body of law which is today the basis of both British and American practice. James Allen Park, in 1786, published, with the approval of Lord Mansfield, a work entitled "A System of the Law of Marine Insurance," which gathered together the English decisions, especially those of Lord Mansfield. This book, in which the decisions are divided into groups relating to the various branches of marine-insurance law, is still a work of great value and constitutes the basis of many of the British and American law books on the subject.

The Marine Insurance Act, 1906. The need of a definite code of marine-insurance law was often brought to the attention of Parliament without any degree of success. As time passed, and the decisions grew in number, inconsistencies crept into the law, and it was difficult indeed to know whether or not one stood on firm ground. The laws that Parliament enacted in regard to marine insurance merely sought to prevent gambling practices or related to stamp taxes. In the latter years of the nineteenth century several efforts were made to pass a bill codifying the British law, and for 12 years the question was before Parliament, various committees considering these measures. Finally, in 1906 the Marine Insurance Act was passed, followed, in 1909, by the Marine Insurance (Gambling Policies) Act. These two Acts are now the controlling law of Britain with respect to marine insurance. The Gambling Policies Act has quite effectually stamped out the dealing in wager policies which, prior to the enactment of the law, was engaged in by all classes of the British people.

Early Underwriting in the United States. The history of marine insurance in the United States is rather colorless. Closely joined to Britain by ties of blood and of custom, it is not surprising that, in the early history of the Colonies, insurance on American risks was placed with British underwriters. Early in Colonial days, however, some effort was made to establish a local market. In 1721, one John C. Capson inserted in the *American Weekly Mercury* of May 25, published in Philadelphia, an intimation that he was about to open an office of public insurance on vessels, goods and merchandise. He stated that "the merchants of this city of Philadelphia and other ports have been obliged to send to London for such insurance, which has not only been tedious and troublesome, but ever precarious, and for the remedy of which this office is opened." In other seaboard cities offices for the underwriting of marine risks were opened during the latter days of the American Colonies. In New York City an insurance office was opened in 1759, and in 1778 the New Insurance Office entered the underwriting field. All these offices were conducted on the English plan of individual or partnership underwriting, incorporated insurance companies being unknown.

First American Insurance Corporation. In 1792 there was organized in Philadelphia, then the commercial metropolis of the United States, the first incorporated company for the transaction of fire and marine insurance, the Insurance Company of North America, to which a formal charter was granted on April 14, 1794 by the General Assembly of Pennsylvania. The early history of this company is closely interwoven with that of the nation itself, and it is greatly to the credit of the management of the company that it was able to survive, notwithstanding the wars and rumors of wars which disturbed the early years of the American Republic. After a very unsatisfactory experience with private underwriters, of whom at least 50 operated in Philadelphia, merchants welcomed the new company, and business flowed to it in a constantly increasing stream.

Corporation Development. The corporate system being initiated, the idea spread rapidly, and soon similar organizations were being formed in Baltimore, Boston, Charleston, New Haven, New York, Newburyport, and Providence. These and other companies, soon after formed, met with a reasonable degree of success for a time, owing to the prosperity which attended shipping interests in the early years of the country's history. The Napoleonic Wars greatly disturbed the peaceful conduct of commerce and caused a great demand for insurance. War has ever been a stimulant to the marine-insurance business, bringing increased hazards and correspondingly increased premiums. It does not necessarily follow, however, that such periods are periods of prosperity for marine underwriters, and these early wars, with their consequent heavy losses, at times brought many insurance companies to the verge of ruin. During the first 10 years of the existence of the Insurance Company of North America the average premium rate was 12 per cent, but the payment of losses absorbed over 91 per cent of the premium income. Periods of partial prosperity followed those of adversity, but with the opening of the War of 1812 the marine market again faced disaster. The shipping of the United States to a large extent having been driven from the seas, marine insurance declined and was not firmly reestablished until 30 years later, when, with the growth of a new merchant marine, insurance again became a profitable employment for capital.

Competition and Failures among Companies. The high premiums resulting from the War of 1812 and those preceding it had attracted into the field many companies that achieved little success. The dawn of peace in 1815, with its attendant loss in war-premium income, inaugurated a period of bitter competition. The volume of business was insufficient to employ the capital invested, and in the endeavor to obtain a share, companies wrote risks at inadequate rates, with the inevitable result that there were many failures. Then, too, those who were managing the companies lacked financial insight and, in an endeavor to pay dividends, neglected the creation of surplus funds to aid in the day of adversity. Lack of governmental control permitted these and other abuses to exist and grow. This was, in fact, a testing time for the whole country. The new nation was suffering its growing pains and making the mistakes of adolescence.

The Clipper Ship and Insurance Frauds. The merchant marine had been gradually reviving, and shipowners were obtaining a new measure of prosperity. With a virgin country amply supplied with woods fit for shipbuilding, it was but natural that from the earliest days the people should turn to shipbuilding. Models were improved as time went on, and finally the clipper ship, the glory of the American merchant marine, was produced and won from the ships of all the world the mastery of the sea. The renaissance of the merchant marine preceded by several years the revival of profitable underwriting. Between 1828 and 1844 the companies were seriously crippled by many fraudulent losses occurring in the West Indies and the Gulf of Mexico. Owing to the lack of cohesion among the companies, however, it was not until 1844 that any concerted action was taken to prevent these losses. In this year the Philadelphia underwriters formed a protective organization, one of the main purposes of which was the prevention of fraudulent claims.

Marine Insurance Revives. Following the panic of 1837, with its attendant failures, those companies which were able to weather the financial storm entered on an era of prosperity which continued for about 20 years. The American clipper ship was now developed to the point where it wrested most of the overseas carrying trade from Great Britain and the Continental countries. The ships and their cargoes being American owned, it was but natural that the marine insurance should be placed with American underwriters. New companies were organized, many of them meeting with phenomenal success. The voyages of the clipper ships, though of short duration judged by standards of that time, were long as compared with later steamer voyages, and the rates of premium accordingly were high. So well built were these ships and so skillful were their masters that the insurance produced a handsome profit to the underwriters.

The Civil War. Great Britain, somewhat baffled by the success of the clipper ship, sought for an antidote and found it in iron as a medium for construction and in coal as a producer of motive power. Soon steam-propelled metal ships were navigating the seas, and the glory of the clipper ship began to fade. Slow in developing her untold resources of iron and coal, the United States began to decline as an overseas carrying nation. Before American shipbuilders realized that iron and coal were to control overseas commerce the nation was engulfed in the Civil War, which added impetus to the decline of the American merchant marine and resulted in the financial embarrassment of most of the insurance companies and the failure of many. Burdened by heavy taxation and deprived of the large overseas traffic in farm products, especially cotton, American shipping and its allied interests were terribly crippled. Great Britain, not slow to grasp her opportunity, entered a new era of shipbuilding and ship operating. Her new metal vessels propelled by mechanical power were soon produced in great numbers and before many years carried much of the overseas trade of the United States.

Mutual Companies. During the 20 years immediately preceding the Civil War, and while the prosperity attending overseas commerce due to the clipper ships was at its height, a curious situation developed in the marine-insurance market. The problems of overseas commerce were relatively simple. Many shipowners were also merchants, and many merchants either owned or partially owned ships. It seemed to them that to the profits they made from their trading ventures they could add the profits which some companies were making on the insurance of these ventures. They accordingly began to organize mutual marine-insurance companies and to pay off stockholders and change stock companies into mutual companies. These men were rugged individualists—capitalists who wished to gain as much of the profits arising from their overseas ventures as was possible. However, they were also willing to accept the losses inherent in venturing if fate should so decree.

Nonassessment Companies. These companies were of a peculiar pattern, totally unlike mutual companies that operate in the fire-insurance business. They did not rely for their security on the power to assess the policyholder in the event of adversity. On the contrary, they raised their initial working capital by taking notes from prospective assured, which notes were paid off by the assured as premiums were charged for insurance purchased for the protection of hull or cargo. If profit resulted, the profit was retained temporarily by the company and the distribution made to the policyholder in the form of a certificate of profits, commonly known as *scrip.* These certificates paid interest until redeemed. However, they were not an irrevocable obligation but by their terms provided that the amount outstanding might be canceled or reduced in amount if the results of the operations of the company were unfortunate. It was also provided by the charter of the typical mutual marine-insurance company that no certificate of profits could be redeemed until $500,000 of free surplus was accumulated. However, when the free surplus reached $1,000,000, the oldest issues of certificates must be redeemed.

A Capitalistic Scheme. By this system a fund of $1,000,000, a huge sum in the 1840's, had to be contributed by the policyholders without hope of return, save in the event of the liquidation of a solvent company. This was surely a more capitalistic operation than paying $1,000,000 into a stock company in exchange for stock certificates on which dividends might be expected in the event of a successful operation.

Unfortunate Experience. At this time there was no state or federal supervision of insurance. Management exercised its powers without let or hindrance. Hence the results were in harmony with the underwriting and financial ability of those in control of the enterprise. Many individuals organized companies without the necessary qualifications, and the mortality among the companies was high. But the business seemed attractive, and mutual companies continued to be organized. In an interesting history of insurance in Philadelphia, the author J. A. Fowler says:[1]

> Mutualism was "in the air." After a series of extraordinary dividends on the stock, the Atlantic Insurance Company of New York, which had the advantage of the commerce of New York in its business resources, became mutual in 1842, and all the stock capital was paid back. The Atlantic Mutual's net earnings or profits for 1843 were 40 per cent. of the determined premiums. Philadelphia marine companies purposing a local business were declining—from the declining commercial prestige of the city rather than otherwise.

This quotation is interesting because over 100 years later the Atlantic Mutual Insurance Company referred to is the only mutual marine-insurance company that continues in business, eminently successful throughout the century. In the first report of the New York Insurance Department that commented on marine-insurance companies, the report of 1864, only 13 marine-insurance companies appeared. Of these nine were mutuals, three combination stock and mutual, and only one a stock company. The only foreign-state company admitted to write marine insurance in New York at that time was the country's oldest company, the Insurance Company of North America, still a leader in the marine-insurance business. At the present time about 150 companies in the United States write marine insurance; all save the Atlantic are stock companies. Today the Atlantic pays its dividends

[1] J. A. Fowler, "History of Insurance in Philadelphia for Two Centuries 1683–1882," Review Publishing & Printing Company, Philadelphia, 1888.

to its participating policyholders in cash, its last outstanding scrip having been redeemed in 1938. A colorful chapter in the story of marine insurance in the United States has thus passed into history.

Foreign Companies Enter the United States. Handicapped by the period of reconstruction following the Civil War and prejudiced by the attitude of foreign classification societies which discriminated against American-built vessels, the American merchant marine steadily declined and with it the fortunes of the marine-insurance companies that had survived the war. To add further to the burdens of the companies, shortsighted legislation permitted the entrance of foreign insurance companies into the American market on terms which militated against the success of the American companies. The first British company entered New York State about 1871 and was quickly followed by many others. These companies had been organized for many years, were carefully managed, had large surpluses, and immediately began a drive for American business by cutting rates. The American companies, not prepared to meet this sort of competition, were gradually forced out of the marine-insurance business. Some were liquidated; others that did both a fire- and a marine-insurance business devoted their efforts solely to fire insurance. When this period had passed, the American marine-insurance market was composed of a very few American companies and a comparatively large number of British companies. Much of the cargo business to and from the United States was insured in the American market, but the hull business was to a great extent placed in the British market, and British underwriters prescribed the form of policy on which such insurance was written. By this time less than 10 per cent of the overseas commerce of the United States was carried in American vessels. As trade follows the flag, so, too, marine-insurance protection, which is but one element in the conduct of trade, is ordinarily furnished by citizens of the same flag, with the result that marine insurance was diverted from the American market.

The Marine-insurance Market Broadens. The last years of the nineteenth century ushered in a new era in the history of the United States. Following the period of depression commencing in 1893, there was a tremendous revival of American trade. After the Spanish-American War the nation found itself a world power with new responsibilities and with new commercial fields to conquer. The coastwise trade of the United States, wisely restricted to American vessels, increased greatly. New vessels were built, both on the seaboard and the Great Lakes. Gradually the American marine-insurance market obtained a greater and greater share of the hull business.

Little American Capital Invested in Marine Companies. Notwithstanding the gradual control which the American market obtained in the conduct of local business, it must not be forgotten that at the beginning of the twentieth century the larger part of the capital employed in the Atlantic, Lake, and Pacific marine-insurance markets was foreign capital, and the profits on this business, in large part, were received, not by American investors, but by foreign shareholders in companies domiciled in this country. In the other branches of insurance, although foreign companies had entered the field, most of the capital invested was American. Profits, though perhaps small, were reasonably certain in all departments of insurance except marine, but the moderate profits of some periods were not sufficient inducement, in view of the history of the business, to attract American capital into the marine field.

Steady Growth of Marine Insurance. A gradual growth and strengthening of the marine-insurance market appear in the first 13 years of the twentieth century. A few new American companies were organized, and the market as a whole reflected in some small measure the prosperity and expansion of the United States. Stricter regulation by the state governments was enforced, but no effort was made either locally or nationally to protect American companies against the encroachment of foreign competition. Neither was any real effort made to foster American shipping by governmental aid. On the other hand, through efforts made to aid seamen, laws were passed which succeeded in driving most of the American vessels in the foreign trade to seek registry under foreign flags. This was, in brief, the condition which existed when World War I commenced.

World War I and New American Companies. Stunned by the outbreak of the world war, all commercial activities were for a time disorganized, but with the gradual recovery of poise, the need for ships and for American insurance became insistent. Bankers were unwilling in many cases to accept the insurance certificates of companies of belligerent countries, and many American companies that formerly had confined themselves to fire insurance entered the marine-insurance field. New companies were organized, and many of Scandinavian, Spanish, and other neutral nationalities established themselves in the American market. The increased value of tonnage and the doubling and trebling of cargo values, with the enormous increase in rates of freight, created a demand for marine insurance that at times taxed to the utmost the insurance markets of the whole world. The New York market, where before the war about 30 companies were actively engaged, expanded until over 100 were writing. Formerly limits of a few hundred thousand dollars exhausted the capacity of this market, but during and immediately following the war, millions of dollars were easily placed. The entrance of the United States into the war, with the attendant commandeering of ships and goods, temporarily depressed the activity of the marine-insurance market. However, the extensive shipbuilding program of the country, presaging a reestablished American merchant marine, indicated a golden future for the practice of marine insurance. This condition continued during World War I. Soon after its end the United States government found itself in possession of an enormous mercantile fleet which it greatly desired to transfer to private ownership. It was necessary to make attractive terms of sale and to arrange adequate facilities for the insurance of the vessels. To provide facilities, the government prevailed upon the American marine-insurance companies to join together under syndicate management for the insurance of vessels sold by the government to private interests. The American Marine Insurance Syndicates, which will be discussed in detail in a later chapter,[1] thus came into being. To protect the companies against the charge of banding together to create a monopoly, a special provision was incorporated in the law exempting the marine-insurance companies from the application of the antitrust laws. The underwriting of ocean hulls by the American insurance offices is, at the present time, practically controlled by the successors of these original syndicates.

The Postwar Period. With the signing of the armistice in 1918 and the cessation of hostilities, a period of depression set in, quickly followed by unprecedented commercial activity. All the pent-up demand

[1] See Chap. 17, p. 281.

of the war years was released, and raw and manufactured commodities were shipped in volume and value which taxed to the utmost the facilities of the marine-insurance companies. It was soon discovered that the hurry and tension of the war years had broken down morale in commercial affairs and that new and unforeseen perils had developed in connection with overseas shipments. Theft and pilferage, improper handling and stowage of cargoes, and faulty and careless packing produced a multitude of relatively small claims which, in the aggregate, used up a considerable part of the premium income of the companies. Before opportunity was had properly to measure these new hazards, the deflation period came with its shrinkage in volume and value of overseas shipments. Claims continued to be presented long after the premium income had been materially reduced, resulting in the embarrassment of many companies and in the decision of others to withdraw from marine underwriting. Notwithstanding the closing and withdrawal of many companies, the marine-insurance facility remaining both here and abroad was much larger than the necessities of commerce required. Cutthroat competition ensued with all its attendant evils of inadequate rates, unwise policy conditions, and other improper inducements granted either to gain or to retain business.

Business Revives. Gradually by the withdrawal of companies and by the prosperity that was worldwide during the 1920's, the marine-insurance business was stabilized and entered a period of satisfactory growth. More and more hull insurance was written, and as the overseas commerce of the United States expanded, a greater volume of cargo premiums was obtained by the American marine-insurance market. This growth trend continued notwithstanding the severe depression of the 1930's. The attitude of the government toward the business was friendly, and although the underwriters neither sought nor received any direct government benefits, nevertheless they were working in an atmosphere of governmental interest in the development of an American marine-insurance market.

Cooperation. Not only was the government's attitude friendly, but for the most part the companies themselves, while actively competing for business, cooperated with each other in solving the broad problems of the business as they developed. The American Institute of Marine Underwriters, the Board of Underwriters of New York, and other organizations of the companies were the channels through which these cooperative efforts were carried on. All these efforts were to the advantage of the merchants and shipowners, for with the growing complications of overseas trade, uniform practices were desirable.

World War II. Not only was the economy of the world depressed, but its political life passed from one crisis to another. The underwriters realized that war was inevitable; when it would come was the unknown factor. Remembering the difficulties that they had encountered in World War I, they decided to be prepared for the coming war with its great demand for marine insurance, particularly against the perils of war. Accordingly, almost every company writing marine insurance in the United States, whether of American or foreign nationality, joined together for the sharing of war-risk liability in the American Cargo War Risk Reinsurance Exchange. This was a wonderful demonstration of the solidarity of the marine-insurance market. The combined surplus of these 150 companies exceeded $1,000,000,000. The Exchange commenced business on June 10, 1939; on September 1, 1939, World War II began. Throughout the dark days of the war years no shipowner or merchant lacked adequate protection for his normal and wartime hazards. Government and companies worked in harmony, and one of the great chapters in the winning of the war was written.

History Repeats. With the coming of peace and the slow restoration of overseas commerce, the many problems with respect to the risks to which cargoes were exposed recurred as after World War I. In addition, many unforeseen difficulties arose owing to delays in transit and lack of transportation. But the cutthroat competition that had followed World War I was not present, as no new companies had entered the field. The same group that had cared for the wartime hazards was working in harmony to solve the postwar problems.

Government Indifference. A new problem soon faced the marine underwriters. With the granting of huge loans to foreign countries and later with the establishment of the Economic Cooperation Administration (ECA), underwriters realized that the beneficent attitude of the government toward the marine-insurance business had changed. Underwriters asked only a fair chance to compete for business that had formerly been theirs under the conditions prevailing previous to the war. The policy pursued by government agencies had the effect, whether intended or not, of building up foreign marine-insurance markets.

New Factors. So the first half of the twentieth century came to an end. The United States is the commercial leader of the world. The marine underwriters, under many handicaps, are fulfilling their mission of making overseas commerce financially safe. Dark clouds of unrest are on the horizon; there are wars and rumors of war. New problems are arising out of the atomic age, not only war problems, but problems of peacetime commerce as the scientific discoveries constantly being made are adapted for use on overseas vessels. The underwriters are prepared to carry on and do their part to enable the United States to take its destined place of leadership in a troubled world. They are slowly creating a world marine-insurance market, just as in the first half of the century they created an adequate domestic market. Nationalistic insurance schemes of many foreign nations pose difficult problems, but marine insurance, now as always, can thrive only in a free international market. There is the long-range hope that the free markets of the past will again be restored and that American marine insurance will be able to compete on fair terms in the markets of the world.

CHAPTER 2

Physical Geography and Marine Insurance

Effect of Natural Conditions on Trade Routes. Marine insurance having been originated for the purpose of distributing losses caused by the physical forces of nature operating on and about the oceans, it is fitting for the student of the subject to acquire at the very outset some general knowledge of these elements. Man from the earliest days has battled with these forces, sometimes going down to defeat only to rise again to devise some new method of conquering them. If he could not overcome these adverse conditions of nature, he sought means to avoid them or to accommodate himself to their effects. The earliest trade routes were overland, following the paths of least resistance. Thus, if there were hills or lakes or forests intervening in the direct path of his journey, primitive man would avoid these obstacles by going round them. Man, however, differing from the beasts of the field in being a thinking animal, soon began to create rude devices for overcoming the obstacles in his commercial paths. A trail would be cut through the forest or a frail craft would be built to cross a lake or river, thus avoiding the necessity of encircling these barriers. His craft, however, encountering the winds, waves, and currents found on the lakes and rivers, soon showed its defects and a stronger vessel was built.

Water Routes. Since water routes offered the easiest means of communication between the settlements of primitive man, it is but natural that he should have discovered ways of navigating these highways. The overcoming of the simple physical forces operating on the inland waterways was a comparatively easy task, and the natural love of adventure, coupled with the desire for barter, in the course of time led man down to the larger seas and finally to the oceans, where he found the mighty forces of the deep aiding him in their periods of calm but, when unleashed, threatening him with destruction. Gradually he acquired knowledge of these physical barriers which hindered the unrestricted use of the waterways, but not having developed sufficiently to devise means of overcoming them, he was compelled to skirt along the shores of the continents, darting from headland to headland, seeking shelter in time of storm and laying to at night. Often, to avoid treacherous stretches of water, he would drag his small vessel overland or transship his cargo over a neck of land to calmer waters beyond.

Natural Law Discovered. The growth of commerce created the desire for easier and safer routes of travel, and men began to study the forces of the universe in order to control them. Certain individuals in advance of their generation began to discover that there was such a thing as law in nature and that these natural forces, untamed as they seemed to be, were but the effects of the sun and the moon and the stars. They discovered the rudiments of astronomy and by means of the stars were enabled not only to navigate at night but to navigate during the darkness away from the coast lines and over the broad expanses of inland seas such as the Mediterranean. It was also discovered that the earth instead of being flat was round, and there were mariners courageous enough to brave the terrors of the unknown oceans in an effort to prove that by sailing west the East Indies, the fabled land of the Middle Ages, could be reached.

Ocean Navigation. Once entering the mighty expanses of the oceans, the hardy mariners discovered that the physical forces which they had encountered on the inland seas were magnified many fold. In these great bodies of water, vast flowing streams were found, and over their surface were belts of wind and sections of calm. At times the physical forces would be unloosed, and the surface of the deep would become a raging maelstrom in which they would be all but engulfed. The faith of these pioneers being vindicated by the discovery of America and of the ocean routes to the East Indies, the overcoming or circumventing of these physical forces became increasingly necessary if man was to obtain the full use and enjoyment of his world. As he gradually gained knowledge by experience, the laws governing the action of these forces of nature were determined and their effects were discovered. When this knowledge was applied to navigation, types of vessels were developed able to resist the action of these forces. As the localities and times of greatest danger became known, they were avoided. Man went even further and adapted these forces to his own use and laid out his water routes over those portions of the oceans where he would be aided by the winds and the currents.

Aids to Navigation. With the development of commerce and the establishment of more stable political control, governments have lent their aid in charting the oceans, in establishing lighthouses on dangerous coasts, and in providing a weather service which warns mariners of impending storms. Scientific societies by many devices and by especially designed and equipped ships have added greatly to the store of knowledge of the ocean, and much has been done to aid in the safety and certainty of ocean navigation. The development of the radio has made possible the broadcasting of weather information, so that mariners are in a better position today than ever before to avoid storms. The use of radar and loran to locate the position of a vessel, when the usual methods are not available because of fog, has eliminated many of the former hazards of navigation. Radar scans the waters near the vessel to detect other vessels or other obstructions to safe navigation. Loran aids in fixing the position of the vessel by radio impulses from shore stations. Sonic depth finders do by electronics what the old-time "lead" did to determine the depth of water under the ship. And then there is the amazing ship-to-shore telephone which enables the master of a vessel so equipped to call port authorities to learn of fog or other conditions that might make navigation into the port extrahazardous. The knowledge now attained and the progress already made in ocean navigation encourage further research in an effort better to comprehend the workings of nature and to overcome or turn to the use of man the powerful forces which nature has let loose on the broad expanse of the ocean.

Effect of Oceans on Climate. That the task is a stupendous one may be appreciated if one considers the vastness of the oceans and the distances covered in the negotiation of the ordinary routes of commerce. Seventy-two per cent of the earth's surface is covered by water ranging in depth from a fraction of an inch to 6 miles and stretching from the equator to the poles. This enormous expanse of water, with its tides and currents, its winds and storms, not only separates the land masses but also determines to a large degree their climates and has influenced man's development to a very great extent. This may readily be seen by comparing land masses in the same latitudes. The British Isles bathed by the warm waters of the Gulf Stream are a veritable garden, while in the same latitude, Labrador, whose coasts are washed by the Arctic Current, is a frozen waste. Not only is climate affected, but the variation of temperature is controlled by the oceans, making life more enjoyable. In far inland sections very wide daily and annual ranges of temperature occur, while in the vicinity of the oceans the slowly heating and cooling water exercises a controlling influence on the temperature.

Ocean Distances. The distances over the routes of commerce between the various centers of human endeavor, following as they do the lines of least resistance, are very great. From Liverpool to New York is about 3,000 miles, while the distance from New York to the River Plate is 5,700 miles. From New York to Sydney, Australia, is 13,000 miles when the Cape route is used and 9,700 miles if the shorter Panama Canal course is followed. A steamer traveling from Seattle to Yokohama covers 4,250 miles, and another 1,725 miles is traversed if it continues on to Manila. Even the distances of inland waters are not often appreciated, the distance from Duluth, Minn., to the mouth of the St. Lawrence being about 1,675 miles, and from the head of navigation on the Mississippi to the Gulf of Mexico 2,150 miles. From New York to Iquitos, Peru, on the Amazon River, is 6,000 miles, and 2,400 miles must be covered in sailing from Seattle to Nome, Alaska.

The Physical Force of Nature. It is with the physical forces of nature that marine insurance is concerned. Were the waters always calm, were there no fogs or currents, there would be little need for insurance except against fire and man's own acts resulting in collisions and war perils. But with the possibility that nature may let loose her weapons at any time, some means of indemnity against the destruction caused by her forces is necessary. A description of these forces will give an indication of the problems with which a marine underwriter is confronted.

The Wind and Storms. First may be considered the wind. The atmosphere is ever in motion, and man has learned to use this movement for the propulsion of his craft. In the earliest times he devised a rude form of sail to aid the oarsman in the movement of his vessels, but soon wind power displaced man power. Atmospheric conditions, however, control the velocity of the wind, and when conditions are ripe, storms break forth under which the sturdiest ships may succumb or may be wrecked or driven on dangerous coasts through the effects of these storms. While there are storms that are sporadic, there are other storms that are periodic. These periodic storms occur most frequently in the tropics, those in the Atlantic Ocean being called *hurricanes* while those in the Pacific Ocean are called *typhoons* and in the Indian Ocean *monsoons.* There are belts of wind known as *trade winds* which blow constantly at a velocity of 10 to 30 miles an hour and are found between 28 degrees north and 28 degrees south of the equator. These winds blow from the northeast in the Northern Hemisphere and from the southeast in the Southern Hemisphere. North and south of the trade winds are other belts known as the *westerlies.* These winds in the Southern Hemisphere are fairly constant between latitude 40 and 50 degrees south, blowing from the southwest, and these latitudes are known to sailors as the "roaring forties."

Effect of Wind on Ocean Routes. The effect of winds on ocean trade routes is shown by the fact that a sailing vessel in going from New York to Sydney, Australia, sails southeast until the island of Tristan de Cunha is reached in latitude 37 degrees south and then, taking advantage of the short lines of latitude and of the power of the "brave west winds" in the "roaring forties," runs before the wind. If the destination is Bombay instead of Sydney, the vessel will turn north at about longitude 80 degrees east, taking advantage of the monsoons, the seasonal winds of the Indian Ocean. In the Northern Hemisphere the westerly winds are not constant and produce the exceedingly severe storms encountered on the North Atlantic. The causes of these winds are many, and these belts of wind move north and south with the changing seasons. In between these wind belts are areas of calm, the *doldrums,* which also move with the seasons, and it is in these sections of calm at the seasonal changes that the hurricanes and typhoons originate. These storms, which at times last for weeks, are of such severity that only the staunchest ships can outride them.

While the wind in the days of sailing vessels was the all-important factor in determining the routes of commerce, it is only to a slightly less extent considered today in laying out steamship courses. The amount of resistance offered to wind pressure by a gigantic steamship is great, and if this resistance can be avoided in the case of head winds or availed of in the event of following winds, fuel consumption will be reduced and an economic gain result, provided the distance between ports is not materially increased. Accordingly, in looking at a map upon which the steamship routes are impressed, the prevailing winds and the ocean currents will be found to have been considered. In the North Atlantic, for instance, will be seen summer and winter tracks for steamers plying between New York and Liverpool. These courses have been determined to some extent by the prevalence of ice at certain seasons but to a greater degree are the result of sailing-vessel experience in choosing the most accommodating routes. The voyage across the Atlantic from New York to the United Kingdom, owing to the prevailing westerly winds and to the current of the Gulf Stream, is a much safer trip than the return passage, where the resistance of both these forces is encountered. For this reason it was said by sailors in the days of the sailing vessel that it was "down hill to Europe." Much progress has been made in recent years in reporting weather probabilities. While this service is of especial value to airplanes, it does furnish invaluable information to mariners, enabling them to avoid many serious weather conditions.

Wave Force. One of the most powerful of the physical forces of nature is the wave. Caused principally by the wind and the tide, this movement of the surface water exerts a power that is beyond measurement. Upon this force to a considerable extent depends the location of harbors. Many otherwise commodious havens have been rendered useless by wave action, and others have been saved only by the building of breakwaters or other devices which curbed this natural force. It will also appear in the consideration of ships and shipbuilding that wave force is, and has been, one of prime consideration in the designing and construction of ships. Although the appearance of the wave from the shore or from the deck of a vessel indicates that a great body of water is rapidly approaching, this is not the case. Were the appearance a reality, ocean navigation would be almost impossible, as the wave would be a current against which a vessel could not sail. On the contrary, vessels ride the waves, the movement continuing under and beyond the vessel, causing some retardation of the vessel's progress but under ordinary conditions offering no serious hindrance to navigation. It is only when waves attain great size, speed, and height that they are a menace to navigation. Then, unless a vessel is skillfully navigated to meet the onrushing waves, serious results will ensue.

When it is considered that in severe storms waves attain a length of 1,000 feet, a height of 40 feet and move forward at the rate of 60 miles an hour, some idea of their power is obtained. Waves have been described as a "transference of form not of substance." This is an accurate description. Wave motion may be likened to a movement of a field of grain in the wind. There is an appearance of wave motion, the heads of grain seem to move across the field but in reality merely crowd together, bend down, and regain their upright position. So an examination of water movement shows that the particles of water move in orbits; each individual particle starts forward, rises, retreats, and falls, completing its orbit during the passage of a single wave.[1] The real menace in wave motion is when the movement is interrupted. When a wave strikes a ship and breaks over it, the weight of water falling on the vessel is measured in tons, and unless the decks are properly constructed quickly to throw off this burden of water, the vessel may sink. Many times a wave breaking against the ship will carry away its upperworks, admitting water into the holds and causing serious damage. Oil is often poured on the water when waves are becoming a menace to a vessel. The effect of oil is to smooth the surface of the water, thus presenting less resistance to the wind and preventing the breaking of the wave, which is the real danger in wave motion. The power of waves when their movement is arrested by harbor works or breakwaters is great beyond description. Waves with a pressure of 3 tons to the square foot have been measured. Their action sets up shore currents which are a menace

[1] Gregory, Keller, and Bishop, "Physical and Commercial Geography," p. 6.

to navigation. The havoc wrought by these storm waves may be seen on any shore. When it is considered that Galveston was destroyed by a 4-foot wave and that the water fronts of Mobile and other Gulf cities have been severely damaged many times by wave action caused by West Indian hurricanes, some conception will be gained of the enormous power of waves.

Seaquakes and Tidal Waves. Another form of wave that has done great damage to harbors and to shipping is that induced by *seaquakes.* When an earthquake occurs, the faulting of the earth may reach out under the ocean, the violent change in the ocean bed producing a difference of level in the water. A wave results which causes the water to regain its level. This wave striking the shore carries all before it, and many times ships have been carried inland so far that, with the receding of the water, it was impossible to restore them to their native element. These waves are usually called *tidal waves,* a term also used to describe the waves produced by the inrushing tide in confined bays. A combination of wind and high tide often produces a water level in a harbor greatly in excess of the normal, overflowing docks and causing heavy losses to marine underwriters.

Tides. The action of the sun and moon working in conjunction on the water masses of the earth produces *tides.* This effect may be noted even in the smaller bodies of water such as the Great Lakes of the American continent. It is with this mighty force of the ocean, however, that marine insurance is concerned. The ocean tide ebbs and flows twice in each 24-hour period. When it reaches the coasts, because of many peculiar conditions, its influence on navigation varies greatly from place to place due to coastal topography. On the broad expanses of the ocean its effect is slight, but when more shallow water is reached, or where the moving masses of water are forced into small bays or through channels, its power is tremendous. Whirlpools, eddies, rushing currents, and in some places high waves result which offer a serious menace to shipping and cause innumerable wrecks. Where the topography of the ocean bed produces bays connected by narrow straits, high tide may occur in one bay at the same time as low tide in the adjoining bay. In the effort to reestablish the water level the water rushes through the connecting channel, producing currents known as *eddies* or *races.* These currents have ever been the dread of navigators. In early history we read of the Maelstrom of the Lofoten Islands and of Scylla and Charybdis in the Straits of Messina which were the terror of the early mariners. Modern seamen still shun the races at Pentland Firth and the Straits of Magellan. Hell Gate, Long Island, taking its evil name from its no less evil reputation, has been made reasonably safe for navigation only by the removal at great cost of large masses of obstructing rock.[1]

Effect of Tides on Harbor Development. The tides serve many useful purposes. They are the scavengers of the harbors, twice each day drawing out the unwholesome water and sending back fresh supplies of ocean water. From the point of view of commerce, the effect of tide on harbor development is important. As will appear later on, some of the most prosperous harbors owe their existence to the tide, whereas other harbors, equally good in their virgin condition, because of lack of tidal flow never rise to positions of commercial greatness. In fact, so important are the tides to the usefulness of harbors that tidal almanacs are published giving navigators information to enable them to approach and enter harbors at the most favorable hour. The sailing and arrival of ocean vessels in most harbors are regulated by the ebb and flow of the tide, not only the depth of water but also the strength of the current produced being determining factors in the movement of vessels. In many harbors ships can enter or depart only at the crest of the tide, while navigation in other ports is possible only at slack water. Not alone is the direct effect of tides of moment to navigators but indirectly the tidal currents quickly produce banks and channels in certain places making the charting of such water impossible and necessitating the use of local pilots familiar with the vagaries of their particular locality.

Ocean Currents. While the ocean water is constantly in motion owing to the tide and the wind, certain well-defined streams move through the ocean following fairly definite courses. These streams of water are known as *ocean currents* and are interesting from the marine-insurance point of view more because of their action on climate, with its resultant productivity or sterility of life, than for any direct bearing that they have on the perils of the sea. These currents by moderating temperature enable men to produce goods

[1] *Ibid.*, p. 11.

thus increasing the subject matter of insurance. The British Isles owe their very existence as a habitable land to the influence of the Gulf Stream. Derelict vessels entering these streams follow their courses for months and years, proving a constant source of danger to navigation and probably accounting for the loss of many vessels posted as missing.

Calms. The absence of wind or atmospheric movement produces calms, and as already indicated, in certain parts of the ocean belts of calm are encountered. To the sailing vessel, this passive force is of the greatest importance. If a vessel unfortunately enters a belt of calm, she may be delayed for days and weeks before being able to extricate herself from its toils. Delay is not the only danger. Lack of propelling power may cause a vessel to run ashore because of the drifting induced by ocean currents. To the steamer, however, under ordinary circumstances, a period of calm offers no danger and causes no delay. With the introduction of auxiliary motive power into sailing vessels, calms have become of less importance as a marine-insurance problem.

Fog. Oftentimes fog, another passive force of nature, accompanies a period of calm. Fog, from the point of view of marine insurance, is one of the most important of natural phenomena. Fog, like other natural phenomena, is intermittent in most places but in some sections of the ocean is more or less constant. Fog is the condensation of moisture in the atmosphere at or near the surface of the ocean and, being caused primarily by the difference in temperature between the air and the water, will be found most prevalent where the climate is moist. Thus conditions tending to produce fog are found around the British Isles, where the atmosphere of the naturally cool latitude is tempered by the moist warm air caused by the Gulf Stream. Likewise, off the Newfoundland Banks in midsummer, the warmer air tempered by the effect of the Labrador Current produces much fog and makes navigation in these naturally treacherous waters doubly difficult. Again, off the west coast of South America the warm air below the equator, affected by the cool water from the Japan Current and the backing up of wind and moisture by the Andes Mountains, produces long periods of fog.

Ice. Ice is also one of the passive forces of nature that is a real menace to navigation. Its effect when held in place may be to stop navigation altogether by closing harbors and preventing access to interior ports through the rivers. The real danger, however, arises with the coming of milder weather and the breaking of the ice. Then its crushing force is given free play, and vessels are strained, causing leaks, or are sunk as the result of the piercing of their hulls. Icebergs present a more insidious form of the same peril, as they are often encountered far from the regions of ice in the well beaten paths of ocean commerce. These huge masses of ice, becoming detached by the spring thaws from the parent icefields of the Arctic, move slowly with the ocean current until they finally melt in the warmer water of the temperate zone. These ice masses, floating six-sevenths submerged and often found in sections where foggy conditions prevail, have caused many ocean disasters, notable among which stands the destruction of the S.S. *Titanic* in April, 1912.

Darkness. The farther north or south of the equator vessels sail in the fall or winter months, the greater the length of the period of darkness. Although darkness cannot be called a force of nature, it is so closely analogous to the physical forces under consideration and so important a factor in ocean navigation that reference to it cannot be omitted. In the early days of navigation it was customary for vessels to lay to in the darkness, and only after some elementary knowledge of astronomy was obtained did mariners venture to navigate at night. With the development of stable governments, lighthouses have been established on dangerous coasts as guides to mariners. Much has been done in this direction, but more remains to be done. In the Baltic Sea and its connecting gulfs, in the North Sea and around the coasts of the Scandinavian Peninsula where there is much trade, the factor of darkness from the viewpoint of marine underwriting assumes a prominent place in determining adequate premium rates. These waters at best afford dangerous navigation, but in the winter months when there are but few hours of daylight, the perils to mariners are greatly increased.

Harbors and Their Development. The question of harbors and harbor development is as important as the consideration of physical forces. In the selection of harbor sites, physical forces and the natural topography of the ocean bed are two of the determining factors. Winds, waves, and ocean currents are of nearly equal importance with shoals, reefs, and bars in deciding whether a particular site is suitable for harbor development. Another factor of vital importance is the relation of the proposed harbor site to the hinterland. If the back country is fertile and access to it physically easy, whether by natural water routes or by the building of railroads or highways, an otherwise unsuitable harbor site may be profitably improved by man. Such harbor development will, however, continue only as long as the artificial improvement is profitable. Thus it happens that several harbors on Long Island Sound which have access to the interior by rivers were prosperous ports as long as small vessels sufficed for water carriage. With the increase in the size of vessels, the cost of removing bars and keeping channels open was greater than the resultant gain, and many ports such as New Haven, New London, and Providence fell behind in the race for harbor prestige.

The topography of the ocean bed in many parts of the world is constantly, though gradually, changing. Shore lines are being elevated in some sections and depressed in others. The coast of Chile has risen from 20 to 30 feet in the last 200 years. Part of the Swedish Coast has risen 3 feet a century, while the Netherlands and our own New York and New Jersey coasts are gradually sinking.[1] When it is considered that in many harbors every foot of depth is vital to the shipping and to the prosperity of the port, the seriousness of this movement will be apparent.

Types of Harbors. Man naturally has followed the lines of least resistance in the selection of harbor sites, and those which he has selected fall into six general classes,[2] *viz:*

1. Drowned-valley harbors, as New York, Norfolk, Puget Sound, San Francisco
2. Barrier-beach harbors, as Galveston
3. River harbors, as New Orleans, London, and Portland, Ore.
4. Coral-reef harbors, as Hamilton, Bermuda, and Key West, Fla.
5. Crater harbors, as Aden
6. Artificial harbors as Port of Los Angeles (San Pedro), Calif., and Manchester, England

[1] *Ibid.*, p. 19.
[2] *Ibid.*, p. 23.

Drowned-valley Harbors. In many places harbors will present a combination of topographical features as in the case of New York, where there is a drowned valley through which a mighty river flows, offering easy access to the interior. Natural harbors such as those of the drowned-valley type are not retarded in their development because of unfortunate natural conditions. San Francisco will always be a leading harbor of our Pacific Coast, regardless of how many times the city may be shaken by earthquake shocks. Nature has here carved out a natural gate of entrance which will always be used even though there is the possibility of heavy toll from earthquake shock. San Francisco not only affords much safe harbor space, but access to the interior is rendered easy by the Sacramento River, which flows into San Francisco Bay. While sufficient depth is essential in a harbor safely to float the largest vessels that will use the port, too great depth may render a harbor less desirable, as vessels will be unable to find easy anchorage ground. This fault is sometimes found in the drowned-valley type of harbor as in the port of Seattle, where vessels moor to anchorage buoys.

Barrier-beach Harbors. The natural flow of shore currents in time produces barrier beaches which afford protection from the force of ocean waves and storms. In many sections these beaches are at the edge of a fertile hinterland, and where sufficient depth is found in the sheltered water between the barrier beach and the mainland, man has built harbors. An example of this harbor type is Galveston, where, at the end of a barrier beach close to an ocean inlet, a great and thriving port has been established. Fed by a back country exceedingly fertile, the development of Galveston has been worth while, and its commercial supremacy has justified the great expense incurred in the building of wharves and in the construction of harbor works and channels.

River Harbors. The river type of harbor is perhaps the earliest form, as before the days of railroads, when overland commerce was carried on by the slow and laborious process of human or animal carriage, the river offered easy access to the interior. Because vessels were of moderate draft, important cities were located at the head of river navigation, cities which now have given place to the larger ports at or near the river mouth. While as a rule the river harbors themselves have ample depth of water, the silt carried down by the river current produces barriers at the river mouth, which, in the case of the larger rivers, may assume the form of a delta. To keep clear the channel of the harbor site, various devices have been adopted. In the case of New Orleans, situated about 100 miles from the Gulf of Mexico, a system of jetties confining and directing the natural flow of the water enables the river itself to keep ship channels clear and deep by forcing the collecting sediment out into the water of the Gulf. In other river harbors artificial banks have been created to control the river. River harbors as a rule are not located on the deltas, since high water and increased currents often shift the course of the stream and may carry the river far away from the established harbor.

Coral-reef Harbors. Coral-reef harbors are comparatively few in number and are of little commercial importance. Located on coral islands they present several forms. The most common are the protecting reef type and the atoll, which afford a circular harbor to which entrance is obtained through a narrow passageway. Situated at places where there is no great back country, these harbors are of little importance, except where they have been developed into coaling or supply stations on the great highways of trade.

Crater Harbors. The crater type of harbor has but few examples and is of little importance commercially. Formed by the submerged crater of an old volcano, the prime requisites of easy access to a fertile hinterland are usually missing, and the port, unless used as a way station on a trade route, develops little commercial importance.

Artificial Harbors. Man has conquered nature not only in the improvement of natural harbors but also in the creation of artificial ports. Whether or not an artificial harbor is economically possible depends on the back country. If there is a prosperous interior containing fertile fields and large manufacturing centers, the need for an ocean outlet will arise, and man will convert an open roadstead into a sheltered harbor by building a breakwater or, by blasting out or dredging a shallow river channel, produce a river port. An example of the first method is seen at the port of Los Angeles (San Pedro), Calif., where the rapid development of Los Angeles and of Southern California created the demand for a convenient point of water contact with the rest of the world. The great shipping port of Houston,

Tex., where a bayou but a foot deep has been developed into a great ocean trade center, illustrates the second method. The expense of constructing these artificial harbors is necessarily great, and their permanence rather uncertain. Situated in naturally unfavorable locations, many artificial harbors, after the incurrence of great expense, have been rendered useless by the forces of wind and wave.

Open Roadsteads. Along many coasts there are no natural harbors, and the back country is not far enough developed to warrant the construction of artificial harbors. In these localities vessels anchor off shore in fair weather and discharge their cargoes into smaller craft which carry them to the shore. These open roadsteads offer no protection from storm, and in the event of storm or heavy weather vessels raise anchor and make for the open sea. The hazards in connection with such anchorages are very great, and with the growth of the shore city and the back country, breakwaters and moles are built, if the coast line and sea bottom will permit, and an artificial port arises.

Tidal Harbors. Many important harbors are so affected by the rise and fall of the tide that tidal basins are built, in which the water is impounded. Vessels enter and leave the basin on high water, and the gates are then shut until the next high tide. In other localities it is usual for vessels to take the ground at low tide, floating again on the next flood tide.

The growth of a country depends largely on its coast line. If there are natural harbors the back country will develop quickly, and the seaboard cities will become rich and prosperous. If, on the other hand, harbor sites are few, development will be retarded.

CHAPTER 3

Commercial Geography and Marine Insurance. Commercial Documents

The Processes of Trade. To the student of marine insurance, commercial geography is no less important than physical geography. While it is necessary for the marine underwriter and the insurance broker to know the physical conditions with which they are confronted, it is also essential that they have some clear idea of the reasons for trade and of its processes. It has been truly said that the successful man must know "everything of something and something of everything." This is especially true of marine underwriting and its kindred activities. Without a reasonable knowledge of banking, foreign exchange, and merchandising, a marine underwriter is not in a position clearly and logically to consider the risks which are offered to him. Some knowledge of the intrinsic qualities of the various commodities offered for insurance, of their mode of packing, of the conditions surrounding their shipment, and of the effect of the elements upon them are absolutely essential in order that intelligent consideration may be given to the question of insurance. It is also important that a very definite knowledge be had of the meaning of the various shipping documents and of their purpose in the completion of a commercial transaction.

Commerce Is the Exchange of Products. The desire of man to exchange products has created commercial activity. That, in truth, is what commerce is—an exchanging among men and nations of the products that they produce. In his original state, each individual provided for his own needs; he fed himself, he clothed himself, he housed himself. In time, groups of people perceived that each individual man had a particular gift and that by using this talent, not only for his own needs but for the needs of others in his group, he was able to produce a better article with less expenditure of effort. Individuals of a group therefore became specialists, providing certain necessary commodities for their own use and for the other members of their group, and thus the exchange of commodities among men originated. However, the specialization in any one group was restricted by the physical environment in which that group lived. Nature finally sets the bounds of man's development. Rubber cannot be grown commercially in the temperate zone, neither is wheat a successful crop in the tropics. The nature of man is determined to a large extent by climate. The heat and moisture of the tropics induce lethargy, while the cool, bracing atmosphere of the temperate zones energizes men and leads them into new and difficult lines of endeavor.

The Demand for Goods. As man has developed, he has acquired new tastes and new desires. Bound down by natural conditions, he soon learned that the cravings of his nature could be satisfied only by bringing from its natural environment the raw or the finished product which he desired. This necessitated the carriage of commodities, and subsequently commercial interchange developed. The law of supply and demand came into play, and commerce increased quickly as new and strange products were brought to the attention of an ever-increasing number of people. The early paths of commerce were overland or across sheltered water. The demand for the products of the East, which the Crusades had introduced, necessitated a new method of supplying the market. Quicker and safer routes of travel became essential. Two solutions of the problem were possible: first, the building of better vessels; second, the establishment of new trade routes.

The Opening of New Trade Routes. Both solutions were adopted. The golden age of discovery dawned when men and nations, after the decay of the Middle Ages, began to take on new life and to read nature's laws. New routes of trade were opened by hardy mariners who built ships staunch enough to withstand the ordinary action of the ocean forces. While civilization originated in the East, it has traveled westward, and its development shows a general westward and southward tendency. Colonization followed the opening of new trade routes. The theory of trade, until comparatively recent times, was not well understood. Barter was looked upon as a one-sided affair where the stronger or wiser trader reaped an advantage at the expense of his weaker or less skillful fellow. If the more powerful trader could not obtain what he wanted by peaceful means, he attempted to take it by force. Trade can be permanently successful only when each trader feels that in the exchange of commodities he has reaped a profit, whether it be measured in a symbol of exchange or in an added benefit acquired.

Primitive Barter. The earliest type of trade of which record exists is silent or dumb barter. Trade of this character arose from lack of trust between the bargainers. Herodotus describes it as practiced by the Carthaginians in their dealings with the African natives. Approaching a trading port, the Carthaginians would go ashore with their goods, build fires to attract the attention of the natives and then return to their ship. The natives would approach and inspect the proffered merchandise, place beside it native products which they considered sufficient payment, and retire. The traders would again go ashore, examine the native goods, and if in their opinion sufficient in quantity and value, take them back to their ship and depart. If not, they returned to their ship empty handed to await further overtures from the natives. This process was continued until the traders were satisfied with the native offer. It is difficult to explain why the natives did not steal the merchandise of the traders and make away with it. Doubtless these early traders had methods of inducing fear that spoke louder than words and made this method of exchange both practical and successful. The Carthaginians pursued these peaceful methods of trade only when forceful measures were not apt to succeed.

Types of Trade. In the development of trade two general types appear, the Mediterranean and the Oceanic. The former is represented by the early Mediterranean and Baltic Sea commerce; the latter by the oversea routes to the Orient. In marine insurance, by custom, a similar classification is made into coastwise and ocean trades. The Oceanic type is the outgrowth and development of that used in the Mediterranean, but each class of trade has exerted and still exerts its influence on commercial development. Indeed, the two types merge into each other and, with their overland connections, cover the earth with a network of routes over which the nations exchange their products.

The Use of Symbols and the Bill of Exchange. Methods of exchanging goods have improved with the passing of time. No longer do individuals, except in rural districts, exchange goods for goods. Early in the development of civilization it was found desirable to have symbols of value which were given in exchange for commodities. The Indian used wampum; other primitive peoples used salt, arrowheads, or gold dust. Later, money, gold or silver, or the baser metals came into use, and among the more civilized peoples barter fell into disuse. With the growth of trade, however, it was found that there was not enough of the precious metals to serve the needs of trade, and their transfer from one individual or one country to another was attended with great hazard. Accordingly, man sought and found a new method of payment by credits. The Jews in the twelfth century devised the bill of exchange or draft, which altered the whole method of conducting commerce and made possible the tremendous growth of international trade.

Marine Insurance Essential to Overseas Trade. At this point marine insurance fits into modern commercial life. That marine insurance in its present form originated about the same time as the bill of exchange seems logical. The bill of exchange when issued in connection with a shipment of goods, on the security of such goods, would become a mere unsecured debt in the event that the goods were lost or destroyed. Some additional guarantee was necessary in order to make the bill of exchange a safe substitute for money. This security was, and still is, provided by the policy of marine insurance. A knowledge of the method of financing commercial transactions therefore becomes an essential part of the education of the student of marine insurance.

Contract of Sale. Prior to the movement of goods in overseas trade much negotiation between buyer and seller takes place. Questions of kind, quality, quantity, packing, and, of course, price and method of financing and of shipment enter into these negotiations. Finally a contract of sale results, and the stage is set for the production and shipment of the goods. The invoice made by the seller at the time of shipment should set forth all the important particulars that have been incorporated in the contract of sale. This contract of sale may be a formal document, or it may be merely a file of correspondence exchanged between seller and buyer. The invoice becomes prima-facie evidence of the *terms of sale*.

COMMERCIAL DOCUMENTS

In the ordinary commercial transaction there are four documents which collectively are known as a *commercial set*. These documents represent and take the place of the goods themselves in the financing of the transaction and pass current in all the markets of the world. They are:

1. The invoice, which is the merchant's bill for the goods and sets forth the terms of sale
2. The bill of lading, which is the carrier's receipt for the goods
3. The insurance certificate or special policy, which is the document of guarantee
4. The draft or bill of exchange, which is the merchant's payment

An insight into each of these documents and its relation to the completion of a commercial venture is essential before any clear understanding may be had of international trade and finance.

The Invoice. First, there is the invoice or bill of goods. A merchant, in making a sale of goods, negotiates with the buyer as to price, discounts, and terms of sale. Having agreed one with the other, the contract of sale is made and the invoice sets forth in writing the terms and conditions of the transaction. The commodities sold are listed one by one, the quantity shown, and the price per unit indicated. Goods are marked and numbered, that is, each package is stamped with an identifying symbol, and, if there is more than one package with the same mark, consecutive numbers follow the marks on these packages. These marks and numbers appear on the invoice. In addition there may be charges for packing, cartage, and consular fees. Whether or not charges for insurance and freight will appear on the invoice depends on the terms of sale. Three general forms of sale are common in commercial transactions, *viz.*, cost (c), cost and freight (c & f), and cost, insurance, and freight (c.i.f.).

Cost Sales, F.O.B. and F.A.S. Cost sales require the seller to provide the goods packed and ready for shipment. The seller may agree to act as agent for the buyer in effecting insurance and in engaging freight space, but these duties are usually performed by a freight broker to whom the goods are delivered by the seller or subject to whose order the seller holds the goods. In any event, no charge appears on the invoice for freight or insurance. In other words, when the merchant ships the goods or delivers them to the buyer's agent, he is out of the transaction except with respect to the payment of the invoice. It sometimes happens that in a cost sale the amount of freight may appear on the invoice, but such entry is merely a notice of the amount of freight that is or will be due the vessel and is not included in the total amount of the bill. The contract of sale may require that the seller of the goods deliver the property at a certain place short of destination where the buyer will take title. In such event, notation is made on the invoice of such terms of sale as "f.o.b. cars Chicago" or "f.a.s. steamer at New York." The letters f.o.b. are a commercial abbreviation for "free on board." A merchant buying goods in various western cities may arrange for carload-lot shipments from Chicago and accordingly agree with each seller that the latter will deliver and be responsible for the property until delivered on board the cars at Chicago. On the other hand, a foreign buyer may wish to have no responsibility until the goods are at the shipside of the steamer that is to carry them to destination, and he accordingly requires the seller to deliver the goods free alongside steamer New York, the seller assuming all charges and risks from the original point of shipment until delivered at the side of the steamer ready for loading. Such terms of sale are indicated on the invoice as "f.a.s. steamer New York."

Cost and Freight Sales (C. & F.). A cost and freight sale (c. & f.) is one in which the seller bills the goods at a price that includes the cost of the goods, the incidental packing, and other charges and the cost of delivering the property at the ultimate destination. No responsibility is assumed for safe delivery at destination, the duty of providing insurance resting on the buyer. If the freight is payable at destination, the amount that will then be due is included in the invoice with the other charges, but this amount of freight is deducted at the foot, credit thus being given the buyer so that he may assume this charge when delivery is made. If the goods are not delivered in specie, the freight will not be due. It will be noted that under a cost and freight sale the seller assumes the responsibility of providing freight room for the goods, which may be difficult in times of shortage of tonnage. In modern practice freight is seldom, if ever, payable at destination. The carrier now requires that freight be prepaid or guaranteed.

Cost, Insurance, and Freight Sales (C.I.F.). Under a c.i.f. sale (cost, insurance, and freight) the seller agrees to furnish the kind of insurance customarily provided by a prudent merchant. He also agrees to set the goods down at the buyer's warehouse free of all charges. If the destination is in the interior, he may agree to assume the transportation and insurance charges only to the port of entry. Deduction may be made of the amount of freight if payable at destination, as in the cost and freight sale, and the buyer may assume responsibility for the payment of duties and other local charges accruing at destination. Whether or not these special charges will be assumed should either be clearly set forth in the contract of sale and noted in brief on the invoice or be so well established by custom and usage as not to require special mention. Custom and usage play an exceedingly important part in the conduct of commercial transactions, and in the absence of evidence to the contrary it will be presumed that a transaction is to be completed in accordance with the customs and usages in vogue with respect to similar transactions. Under c.i.f. terms the seller not only is obligated to provide freight space but must protect the goods by insurance, obtaining coverage in the usual form provided for the insurance of such goods with respect to particular average (partial loss), war risk, and geographical limits. If the seller has quoted a lump-sum price on the c.i.f. basis, he will be liable for fluctuations in the freight and insurance markets. Because of this, it is quite common when unusual conditions prevail, as in wartimes, merely to fix a price for the goods themselves in the contract of sale, to which would be added on the invoice the cost of insurance, freight, and other charges at the rates prevailing at the date of shipment.

Sales Contract Determines Relation of Buyer and Seller. The foregoing explanation of terms of sale (and there are many modifications of the three forms mentioned) will indicate the importance of the invoice in settling the relations of the parties to a commercial transaction. Its importance from the point of view of insurance will be evident when it is considered that in a cost and freight sale "f.a.s.

ship" or "f.o.b. ship" the seller provides insurance until the goods are alongside ship or until on board ship while the buyer must provide protection from that time on. In the event that loss occurs at the port of loading, the invoice will determine at whose risk the property was and upon which set of underwriters, those of the buyer or the seller, the burden of responding for the loss will fall. A consular invoice accompanying the shipping documents may be required in the shipment of goods between foreign nations. In such case, the seller, having made out his invoice, presents it to the consul of the country to which the goods are consigned or through which they may pass or to both. Each certifies that the invoice is proper and signs and attaches the seal of his office to the document. This visa by the consul indicates that the shipment has been made in proper form, that the price for customs purposes is fair, and that the rules and regulations respecting such shipments have been complied with. In any disturbed state of the world's commerce, this visa of the consul is of the greatest importance. When war conditions exist, various forms of export and import licenses may have to be obtained and other unusual requirements complied with before shipment may be made.

The Charter Party. Before proceeding to the consideration of the second document in the commercial set, the bill of lading, it will be necessary to gain some idea of an agreement which, in many cases, underlies the bill of lading. This is the charter party, a document embodying the terms of a contract for the hire of the whole or a part of a vessel. The charter party and the bill of lading, while both relating to the ship itself, may be differentiated by describing the charter party as a contract for the hire of the vessel as a carrying medium, whereas the bill of lading is a contract of transportation. Owners of vessels may be divided into three classes: first, those who have vessels specially designed and constructed for the carriage of their own property, such as the oil tank lines; second, companies organized for the transportation as common carriers of goods over certain definite routes and owning *liners*; third, individuals or companies who enter the ship business as owners but not with any definite employment for the vessels that they own. Their vessels are for hire and will enter any trade for which they are adapted as the commercial demand requires. These vessels are *tramps*, and the document setting forth the contract by which the vessel is rented is the *charter party.* Two general forms of charter party exist, but there are many modifications of these general forms. Under the first and more common form, the vessel owner hires his vessel to the charterer for a definite period or for a described voyage at a definite rate of compensation, the charterer to have the entire use of the vessel, but the owner to operate and be responsible for the conduct of it. Under the second general form of charter, the owner transfers his vessel as a bare ship, that is, without captain, crew, fuel, or provisions, to the charterer, upon whom falls the entire burden of the operation of the vessel and the entire responsibility for its preservation and safety. By a *bare-boat* charter the owner transfers to the charterer everything but the legal title to the vessel.

Forms of Charters. As a general rule, vessels are chartered for one of two purposes. The charterer may be engaged in a specific line of trade where vessel space in large quantities is needed, as in the shipment of bulk cargoes, such as grain or coal, or of baled or bagged goods, such as cotton, coffee, or sugar. For these cargoes the merchant could not rely on obtaining sufficient space on liners, and so, through vessel brokers who are in touch with the freight markets of the world, he will engage one or more entire ships on a basis of payment of so much a day, so much a voyage, or so much a unit of cargo carried. Such charters are made in various forms, each particular trade having a special form, some associations of merchants engaged in the same trade having standard forms for the chartering of vessels for their particular trade. The second general reason for chartering a vessel is the necessity of additional tonnage for a line operating vessels over definite routes. In many cases where a line charters a ship, especially if it is a long-time charter, the vessel will be taken over on the bare-boat form. During the world wars much of the chartering done by the governments was on the bare-boat form.

The Bill of Lading. If the vessel owner or the charterer "puts his vessel on the berth" to load cargo for whosoever may offer it for transportation, he must give a receipt for the goods that he accepts for carriage, setting forth in this document the rate of freight and the terms and conditions under which the property will be carried. This receipt is the bill of lading, which, in its many forms, is basically a document older by far than the marine-insurance policy and is said to have changed little in 2,000 years. It contains a mass of terms and conditions, usually printed in such small type as to make the reading of it a difficult operation. These clauses are the result of years of legal adjudication and have been added to from time to time, frequently in an effort to lessen the liability of the shipowner or charterer. The ordinary bill of lading is so worded as to relieve carriers from all obligations except those which the law insists that they retain. As decisions have been rendered holding carriers liable for this or that risk to which the goods may be subject, the carriers have, as far as law permitted, inserted new words adding such risks to the list of exceptions contained in the bill of lading. In most countries water carriers have been permitted by statute to be relieved of many of their common-law obligations, whereas land carriers as a rule still are held to a high degree of responsibility for property in their custody. The Carriage of Goods by Sea Acts, now in force in the leading maritime nations, regulate the obligations of carriers by sea.

Bill of Lading a Contract of Carriage. The bill of lading is the contract of carriage wherein the master of the vessel or the owner or agent not only receipts for the goods but also agrees to carry them to the port or place named and deliver them in the same condition unless prevented by one or more of the long list of excepted causes. In the bill of lading are noted the marks and numbers of the packages received, which are receipted for in "apparent" good order. If, however, any unusual condition of the package is observed, as moisture or breakage, a note is made of this to prevent claim being made on the vessel at destination for the improper condition of the package. The document also calls for delivery to some named individual or firm, or the goods may be consigned simply "to order, notify ...." The bill of lading thus takes on the character of a quasi-negotiable instrument and by endorsement passes title to the property that it represents. This negotiability is necessary if the commercial set is to serve its purpose in trade.

Liability of Carrier Determined by Bill of Lading. The bill of lading serves a further purpose in that it determines the respective responsibilities of the carrier, the shipper, and the consignee, enabling the owner of the goods to arrange insurance against the risks excepted in the bill of lading, in so far as underwriters will assume liability. In early forms of "ladings" carriers assumed responsibility for practically everything except losses caused by acts of God, the King's enemies, and perils of the sea. Underwriters generally accepted these risks so that the owner of the goods could fully protect himself against all liabilities other than the minor damages excepted in insurance policies. With the adding of exceptions in the bill of lading, and with the general willingness of underwriters to assume responsibility for most of the excepted risks, it is usually possible at the present time for a merchant to relieve himself of most of the risks to which the goods may be subject during transportation.

Uniform Bill of Lading. For years past an endeavor has been made to draw up a uniform bill of lading that would be acceptable to all commercial interests in all maritime countries. Many conferences have been held without definite result. In 1921 a conference was held at The Hague at which representatives of the leading maritime nations drew up and recommended to their respective governments for acceptance a set of rules for the carriage of goods by sea which took the name of the "Hague Rules." These rules were considered by commercial bodies in the various countries, and recommendations were made for their clarification and improvement. A further international conference was held at Brussels in 1922, at which these suggested changes were considered and a few of them adopted. The revised rules were then recommended back to the participating governments for adoption. Great Britain, taking the lead, diplomatically accepted the rules and later passed the Carriage of Goods by Sea Act to provide for their enforcement. Other nations have accepted the rules, including the United States in 1936. Although the Hague Rules are not perfect, they are a very great improvement over any international agreement heretofore offered and indicate a marked advance in the progress toward a uniform bill of lading placing a proper measure of responsibility on the carriers.

Letters of Indemnity. It has been mentioned that, in issuing bills of lading, notation is made of any defect in package or any apparent fault in the condition of the shipment. A bill of lading with such a notation is not "clean" and ordinarily will not meet the conditions required in a letter of credit used to finance overseas shipments. To overcome this difficulty, shippers sometimes resort to the vicious practice of issuing to carriers letters of indemnity holding the carriers harmless for issuing clean bills of lading against shipments received by them in bad order. The clean bill of lading is attached to the commercial set and forwarded. On arrival of the goods at destination, their imperfect condition is noticed, and notation thereof is made on the receipt. When effort is made to recover against the carrier for damages incurred in transit, the letter of indemnity is produced showing that the goods were actually received by the carrier in bad order and holding him harmless from claim. Such letters of indemnity, when not disclosed in advance to the underwriter, are tantamount to fraud and in any event are against public policy.

The Manifest. The manifest is a ship's document giving in brief a list and description of all the property for which the vessel has issued bills of lading, showing shippers' or consignees' names or initials, marks, and numbers and other descriptive information. This document is of great value in determining whether packages of goods are on board a vessel when the bill of lading is not available. Bills of lading are usually issued in triplicate, and several nonnegotiable copies may be issued if required. Additional copies of the manifest are also made so that, in the event of disaster, particulars of the vessel's cargo may be quickly obtained. A copy of the manifest is also lodged in the customhouse, and another copy is on board the vessel to present to the custom or port authorities at the port of destination.

The Marine-insurance Policy or Certificate. The marine-insurance policy is the document that makes possible commercial transactions on a basis of credit rather than by the actual exchange of goods or money. Marine insurance may be arranged specially for each individual transaction, but it is more usual for merchants to negotiate in advance with underwriters for a contract which will protect all their shipments made within a specified time or over definitely described commercial routes. This contract is an *open policy,* and the assured is usually given the privilege of issuing under such a policy, on specially prepared forms embodying the salient conditions of the policy, *certificates* or *special policies* of insurance. These special documents certify that there have been insured with the named insurance company in the name of the assured certain packages of goods marked and numbered as indicated in the margin, for a specified amount of money, by named or described conveyances from the point of shipment to the point of destination, against the perils enumerated therein or in the parent policy to which reference is made. The important point in the present connection is that the document goes on to state that loss, if any, is payable to X.Y.Z. or order at a named place and, if a certificate or special policy is payable abroad, at a fixed or determinable rate of exchange. This document, like the bill of lading, is a quasi-negotiable instrument and passes the insurance to the holder to whom by the endorsement it has been transferred in good faith. The holder of the document, however, takes it subject to any obligations of the original assured to the underwriter and to any defenses of the underwriter against the original assured or against the holder of the document rising out of that particular transaction. These documents of insurance provide for payment of loss in all parts of the commercial world and, when issued by responsible underwriters, are accepted at their face value in all the banking centers of the world.

Special Policies of Insurance. For many years, certificates of insurance were accepted as satisfactory evidence of insurance and as sufficient compliance with the requirement of the sales contract or letter of credit that insurance be provided by the seller. During the postwar deflation period, following the end of World War I, when every possible loophole was availed of to avoid contracts, an English merchant refused to accept a shipment, claiming that the requirements for insurance were not satisfied by the certificate of insurance, in that this document was not complete in itself but referred to another document, the open policy of insurance, which contained other terms and conditions governing the insurance. The English courts, both of original instance and of appeal, accepted this view and declared the contract void. Special policies of insurance were thereupon demanded by many shippers. A new form of document, a special policy[1] issued in the same manner as a certificate of insurance but embodying the full terms and conditions of the open policy and making no reference to that policy except by number, was devised and is now in general use, thus fully meeting the technical requirements of British law. The certificate of insurance is seldom used today.

The Symbols of Ownership. The merchant who has made a shipment of goods has at this point three documents: first, an invoice

[1] See Appendix D.

showing the purchase price of the goods sold; second, a bill of lading indicating that the goods described in the invoice have been shipped and are in the possession of a common carrier on their way to the buyer; third, an insurance policy certifying that these goods are insured as specified against the perils of transportation. He thus has parted with his property and has in its place certain documents that will entitle him or the legal holder thereof to the property at destination or, in the event of its damage or loss, to recompense by insurance. This, however, from the merchant's point of view, is but one of many transactions of a similar nature in which he is involved, and he is primarily interested in receiving payment for the goods sold and closing out the transaction.

The Draft or Bill of Exchange. When making a contract of sale, arrangements are made between buyer and seller regarding the method and terms of payment. In overseas trade this is usually arranged by draft payable on sight or a definite number of days, 30, 60, or 90 as the case may be, after sight or presentation of the draft, accompanied by invoice, bill of lading, and insurance documents. The seller of the goods has banking connections who have agreed to pay his drafts or to accept them for collection. The merchant accordingly having made his invoice and obtained the bill of lading and insurance documents, draws on the purchaser in the following form:

FIRST

No. 1128

£2000. Abilene, Tex. Feb. 15, 1951

Thirty days after sight of this First of Exchange (Second Unpaid) Pay to the order of COX & Co. Two Thousand Pounds Sterling, value received and charge same to account of

(100 Bales Cotton T S R).

Cox & Co.

To—JAMES TURNBULL & Co.
Liverpool, England.[1]

[1] During World War II and since, Great Britain has controlled the purchase of raw cotton, and manufacturers buy their cotton from the government agency. It is hoped that the normal system outlined above will be reestablished when the dollar problems are solved. Now it is also quite usual, because of fluctuating currency values, to insist that drafts and payments be made in United States dollars.

Endorsing the draft in blank and attaching it to the other three documents, the bill of lading and special policy also having been endorsed in blank, the merchant presents the commercial set to his bankers, who put the draft in process of collection and set up as a credit to the seller the whole or a part of the amount of the draft. The merchant is now in funds and is practically out of the transaction.

Method of Collection of Draft. The process of collection of this draft, which we will assume represents reimbursement for a shipment of 100 bales of cotton marked T S R by Cox & Co., Abilene, Tex., to James Turnbull & Co., Liverpool, England, will serve to illustrate how an overseas shipment is made and financed and the important part marine insurance plays in these transactions. The Farmers & Merchants Bank at Fort Worth, with which Cox & Co. do their banking and which has accepted the draft for the 100 bales of cotton, is a country bank and does its banking with a larger bank at New Orleans to which it passes on this commercial paper, receiving credit for the amount advanced. The New Orleans bank is a correspondent of a New York bank to which it sends this commercial paper for collection and receives credit therefor at the New York bank. In Liverpool the New York bank has a correspondent to which it sends the documents, and this bank sends its representative to James Turnbull & Co. with the documents. They carefully examine them to see that the shipment against which the draft is drawn corresponds to the contract of sale into which they have entered with Cox & Co., and if it does, they write across the face of the draft,

Accepted Mar. 15, 1951.
Payable at Security Bank.

and sign their name. The documents which are the symbols of the goods are retained by the bank that presented the draft for acceptance. Assuming that the bill is payable 30 days after sight, this means that 30 days from Mar. 15, 1951, or on Apr. 17, 1951, 3 days of grace usually being granted, the holding bank will present the draft at the Security Bank for payment, and James Turnbull & Co.'s account will be charged with the amount, and the bill of lading, special policy, and invoice will be delivered to them. If James Turnbull & Co. so desire, they may discount the bill when presented for acceptance or at any time prior to the due date. If the 100 bales of cotton arrive prior to the due date, James Turnbull & Co. will probably wish to discount the bill in order to obtain the documents and so obtain delivery of the goods upon the surrender of the bill of lading. The draft having been paid by James Turnbull & Co., the transaction is completed, and the credits, set up in the various banks through which the documents have passed, are confirmed. If James Turnbull & Co.'s credit is high, the shipping documents may be surrendered to them when they accept the draft.

Trading in Bills of Exchange. It may be that Cox & Co., instead of depositing their documents with their local bankers at Abilene, will send them on to New York City to a bill broker. These bill brokers deal in commercial paper, just as stock brokers deal in stocks and bonds. If Cox & Co.'s financial and moral reputation is high, the bill broker will buy their commercial paper at the prevailing rate for exchange on London, and they will receive credit in full for the amount of the draft and will be absolutely out of the transaction, except under their liability as the drawer and/or endorser of the bill in the event of its nonacceptance by the drawee. The bill broker in turn sells this exchange to a bank which sends the draft on to Liverpool for collection, where the process of acceptance and payment is conducted as outlined above. Bankers, in buying commercial paper, carefully examine the documents, paying especial attention to the special policy to see that it is in proper form and that the company or underwriter with whom the insurance is placed is one whose security can safely be accepted.

Letters of Credit. The foregoing description of the use of the commercial set is merely an outline and does not attempt to go into the details of these transactions. A similar process is involved when shipments are made under letters of credit. In such cases the buyer purchases a letter of credit from his bank, by virtue of which there is established in some foreign banking center a fund to the credit of the buyer, against which he may authorize the seller to draw drafts for goods purchased by the buyer. The seller draws the draft, attaches the invoice and bill of lading thereto, and presents it to the firm or bank in whose favor the letter of credit is issued. They accept and pay the draft, charging the amount so paid against the letter of credit. In such cases, it is usual for the buyer to have an open policy of insurance payable to the bank issuing the letter of credit, which covers all shipments made under such credit, so that no insurance document is attached to the commercial set. The invoice, however, indicates that the terms of sale provide for buyer's insurance and that the sale is one made on cost or cost-and-freight terms already described.

The Balance of Trade. These transactions in their various forms establish the basis of international trade and credit. Countless in number, it will readily be seen that there are always in the banking centers of the world large amounts of commercial paper, drawn on foreign merchants, which eventually must be paid. The large banks in the great commercial centers of the world run debit-and-credit accounts with one another, a New York bank crediting itself with commercial paper that it sends to its London correspondent for collection and debiting itself with paper drawn on American firms sent to it by its London correspondent for collection. This process of debiting and crediting continues on each side until the balance of trade becomes so much in favor of one country that all bankers in that country do not hold sufficient credits to offset the debits against the bankers in another country. To reestablish the financial equilibrium the debtor nation must ship gold to the creditor nation and so again restore the balance of trade. Here again marine insurance is called upon, for without insurance the gold would not be shipped.

Goods the Basis for Exchange. It must not be supposed from this general description of the process of financing overseas shipments that all drafts are accompanied by shipping documents. But underlying the major portion of bills of exchange there is the buying and selling of goods, and because of the existence of the goods and of the negotiable documents which represent the goods, the transference of credits by the bill of exchange or draft is possible. Banking, transportation, and insurance are a trinity so closely interwoven that one cannot fully function if dissociated from the other two.

Temporary Problems. Some of the procedures described in the foregoing paragraphs are temporarily suspended. As a result of the monetary difficulties and the reconstruction problems resulting from

World War II, many of the normal trade processes have been interfered with. Trading is not free but is conducted in many parts of the world under government permits and licenses and controls of various kinds. At the root of the problem is the inability of countries to settle their trade balances with other countries. Until this balance can be restored, it will not be possible to resume the normal flow of international commerce.

CHAPTER 4

Ships and Shipbuilding

A Vessel the Basis of All Marine Insurance. Every marine-insurance transaction involves some type of vessel. Whether the insurance be on hull, freight, or cargo, a vessel is the basis of the insurance, and whether the risk is a good one or a bad one from the underwriting point of view depends largely on the character and condition of the vessel. Marine insurance is general in its application. From the slow man-propelled canoe of the Indian on the upper reaches of the Amazon River up through all the intermediate stages to the colossal ocean greyhound driven through the waves at a tremendous rate of speed by the propelling power of the latest type of turbine or diesel engine, marine insurance plays its part in assuming the hazards of navigation and in distributing losses over the whole consuming public. It therefore becomes essential, before attempting any general discussion of the principles of marine insurance, to obtain some general idea of vessels, their types, their structural qualities with respect to the natural forces with which they must contend, and their suitability as carriers of the many and varied commodities with which transportation has to deal.

Mediums Used in Construction of Vessels. Perhaps the best avenue of approach to this subject is to consider first the mediums which are used in the construction of vessels. These are in general three in number, *i.e.*, (1) wood, (2) wood and metal for composite vessels, and (3) metal.[1] Vessels may also be considered from the point of view of their propelling power: first, the man-propelled vessel, now fast disappearing except among the most primitive tribes; second, vessels propelled by the wind; third, vessels whose motive power is purely mechanical; fourth, vessels propelled by a combination of wind and

[1] Reinforced concrete was used in the construction of a few vessels during the two world wars; it proved unsatisfactory.

mechanical power which are known as auxiliary vessels; and fifth, vessels without motive power, such as harbor barges.

Modern Construction. Relatively few vessels, except small ships for special trades, are constructed of wood, and except for special harbor, short voyage, or fishing services, few sailing vessels are built. Even in the fishing trade the trend is toward diesel-propelled steel vessels. The first vessels, however, were built of wood and were propelled by sail power. Marine insurance developed in a world of wooden sailing ships, and in order to appreciate the marine-insurance problems consideration must be given to this fast-disappearing class of vessels.

Wooden Ships. Difficulties in Construction. Wood was the original material from which large sailing vessels were built. This type of ship may, roughly, be divided into two classes, the square-rigged and the schooner, or fore-and-aft-rigged, types. Among the square-rigged vessels are found barks, barkentines, brigs, and full-rigged ships, each named for its special arrangement of masts and sails and each possessing its peculiar advantages in connection with certain routes of trade. The square-rigged vessel, to a considerable degree, gave way to the simpler form of fore-and-aft-rigged schooner. In this latter type the sails are less difficult to manipulate. Mechanical power was sometimes used in raising and lowering the sails of the schooner-rigged vessels, thus materially reducing the cost of operation. The schooner type may again be subdivided into classes according to the number of masts with which the vessel is equipped, the rigging of the vessel being determined to a large extent by the trade for which it is designed. In connection with the construction of wooden vessels, whether for sail or steam power, it should be borne in mind that beyond a certain length, say 200 feet, the parts of a vessel become increasingly difficult to fasten together so that it will be able to withstand the severe strains to which it will be subjected when exposed to ocean storms. Furthermore, the increase in the number of masts, with the consequent added sail area, or the installation of propelling machinery subjects the vessel to unusual stresses. These stresses so strained vessels in many cases that seams opened up, permitting water to enter and damage cargo and frequently causing the whole hull structure to be thrown out of alignment. This was particularly likely to be the case when vessels constructed for a certain trade were transferred to more difficult routes for which they were not designed.

The Fastenings of Wooden Vessels. Not the least of the problems the wooden shipbuilder has to meet is that of fastening the various component parts of the vessel into one harmonious whole. This problem becomes more difficult as the length of the vessel is increased and the sail or engine equipment enlarged. The amount of wind pressure exerted against the sails of a five- or six-masted vessel is enormous in moderate weather, and when atmospheric conditions produce storms, unless such vessels have sufficient metal and wooden fastenings (treenails), something will give under the strain with consequent loss of life and property. Not a few of the wooden vessels launched during World War I were returned, after their first trip, to the shipyards for the insertion of additional material and the refastening of the whole structure.

Composite Ships. During the decline of the wooden vessel in the second half of the nineteenth century and before the metal ship had come into its own, composite ships were produced, built partly of wood and partly of metal. In these vessels the usual construction called for a metal framework and deck beams with wooden sheathing and decks. Vessels of this type of construction are no longer built. A very few of the old composite ships are still operated on the Great Lakes, and here and there vessels of this type can still be found in active service. The vessel of wood construction and the vessel depending for its motive power on the wind have practically disappeared from ocean routes. The competition of the metal vessel and of the mechanically operated craft has driven the wooden steamer and the wooden sailing vessel off these routes. With their passing much of the glamour of the sea has departed.

Steel Vessels. Steel has taken the leading place among shipbuilding materials. When metal ships were first introduced, iron was used almost exclusively. With the development of the iron industry and the production of new forms of the metal it was found that steel lent itself more readily to the construction of the hull and contained qualities which offered better resistance and accommodation to the various stresses and strains to which the structure was subjected when the vessel was in operation. Iron, however, offers more resistance to the corrosive action of sea water, and a few of the old iron vessels built more than a half century ago are still in service, their hulls tight and sound after their long and arduous careers. Great Britain was the pioneer nation in the development of the steel vessel, and to this fact her leadership in the overseas carrying trade may, in no small measure, be attributed.

Modern Steel. Much research work has been done in recent years in producing formulas for better steel for use in shipbuilding. The steel used in the modern ship has qualities unknown a few years ago. Not only in the structure of the vessel are benefits gained, but in the working parts—rudder and tail shaft, for example—better material is being used. By the use of X-ray technique castings are tested for latent defects. Less and less inflammable material is being used in the interior fittings of vessels. Both from a seaworthy point of view and with respect to fire safety standards, modern vessels, particularly those built to comply with the stringent standards set forth in United States laws, provide the safest marine transportation ever known.

Welding. Formerly steel vessels were constructed by joining the steel plating together by rivets. As the use of electricity developed, it was found that metal could be joined to metal by welding, using a fusible metal binder. This process in time was applied in the building of small craft. By 1940, when the great war shipbuilding program was commencing in the United States, the technique of building large vessels by the welding process had been perfected. Welding was the established practice in the building of the wartime fleet. As usually happens when speed is the controlling factor in construction, difficulties arose. Proved practices were not always followed, and stresses, due to the high heat necessary in the welding operation, unwittingly were built into the ship structure. Later, owing to these stresses, a number of these ships developed fractures of sides and deck, and one or two ships broke in two. The remedies for these defects were found, and later ships were built that were free of welding defects. A combination of welding and riveting has in general been found more satisfactory than completely welding the structure.

The Marine Engine. The construction of metal vessels naturally led to the development of the marine engine. Steamers have been in operation for a century, the side or stern paddlewheel type of propulsion first being used. This system of propulsion was not well adapted to the severe storms encountered on the oceans, and the screw propeller came into use. Since the adoption of this latter method of applying the power generated by the engines, the development of the steamer has been one of form rather than of method. How great this progress has been will appear from a comparison of the first Cunard liner with the modern ocean greyhound. In the field of ship propulsion rapid advances have been made in recent years. High-temperature and high-pressure steam has greatly increased the power developed. This has resulted in a considerable saving of space, since fewer boilers are necessary to produce the same amount of power. New engine designs have greatly increased the available speed and at the same time are more economical in fuel consumption. Thought is being given to the use of turbogas engines, and the use of atomic power is possible in the not-too-distant future.

Liners and Cargo Vessels. Various types of construction have been devised to meet the needs of the varying conditions found in the different commercial trades, but in a very general way steel steam vessels may be grouped under two heads: the passenger liner and the cargo steamer. The liner is designed primarily for speed; the cargo vessel for utility. The modern leviathan would be a commercial failure were the traveling public not willing to pay large amounts of passage money for the extra speed, comfort, and luxury that these steamers afford. So much room is occupied by passenger, engine, and bunker accommodation that little cargo space remains. In the modern cargo steamer, on the other hand, cargo space is the primary object, and speed usually is a secondary consideration. In the building of the cargo steamer, the endeavor is to produce as large a vessel as is practicable, considering the routes of trade for which it is designed, the size of the harbors which will be used, and the possibility of obtaining cargoes sufficiently large to occupy the cargo space provided. It is considerably cheaper to build one large steamer than to build four small ones of equal aggregate carrying capacity. It is also much cheaper from the point of view of both fuel and crew to operate the large vessel than it would be to operate the four small ones. However, if the large vessel cannot obtain full cargoes or if her size restricts her use to a few harbors or to a few trades that are relatively unprofitable, she will be a commercial failure. Every additional ton of weight in the structure of the vessel itself reduces by 1 ton the weight of the cargo to be carried. Hence, the principal consideration in the building of the cargo steamer is the reduction of the vessel weight to the point where all the requirements of safety have been met but where all unnecessary parts have been eliminated. The endeavor is also made so to design the shape of the vessel that the maximum of cargo space is provided with the minimum retardation of speed.

Longitudinal Framing. One great advance in this direction was the invention of a practical system of longitudinal framing. This system, known as the *Isherwood system* after the name of the inventor, reduces the weight of the material in the ship itself without any loss of strength and at the same time increases the cargo space. Under the older system of transverse framing, the frames were placed so close together that it was impossible to stow the ordinary cargo between them. In the longitudinal system, the transverse framing is replaced by great transverse bands which undergird the body of the vessel, placed at intervals of 12 to 20 feet. In them are notches in which are set longitudinal frames to which the steel plating is riveted. Between these frames cargo can be placed against the side of the ship or against the cargo battens, thus greatly increasing the capacity for a light cargo such as cotton. For heavy, dense cargoes the capacity is also increased, since the weight of the vessel itself is reduced. This system of construction has lent itself successfully to all types of shipbuilding, both sail and steam, and is also used in the building of bulk carriers and in the construction of passenger vessels. Certain modifications of the original system of longitudinal framing have been introduced in recent years, reducing further the material used in constructing this type of vessel.

Bulk Carriers. The carrying of bulk cargoes presents various difficulties, and special types of vessels have been devised to meet the peculiar conditions created by the overseas trade in such commodities. The tendency of grain and coal cargoes to shift and to render a steamer unstable has led to the production of *self-trimming* steamers. The carrying of petroleum in bulk has produced problems which are successfully met in the modern tank steamer. On the other hand, the use of crude oil as a fuel presents special problems, especially from the underwriting point of view. Fuel oil is ordinarily carried in the ballast tanks or the double bottom of a steamer. If the vessel grounds and injures her bottom so that repairs must be made, the fuel oil is necessarily drawn out. Before mechanics can safely enter the tanks, they must be thoroughly cleansed and a chemical test made for poisonous gas. This process is one entailing considerable expense and adds materially to the cost of bottom-damage repairs.

Special Designs. Experiments are made from time to time in building steamers to meet special needs. During World War I a self-trimming ship, equipped with small unloading elevators, made its appearance. This entirely new type of vessel was designed to afford speed in the unloading of bulk cargoes of grain, ore, or coal. The ship was self-trimming in design, and at the bottom of the ship in long chambers running the length of the vessel was laid a miniature railway on which small cars ran. These were loaded through chutes at the bottom of the holds and were drawn to the elevator wells. They were then lifted up above the deck, and their contents dumped through discharge pipes into receiving barges or on the discharging dock. This type of vessel was designed by the Italians, and the first vessel produced, the steamer *Milazzo*, had a short but eventful career. Loaded with a general cargo, the vessel took fire in her cotton cargo, the fire spreading to barrels of oil in the bottom of the hold. The burning oil, floating on the water which was poured into the hold to extinguish the fire, found its way along the railway trunk to the openings into adjoining holds, thus communicating the fire to the rest of the ship. The fire was extinguished, but not until great damage was done, and after temporary repairs at the Azores, the ship reached her Italian port of destination where permanent repairs were made. But ill luck pursued her, for soon after reentering commercial service she was sunk by a submarine. The case of the *Milazzo* is especially interesting from the point of view of marine insurance in that it indicates how new types of vessels produce new problems and create unsuspected hazards for the underwriter. Another experiment which has met with considerable success is the *sea train,* especially designed and constructed to carry loaded railroad cars from one rail terminal to another. Loading cranes at loading and discharge ports lift the cars, which are loaded on several decks on railroad tracks.

Lake Vessels. The lake type of vessel is worthy of notice, since a considerable portion of American marine premiums is derived from the insurance of these vessels and their cargoes. Built for quick loading and discharging, with many large hatches and with engines located in the after end of the vessel, a distinctive type of steamer has been developed. Operated in fresh water, these steamers are furnished in most cases with fresh-water engine equipment. They are of comparatively light construction, since they do not encounter, except on rare occasions, storms of the severity of those experienced on the oceans. These vessels are admirably adapted for their particular service but are not suitable for ocean trade. Only by rebuilding and refitting can the lake type of steamer be made fit for ocean trade, and even then it is suitable for only the least hazardous coastwise service. The distinction should be observed, however, between steamers built for lake service and lake-built steamers for ocean service. Many of the Great Lakes shipbuilding yards have built steamers suitable for ocean operation.

River and Harbor Craft. The various types of river and harbor craft are worthy of notice and study. Each serves a particular purpose and produces its own peculiar problems. The opening of the new and enlarged Erie Canal in 1918 led to the endeavor to design a type of vessel suitable for navigating the Great Lakes, the Erie Canal, and the coastwise waters of the Atlantic Ocean. Several such vessels were constructed, but they have not been too successful in meeting the varying conditions found on these three waterways. These vessels must be so built as to suit the limitations of the most restricted waterway, the Canal, and accordingly are not proper models for lake and ocean service.

Types of Marine Engines. The motive power of vessels must also be studied by those who would be proficient in marine insurance. The reciprocating engine was superseded by the turbine type. The internal-combustion engine opened up an entirely new field of power design. Internal-combustion engines are used in the largest vessels, with a resultant saving in cargo space and economy in operation, which are two factors of the first importance in profitable ship owning. Electric-drive engines are also used to some extent. In this type, the power developed from the fuel is not applied directly to the turning of the propeller shaft. Instead it is used to produce electricity which, in turn, is used to turn the propeller.

Why Does a Vessel Float? It is also important that at least a theoretical knowledge be acquired, particularly by the underwriter, of the natural laws that make it possible for a vessel built of a material heavier than water and loaded with a full cargo to float. Whether or not a ship when ready for sea is seaworthy depends not a little on her loading and stability. How much cargo a vessel can safely carry and how that cargo must be loaded in order to produce a stable ship are questions that involve many difficulties and can be satisfactorily answered only by those who are expert in such matters. But underwriters and shippers may obtain some idea of the underlying principles of these subjects, sufficient at least to enable them to ask intelligent questions of experts.

Displacement. Displacement is the name given to the weight of the ship when empty or of the ship, its stores, and cargo when the vessel is fully loaded. It is measured by determining the weight of the mass of water displaced by the floating vessel, measured in cubic feet or in tons. A cubic foot of salt water weighs 64 pounds; thus 35 cubic feet exactly equal 1 long ton of 2,240 pounds. It can be practically demonstrated that a tin watertight box 1 foot long, 1 foot wide, and 1 foot high, measuring exactly 1 cubic foot and weighing 1 pound, will float on the water. If, however, 62 pounds of weight are put in the box, it will almost submerge. If 1 pound more is added, making a total weight of 64 pounds, the box will submerge. The slightest additional weight will cause the box to sink. The amount of water displaced by this submerged box is 1 cubic foot, and as its total weight is 64 pounds, it is fairly demonstrated that the displaced water also weighs 64 pounds. The same fact could be proved by actually weighing 1 cubic foot of sea water. This being so, if the exact quantity of the water displaced by the ship could be measured in cubic feet and divided by 35, the weight of the ship in long tons would be obtained. The formula for obtaining this weight or the displacement in long tons is therefore

$$\frac{\text{Length} \times \text{breadth} \times \text{immersed depth (draft)}}{35}$$

Displacement Curve. In the case of a cubical box as used in the foregoing illustration, the application of the formula is a simple matter, but in the case of an irregular object such as a ship, the figuring of displacement introduces many complications. To facilitate this process there has been devised a *displacement curve*, specially designed for each vessel, which enables one to read off the displacement when the draft is known.[1]

The importance of this ability to measure the weight of a vessel becomes apparent in the loading and discharging of cargo. The weight of a vessel in an unloaded condition being known, from the displacement shown at that point in the displacement curve, every inch of increase in draft will indicate the number of tons of weight loaded. Likewise, in the discharge of cargo or in the burning of fuel, each inch of decrease in draft will indicate the weight of cargo discharged or of fuel consumed. The difference between the displacement of a vessel when light (unloaded) and the displacement fully loaded is the *dead-weight* capacity. If the displacement curve is figured on the basis of sea water, which offers a buoyancy of 64 pounds to the cubic foot, allowance must be made in the case of a vessel lying in a fresh-water river, where the buoyancy of the water will be only 62½ pounds to the cubic foot.

When Will a Vessel Float? Buoyancy. The question is naturally raised, what is buoyancy and why does a vessel float? *Buoyancy* is the power to float. A vessel will float when its enclosed watertight volume in cubic feet is greater than its total weight (displacement) in tons multiplied by 35. The supporting pressure of water is all exerted vertically or obliquely and increases in proportion to the depth. At 1 foot depth there is 64 pounds pressure to the square foot, at 2 feet depth there is 128 pounds pressure to the square foot, and so on. The pressure exerted horizontally is just as great proportionately but has no lifting power. Thus, in the illustration of the cubical tin box cited above, which was watertight and weighed 1 pound, it appeared that with 62 pounds weight therein the box would just float, but if more than 1 pound were added, the box would sink. It should also be noted that, once having become submerged, the box would continue to sink until it rested on the water bed, the increased lifting power at the lower depth being exactly offset by the downward pressure exerted by the weight of water above the box. Applying the same principle to a ship, it will float up to the point where its own weight,

[1] A detailed explanation of how this curve is designed may be found in "Know Your Own Ship" by Thomas Walton.

in tons, plus the dead weight contained in it, multiplied by 35, equals its enclosed watertight volume measured in cubic feet. Of course, a vessel so loaded would not be seaworthy, because the least additional weight, such as that of a wave breaking on the deck, would cause the vessel to sink, and it would continue to sink until it rested on the ocean bed. For safety, it is essential that a considerable portion, say 25 per cent, of her total dead-weight capacity be not used in order to provide a margin of safety, known as *reserve buoyancy.*

Freeboard and Load Lines. Buoyancy naturally leads to a consideration of freeboard and load lines. The *freeboard* of a vessel is the distance measured at the middle of the length of the ship from the top of the main or upper fully enclosed deck to the water line. The freeboard is the measure of the reserve buoyancy of the vessel. How great the freeboard in any given ship should be is a matter of very careful measurement depending on its design, its structural strength, and the trade for which it is intended.

The load line may be thought of as the normal depth to which a vessel is submerged when safely loaded with a complete cargo. Usually the hull below this depth is painted one color and the hull above another color. A partially loaded ship usually shows a line where the two colors meet. This line is not the legal load line, which is indicated by the *gridiron* shown in Fig. 1 on pages 76 and 77.

Load-line legislation in the United States is relatively new, the first Load Line Act having been approved March 2, 1929, to become effective 18 months thereafter. This law applied to vessels of 250 gross tons or over loading for foreign voyages by sea. A number of amendments and exceptions to the United States load-line legislation have been made so that at the present time it is required that load lines shall be established:

1. For merchant vessels of 150 gross tons or over engaged in a foreign voyage by sea
2. For merchant vessels of 150 gross tons or over engaged in a coastwise voyage by sea
3. For merchant vessels of 150 gross tons or over engaged in a voyage on the Great Lakes
4. For passenger vessels operating on the sea or on the Great Lakes

General authority over and responsibility for the enforcement of the laws and regulations governing load lines in the several Coast Guard districts are vested in and imposed upon Coast Guard district commanders. The American Bureau of Shipping is the agency of the

LOAD LINE MARKINGS

FOR

OCEAN-GOING VESSELS

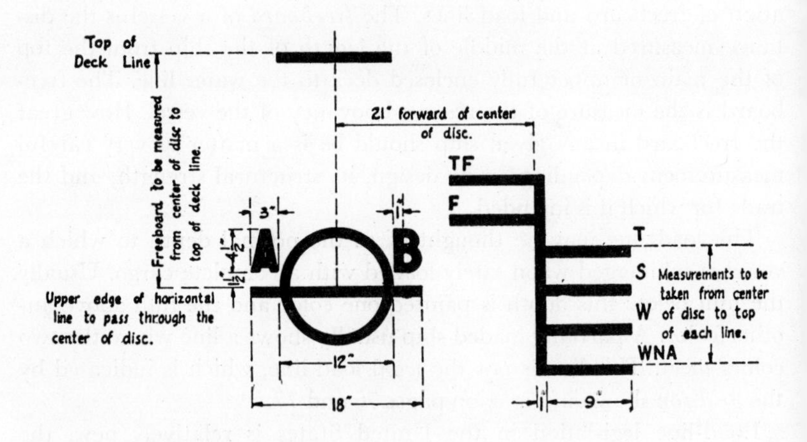

The Center of Disc to be placed on both sides of vessel at the middle of the length on the load line. The disc and lines must be permanently marked by center punch marks or chisel, and the particulars given in the Load Line Certificate are to be entered in the official log.

The markings shown are for the starboard side; on the port side the markings are to be similar, and forward of disc.

The letters	**A B**	**signify**	**American Bureau of Shipping.**
"	**T F**	**"**	**Tropical Fresh Water Allowance.**
"	**F**	**"**	**Fresh Water Allowance.**
"	**T**	**"**	**Load Line in Tropical Zones.**
"	**S**	**"**	**Summer Load Line.**
"	**W**	**"**	**Winter Load Line.**
"	**W N A**	**"**	**Winter North Atlantic Load Line.**

FIG. 1.

Coast Guard which surveys the vessels for load lines, determines them, and sees that they are painted on the side of the vessel. Two copies are reproduced in Fig. 1: one of the American Bureau load-line markings for ocean vessels, the other for lake vessels, with an accompanying explanation of the various prongs of what is sometimes termed the "gridiron."

Further steps have been taken for safety at sea by the adoption of the International Load Line Convention which was approved by

LOAD LINE MARKINGS

FOR

GREAT LAKES VESSELS

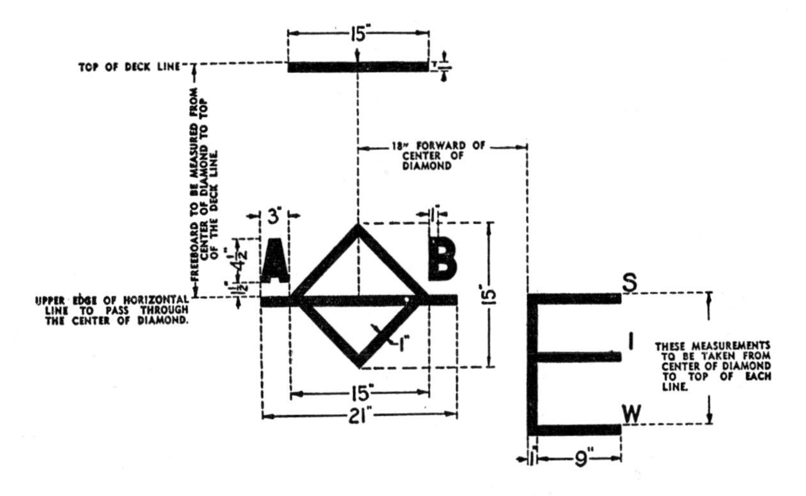

The Center of Diamond to be placed on both sides of vessel at the middle of the length on the load line. The diamond and lines must be permanently marked by center punch marks or chisel, and the particulars given in the Load Line Certificate are to be entered in the official log.

The markings shown are for the starboard side; on the port side the markings are to be similar, and forward of diamond.

The letters A B signify American Bureau of Shipping
" S " Summer Load Line
" I " Load Line in Intermediate Seasons
" W " Winter Load Line

FIG. 1 (*Continued*).

delegates from various maritime nations at a convention held in London in 1930. Several nations having signed the convention, the United States government proclaimed it effective with respect to the United States on January 1, 1933.

During World War II, in order to facilitate the conduct of the war, by presidential proclamation the load lines on coastwise steamers, particularly oil tankers, were slightly modified so that they could load a few inches deeper but still well within the margin of safety in order that a greater amount of cargo, especially oil, could be carried in these vessels.

In other countries load-line legislation has been in effect for many years. Credit for the first legislation rightfully belongs to Samuel Plimsoll, an Englishman, who after much educational work impressed on members of the English Parliament that vessels were putting to sea dangerously loaded, with consequent loss of life and property. Legislation was finally passed providing that all British vessels over a certain size should be measured for freeboard and a mark, now known as the *Plimsoll mark*, be cut in and painted on the side of each vessel at the middle of its length.

Stability. The Centers of Buoyancy and Gravity. The seaworthiness of a vessel does not depend altogether on the depth to which it is loaded. The stability of the vessel is of equal importance. Stability may be defined as the ability of a vessel to retain or regain a position of equilibrium. This ability depends on the design and loading of the vessel. In the consideration of the watertight tin box weighing 1 pound and containing 1 cubic foot of watertight space, it was observed that any weight greater than 63 pounds sank the box. The cause of the sinking was that two forces, that of buoyancy and that of gravity, had first become neutralized and then by the addition of the last pound of weight the force of gravity had overcome the force of buoyancy. The forces of buoyancy meet at a point within a ship called the *center of buoyancy*. Where the forces of gravity meet is the *center of gravity*. If these two centers are in the same vertical plane, the vessel will be in a state of equilibrium, the forces of gravity being exerted downward directly against the forces of buoyancy, which are exerted upward. The stability of the vessel depends on the relative positions of the two centers. The fact that these two forces are opposed one to the other, counterbalancing each other, explains why a vessel rests after rolling or pitching.

Why a Vessel Rights after Rolling. The action of buoyancy and gravity is illustrated in Figs. 2 and 3. The position of a vessel when in a state of rest is indicated in Fig. 2, which shows the cross section of a vessel. *WL* is the water line, the point *G* the center of gravity, and the point *B* the center of buoyancy, the dotted line *XY* showing the median line of the cross section, indicating that the two centers are in the same vertical plane. Figure 3 shows the same cross section, the vessel having rolled with a wave. It will be observed that the center of gravity *G* remains stationary, provided the cargo does not shift, while the center of buoyancy *B* moves over toward the heeling of the ship. This center moves because the immersed portion of the ship, that part below the new water line *W′L′* is of a different shape from the immersed portion in Fig. 2, that part below the water line

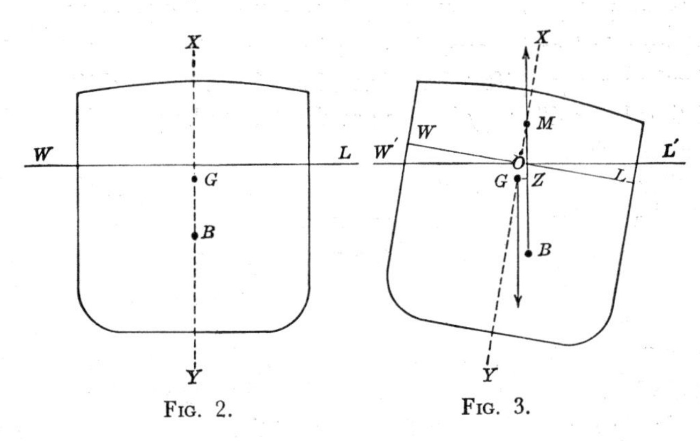

Fig. 2. Fig. 3.

WL, and the center of buoyancy naturally is found where the forces of buoyancy meet in this new shape. The effect of the moving of the center of buoyancy is to throw out of line the center of the force of gravity *G* and the center of the force of buoyancy *B*, thus creating a lever of stability indicated by the line *GZ* in Fig. 3. This lever, acting with a force measured in foot-tons equivalent to the weight of the ship and its cargo in tons (displacement) multiplied by the length of the lever in feet, operates to draw the ship back to its original position.

The Law of Inertia. At this point the law of inertia enters. The tendency of the vessel is to continue to roll in the direction of the pull of the lever *GZ* until, by the shifting of the center of buoyancy toward the new heeling of the ship, another lever is created, which pulls the ship back again. This movement will continue until the friction of the air and the water counteracts the force of the lever and the vessel again comes to a state of rest as in Fig. 2.

Shifted Cargoes. In the loading of bulk cargoes such as grain, coal, ore, or bulk oil, great care is used to prevent shifting of the cargoes during the rolling to which a vessel is subjected. If a cargo such as grain does shift with the rolling of the vessel, the center of gravity will shift toward the heeling of the ship, and the vessel will right herself with a shortened lever of stability only to the point where the two centers *G* and *B* are again in the same vertical plane. This will not, of course, be in the median line of the cross section but to one side of it, and the vessel will float with a list. In this position, when buffeted by wind and wave, the vessel will regain her listed position if no further cargo shift takes place, but if the cargo shifts further, the righting lever *GZ* may become so short as to be powerless and the vessel will capsize.

The Metacenter. Stiff and Tender Vessels. Again referring to Fig. 3 it will be noticed that the vertical line drawn through the new center of buoyancy *B* intersects the medium line *XY* at point *M*. If the roll of the vessel does not exceed, say, 15 degrees, this point will remain the same for all rolling less than 15 degrees, because the wedges *WOW′* and *LOL′* are equal in size. They are really sectors of a great circle, and their centers of gravity when the wedges are small are practically equal distances from the vertical line through the center of buoyancy. It is the position of this point *M*, with respect to the center of gravity *G*, that is the controlling factor in the stability of a vessel. The point *M* is the *metacenter*, and the distance between the point *M* and the center of gravity *G* the *metacenter height*. If this distance is great, the vessel is said to be *stiff*, the length of the lever *GZ* will be long, and the vessel will roll back quickly. If the metacenter height is short, the lever *GZ* will be short and the vessel will roll back slowly and is said to be *tender*. It is apparent, therefore, that, if a vessel is stiff and rolls back quickly, the shock to the structure of the vessel is exceedingly great. In the case of sailing vessels when the metacenter height is very great, owing to the low center of gravity, the quick return from a roll has frequently resulted in the snapping off of the masts. On the other hand, a tender vessel owing to her slow righting power in heavy weather may suffer greatly or, in extreme cases, may capsize.

The Control of Metacenter Height. As the metacenter height is the important factor in the stability of vessels, it is necessary to know how to regulate this height. This is done in two ways: first, by constructing vessels with sufficient breadth of beam, which has the effect of lowering the metacenter and thus decreases the metacenter height; second, by so stowing the cargo that the weight is well distributed and the center of gravity properly placed. Stowing cargo, or stevedoring, is an art in itself. The method of stowage is important in all cases but requires unusual attention in the case of a very light cargo, such as cotton, or a very heavy cargo, such as nitrate. In the former case it is necessary to stow heavy dead-weight cargo, such as steel or spelter, in the bottom of the holds to lower the center of gravity and prevent tenderness. In the case of heavy cargoes it is essential that the cargo be well distributed in the middle of the ship and built up high in bins if necessary, in order to raise the center of gravity and prevent stiffness.

Loading Problems. In the case of coal- or oil-burning vessels, as the fuel is consumed, the position of the center of gravity may change and shift to one side if the fuel is not evenly consumed, thus greatly affecting the stability of a ship that has little margin of safety through excessive loading under- and on-deck. The disregard of these various factors results in marine losses for which underwriters are called upon to respond, and some slight knowledge of the principles underlying them is essential for all interested in maritime affairs. The present book can merely mention these questions without fully considering them, but a very complete discussion of these and other kindred problems may be found in "Know Your Own Ship," by Thomas Walton.

Stresses and Strains. Consideration must be given to the stresses and strains to which a vessel in operation is subjected. It is to withstand these that vessels are designed. Ships are built to earn freight money, and since they have a limited amount of buoyancy, each additional ton of weight in the ship structure itself reduces the dead-weight capacity 1 ton. Herein lies the danger to passenger, shipper, and underwriter. Vessel owners naturally wish to make their vessels light in weight, and were it not for stringent rules of classification societies, the dangers of travel by sea would be increased for passenger, crew, and cargo.

Strain of Unequal Weights. If an unloaded steamer could be divided into five sections as in Fig. 4, each of exactly the same weight, it would be found that the supporting surfaces of these sections would be unequal in size. That is, the section containing the machinery would be smaller than that comprising one of the holds, although both sections would be equal in weight and when immersed in water each would displace the same volume, as was demonstrated in the con-

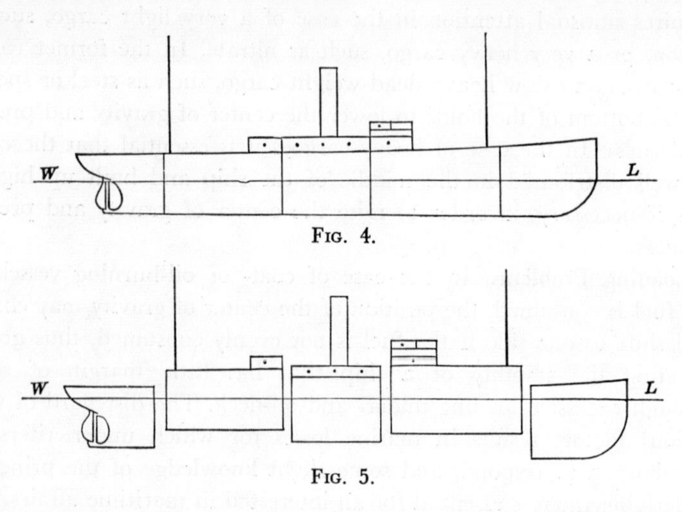

Fig. 4.

Fig. 5.

sideration of displacement. Therefore, different sections of the steamer would sink to different depths in the water as shown in Fig. 5. However, the steamer is not in five separate pieces but is one inseparable whole. While the total weight is supported by the total volume of water displaced, nevertheless the pressure is greatest at those points where a greater weight is contained in less space. The steamer must therefore be constructed to take up the strain caused by this unequal distribution of weight. Part of this strain is taken up when the vessel is laden with her cargo, because with careful stevedoring the weight of the steamer and her cargo can be fairly evenly distributed over the entire length of the ship. As steamers are quite often light, *i.e.* without cargo, and sometimes make considerable trips in ballast, this particular condition must be compensated for in ship structures.

Strain of Lateral Pressure and of Wave Action. A vessel is also subjected to strain caused by the lateral pressure of water, it being remembered that the pressure exerted at right angles to the submerged surface of a vessel in a horizontal direction is equal to the pressure exerted at the same depth vertically or obliquely against its bottom. The greater the draft of the vessel, the greater this crushing pressure becomes, since the whole tendency of the displaced water is to regain its former place. Also, vessels must be built to withstand the strain of riding the waves. They should be so constructed as to be at least twice the length of the average wave that they will encounter. If a vessel is caught on the crest of a wave so that her bow and stern are out of water, she has a tendency to bend or break at the point of support. Sometimes wooden vessels are *hogged*, a condition caused by structural weakness appearing when the vessel was so caught on a wave. On the other hand, if the bow and stern of a vessel are each resting on the crest of a wave while the center of the ship has but little water under it, there is a tendency for the vessel to sag at the middle and possibly to break at this point. One of these causes was doubtless the reason for the loss of the tank steamer *Oklahoma* many years ago. The experience gained by disasters occurring to vessels through the effect of the various kinds of strains has led to improved types designed to meet such stresses and strains with safety.

Panting Strains. Another strain that vessels must be constructed to withstand is the pressure against the bow of the ship as it rushes through the water or as it plunges up and down in riding the waves. This causes *panting strains*, the tendency of the shell of the vessel being to work in and out as it passes through the water. There are also strains caused by vibration due to the propelling machinery of the vessel. In the case of sailing vessels peculiar stresses are encountered owing to the power of the wind on the sail surface. In auxiliary sail vessels, a combination of engine strain and wind strain is encountered, necessitating especially strong construction in this type.

Other Strains. Shipbuilders must also counteract the strains caused by the heavy permanent weights carried on the deck, such as the winches and, if necessary, guns carried for defense. The shock caused by the firing of these guns also produces unlooked-for results, as in a case where the gun practice on a merchant ship developed a crack in the stern frame. It is customary in some trades to carry heavy deckloads, and this added pressure must be compensated for as well as the enormous strain on the deck caused by the shipping of heavy seas. It is necessary, from time to time, to put vessels in dry dock for repairs and cleaning. In such cases the vessel is subjected to extraordinary strains, the customary support of the vessel being removed, all the weight being carried at a few supporting points. Vessels must be so constructed that they can withstand unusual conditions.

Vessels in Ballast. In insuring tank and cargo steamers it must be remembered that these vessels, in order to secure cargoes, make long voyages in ballast, that is, without cargo, but with a certain amount of dead-weight load or ballast sufficient to submerge the vessel to a reasonable depth. Usually the propeller blades of steamers in ballast are not fully immersed, and the working of the propeller, partly in the water and partly out, causes undue strain on the blades. Furthermore, with the pitching of the vessel, the propeller at times will be entirely exposed, and unless great care is taken in the engine room, this will cause the engines to race, thus subjecting the power plant to unusual stresses. The exposed surface of the vessel when in ballast being greater than when loaded, the pressure of the wind and the force of breaking seas are felt with greater severity than in the case of a deeply laden vessel. The fact that the vessel is so far out of the water also makes her less easily managed, and she will not answer her helm with the same degree of precision as when fully laden. Added to this, in many cases care is not taken in the stowage of ballast to secure it so that it will not shift. The proper way to stow ballast is, first, to distribute the weight in such manner that the center of gravity will be as high as possible and, second, to make sure that it is so stowed that it will not shift during the voyage. The metacenter height is usually great in vessels in ballast, and they are consequently stiff and snap back and forth in heavy seas, subjecting the structure of the vessel to severe strains. While it is true that the modern steamer is equipped with ballast tanks, it must not be assumed that these are built into the vessel to enable it to go to sea without cargo. These tanks when full of water (and they should be either absolutely full or absolutely empty in order to prevent water from sloshing around in stormy weather and affecting the stability of the vessel) are a great aid to a vessel sailing in ballast. The primary purpose of the tanks, however, is to give the vessel proper trim when loaded with light cargoes. The trim of a vessel is her position in relation to her load line. Perhaps for special reasons a captain will wish the bow of the vessel to be up a few inches and the stern down a few inches and so trims the ship when it is being loaded.

CHAPTER 5

Introduction to Marine Insurance

Commerce is conducted for the purpose of placing commodities where they can be most advantageously used. If for any reason the commodity does not reach that place or arrives in a damaged condition, then to that extent the orderly flow of commerce has been interrupted. If this interruption has been caused by a fortuitous event, that is, an event occurring by chance and not by design, no one is to blame. It must always be remembered that this fortuitous happening, this misadventure, was not looked for. It was the hope and expectation that the venture would be completed without mishap, as is usually the case. But there is always the possibility that a casualty may occur and the successful completion of the undertaking be interrupted or the voyage ended. On the other hand, the goods may not arrive at destination or arrive in a damaged condition owing to causes that might have been avoided by greater care on the part of the merchant in the packing of the goods or of the ship in the stowing of the cargo. Such losses are not inevitable, and efforts should be made by merchants and transportation companies to prevent their occurrence. The loss of any useful property is a loss to the world's wealth that can never be replaced.

One who would venture in overseas or domestic trade, whether as merchant, banker, or transportation operator, should clearly understand the economic and financial problems involved. Also he must be aware of the physical hazards to which his property will be subjected. These hazards should be clearly recognized for two reasons: first, so that they may be avoided if possible and, second, so that compensation may be provided if they result in damage. Insurance is the commercial answer to this problem and for centuries has removed the risk of fortuitous loss which, if not compensated for, would deter adventurous merchants and vessel owners from embarking on perilous undertakings.

Reasonable Care Essential. It is fair to assume that both the merchant and the vessel owner, realizing the known hazards of the voyage contemplated, will use all practical measures so to prepare the merchandise and the carrying vessel that the venture may be completed safely. The words "practical measures" are used advisedly, for there are hazards that might be eliminated at a cost out of proportion to the result accomplished. A merchant or vessel owner by so doing might price himself out of the competitive market. Therefore, as in all areas of human activity, the rule of reason must be applied, and a prudent rather than a foolish course be adopted.

Standards. Even the seemingly prudent course may result in establishing commercial standards through competitive price cutting that approach a situation which is against public policy. For instance, many years ago no underwriter ever considered insuring against petty thievery, now commonly known as *theft and pilferage.* The underwriter was willing to protect a merchant against assailing thieves, against whose activities he was powerless to protect himself. However, by proper packing, the merchant could largely eliminate the hazard of petty thievery. Some underwriters, eager for premium, offered to assume the hazard of pilferage. Some merchants accepted the offer, and the problem developed. If the premium charged was less than the extra cost of good packing, the imprudent merchant paid the premium and shipped his goods in inferior packages. Goods that arrive at destination in imperfect condition do not cultivate good relations, and if many shipments so arrive, a merchant may lose his markets to those merchants of his own or other countries who seek to carry out their commercial obligations on a high level of business conduct. Any system relieving a merchant or a shipowner of any obligations that he should assume tends to break down those standards of commercial practice the observance of which creates international commercial good will.

Hazards. Before considering the marine-insurance contract it will be profitable to examine some of the hazards of overseas commerce.

This should make easier the understanding of the insurance contract. It has been devised and developed for the purpose of assuming the risk of the fortuitous losses of transportation and of leaving, in so far as is practicable, the preventable losses and normal expected losses at the risk of the merchant or vessel owner. There are hazards peculiar to cargoes and others to which the hull and machinery of the vessel are subject. In addition there are hazards common to both cargo and hull. It will not be feasible to consider all hazards, but those of major importance will be discussed.

Cargoes. Consideration will be given first to transportation hazards peculiar to cargo. First, when do these hazards commence and for how long do they continue? As the goods leave the warehouse, at either the port or the interior, the transportation venture begins. A railroad car or a motor truck may be the initial carrier. If the point of shipment is on an inland waterway or on a lake shore, the initial carrier may be a vessel either self-propelled or towed, as in the case of the vast tonnage moving down the Mississippi River and its tributaries. Direct loading to the ocean vessel may be made from car, truck, or barge, or an intermediate transfer may be made one or more times before the shipment is loaded on board the ocean vessel.

General Cargoes. In the case of ordinary merchandise, apart from bulk cargoes, the shipment will usually be loaded with a variety of other goods in a general-cargo ship specially designed for the carriage of general cargoes. On the other hand, when vessel tonnage is scarce, ships that were not designed for such cargo may be chartered to load general commodities. A single-deck vessel with deep holds is not so suitable for loading general assorted cargo as is a vessel with intermediate decks which tend to lessen pressure on the cargo.

Transshipments. Before reaching the final port of destination the cargo may be transshipped one or more times via lighters at an intermediate port or ports. Or it may be transferred by rail, cart, motor truck, or lighter from one port or district of a port to another port or district. When the final port of discharge is reached, a whole new series of transportation problems may ensue, depending on the hinterland of the port that must be traversed to reach the warehouse of the consignee. Shipments to the interior may move by rail, motor truck, airplane, cart, river vessel, canoe, muleback, or even human carriage. To pack goods in a package that weighs 500 pounds that must finally be carried by muleback or by coolie can result only in the package being broken down and repacked in suitable size. Damage will almost inevitably result. Similar transportation problems in reverse will occur if the shipment is an import from a foreign country.

Exposures. This somewhat detailed description of an overseas venture is cited in order to make clear the variety of exposures to which the shipment is subjected. If these exposures and their effect on the shipment are not understood and measures taken to pack the goods properly to withstand them, it cannot be expected that the shipment will arrive safely at its desired destination. General cargo may consist of anything from the heaviest machinery to the most fragile X-ray tubes, from shipments of little value and great bulk to those of little volume but of great value. One whose shipping ventures have been confined to the movement of goods in local or domestic transportation may lack the experience that will enable him to enter successfully the field of overseas commerce. By trial and error such experience is gained.

Problems. Having outlined the voyage in general terms, an examination of some of the hazards to which the shipment is exposed on each section of the journey is in order. Beginning at the shipping door of the interior warehouse, there are risks such as fire, flood, windstorm, rain, collapse of platforms, and perhaps earthquake. If the shipment moves by rail, there are risks of fire, collision, and derailment, in addition to flood and storm. These same risks are intensified to a considerable degree in the case of transportation by motor truck, as the movement is over public highways and not a private right of way as in rail transportation. Motor trucks are also subject to the serious hazard of the overturning of the vehicle. Furthermore, the legal liability of the warehouseman, the rail carrier, and the motor trucker must all be considered, since it is not the same. Familiarity with legal-liability statutes is of the greatest importance so that receipts or bills of lading improperly limiting the responsibility of warehousemen or carriers may not be unintentionally accepted. A responsible warehouseman or carrier will use proper documents. Warehousemen or carriers who issue unusual document forms should be avoided. The legal remedies a merchant has against warehousemen or carriers for losses due to negligence are valuable and should be jealously guarded.

Loading Hazards. At the port of loading, new hazards present themselves. At some ports, such as those on the Gulf Coast of the United States in summer and early fall, there is the threat of hurricane damage and water damage due to high water caused by wind. In the north in midwinter there is danger of freezing, especially of perishable liquids. In other areas there are threats of flood, wind, or earthquake. Danger of fire is always present. Various loading and unloading problems arise at foreign ports due to lack of building protection or the necessity of loading by lighters with attendant damage by exposure to the elements, by theft and pilferage, by breakage, or by leakage.

Sea Perils. Once on the overseas vessel the perils are more easily defined and affect cargo and vessel in varying degrees. These perils are of the sea, such as wind, waves, and the hazards of stranding and collision. Also perils such as fire and lightning are encountered on the sea. Sea-water damage, damage to machinery of a steamer, and sinking are classed as perils of the sea. Sometimes a peril may cause loss to the vessel and not to the cargo, as in the case of a collision that damages the bow of the vessel but does not affect the collision bulkhead. Frequently damage occurs to rudder or propeller with no damage to the cargo. On the other hand, heavy weather may cause water to enter the hatches, or fire in the cargo, though controlled by a modern fire-retarding device, may seriously damage the cargo and not harm the vessel. Cargo laden on deck may be washed overboard or may be jettisoned to relieve a vessel in distress. If heavy weather is encountered, causing the vessel to roll or pitch, shifting of cargo may result in heavy damage through breaking and crushing of packages. A serious fire, stranding, or collision may put the refrigeration system of a ship out of commission, spoiling the cargo in the freezers.

Shipper's Responsibility. There is another group of hazards that in many cases are in the twilight zone between necessary risks and those which are preventable by the exercise of reasonable care. In the case of cargo, the principal hazards of this kind are theft and pilferage, leakage and breakage. Under normal conditions no loss should occur from such causes if the merchant has used reasonable care in the packing of the commodity. A good container, properly strapped with steel bands and so constructed as to prevent the slipping of its individual boards, will discourage the casual thief. Absence of advertising on the case leaves the thief in a quandary as to whether broaching the case is worth the risk of being detected. In the case of liquids, the container, whether wooden cask, tin, or glass, must be sufficient to withstand the severe pressures that are inevitable in the varying weather conditions encountered by a vessel on a normal voyage. The same is true with respect to breakage, whether the commodity is a heavy piece of machinery or fragile chinaware. The burden is on the merchant so to pack his goods that they may be expected in the ordinary course to reach the intended destination in sound condition.

Vessel's Responsibility. The merchant has a right to expect that the carrier he engages to transport his goods, whether by land, air, or water, will use reasonable care in the stowage of the cargo. Therefore it is essential that the bill of lading show the kind of commodity being shipped and how it is packed, whether in cases, barrels, bales, or otherwise. This enables the carrier to load the car, truck, or airplane and, more important, to arrange the stowage of the ocean vessel so that the goods may be expected to withstand the hazards of the journey. Much time and thought have been given by carriers and by underwriters, and by both cooperating with government agencies, to make the stowage of cargo proper not only for its own safety but also, more important in the case of water transportation, for the safety of the ship and her crew and passengers. A ship may be constructed so as to be seaworthy and reasonably fireproof, but the cargo may be so loaded as to make useless all the care taken in the construction of the vessel. The load line is one of the many means to ensure safety from a seaworthy point of view. The many devices to aid in navigation and to prevent, detect, and extinguish fires are designed to meet some of the multitude of problems in the carriage of goods by sea. If a vessel owner or operator does not use reasonable care in the preparation of his vessel for the intended voyage and for the stowage of its cargo, he may become legally liable if damage results. Bad stowage may result in damage caused by breakage and leakage or by sweat, heat, dust, or dirt, or by the crushing or chafing of the cargo. In the case of oil-burning vessels, fuel oil may, through negligence, come in contact with the cargo. Lack of care in maintaining proper temperatures in refrigerated spaces may result in heavy cargo losses.

Transit Interruptions. It is assumed, under ordinary world conditions, that a shipment will move from point of origin to place of destination without undue interruption. There is no fixed standard for this normal movement. The world and its trade relations grow more complicated as time moves on. Nationalistic aspirations impose requirements with respect to the movement of commodities that may and do change the conduct of commercial activities. The merchant and the vessel owner must keep abreast of these changing conditions. So-called paper requirements, due to the necessity of providing the necessary permits and other documents required to allow the entrance of goods into a foreign country, must be met; otherwise transit will be stopped, and the shipment left in a port customs or shed or, perhaps, in an open, fenced-in space. This necessarily subjects the shipment to many of the hazards previously referred to, but in a more intensive way. It must be remembered that in the course of a long voyage ports in many countries will be visited, and if misfortune overtakes the venture, it may become involved in local legal problems.

Value or Valuation. The words *value or valuation* are used many times in the consideration of the practice of marine insurance. The word value or valuation is not used in the sense of exact value or exact valuation. In the course of a year the value of the vessel and the value of the cargo are constantly fluctuating. The only international measure of value that has been found of practical use is gold. All other commodity prices fluctuate in terms of gold.

In property insurance, other than ocean-marine, the amount for which a policy is written is usually the limit for which the underwriter is liable in event of loss. Any claim is predicated on the value at the time and place of the loss. The underwriter usually reserves the right, instead of paying the claim, to restore or replace the property with property of like kind and quality.

In ocean-marine insurance the assured and the underwriter agree at the inception of the risk on a value for the property, whether hull or cargo. Both parties thereafter are bound by this agreed value, which should bear a reasonable relation to the true value of the property. In the case of a ship this should be the reasonable market value at the time the policy attaches. In the case of cargo the value should be the expected market value of the goods when they arrive at their intended destination. The value once agreed upon, if not fraudulent, controls the relationship between underwriter and assured throughout the entire term of the policy. Premium is paid on this agreed value. Claims for loss are adjusted on this agreed value. No right is reserved to replace damaged or lost goods or vessel, although in many cases this could be done at a great saving to the underwriter. It is a basic principle of ocean-marine insurance that a policy is a valued policy.

From the point of view of general average, which will be considered later, it is most important that the property, whether hull, cargo, or freight, be properly valued in the insurance policy. If this is not done, when the general-average adjustment is made, the assured may find himself underinsured and therefore liable for the general-average contribution due on the uninsured amount. In making up a general-average adjustment, the adjusters call in an outside appraiser who fixes a value for the vessel. With respect to cargo, contributions are made upon the net values of the property at the termination of the venture, to which values are added the amount made good as general average for property sacrificed, less certain deductions with respect to freight and other charges. It is a well-settled rule that an insurance policy is not liable to contribute in general average for a greater amount than the insured value stated in the policy. If this amount is less than the value determined by the adjusters, the assured becomes a coinsurer to the extent of any difference between the insured amount in the policy and the contributory value fixed by the general-average adjusters.

Average. The word *average* is perhaps the most important single word in the whole vocabulary of marine insurance. It has a special meaning. Gow[1] discusses the etymology of this word and cites the medieval Latin word *averagium* signifying loss in transit, such as by leakage, and the medieval legal English word *aver* used to denote the best live beast due to the feudal lord on the death of a tenant as a tax or impost. Gow suggests that from this original was formed the word average, signifying the rendering of a service or the payment of a tax or contribution. As far as insurance is concerned, the origin of the

[1] "Marine Insurance," 5th ed. p. 288, 1931.

word is obscure but, in the early development of marine insurance, may have taken its meaning from the French word *avarie*. It means loss or damage less than a total loss. Two types of average occur: particular average relating to loss to and borne by a particular interest and general average referring to a partial loss due to a sacrifice of vessel or cargo or of an expense incurred for the purpose of saving all the interests involved in a maritime venture.

Losses. The hazards that have been considered may produce losses. These may or may not be covered by the marine-insurance policy, depending on the nature of the damage and on whether the loss suffered comes under the risks assumed by the underwriter in his policy issued to the merchant or vessel owner. In general, losses fall into the following categories:

Particular average
Total loss (actual or constructive)
Total loss of a part of a shipment
General average

Each type of loss will be considered in detail in later chapters, but it will be profitable at this point briefly to consider general average.

General Average. *History.* From the earliest records of overseas commercial voyages, there is evidence that the sacrifice of cargo for the safety of the vessel posed a problem as to who should bear the resultant loss. It seemed then, as it does now, inequitable that the owner of the sacrificed commodity should alone bear the loss. So the practice developed of making all the interests involved in the venture, whether ship, cargo, or freight (the earning power of the ship), contribute ratably, in proportion to the values saved by the sacrifice, to make good the loss of the sacrificed cargo. Jettison, the voluntary throwing overboard of cargo to lighten the ship, was the customary sacrifice. As the centuries passed, marine ventures became more complicated, ships more highly developed, and the use of sails and, later, mechanical means of propulsion were devised. As a consequence, many new types of sacrifice both of ship and of cargo were made, and the scope of the practice of general average was greatly broadened.

Not Insurance. General average will be examined later in connection with loss adjustments. For the present it is important to realize and to remember that general average is not insurance or the outgrowth of insurance but a part of the provisions of national and international law. It is provided for by the maritime law of practically all countries. Its principles apply generally in connection with all transportation by water, whether on the ocean, in harbors, or on navigable lakes and rivers.

Average Adjusters. The practice and the preparation of the very involved statements apportioning the liability over the various interests are in the hands of average adjusters. These men are expert in the interpretation and application of the law and the rules of practice and occupy a quasi-judicial position. They should be just as free of prejudice as is a justice of the courts. As the shipowner is in control of the cargo during the voyage, he appoints the general-average adjuster.

General Average and Insurance. When a general-average sacrifice of ship or cargo is made, if the marine-insurance policy covers the resultant physical loss, the underwriter promptly reimburses his assured for the loss or damage. Subject to the limitation of liability due to the question of valuation, referred to on page 93, responsibility for the payment of any general-average *assessment* (contribution) is assumed by the underwriter. General-average sacrifices are of relatively frequent occurrence, and oftentimes the respective liabilities of the various interests are not determined for years after the happening of the event. In the meantime any merchant actively engaged in overseas trade and any shipowner may be involved in a number of such cases. The underwriter, by assuming responsibility for the ultimate settlement of the case, relieves the merchant or owner of a very heavy burden.

Why Have General Average? Throughout the years an endless debate has gone on as to whether in a modern age the somewhat archaic system of general average can be justified as a method of distributing loss. Would it not be better to let the loss lie where it falls in the first instance? In most cases the property is insured, and the underwriter pays the loss. Why not let the whole question end at this point and let the underwriter adjust his rates to meet this initial burden? Superficially the argument urging the discontinuance of general average seems logical. Human nature, however, has not changed as civilization has progressed. If the master of a vessel, who is in control of the venture, realized that his owner would not suffer by the sacrifice of cargo to save the ship, he might jettison more cargo than was necessary to relieve the ship or pump more water or steam into a hold on fire than conditions warranted. The same danger pointed out in the insurance of hazards that can be controlled by proper packing and handling of cargo applies in the case of general average. The mental attitude of men is largely influenced by financial results. No better system than general average has yet been suggested to minimize sacrificial losses during water transportation. It is safe to predict that general average will continue to be part of maritime law for many years to come.

Effect of Insurance. The procurement of marine insurance by the assured results in the sharing by the ultimate consumer of the losses that overtake property in overseas and overland commerce. The underwriter charges a premium for the insurance of the risks that he underwrites. This premium charge becomes one of the items in the invoice for the sale of the goods, and in the freight rate which is also an item in the invoice there is indirectly included part of the cost of insuring the hull of the vessel. In this way the cost of insurance becomes part of the price of goods and is an indirect charge on the consumer. The underwriter assumes the burden of the losses and thus stabilizes prices and makes possible large commercial transactions.

Averages. Competition. In fixing rates adequate to compensate him for the losses paid and the expenses incurred and to produce a profit on the capital invested, the underwriter works on the basis of averages. A dependable average is not the result shown by the outcome of a few risks, but the result shown by many risks of the same kind over a period of many years. Ten years is a fair period from which to draw deductions, for in this length of time, practically every condition peculiar to a given trade will appear and the number of risks run in such a period will be sufficiently great to enable fairly accurate conclusions to be drawn. But in the last analysis, such deductions are not more than an approximation to scientific accuracy. Competition serves to hold rates down to the point where there is only a fair margin of profit on the capital invested. If the rates on a certain line of insurance are such that an undue margin of profit results, underwriters who are not actively engaged in this particular branch of the business will cut rates in order to get a share of the good business, and those who are underwriting this particular kind of risk will necessarily be forced to meet the competition. On the other hand, if a certain line of business proves unprofitable, underwriters will forego this class of insurance unless higher rates are paid by merchants or shipowners. So rates fluctuate within narrow limits. In addition, underwriters always face the possibility that, if undue profits are made on any particular class of business, self-insurance will result, merchants and shipowners figuring that, if the underwriter can make money by assuming the risk, they can save money by carrying it themselves. But unless they have a very large and diversified business, such reasoning is fallacious, as they will not have sufficient distribution of risk to permit the law of large numbers to play its part, and a severe total loss may furnish a pointed object lesson of the folly of self-insurance under ordinary conditions.

CHAPTER 6

Factors in Marine Underwriting

The Classification Societies. Most vessels are built according to the rules and under the supervision of the classification societies. The primary object of these societies is to see that the vessels built under their supervision are fully seaworthy, as far as construction is involved, for the particular trade for which they are designed. It is in no sense compulsory that vessels be built under the supervision of the classification societies, though it might be desirable. However, a shipowner will experience considerable difficulty in procuring insurance on his vessel if it does not appear in the book of some recognized classification society with a mark indicating that it has been classed by that organization. The classification societies promulgate rules for the building of wooden and metal ships. At the principal ports of the world where shipbuilding is carried on, they have agents who are experienced ship constructors or naval architects, who are familiar with the societies' rules and regulations, and who are competent to oversee the construction of vessels.

What a "Class" Signifies. If a man intends to build a vessel, he will go to a marine architect and say that he wants a steamer of a given dead-weight capacity, suitable for a named trade, to be built in such manner that it will receive the highest class in *The American Record* or at Lloyd's. The new owner may not be particular about the type of steamer that he gets if it will perform the service for which he needs it, obtain the desired speed, and not exceed in cost the amount that he desires to spend. The architect accordingly designs a steamer to be built to the requirements of the American Bureau of Shipping or Lloyd's Classification Society. These classification societies in their rules set forth in great detail standards of construction, material, and workmanship that they require in a vessel before they will grant their class. If the steamer is to be built under their supervision, the plans and specifications will be submitted to them for examination. If the plans are approved, construction will be commenced, and from time to time their surveyors will examine the work done and make tests of the materials used in the construction of both the hull and machinery. When the vessel is completed, a class will be assigned to it, requirement being made that, as a condition precedent to the continuance of such class, periodical surveys shall be made and such repairs and replacements made as the surveyors of the society may demand. These periodical surveys may be made at any port where there is an authorized surveyor of the society and where proper dry-docking facilities are obtainable.

Lloyd's Register. Classification societies play an important part in marine underwriting. In fact the earliest "books" were those compiled by British underwriters setting forth in brief and coded form their opinion of the vessels then in existence. The first books were brought out in 1764, 1765, and 1766 and were very carefully guarded by their possessors. The paucity of information given, compared with the wealth of facts set forth in the modern book, shows the gigantic progress made in such matters in the last 150 years. The volumes issued by the underwriters at Lloyd's continued to be published from year to year, but in 1799 a rival register was set up by shipowners who were dissatisfied with the treatment accorded by Lloyd's. The two registers continued to be published until 1833, when they were combined in one volume, the "Register of British and Foreign Shipping." The following year the book appeared as "Lloyd's Register of British and Foreign Shipping" which has been published continuously until the present day. The organization publishing this book is entirely distinct from the Underwriting Association of Lloyd's, London, and has on its managing board underwriters, shipowners, merchants, and shipbuilders. It is perhaps fair to assume, however, that the underwriting fraternity is the dominant factor in the organization. They pay for the mistakes of merchants, architects, and shipbuilders, and it is but natural that they should be the chief advocates of better built ships.

Rival Organizations. Rival organizations were started in other countries because it was felt, and with reason, that Lloyd's discriminated against vessels of other than British build. Now there are a number of societies performing the same kind of service and, naturally, in the bidding for business, modifying the stringency of their requirements, with consequent detriment to the soundness of the vessels constructed under their supervision. Underwriters soon discover, however, whether the requirements of the societies are as stringent as they should be and do not consider classification in all societies of equal value. The fact that a ship has a class in one of the less respected societies warrants the natural inference that her construction is such that the better societies would not class the vessel. The mere fact that a vessel is unclassed does not necessarily condemn it. Lack of class usually indicates one of two conditions: either the vessel is of such inferior construction that no classification society would be sponsor for the ship, or the vessel may be constructed to a standard so much in excess of the requirements of any society that the owners are not warranted in incurring the additional expense to have it classed. This latter condition exists with some steamers of the first-class passenger and freight lines.

Necessity for Understanding Classification-society Codes. It is absolutely necessary for marine underwriters and important for merchants to be able to read intelligently the books of the classification societies. The information is printed in coded form, each book having its own code which appears translated at the opening of the volume. It must be remembered that each organization has classes of different degrees, and it should not be inferred, simply because a named steamer is classed in *The American Record,* for instance, that it is fit for the intended employment. Classes are given for harbor, river, lake, coastwise, ocean, and other services, and unless the class marks are understood, underwriters in insuring and merchants in engaging freight space may be led into serious error. A portion of a page out of *The American Record,* which is reprinted in Fig. 6, will give an indication of the wealth of information furnished in small compass by these volumes.

The American Record. *The American Record* is published by the American Bureau of Shipping, an organization started many years ago to foster American shipping and reorganized in 1916 on a plan

1 No. Off. No. Sig. Ltr.	2 Name of Vessel Former Name Owner Flag Port of Registry	3 Type Water Ballast Size Tank Tons	4 Construction Bulkheads No. of Hatches Largest Hatch No. of Holds Longest Hold	5 Fuel and Capacity Appliances Fire Protection Apparatus Equipment	6 Dimensions Molded Registered Lgth. Bdth. Dpth. Deck Erections Draft Bale Cub. Freeboard Deadrise	7 Tonnage Gross Net Dead Wgt. Displ.	8 Builders Ship Hull No. Place Date Built Engine Date Built Boiler Date Built	9 Type and Particulars of Machinery	10 Hull: Classification; Date of Last Survey; No., Port and Date of Last Periodical Survey Machinery: Classification; Date of Last Survey Mchy. and Boilers; Date Tailshaft Drawn; Etc. Other Classification
719 245,351 KWXM	**AMERIGO VESPUCCI....** **U.S. Maritime Commission** **Washington, D.C.** **United States San Francisco, Cal.**	**Sgl Sc** AP 152 DTa 20' 762 DB 345'9" 1258 DTf 60'9" 652 FP 138	**Steel; 2 Dks** Orlop Dk f Metal Arc Welded (Frames riveted) Trans Frmg 7 WT to Fbd Dk 1 WT to 2nd Dk 5 Ha 35'x20' 5 Ho 72'6"	**Oil** 1834 tons Rad Tel Rad DF DS; GC **C-38**(S)	**417'8¾" 56'10½" 37'4"** 422.8' 57' 34.8' Dft 27'8¾" 468M Fbd 9'8¼" **Dr 6"**	**7212** 4380 10500 14100	**Permanente Metals 2767 Corp.** **Shipbuilding Div.Yd.No.2** Richmond, Cal. 3-1944 Joshua Hendy Iron Works 3-1944 Puget Sound Machinery Depot 3-1944	**3 Cyl TE 24½" 37" 70"x48"** IHP 2500 2 WTB;HS 10232;WP 240 Lbs FD;SH SBP;CL 2	✠A1Ⓔ **9-45** AS 2-45;Dkd 2-45 ✠**AMS 2-45** BS 2-45 An MS 2-45 **EAC** (Laid up)
720 SV2Q	**AMERIKI....................** **ex William H. Todd** **Marathon S.S. Co.** **London, Eng.** **Greek Piraeus, Greece**	**Sgl Sc** AP 152 DTa 20' 762 DB 345'9" 1258 DTf 60'9" 652 FP 138	**Steel; 2 Dks** Orlop Dk f Metal Arc Welded (Frames riveted) (Gunwale Strap riveted) Trans Frmg 7 WT to Fbd Dk 1 WT to 2nd Dk 5 Ha 35'x20' 5 Ho 72'6"	**Oil** 1734 tons Rad Tel Rad DF DS **C-38**(S)	**417'8¾" 56'10½" 37'4"** 422.8' 57' 34.8' Dft 27'8¾" 500M Fbd 9'8¼" Dr 6"	**7176** 4380 10916 14245	**New England S.B. 242 Corp.** So. Portland, Me. 9-1943 Harrisburg Machinery Corp. 9-1943 **Henry Vogt Machine Co. 9-1943**	**3 Cyl TE 24½" 37" 70"x48"** IHP 2500 2 WTB;HS 10232;WP 240 Lbs FD;SH SBP;CL 2	✠A1Ⓔ **11-49** SS No. 1 Newport News 9-47 AS 11-49;Dkd 11-49 ✠**AMS 11-49** MS 9-47;BS 11-49 TS Drn 12-48 **EAC**
721 247,292 KCLJ	**AMES VICTORY..........** **Victory Carriers, Inc.** **New York, N.Y.** **United States New York, N.Y.**	**Sgl Sc** AP 34 DTa 132' 1648 DB 306'6" 1524 FP 106	**Steel; 3 Dks** Metal Arc Welded (Gunwale Bar riveted) Trans Frmg 7 WT to Fbd Dk 2 WT to 3rd Dk 5 Ha 36'x22'4" 5 Ho 81'	**Oil** 2882 tons Rad Tel Rad DF DS; GC **C-39**(S)	**436'6" 62' 38'** 439.1' 62.1' 34.5' F87' Dft 28'6½" 453M Fbd 9'7" Dr 0"	**7606** 4549 10767 15199	**Oregon S.B.Corp. 1217** Portland, Ore. 2-1945 General Electric Co. 2-1945 Babcock & Wilcox Co. 2-1945	**3 Cyl Stm Turb** SHP 9350;DR Gears 2 WTB;HS 16260;WP 525 Lbs FD;SH SBP;CL	✠A1Ⓔ **1-50** SS No. 1 Mobile 7-49 Dkd 7-49 ✠**AMS 7-49** MS 7-49;BS 7-49 n TS 7-49 **EAC**
722 231,094	**AMETHYST................** **ex Samona II** **S. K. Rindge** **Los Angeles, Cal.** **United States** **Now n**	**Tw Sc MV** ex Yacht **amed: "SAMO**	**Steel; 1 Dk** 6 BH **NA II" see Supp**	**Oil** Rad Tel **le 1**	136.8' 23.6' 12.9'	350 159 — —	**Craig S.B. Co.** Long Beach, Cal. 7-1931 Winton Engine Co.	**2 Oil Engs 6 Cyl 14"x16"** 4 Cyc BHP 1000	
723 HPFU	**AMIENS....................** **Overseas Tankship Corp.** **Panama, R. P.** **Panamanian Panama, R.P.**	**Sgl Sc Tanker** **Mchy Aft**	**Steel; 1 Dk** Metal Arc Welded (1 Dk, 1 Side & 1 Btm Shell Seams each side riveted) Long Frmg 15 OT to Fbd Dk 2 OT Long BH 1 Ha;SC; 11'3"x15' 8 CT p, c&s 36'6" 1 CT p&s 13'6"	**Oil** 1460 tons Rad Tel Rad DF DS; GC Sub Sig **C-43**(S)	**503' 68' 39'3"** 504' 68.2' 39.2' P107'6½" B35'9" F52'7½" Dft 30'2" Fbd 9'2½" Dr 9"	**10296** 6154 16282 21880	**Sun S.B.& D.D.Co. 464** Chester, Pa. 3-1945 Westinghouse Electric & Mfg. Co. 3-1945 Westinghouse Electric & Mfg. Co. 3-1945 Babcock & Wilcox Co. 3-1945	**Stm Turb;Elec Mot** SHP 7240 2 WTB;HS 11552;WP 500 Lbs FD;SH SBP;CL	✠A1Ⓔ **Oil Carrier 11-49** SS No. 1 Philadelphia 10-48 AS 11-49;Dkd 11-49 ✠**AMS 11-49** MS 10-48;BS 11-49 An MS 11-49 TS Drn 1-48 **EAC**

The ✠ and ☪ prefixed to the Classification symbols denote vessels built under the supervision of the Bureau, the latter being applicable only to Great Lakes Vessels. The publication of the particulars of unclassed vessels is for general information only. While extreme care is used in the preparation of all information, the Bureau accepts no responsibility for any errors or omissions.

Fig. 6.

commensurate with the position of the American merchant marine in the world's commerce. Its success depends largely on the support and encouragement that it receives from government and from underwriters, merchants, shipowners, and shipbuilders of this country. All the ships constructed for the Federal Maritime Commission are built under the supervision and according to the rules of this Bureau, and most of the other new tonnage built in this country is so constructed. Since the close of World War II, the Bureau has extended its activities in the foreign field. Many of the new vessels being built in Germany, Italy, Japan, and other foreign shipyards are being built to American Bureau class.

Underwriters' Surveyors. The well-organized underwriting office, although depending in large measure on the records of vessels as shown in the classification-society books, often has competent surveyors of its own. A steamer in first-class condition, according to the society's book, may have experienced disaster or may have been permitted to run down since her last classification survey. It is prudent for the underwriters as far as possible to keep their own vessel records and to have their own surveyors, in whose judgment they have confidence, make special reports on vessels offered for insurance.

Underwriters' Organizations. The marine-insurance business is well organized, and to aid and protect underwriters, societies have been established here and abroad, the purpose of which is to foster the business and to improve its service to the assured. In this country the American Institute of Marine Underwriters was organized in 1898. Its purpose is to formulate policy clauses to meet special conditions, to follow and recommend or oppose proposed legislation in regard to marine insurance, and to keep in close touch with similar organizations in Great Britain and other foreign countries.

Underwriters' Boards and Loss Agents. On the loss side of the business there are underwriters' boards, such as the Board of Underwriters of New York and the San Francisco Board of Marine Underwriters, which have representatives at the principal ports of the world. They send prompt reports of disasters occurring within their territory and are competent to take charge of operations looking to the safeguarding of imperiled property. They survey damaged goods and issue certificates showing the nature and extent of the injury suffered.

These boards also supervise the loading of vessels and promulgate rules for the proper stowage of bulk and other extrahazardous cargoes. Their representatives grant certificates showing that vessels are fit to load the proposed cargoes and certify that the loading is proper when the vessel is loaded. Such organizations are merely voluntary and are powerful protecting factors in overseas commerce only in so far as they receive the support and encouragement of underwriters, shipowners, and merchants. A similar service with respect to hulls is provided by the United States Salvage Association, an organization supported by the underwriters comprising the American Marine Hull Insurance Syndicate. It is not a salvage association such as is described in the next paragraph.

Salvage Associations. Salvage associations are usually privately organized but sometimes have on their board of managers representatives of the underwriters. Such organizations attend to the salvaging of both ships and cargo when damaged or in a position of peril. Some organizations, like the Liverpool and Glasgow Salvage Association and the Merritt-Chapman & Scott Corporation in this country, have their own wrecking departments fully equipped with vessels and machinery suitable for salvage operations. Other organizations call in, when needed, private wrecking companies who are experienced in salvage work. These associations do much to reduce marine losses and are of value not only to the underwriters but to merchants and shipowners as well.

Maps, Charts, and Port Books. The underwriting office itself must be equipped with or have access to maps, charts, and port books showing the ocean tracks, paths of the winds, currents, lighthouses, radio stations, particulars of ports with respect to depth of water, berthing accommodations, facilities for supplies of fuel and stores, and the numberless other items of information that an underwriter must have in order to consider a risk intelligently from the geographic point of view. Improvement in port conditions and changes in commercial methods are so rapid that an underwriter must keep abreast of the times and be informed as to present conditions with respect to shipping and commerce, not only in his own country but also in foreign nations.

Nationality. An underwriter must take into account many factors in deciding whether a risk offered is acceptable. First of all, the nationality of the vessel is of great moment. In wartimes its importance is apparent, but in times of peace, while this factor is of only slightly less importance, its bearing on the risk lies beneath the surface. Certain nations have produced more skillful mariners than others. The adaptability of a people to a seafaring life is largely a matter of temperament. This fact is of no little importance to underwriters, because at a time of crisis, when the captain and crew have to think clearly and act quickly, the citizens of those nations whose heritage has been connected with the sea seem to have the innate ability to do the right thing at the right time and to take advantage of every opportunity to preserve the ship and the cargo.

Owners, Managers, and Masters. The ownership of a vessel is also a matter of much concern. Some owners run their vessels without incurring many accidents, while others, born perhaps under less lucky stars, are always in trouble. An underwriter is not so much interested in why one ownership is good and another bad as he is in the fact itself. An owner or a line may innocently acquire a bad reputation, but more often such a reputation is the result of incompetent management. Poor management results in deteriorated, insufficiently equipped vessels, often incompetently officered and manned. Truly, in shipowning and ship managing "a good name is rather to be chosen than great riches."

The question of "riches" is, nevertheless, of considerable importance, since the financial position of the owners is of real consequence in the event of loss or other untoward event, when the owner may be suddenly called upon to disburse considerable sums in order to extricate a vessel from a position of difficulty. If the owner is without available funds, valuable time may be lost in commencing salvage operations.

There is another side to the question of ownership. An owner may keep his property in good condition and employ competent officers and crews, but his reputation for unfair dealing in cases of disaster, when so much depends on his attitude, may make underwriters wary of accepting risks on his vessels. Lloyd's, London, formerly published volumes for the confidential use of underwriters, one showing the record of vessels registered under the British flag, the other, vessels registered under foreign flags. The vessels in each volume were grouped under their respective ownerships, so that some evidence of the success or failure of any ownership could be obtained, for the lists contained not only all vessels owned, but all vessels formerly owned that had met an untimely end through disaster or terminated their career in the scrap heap. These volumes gave a concise history of the voyages of the vessels, showing the various disasters to hull and machinery and where they had occurred. The same organization also published for the confidential use of subscribing underwriters a port record giving a concise description of the physical and moral hazards peculiar to each port. Lloyd's, London, also had a record containing in brief form statistics on the life career of all British shipmasters, showing the ships that they had commanded and what misfortunes they had experienced with their vessels. The nature of a risk is influenced not a little by the character of the master to whom the venture is entrusted. It is to be hoped that as soon as practicable these records will be made available again.

Structural Characteristics of Ship and Its Physical Condition. The material of which a vessel is built, her structural plan, her engine, horsepower, and interior condition with respect to the protection of cargo that may be carried in her hold are all matters of moment to underwriters. If a great single-deck bulk freighter is put on the berth to load a general miscellaneous cargo, the underwriter must think of the effect on barrels of wine or other cargo, placed in the bottom of the hold, which will have to sustain the pressure of the weight of cargo loaded above. Or if it be a tank steamer that has carried bulk petroleum to Cuba and is to return to the United States with a cargo of molasses, the underwriter will be interested in knowing if the hold has been steamed or otherwise cleansed before the molasses is loaded. If the vessel is to carry a perishable cargo, such as green coffee or cocoa beans, it is pertinent to inquire whether the holds are fitted with cargo battens and properly dunnaged to protect the cargo from the moisture that may condense on the inside of the vessel. If a full cargo of grain is to be loaded, question will arise as to whether the vessel has been properly equipped with shifting boards and wing feeders. These illustrations will serve to indicate the trend of an underwriter's thought in considering the physical condition of the vessel.

Other Considerations. Again, the season of the year during which the voyage is to be made becomes of interest when the periodic storms that run their courses on the ocean and the ice conditions that exist at certain seasons on the Great Lakes and in other places in the cooler latitudes are considered. In the case of cargo insurance the kind of goods to be insured is important, considered not only for their intrinsic qualities but also for their usefulness at the port of destination. It may be that in the event of disaster there will be small salvage to the goods, or there may be no market at the port of destination or at an intermediate port of refuge for damaged goods of the particular character in question.

Measurement of Ships. An underwriter is often asked to quote on a full cargo of grain or other bulk cargo without any definite information being given as to the quantity to be laden. It is important that he have some rule by which he can quickly estimate the quantity the vessel can carry and from this quantity arrive at the approximate value of the cargo. In the books of the classification societies two figures are usually given in the tonnage column, one larger than the other. In a previous chapter the displacement of a vessel was defined as the weight of the vessel in tons. The tonnage of a vessel as shown in the classification-society books is not displacement tonnage but measurement tonnage. Many years ago, in order to gain uniformity in the measurements of vessels, there was arbitrarily adopted in Great Britain a measurement ton of 100 cubic feet, and this unit of measure has generally been accepted by other nations. The tonnage shown in the classification books therefore indicates the number of tons of 100 cubic feet each contained in the boat, the larger figure indicating the number of measurement tons in the enclosed watertight portion of the ship, without any allowance being made for necessary engine, crew, fuel, and store space; the smaller figure showing the measurement tonnage with these spaces deducted. The larger figure is known as the *gross* tonnage; the smaller, the *net* tonnage. Sometimes in the case of passenger vessels an intermediate measurement, before the passenger accommodations are deducted, is shown. There are elaborate rules for the measurements of gross, intermediate, and net tonnage, which vary in different countries and in connection with the tonnage dues at the Panama and Suez Canals.

Measurement of Cargo Capacity. While the measurement ton is 100 cubic feet, a ton of average dead-weight cargo occupies only about 40 cubic feet. This is true of grain and many other bulk cargoes. It is therefore possible in such cases to load about 2½ tons of cargo in one measurement ton of space, and as each 35 cubic feet of water will support 1 ton,[1] it will be quite possible to load more than twice the net registered tonnage with grain and still not have exhausted the supporting power of the water. Whether or not this quantity of grain could be loaded would depend somewhat on the structural arrangement of the particular vessel and the necessity of having adequate freeboard. In this connection Prof. Emory R. Johnson cites the following rule in regard to loading: "The ratio of net register to . . . cargo tonnage of a modern freight vessel loaded with general cargo is as 1 . . . to 2¼ . . . In the large modern sailing vessel . . . the cargo tonnage of the loaded vessel will average about 1⅔ times the net register."[2] To apply this rule to the proposed full cargo of grain, the underwriter would multiply the net registered tonnage by, say, 2¼ and, multiplying this result by the value of the grain per ton, obtain a fair approximation of the value of the contemplated cargo. A graphic idea of the cargo capacity of a freight steamer of, say, 4,000 net tons may be gained by considering how much bulk there is to 9,000 tons of wheat, the quantity that such a vessel could carry under the above-cited rule. Each ton of wheat consists of approximately 40 bushels, so that this vessel could carry 360,000 bushels. The average yield per acre is, say, 30 bushels, so that this cargo will represent the yield of 12,000 acres, or about 20 square miles of land. To carry this grain to the vessel will require a train of 180 cars, each carrying 50 tons and stretching over a mile in length. Such are the giant freight vessels that enable this country to be the granary of the world.

Cargoes and Shipping Packages. While it is true that the physical condition of the ship itself must be considered, it is no less true that

[1] See p. 73.

[2] "Ocean and Inland Water Transportation," p. 11.

the underwriter must give thought to the intrinsic qualities of cargo that is offered for insurance and to the nature of the package in which such cargo is shipped. In some countries it is a difficult and expensive matter to obtain wood to make packing cases, and accordingly easily damaged articles are packed in inferior containers and place an additional burden on underwriters. Packing cases or barrels used in importing goods into a foreign country may again be used in the export of goods. In recent years cartons have been used to pack goods for export. Considerable improvement has been made in these packages, but they rapidly disintegrate when submerged. In the event that a hold is flooded through collision, the loss will usually be much greater than if the goods were packed in wooden containers.

An underwriter's education is never completed. Day by day he must keep abreast of new conditions in all parts of the world and be able to deduce the effects which these new conditions will have on marine underwriting.

The Moral Hazard. Before passing from the consideration of the factors that are important in the judging of risks, mention must be made of what is undoubtedly the primary and most important factor in marine underwriting. As will be pointed out in subsequent chapters, the whole fabric of marine underwriting is based on good faith and fair dealing between underwriter and assured. This element in the marine contract is little talked of but is ever present and is known as *moral hazard*. An underwriter must rely to a very large extent on the statements made by a merchant or shipowner with respect to the risk offered for insurance. To be sure, the underwriter has some documentary evidence in the classification books respecting the vessel, but in many cases he knows nothing definite regarding its present condition. When the subject matter is cargo, the underwriter must rely almost entirely on the integrity of the insured and his willingness to tell of any unusual circumstances connected with the shipment. The underwriter is presumed to know all the usual conditions in regard to various kinds of goods and their mode of shipment, but as a rule he is working on theory alone and has no opportunity actually to view the goods. The result is that an underwriter must be a reader of character and a judge of the hearts and intents of men. After a loss has occurred, it is too late to discover that an assured or his broker is a deceiver or a skillful talker, perhaps telling the truth in regard to the risk, but not the whole truth. The experienced and careful underwriter must be able to judge the character of a man at sight, instead of discovering his deficiencies in the expensive and bitter school of experience. And so in the consideration of marine insurance principles and practice, it is well to understand that the profession of marine underwriting is a serious one, calling for the greatest degree of skill and knowledge and for a more than ordinary equipment of common sense and ability to judge men.

CHAPTER 7

Brokers and Managing Agents

Before proceeding to a consideration of the insurance-policy contract that has been devised to protect merchant and shipowner against losses due to the hazards of transportation discussed in the previous chapters, it will be desirable to consider how he obtains this protection. In the early commercial history of the United States, overseas commerce, though subject to grave physical risks, was quite simple in operation. Oftentimes the shipowner was also a merchant. He ran his ships primarily to carry his own cargoes. He had all his overseas problems at his finger tips, and so in most cases he sought out an insurance company in whose management he had confidence, discussed his problem face to face with the underwriters, and arranged what protection he desired and could obtain. A very considerable part of the marine underwriting in the United States was done by mutual companies, and each had its followers among the merchants and shipowners.

THE BROKER

While the clipper-ship era was at its height, a few men of imagination decided that they could perform a useful service by establishing themselves as experienced intermediaries between merchant or shipowner and underwriter. Many of these men had received their training with the marine-insurance companies and could demonstrate their competence to undertake this important service. And so the *broker* entered the marine picture as the middleman of the marine-insurance market, knowing market conditions accurately and acting as the distributing medium between the underwriter and the merchant or shipper. His progress was relatively slow, and merchant and shipowner had to be persuaded that the broker could serve them as well or better than they could be served in dealing directly with the underwriter. In time the idea received general acceptance as the problems of overseas commerce became more and more complicated. By the beginning of the twentieth century most of the marine-insurance business in the United States was negotiated through brokers.

He Is Not a New Factor. While the broker was late in establishing himself in the United States, he is in no sense a new factor in the marine-insurance business. As early as the fifteenth century reference is found, both in England and in Continental countries, to the activities of insurance brokers. Individual underwriting probably created the condition that made the work of the broker useful. In England, at least, for some time private underwriters conducted their business in their own homes. It was a great aid to the merchant to be able to engage the services of one who knew where the underwriters lived and who would take the policy from house to house, obtaining the signatures of various underwriters, until the whole amount was taken and the policy of insurance completed. With the gathering of the individual underwriters under one roof, the same need of an intermediary between assured and underwriter continued, and the broker passed from desk to desk obtaining signatures. Even today, at Lloyd's the underwriting room is not open to the public, but authorized brokers, some of whom are themselves underwriting members of Lloyd's, perform this important and necessary work in the placing of marine risks.

He Is Indispensable. In this country the broker has grown with the development of the business and now performs an indispensable service in the placing of marine risks. His work has, in principle, changed little. As it was necessary 400 years ago to visit 50 individual underwriters to place a risk of £10,000, so today it is sometimes necessary to obtain the aid of many incorporated insurance companies in order to place a risk of $5,000,000. The values coming into the market are proportionately larger, but the law of supply and demand works inexorably, and the market rarely becomes larger than is needed for the ordinary line, so that, as in olden days, brokers still beat a path between the offices of the underwriters.

He Occupies an Anomalous Position. The broker occupies a somewhat anomalous position in the field of agents. Ordinarily an agent is paid by his principal. With the insurance broker, however, this condition is reversed. He is engaged by and acts as the agent of the assured but is compensated by the underwriter. It is, of course, true that the merchant indirectly pays for the service rendered in the increased cost of insurance; nevertheless, it is an indirect charge which does not make the same mental impression as would an item of broker's commission if added to the bill for insurance premium. If the charge were so made, it would doubtless result in more direct transactions between assured and underwriter, but whether this would work to the advantage of either assured or insurer is altogether problematical. The average assured needs the services of a highly trained expert in whom he has a confidence that he will not have in an underwriter who is one of the parties to the contract. A disinterested intermediary serves, at least, to calm the mind of the assured, who, as a rule in this country, has little technical knowledge of the principles of this exceedingly important part of his commercial transactions. An expert broker not only is of value to the assured but performs a distinct service to the underwriter in relieving the latter of the necessity of explaining to inexperienced assured their policy obligations and in preparing for him proper declarations of insurance from the inadequate reports too often submitted by the assured.

He Offers a Service. The broker, then, offers himself for employment as a specialist or an expert in the principles and practice of marine insurance. A broker has but one thing to offer the assured, and that is service. Service, in its broadest meaning, is the sole logical reason for the existence of the able group of brokers in the marine-insurance market. The comparative success or failure of individual brokers or of firms of brokers rests in large part on the interpretation they give to the word *service*. It is not enough that the broker place the risk which his client sends him. He must place it with the underwriters having the best security and the best reputation for fair dealing with the assured. This, however, represents in its barest outline the duty of the broker.

He Is a Trained Expert. In soliciting business, the broker presents himself to a prospective client as a trained expert in the business of marine insurance. He may offer to obtain the kind of insurance which a merchant or shipowner needs at less cost than he is paying or to provide insurance broader in its protection at the same cost. Furthermore, he may promise, if employed, to take better care of the client's interests, to relieve him of all responsibility in regard to the insurance except the duty of promptly reporting the facts necessary to enable the broker to place the insurance. In addition he may agree, in the event of loss, to conduct the negotiations relating to the adjustment and payment of the loss without trouble to the assured. The discharge of these duties and others unnamed, but which are inseparably bound up in the complete execution of those which are named, constitutes service. Success will inevitably come to those brokers who make good their promise by caring for their clients in a manner superior to that of their fellows.

He Knows the Market. The broker, as an expert, requires a degree of knowledge approximating that of the trained underwriter or loss adjuster. The broker obtains from his client a bare statement of facts concerning his commercial operations, the kind of goods in which he trades, the routes of shipment, and other items necessary to enable him to gain a clear insight into the kind of risks upon which he must obtain insurance. Having this information in hand, he applies his knowledge of marine insurance to the facts, deciding what form of protection is best suited to the particular case. He carefully weighs the comparative gain in the use of clauses granting a high degree of protection, with respect to average, for instance, against the increased cost of such protection. Having reached a conclusion, he may first submit and explain to his client the form of insurance that he would advise and obtain the consent of the client to accept such a policy. Of course, if there should be any doubt in the mind of the broker as to the possibility of obtaining the kind of protection that he thinks the client needs, he will first test the market to learn if there are underwriters who will accept the proposed policy and, if so, at what rates. The suggestion that he obtain a certain form of insurance may appeal strongly to a new or prospective client, but if the proposal cannot be underwritten, little credit will result to the broker. A broker must have a working knowledge of what the market offers and at what cost.

Progressive Underwriting. However, it must not be presumed that the broker should limit his efforts to obtaining conditions or rates that he knows are readily granted. If he believes that his client needs a form of protection not heretofore offered by underwriters, or if his client demands a certain form of protection that he believes can be consistently underwritten, it is his duty as an intermediary to use his efforts to obtain such form of policy. Much of the progress that has been made in the broadening of the marine-insurance contract is due to the honest efforts of experienced brokers to obtain better protection for their clients. At this point, however, the broker is treading on dangerous ground. In his desire to gain business he may advocate the granting of conditions that, on sober second thought, he may realize are fraught with peril to the careless underwriter. Nevertheless, his desire for business may warp his judgment, and he will seek to obtain these unwise insurance conditions and perhaps succeed. If the underwriter is induced to grant unsound conditions and consequently suffers heavy losses, he will be apt to consider, with more than ordinary caution, future proposals from this source. To be sure, competition often compels a broker to ask an underwriter to grant conditions that the broker believes to be unwise, but if in such cases he will take the trouble to explain that competition is causing him to plead against his better judgment, the underwriter will be more disposed to treat with him and probably will not later feel that the broker has taken an unfair advantage.

Twofold Duty. It may be thought that an underwriter should be competent to take care of himself and that, if he does poor underwriting in the granting of unwise conditions and inadequate rates, he alone is responsible. This is not altogether the case. It frequently happens that a broker controlling a large volume of business will obtain a powerful position in the underwriting market, and underwriters will seek his favor in order to obtain a share of the business that he controls. When such a condition exists, a broker, in order to obtain from a prospective client an account controlled by another broker, may offer to furnish a policy containing conditions that appeal to the client but that the broker knows are not in harmony with sound underwriting. Having obtained the account under such promise, he will use his power, indirectly it may be, but nevertheless effectively, to induce one or more underwriters to grant the required conditions.

The broker owes a duty, not only to his client but also to the underwriter, to foster and conserve in every practicable way the stability of the latter, in order that the security behind the policy may continue to be of the best. Brokers should realize that the success of the insurance companies makes possible the continued existence of their own business. In this country, the broker has no capital at risk that will be affected by the success or failure of the underwriter. Nevertheless, it is just as much his duty to refrain from asking unwise insurance conditions of underwriters as it is to see that his client obtains the fullest measure of protection consistent with safe underwriting. The broker should realize that, in the last analysis, his interest and that of the underwriter are one.

Attitude toward Losses. It is not only in the placing of risks that the broker has this twofold duty. The same obligation exists with respect to the collection of losses. Notwithstanding the efforts that the broker may make to explain to the assured the measure of protection that he is receiving under the policy of insurance in regard to perils covered and to average conditions granted, some assured feel that, in the event of loss, the underwriter should recompense them regardless of the nature or extent of the damage suffered. Accordingly they will present a claim to the broker. In cases where the facts presented indicate clearly that no liabilty exists on the part of the underwriter, the claim should never reach him. The broker should return it to the assured and explain to him why no liability rests upon the underwriter. If, on the other hand, there is a reasonable doubt as to the question of liability, or if the facts as presented are unusual and give rise to the question whether, as a matter of equity rather than as a matter of legal right, the assured may be entitled to a hearing with respect to the claim, the broker should present the case to the underwriter, pleading the cause of his client but leaving the question of settlement to the judgment of the underwriter. The broker's position is not always an easy one, and in many cases, no little degree of tact is required in order amicably to satisfy both assured and assurer. His position is often that of a buffer, taking up the blows delivered both by assured and underwriter.

Arranges Settlement of Losses. The duty of a broker does not end with the presentation of claim for loss. Sometimes he actually makes an adjustment of the loss, presenting the completed claim for the approval of and settlement by the underwriters. Some underwriters prefer to make their own adjustments, and in such cases the broker collects the necessary documents in order to prove the claim, presenting them to the underwriter for his consideration. The underwriter then makes up the adjustment. It is the duty of the broker to scrutinize this statement of loss carefully and to make certain that his client is receiving the full measure of recovery afforded by the policy.

Services in General Average. If the casualty in which the property is involved results in a general-average sacrifice, the broker makes the necessary arrangements for the release of the goods, advises with respect to the general-average bond, and obtains the general-average guarantee from the underwriters.[1] The amount of time and trouble expended in the collection of losses is sometimes very great, especially when intricate questions of liability arise. Brokers in the United States perform this labor without extra charge, considering that this is part of the service they have agreed to give their client.

Commissions. The question of commissions should be the last thought of the broker. It is true that they are the source of his income, yet the main consideration for the broker is to give the best quality of service to his clients and so to conduct his operations with the underwriters that both client and underwriter will wish to do business with him again. If the broker successfully meets this twofold obligation, the matter of commission will take care of itself, and his financial success will be assured. To the conscientious and skillful broker, the business is very lucrative. In the brokerage field, a good reputation spreads quite as quickly as a bad one, and clients will come to the broker who consistently furnishes the best service and who, because of his relations with the underwriters, can obtain policies backed by the best security that the market affords.

Does Not Guarantee Payment of Premiums. In this country, the broker in the ordinary case does not guarantee the solvency of his client; that is, he is not a guarantor for the collection of the premiums. It is his duty, however, to use all reasonable efforts to make collection of the premium, but if his client becomes financially em-

[1] See Chap. 25.

barrassed and fails to pay, this does not create any financial obligation on the part of the broker to the underwriter. It sometimes is the case, however, that an underwriter may be unwilling to write an account because of lack of faith in the financial standing of the assured, in which event the broker may guarantee the payment of the premiums. Such agreement should not be left to inference but should be expressly made in writing by the broker. While there is no financial obligation on the part of the broker in the ordinary case with respect to the payment of premium, there is a moral obligation on his part not to offer business to an underwriter unless he is reasonably certain of the financial integrity of his client. Furthermore, the broker's own reputation with the underwriter is in a large measure determined by the character of business offered. If he constantly offers business where the moral hazard is bad or business which proves unprofitable because of careless packing or handling of goods or of lack of skill in the operation of vessels, he will soon find that the first-class market is closed to him and that all risks offered by him are looked upon with suspicion. A broker's reputation will depend in no small measure on the reputation of his clients. It is customary for the assured to pay the premium to the broker. It is his duty to remit the premium promptly to the underwriter. In many states it has been held that, if the premium is paid to the broker, he receives it as agent of the underwriter.

The Broker as an Underwriter. During and following World War I a new situation developed in the marine-underwriting field where brokers entered upon the dual career of broker and underwriter. This form of operation was not very successful and has practically disappeared. Large broker firms or corporations, which formerly confined their operations to the placing of risks and the adjusting of losses, opened separate departments for the underwriting of risks, receiving appointment as general or special agents of important marine-insurance companies. In some cases the underwriting was conducted under the same name as the brokerage portion of the business; in others a separate firm or corporation was organized for the conduct of the underwriting section of the business. Although there was an apparent separation of interest, there was nevertheless unity of control. If a complete separation between the two branches of the business existed, there was no good reason why a broker should not extend his activities to the underwriting field. The principal difficulty in the situation was one that could not be removed—human nature. It is a difficult matter for two phases of a business, which in a measure are opposed to each other in their method of approaching the problems of that business, to be conducted by one person or by the same group of persons with proper consideration for the interest of each.

A Difficult Relation. There are two chief dangers in such a complicated system. First, the aid of the underwriting branch of the business will be given to the brokerage branch in order to create a lead. That is, the underwriting branch may grant conditions and rates that are necessary for obtaining a new account, and if the companies represented are of sufficient reputation, other underwriters may follow the lead. In the second place, a broker, acting as an underwriter, obtains valuable information regarding the business connections of other brokers. The underwriter occupies a confidential relation both to broker and to assured, and if a broker acting as underwriter abuses this confidential relation, the result will be that other brokers will not avail themselves of his underwriting facilities, except in case of urgent necessity, and there will be a consequent loss of business to the insurance company that has entrusted its underwriting agency to a broker. From the company standpoint, however, this may possibly be offset by a consideration of the fact that a large brokerage concern, controlling a great amount of business, may bring to the company a volume of premium income that might not otherwise be obtained. While the entrance of the broker into the underwriting field revealed no considerable abuse of the dual relation, it was a condition fraught with dangerous possibilities and one which, in the hands of unscrupulous persons, might have led to serious consequences. In principle, a complete separation of broker and underwriter will do most to foster the growth of the marine-insurance market and will leave competition free and open with resultant benefit to the insuring public.

MANAGING AGENTS

Many of the companies that tried to operate through brokerage offices on an agency basis have withdrawn from the market. Others have transferred their facilities to the offices of *underwriting agents* and *managers,* who conduct a very large portion of the marine-insurance business in the United States. The marine-insurance activities of many companies, both domestic and foreign, are a very special line of relatively small volume, and they find it economical and profitable to place their facilities in the hands of experienced marine underwriters and loss adjusters. Thus one managing office may underwrite for a number of companies, conducting and supervising their marine-insurance underwriting throughout the United States and sometimes abroad. On the other hand, the old insurance companies that were organized for the primary purpose of underwriting marine risks maintain their own offices throughout the country.

Local Agents. While a very large percentage of the marine-insurance business is placed by brokers, there are, particularly in some major inland cities, qualified local agents who do a substantial marine business. In these marine-insurance operations they act more in the nature of brokers than agents. Technically they are agents of the company; practically they are representatives of the assured.

BROKERS IN GREAT BRITAIN

Although there is an intimate connection between the British and American marine-insurance markets, the methods of conducting brokerage operations here and in England are quite different. There the broker occupies a position that, to a certain extent, is fiduciary in its nature. The ordinary form of the British policy, by its terms, confesses payment of premium. The Marine Insurance Act of Great Britain provides that, when a marine policy, effected by a broker on behalf of the assured, acknowledges receipt of the premium, such acknowledgment is, in the absence of fraud, conclusive as between the insurer and the assured but not as between the insurer and the broker. This seems to free the assured from any liability for premium under such a policy. Another section of the same Act provides that, when a policy is placed by a broker, the broker is responsible to the underwriter for the premium but he has a lien on the policy for the premium plus his charges for effecting the insurance. Under the system in use in Great Britain the broker makes monthly remittances to the underwriters for premiums due, the broker receiving the policies and retaining them until payment is made by the assured. The assured is also expected to make monthly remittances to the broker. The broker is allowed a 5 per cent placing commission on the gross amount of the premium. The assured customarily is allowed a 10 per cent discount from the net amount after deducting the broker's commission provided he pays the premium by the tenth of the month.

Losses and Return Premiums. While the payment of premium is, in Great Britain, a matter that rests between the underwriter and the broker, the underwriter is directly responsible to the assured for the payment of losses and for the payment of return premiums. The broker is thus placed in the peculiar position of being liable for the premium, but in the event of nonpayment by the assured, he is not able to lay claim to a loss payment out of which he might reimburse himself for the premium paid. However, if the broker retains possession of the policies as is his right under the law until the premium is paid, he will be in the position of preventing the assured from collecting a loss or a return premium owing to the inability of the latter to produce the policy. The broker's position is therefore not quite so precarious as the bare statement of the rule would seem to indicate. Furthermore, the lien that the broker retains by the possession of the policy does not apply to the particular policy alone but to any other unpaid balance arising out of an insurance account between the broker and his client.

Current Accounts. In practice the broker usually attends to the collection of return premiums and losses and runs a credit-and-debit account with his client, charging the account with premiums due and crediting it with return premiums and losses recovered, the debit or credit balance being settled from time to time by the assured or the broker. This bare outline of brokerage practice in Great Britain will serve to indicate the more responsible position of the broker in the British marine-insurance market as compared with that of his American contemporary.

CHAPTER 8

The Contract of Marine Insurance

Definition of Marine Insurance. Marine insurance is the method whereby one party, called the *assurer* or *underwriter,* agrees, for a stated consideration known as the *premium,* to indemnify another party, called the *insured* or *assured,* against loss, damage, or expense in connection with the subject matter at risk if caused by perils enumerated in the contract known as the *policy of insurance.* A policy of insurance insures the person or persons interested in the subject matter and not the subject matter itself. The policy promises to indemnify the assured for damage arising out of the loss of or injury to the property insured but does not guarantee the continued existence or replacement of the thing itself.

Not a Perfect Contract of Indemnity. A marine-insurance policy is a contract of indemnity, but not a perfect one. To indemnify means to make good, to put a person back in his original situation with respect to a specified thing or a certain condition. Insurance strives, as far as possible, to make good whatever financial loss a person may have suffered through the destruction or depreciation of the true value of the commodity to which the insurance relates but does not endeavor to reimburse the assured for any sentimental or aesthetic value unless it is definitely possible financially to measure such value and the underwriter and assured have mutually agreed that such value shall be insured.

Only Fortuitous Losses Covered. Marine insurance was never devised to protect the assured against all loss or damage that may overtake his property, but only against those losses which are fortuitous and beyond the control of the assured. The policy will not cover losses that are inevitable or usual because of the nature of the goods, the shipping package, or the voyage. Competition, it is true, has greatly modified this rule, but the principle remains and should always be enforced in the case of *vice propre* losses, that is, losses which are the result of the inherent qualities of the subject matter insured and not the result of a casualty. An illustration of a *vice propre* loss is that of the heating of improperly cured skins, resulting in their rotting in the inside of the bale. Given the proper conditions of heat and moisture, bacterial action will commence in any animal or vegetable product. Unless such action is caused directly by an outside force, against whose action insurance is provided under the policy, the underwriter is not liable for the resultant damage. For this reason, deterioration of a commodity, due solely to delay or prolongation of transit, is not covered under a marine-insurance policy in its ordinary form. In the United States the courts, while confirming this general rule, have held that, where the delay resulted from a marine peril and, as a consequence of such delay, deterioration commenced, the underwriter is liable for the resultant loss, the proximate cause of the loss being the marine peril and not the delay. However, underwriters are customarily unwilling to assume losses due to delay, even if the delay be caused by an insured peril. Accordingly the following Institute clause is usually inserted in the American cargo-insurance policy:

> Warranted free of claim for loss of market or for loss, damage or deterioration arising from delay, whether caused by a peril insured against or otherwise, unless expressly assumed in writing herein.

It is usual in some trades, such as the importation of fresh fruit, specifically to cover loss or deterioration resulting from prolongation of the voyage due to breakdown of the propelling machinery, rudder trouble, or other named causes, provided the prolongation equals or exceeds an agreed number of days.

Negligence Should Not Be Covered by Policy. Neither should marine insurance agree to indemnify the assured against losses that are the result of the negligence or carelessness of those into whose custody the property is given. That is, the insurer should not assume liability for loss or damage caused through the neglect of carriers, whether private or common. The law charges the carrier under the bill of lading with certain duties that he should be compelled to perform, and the assured should not be permitted, because of insurance, to become remiss in his duty of enforcing carriers to comply with their obligations. True, it is often easier to insure against a risk that is an obligation of the carrier than it is to enforce the obligation without the use of legal pressure, but the inevitable result of such a course over a period of years is detrimental to all concerned. This is abundantly shown in the matter of pilferage claims. Such losses are the result of negligence on the part of those to whose custody property is entrusted. Through lack of protection packages are opened and part or all of the contents removed. The carrier responds for this loss if it can be shown that the pilferage took place while the goods were in his possession. Owing to the delay in collecting such losses, underwriters were urged to give protection against such losses so that the assured might be promptly reimbursed and not have to wait on the convenience of the carriers. Some underwriters consented, with the result that the writing of pilferage insurance became general. The carriers, knowing that the shipper could obtain protection against such losses, were less ready to settle these claims, practically denying liability in many cases and interposing all sorts of objections to the claims presented.

Agreed-value Clauses. Where legally possible, carriers have inserted in their bills of lading clauses limiting their responsibility to a named sum per package or per shipping unit, say $50 per package or $10 per cubic foot. One of the great advantages of the Carriage of Goods by Sea Acts or the Hague Rules[1] is that the carriers are not permitted, except in certain specified cases, to insert any limiting valuation less than $500 per shipping package or customary cargo unit. The insurance of negligence risks has increased very materially in recent years, so that it is now not unusual for an underwriter to cover practically all these risks, such as bad stowage, contact with other cargo, oil damage, chafing, hook hole, and other similar losses due almost entirely to causes within the control of the carrier and his servants. The ill effects of insuring against pilferage risks appear only in lesser degree in connection with the insurance of these other negligence risks. Such insurance is theoretically unsound, in that it is really an

[1] See Appendix O.

insurance against a person's (the carrier's) own acts even though it be written in the name of a third party (the shipper). The general acceptance of the Hague Rules, with the increased-valuation clause required, has done much to induce more careful handling of cargo on the part of the carriers and thus in a measure to offset the bad effect of the insurance of negligence risks.

Modern Policy Broad in Its Protection. Transportation insurance would probably be a better modern name for so-called marine insurance. The present-day marine-insurance policy on goods covers property from the time it leaves the shipper's warehouse until, in due course of transit, it is delivered, by air, land, and/or water conveyances to the consignee's warehouse. It is, in its broadest sense, transportation insurance by air, land, and/or water, and, consequently, merchandise should never be covered by a marine policy after transit has ceased or after the property has been placed in the custody of the owner.

This general rule has been somewhat modified, and insurance has been extended to cover goods which, in their transit from the warehouse of the original shipper to the consignee, are temporarily delayed or of which the transit is interrupted to enable the owner to examine, repack, or break up a large shipment into smaller lots and then reship to various destinations. Other shipments may be delayed in transit and warehoused, awaiting a more favorable market, as in the case of imported goods arriving too early for the Easter or Christmas trade, which are placed in bonded warehouses or in free ports awaiting withdrawal at the convenience of the owner. It is not unusual for the marine-insurance policy to continue to cover such goods until they are received in the consignee's own warehouse. If the policy was not so extended and goods, after being received in the consignee's own warehouse, were found to be pilfered or broken, the underwriter might question a claim for loss, on the ground that the loss might have occurred during the interruption of transit when the goods were not insured. To guard against the possibility of dispute arising in regard to "concealed" damages, that is, damages not discoverable until the cases are opened, it is always prudent to provide continuous insurance notwithstanding a possible warehousing in transit.

It is not unusual, even after goods have reached the consignee's warehouse and while they remain in the original package, to extend the policy to cover such goods in the consignee's warehouse. In other cases, fire insurance may be placed on the packages, but the other risks that may develop concealed losses continue to be covered under the marine policy until the packages are opened. In like manner with respect to export shipments, the marine underwriter will cover, for not exceeding 30 days prior to actual transit, goods that are in warehouse ready for shipment.

Good Faith. In no branch of insurance does good faith play so large a part as in the marine field. An underwriter is often asked to insure a ship or a cargo, thousands of miles away, without an opportunity to inspect the risk. In such cases he must rely absolutely on the statements made by the applicant in so far as they relate to matters that cannot be confirmed by the information which the underwriter has at his disposal in the classification-society books and in the shipping papers. He is, it is true, protected in a measure by the implied warranties which are read into the contract, but to a great extent he must rely on information that he cannot confirm. Good faith and fair dealing are the cornerstones on which the marine-insurance business is founded.

Elements of a Contract. To have a valid contract of insurance the following elements must appear, *viz.*,

1. The parties to the contract must be legally competent to make a contract.
2. The assured must have an insurable interest.
3. A valid consideration must pass (the premium) or a promise to pay the premium.
4. There must be a meeting of the minds of the contracting parties.
5. The contract must have a legal purpose.

Corporate and Individual Underwriters. Basically, a marine-insurance contract is no different from any other contract. The legal safeguards surrounding contracts in general are applicable to insurance contracts, and in addition, many conditions have been read into the latter for the protection of both assured and underwriter that are not included in other forms of agreement. In this country marine insurance is conducted almost exclusively by incorporated companies. These corporations, chartered by the various states, are legally competent to engage in the business of insurance as far as they are given authority under their charters. There seems to be no valid reason, however, why individuals should not engage in business as underwriters. Formerly this was done, but the American mind has turned more readily to the corporate form of underwriting with its published statement of assets, liabilities, and surplus. This condition contrasts greatly to the composition of the British insurance market, wherein individuals, underwriting at Lloyd's and elsewhere, form an important part of the market. Anyone may be an assured if he is legally competent to enter into a contract. That is, he must be of legal age, of sound mind, and otherwise within the rules that the law prescribes for contracting parties. A legal agent may act for a minor.

An Insurable Interest Necessary. No person may become a party to a marine-insurance contract unless he has an insurable interest. That is, the assured must bear such a relation to the insured subject that, directly or indirectly, he may be benefited by its safe arrival or continued existence and be injured by its damage or loss. In other words, a person may not legally take out insurance on certain property for his own benefit merely because such property is subject to marine hazards. The party seeking insurance must bear some provable relation to the property itself in order to insure it for his own benefit, or a legal relation of agency must exist to enable one to take out insurance for the benefit of another who has a valid insurable interest. Insurance which does not stand the test of these two conditions is void in law and is prohibited by statute in some of our states and in Great Britain.

The Premium a Valid Consideration. The third requirement of the marine-insurance contract is that there be a valid consideration. In every legal contract it must be possible to show that the person who performs or agrees to perform a service receives or will receive adequate compensation. The parties themselves are, however, the judge of the adequacy of the compensation, and its intrinsic value is not so important as the fact that the parties agreed to some measure of compensation. Accordingly, provision is made in all insurance contracts for the payment by the assured to the underwriter of a sum of money called the *premium.* How large or how small this amount may be is legally of no consequence if the assured and the underwriter have mutually agreed on the amount charged. If the insured subject is lost, the underwriter may not refuse to pay on the ground that the premium was too low, neither may the assured, if the risk has commenced or in the event of safe arrival, legally demand the return of any part of the premium.

The Minds of the Contracting Parties Must Meet. It is a basic principle of the law of contracts that the minds of the parties must meet. If the assured and the underwriter enter into negotiations for insurance relating to a certain subject or condition, and if the assured has one subject or condition in mind while the underwriter has in mind a similar but entirely different subject or condition, even should they complete their negotiations and a policy be issued, it will not be valid or enforceable in law. The contract as issued does not relate to anything common to the thought of both parties and therefore is null and void and of no effect. It is of the highest importance in the procuring of marine insurance that a full disclosure of all pertinent facts be made, so that no misunderstanding may exist as to the amount to be insured, the quantity and kind of property, the carrying conveyance, the voyage to be run, and the date of sailing or shipment. How important each of these elements of an insurance contract is will appear in a subsequent detailed discussion of these phases of the insurance policy. Fair dealing plays such an important part in marine insurance that the law requires a fuller disclosure of the facts relating to these contracts than it does with respect to other contractual relations.

A Legal Purpose Necessary. A contract must have a legal purpose. The law will not tolerate practices against public policy under the guise of insurance. Gambling done in the form of insurance is as injurious to the public morals as is gambling done in a less respectable way. The issuance of insurance in connection with transactions that are contrary to law is tainted with the same defect as is the transaction to which the insurance relates. Insurance is a necessary part of the commercial life of the nations but aids in the conduct of commerce only in so far as it complies with national and international law.

Direct and Indirect Placing of Insurance. Two methods of placing insurance are in vogue. A merchant may treat with an underwriter directly or, as is the customary practice, he may turn over to an insurance broker, who is trained in the practice and principles of marine insurance, the placing of his insurance for him. The first method has, in rare cases, some advantages. An insured, in dealing directly with an underwriter, may be able to present his risk in a more favorable light than the broker, because he has a fuller knowledge of the peculiar character of the property that he is insuring and can in many cases demonstrate to the underwriter the result of the action of sea water and the effect of handling on the commodity on which insurance is desired. On the other hand, if the merchant has not a fair understanding of insurance principles, he may greatly harm himself by asking for and accepting insurance that does not fully protect his property. Thus frequently an assured unwittingly assumes that the ordinary form of marine policy covers the risks of war.

Brokers. If the business of a merchant or shipowner is so large and diversified that he has to deal with many underwriters, or if his business is smaller but he has little knowledge of the intricate problems involved in marine insurance, he will do well to give the placing of his insurance into the hands of some competent broker. The subject of brokers has been considered in some detail in an earlier chapter.[1] It will suffice to remark here that a competent broker should have the same technical knowledge and training as an underwriter. Much progress in underwriting has resulted from the demands of brokers for new forms of protection, but on the other hand, the demands of brokers controlling large volumes of business have caused underwriters at times to depart from sound underwriting principles. The broker is employed by the assured but is paid by the underwriter and accordingly occupies the invidious position of trying to please both parties to the insurance contract.

The Insurance Application. In placing insurance, the basis of the contract is the insurance application. If a merchant wishes to insure 100 cases of dry goods from New York to Bombay, he gives the particulars about the shipment to his broker, who fills out a printed form containing spaces for the name of the assured, for the account on

[1] See Chap. 7.

whose behalf the insurance is desired, and for the payee of any possible loss. Spaces are also provided for the amount of insurance desired, the number of packages and kind of goods, the name of the carrying vessel, the points of shipment and of destination. The approximate date of shipment or of the sailing of the vessel should also be given.[1]

Binders and Inquiries. Having filled out this application form in duplicate, the broker presents it to the underwriter, who considers the facts presented and turns to the classification-society books or to his own private records for a description of the vessel. He then either names a rate and indicates the conditions under which he will grant insurance or declines the risk. If the rate and conditions are acceptable to the broker, he will sign the original application and hand the forms to the underwriter, who initials the duplicate, returning it to the broker. Thus a binding contract of insurance has been entered into. All that now remains to be done is the preparation by the underwriter, in accordance with this signed application, of the formal policy of insurance, which he signs and delivers to the assured or his broker. The assured or his broker may wish time in which to consider the rate and conditions quoted, in which case the application forms will not be signed, but one copy will be retained by the underwriter in a "not binding" file. This is merely an inquiry for and a quotation of a rate and is known as an *inquiry*. This quotation, like any other offer, must be accepted within a reasonable time, or the underwriter may limit the time within which acceptance may be made. The underwriter may withdraw the quotation any time prior to acceptance. The same procedure is followed whether the insurance desired relates to hull, freight, or cargo; whether it is for a special risk or for contemplated risks to be insured under an open contract.[2]

Cancellation and Modification of Contracts. Contracts of insurance being entered into by mutual agreement of the parties may be canceled or modified only by their mutual consent. Such consent should be in writing and may be shown either by having a cancellation clause written across the original application and signed or initialed by the assured or the broker and the underwriter or by having a reg-

[1] See application form, Appendix A.

[2] See p. 149.

ular form of cancellation[1] filled out in duplicate by the assured or his broker, setting forth the reason for the cancellation and outlining the particulars of the original insurance so that no doubt may exist as to the insurance to which the request for cancellation refers. One copy of the cancellation notice is signed by the assured or the broker and retained by the underwriter, and the other is signed by the underwriter and retained by the assured. If the policy has been issued, it is surrendered to the underwriter, who then makes the necessary cancellation on his records. In some instances, the cancellation clause may be written across the face of the policy, both parties signing it, although the policy itself is signed only by the underwriter. Alterations in the contract are similarly made. No writing on the policy, other than such as is assented to and initialed by the underwriter, is of any force or effect as against him, although it may result in voiding the contract with respect to the rights of the assured. When a contract has been made but has not become operative, the assured may, by preventing the commencement of the risk, in effect dissolve the contract. In no other way can the assured, without the consent of the underwriter, release himself from his bargain. The underwriter, on the other hand, may prevent such a result by requiring the assured to agree that there shall be no return premium for cancellation or short interest. Such an agreement is justifiable because the underwriter, in accepting insurance by a named vessel for one merchant, restricts to that extent his underwriting capacity available for others.

In the case of open cargo policies and of hull policies written for a period of time, a cancellation clause is part of the contract and sets forth the terms and conditions under which cancellation may be asked by either the assured or the company. Cancellation clauses will be discussed later.

Usage. When it is recalled that the law relating to marine insurance is largely an acceptance and adaptation of the customs of merchants, it is not strange that usage controls to a great extent the meaning of marine policies. The parties concerned may, of course, so draw the contract that its obvious import is to override the ordinary usage in connection with similar transactions, and as far as such contracts do not conflict with the law, they are perfectly proper and will be enforced

[1] See Appendix B.

as written. That is to say, usage is brought into evidence only where it is required to give proper meaning and force to the contract.

Mercantile Customs. Owing to the fact that custom plays such an important part in mercantile transactions and especially in marine-insurance contracts, it is necessary in many cases to go outside the contract itself to determine the intention of the parties. It would be manifestly impracticable to incorporate into each policy the customs and usages of the particular trade to which the insurance relates, and in the absence of affirmative evidence indicating that the voyage was to be conducted in some particular way, it will be presumed that the usual course and customs of the trade are to be followed. This does not mean, however, that extrinsic evidence is to be read into a marine-insurance policy to show that the intent of the parties was different from the fair meaning of the words used. It does mean, for instance, that a short phrase describing a voyage as "a trading voyage to West Africa" carries with it liberty to touch and stay for the purposes of ordinary trading at the usual trading stations along the West African Coast.

Printed, Written, and Stamped Words. All policies consist in part of printed and in part of written or stamped words. The basic part expresses that which is common to all marine-insurance policies. The added portions set forth those facts and agreements peculiar to the particular policy. It therefore is presumed that the added portions were the subject of special consideration by the parties. When these portions are in conflict with the basic form, they overrule or control it. It is these added words and clauses which give rise to most of the disputes in the interpretation of policies. The meaning of the basic form is well known, but who can know what will be the effect of some ill-considered clause which is demanded by an assured because he thinks it gives him increased protection? It may be so worded as to invalidate some of the basic or implied terms of all marine-insurance policies and leave him with less protection than he would have had with a policy in the usual form.

The Intention of the Parties. *Technical Words.* The intention of the parties to the contract should govern the meaning of the contract. This intention must be determined from the words as expressed. The words used may permit of more than one interpretation, and it must be determined which of the several meanings was the one intended by the parties. Policies should not be construed contrary to the fair meaning of the words and expressions used, but if it can be clearly established that the words and expressions used do not embody the intention of the parties, the contract may be reformed so as to express that intention. The meaning of technical or peculiar words is presumed to be the significance which those words have acquired by usage in similar commercial transactions.

Extrinsic Evidence. The question is often raised whether oral or written negotiations, entered into before the formal written contract was executed, shall in any way be read into the contract to explain the intention of the parties. The common rule, and the only safe one to follow, is that all negotiations prior to the issuance of the formal contract are waived and that the policy as written and accepted by the assured stands as the embodiment of all the terms and conditions of the contract. It is, however, possible, by reference, definite and descriptive, to make the policy subject to some extrinsic document containing material facts relating to the risk. Such references are scrutinized with the greatest care and are admitted as evidence only where it is clearly the intention of both parties that this evidence be admitted. Oral evidence is never admitted to vary the terms of a contract, but in some cases it may be received to explain the meaning of the words used.

Does the Application Control the Policy? The basis of the policy, as already explained, is the insurance application signed or initialed by both parties. The question naturally arises whether this application in any way controls the formal policy when issued. In the ordinary transaction, an application is made on a form furnished by the underwriter, containing in part the printed clauses appearing on the policy. In such case the only conflict between policy and application would be a mistake in transferring the information on the application to the policy. Underwriters are usually prompt in correcting such errors and, if they should object, would be judicially compelled to make the correction. If, however, the application has been bound on a form, prepared by the broker, containing strange or unusual clauses but the policy when issued is on the underwriter's customary form, it is more difficult to determine whether the application may be read in to change the terms of the policy. As a matter of equity, it seems fair that an underwriter should be bound by the application which he signed; as a matter of pure law the question is doubtful. A court of equity would probably decree that the policy be changed to conform to the terms of the application unless the underwriters could show that their attention was not directed to these strange and unusual clauses and that they had not noticed them. In such case it might be decreed that the minds of the parties had not met and that there was no valid contract.

The Law of the Place. It is a general rule of the law of contracts that an agreement is held to be made in accordance with the laws of the place where the contract is drawn and is to be interpreted in conformity with such laws. This rule becomes important in the consideration of contracts made in one state or country but to be performed in another. It has been held by the Supreme Court of the United States that an insurance company in one state may make contracts by mail with persons in other states and that such contracts are not amenable to the law of the state where the contract is to be performed. Several of the states have endeavored to bring such insurance contracts under their control for purposes of taxation, but the law would seem to be clear in this respect. This question of jurisdiction arises in connection with certificates or special policies issued under contracts of marine insurance countersigned by the assured who is domiciled in another state. If the issuance of the document were the actual making of the contract, it might be subject to the laws of the state where the countersignature is affixed. The countersignature of the certificate or special policy is, however, in no sense the making of a contract, nor is it a necessary act in the completion of a contract. It is merely an act in connection with the issuance of the formal evidence of a contract already made, namely, the open policy. It therefore seems clear that the laws of the state where the open policy was issued control the contract.

Clarity Essential in the Writing of Policies. The only safe rule to follow in the writing of insurance contracts is to have the facts in relation to the insurance so clearly set forth in the policy that it is not necessary to have recourse to the rules of construction for explanation. Inconsistencies should be reconciled and ambiguities clarified at the time of issuing the contract so that, in the event of loss, the only necessary acts to be performed will be the presentation of proofs of loss, the adjustment of the claim, and the drawing of the check in payment thereof. It is very unusual for a dispute involving a marine-insurance policy to reach a court of law. Most differences of opinion are amicably settled by negotiation between the underwriter and the other parties involved, whether original assured or assignees. This is the best evidence of the good faith in which these transactions are consummated. It also is evidence of the high degree of confidence which exists between assured, broker, and underwriter.

Insurance Interest Must Be Actual. The insurable interest must be such that the happening of any of the perils insured against might directly affect the interest of the assured rather than have merely a remote or consequential effect. For instance, the loss of a full cargo of grain might disturb the grain market, yet this fact would not give an insurable interest in the grain at risk to any except those who would be directly affected by loss of that particular grain. This does not mean that one whose relation to the subject matter is conditional does not have an insurable interest, for an interest is insurable that is real and exists when the insurance is applied for, but that may be defeated by a contingent happening. Such an interest, however, should be definitely described. Several different persons may have insurable interests in the same subject matter, each having a different interest not conflicting with the interests of the others. A mere expectant interest in the subject matter, not founded on any legal right or title, does not give a person such an insurable interest in property as may be covered by a policy of insurance.

Extent of the Insurable Interest. The insurable interest need not exist at the time the insurance contract is made. Merchants make contracts to cover automatically their future transactions, but it is essential to a recovery under the policy that the assured have an insurable interest at the time of the loss. While it has been stated that an insurance policy insures the person and not the thing, the policy protects the person only with respect to his pecuniary interest in the thing itself. Without the existence of the thing and without a definite relation between the person and the thing, there is no insurable interest. It is not necessary that the assured be interested to the extent of the whole value of the subject matter. Any interest, however slight, if definite and legal, may be insured, as, for instance, the commissions which a commission merchant will earn if the goods arrive safely so that he can attend to their distribution. The number of insurable interests which exist with respect to the same subject matter may be numerous, but the sum total of all the insurance on these various interests should not exceed the total pecuniary value of the property itself or the value contingent upon its continued existence. This sum should be the total amount recoverable in the event of the destruction of the subject matter of the various insurances. It should never be possible for two parties each to collect the value of the same destroyed property. It is therefore necessary so to provide that the policies covering different interests do not overlap, otherwise double insurance will exist.

Persons Who Have Insurable Interests. Among the many classes of persons who may have an insurable interest in property, and who may therefore effect insurance in their own names, or those on whose behalf valid insurance may be written in the name of a duly authorized agent, the following may be mentioned, *viz.,*

Owners. He in whom the legal title is vested may insure the property.

Managing Owners. In many cases in the past and in some cases at present, the ownership of sailing vessels and steamers is divided into 64 or 256 or some other number of shares. The individual owners may have no voice at all in the management of the vessel, but one of the part owners may be entrusted by the others with the conduct of the property. To avoid detail, this managing owner may be charged with the duty of insuring the vessel and take insurance in his own name for account *of whom it may concern,* an expression which presently will be explained, but in this particular case referring to himself and his coowners.

Mortgagee. Commercial transactions are conducted largely on credit, and vessels, like other forms of wealth, are often mortgaged for a considerable part of their value. The lender of money either on cargo or on vessel has an insurable interest in the property to the amount of his loan but may effect insurance for the full value for the benefit of all concerned.

Consignee. Goods are often shipped on consignment for sale, the property being at the risk of the consignee, the latter paying for the property, not a fixed sum determined by an invoice, but a definite percentage of the proceeds. In such cases the consignee has an insurable interest to the extent of the full value of the goods.

Factor or Commission Merchant. Factors or commission merchants have an insurable interest to the extent of their contingent profits or commissions if these are dependent on the continued existence and safety of the property.

Trustee for Creditors. The owner of property may become bankrupt or may make an assignment for the benefit of creditors, in which case the trustee in bankruptcy or the assignee has an insurable interest for the benefit of all concerned.

Agent. An agent, provided his authority is broad enough, always has such an insurable interest that he can take insurance in his own name, but the policy should set forth the agency.

Charterer. A vessel may be chartered under an agreement that the charterer assumes full responsibility for the vessel, as in the case of a "bare-boat charter." In such case the charterer has an insurable interest and may insure in his own name. The charterer always has an insurable interest in the earnings of the vessel, depending on the terms of the charter. The charterer also has an insurable interest in the "profits on charter," the difference between the hire he pays for the use of the vessel and the amount he will earn by the carriage of goods under bill of lading.

Repair Yard. When a vessel is sent to a yard for repairs, the contractor may assume responsibility for certain perils that may overtake the vessel while under his control. He has an insurable interest in the vessel with respect to these perils.

Common Carrier. A common carrier transporting property is responsible under the law for the safe delivery of goods to the consignee, except in so far as he may be relieved of this responsibility by law, as in the case of the Harter Act and the Carriage of Goods by Sea Act with respect to ocean commerce. For an increased rate, a carrier may agree to assume liability for loss caused by risks for which he is not legally responsible, or he may agree, upon the order of the shipper or consignee, to procure insurance on the property while in transit over his lines or those of connecting carriers. A carrier, therefore, by virtue of his legal responsibility or his assumed responsibility, has a valid insurable interest in the property in his custody.

Bottomry and Respondentia. The lender under a bottomry or respondentia bond has an insurable interest in the property to the extent of his loan, since in the event of the loss of the property the debtor will be discharged from his obligation to repay the loan.

The borrower under a bottomry or respondentia bond also has an insurable interest, but only for the amount by which the value of the property exceeds the amount borrowed, since in the event of loss he will not suffer with respect to the amount borrowed, this loss falling on the lender. If, however, the bond provides that the borrower shall be discharged from his debt only in the event of loss caused by certain specified perils, he has an insurable interest to the full value of the property against all other perils.

Bottomry and respondentia loans are very rare in modern practice and are confined to loans made at a port of refuge to pay for disbursements made to enable the vessel to continue her voyage. The loan is made to the master of the vessel on the security of the vessel or the cargo or both and does not as a practical matter affect the insurable interest of the hull or cargo owner.

Reinsurance. An underwriter, having assumed the risks to which the assured's property is subject, has a valid insurable interest in such property, and may reduce his liability by reinsuring the whole or any part of it against all or part of the risks for which he has assumed liability. The original assured, however, has no right to or interest in such reinsurance.

Definition of Marine Insurance. The development of new methods of transportation and the devising of new kinds of insurance that afford protection against practically all hazards have given rise to policy forms that come within the scope of what is improperly, for lack of a better name, known as *inland-marine* insurance and that are therefore not within the purview of this book. These new types of insurance have made it necessary to amplify the meaning of marine insurance. Accordingly, the New York Insurance Law[1] now defines marine insurance as insurance or reinsurance against any and all kinds of loss or damage to:

[1] Art. IV, Sec. 46, Pars. 20, 21, and Sec. 60.

(a) Vessels, craft, aircraft, cars, automobiles, and vehicles of every kind, as well as all goods, freights, cargoes, merchandise, effects, disbursements, profits, moneys, bullion, precious stones, securities, choses in action, evidences of debt, valuable papers, bottomry and respondentia interests and all other kinds of property and interests therein, in respect to, appertaining to or in connection with any and all risks or perils of navigation, transit, or transportation, including war risks, on or under any seas or other waters, on land or in the air, or while being assembled, packed, crated, baled, compressed, or similarly prepared for shipment or while awaiting the same or during any delays, storage, transshipment, or reshipment incident thereto, including marine builder's risks and all personal property floater risks, and

(b) Person or to property in connection with or appertaining to a marine, inland marine, transit or transportation insurance, including liability for loss of or damage to either, arising out of or in connection with the construction, repair, operation, maintenance or use of the subject matter of such insurance (but not including life insurance or surety bonds nor insurance against loss by reason of bodily injury to the person arising out of the ownership, maintenance or use of automobiles), and

(c) Precious stones, jewels, jewelry, gold, silver and other precious metals, whether used in business or trade or otherwise, and whether the same be in course of transportation or otherwise, and

(d) Bridges, tunnels and other instrumentalities of transportation and communication (excluding buildings, their furniture and furnishings, fixed contents and supplies held in storage) unless fire, tornado, sprinkler leakage, hail, explosion, earthquake, riot and/or civil commotion are the only hazards to be covered; piers, wharves, docks and slips, excluding the risks of fire, tornado, sprinkler leakage, hail, explosion, earthquake, riot and/or civil commotion; other aids to navigation and transportation, including dry docks and marine railways, against all risks.

The broadening of the marine-insurance policy has created a situation where the risks by land, by interior water conveyance, or by air are generally covered. Thus in the shore-transportation field the actions of the ocean-marine and the inland-marine underwriter frequently overlap. Furthermore, since the same companies usually engage in both types of insurance, it is customary for the broker to provide insurance for his client so that the ocean- and inland-marine policies dovetail one with the other and no uncovered risks fall between the two policies.

CHAPTER 9

The Policy

ASSURER AND ASSURED

The Policy. The policy issued by the underwriter as the formal evidence of the contract is one of the quaintest documents in existence. For over 300 years the basic or skeleton form of this contract has changed but little. Additions have been made, it is true, but these to the lay mind have tended rather to confuse than to clarify its meaning. The present Lloyd's form differs little from the "Tiger" policy issued in 1613, now in the Bodleian Library at Oxford. The basic forms used in the United States are similar to Lloyd's policy but modified to meet American law and practice. The form of expression is that of an age long past, and the enumeration of the perils insured against is evidence that they were added one by one as occasion demanded. They follow one another in no logical order, war and marine perils appearing in indiscriminate sequence. Much as the form has been amended by the addition of modifying clauses, no one has attempted to change its basic wording. It may be said, without undue violence to the truth, that every word in the basic form has been weighed in the judicial balance and its significance, both by itself and in relation to the context, legally determined. Quaint as the document is, there is no doubt as to its meaning, and any material change might greatly weaken its force.

Types of Policies. There are many types of policy in use in the insurance of marine and other transportation risks. These various forms differ widely in much of their phraseology, yet all are merely the outgrowth and development of the original form of marine-insurance policy which has been in use for centuries. This fact will readily appear from an examination of several types of policy, in each of which will be found phrases and clauses common to all. Among the types of policy in use are those for insuring a single cargo risk, known as *special* policies, and those for insuring a number of cargoes to be shipped in the future, called *open* policies. Special types of cargo policy are used for the insurance of certain commodities such as cotton, grain, or refrigerated products. Other types of cargo policy are the *blanket* and *transit floater* policies which are in general use in connection with coastwise and inland-marine insurance.

The insurance of vessels, or *hull insurance,* has developed numerous types of policy. Some of these are general in their application, being used for all kinds of hull risks, while others are limited in their scope. Some are adapted to special trades such as Great Lakes or river traffic, while in the insurance of sailing vessels different forms are provided for vessels depending for power on their sails alone and for those equipped with auxiliary engines. There are also forms for the insurance of *disbursements*[1] in connection with hull insurance. Special forms are provided for the insurance of yachts and motorboats. There are hull forms for the insurance of port risks and for the insurance of vessels while being built or repaired.

The insurance of freight, commissions, profits, and other special interests requires special clauses which may be embodied in separate forms of policies, or these interests may be insured under cargo forms containing modifying clauses. Liability forms are issued to common carriers under which the insurable interest is not cargo but the liability, either imposed by law or assumed by contract, of the carriers for cargo in their custody.

Form of Policy. There is, in the United States, no standard form of policy required by law for marine-insurance contracts. Each company has its own skeleton forms, differing from one another in some words or expressions, but all essentially alike and closely following the forms of expression that have stood the test of time and have received judicial interpretation. The mere fact, however, that the skeleton forms of the various companies do differ makes it necessary for the assured or his broker to have a thorough knowledge of the different forms in use, so that in accepting many policies of different companies, each covering part of the same risk, no conflict may exist

[1] See Appendix H, p. 466

between the several policies in the printed, written, or stamped portions. The form of policy used as the basis of discussion in the following pages is the special cargo skeleton form in use by one of the New York companies and is chosen because it has changed but little in the past 100 years and furnishes a good text for the discussion of the underlying conditions of all marine insurance.[1] The cargo form is taken because it is more generally used than the hull form, but the basic parts of policies used for hull, cargo, and freight are alike. The modifications necessary for the insurance of these different interests will be discussed in their proper places.

British Form of Policy. The relations between the American and the British marine-insurance markets being so close, attention will be called from time to time to the salient differences between American and British policies. As already indicated, the British marine-insurance law has been codified, and in the Marine Insurance Act of 1906, the rules under which marine insurance is written in Great Britain are set forth in considerable detail. No definite form of policy is required by the Act, but the form of policy in general use in Great Britain, with rules for its construction, is appended to it.[2]

The Assurer. The first item in the policy is the name of the insurance company, the party of the first part to the contract. Underwriting in the United States is conducted almost exclusively by incorporated companies, acting through their duly elected officers or their appointed agents. Individual underwriting has fallen into disuse. The underwriting scope of a corporation is strictly limited by its charter, but ordinarily a company's activities are not confined to any one branch of insurance. In New York State, at least, the companies are not limited by law with respect to the amount that they may carry on any one marine risk, but prudence naturally sets conservative limits which a company will assume for its own account on any one risk.[3]

The Assured. The name of the assured follows the name of the company. It should not be inferred that the person, firm, or corporation named as the assured is necessarily the real party at interest, as insurance may be taken out in the name of an agent. However, a

[1] This form is reproduced on pp. 142, 143.

[2] See Appendix I, p. 468.

[3] See Reinsurance, Chap. 21.

SPECIAL CARGO POLICY FORM

By Insurance Company. **[No.]**

ON ACCOUNT OF

In case of loss to be paid in funds current in the United States, or in the City of New York to

Do make Insurance and cause **to be insured, lost or not lost, at and from**

the good........................called the **upon all kinds of lawful goods and merchandises, laden or to be laden on board**........................ whereof is master for this present voyage. or whoever else shall go for master in the said vessel, or by whatever other name or names the said vessel, or the master thereof, is or shall be named or called.

Beginning the adventure upon the said goods and merchandises, from and immediately following the loading thereof on board of the said vessel, at as aforesaid, and so shall continue and endure until the said goods and merchandises shall be safely landed at as aforesaid. AND it shall and may be lawful for the said vessel, in her voyage, to proceed and sail to, touch and stay at, any ports or places, if thereunto obliged by stress of weather or other unavoidable accident, without prejudice to this insurance. The said goods and merchandises, hereby insured, are valued (premium included) at

Touching the adventures and perils which the said **Insurance Company** is contended to bear, and takes upon itself in this voyage, they are of the *seas, men-of-war, fires, enemies, pirates, rovers, thieves, jettisons, letters of mart and countermart, reprisals, takings at sea, arrests, restraints and detainments of all kings, princes or people, of what nation, condition or quality soever, barratry of the master and mariners*, and all other perils, losses and misfortunes, that have or shall come to the hurt, detriment or damage of the said goods and merchandises, or any part thereof. AND in case of any loss or misfortune, it shall be lawful and necessary to and for the assured, factors, servants and assigns, to sue, labor, and travel for, in and about the defence, safeguard and recovery of the said goods and merchandises, or any part thereof, without prejudice to this insurance; nor shall the acts of the insured or insurers, in recovering, saving and preserving the property insured, in case of disaster be considered a waiver or an acceptance of an abandonment; to the charges whereof, the said Insurance Company will contribute according to the rate and quantity of the sum herein insured, having been paid the consideration for this insurance, by the assured or assigns, at and after the rate of

Sum Insured.

$

And in case of loss, such loss to be paid in thirty days after proof of loss, and proof of interest in the said (the amount of the Note given for the premium, if unpaid, being first deducted), but no partial loss or particular average shall in any case be paid, unless amounting to *five per cent.* PROVIDED ALWAYS, and it is hereby further agreed, That if the said assured shall have made any other assurance upon the premises aforesaid, prior in day of date to this policy, then the said

if there be one at the place such proofs are taken.

INSURANCE COMPANY shall be answerable only for so much as the amount of such prior assurance may be deficient towards fully covering the premises hereby assured; and the said INSURANCE COMPANY shall return the premium upon so much of the sum by them assured, as they shall be by such prior assurance exonerated from. AND in case of any insurance upon the said premises, subsequent in day of date to this policy, the said INSURANCE COMPANY shall nevertheless be answerable for the full extent of the sum by them subscribed hereto, without right to claim contribution from such subsequent assurers, and shall accordingly be entitled to retain the premium by them received, in the same manner as if no such subsequent assurance had been made. Other insurance upon the premises aforesaid, of date the same day as this policy, shall be deemed simultaneous herewith; and the said INSURANCE COMPANY shall not be liable for more than a ratable contribution in the proportion of the sum by them insured to the aggregate of such simultaneous insurance. IT IS ALSO AGREED, that the property be warranted by the assured free from any charge, damage or loss, which may arise in consequence of a seizure or detention, for or on account of any illicit or prohibited trade, or any trade in articles contraband of war.

Warranted not to abandon in case of capture, seizure, or detention, until after condemnation of the property insured; nor until ninety days after notice of said condemnation is given to this Company. Also warranted not to abandon in case of blockade, and free from any expense in consequence of capture, seizure, detention or blockade, but in the event of blockade, to be at liberty to proceed to an open port and there end the voyage.

In witness whereof, the President or Vice-President of the said **Insurance Company** hath hereunto subscribed his name, and the sum insured, and caused the same to be attested by their Secretary, in **New-York**, the day of one thousand nine hundred and

Memorandum. It is also agreed, that bar, bundle, rod, hoop and sheet iron, wire of all kinds, tin plates, steel, madder, sumac, wicker-ware and willow, (manufactured or otherwise), salt, grain of all kinds, tobacco, indian meal, fruits, (whether preserved or otherwise), cheese, dry fish, hay, vegetables and roots, rags, hempen yarn, bags, cotton bagging and other articles used for bags or bagging, pleasure carriages, household furniture, skins and hides, musical instruments, looking-glasses, and all other articles that are perishable in their own nature, are warranted by the assured free from average, unless general; hemp, tobacco stems, matting and cassia, except in boxes, free from average under *twenty per cent.* unless general; and sugar, flax, flax-seed and bread, are warranted by the assured free from average under *seven per cent.* unless general; and coffee in bags or bulk, pepper in bags or bulk, and rice, free from average under *ten per cent.*, unless general.

Warranted by the insured free from damage or injury, from dampness, change of flavor, or being spotted, discolored, musty or mouldy, except caused by actual contact of sea water with the articles damaged, occasioned by sea perils. In case of partial loss by sea damage to dry goods, cutlery or other hardware, the loss shall be ascertained by a separation and sale of the portion only of the contents of the packages so damaged, and not otherwise; and the same practice shall obtain as to all other merchandise as far as practicable. Not liable for leakage on molasses or other liquids, unless occasioned by stranding or collision with another vessel.

If the voyage aforesaid shall have been begun and shall have terminated before the date of this policy, then there shall be noreturn of premium on account of such termination of the voyage.

In all cases of return of premium, in whole or in part, *one-half per cent.*, upon the sum insured, is to be retained by the assurers.

Proof of loss to be authenticated by the Agent of the Company,

Premium

$

Secretary. **President.**

policy must be taken out in the name of a person, firm, or corporation who directly or indirectly has an insurable interest. One who has a legal interest in the subject matter, whether vested or contingent, in consequence of which he may be benefited by its preservation or injured by its loss or damage, has an insurable interest in the property. Only those interested in the subject matter at the commencement of the risk under the policy may be original parties to the policy, and they continue to be parties only while they have an interest. The appointment of one person as the agent of another for the placing of insurance gives that person sufficient insurable interest in the property to enable him to effect insurance in his own name as agent. A policy placed by an agent for a principal without the latter's consent may be ratified and adopted by the principal at any time, even, it would seem, after loss is known to have occurred. Insurance placed by agents, however, will be applied only to such principals as were intended at the time the insurance was effected.

"For Account of." No part of the marine-insurance policy is more important, or requires greater care in its wording, than does the phrase following the name of the assured and reading "for account of." In this blank space should be inserted, by name or by description, all the parties who are interested in the insured subject. In the case of individual or special insurance, the problem is often very simple, as the assured may desire the protection to be merely for account of himself, no third party or parties being interested in the transaction. Where, however, an open contract, which will cover all property that may be received by a merchant, is desired, the most careful wording is necessary in order to make the contract cover all the property in which the merchant, as owner or as consignee with orders to insure, is interested or for which he may be directly or indirectly responsible. It is equally important that the policy be not made a "catchall," apparently covering property to which the relation of the assured is not clearly defined. It often happens that a merchant will wish to cover under an open policy only a portion of the merchandise that may be shipped to him or only such goods as may be shipped under special conditions, as, for instance, merchandise purchased under letters of credit issued by a named bank. In such circumstances it is necessary that the policy be so worded as to provide for nothing but the shipments on which insurance is desired. A considerable degree of skill is required so to word this portion of the policy that dispute will not arise in determining whether the assured is entitled to receive reimbursement for a loss which may have occurred or whether the underwriter is entitled to premium on risks which the assured has failed to declare.

Attachment of Policy. As the question of the passing of title is often one of considerable importance and may be difficult of proof, it is, in many cases, prudent to insert at this point in the policy a definite description of the time at which the policy will attach. For instance, in raw-sugar trade the policy may be made to attach when the sugar is bagged and set aside for the assured, while in the raw-cotton trade it may be made to attach

> . . . from the moment the cotton becomes the property of the assured or legally at their risk, provided, however, that no cotton shall be covered hereunder prior to actual delivery to the assured or their agents, unless specifically identified by marks and numbers or other designation in possession of the assured or mailed to the assured prior to loss.

Description of Parties and Property Should Be Definite. If the assured wishes to cover property of others that he may be ordered to insure, provision should be made that such orders be in writing and mailed to the assured prior to the time the shipment is made. By insisting on a careful description of the interested parties, of the property insured, and an exact statement of the time at which the goods are to come under the protection of the policy, underwriters are not endeavoring to insert technicalities of which they may avail themselves to avoid payment of loss. They are merely trying so to write their policies that there may be no question of the risks for which they are liable to the assured or of the premiums for which the assured are liable to the underwriters. Often an assured, perhaps through an honest misconception, fails to declare risks under an open policy to an underwriter and to pay premiums thereon. In the event of loss on a similar risk he will declare it, make claim under the policy, and insist on payment of the loss. In such cases, of course, payment of the premium on the unreported risks can be claimed by the underwriter, but where a loss does not reveal the mistake or omission, the underwriter suffers. It is only by the continuous flow of premium to the underwriter that he can respond for losses, and policies should be so clearly drawn that no doubt can exist in the mind of either the assured or the underwriter as to their respective duties and liabilities.

An Insurable Interest Must Exist. There is another problem in connection with the description of the assured which cannot be ignored in view of a situation that developed during World War I. It was then possible, in New York State at least, for a broker or ship agent to contract for large amounts of insurance on cargo by a named vessel when the so-called assured had no property at risk and had no intention of shipping goods by the vessel in question. Having obtained advance information that a certain steamer was to load for a port for which freight space was in great demand, this broker or ship agent would enter the marine market and bind at low rates all the available underwriting capacity. When the vessel arrived and began to load her cargo, the legitimate shipper would discover that the market was "full" by this vessel. The broker who had bought up the market would then approach the shipper, offering to transfer insurance to him at a rate greatly in advance of the original rate charged by the underwriter. Such practices were obviously unfair and could have been prevented in large measure had underwriters insisted on having insurance placed only in the names of legitimate shippers who had definite freight engagements for the vessel named. The law of New York has since been amended, making it unlawful to issue insurance to anyone who does not have a valid insurable interest and for anyone who does not have a valid insurable interest to apply for insurance. It also becomes unlawful to transfer insurance at a rate higher than its original cost unless the buyer is informed of the original rate and consents to pay the higher charge. Underwriters, by issuing policies only to those whom they know to be legitimate shippers or authorized brokers, can most effectively stamp out unethical practices. In Great Britain, underwriters have been deceived in the same way and now insist that the names of the real parties in interest be declared when insurances are made binding. The wording of the Lloyd's policy[1] is so indefinite and comprehensive with respect to the persons insured

[1] See Appendix I, p. 468.

that underwriters have readily been imposed upon by those who sought unlawfully to "corner the insurance market."

"Whom It May Concern." Before passing from the subject of the assured, reference must be made to an expression, common to most marine policies, which leads to some confusion in determining the actual parties at interest. This expression, *for account of whom it may concern,* is somewhat peculiar to American policies, but similar expressions are found in British and Continental insurance contracts. The original purpose of these expressions is doubtful, but as Emerigon, the French author, suggests, they may have been introduced in order to conceal the identity of the real party at interest and to keep his commercial enterprises secret. However, their use caused British underwriters in the eighteenth century to complain "that policies were so loose that an underwriter had no opportunity of knowing who the persons were for whom he insured." A statute accordingly was passed setting forth how the assured should be described in the policy, and an underwriter promptly took advantage of the law in declining payment under a policy issued in the name of an agent who was not described as such. Other similar cases occurred, and a new statute was enacted, virtually repealing the former. The use of these expressions is now firmly established, and their meaning is well understood.

"Whom It May Concern" Is Not All-inclusive. The expression *for account of whom it may concern* has not the all-inclusive meaning the words would indicate. Phillips states that a policy written with these words or "any equivalent clause will be applied to the interest of the party or parties, and only the party or parties, for whom it is intended by the person who effects or orders it if such party has authorized its being made beforehand, or subsequently adopts it."[1] The use of this expression, which is a technical one, presupposes an agency and refers only to the person or persons whom the agent had in contemplation when he effected the insurance. Such person or persons are the "concerned" in the transaction, and not all persons who might possibly have an interest in the subject matter of the insurance. It is not essential that these parties be definitely known to the assured, but they must be embraced within a certain class of persons for whose account the assured intended to effect insurance.

[1] Phillips, "A Treatise on the Law of Insurance," Sec. 383.

The Payee of Loss. In the policy form under consideration, the wording continues: "In case of loss, to be paid in funds current in the United States, or in the city of New York to............" Ordinarily a policy is made payable to the assured or order, but loss may be made payable to any interested third party or parties. On shipments that are financed under letters of credit, it is customary to have the loss made payable to the issuing bank in order that its advances on the shipment may be protected. In the case of hull insurance where there is a mortgage, the loss is usually made payable to the mortgagee and the assured "as their respective interests may appear." The expression "as their interests may appear," though in general use, is technically objectionable in that it may put on the underwriter the burden of deciding what the respective interests of the parties are. However, in case of a dispute, it would be possible for the underwriter to pay into court the amount of the loss, and permit the claimants to settle their differences there. It must of course be remembered that, in order to establish a valid claim for loss, certain documentary evidence must be presented, showing that such loss has actually occurred and that the claimant is entitled to payment of the amount due under the policy.[1]

The Special Policy Transfers the Payment of Loss. The special policy has largely supplanted the open policy in the negotiation of documents relating to cargo shipments. The use of this special policy has already been explained, but its consideration at this point is pertinent, since its purpose is primarily to transfer to the holder the benefit of the insurance, *viz.*, in the event of loss, the right to claim the indemnity that the insurance provides. As most merchants have open policies covering all shipments at their risk, the special policy provides a simple and convenient method of evidencing the insurance and of making possible the payment of loss to the bona fide holder of the commercial documents. These policies, when negotiable, provide that loss shall be payable to a designated person or order, the last two words enabling the payee to transfer the right to payment of loss. This he may do in one of two ways: either he may specially transfer the special policy by endorsing it "Pay to the order of...........," inserting a definite name, or he may, by merely signing his name, make the instrument a "bearer" document. In the first case, loss will

[1] These proofs of loss will be considered in Chap. 12, p. 199.

be payable only to the person indicated or one to whom he may order the loss payable; in the second case, any person producing the special policy, with the supporting documentary evidence of ownership and loss, would be entitled to payment. By the omission of the words "or order" or "to the order of" the endorser can destroy the negotiability of the document, it being transferable from that time on only by assignment.

Loss May Be Made Payable in Foreign Countries. The custom of providing that loss may be payable in foreign countries, while essential in the conduct of commerce, is not a new departure, as this provision was in vogue at least as early as the sixteenth century. Underwriters either carry funds in the larger banking centers or have arrangements by which drafts drawn on them are honored by their own bank. This enables the holders of special policies, after proper adjustment has been made by the local representative of the underwriters, to receive prompt payment and thus to be put in funds to continue their commercial transactions. Were it necessary in each case to return the loss papers to the underwriter for payment, much time might elapse before the holder of the insurance document could, in the ordinary course of the mail, receive reimbursement for his loss. With the use of air mail this problem is greatly simplified.

Loss Orders. The payee specified in the policy or the payee under the special policy, if one has been issued, may, by a written order in proper form, instruct the underwriter to pay the loss to a third party. Such orders are principally used in connection with policies in which loss is payable to a bank to protect its advances on the shipment, and these advances having been paid by the assured, the bank is out of the transaction and quite willing that the loss be paid to the assured. To accomplish this end, a formal order of payment is executed by the bank.

Open Policies. It may be well at this point to give consideration to the subject of open policies. The word *open* in connection with marine-insurance contracts has a double meaning. Sometimes it is used to describe the insurance on a specific risk where the exact amount needed has not been determined and the transaction is, therefore, an open or uncompleted agreement. A broader meaning, which, however, is merely an enlargement of the primary definition, is given to the term when used in connection with open policies. These policies are contracts which may be issued for a definite or indefinite period of time, there being no restriction in the United States as to the duration of a marine policy. They cover the assured with respect to all his shipments as described in the policy within the named geographical limits. Amounts applicable to the contract are to be reported from time to time as information of shipments is received and therefore are open. Such policies usually have a limit of liability on any one risk, but the actual amounts on which premium is to be paid, though undetermined, are definitely controlled by the limit of liability and by the valuation clause which will be explained later. Open policies, covering as they do all goods as described which may be afloat or in transit, make possible the great commercial transactions of the present day. Were it necessary specially to insure in advance each individual shipment, commerce on its present gigantic scale would be impossible, since, in many cases, goods are shipped and may even have arrived before the assured has knowledge that property at his risk has been exposed to the perils of transportation.

Book Policies. Overseas commerce has become more and more complicated, and practices in its operation are constantly changing. Open policies are usually "tailor-made" to meet the requirements of the individual business of the merchant. Much thought has been given to the modernization of the marine-insurance policy, but underwriters hesitate to introduce new words and expressions lest they be found to be out of harmony with the old legal decisions. In the very recent past some companies, in the interest of clarity, have reorganized their open-policy forms in view of the fact that most open policies are tailor-made. The various clauses of the basic policy and the modifying clauses approved by the American Institute of Marine Underwriters have been arranged in a new order, clauses following one another in logical sequence and the various pages of the form bound in a formal cover, the new format being known as a *book policy.* While some companies have retained all the clauses of the basic form, others have omitted clauses that have fallen into disuse.

Blanket Policies. However, the distinction cannot be too closely drawn between open policies and the so-called blanket policies, which are similar in their nature but entirely different in their mode of operation. The purpose of the blanket policy is similar to that of the open policy but is a closed instead of an open contract. The blanket policy describes the geographical and time limits of the contract, the payee of loss and the kind of goods to be insured and always has a fixed limit of liability on any one vessel or in any one locality at one time. The principal distinction between the open policy and blanket policy is that in the former type of contract the assured pays the premium on the actual amounts at risk while under the latter form a lump-sum premium is charged. This premium is based on the estimated total amount that will come under the protection of the policy during the contract term and may be subject to readjustment at the end of the term by the payment of an additional premium at a fixed rate if the books of the assured indicate that the amount was greater than that estimated. By the same terms of agreement, a return of premium may be made at a fixed rate if the actual amount at risk fell below the estimated amount. Many of these policies contain a provision that, if loss is paid, the policy must be reinstated for the amount of the loss by the payment pro rata of the annual premium on the amount so paid for the unexpired period of the policy. This reinstatement clause may make such policies very costly if an assured has a series of losses.

Advantages of Blanket Policies. From the underwriter's point of view, a blanket policy, properly worded, has the advantage of securing the premium for the risks that he assumes. Too often, in the case of open policies, the assured forgets to report shipments to which the policy is applicable or has the mistaken notion that it is necessary to report only shipments on which loss has occurred, forgetting that the underwriter is entitled to premium on every dollar that has been at risk under the policy. Under the blanket form, the assured avoids the necessity of making these detailed reports of shipments.

Transit Floaters. Blanket policies, under the name of *transit floaters*, are in common use to cover local shipments made by merchants where it would be impracticable to make specific reports of the individual items. These policies are also frequently used by common carriers to protect shipments moving over their lines. Policies are sometimes issued by which the interest insured is the liability of a common carrier for loss suffered to property in his custody. The subject of insurance is not the property itself but the liability of the carrier, whether this be implied by law or assumed by contract. Such a policy is unvalued, the responsibility of the underwriter being limited only by the amount expressed in the policy and not by the value of the property to which the liability relates. The great bulk of cargo insurance, especially in the overseas trade, is written in the form of open policies or, as they are called in Great Britain, "permanent covers." The Marine Insurance Act of Great Britain limits the term for which a policy may be written to one year, and owing to the "Stamp Act," these "permanent covers" are merely agreements on the part of the underwriters to cover the shipments described and to issue properly stamped evidence of the individual insurances when declarations of amounts are made. Blanket policies and transit floaters are in common use to cover transit risks on shore.

CHAPTER 10

The Policy

DURATION OF RISK AND VALUATION

"Lost or Not Lost." After laying such great stress on the fact that to have a valid insurance there must be an insurable interest, that is, a subject matter to which the assured bears such a relation that he may be benefited by its continued existence or injured by its damage or destruction, it is somewhat disconcerting to find the following words in the policy form, "Do............make insurance, and cause............to be insured, lost or not lost." If the subject matter is lost, there would seem to be no insurable interest, but it must be remembered that the assured and his underwriters may incorporate into the policy any conditions that are legal. Were the subject matter known to either party to have been lost, a policy issued with respect to it would then be void. There must, therefore, be read into this phrase the words "without the knowledge of either party."

"Lost or Not Lost" a Necessary Condition. The words *lost or not lost* appear in policies issued as early as 1613, but their use has become so general that they are now found in practically all forms. A merchant ordering goods from a distant place may experience delay in obtaining information as to the shipment. When advices are received, the vessel may have sailed and in fact may have been lost. Were the merchant to insure the goods under a policy not containing these words, and the underwriter could establish that at the time the policy was issued the goods were damaged or had ceased to exist, payment of loss could be resisted on the ground that there was no insurable interest to the extent of the damage or loss. Such a situation would be intolerable in mercantile transactions, and over 300 years ago, when the means of communication between countries were very slow, this provision was first incorporated in the policy form. Of course, these words can be construed only in the light of that underlying principle of all marine insurance, that the utmost good faith must exist between the assured and the underwriter. If the assured knows that disaster has overtaken the vessel or its cargo, the concealment of this knowledge would amount to fraud and the insurance would be void. In the absence of such knowledge, this clause permits the valid insurance of goods or vessel which, at the time of insurance, may be lost or damaged. It sometimes happens that the merchant or his underwriter has heard rumors that disaster has overtaken the venture, but by mutual consent the assured warrants that the property was in good safety on a given date, and in the event of loss, the assured may recover if it can be established that at any time on that particular day the venture was in existence and undamaged. On the other hand, it may be known that disaster has overtaken the venture, but the extent of the damage or loss is unknown. The assured, however, wishes the remnant of his property then existing to be insured, and the underwriter who is willing to assume such a risk will insert a warranty of the following tenor: "Warranted free from loss, damage, injury or expense arising out of casualty of . . . .," inserting in the blank space the date of the disaster. This makes the underwriter liable for damage caused by a new casualty, but not for that resulting directly or indirectly from the original disaster.

The Termini. The words "at and from" follow "lost or not lost" in the form, and a blank space is provided in which the geographical or time limits of the policy are inserted. These limits are known as the *termini* of the insurance, the *terminus a quo* being the place or time of the inception of the risk, the *terminus ad quem* the place or time of the termination of the risk. No insurance policy is valid unless these termini are mentioned. The *terminus a quo* must be specifically indicated. The *terminus ad quem* may be subject to determination. For example, in an open policy the time of the termination of the contract is not usually stated, because the policy, though continuous, may be terminated by either party's giving notice of cancellation as provided in the contract. In the case of open policies, however, the geographical termini are definitely described. In these policies, and usually in the case of hull insurances on time, both geographical and time limits appear in the terms of agreement.

The Subject Matter of Insurance. The policy continues "upon all kinds of lawful goods and merchandises." The subject matter of the insurance must be distinctly set forth. If the policy is on a specific lot of goods, the property should be described by marks and numbers if possible—the number of packages and kind of goods at least should be noted. In open policies, general words are used, such as goods, cargo, merchandise, but in the declarations of shipments under the policy, a definite description of the kind and quantity of goods is given. In cases where special policies of insurance are issued, it is very important that the description of the goods be exact, so that the property covered by the insurance document will fit the description of the goods for which the corresponding bill of lading is issued. If the policy covers only a part interest in the insured subject, such fact should be noted at this point in the policy, as for instance, "on one-half interest in 100 Bales Cotton marked KITE." While the printed words in the policy are general in their meaning and would cover any goods, it is customary to insert in the blank space preceding these words the definite description of the property. The word "lawful" found in the printed form is inserted merely to protect the underwriter from the inclusion, under general words, of property not lawful to be traded in and does not necessarily refer to contraband of war.

Goods Presumed to Be Laden under Deck. It is a well-understood and well-established rule of marine insurance that goods are presumed to be shipped under deck, that is, below the weather deck of the vessel. If the goods are shipped on deck, they are not covered by the policy unless special notice of the stowage is given to the underwriter and he accepts the enhanced risk. The reason for this presumption is that the deck of a vessel is not designed to carry goods. Its primary function is to make the holds watertight and to protect the cargo laden in the holds. Goods carried on deck are subject to weather damage, sea damage, and the hazard of being washed overboard. Shipowners have no legal right to load goods on deck, and if they do, such goods are at the shipowner's risk unless he has obtained the consent of the cargo owner to such stowage. Accordingly, underwriters cannot be expected, without special notice, to assume the risk of goods laden on deck and will be released from their contract if the insured subject is so loaded. There are certain cases, however, which may furnish an exception to this rule. Certain kinds of goods, dangerous in themselves, are by custom, and sometimes by law, required to be shipped on deck so that they will not endanger the other cargo and can, if necessity arises, be quickly thrown overboard. Underwriters are presumed to know of these customs and legal requirements. If, therefore, an underwriter accepts a risk on one of these unusual commodities and the assured does not specify that the property is to be shipped on deck, the underwriter might be precluded from urging that the insurance was invalid because the property was laden on deck. Either the custom of carrying such goods on deck or a legal requirement necessitating such stowage would have to be clearly shown in order to create such a presumption of knowledge on the part of the underwriter. Under present-day conditions where a shipper in the interior, engaged in exporting merchandise, or a merchant importing goods does not receive his bill of lading until the shipment is afloat, it seems reasonable that he should have protection in the event of goods being stowed on deck without his knowledge or consent. If the goods so stowed are safe goods to be laden under deck, and if the carrier places them on deck without the knowledge or consent of the shipper or consignee, the carrier is liable for loss of or damage to the shipment. If, on the other hand, the goods are such that on-deck stowage is proper or customary, the carrier is within its rights in issuing an "on-deck" bill of lading. Until the bill of lading was received, the merchant might be in ignorance of the fact that his goods had been stowed on deck. It is therefore not unusual for open policies to contain a clause granting a limited amount of insurance on cargo laden on deck, such insurance, of course, not covering losses inevitably resulting from such stowage. Some underwriters definitely exclude from the protection of their policies cargo laden on deck. However, in the absence of "including" or "excluding" clauses, the weight of opinion indicates that on-deck cargo is not covered by a marine-insurance policy.

Some Kinds of Property Should Be Specifically Mentioned. There are other kinds of property which are not included in the general words "goods" and "merchandises," and among these may be mentioned livestock and goods shipped in refrigerators. Livestock, such as horses and cattle, must be specially declared to an underwriter, since the special hazards to which such property is subject could not be presumed to be contemplated by an underwriter when he accepted insurance on goods and merchandise. The same remarks apply to shipments of refrigerated and frozen goods such as meats, poultry, fish, and game. When marine insurance was first devised, and when the printed form of policy was first adopted, the modern method of preserving perishable articles by refrigeration was unknown. Question has also been raised as to whether specie, bullion, securities, and like articles come within the scope of the general words. The surest rule to follow is specifically to describe the property to be insured so that no doubt of the intention of the parties may exist. Whether the insurance is on cargo, hull, profits, commissions, or freight, the interest to be insured and the subject matter to which it refers should be adequately described.

The Vessel and Its Master. The printed form of policy continues:

.............laden or to be laden on board the good............called the............whereof is master for the present voyage............or whoever else shall go for master in the said vessel, or by whatever other name or names the said vessel, or the master thereof, is or shall be named or called.

These are quaint words referring to matters which are of vital importance to the risk, but some of the blank spaces are rarely filled in when the policy is issued. The name of the carrying vessel is, of course, mentioned, but while it has been pointed out that much depends on the experience and skill of the master, it seldom happens that his name appears in the space provided. The words "laden or to be laden" do not refer to the attachment of the risk but are descriptive of "lawful goods and merchandises" which are "laden or to be laden on the good ship *Atlas*," for instance. The word "good" is not a warranty that the vessel is seaworthy but is merely a descriptive adjective. There is, however, an implied warranty of seaworthiness which will be explained.[1] The name of the vessel is of the utmost importance because this is really the crux of the whole insurance. The underwriter's willingness or unwillingness to write the risk is dependent in large part on the suitability of the proposed vessel for the voyage to be run, and no other vessel may be substituted without the consent of the underwriter. The name of the vessel may be changed,

[1] See p. 215.

the master may be changed, but the vessel itself may not be changed without voiding the insurance. It will be noticed that it is not sufficient to give merely the name of the vessel; a description of her type must also be given such as "ship," "steamer," "motor vessel," "auxiliary sailing vessel," etc., so that the underwriter can identify the particular vessel intended.

Attachment of the Risk. The name of the assured, the payee of loss, the description of the voyage, and the name of the vessel having been set forth, the next paragraph of the form tells when the risk attaches and how long it endures. It also introduces some fine points of interpretation. The first sentence of this paragraph reads:

> Beginning the adventure upon the said goods and merchandises, from and immediately following the loading thereof on board of the said vessel, at............as aforesaid, and so shall continue and endure until the said goods and merchandises shall be safely landed at............as aforesaid.

It should be remembered that a policy of marine insurance is a transit policy and should cover goods only while in course of transportation and while out of the custody of the owner. Notwithstanding the provision given above for the attachment of the risk, the policy will be of no effect until the assured has an insurable interest, and while it does not, under the wording given, attach until the actual loading on board the said vessel, it will not attach then unless the insurable interest exists.

Date of Attachment. The wording of this form, of course, refers to cargo insurances insured on special voyages. Hull policies, which are in many cases written "on time," attach from the day and hour named in the policy, but if no hour is named, the policy will attach from midnight of the day before. It is customary to name an hour, and in order to make certain what hour is intended, the standard time of some named place is used, as "noon Washington standard time." Open policies on cargo are written to attach from a named date. The policy, as a contract, "covers all shipments as herein described made on and after" the date indicated, but the insurance on each individual shipment made under the policy will attach only in accordance with the printed form, that is, "immediately following the loading on board" the specific vessel, unless the policy has been so worded as to provide an earlier point of attachment, as under the warehouse-to-warehouse form.

Time of Attachment. The words "from and immediately following" give the barest form of protection and, as the words imply, will provide insurance only from the actual loading of the goods. What constitutes actual loading has been a matter of some controversy, but it seems to be a well-settled principle that, from the moment the slings of the vessel lift the goods clear of the wharf or other place of deposit, the risk attaches. If, on the other hand, the goods are lifted on to the vessel by the slings of a delivering lighter or by a crane on the wharf, it would seem to be equally clear that there is no loading until the slings have released the goods on the deck or in the hold of the vessel. In case the *terminus a quo* is a port or place where it is customary, or in fact necessary, that goods be lightered from the shore to the vessel, as is the case at some ports or roadsteads along the West Coast of South America, doubt may arise as to what the words "laden on board" mean. It has been held in certain instances that "laden on board" means laden on board the vessel carrying the goods from the shore where the loading conditions have required this mode of transit. Such decisions would seem, however, to read into a policy a risk which may not have been contemplated or desired by the underwriter. If the lighterage risk is to be included, provision therefor should be made, as is done in the American Institute form of craft clause, reading:

> Including transit by craft, and/or lighter to and from the vessel. Each craft and/or lighter to be deemed a separate insurance. The assured are not to be prejudiced by any agreement exempting lightermen from liability.

In Great Britain this question is settled, as, in the rules of construction accompanying the Marine Insurance Act, it is stated that, where goods are insured "from the loading thereof," the risk does not attach until such goods are actually on board and that the insurer is not liable for them while in transit from the shore to the ship.

Insured until Safely Landed. As the insurance continues until the goods "shall be safely landed at. . . . . ," the *terminus ad quem*, the same necessity arises to determine whether delivery into a lighter or other shore vessel constitutes a safe landing. The answer to this question depends on the hydrographic character and the custom of the port, and a safe landing will not have been accomplished until the goods have been landed in the customary manner and within a reasonable time after arrival at the port. If the only method of landing merchandise is by lighters or surfboats, the risk will continue in such craft until the property is deposited in a safe place on shore. If discharge is made into a floating receiving hulk, and this is the customary place of discharge, a safe delivery has been made. The facts in each particular case will control, though borderline cases will arise where it will be difficult to determine when the risk under the policy ceases.

Warehouse-to-warehouse Clause. The protection afforded by the basic printed form of policy is the minimum. Since it leaves many risks uninsured, various clauses have been devised to enlarge its scope. One of the broadest and perhaps the most usual form of protection afforded in the case of cargo insurance is that of the *warehouse-to-warehouse clause.* This clause does not by any means represent the extreme limit to which underwriters go in the insurance of cargo, since policies are written covering raw materials direct from the farm or from the mine or forest. Insurance policies have, in some cases, been so broadened that they covered agricultural products while growing in the field and wool while it was still on the back of the sheep. Bulk cargoes are usually insured under special clauses that are peculiar to these trades.

The warehouse-to-warehouse clause, although a modern development of marine insurance, is now found in almost every cargo policy covering goods that are shipped in packages. This clause, in the American Institute form, reads as follows:

This insurance attaches from the time the goods leave the Warehouse and/or Store at the place named in the policy for the commencement of the transit and continues during the ordinary course of transit, including customary transhipment if any, until the goods are discharged overside from the overseas vessel at the final port. Thereafter the insurance continues whilst the goods are in transit and/or awaiting transit until delivered to final warehouse at the destination named in the policy or until the expiry of 15 days (or 30 days if the destination to which the goods are insured is outside the limits of the port) whichever shall first occur. The time limits referred to above to be reckoned from midnight of the day on which the discharge overside of the goods hereby insured from the overseas vessel is completed. Held covered at a premium to be arranged in the event of transhipment, if any, other than as above and/or in the event of delay in excess of the above time limits arising from circumstances beyond the control of the Assured.

It is necessary for the Assured to give prompt notice to these Assurers when they become aware of an event for which they are "held covered" under this policy and the right to such cover is dependent on compliance with this obligation.

Marine underwriters have endeavored, in this clause, to extend the protection of the policy on shore without sacrificing any of the fundamental principles of marine insurance. Thus, the risk under the clause continues only while the property is out of the custody and control of the assured and only while it is in the ordinary course of transit. The primary purpose of the clause is to change the *terminus a quo* and the *terminus ad quem* of the insurance.

New Factors. Nevertheless, in accomplishing this purpose, many new factors appear that are not present in an ordinary marine risk. There may be a truck or motor risk from the shipper's or manufacturer's warehouse to the railroad car, a rail risk to the port, a risk from the cars to the steamer, by truck, motor, lighter, or other conveyance, after the ocean passage is completed. A similar group of risks may be incurred during the transit to the consignee's or other warehouse at an interior destination in a foreign country. Part of the transportation may be by aircraft. The underwriter should also consider the delays incidental to the clearing of the goods through the customhouse or the appraisers' stores. At many places, especially in South America, considerable time is used in passing goods through the customs. Goods imported from the United States are often placed in general order stores while awaiting the arrival of the commercial documents relating to the shipment, or the owner may place the goods in bonded warehouses to avoid the prompt payment of duties. Unless specifically provided for in the policy, goods are not covered while in general order stores or in bonded warehouses.

Delays in Transit. At each transfer point and on each separate portion of the route, there is the possibility of unforeseen delay. The underwriter, in naming his premium charge, is presumed to have in mind the ordinary and customary course of transit from the point of shipment over the named route to the point of destination. If there should be an unexpected, unusual, and unforeseen delay not caused by the insured perils, it would appear that the insurance under the warehouse-to-warehouse clause would cease, since a deviation would have taken place. The cessation, however, would not become effective, because the *deviation clause*[1] would immediately become operative, thus automatically continuing the protection of the policy. Whether any particular delay is of such an unusual character as to void the policy is a question of fact which can be decided only in the light of all the conditions at any place at any given time. In other words, ordinary transit is not always the same in the same place. The present American Institute clause endeavors to eliminate some of the ambiguity in the clause by fixing limits at destination. The strength of the clause, however, lies in this very weakness of its generality and assumes a fair and reasonable attitude on the part of both assured and underwriter. Applied in this spirit, the warehouse-to-warehouse clause with the deviation clause under normal conditions meets the commercial need of continuous insurance from point of shipment to point of destination.

Marine Extension Clauses. During and following World War II the usual channels of overseas commerce were so congested, and in many cases so disrupted, that the Institute warehouse-to-warehouse clause left the merchant in a very difficult position. It was not possible for him to know or to find out whether his shipments were proceeding to their destination in an orderly manner or were being subjected to unusual delays or being forwarded over unusual routes. To assure the merchant that his shipment would continue to be covered notwithstanding such interruptions, underwriters agreed, for an additional premium, to protect the shipment during such interruptions under the terms of the following *marine extension clauses.* Often the rate charged for this additional protection was much greater than the basic rate charged for normal transits.

Notwithstanding anything to the contrary contained in or endorsed on this policy it is understood and agreed that in consideration of an additional premium the following terms and conditions shall apply to all shipments which become at risk hereunder on and after............, 19............

1. This insurance attaches from the time the goods leave the warehouse

[1] See p. 169.

at the place named in the policy, certificate or declaration for the commencement of the transit and continues until the goods are delivered to the final warehouse at the destination named in the policy, certificate or declaration, or a substituted destination as provided in Clause 3 hereunder.

2. This insurance specially to cover the goods during,

(i) deviation, delay, forced discharge, re-shipment and transhipment.

(ii) any other variation of the adventure arising from the exercise of a liberty granted to the shipowner or charterer under the contract of affreightment.

3. In the event of the exercise of any liberty granted to the shipowner or charterer under the contract of affreightment whereby such contract is terminated at a port or place other than the original insured destination, the insurance continues until the goods are sold and delivered at such port or place; or, if the goods be not sold but are forwarded to the original insured destination or to any other destination this insurance continues until the goods have arrived at final warehouse as provided in Clause 1.

4. If while this insurance is still in force and before the expiry of 15 days from midnight of the day on which the discharge overside of the goods hereby insured from the overseas vessel at the final port of discharge is completed, the goods are re-sold (not being a sale within the terms of Clause 3) and are to be forwarded to a destination other than that covered by this insurance, the goods are covered hereunder while deposited at such port of discharge until again in transit or until the expiry of the aforementioned 15 days whichever shall first occur. If a sale is effected after the expiry of the aforementioned 15 days while this insurance is still in force the protection afforded shall cease as from the time of the sale.

5. Held covered at a premium to be arranged in case of change of voyage or of any omission or error in the description of the interest vessel or voyage.

6. This insurance shall in no case be deemed to extend to cover loss damage or expense proximately caused by delay or inherent vice or nature of the subject-matter insured.

7. It is a condition of this insurance that there shall be no interruption or suspension of transit unless due to circumstances beyond the control of the Assured.

All other terms and conditions of the policy not in conflict with the foregoing remain unchanged, it being particularly understood and agreed that the F.C. & S. clause remains in full force and effect, and that nothing in the foregoing shall be construed as extending this insurance to cover any risks of war or consequences of hostilities.

The foregoing clauses do not apply to the following shipments:
(a) Between ports in the Continental United States (excluding Alaska);
(b) Continental United States (excluding Alaska) to/from Canada;
(c) Canada to Canada;
(d) Newfoundland to Newfoundland;
(e) Shipments by air conveyances.

Since the close of the war exceptions (a), (b), (c), (d), and (e) have been deleted, and the charge for the additional protection is included in the basic rate.

At and From. Between the restricted protection afforded by the printed form and the broad coverage granted in the marine extension clauses many intermediate forms of insurance are found. The policy reads "at and from," but these words indicate merely that the insurance attaches when the goods are loaded on the vessel *at* the port and continues there until the vessel sails, when the word "from" becomes effective. The words "at and from" can be construed only in connection with the other words of the contract. Under modern insurance practice, question is more likely to arise as to the meaning of the words "at and from" in connection with hull insurance written on the voyage basis.[1]

Attachment of Cargo Insurance. Often policies will be worded to attach when the goods are receipted for by the transportation company, in which case dock insurance is provided. Such protection may have a time limit in order to guard the underwriter against a long wharf risk. Likewise, at the point of destination, the insurance may be continued for a stated period after discharge from the steamer or lighter, or it may cover in custom stores or other places of deposit for definite periods while awaiting acceptance by the consignees. The granting of such extended shore risks, however, should be closely watched, as an underwriter may thus assume risks that, because of congestion, may greatly exceed his carrying capacity. Clauses of this description may also grant protection much beyond that afforded in the ordinary warehouse-to-warehouse clause, since, under the latter form, the risk ceases when the goods are delivered into *any* store or warehouse at destination whereas the shore insurance on time, if not

[1] See p. 166.

restricted by modifying words such as "for thirty days unless sooner warehoused," may give the underwriter an extended risk in an undesirable place of storage after transit has ceased.

Risk after Discharge from Vessel. It is important to observe a distinction in meaning between a policy reading "including the risk on the wharf after discharge from the steamer for not exceeding ....days, commencing upon discharge," and one reading "including the risk on the wharf for not exceeding............days after commencement of discharge." In the first policy the specific time on the wharf begins to run from the moment each individual package is discharged, a moment in most cases difficult of determination, whereas in the second policy the time begins to run from the moment the vessel begins to discharge or "breaks bulk," the time of discharge of the particular goods insured under the policy being of no consequence.

Ex-dock Sales. The *ex-dock* sale is usually made in connection with importations of raw commodities. Under this form of sale contract, the importer assumes responsibility for the goods until he has made delivery of the goods to the purchaser. This delivery is usually accomplished when the goods have been turned over to the purchaser's agent on the dock, if for local delivery, or to the lighterman or connecting carrier, if for delivery beyond the port of discharge. Furthermore, in many cases, raw commodities arrive unsold, but with a good prospect of immediate sale, so that the importer prefers to leave the goods on the wharf temporarily while endeavoring to dispose of them. In this and other similar cases, the assured (importer) elects to use the dock as his warehouse, and the insurance risks cease when the goods are discharged on the dock, as delivery has been made to a warehouse. In order to meet the various phases of such ex-dock transactions, clauses have been devised to extend the protection of the importer's policy until he has sold and made delivery of his cargo. In these cases the goods are, technically, in the assured's possession, are not in transit, and should therefore be protected by a fire-insurance rather than a marine-insurance policy. A form of clause used to cover ex-dock sales reads as follows:

On merchandise which for any reason may be sold ex dock at destination, this policy to continue in force until delivery is taken by the buyer and/or his agent or assignee and until goods cease to be at the risk of this assured, but not exceeding fourteen (14) days or held covered at a rate to be arranged. On merchandise which for any reason is held on dock, quay or wharf at destination by the order of the assured or for their convenience whether in due course of transit or otherwise, this policy is to continue in force for not exceeding fourteen (14) days from the date of landing of the last package of the shipment or held covered at a rate to be arranged. If such merchandise be still at the risk of the assured, this policy to cover thereafter in due course of transit until safely delivered into store, warehouse or factory at final place of destination.

This is but one more evidence of the desire of underwriters to broaden the marine-insurance policy so as to adapt it to new trading methods.

Attachment of Hull Risks on Time. To determine the point of attachment of hull insurance presents some peculiar difficulties. If the insurance is written on time, the point of attachment is determined. In such cases it is usually presumed that the vessel is in port and in good safety, but this is not necessarily so. When single-vessel risks are under consideration, it should be insisted that the vessel be in port and in good safety at the date of the attachment. This requirement imposes no hardship on the assured, as all hull time policies contain a clause similar in import to the following:

Should the vessel at the expiration of this policy be at sea, or in distress, or at a port of refuge or of call, she shall, provided previous notice be given to the underwriters, be held covered at a pro rata monthly premium to her port of destination.

There would seem to be no sufficient reason, in the case of a single-vessel risk, why the attachment should take place while the vessel is at sea. In the case of fleet insurance a different condition exists. In this case, the insurance usually attaches at the same date on all the vessels of a fleet, and naturally some of the vessels will be at sea while others are in port. Custom has established the practice of disregarding the position of the vessels of a fleet at the time of attachment. The question which of two policies should respond for the loss of a vessel that sailed before the date of attachment of the second policy but was never heard of again would have to be determined by the circumstances in each particular case.

Attachment of Voyage Risks on Hull. In voyage insurance on hulls, the time of attachment is determined by the wording of the policy. If the contract reads "from" a port, the risk will attach from the moment the vessel sails, or "breaks ground" as it is technically called, with the intention of proceeding on the insured voyage. If the insurance is written "at and from" a port, the time of attachment is more difficult to determine. It would seem to be the fair meaning of the words, and there are decisions supporting this view, that the risk attaches when the vessel is at the port and is either in readiness to take cargo for the proposed voyage or the captain or the vessel's agents have made some preparation looking to the prosecution of the voyage. The mere fact that a vessel is in port with no definite employment or with no preparation being made to fit her for proposed employment will not cause a policy reading "at and from" to attach. The safest practice is to consider that, under a voyage hull policy reading "at and from," the insurance attaches only when the vessel goes on the berth to load. In order that there may be no overlapping of voyage policies, a clause reading "this policy not to attach until expiry of previous policies" may be inserted in the contract. It is customary for a voyage policy on hull to terminate 24 hours after arrival in good safety at the port of destination or, as the Lloyd's form of policy reads, "until she hath moored at anchor 24 hours in good safety." The intent of either clause is that the risk shall continue not only for 24 hours after mere arrival, but a full 24-hour period after arrival at the customary anchorage or harbor, in the particular port, where the vessel is not exposed to the perils of the voyage.

Policy May Terminate by Breach of Contract. While the *terminus ad quem* is dependent on the wording of the policy, the assured may terminate the insurance short of its ultimate time or place of expiration by breach of any of the express or implied terms of the contract. The discussion of express and implied warranties is reserved for a later chapter, but reference to these warranties is necessary at this juncture, because the breach of one of them will vitiate the insurance and thus introduce a new *terminus ad quem*. So the abandonment, by the assured, of the insured voyage or the substitution of another voyage will terminate the insurance.

The Doctrine of No Deviation. The second sentence of the paragraph of the printed form referring to the inception and duration of the risk reads, "and it shall and may be lawful for the said vessel, in her voyage, to proceed and sail to, touch and stay at, any ports or places, if thereunto obliged by stress of weather, or other unavoidable accident, without prejudice to this insurance." No mention has yet been made of the *doctrine of no deviation*, that is, the implied condition that there shall be no departure from or variation of the insured voyage after the risk has attached. Any inexcusable violation of this implied condition will terminate the insurance. This being so, the words quoted from the printed form are introduced in order to excuse certain forms of deviation so that the insurance may not be automatically terminated. This exception to the rule of no deviation is made as a practical matter and as an inducement to the captain of a vessel to exercise supreme care in order to effect the safety of the venture. Were such deviation to make void an insurance, the captain might delay making for a port of refuge in the event of threatening weather, thereby unnecessarily exposing the venture to loss or damage. However, the facts in a given case must show the necessity for the deviation; otherwise this clause could be used as a cloak for unlawful acts.

Conduct of the Voyage. The implied conditions with respect to deviation require that the voyage be commenced within a reasonable time, that it be pursued over the usual and direct route between the termini, and that the cargo be discharged from the vessel with customary dispatch. If it is a well-established usage of a particular voyage that certain places be used as ports of call, the use of such ports will not be considered a deviation. If the policy provides that the destination shall be ports in a given locality, they must be visited in their geographical order unless there be well-established usage to the contrary. If, on the other hand, the ports of destination are specifically enumerated in the policy, they must be visited in the order named.

When Does Deviation Occur? Deviation may occur at any time after the inception of the risk and voids or suspends the insurance from the moment the deviation commences. As a general principle, any deviation voids the insurance. Nevertheless, a deviation may be held only to suspend the insurance where the deviation is of such short duration as to be negligible, as a delay of an hour or a deviation of a mile. The underwriters would, however, be discharged from liability for any loss happening during such temporary deviation.[1] The mere intention to deviate does not void the policy; there must be an overt act putting the intention into operation. Deviation is excusable, not only in the cases enumerated in the printed form, but also when the vessel leaves her course in order to save life. It has been held that deviation to save property alone is not excusable, but hull policies ordinarily expressly permit such deviation. The extent of the deviation or the fact that it does not materially enhance the risk is of no moment in deciding whether a breach has been committed. The mere fact that a different voyage has been substituted, after the commencement of the risk, is sufficient. In order to avoid the hardships that the doctrine of deviation imposes on innocent cargo owners, who have no voice in the conduct or management of the vessel, it is customary to insert in cargo policies the *deviation clause,* which holds the assured covered in the event of deviation or change of voyage, the assured agreeing to notify the underwriter as soon as knowledge of the deviation is brought to his attention and to pay such additional premium as may be required. A deviation clause in common use reads:

> Held covered, at a premium to be arranged in case of deviation or change of voyage, or other variation of the risk by reason of the exercise of any liberty granted to the shipowner or charterer under the contract of affreightment, or of any omission or error in the description of the interest, vessel or voyage.

This clause ordinarily does not extend protection in the event of substitution of a different vessel. As deviation in the case of time hull insurance would automatically void the policy for the remainder of the policy term, a deviation clause similar to that in cargo policies is inserted, or it is provided that in the event of deviation the underwriters shall not be liable for loss occurring while the vessel is out of the policy limits. It will be observed that the clause quoted above provides for contingencies, other than deviation, that may happen through the exercise of rights reserved by the shipowner or charterer under the contract of affreightment. It also provides that the risk will be held covered, notwithstanding the occurrence of unintentional clerical errors.

[1] See Phillips, "A Treatise on the Law of Insurance," Sec. 989.

The Valuation. The final sentence in the paragraph under consideration reads, "The said goods and merchandises hereby insured, are valued (premium included) at............" In general, policies may be divided into two classes: *valued* and *nonvalued*. Nonvalued policies are rather rare except in the case of carriers' liability policies. The purpose of the valuation clause is to predetermine the worth of the property insured, so that in the event of loss this will not be an open question. Herein is one of the principal differences between marine-insurance and other forms of indemnity contracts. In marine insurance, from the earliest times it has been customary for the underwriter and assured mutually to agree on the value of the insured subject. Having decided on this value or basis of valuation, neither party to the contract may raise objection, after loss, on the ground that the value is too low or too high unless it should appear that a fraudulent valuation has been imposed on either party.

Determination of Value. Marine insurance endeavors, as far as is humanly possible, to give perfect indemnity to the assured. The assured ships goods to a distant port with reasonable expectation that he will realize a certain price, perhaps greatly in excess of their cost to him. To place the goods in this particular market will necessitate the incurring of various expenses, such as freight, insurance premium, packing, cartage, customs charges, and agent's commissions, so that the value may be a constantly changing one. Were it not possible to predetermine a value, many intricate questions would arise as to the real value at the time of loss, which might occur at any point on the proposed passage. It is far simpler, and in practice works a fair measure of justice, to fix a reasonable value and adhere to that.

Valued Policies Justified. Perhaps in fire and other branches of insurance, the chief objection to valued policies arises out of the moral hazard. A man is in possession and control of his fixed property, and the possibility of obtaining insurance at a determined valuation might induce him to effect the destruction of his property in order to obtain this fixed value from his underwriters. Human nature being what it is, the practice of having open values on fixed property is manifestly sound. On the other hand, valued policies in marine insurance are justified by the fact that the subject matter is movable property and, in the case of merchandise particularly, is out of the custody and control of the assured. The assured cannot compass the destruction of his property without collusion on the part of those in custody of the property. In the case of hull insurance in a time of commercial stagnation, when there are more ships than there is employment for them, the valued policy, especially the high-valued policy, is a real menace to the underwriters. The insured subject in such cases is under the control of the assured, and an unscrupulous owner may endeavor to insure the vessel for an amount greatly in excess of its true market value. If he is successful in insuring the vessel for this unfair value, he may, in collusion with the captain, try to destroy the vessel. It is therefore important that underwriters at all times have reasonable knowledge of the value of ocean tonnage.

Basis of Valuation. In a single-risk policy the valuation may be expressed as "valued at sum insured," or "valued at $. . . . ." In open policies, however, it is possible to have only a *basis* of value, such as "valued at invoice cost plus 10 per cent plus prepaid or guaranteed freight," or in the case of imported goods "valued at $. . . . . the £ sterling (or the franc) of invoice." Because the currencies of many countries are unstable, it is usual to provide in the valuation clause for the conversion of the foreign currency of invoice into United States dollars at the current sight rate of exchange for bankers' demand drafts on the date of the bill of lading. This clause is reasonably safe in the case of pegged currencies, such as sterling. However, where there is no peg and the currency quotations fluctuate greatly, the underwriter may insist on a fixed rate for the conversion of the foreign currency of invoice. Under this form of policy it happens many times that the individual shipments, to which the open policy is applicable, are not known until after the risk has terminated by arrival or by the loss of the vessel. In either case, were the basis of valuation not determined in advance, endless disputes would arise as to the amount of loss suffered by the assured or as to the amount of premium to which the underwriter is entitled, since the premium is charged at predetermined rates applied to the insured amounts.

Market-value Clauses. The modern tendency in overseas trading is for the merchant to place on the underwriter the burden of carrying the risk of fluctuating values due to market conditions. To illustrate, a merchant buying rubber in the Straits Settlements is no longer content to have an open policy covering his purchases for invoice cost plus 10 per cent. During the long voyage to the United States the value of the rubber may increase considerably, and constant attention would be required to place additional insurance to protect the increased value. To avoid this difficulty it is now customary for underwriters to issue policies wherein the commodity insured is valued at the highest market value attained during the insured voyage or at invoice plus 10 per cent, whichever is higher. Premium is charged on this value, and losses are adjusted on this basis. Of course, such valuation clauses are feasible only where there is an independent trading market where the market value can be determined, as in the case of cotton, coffee, rubber, sugar, and certain other raw commodities.

Additional Insurance. In many cases of commodities other than those named in the preceding paragraph, increases in market value that occur during the insured voyage make it desirable for the shipper or the consignee to procure additional insurance to cover such increase in value. In such situations it is desirable, if possible, to have the underwriter who has insured the original risk accept the additional insurance required, making it part of the original contract and amending the policy valuation to conform to the new value, so that, in the event of claim for loss, there would be but one underwriter with whom to negotiate. Frequently, however, this is not possible. When goods are sold on c.i.f. terms, the shipper is required to provide the usual form of insurance, for the customary amount, say invoice plus 10 per cent, but is not interested in providing insurance to cover a subsequent increase in the market value of the commodity. The buyer of the goods, therefore, will endeavor to obtain the additional insurance from his own underwriter.

Without Benefit of Salvage. If there is no information that a casualty has overtaken the shipment, the underwriter will probably cover the additional insurance subject to the same terms of average as the original insurance, but "without benefit of salvage." The reason for using this latter phrase is that the original insurance is customarily valued at sum insured. It therefore follows that, after the payment of loss, any salvage recovered from the sale of the damaged goods, which may have been abandoned to the underwriter, or through the enforcement of claims, under the right of subrogation, against third parties such as rail or ocean carriers, would be received by the original underwriter. The underwriter on the additional insurance admits this situation by the use of the words "without benefit of salvage" and accordingly charges a higher rate of premium than that assessed on the original insurance.

Prior-loss Clause. Should a casualty have overtaken the vessel or the goods before the additional insurance is requested, the underwriter, if willing to accept the insurance, would probably add a warranty to prevent claims, arising out of such casualty, being made under his policy. One form of this warranty reads: "Warranted free of claim for loss, damage, injury or expense arising from (here the casualty is named) occurring on or about (here the approximate date is inserted)."

Hull Values. In the case of hull insurance, the valuation is always expressed in dollars or other currency. Owing to the large values involved in the modern cargo or passenger steamer, it is usual to divide the valuation into parts, one applying to the hull, tackle, and furniture of the steamer, the other to its machinery. In the case of expensively fitted passenger steamers or of refrigerated vessels a further separation may be made showing the value of the cabin outfit or the refrigerating plant. No problem is more difficult than that of determining a fair insured value for a vessel, nor is any problem more important from the point of view of sound and conservative underwriting. The purpose in separating the value of a steamer into parts is to permit of claims for smaller losses being made, the percentage of loss necessary to make a claim being applied to each separate valuation or to the whole value, whichever method is most advantageous to the assured.[1]

[1] A more detailed explanation of separate values appears on p. 385.

CHAPTER 11

The Policy

THE PERILS CLAUSE

Perils Insured against. The quaintest portion of the marine insurance policy, and the part that most clearly indicates it to be a document that originated many years ago, is the paragraph dealing with the perils insured against. These hazards are not listed in any logical order. Marine perils and war perils follow each other indiscriminately, indicating that this portion of the policy at least was the result of evolution, new perils being added as commerce developed and as new difficulties were encountered by mariners in extending the scope of their commercial activities. Words are used that have become obsolete and leave in doubt the precise form of peril that the early underwriter and merchant had in mind. General words follow the specific enumeration of hazards, making obscure the true intent of the policy. Read without reference to the wealth of legal lore referring to this particular part of the policy, the document is vague, misleading, and perhaps unintelligible. But practically every word in the paragraph has been weighed in the judicial balance, and its own meaning, as well as its meaning in relation to the context, has been determined. Therefore, this particular wording has continued through the centuries, slight modifications appearing in the various forms of the individual companies, but in general the same wording being followed in all. The very modern book form of open policy[1] attempts to remedy this situation.

The enumeration of the perils in the printed form under consideration is worded as follows:

[1] See p. 150.

Touching the adventures and perils which the said............Insurance Company is contented to bear, and takes upon itself in this voyage, they are of the seas, men-of-war, fires, enemies, pirates, rovers, thieves, jettisons, letters of mart and countermart, reprisals, takings at sea, arrests, restraints and detainments of all kings, princes, or people, of what nation, condition or quality soever, barratry of the master and mariners, and all other perils, losses and misfortunes that have or shall come to the hurt, detriment or damage of the said goods and merchandises, or any part thereof.

Truly, this is a formidable list of calamities and seems to afford little hope of escape for the underwriter. The courts, however, have applied the rule of reason in their interpretation of these perils, so that, in reality, the protection afforded is not so all-inclusive as the words of the clause would seem to indicate.

Doctrine of Proximate Cause. The policy applies only on the voyage insured and covers only losses occasioned by the perils stipulated, provided these hazards, or any one of them, should be the *proximate cause* of the loss. The doctrine of proximate cause is in no way peculiar to marine insurance, since it is a familiar principle of all law concerning the liability of one person to another for injury suffered. This principle of fixing liability by considering the direct, primary, and immediate cause of the injury suffered, and not the remote and indirect cause, is of the greatest importance in determining liability under marine-insurance policies. Phillips, in his admirable work on the law of marine insurance, sets forth the determination of the proximate cause in these words:[1]

In case of the concurrence of different causes, to one of which it is necessary to attribute the loss, it is to be attributed to the efficient predominating peril, whether it is or is not in activity at the consummation of the disaster.

That is, if at the time of disaster there are in operation two perils, one of which is covered under the policy while the other is impliedly or expressly excepted, as in the case of a marine peril operating at the same time as a war peril, it must be determined which of the two perils is the all-efficient and predominating one that caused the re-

[1] "A Treatise on the Law of Insurance," Sec. 1132

sultant loss. The fact that the hazard which was the proximate cause was not in activity at the moment of destruction would not preclude that peril from being the actual and efficient cause of disaster.

To illustrate, a steamer is torpedoed, but nevertheless still floats and has a reasonable chance of making port. Listing heavily because of the entrance of water, the vessel is partially out of the control of the master who, in endeavoring to make port, misses the channel and runs his vessel aground so that she becomes a total loss. The immediate cause of the total destruction of the vessel is undoubtedly the stranding, a marine peril, but the proximate cause is the torpedoing, a war peril. The loss should be claimed from underwriters covering war risks.

Loss Not Covered. It must be borne in mind that, although an underwriter is liable for losses caused by perils of the sea, the meaning of which will be explained presently, he is not necessarily liable for perils *on* the sea. The underwriter is not liable for the ordinary and inevitable action of the forces of nature causing ordinary wear and tear to the vessel. He is not liable for the natural decay of the vessel due to the passage of time. He is not liable for loss arising from the subject itself because of its inherent qualities, nor is he liable for a fire arising from the improper preparation of a commodity as, for instance, the occurrence of spontaneous combustion in a cargo of soft coal which was shipped in an improper condition. Neither is the underwriter responsible for loss caused by the ordinary leakage of liquids. But it seems he may not deny liability for consequent damage to property insured by him, belonging to another, which is part of the same venture. His responsibility continues during events that, through no fault of the assured, enhance the risk, as, for instance, unavoidable delay in the prosecution of the voyage due to fog, wind, or storms, by which the time at risk under the policy is increased beyond that in contemplation by the underwriter at the time of accepting the risk. So, too, if a policy in time of peace covers the risks of war at a determined rate for a named period and war suddenly breaks out, the underwriter is not relieved of his responsibility, notwithstanding the fact that the compensation he is receiving, through the occurrence of an unforeseen event, is inadequate.

Fraud or Misconduct. An underwriter is not responsible for losses caused by perils insured against that are directly incurred by fraud or misconduct on the part of the assured or his representatives, but it must be shown that such fraud or misconduct is the proximate cause of the loss. Negligence, in order to void the policy, must amount to gross negligence or to willful misconduct. Errors of judgment on the part of the captain of a vessel will not forfeit the insurance, but willful misconduct done in bad faith and illegally, or gross carelessness of the captain, showing culpability, will not be covered by the policy unless barratry[1] is also covered.

In order to promote the overseas commerce of the United States, Congress, in 1893, passed the Harter Act.[2] This statute relieves the owner of a ship from the consequences of careless or negligent acts in the navigation or in the management of the vessel, and from liability for losses caused by inherent defects or weakness in the vessel itself, provided the owner or his manager has taken all precautions to furnish a seaworthy vessel that has been adequately equipped and manned by a competent master and crew. Similar statutes are found in the laws of other maritime nations. The Carriage of Goods by Sea Acts further define the relationship between carrier and shipper.

Perils of the Sea. In the enumeration of the hazards against which protection is afforded by the policy, perils of the sea are first mentioned. These are the general words used to include losses that are the result of unusual action of the forces of nature operating in and about navigable waters. A careful distinction must be made, however, between perils *of* the sea and perils *on* the sea. The policy does not, under the form of wording used, cover all perils that may overtake the venture on the sea, but only those which are the direct result of actual perils of the sea. Included in these general words are losses resulting from the unusual action of the wind, not the ordinary wear and tear caused by the ever-moving atmosphere, but losses resulting from the tempestuous action of this force. It is not necessary that the resultant loss be an immediate effect of wind, such as the loss of sails or the snapping of a mast. It may be a consequential loss occasioned by the wind, such as the leaking of the seams of a vessel through unusual strain on sails and masts by excessive wind pressure.

[1] See p. 183.
[2] See Appendix N.

Enumeration. The tempestuous action of the *waves*, causing a vessel to be buffeted and battered by the force of the water, is a peril of the sea, as are also the risks of *stranding* on reefs, rocks, and shoals, even when it results from negligent navigation. Loss caused by the action of *lightning* is a peril of the sea, lightning being distinguished from fire in that loss may be occasioned by the action of lightning without any fire resulting. *Collision* is one of the perils of the sea, occasioned as it often is by the presence of fog, darkness, ice, or other natural conditions interfering with the navigation of the vessel. Collision may involve the coming together of vessel with vessel or of the vessel with an iceberg or with some other floating or stationary object. The use of the word "collision" as a peril of the sea should not be confused with the protection provided under marine policies on hulls, whereby the underwriter assumes responsibility for the liability imposed upon the owner of a vessel for loss caused to innocent third parties by the negligent collision of his vessel with another.

Unavoidable Accident. "Perils of the sea" will also cover unavoidable accident, the result of the physical topography of the ocean shores and the ocean bed. For instance, a vessel in a properly equipped tidal harbor may take the bottom in a place where, through action of the tide or through some other unavoidable cause, the bottom is uneven, causing the vessel to tip with resultant damage to the hull or cargo. Derangement of or damage to the machinery of a steamer or mechanically propelled vessel, through stress of weather, is also covered under the general words "perils of the sea."

Other Perils of the Sea. The policy covers sea-water damage due to an insured peril, and it has been held that injury caused by rats on board ship is also due to a peril of the sea, provided the owner and captain have exercised reasonable care to rid the vessel of these pests. It would seem, however, that damage by rats is rather a peril *on* the sea than a peril *of* the sea and that underwriters should not be held liable for losses of this nature unless they have been specially insured against. In fact, it is so stated in the Marine Insurance Act of Great Britain.[1] Sinking is also a peril of the sea. It may result from unseaworthiness, from overloading or improper loading, or from uncontrolled leaks caused by heavy weather. Sinking is often the ulti-

[1] Paragraph 55, Sec. (*c*); Appendix I, p. 468.

mate result of other perils of the sea. Stranding or collision may puncture the shell of the vessel so that sinking results. Frequently a vessel is sunk from the efforts made to extinguish a fire on board.

Casting Away. At the end of the period of inflation immediately following the close of World War I, ocean tonnage values disappeared like mist before the rising sun. Hull policies being written for a definite period of time, usually one year, it happened in many cases that underwriters had policies outstanding at wartime valuations on tonnage the market value of which was but a fraction of the policy value. To an unscrupulous owner, the temptation to cast his vessel away proved irresistible, and vessel after vessel was lost under most suspicious circumstances. Where this condition appeared, underwriters refused to pay, claiming that the vessel was not lost through an insured peril. True, the vessel had been lost by sinking, a marine peril when the result of fortuitous causes, but it was claimed that the proximate cause of the destruction was the intentional casting away of the vessel by her owner or his agent. A number of such cases came before the courts, and in the most noted of them, that of the *Gregorios*, it was held that the vessel had been lost through the intention of the owners and not through an insured peril. Many similar cases were tried, the greater number being decided in favor of the underwriters. Other cases the underwriters lost through lack of sufficient evidence implicating the owners.

Third-party Interests. The *Gregorios* case was important, in that there was a mortgaged interest insured. It was claimed on behalf of the mortgagees that they were innocent of wrongdoing, even if the owners were guilty, and that they, as innocent insured, should recover their loss from the underwriters. The House of Lords, however, dismissed this claim on the ground that no insured peril had occurred, that the policy did not include the risk of casting away, and that the underwriters therefore were not liable. This decision placed innocent mortgagees in an impossible position, and underwriters immediately devised clauses to protect such innocent beneficiaries against the wrongdoing of the assured. As the cargo owners were in an equally embarrassing situation under the application of this decision, clauses were also devised to protect them under such circumstances. The American Institute clause reads:

The Assured are not to be prejudiced by the presence of the negligence clause and/or latent defect clause in the Bills of Lading and/or Charter Party. The seaworthiness of the vessel as between the Assured and these Assurers is hereby admitted and the wrongful act or misconduct of the shipowner or his servants causing a loss is not to defeat the recovery by an innocent Assured if the loss in the absence of such wrongful act or misconduct would have been a loss recoverable on the policy. With leave to sail with or without pilots, and to tow and assist vessels or craft in all situations, and to be towed.

Inchmaree Clause. A somewhat similar situation arises when damage to cargo results from the bursting of boilers or the breakage of shafts, perils held in the *Inchmaree* case[1] not to be covered by a marine-insurance policy. To protect the cargo owner in such case, the following clause is incorporated in the Institute policy form:

This insurance is also specially to cover any loss of or damage to the interest insured hereunder, through the bursting of boilers, breakage of shafts or through any latent defect in the machinery, hull or appurtenances, or from faults or errors in the navigation and/or management of the vessel by the master, mariners, mates, engineers or pilots.

Fire. It will be more logical to ignore the sequence of the hazards as they appear in the printed form and consider, first, the perils that are marine in their nature and then those which are the result of the acts of individuals or of nations. Fire is specifically mentioned, since this is not a peril of the sea but a peril on the sea. The underwriter not only is liable for the cargo or the part of the vessel destroyed by fire but is also liable for consequential losses resulting from the fire. Thus, the underwriter assumes responsibility for damage caused by water or steam used in the hold of a vessel in an endeavor to smother the fire or by the action of smoke damaging cargo not touched by the fire or penetrating other holds not involved in the fire.[2] The underwriter is also liable for the action of chemicals or gases used in an endeavor to smother the fire.

Fire Protection. Fire is one of the greatest and most feared dangers that mariners face. A great deal has been done by the installation of fire-fighting devices and fire detectors to prevent and control fires at

[1] See p. 271.

[2] See General Average, p. 415.

sea, but much still remains to be done. Perhaps no problem connected with marine perils offers a more fertile field for the inventor than this. Fire control on the sea is materially different from that on land and yet in some respects is essentially the same. Steam injectors take the place of standpipes in buildings. Fireproof and watertight bulkheads correspond to the fire walls in land structures, while sprinkler systems, so common in buildings, have been installed in but few steamers. When the depth of a steamer's hold is considered, the futility of the ordinary form of sprinkler will be seen. A fire starting at the bottom would probably attain such headway before the sprinkler would work that it would be useless, even if it were possible, for the water to reach the seat of the fire. It must be remembered that at sea the hatches of a vessel are usually closed, so that a fire may smolder and gain a firm hold on the cargo some time before it is detected. Steam introduced into the hold by means of steam pipes so installed as to give a good distribution of steam over the entire hold is very effective in the control of fire. Other devices introducing gases which absorb the oxygen in the hold and thus smother the flame are also effective. While the fire hazard does not affect the seaworthiness of the vessel, in the ordinary meaning of that term, from the point of view of the marine underwriter, the design, equipment, and loading of a vessel with respect to the fire hazard have a material bearing on the seaworthiness of the vessel.

The diesel-engined type of ship is without steam for fire lines unless an auxiliary boiler is provided for this purpose. Such a boiler is usually cold, and considerable time is required to get up a head of steam sufficient to feed the fire lines. These auxiliary boilers often are used while in port to work the winches and, though of sufficient capacity for this purpose, are inadequate to care for the steam lines in more than one hold. Many diesel-type vessels are now equipped with carbon dioxide systems. This fire-extinguishing gas is carried in cylinders connected with the fire lines which introduce it into the holds.

Many vessels are now equipped with smoke-detection systems. By a series of pipes running from the holds and other enclosed spaces to a control box on the bridge, air is continuously drawn to the control box. If smoke appears, it is immediately detected, and a fire-extinguishing gas, usually carbon dioxide, is released into the space from which the smoke has come. In this manner a fire can be controlled quickly. Although the gas may not extinguish the fire, it can control its spread so that the vessel can reach port, where more intensive methods can be used to extinguish the fire.

The use of oil as a fuel in steamers has also presented a new fire problem in that water will not put out an oil fire but, on the contrary, has a tendency to spread it. This difficulty has been quite satisfactorily met by the invention of special chemical systems for extinguishing oil fires, but comparatively few oil-burning vessels are adequately equipped with these systems. During World War II experiments were made with cold fog to extinguish oil fires, particularly in engine-room spaces. Through a specially designed nozzle, water under high pressure was broken up into a very fine mist. This in a short time reduced the temperature in the space on fire so that men could enter and extinguish the fire by the use of fire foam or other chemicals.

Jettison. Jettison is another peril on the sea, but not of the sea, that is specially covered by the policy. Jettison is defined by Phillips[1] as

> . . . the throwing overboard of part of the cargo, or of any article on board of a ship, or the cutting away of masts, spars, rigging, sails, or other furniture for the purpose of lightening or relieving the ship in case of necessity or emergency.

Jettison must be distinguished from "washing overboard," which is a peril of the sea with respect to cargo that is laden and specially insured on deck. Jettison is a voluntary act done for the purpose of saving the general interest. The early mariners in their frail craft found that the best way to save lives and their ships, in the event of storm, was to throw cargo out of the ship to lighten it. Jettison, therefore, was the cause of many of the early losses and proved a great burden to the merchants. At a very early period in commercial history, losses by jettison were considered as sacrifices made in the common interest and were treated as general-average losses for which contribution was made by all interested parties. When insurance was

[1] Phillips, *op. cit.*, Sec. 1278.

devised, this practice of contribution was already firmly established. Therefore, in cases where the jettison results in the saving of the venture, underwriters are more interested in the method of contributing for the loss by jettison than in the jettison itself.[1]

Barratry. While jettison is a voluntary, justifiable act of the master of the vessel, barratry is occasioned by the willful misconduct of the master or the mariners. Barratry is defined as a fraudulent breach of duty or a willful act of known illegality on the part of the master of a ship, in his character of master, or of the crew to the injury of the owner of the ship or cargo and without his consent. It includes every breach of trust committed with dishonest purpose, as running away with the ship, sinking or deserting her, or embezzling the cargo. At the present time, with the rapid means of communication existing between the ends of the earth, barratry has become a rather unprofitable and dangerous occupation. In former times, however, when a vessel would be unheard of for months at a time, it was not unusual for the captain to use the ship for his own purposes. Such unlawful act was barratry, and a loss occurring during such misuse of the vessel would not be covered unless barratry was included among the insured perils. Therefore, willful violations of law, such as the violation of a blockade or an embargo or trading with the enemy, even though done for the purpose of benefiting the owners, are barratrous acts. The willful action of the master or the mariners in putting the vessel in a position of peril by disobeying the instructions of an authorized pilot or cutting a cable so that the vessel would run ashore, proceeding on a voyage when capture by the enemy was certain, and other like cases have been held to be barratrous acts. In any particular case, it is necessary to distinguish between willful misconduct and errors of judgment, although gross ignorance and recklessness on the part of the master may amount to barratry. As the master is the agent of the owner in the management of the vessel, it is quite proper to exclude the risk of barratry of the master in an insurance on the hull. It is rather illogical to insure the owner of a vessel against the wrongful acts of one whom he himself has entrusted with the care of the ship. With respect to the mariners, the case is different in that these men are not directly chosen by the owner but rather by

[1] See p. 415.

the master. It is quite reasonable, however, that the cargo owner who has no voice in the selection of the master or crew should have protection against their wrongful acts. As a matter of practice it is usual to insure the hull owner against the risk of barratry.

Lawless Acts and War Perils. The remaining perils, specifically enumerated, refer to the overt acts of persons or peoples who are not connected with the venture but who, from either personal or national motives, seek to injure, appropriate, or destroy the ship and its cargo. These perils naturally group themselves into two classes. The first class includes perils which are the result of the acts of individuals or groups acting on their own responsibility and without the sanction of any recognized government. These hazards are described as those of *pirates, rovers,* and *thieves.* The second class is composed of those perils which are the results, directly or indirectly, of the belligerent acts of hostile governments. These latter acts are supposed to be executed in accordance with the principles of international law, and in wars previous to 1914, that law was generally observed. In World War I, however, at least one of the belligerents set up a new standard of conduct, claiming that might is more powerful than right, with the result that marine underwriters had to revise their preconceived notions of the hazards which belligerent action involved. This ignoring of the principles of international law was common practice in World War II. The peril of *thieves* refers to those acts of an individual or a band of individuals done in contravention of the law of the place where the criminal act of theft is committed. Rovers and pirates may commit similar acts on the high seas under the sanction, it may be, of an unorganized or unrecognized government acting in defiance of international law.

Thieves. The peril of *thieves,* as covered by the marine-insurance policy, is generally recognized by merchants and by the textbook writers as that of the taking of property by force, as distinguished from taking by stealth, which latter form of larceny is known by the specific term *pilferage.* It was always the intention of underwriters to protect property on vessels from losses occasioned by the criminal acts of those who obtained access to the property by force. Pilferage, however, was not contemplated by the underwriter when property was insured, because such loss was supposed to be the result of the criminal acts of those who had a right to be with the property, such as stevedores or others who by stealth mingled with them and thus had access to the goods. Unfortunately, this theory and practice were overridden in certain state courts, where the judges, in an academic discussion of the meaning of the word "thieves," ignored for the most part the practice of merchants and underwriters which, of old, was the basis on which marine-insurance law was determined and held that the word "thieves" covered what is commonly known in marine circles as pilferage. Accordingly, most policies in use in the United States have inserted the words "assailing thieves" in order to make clear the original and present intention of underwriters in insuring against thieves. No such interpretation has been given to the word "thieves" in the English courts, but in the Marine Insurance Act, Par. 9 of the rules for construction reads: "The term 'thieves' does not cover clandestine theft or a theft committed by any one of the ship's company, whether crew or passengers." Such clandestine theft, under the term *pilferage,* is now commonly included in marine policies. The results of including this hazard in the years immediately following the two world wars were very disastrous to underwriters. The granting of pilferage insurance meets a need of the merchant but is unsound in principle in that it creates a tendency to lessen the care of the shipowner for property in his custody. It also has a tendency to make the merchant less careful in packing his goods for shipment.

Nondelivery Risks. Closely akin to the pilferage risk is that of *theft and/or nondelivery.* This term is used to denote the nondelivery of an entire shipping package at destination. It does not relate to the delivery of a package empty, its entire contents having disappeared, but only to missing packages. There should be no question but that a carrier is liable for packages which he receives but fails to deliver. A variety of causes may account for nondelivery, such as wrong delivery where packages are carried beyond the port of destination or are discharged at an earlier port of call or where the package is overlooked and not loaded. Nondelivery may also be caused by clandestine theft of the entire shipping package. Insurance against pilferage is not intended to cover such loss, and underwriters assume liability for missing packages lost by such theft only when the risk of theft and/or nondelivery of an entire shipping package has been specially written into the policy.

Pirates and Rovers. The two expressions *pirates* and *rovers* are hard to distinguish, both terms referring to depredations committed on the high seas in violation of the laws of nations and of such a character that, if committed on land, the crime would amount to a felony. Pirates and rovers are the outlaws of the high seas and the enemies of society, owing allegiance to no authorized government. It may be that the word "pirates" originally referred to those who lay in wait on the high seas, hoping to entrap their victims, while the word "rovers" referred to those who sailed the high seas seeking their prey. Such inferences are, however, conjectural. Gow suggests that the word "rovers" may have been added to include specially the Mohammedan sea robbers of North Africa. These two perils, with the exception of the Chinese pirates, have become obsolete since the United States cleared the sea of the Barbary pirates, in the early part of the nineteenth century, though many acts committed in the world wars amounted to piracy, notwithstanding the fact that they were committed under the authority of a so-called established government.

War Perils. The remainder of the perils enumerated in the policy are true war perils, and it was insuring against these risks that caused the gigantic development of insurance in England in the latter part of the eighteenth and the beginning of the nineteenth century. History has repeated itself, and again an unprecedented expansion in marine insurance resulted from the exigencies of the world wars and the enhanced risks to which property at sea was exposed. In the enumeration of these war perils, difficulty is experienced in determining what is the real meaning of the words. Some of the words used to describe perils have become obsolete, and others are so alike in meaning as to make difficult any differentiation in the perils to which they refer. Piracy is now considered a war peril.

Men-of-war. The first of the war perils, *men-of-war,* is an elastic term general enough in its meaning to include all the new devices that new wars produce. "Men-of-war" refers to the aggressive acts of a belligerent government committed on the seas by means of war machines. In the early days of international strife, "men-of-war" was a term which adequately described the only marine offensive weapon. Today, however, the words refer not only to battleships, the successors of the former men-of-war, but to submarines, airplanes, destroyers, and the equipment of these devices in the form of torpedoes, mines, and bombs. Mines, stationary or floating, and all other mechanical devices used by belligerents to effect the destruction of property on the sea are included in the term men-of-war.

When peace follows a state of war, many derelict mines and torpedoes remain as a menace to navigation. While it would seem evident that the wording of a policy covering war perils is sufficiently broad to cover this hazard, it is customary to eliminate any possible doubt with respect to this peril by the insertion of the words "including the risk of floating or stationary mines and stray or derelict torpedoes, floating or submerged."

Enemies. If there be question whether any particular warlike device is included under the term "men-of-war," the next peril, that of *enemies*, is broad enough to include that device. Doubt has been expressed as to whether cruisers are men-of-war, but if they are not, they certainly are enemies and can find refuge under that term. The peril of enemies would seem to be embraced by the peril of men-of-war, but it may be that the word "enemies" was introduced into the marine policy to protect the assured against losses occasioned by the acts of privateers and other openly declared foes under a belligerent flag, who are authorized to carry on warfare but who do not belong to the government whose flag they fly.

Letters of Mart and Countermart. While privateering was formally abolished by civilized nations by the Treaty of Paris in 1856, references to this mode of warfare still remain in the policy. *Letters of mart and countermart* were issued to privateers. These letters were granted by belligerents to their citizens who had suffered loss at the hands of the enemy, in order that they might recoup their losses. Letters of mart are the commissions granted by one of the belligerents to its citizens, while letters of countermart are the commissions granted by the opposing belligerent to its citizens as a retaliatory measure. Such letters granted a limited commission to the privateer, who should be distinguished from the pirate, as the former sails under a national flag, is under governmental commission, and operates only against the declared enemies of his own nation. The practice of issuing these letters is now condemned; hence, these terms are relatively unimportant to the student of marine insurance.

Reprisals. It is difficult to distinguish reprisals, the next war peril enumerated, from letters of mart and countermart, but the word may have been inserted in the policy to cover losses occasioned by acts done in retaliation for wrongs against one nation or its subjects committed by another nation or its subjects, short of actual war. The word was in common use during the world wars with reference to acts of retaliation against one of the belligerents for crimes committed in violation of international law. Whether or not a similar meaning is intended in the insurance policy is a matter of conjecture. In the Lloyd's form of policy, the word "reprisals" does not appear, but in its place is found the word "surprisals," which would seem to be synonymous with takings at sea, the next peril enumerated in the American form.

Takings at Sea. Arrests. The expression "takings at sea" is equivalent to the modern word "capture" and means the forceful taking of a vessel or its cargo with the intention of retaining possession of it. In World War I "capture" was the principal peril to which property of the Teutonic allies or their sympathizers was subject, while "men-of-war" describes the principal peril to which the property of the rest of the world was exposed. The word "arrests," though similar in meaning to "takings at sea," refers more particularly to the stoppage of a ship at sea or in port for the purpose of making an examination of her papers or cargo, but without any intention of appropriating either the ship or the cargo.

Restraints and Detainments. Restraints are the action of a government in establishing an embargo or other restrictive measure, thus preventing the free use of its ports by commercial vessels, causing the interruption and possible loss of voyages involving such ports and perhaps consequent sacrifice of cargo. The term *detainments,* on the other hand, covers losses resulting from the detention of a vessel and its cargo by blockade or possibly quarantine regulation or other interference by the police power of a nation while a vessel is in port. In this connection, however, the use of the word detainment does not cover losses which are the result merely of delay or interruption of the voyage and cause injury, for example, through loss of market or some other remote result.

Kings, Princes, or People. The modifying words "of all kings, princes, or people of what nation, condition or quality soever" are introduced to show that the perils intended to be covered are not the mere acts of individuals, but the acts of groups of individuals organized into governments, whether such governments be duly constituted or not. The rules of construction of the Marine Insurance Act of Great Britain, Par. 10, state that this phrase refers to political and executive acts and does not include a loss caused by riot or ordinary judicial process.

All Other Perils. The closing words of the perils clause reading "and all other perils, losses and misfortunes, that have or shall come to the hurt, detriment or damage of the said goods and merchandises, or any part thereof," if unexplained, are exceedingly misleading. If the words mean what they state, the enumeration of specific perils would seem to be needless, but the very fact that specific perils have been enumerated gives the key that unlocks the meaning of these words. It has been decided more than once that there must be read into this clause after the words "and all other perils," the words "of the same nature." This is called the doctrine of *ejusdem generis.* Only fortuitous perils, happening while the property is under the protection of the policy, are covered by these general words, and not every conceivable injury that may come to the hurt, detriment, or damage of the property. Had such construction not been given to this clause, underwriters would have been compelled either to revise the basic wording of their policy or burden the document with exceptions. This part of the perils clause is sometimes called the *omnibus clause.*

The Free-of-capture Clause. Although the policy covers war perils, it is customary, in view of the hazards to which property is suddenly subjected by the declaration of war, to incorporate into marine policies the *war clause* or *free-of-capture and -seizure* clause, by which the underwriter is relieved of all purely war perils. Various forms are used to accomplish this end, but they are all alike in their purpose. By the deletion of this clause, the policy is automatically restored to its original condition, but the underwriter is then in the position of being able to charge adequate rates of premium for the increased hazard assumed. Since 1938 it has become the practice not to delete the clause but to issue a separate war-risk policy setting forth in detail the war perils covered and the other conditions applicable to war-risk insurance.

Explosions. In the application of scientific knowledge in the past quarter century, the risk of explosion has greatly increased. There was little doubt that an explosion on board a vessel damaging hull or cargo or both could be construed as a peril on the sea. Explosion in many cases did serious damage beyond the place of the explosion. An explosion on a ship might damage cargo on lighters alongside or on the dock. Likewise an explosion on shore might damage a ship or its cargo. Were such remote losses covered? In World War I the explosion of a munitions ship in the harbor of Halifax, Nova Scotia, did terrible damage to the nearby shipping and to the city itself. In this case a collateral question arose as to whether the damage, if insured, was covered under the marine or the war-risk policy. Accordingly, marine cargo policies were amended to include the risk of explosions not clearly caused by war perils. The explosion clause in common use today reads:

> Including the risk of explosion, howsoever or wheresoever occurring during the currency of this insurance, unless excluded by the F.C. & S. Warranty or the S.R. & C.C. Warranty set forth herein.

Such insurance may involve an underwriter in very heavy loss as, for instance, in the case of the explosion in 1947 in Texas City, Tex. The atomic age also poses grave problems.[1]

In hull policies the risk of explosions "on shipboard or elsewhere" is covered in the amended *Inchmaree* or negligence clause.[2]

Strikes, Riots, and Civil-commotions Clause. Owing to the fact that marine insurance on cargo is usually extended to cover from warehouse to warehouse or otherwise insures the goods on shore prior to shipment and after discharge, the danger of underwriters being held liable for losses resulting from the unlawful acts of strikers or from riots or civil commotions is materially enhanced. In such cases the loss is usually due to fire, but it is often difficult to prove whether the proximate cause of the fire was a natural cause or was the result of an

[1] See p. 31.
[2] See p. 271.

unlawful act. Underwriters are unwilling to assume liability for losses due to such unlawful acts unless opportunity is afforded for the special consideration of these risks. Most cargo policies contain a clause similar in import to the following:

Warranted free of loss or damage caused by or resulting from strikes, lockouts, labor disturbances, riots, civil commotions or the acts of any person or persons taking part in such occurrence or disorder.

As in the case of the free-of-capture and -seizure clause, underwriters will, as a rule, waive the strikes, riots, and civil commotions clause in consideration of the payment of additional premium. The clause recommended by the American Institute for this purpose reads:

This insurance also covers damage, theft, pilferage, breakage or destruction of the property insured directly caused by strikers, locked-out workmen, or persons taking part in labor disturbances or riots or civil commotions and destruction of or damage to the property directly caused by persons acting maliciously; but the foregoing shall not be construed to include or cover any loss, damage or expense caused by or resulting from (a) delay, deterioration or loss of market, or (b) hostilities, warlike operations, civil war, revolution, rebellion or insurrection or civil strife arising therefrom; or (c) any weapon of war employing atomic fission or radioactive force.

While the property insured is at risk under the terms and conditions of this insurance *within the United States, its incorporated territories and its possessions in the Western Hemisphere, Canada and Newfoundland,* this insurance is extended to cover damage, theft, pilferage, breakage or destruction of the property insured directly caused by "Vandalism," "Sabotage" and "Malicious Mischief," and as so extended shall include such losses directly caused by acts committed by an agent of any government, party or faction engaged in war, hostilities or other warlike operations, provided such agent is acting secretly and not in connection with any operation of military or naval armed forces in the country where the described property is situated. Nothing in the foregoing shall be construed to include or cover any loss, damage or expense caused by or resulting from (a) delay, deterioration or loss of market; or (b) hostilities, warlike operations, civil war, revolution, rebellion or insurrection, or civil strife arising therefrom, excepting only the acts of certain agents expressly covered above; or (c) any weapon of war employing atomic fission or radioactive force.

The Assured agrees to report all shipments attaching under this cover and to pay premiums therefor at the rates established by the Company from time to time.

This endorsement may be canceled by either party upon forty-eight hours written or telegraphic notice to the other party, but such cancellation shall not affect any risks which have already attached hereunder.

Cancellation Clause. To enable the underwriter to have well within his control the special hazards of war, strikes, riots, etc., he customarily reserves the right to cancel these special covering clauses upon giving short notice of his intention so to do. This notice period formerly varied from 48 hours to 10 days, the period depending somewhat on the seriousness of the conditions existing, or expected, at the time the free-of-capture and the strikers clauses are deleted. The tendency has been to shorten the notice time, particularly with respect to the war-risk cover. The present American Institute clause reads:

This insurance may be canceled by either party upon forty-eight hours written or telegraphic notice to the other party, but such cancellation shall not affect any shipment on which this insurance has attached under the terms of Clause 4 hereof prior to the effective date of such notice. Shipments on which this insurance has not so attached but for which, prior to the effective date of such notice, bills of lading have been issued and (in the case of exports) Special Policies have been issued and negotiated, shall be covered from the time of loading on the overseas Vessel, as provided in Clause 4, at the rates of this Company, provided that, prior to said effective date, such shipments were at the risk of the Assured and were covered under said policy against marine risks.[1]

Risks on Shore. The extension of marine insurance to provide protection on goods during land transit has made necessary the insertion in policies of clauses enumerating the perils covered while the goods are on shore. Various types of conveyances are used in on-shore transportation, such as railroads, motor trucks, aircraft, and horse-drawn vehicles. Again, goods while in transit to the steamer may remain for a time on wharves, piers, or other places of temporary deposit. The American Institute clause detailing the various hazards assumed on shore, which is self-explanatory, reads as follows:

Where this insurance by its terms covers while on docks, wharves or elsewhere on shore and/or during land transportation, it shall include the risks

[1] See war-risk policy, Appendix E.

of collision, derailment, overturning or other accident to the conveyance, fire, lightning, sprinkler leakage, cyclones, hurricanes, earthquakes, floods (meaning the rising of navigable waters), and/or collapse or subsidence of docks or wharves, even though the insurance be otherwise F.P.A.

Broad Forms. Broader forms of policies are being demanded by merchants who seek to eliminate any insurable hazard in connection with their operations. Accordingly, it is not unusual to find policies specifically covering the risk of fresh-water damage, sweat damage—meaning damage occasioned by the condensation in the hold of moisture which drips from the vessel structure on the cargo—damage caused by fuel oil or by oil carried as cargo, damage caused by contact of the insured goods with other cargo, chafing of cargo by rubbing against other cargo, hook-hole damage caused by careless use of hooks by longshoremen, heating of cargo caused by its being placed in too close proximity to the engine room, bad stowage, damage due to the improper stevedoring of cargo, and taint damage (on tea, for example) due to contact with other cargo or caused by odors from other cargo in the same hold.

In other cases, instead of specifically enumerating perils, general clauses are used, covering "all hazards and dangers of transportation" or "all risks of transportation and navigation," or the external cause clause is used, reading:

> To pay for physical loss or damage from any external cause (but excluding those risks excepted by "F. C. & S. & S. R. & C. C." clauses, unless otherwise provided herein) arising during transportation between the points of shipment and of destination named in the policy irrespective of percentage.

Many of the risks specially enumerated above or included in the broad words of the clauses referred to are true liabilities of the carriers for which they are liable under their bill of lading. The inclusion of these hazards in the policy permits claim for such losses directly upon the underwriter, who, through his right of subrogation,[1] is placed in a position to claim against the carrier in the name of the assured.

Theoretically, the practice of insuring these "carrier-liability losses" for the cargo owner is sound, in that it permits the assured to relieve himself of an insurable risk. Practically, however, it is unsound because

[1] See p. 423.

the merchant, knowing that these risks are insured and having paid a premium for such insurance, is disinclined to give the necessary legal notice to the carrier and to take the legal steps necessary to protect his rights against the carrier. Accordingly, the underwriter often finds, upon paying such claims, that his rights under subrogation have been impaired or lost through the inactivity of his assured. Only by acting in the same manner as if he were uninsured can the merchant protect the interest of the underwriter and make possible the satisfactory underwriting of carriers' liability risks. The assured should not expect that this type of insurance will furnish him anything more than a prompt settlement of his loss, which is equivalent, on the part of the underwriter, to a guarantee of solvency of and collection from the carrier. Any action or inaction on the part of the assured that relieves or tends to relieve the carrier of his legal obligations will, in the long run, prove disadvantageous to the assured for the reason that less care will be exercised by carriers in the handling of goods and increased rates will be charged by underwriters to pay for the increased and unrecoverable losses.

Modifying Clauses. Much of an underwriter's time is consumed in preparing, and inserting in policies, clauses that restrict or enlarge the protection afforded by the basic form of policy, but the contract as originally worded has stood the test of time and offers a fair measure of protection against the perils to which property in transit over water routes is exposed.

CHAPTER 12

The Policy

MISCELLANEOUS PROVISIONS

Sue-and-labor Clause. The *sue-and-labor clause* immediately follows the enumeration of the insured perils and is found in all marine-insurance contracts. It is not known when the words were first inserted in policies, but a clause of similar import appears in the "Tiger" policy, dated 1613. The latter part of the clause, the "waiver," is of later origin and may have been introduced, in part at least, to make clear the privilege of the underwriter himself to step in and protect the insured property. The sue-and-labor clause reads:

> And in case of any loss or misfortune, it shall be lawful and necessary to and for the assured, ... factors, servants and assigns, to sue, labor and travel for, in and about the defense, safeguard and recovery of the said goods and merchandises, or any part thereof, without prejudice to this insurance; nor shall the acts of the insured or insurers, in recovering, saving and preserving the property insured, in case of disaster, be considered a waiver or an acceptance of an abandonment; to the charges whereof, the said Insurance Company will contribute according to the rate and quantity of the sum herein insured . . .

Purpose of Clause. In the early days of overseas commerce, voyages were of long duration and means of communication between the ports of the known world were slow and unreliable. It was necessary for the assured and his underwriter to agree that, if misfortune overtook the venture, it should be the duty of the assured—who then either accompanied the ship or the cargo himself or sent as his representative an agent known as the supercargo—to use every means within his power to protect the property and save it from further damage after loss had occurred. He was authorized to incur expenses for this purpose, and the measure of his duty was the care a prudent uninsured owner would exercise in regard to his property. This was the origin of the sue-and-labor clause under which the assured and the underwriter agree that their legal position, with respect to loss recoverable under the policy, will in no way be affected by any acts that either may perform looking toward the safeguarding and recovery of the imperiled goods or ship. This clause becomes operative only after loss or misfortune has occurred and is not merely a statement of the duty with which the law would naturally charge an assured but is an affirmative agreement that the assured shall perform the duty of saving and preserving the property.

Applies to Specific Property Insured. The sue-and-labor clause is strictly limited, in its application, to the specific property or interest to which the policy relates and to the expenses incurred in relation to such property or interest. Efforts may be put forth and expenses incurred which, in a measure, benefit the insured interest but are not of exclusive value to this interest, since in their nature they are common benefits and thus partake more of the character of general-average charges. Such efforts and expenditures do not come within the meaning of the sue-and-labor clause, and the underwriter assumes no direct responsibility for them.

Assured Must Enforce His Rights against Third Parties. The original purpose of the sue-and-labor clause has become more or less obsolete owing to the present rapid means of communication between different parts of the world by way of the submarine cable, the radio, and the telephone, it now being customary for the underwriter to give specific instructions as to salvage measures to be undertaken and as to expenses to be incurred. Nevertheless, the clause is still of vital importance. Many losses which overtake property, especially cargo, are due to negligence or breach of duty on the part of some third party. The enforcement of claims against such negligent persons and the collection of damages for injury to the property are in many cases troublesome, in consequence of which the assured is inclined to ignore his legal remedies and to fall back on the protection of his insurance policies. Especially is this the case since underwriters have been affording protection against the carriers' liability risks. The underwriter has no direct recourse against such third parties, but by invoking the requirements of the sue-and-labor clause, he is enabled to hold the assured to his duty of taking the necessary measures to protect and enforce his legal rights with respect to the damaged property.

The Premium. The sue-and-labor clause is followed by the words, "having been paid the consideration for this insurance by the assured or. . . . . .assigns, at and after the rate of. . . . ." The premium furnishes the valid consideration without which the policy would not be an enforceable contract, but the wording as given in the policy form must not be construed as a confession on the part of the underwriter that the premium has been paid by the assured. It is rather a condition upon the fulfillment of which the underwriter will carry out the agreements to which he has obligated himself. The Lloyd's form of policy reads: "Confessing ourselves paid the consideration due unto us for this assurance by the assured, at and after the rate of. . . . ." Even this has been held to be only prima-facie evidence of payment, and the question whether the payment has actually been made may be opened up in a court of law and the facts determined.

Competition Affects Rates. No part of the policy is of more interest to the underwriter than the rate of premium. Upon the proper determination of this rate depends his success or failure. Rates that are too high drive business to others; inadequate rates invite failure. The question of premium is much more vital to the underwriter than to the assured, for the latter should be interested primarily in the security of the insurance company and secondarily in the rate of the premium. It is axiomatic in insurance that the best is in the long run the cheapest. Rates are, as already indicated, based on averages and tested by the experience of a period of years. The law of supply and demand, or, in other words, the presence or absence of competition, as in other lines of commercial activity, has an important bearing on the cost of insurance.

Premium Charged on Amount Insured. The amount of premium appears in the margin of the policy and is determined by multiplying the sum insured by the rate of premium. The rate of premium is expressed ordinarily as so much per cent; that is, 1 per cent indicates that the cost of the insurance is $1 for each $100 insured; 0.5 per cent indicates that 50 cents is the cost of each $100 of insurance. The amount insured in a special policy is determined by agreement at the time the risk is insured. Under an open policy, this amount is calculated by applying the basis of valuation to the invoice or quantity insured, depending upon whether the invoice or a unit of measure, such as the pound, ton, or barrel, is specified by the open policy as the basic measure of value. Of course, under an open policy the amount insured on any one risk cannot, in the absence of special agreement, exceed the limit of liability expressed in the contract.

Rates of Premium Used in Great Britain. The method of quoting rates in Great Britain, while similar to the American system in principle, is different in expression. In Great Britain, £100 sterling is the basic unit of insurance, so that we find rates expressed as £1 per cent, £2 per cent, etc., indicating that the cost of insurance per £100 sterling is, respectively, £1 and £2. When the rate is less than £1 per cent, a different set of symbols is used. As there are 20 shillings in a pound sterling and 12 pence in the shilling, small rates are expressed as so many shillings or pence per cent. For instance, a rate of one-twentieth of 1 per cent in an American policy would be expressed in the English form as 1 shilling per cent, while a rate of 1/16 per cent or 6¼ cents per $100, would appear in the English policy as 1 shilling 3 pence per cent or ⅓ per cent, as it is usually written. This method of rating is very confusing at first, but if the relative values of the pound sterling, shilling, and pence are kept in mind, and the fact that the unit of insurance is £100 sterling, this confusion of thought will soon disappear and the English rates will be as readily understood as are the American.

Return Premium. Closely associated with the subject of premium is that of return premium. It has been held that there can be no return premium after a risk has once attached unless it can be shown that the risk insured is divisible and that the premium as quoted is also divisible, that is, a definite part of the premium charged is to apply to each portion of the risk insured. For instance, a vessel might be insured for a voyage from New York to Buenos Aires and return to New York at a premium of 4 per cent. Suppose the vessel becomes a total loss on the way to Buenos Aires. It might be reasoned that the premium was divisible and that one-half of the premium should be returned. The underwriter could properly claim that he had quoted a round-voyage premium and refuse to return any part of it. If he had quoted 2 per cent for the outward trip and 2 per cent for the homeward trip, a claim for a return of 2 per cent would be justified. The reason for permitting an underwriter to retain full premium after the risk has once attached, even though only a portion of the voyage is accomplished, may be further explained by considering the case of an annual hull insurance. It has been held by the courts that the premium charged for such insurance is an annual premium, not based on so much premium for each day's risk or each month's risk, but an indivisible charge adequate for the year's risk. The courts, therefore, have held that, since they cannot determine justly what portion of the premium should apply to the part of the risk actually incurred in case the vessel is destroyed during the insured period, the underwriter is entitled to retain the whole premium. That this reasoning is sound will be apparent when one considers that, under an annual policy covering a vessel operating over a route subject to seasonal hazards, the major part of the total hazard incurred during the policy term may be encountered in 3 months while during the remaining 9 months the vessel is operating over comparatively safe waters. To determine how much of an annual premium applied to any portion of the annual period would be merely an estimate, the underwriter having charged a premium for the entire year. The same reasoning is applied to other forms of policies. It is upon this theory that return premiums are not allowed when the insured subject is destroyed during the policy term by a peril not insured against. Thus, in the case of an annual marine policy on a hull, no return premium is allowed if the insured vessel is destroyed by a war peril. To avoid this rule of law, specific provisions for the return of premium, under certain circumstances, are found in hull policies, but these clauses will be considered in the special discussions of hull insurance.

Proof and Payment of Loss. The next subject referred to in the policy is that of losses, the form reading:

> And in case of loss, such loss to be paid in thirty days after proof of loss, and proof of interest in the said (the subject matter of the insurance) ....(the amount of the note given for the premium, if unpaid, being first deducted), but no partial loss or particular average shall in any case be paid, unless amounting to five *per cent.*

Two requirements are imposed upon the claimant before there is any obligation on the part of the underwriter to make settlement of loss. First, the claimant must furnish proof of loss, and second, he must prove an interest in the insured subject. The usual form of proof to establish the first point is the *protest* of the master of the vessel. This document is in affidavit form, in which the master sets forth, before a notary or other person commissioned to administer oaths, the incidents of the voyage, laying special stress on particular perils encountered that would probably result in damage to the vessel and its cargo. This protest is usually made in short form immediately on arrival at the first port after disaster has occurred, the protest, if necessary, being "extended" later when a more detailed description of the events occurring at the time of the casualty is given. The protest receives its name from the fact that, in the document, the master protests that whatever damage may have been sustained happened through no fault or breach of duty on his part. The log of the vessel may also be examined to establish the facts in regard to the cause of loss.

Proof of Interest. Proof of interest is ordinarily made by offering to the underwriter the invoice and the bill of lading, the former document determining the basic value of the commodity and showing by the terms of sale in whom the insurable interest rests, the latter proving that the goods were actually on board the vessel that has been overtaken by disaster. The bill of lading is only prima-facie evidence that the goods are on board the named steamer. Goods oftentimes are shut out of the vessel after the bill of lading has been issued, and the manifest or the master's receipt may be called for to establish definitely that the goods were on board. For instance, unless the bill of lading specifies "on board," the underwriter may require a letter from the steamship company certifying that the goods were on board. If a special policy has been issued, this document is offered as a proof of insurance, or if there is no special policy, the open policy itself is presented to the underwriter in evidence. Other documents may also be required. In the case of hull insurance, the certificate of enrollment may be presented to prove by a governmental document the ownership of the vessel, or in the case of freight insurance, the freight list or the charter party may be offered to prove the amount of freight at risk.

Adjustment of Loss. Having presented these proofs of loss and proofs of interest in proper form, the loss, if a valid claim under the policy, is due and payable 30 days after such presentation. Whether the loss is a claim under the policy is determined by the underwriter's adjustment, the method of preparing which will be considered in the discussion of losses.[1] This adjustment may be made by the underwriter himself, or if loss happens at a distant place, the documents may be presented to the underwriter's agent, who may make the adjustment. Sometimes the agent will give a certificate merely showing the apparent cause and extent of the damage. This document is attached to the other proofs of loss, and the claim is sent to the underwriter for adjustment. Whether the adjustment will show a valid claim under the policy depends primarily on two facts. First, was the proximate cause of the damage or loss suffered one of the perils insured against, and second, does the amount of the loss equal or exceed 5 per cent? If both these facts cannot be established, there is no claim under a policy issued in the form under consideration. If both these facts are established, then, if the premium is unpaid, or if the note given for it is unpaid, the premium will be deducted from the amount of the loss and the balance, if any, will be due and payable 30 days from the day complete proofs were presented to the underwriter.

Average Clauses. *The Franchise.* The words in the loss clause reading "unless amounting to 5 per cent" open up one of the most interesting and important questions in the realm of marine insurance. The fixing of the percentage of average or loss, sometimes called the franchise, requires a considerable degree of skill and an intimate knowledge of the intrinsic qualities of property to be insured. Five per cent in most American policies or three per cent in the English form is fixed as the general minimum damage that must be incurred to permit a valid claim under the policy, but this percentage having been reached, the underwriter assumes liability for all the damage suffered through a peril insured against. The modern tendency is to waive the franchise requirement and to pay insured cargo losses irrespective of percentage.

Deductible-average Clauses. The average clause may, however, be so worded that the minimum percentage or amount when reached is

[1] See Chap. 22.

not allowed as a claim but is deducted from the total amount of the claim, the excess over and above this deductible franchise being paid. These deductible-average clauses are worded in a variety of ways, such as: "Subject to a deductible average of........... per cent or $..........." or "Free of particular average under........... per cent, which is deductible." Deductible-average clauses naturally result in lower rates, as a greater measure of responsibility remains with the assured than is the case with the ordinary form of average clause.

Purpose of Average Clauses. The reasons for inserting average clauses in policies are, in the main, twofold. The principal reason is to relieve the underwriter of the inevitable losses to which certain property, from its very nature or mode of shipment, is subject, thus preventing a multiplicity of petty claims. These clauses also relieve underwriters from the annoyance and expense of adjusting claims that, while fortuitous in their character, are trifling in amount. The elimination of these claims results in a net saving to the assured, as the increased cost of insurance necessary to provide for the expense of making such adjustments would far exceed the amount of the losses themselves. This will be evident when consideration is given to the files of documents which transportation companies have in connection with some petty claims, the postage alone on which is often many times the amount of the claim itself. When to this expense are added the costs of paper, notary fees, and the salaries of those who are charged with the adjustment of the losses, the economic advantage of eliminating petty claims in marine insurance will be apparent.

Average Clauses Reduce Cost of Insurance. The second reason for inserting average clauses is to reduce the cost of insurance. An underwriter may be willing to grant a minimum average of, say, 5 per cent on a certain commodity, but the cost of such insurance from the standpoint of the merchant is prohibitive. He accordingly is oftentimes willing to assume a greater percentage of partial loss in order to obtain a lower rate which will enable him to carry out his contract without financial loss. Or the merchant, from his intimate knowledge of the commodity and its mode of shipment, may be confident that it will result in a net saving to him to pay a reduced rate for insurance and to assume the liability for small losses. The method used to amend policies so as to relieve underwriters of a measure of their customary liability is to insert in the contract an average clause which modifies or overrides the average clause in the printed form. Such clauses may contain a franchise as high as 10, 20, or even 50 per cent. They may be deductible in form or so worded as to eliminate all claims unless a definite, named casualty occurs, as in the case of the common F.P.A.A.C. (free of particular average American conditions) clause, reading: "Free of particular average unless caused by stranding, sinking, burning, or collision with another vessel."[1]

Double Insurance. The next section of the printed form deals with the subject of prior, simultaneous and subsequent insurance. Herein is found one of the principal differences between American and British insurance practice. The clause reads:

> Provided always, and it is hereby further agreed, that if the said assured shall have made any other assurance upon the premises aforesaid, prior in day of date to this policy, then the said............Insurance Company shall be answerable only for so much as the amount of such prior insurance may be deficient toward fully covering the premises hereby assured; and the said............Insurance Company shall return the premium upon so much of the sum by them assured, as they shall be by such prior assurance exonerated from. And in case of any insurance upon the said premises, subsequent in day of date to this policy, the said............Insurance Company shall nevertheless be answerable for the full extent of the sum by them subscribed hereto, without right to claim contribution from such subsequent assurers, and shall accordingly be entitled to retain the premium by them received, in the same manner as if no such subsequent assurance had been made. Other insurance upon the premises aforesaid, of date the same day as this policy, shall be deemed simultaneous herewith; and the said ....Insurance Company shall not be liable for more than a rateable contribution in the proportion of the sum by them insured to the aggregate of such simultaneous insurance.

Little need be said in explanation of this portion of the policy. The American theory of double insurance, as therein set forth, is that, if insurance has been effected prior in day of date to the policy in question, the second underwriter shall be relieved of all liability for loss except in so far as the prior policy is deficient in amount, not

[1] A more detailed discussion of average clauses will appear in Chap. 14.

fully protecting the property insured. The insurance company agrees to return premium on so much of the amount as is overinsurance. If there are two or more policies on the same property, aggregating in amount more than the insured value of it and simultaneous in day of date, then the various underwriters become coinsurers, each agreeing to be responsible for his prorata share of the loss and each retaining his prorata share of the premium. If the policy in question, however, is prior in date to all other policies, the underwriter agrees to assume full responsibility for loss to the amount of his policy and is entitled to retain the full premium charged.

Theory of Double Insurance Different in Great Britain. This principle of double insurance is quite different from the practice in Great Britain, where the priority of the date of a policy has no control over its validity. An assured may be very much overinsured; in fact, after having placed the risk in full with one underwriter, he may again insure it with a second underwriter, each of whom is liable in the event of loss for the entire amount of his policy. The assured, however, cannot collect his loss twice, and the two underwriters stand in the position of sureties, one for the other, he from whom the loss has been collected having a valid claim upon the other underwriter for a ratable contribution to the loss. The English doctrine is set forth in the following words in Sec. 80 of the Marine Insurance Act:

> 80. (1) Where the assured is overinsured by double insurance, each insurer is bound, as between himself and the other insurers, to contribute rateably to the loss in proportion to the amount for which he is liable under his contract.
>
> (2) If any insurer pays more than his proportion of the loss, he is entitled to maintain an action for contribution against the other insurers, and is entitled to the like remedies as a surety who has paid more than his proportion of the debt.

Double Insurance Unusual. In actual practice few cases of double insurance arise. In a previous chapter it was pointed out that terms of sale, *viz.*, cost, cost and freight, and cost, insurance, and freight, placed the responsibility for obtaining insurance on either the buyer or the seller. Therefore, if attention is paid to these terms of sale and they are understood, only one party to the contract will take out insurance.

Only when there is misunderstanding or confusion as to where the responsibility rests for obtaining insurance does double insurance occur. If through mistake or inadvertence both parties to the contract have placed insurance, the underwriter whose client has no responsibility for placing the insurance is usually willing to cancel his insurance and return the premium in full when the terms of the contract are disclosed.

Underinsurance. Closely analogous to the subject of double insurance or overinsurance is that of underinsurance. Here the rule in America and Great Britain is the same and is succinctly stated in Sec. 81 of the Marine Insurance Act in the following words:

> 81. Where the assured is insured for an amount less than the insurable value or, in the case of a valued policy, for an amount less than the policy valuation, he is deemed to be his own insurer in respect of the uninsured balance.

This rule is peculiar to marine insurance. The insurer in the case of fire insurance, where the customary form of unvalued policy is used, is liable for the entire loss not exceeding the amount of his policy or not exceeding the value of the insured subject, whichever amount is the smaller. Fire insurance has, in certain cases, adopted marine-insurance practice, inserting in policies coinsurance or average clauses, by which under certain conditions the assured becomes a coinsurer with his underwriter. The motive for using such clauses in fire policies is primarily to produce adequate premium income in that, to escape the effect of the coinsurance clause, the assured must carry insurance equal in amount to a certain fixed percentage of the value of the insured property. The higher this percentage is, the lower the rate of premium. The principle of coinsurance in marine underwriting, however, is fundamental and applies in all cases.

Insurance on Same Property Covering Different Risks. Careful distinction should be made between double insurance and insurance under two or more policies, each of which, while relating to the same property, covers different risks to which that property is subject. Thus, in the case of three policies, the first covering total loss and liability under the free-of-average-English-conditions clause; the second, other partial losses or "difference in conditions"; and the third, war risks, each underwriter is responsible for the particular losses against which he has provided insurance. In like manner additional insurance placed to keep property insured up to its value in a rising market is not double insurance.

Carrier's Liability. At this point there are inserted in many of the printed forms in use by the companies clauses worded in various ways, the general intent of which is to make the policy null and void in the event of there being other insurance on the property, furnished by a transportation company under its bill of lading or otherwise, except in so far as such carrier's insurance may be deficient to cover the loss incurred. Similar provision is made in regard to fire insurance prior to loading on or after discharge from the vessel.[1]

Illicit or Prohibited Trade. Insurance companies, in order to protect themselves from unwittingly assuming liability for losses caused by perils against which they do not wish to give protection, have inserted in the printed policy certain modifying clauses which except them from such liability. The first of these clauses reads:

> It is also agreed, that the property be warranted by the assured free from any charge, damage or loss, which may arise in consequence of a seizure or detention, for, or on account of any illicit or prohibited trade, or any trade in articles contraband of war.

This clause refers only to losses occasioned by seizure or detention due to illicit or prohibited trade or to trade in articles contraband of war and does not refer to seizure or detention in general. It would also appear that there must be read into this clause "loss........... which may arise...........for, or on account of any........... trade in *the goods hereby insured*"; otherwise, an innocent shipper might be prejudiced by the seizure and detention of his goods merely because they happened to be in the same vessel with other goods liable for seizure or detention on account of illicit, prohibited, or contraband trade. Trading in contraband presupposes a state of war, but an illicit or prohibited trade may exist in time of peace. Such illicit or prohibited trade refers particularly to traffic which is illegal under the laws or regulations of foreign ports. In addition to this specific warranty against illicit, prohibited, or contraband trade, there is in marine in-

[1] The purpose of these clauses will be considered when the question of carriers' liability is discussed (see p. 259 and Chap. 26).

surance, as in all contracts, an implied warranty that the laws of the land will be observed. Both the express and implied warranties, while extending to the foreign and domestic laws of the country where the contract is executed and to international law and to treaties to which that country is a party, do not prevent the assured and assurer from bargaining with respect to voyages contrary to the domestic laws of foreign countries. This will explain why legal foreign insurance was available on the rum-running fleet which violated the Eighteenth Amendment to the United States Constitution before its repeal.

Abandonment. The second of the modifying clauses reads:

> Warranted not to abandon in case of capture, seizure, or detention, until after condemnation of the property insured; nor until ninety days after notice of said condemnation is given to this Company. Also warranted not to abandon in case of blockade, and free from any expense in consequence of capture, seizure, detention or blockade, but in the event of blockade, to be at liberty to proceed to an open port and there end the voyage.

The subject of abandonment is one that may be considered more logically in connection with the discussion of total losses. It will be sufficient at the present time to state that, by an abandonment, the assured transfers to the underwriter his right, title, and interest in whatever remnant of property may remain after an insured peril has occurred. The underwriter receives the property, if abandonment is accepted, subject to all liens, encumbrances, or benefits that may have attached to it. When the underwriter pays the insured value to the assured, he is subrogated to all benefits or claims against third parties arising out of the loss of the property, but only to the extent of the amount paid to the assured. This distinction between abandonment and subrogation should be carefully observed. Abandonment transfers what is left of the thing insured but does not transfer rights of action against third persons that grew out of ownership of the property but that are vested in the owner personally. By payment of claim under the policy, however, the underwriter is subrogated, to the amount of his payment only, to such rights against third persons arising out of the accident that caused the loss. The claim against the third person is enforced in the name of the assured.

Purpose of Abandonment Clause. The primary purpose of the abandonment clause is to make it impossible for an assured, when his vessel or cargo is taken by a belligerent, to avoid the obligation that he owes to his underwriter to use all means to obtain the release of the vessel or cargo. He cannot consider that his property has become a total loss and abandon it to the underwriter. This is merely a further illustration of the general principle that marine insurance seeks to indemnify the assured for actual losses suffered but does not purpose to relieve the assured of the care that a prudent uninsured owner should exercise with respect to his property under similar circumstances. Even if condemned under legal proceedings, the assured agrees in this clause not to abandon until the expiration of 90 days from the time that notice of such condemnation is given to his underwriter. This precaution is taken in order that appeal may be made from the judgment of condemnation and that additional efforts may be made to effect the release of the insured property.

Liability for Expenses. The underwriter also expressly stipulates that he will not be liable for an expense that may be occasioned to the assured in consequence of capture, seizure, detention, or blockade. Such expenses remain at the risk of the assured, notwithstanding the fact that the policy covers the peril with which such expenses are associated. The mere fact of capture, seizure, detention, or blockade does not imply that the property is lost. The subject of insurance is lost and the loss is recoverable under an insurance policy only when the property is legally condemned and permanently taken from the assured. Up to this point the underwriter is only indirectly concerned, in that the preliminary seizure may result in the condemnation and loss of the property. Being thus interested, it is customary for him to lend his aid and give his advice concerning ways and means of obtaining release of the insured property and thus preventing the consummation of the loss.

Liberty to Deviate in Event of Blockade. In order that the policy may not be voided by the application of the doctrine of no deviation, liberty is expressly granted for a vessel, in the event of blockade, to proceed to an open port and there end the voyage. Here again, the way is made clear to effect the saving of imperiled property by providing a way of escape which will in no wise invalidate the insurance. However, a deviation made to escape the peril of blockade must be a reasonable one, the assured not being permitted under cover of this clause to substitute an entirely new voyage.

The Attestation Clause. Following these modifying clauses there appears in the printed form under consideration the attestation clause reading:

> In witness whereof, the President or Vice President of the said............ Insurance Company hath hereunto subscribed his name, and the sum insured, and caused the same to be attested by their Secretary, in New York, the............day of............one thousand nine hundred and ....

The policy, in which both the assured and the company agree to perform certain obligations or to refrain from committing certain acts, is signed only by the authorized officials of the company. The assured, or his broker, by signing the preliminary application and by the acceptance of the formal contract as embodied in the policy, assents to the obligations that the contract imposes upon him.

Memorandum Clause. The signatures of the officers of the company do not immediately follow the attestation clause, for a clause headed "Memorandum" materially modifies the contract terms and incidentally gives the first intimation that the marine-insurance policy is concerned with general-average losses. The memorandum clause was first introduced into London policies in 1748 but is now more important historically than practically. Its consideration will be reserved for the following chapter so that it may receive the attention that it deserves.

Underwriter Retains Premium on Risk Unwittingly Insured after Arrival. The last two sentences of the policy, however, may be considered at this point. The first is the complement of the phrase "lost or not lost" and reads:

> If the voyage aforesaid shall have begun and shall have terminated before the date of this policy, then there shall be no return of premium on account of such termination of the voyage.

Here again, there must be read into the contract modifying words to the effect that the voyage has been begun and ended "without the knowledge of either party." It seems only fair that, if the underwriter assumes, as he does under the "lost or not lost" clause, a risk on property which, at the date of the policy, may have ceased to exist, he should be entitled to retain premium on a policy innocently issued on a terminated risk. Were this not so, the underwriter could be held for a loss that happened prior to the date of the policy, under the "lost or not lost" clause, but would receive no premium on a risk that terminated without loss prior to the date of the policy.

Résumé. The final sentence reads: "In all cases of return of premium, in whole or in part, one-half per cent upon the sum insured, is to be retained by the assurers." This provision is obsolete. Its original purpose may have been to afford the insurance company, in the event of cancellation, some remuneration for the time and expense involved in the issuance of the policy. The absurdity of this clause in modern practice will be apparent when it is considered that, in many cases, the rate of premium is considerably less than one-half of 1 per cent, and were the clause to be enforced literally, the cancellation of the policy would result, not in the payment of a return premium to the assured, but in the payment of additional premium *by* the assured.

After the amount insured has been entered both in figures and words on the last line of the policy, the signatures are affixed and the document becomes a formal policy of marine insurance.

The subjects which have been considered in this and the preceding chapters are merely the customary clauses which are found in all cargo policies. There is no limit to the modifying stipulations and warranties that may be added to a policy to change the printed form. In fact, in many cases the modifications take more space than the original matter. Added to these written variations, there are the implied warranties which, unless waived, apply to all policies. In the following chapters, consideration will be given to such modifications as they apply to policies generally and to specific forms of insurance on cargo, hull, freight, and other insurable interests.

CHAPTER 13

Basic Conditions

All Goods Not Equally Susceptible to Damage. It will have been observed that a policy form which, on first reading, seemed to give protection against practically all misfortunes to which property at sea may be subjected is, by interpretation, more or less restricted with respect to the nature of the casualties against which it provides indemnity and as to the minimum amount of loss for which responsibility is assumed. Notwithstanding these restrictions, underwriters early discovered that, while the protection afforded might be suitable for some subjects of insurance, with respect to others it merely resulted in the underwriter's assuming responsibility for losses which, although the result of insured perils, produced claims out of all proportion to the severity of the casualty suffered. In other words, experience demonstrated that certain kinds of goods, when exposed to sea perils, deteriorate rapidly, causing unlooked-for losses which it was not prudent for an underwriter to assume. It was often difficult, with such goods, to determine whether, in the event of a minor casualty, the consequent loss was due to the inherent qualities of the article itself or the deterioration was the proximate result of the casualty.

A Uniform Rate of Premium Desirable. In the early days of marine insurance, clauses were devised that relieved underwriters of all partial loss on certain goods and of small partial losses on other goods less susceptible to damage, the apparent purpose of this being to arrive at a basis of insurance which would make the liability under the policy on all kinds of goods as nearly equal as possible, permitting the charging of a uniform rate. Whether or not this was the primary purpose of these clauses, the fact remains that it is impracticable to devise any system of insurance that will result in the underwriter's assuming the same degree of risk, no matter what the insured subject may be.

The Memorandum Clause. It is possible that the clauses of this nature, in use in the eighteenth century, were combined in 1748 when the first memorandum clause appeared in London policies. Today, the clause appearing in the Lloyd's form is comparatively short but general in its terms, whereas in the memorandum clauses found in American policies, a more specific enumeration of commodities is found. Some of the lists are exceedingly long and embrace most of the common and uncommon articles of commerce. These lists are followed by general words intended to include all other articles of the same general characteristics and susceptibility to damage that may by chance have been omitted in the specific enumeration. The memorandum clause appearing in the printed form that was considered in the previous chapters is in the following words:

Memorandum. It is also agreed, that bar, bundle, rod, hoop and sheet iron, wire of all kinds, tin plates, steel, madder, sumac, wicker-ware and willow (manufactured or otherwise), salt, grain of all kinds, tobacco, Indian meal, fruits (whether preserved or otherwise), cheese, dry fish, hay, vegetables and roots, rags, hempen yarn, bags, cotton bagging, and other articles used for bags or bagging, pleasure carriages, household furniture, skins and hides, musical instruments, looking-glasses, and all other articles that are perishable in their own nature, are warranted by the assured free from average, unless general; hemp, tobacco stems, matting and cassia, except in boxes, free from average under *twenty per cent* unless general; and sugar, flax, flaxseed and bread, are warranted by the assured free from average under *seven per cent* unless general; and coffee in bags or bulk, pepper in bags or bulk, and rice, free from average under *ten per cent* unless general.

Warranted by the insured free from damage or injury, from dampness, change of flavor, or being spotted, discolored, musty or mouldy, except caused by actual contact of sea water with the articles damaged, occasioned by sea perils. In case of partial loss by sea damage to dry goods, cutlery or other hardware, the loss shall be ascertained by a separation and sale of the portion only of the contents of the packages so damaged, and not otherwise; and the same practice shall obtain as to all other merchandise as far as practicable. Not liable for leakage on molasses or other liquids, unless occasioned by stranding or collision with another vessel.

General Average Introduced into Marine Policy. Some of the articles mentioned in the memorandum clause are, by inference only, insured against total loss, that is, they are "free from average," while other articles, considered less susceptible to damage, are subject to partial loss if such partial loss amounts respectively to 20, 7, or 10 per cent of the insured value. But whatever may be the percentage of damage due to partial loss that is necessary to permit claim under the policy, one kind of loss is unrestricted and is payable irrespective of percentage. Each free-from-average exclusion is qualified by the words "unless general." This, the first reference in the policy to general average, gives notice that losses of the nature of general average will be paid in full by the underwriter.

Excepted Risks. The second paragraph of the memorandum clause is more modern, and no words of similar import appear in the Lloyd's form of policy. It was discovered that certain commodities, because of their nature, readily absorbed odors which might be given off by the cargo, and in the case of extremely perishable articles, their value in the market was completely destroyed. Other goods would become spotted, discolored, musty, or moldy or might be damaged merely because of moist atmosphere in the hold. Or the vessel might leak and damage certain cargo, such as hides or skins. These would quickly begin to rot and give off offensive odors which would penetrate the vessel and be absorbed by other articles not directly affected by the casualty. Underwriters having been held liable in certain cases for such consequential loss, the clause under discussion was inserted to restrict their liability (for losses of this nature) to such as are the direct result of the insured subject itself being in actual contact with sea water, the sea water obtaining entrance to the cargo through a sea peril.

Separation of Damaged Goods. Furthermore, the underwriter requires that, in case of damage to property which is capable of being separated into units, such segregation must be made, and the assured must be content with an adjustment of the loss, in accordance with the terms and conditions of the policy, on the damaged portion only. Thus, in the case of cutlery—each piece of which is ordinarily wrapped separately and placed in a small package which, in turn, is combined with others in a large shipping case—if the case is damaged through a peril insured against, the individual units must be separately handled, the sound separated from the damaged, and claim made on only the pieces actually damaged. The underwriter, of course, assumes the expense of making the separation. The same procedure is required in the case of other articles which can be treated in a similar manner. The underwriter also provides in this paragraph that there shall be no liability on his part for loss on molasses or other liquids through leakage unless such leakage is the direct result of stranding or of a collision with another vessel.

As previously stated, the memorandum clause is falling into disuse. The present tendency is to insure goods irrespective of the percentage of loss or to specifically insert clauses with respect to items referred to in the memorandum clause, voiding or modifying the effect of the memorandum clause.

Insurance Does Not Restore Property. It must ever be remembered that the loss of property is an economic loss to the world. Marine insurance does not make good that loss; it serves merely to distribute the shock caused by the loss. It therefore is the duty of the assured, as well as of the underwriter, to use every means to preserve property from damage and to restore it, when injured, to a state of commercial usefulness if such preservation or restoration can be accomplished at a cost which will result in a net economic gain. Too often it is felt that the destruction of property, if insured, is of little moment to the assured or to the public in general, the fact being lost sight of that every destruction of property reduces by that amount the total wealth of the world. Compensation made by an insurance company for such loss does not create new wealth to offset the loss; it merely transfers from the underwriter to the assured a sum which has been set aside from the wealth of the world to aid the particular individual who has suffered. Thus, the assured, from the point of view of public policy, is bound to take every precaution to prevent loss, and to minimize it if it does occur, and the underwriter is under no less obligation to insist that the assured perform his duty in this respect. Many assured have the mistaken notion that insurance relieves them of any further concern in regard to their property, entirely losing sight of the part which insurance plays in commercial life.

IMPLIED WARRANTIES

While the printed and written form of policy sets forth the terms of the contract between the assured and the underwriter, this agreement is subject to *implied warranties*. These implied warranties are agreements not embodied in the terms of the policy, but read into it by law. That is, the parties to the contract agree by implication when making the insurance that certain conditions exist and that certain well-defined rules will be followed in the conduct of the voyage. These implied warranties are the result of court decisions of the preceding centuries with respect to marine-insurance policies, decisions which are, in many cases, merely the embodiment, in legal form, of the customs and usages of merchants and just as binding on the assured and on the underwriter as are the conditions definitely expressed in the body of the policy.

Legal Conduct. There is usually included in the list of implied warranties the agreement that the voyage will be legally conducted. This is not an implied warranty in the strictest sense of the word, since it is common to all contracts that the law of the land in which the agreement is made will not be contravened in the carrying out of the contract terms. The law of the land not only consists of the domestic laws of the country but also includes international law and agreements and regulations laid down in treaties to which the nation is a party. Commercial ventures during their course may come within the protection or the restrictions of the laws of foreign governments, but it is within the rights of the assured and his underwriter to bargain in regard to a voyage or shipment that may be made in violation of foreign edicts, and there is no implied warranty to prevent it. This warranty of legality differs from all other implied warranties in that the parties may not mutually agree to waive the warranty and make it of no effect. The waiver of the implied warranty of legality is against public policy and will not be tolerated. Insurance that involves the illegal conduct of the assured or of the underwriter must not be confused with insurance against the illegal conduct of third parties, as in the case of barratry, theft, pirates, or rovers. Such insurance is, of course, valid.

Seaworthiness. The most important of the implied warranties is that of seaworthiness. In order that this implied warranty may be complied with, it is necessary that the vessel, at the commencement of the voyage (or of any separate part of the voyage, if divisible) be suitably constructed and equipped, properly officered and manned, and sufficiently fueled and provisioned to carry the specified cargo insured on the particular voyage described. Nothing is more difficult than to determine that a vessel is unseaworthy in advance of its destruction. Underwriters' surveyors may think that one vessel is seaworthy and another is unseaworthy. The first vessel may make her passage in safety, while the second may be lost. Such judgments are mere matters of opinion, and while underwriters, to a certain extent, give weight to these opinions in forming their judgment, nevertheless they are not conclusive or presumptive evidence of either the seaworthiness or unseaworthiness of the vessel.

Tests of Seaworthiness. The question is deeper than any mere matter of opinion. Seaworthiness involves questions that a survey of the vessel may not reveal. The strength and intrinsic qualities of the material used in the construction of the vessel, the fastenings, the workmanship, the model of the vessel, the engine equipment, the fuel and food supply, the competency and experience of the master and the crew, the suitability of the vessel at the particular season of the year for carrying the particular kind of cargo in question on the proposed voyage are some of the many elements that may be involved in the question of seaworthiness. Often, the best evidence of unseaworthiness is the fact that the vessel, without apparent external cause, is lost. Seaworthiness is a question of fact that in the last analysis can be determined only in a court of law.

No Fixed Standard of Seaworthiness. The standard by which seaworthiness is judged is a changeable one and may vary with any particular vessel at different periods of the same voyage. A vessel might be perfectly seaworthy to load and carry a cargo while lying safely in a sheltered port. In fact it might be perfectly seaworthy to carry the cargo from a river port at which it was loading down to the open sea but, having reached the open sea, be absolutely unseaworthy for the remainder of the proposed voyage. There is a different standard for every ocean, and the same measure of seaworthiness will not apply to all parts of a given ocean or to all times in the same part of the ocean. A vessel fit for Atlantic coastwise trade may be unseaworthy for trans-

Atlantic trade. So, too, a vessel suitable for trans-Atlantic trade in the summer season may be an unseaworthy risk in the winter months. Again, a ship might be considered fit to carry a light, nonperishable trans-Atlantic cargo in the winter and yet be absolutely unfit to carry a heavy perishable cargo over the same route at the same season. There is no fixed and predetermined standard for any particular vessel, trade, or route, except in so far as the necessity of being suitably constructed and equipped, properly officered and manned, and sufficiently fueled and provisioned may be considered as a fixed standard. Of course, a vessel, if the law so requires, must have the Plimsoll mark or the load-line mark painted on each side so that loading to an unsafe depth can be immediately noticed by any observer.[1] To load below the legally permitted depth would be prima-facie evidence of unseaworthiness.

Seaworthiness Refers to Inception of Risk. The implied warranty of seaworthiness extends not alone to those qualities and defects which are apparent but also to qualities and defects that are unknown to the assured and refers primarily to the inception of the risk. It is the condition of the vessel at this time, judged in the light of the cargo it is to carry and the voyage upon which it is about to enter, that determines seaworthiness. If, however, the voyage is divisible into stages and a different standard applies to each stage, then it may be that each particular portion of the risk would be separately considered. The risk having commenced, and the vessel being in a seaworthy condition, the happening of some fortuitous event rendering the vessel unseaworthy will in no wise void the policy.

Implied Warranty of Seaworthiness Not Applicable to Hull Time Risks. The doctrine of seaworthiness applies equally to cargo, freight, profit, and other forms of marine insurance and to hull insurance written on the trip or voyage basis at the inception of the trip or voyage. The courts have decided that, in general, there is no implied warranty of seaworthiness with respect to hull insurance written on time. In England this principle is settled, but in this country there are exceptions to the general rule. However, it is generally required in this country that, when a vessel in an unseaworthy condition arrives at any point where repairs can be made or equipment or supplies obtained, the assured must there use due diligence to make the vessel

[1] See pp. 76, 77.

seaworthy. This exception to the general rule with respect to seaworthiness is made because in many cases, in the placing of hull insurance, especially when whole fleets are placed at one time from a named date, many of the vessels are at sea when the insurance attaches, so that, at that time, there would be no possibility of the owner's knowing the condition of his vessel. The facts upon which an implied warranty of seaworthiness would depend, in such cases, might not be provable. However, there would seem to be no sufficient reason why the courts should not have applied the warranty in cases where hull insurance, on time, attached while the vessel was safely in port. It is possible for an underwriter to make any implied warranty an express warranty. An express warranty of seaworthiness in a time hull policy would be proper, but if the vessel were at sea at the inception of the risk, there would be great difficulty in establishing by proof its unseaworthiness.

Waiver of Warranty of Seaworthiness. In the days when it was usual for a shipowner to load his vessel with his own cargo, or when the cargo owner chartered a vessel to carry his goods, it seemed natural and justifiable that the warranty of seaworthiness should be read into the insurance contract. The cargo owner chose the vessel which was to carry his goods, and it was a fair presumption that he knew its condition and equipment. Now, however, with the establishment of steamship lines and with the great increase in size and carrying capacity of vessels, it is a hardship for the cargo owner to receive insurance subject to an implied warranty of seaworthiness when he knows little about the carrying vessel and is not in so good a position as is the underwriter himself to find out about its condition and equipment. Many bills of lading contain a clause relieving the carrier from liability for unseaworthiness if he has used due diligence to see that the vessel is seaworthy. The courts have held this clause to be valid. Accordingly, it is not unusual to find in cargo policies a clause reading "Seaworthiness of the vessel as between the assured and the underwriter is hereby admitted." This clause should never be used in a policy covering cargo by a vessel wholly chartered by the cargo owner. In such case, it should remain his responsibility to determine that the vessel is seaworthy. The admission-of-seaworthiness clause in no way waives the implied agreement between the assured and the carrier that the latter will furnish a seaworthy vessel, and the underwriter, under his right of subrogation, will, in the event of loss being paid, receive the assured's right of action against the carrier if the implied agreement is not performed.

Implied Warranty of Seaworthiness Refers to Vessel, Not to Cargo. There is no implied warranty of seaworthiness with respect to the cargo itself; the warranty runs only against the vessel. A cargo may be shipped in such bad condition that it may imperil the ship. Thus, in the case of soft coal, which heats readily, or in the case of improperly cured vegetable fiber such as hemp, which may be subject to spontaneous combustion, the mere shipping of such cargo would not void the policy, but the underwriter would not be liable for loss by fire if it could be established that the assured, while aware of the condition of the cargo when shipped, nevertheless negligently permitted its loading in such condition. Nor would he be liable if it could be shown that the fire was due to the inherent qualities of the cargo itself. Losses that result from the improper condition of cargo at the time of shipment or from its inherent qualities are the only ones from which the underwriter is exonerated, other perils insured against remaining at his risk.

Proof of Breach of Warranty of Seaworthiness. While it is true that the implied warranty of seaworthiness is the most important and far reaching of all the implied warranties, it is equally true that it is more difficult to prove a breach of this warranty than it is to prove a breach of the others. Some cases readily demonstrate a condition of unseaworthiness, as when a vessel, shortly after leaving port, founders in clear weather and a calm sea. But in the vast majority of cases some disturbed condition of the sea or of the elements exists at the time the vessel is lost, and to prove that the loss was due to the unseaworthiness of the vessel and not solely to the unusual action of the forces of nature on a seaworthy vessel is a matter of no little difficulty. The safe rule for the underwriter to follow is to insure only vessels that he is reasonably sure are fit for the proposed work, and not to insure doubtful vessels and then rely on a breach of an implied warranty to make void the policy and prevent the collection of a loss. It is imprudent for an underwriter to state that a vessel is unseaworthy, even if he believes such to be the case, as the owner of the vessel may sue him for damages occasioned by the publication of such adverse opinion, and the underwriter may be unable to establish, in defense, that his opinion was justified by the existing facts.

Implied Warranty of Prompt Attachment of Risk. There is in all policies, except those written on time, an implied warranty that the risk will attach within a reasonable time. The insurance does not necessarily attach from the time the policy is issued. It may relate to a prospective voyage. Nevertheless, in the absence of specific information to the contrary, the underwriter is justified in assuming and usually does assume that the proposed venture will commence with due dispatch. It has already been suggested that the measure of risk existing in a given port or over a named route is not the same at all seasons of the year, and in taking a risk, an underwriter has in mind, and bases his rate of premium on, the conditions existing or likely to exist at or about the time the hazard is accepted. If, for instance, an assured places in the month of October a risk on a vessel to sail from Montreal to Europe, the underwriter who assumes the risk has in mind the hazards existing in the port of Montreal and in the river and Gulf of St. Lawrence during the month of October. If the sailing is delayed by the assured until the latter part of November, when conditions with respect to navigation in these waters become extra-hazardous, a different risk has been substituted for the one the underwriter assumed and he should be, and is, relieved by law from the execution of his contract. Again, an assured, obtaining insurance on a cargo, may for some reason, market or otherwise, delay the sailing of the vessel after the loading is completed, thus imposing on the underwriter a longer and different risk from the one contemplated by him when the risk was assumed. Under such a state of facts the underwriter will be relieved of his obligation.

Delay Must Be Unreasonable to Void Contract. Of course, in all such cases, the test of whether the delay incurred is sufficient to void the contract is the reasonableness or unreasonableness of the delay. This is a question of fact, determined in the light of all the circumstances surrounding the case. If the delay is the result of interference or other overt act on the part of the assured, a clearer and more easily determined case is found than where such delay is solely the result of the action of others or of circumstances over which the assured had no control. This warranty is one that works justice both to assured and underwriter. On the one hand, the assured is not prevented from arranging his insurance in advance of the attachment of the risk; on the other hand, the underwriter cannot be led unwittingly into assuming a risk different from or greater than the one to be presumed from conditions that exist at the time the risk is taken or are likely to exist in the immediate future.

Implied Warranty of No Deviation. Closely connected with the implied agreement that the voyage will be commenced within a reasonable time is the implied warranty that there shall be no deviation. The doctrine of no deviation has already been considered.[1] No further discussion is necessary here except to reiterate that the assured, after the risk has once attached, may not substitute a different risk, no matter how slight the difference may be or whether or not the substituted risk involves a greater or less hazard than did the original voyage, save only in the case of excusable deviation. This doctrine is merely the statement, in specific form, of the general legal principle that a formal contract cannot be varied without the mutual consent of the parties to the contract.

Other Implied Warranties. The foregoing are the principal implied warranties, although included under this head are sometimes found implied conditions such as, "that the assured shall have an insurable interest," "that the assured shall not be guilty of negligence," and "that the assured shall make a full disclosure of all the pertinent facts in connection with the risk," all of which are more in the nature of conditions that must exist in order to have a valid contract than warranties the breach of which will void the contract. Formerly, there seems to have been an implied warranty of neutral character and conduct of the voyage, but owing to conflicting authority on this question it is best to insist on an express warranty of neutrality if the underwriter wishes to avoid liability for a breach of neutrality.

Breach of Warranty May Be Excused. As has already been suggested, the underwriter may agree to waive any of the implied warranties except that of legal conduct, or he may insist on making the implied warranty an express condition in the policy. Furthermore, he may excuse the breach of any of the implied warranties, since all of them are read into the policy by law as a measure of protection to

[1] See p. 167.

the underwriter, which protection he is at liberty to claim or not as he may choose.

EXPRESS WARRANTIES

As the breach of one of the implied warranties, unless excusable, will void the policy from the date of the breach, so the failure to observe the conditions of an express warranty will also void it. Express warranties are of the same nature as implied warranties but are different in their form and origin. The implied warranties are read into the policy by law; the express warranties are written into the policy by the intention of the parties. The implied warranties are few in number; the express warranties are without number and may relate to any matter whether it be vital to the contract or not. Express warranties must be strictly and, it may be said, literally complied with.

Warranties and Stipulations. An express warranty may relate to a present, past, or future condition. It is a written agreement that certain facts are or were or shall be true or that certain acts have been or shall be done. It is not essential that the word "warranted" be used; it is sufficient that there be an allegation of a fact relating to the risk. Thus, the expression "American ship *Atlas*" is an express warranty that the ship *Atlas* is under the American flag. So, too, the statement that a vessel is in port on a named day is a warranty of that fact. However, it must not be inferred merely because the word "warranted" is used in a clause that the expression is an express warranty. Thus, the common clauses appearing in policies such as "warranted free of particular average," "warranted free of capture, seizure, etc.," are not express warranties, but merely stipulations in regard to the extent of the underwriter's liability. This will be apparent when it is considered that, if such clauses were express warranties, the occurrence of a partial loss or the mere fact of a capture or seizure taking place would absolutely void the policy.

Express Warranties Usually Relate to Material Conditions. Express warranties may relate to any matter, whether material or not, if the underwriter insists on the warranty and the assured is willing to have the validity of the insurance depend on a strict compliance with it. As a matter of practice, however, express warranties are inserted only in regard to matters of really vital concern. Thus, express warranties relative to sailing are often inserted in policies, since much depends on the particular period during which a risk is exposed to sea perils. Warranties are also inserted agreeing to the classification of the vessel by one of the classification societies. If such class cannot be obtained, the insurance will not attach. Warranties in regard to loading are also found, as, for instance, that a vessel will not load more than a certain percentage of her cargo on deck or that her loading will be in conformity with the rules of a certain underwriters' board. There are many warranties in regard to war insurance, such as those of neutral ownership and consignment, or warranties of convoy. Underwriters usually insert only warranties relating to matters under the control of the assured or within the knowledge of the assured.

REPRESENTATION, MISREPRESENTATION, AND CONCEALMENT

Marine insurance being founded on the fullest good faith between the contracting parties, it is not surprising that we find many decisions relating to marine insurance which refer to representations, misrepresentations, and concealments. Phillips defines these words as follows:[1]

SECTION 524.—A representation in insurance is the communication of a fact, or the making of a statement, by one of the parties to a contract of insurance to the other in reference to a proposal for their entering into the contract, tending to influence his estimate of the character and degree of the risk to be insured against. To constitute a representation, says Mr. C. J. Marshall, there should be an affirmation or denial of some fact, or an allegation which plainly leads the mind to an inference of a fact.

SECTION 525.—A fact or statement having such tendency is called a *material* fact or statement. One having no such tendency is called *immaterial.*

SECTION 529.—A misrepresentation is a false representation of a material fact, by one of the parties to the other, tending directly to induce the other to enter into the contract or to do so on terms less favorable to himself, when he otherwise might not do so, or might demand terms more favorable to himself.

SECTION 531.—Concealment in insurance is where, in reference to a negotiation therefor, one party suppresses, or neglects to communicate to the other,

[1] "Treatise on the Law of Insurance."

a material fact, which, if communicated, would tend directly to prevent the other from entering into the contract, or to induce him to demand terms more favorable to himself; and which is known, or presumed to be so, to the party not disclosing it, and is not known, or presumed to be so, to the other.

The Avoidance of Contracts—Fraud. These quotations give in brief and lucid terms the underlying conditions with respect to these three important elements in the negotiation of insurance contracts. If, through representations, misrepresentations, or concealments, the underwriter or the assured is induced to enter into a contract that is different from that which, under the circumstances, he was justified in supposing it to be, the law will relieve him of the burden of the agreement on the ground that the minds of the contracting parties did not meet and that therefore there could be no contract. It is not necessary that representations, misrepresentations, or concealments be made with fraudulent intent; the mere fact that certain conditions are misrepresented or concealed and exercise an improper influence is sufficient to exonerate the offended party from his contractual obligations. The law of representations, misrepresentations, and concealments not only applies to direct insurance but is of equal force and effect in reinsurance.

What Must Be Disclosed. All material information, whether the result of knowledge or rumor, should be disclosed. Thus, if the assured has heard that the vessel by which he desires insurance has met with a disaster, however slight, he must disclose this information to the underwriter. So too, the underwriter, if he knows or has reason to believe that the vessel has completed the voyage on which insurance is desired, must inform the assured of such knowledge or information. A misrepresentation or concealment made by an agent without the knowledge or consent of the principal is binding on the principal. In this manner an insurance broker may prejudice the position of his principal. It has been held that a material representation by the assured, through misconstruction of information, is a misrepresentation and that unwittingly omitting to state a material fact is a concealment.

The Effect of a Representation. A representation differs from an express warranty in that a literal compliance with the representation is not essential. It is enough that there be a substantial compliance with the conditions represented. A representation continues to be binding until it is revoked. All material facts must be revealed, and it is wise to reveal all apparently immaterial facts that might have a bearing on the risk, as the underwriter may consider such facts of greater weight than does the assured. The underwriter is at liberty to ask any question he sees fit in regard to the risk, whether the question seems material or not. Oftentimes, questions that seem trivial are asked by an underwriter merely as test questions if he suspects that the assured or his agent is withholding material information. As it is the underwriter's capital that is to be put at risk, it is proper for him to endeavor to obtain any information that he considers necessary in order to determine whether the risk is one he cares to insure and, if he does, to decide what rate is adequate to compensate for the protection to be afforded.

Certain Facts Need Not Be Disclosed. There are, of course, limitations to the extent to which the disclosure of material facts is necessary. The assured is not bound to divulge facts that are matters of common knowledge. Thus, it is not necessary to disclose usages of trade common to risks similar to the one under consideration, but conditions peculiar to the particular risk, not matters of common knowledge, must be revealed. The assured need not state that other underwriters have declined the risk, although the underwriter might consider this an important fact. However, if the assured states that other underwriters have accepted part of the risk at a certain rate, he will be bound by his representation. If, by statements of the assured, the underwriter is put on inquiry and fails to investigate further into the matter, he will be bound by the policy.

What a Representation Implies. A representation is construed in accordance with the ordinary meaning that the words imply, and the natural inferences drawn from such representation are presumed to be implied. Thus, if the assured states that a vessel was in a certain port on a certain day, it will be presumed that the vessel was there and in good safety at some time during that day. An unusual meaning may not be read into a representation made by an assured. The mere statement by him of an expectation, opinion, or belief must be distinguished from a representation of a definite fact or condition. If the assured states a fact in regard to a risk in such manner that the underwriter naturally infers a meaning different from the true meaning, it is a misrepresentation. So, too, if the assured willfully and fraudulently avoids learning material facts, such action amounts to a concealment.

Fraud. The subject of fraud is closely connected with that of representation, misrepresentation, and concealment. While representation, misrepresentation, or concealment may be due to an innocent mistake or to ignorance on the part of the assured, sometimes the withholding of information or the giving of incorrect or misleading information is intentional on the part of the assured or his agent. If it can be proved that fraud exists, the policy will be void from its inception, since the minds of the contracting parties cannot be considered to have met. On the other hand, if the giving of material misinformation or the withholding of material information has been the result of an innocent mistake, the policy will be affected only with respect to consequences arising from such innocent action.

CHAPTER 14

Cargo Insurance as an Underwriting Problem

Basic Form of Policy Necessary. The consideration of marine insurance up to this point has been theoretical. The basic form of policy common to all branches of the business has been analyzed, but little consideration has been given to the practical application of the underlying principles governing the practice of this particular branch of the insurance science. While it is necessary that there be a basic form of contract adaptable to all the particular forms of marine insurance, it is equally necessary, since this branch of insurance is concerned in transactions involving all types of vessels, all kinds of commodities, and all parts of the civilized and uncivilized world, that the form be sufficiently elastic to accommodate itself to the peculiar problems and the individual conditions that surround each particular venture. That the basic form is admirably adapted for this purpose has been adequately demonstrated by its continued use during the long period in which the commerce of the world has been developing. Many times, it is true, the basic form is buried under a mass of modifying clauses, but out of the apparent confusion of words, a definite and understandable contract of indemnity appears.

Cargo, Hull, and Freight Insurance. Marine insurance may be divided into three general sections, namely, cargo, hull, and freight insurance. The practice of insurance as applied to each of these three great branches of maritime commerce differs so widely that they must be considered separately. In point of volume and diversity, cargo insurance stands preeminent. The ordinary cargo risk being of comparatively short duration, an underwriter may have several cargoes at risk in the same vessel in a single year. In a single venture there will be but one vessel, and ordinarily but one freight interest, but if the vessel is a cargo ship, there may be hundreds of cargo interests involving many different kinds of goods, all exposed to the same general hazards but each presenting its special peculiarities as an underwriting problem. In discussing the great interest of cargo, it will be best, in the first place, to treat it as a general problem and then to give special consideration to individual cargo interests.

General and Full Cargoes. In general, cargoes may be divided into two broad classes: *general cargoes* and *full cargoes.* The general cargo is one consisting of a variety of commodities shipped by one or by many merchants, while the full cargo consists of a single commodity which is sometimes in bulk and shipped in its entirety by one merchant, though it may be made up from the property of several shippers. A vessel taking on a general cargo ordinarily loads at the berth and accepts any cargo offered for the ports for which the vessel is destined. On the other hand, full cargoes are ordinarily loaded under charter, where the entire capacity of the vessel is hired out to one merchant, who for the time being controls the use of the ship.

Under- and On-deck Cargoes. Cargoes may again be subdivided into *under-* and *on-deck* cargoes. Under-deck cargo includes all goods loaded below the main deck of the vessel; on-deck cargo in its strictest sense consists of all goods loaded above this deck whether under cover or not. By custom, all cargo stowed below the weather deck is considered to be under-deck cargo, as it is no more exposed to the elements than is cargo in the hold. Theoretically, on-deck cargo is not covered by marine insurance unless specifically mentioned as being on deck; practically, certain cargoes, from their very nature or from the custom of the trade, put an underwriter on inquiry to learn whether or not all or part of such cargo is on deck. Thus, sulfuric acid —because of its hazardous nature—is shipped only on deck, while a full cargo of lumber in the ordinary case presupposes a part of the shipment on deck, as usually a vessel loaded with lumber will not be in proper trim unless a considerable portion of the cargo is on deck.

A General Knowledge of All Commodities Essential. Each particular commodity has its own peculiarities, and a full knowledge of all is essential in order that proper consideration may be given to each. Some raw products are shipped in their original condition, while others are put through a preliminary process before shipment. Some commodities are shipped in bulk, while others are forwarded in packages or wrappers. The same commodity coming from two different parts of the world will present two entirely different types of risk. Cotton exported from the United States is usually shipped in a poor package, the bale being improperly protected by burlap, with the result that it is apt to arrive at destination in bad condition. On the other hand, cotton exported from Egypt is in a smaller bale, completely protected by burlap, and in the usual course will arrive in perfect condition. So we find that rubber shipped from Brazil is in balls, while the same commodity imported from the Far East is partially refined and fashioned into slabs or chunks known as "bare backs." Some Far Eastern rubber has a matting covering. It is not enough for the underwriter to know that the risk offered to him is cotton or rubber; he must be able to look behind the mere commodity and know its peculiarities, its physical condition, and the nature of its shipping package.

Marine Insurance Conforms to Trade Customs. But this is not all. Marine insurance does not as a rule create new conditions. Marine underwriters may—and do—strive to improve local conditions, but they adapt their form of protection to the customs of the country, the usages of the trade, and the physical conditions existing in the various parts of the world. If the custom of the trade or of the country is to sell goods to exporters at the farm or the plantation, insurance will be furnished to attach at the farm or plantation. If, on the other hand, the raw commodity is brought to the ports and sold there, insurance will be furnished attaching at the port. In the raw-cotton business of our own country the marine underwriter furnishes protection from the moment the cotton is ginned and weighed, whereas in the exporting of grain the marine underwriter customarily assumes no risk until the grain is water-borne. Each particular trade has its peculiar customs, and the marine underwriter conforms to them as far as prudent underwriting will permit. An underwriter is presumed to know the ordinary customs of trade or, if he does not, is at least put on inquiry as to what these customs are.

Methods of Shipment Controlled by Physical Environment. The customs of trade are in part controlled by the physical environment. Therefore, the methods of shipment at deep-water ports fed by a fertile and well-developed hinterland will be entirely different from those at shallow and unprotected ports where access to the interior is difficult or where the back country is not fertile or is a desert. Thus, at the North Atlantic ports of the United States, raw commodities are partially processed before export, iron, for instance, not being shipped as ore but after being partially refined and converted into pigs. This is true of most of the products of the mines. The products of the forests are converted into commercial lumber before being shipped. The products of the farm are in some instances shipped in their natural condition, as in the case of grains, while perishable commodities are processed in order to preserve them and ensure safe carriage. The country back of these ports is often well wooded, making possible the shipping of manufactured goods in substantial packages, and the means of transportation to the ports are such that the commodities may be expected to arrive at the ports in good condition.

Knowledge of Trade Customs Important. On the other hand, the Pacific ports of South America have an entirely different environment, resulting in customs of trade that present a wholly new problem to the underwriter. Manufacturing is not developed along this coast, with the result that the raw products of the mines are shipped in the form of ore, shipments of copper ore and of nitrate constituting a considerable part of the export trade. These commodities are brought from the mines to the shore, where they are taken by lighters to the steamers, which, on account of the conformation of the coast line, are compelled to lie in open or partially sheltered roadsteads to receive their cargoes. Imports are handled in much the same way, being exposed to risks peculiar to the locality. The route into the interior is in many cases extremely hazardous, involving carriage by rail, by water, by wagon, by mule, or by air. Often, property is transshipped or transferred from one mode of conveyance to another several times before the final destination is reached. Conditions are improving in these newer and less-developed parts of the world, and the underwriter must keep himself fully informed of progress made or of hazards increased through some local disturbance or through the neglect of some decadent government.

Racial Characteristics Affect Marine Insurance. In every country the natural environment and the peculiar national characteristics of the people have developed customs that show their influence on the commercial activities of the people and on their modes of conducting their business enterprises. Marine insurance is in no sense provincial. It is as cosmopolitan as any business can be and is essential to the life and growth of humanity. But this very fact makes necessary, on the part of the underwriter, a knowledge of these racial characteristics and customs. An underwriter can, if he will, limit his business to routes of trade between the highly civilized nations, but if he is to fulfill his true mission he must be content to assume risks in all trades, making his rates in harmony with the degree of hazard that each particular trade involves. Some races are noted for their low commercial ethics, and the moral hazard in the trade with which they are concerned is naturally great. Other races have a high sense of commercial honor and integrity, and trading with these races involves merely a consideration of the physical hazards involved. It is in this respect that organizations of underwriters have done much to raise the standard of commercial ethics. Their representatives in foreign ports have insisted on a degree of honesty in connection with transactions involving damaged property that has presented to the native peoples an entirely new standard of business ethics. Even today some nations have not progressed much beyond the original theory that might makes right and that possession is better evidence of ownership than is any legal title to property.

Sale of Goods at Port of Refuge. Among some races and in some ports, there are found a sense of clannishness and a desire to band together to outwit and despoil the foreigner which have no little bearing on the fortunes of marine underwriters. Casualties happen in unexpected places, and the master of a vessel in distress cannot always choose his port of refuge. Consequently where goods arrive at a port of refuge in such condition that they must be sold to prevent their total destruction, the local merchants sometimes will come to an understanding one with another that, when the goods are offered for sale in the open market or at auction, there will be no competitive bidding or bidding of the most perfunctory sort only, so that the goods will have to be sacrificed. After this worthy end has been attained, distribution of the goods will be made among the merchants, and another commercial victory over the foreigner will be recorded.

These conditions cannot be avoided, and the rates over such commercial routes will naturally reflect the increased hazards.

Falling Markets. Another serious problem that underwriters face in the writing of cargo risks is that of falling markets. When a consignee is tendered goods at a time when the market price has declined materially from his purchase price, he may be much inclined to find an excuse for breaking his contract and refusing delivery of the goods. If he is unable to find in the shipping documents any flaw that will furnish a technical excuse for refusing the shipment, his next move may be to endeavor to find damage to the shipment for which claim might be lodged with underwriters. It has happened, especially at smaller ports where there is not careful supervision of the underwriters' agents, that claims have been certified by the agents for damage that seemed greater in degree than any conceivable circumstances could have produced. Nevertheless, unless there is some legal evidence of fraud, underwriters pay such claims, knowing full well that they have been imposed upon, but without legal defense against the claimants. During the deflation period in 1921 thousands of dollars were paid by underwriters for claims that had been fraudulently bolstered up to make allowance for the decline in the market price of the damaged commodity.

Effect of Vessel Types on Cargo Insurance. The problem of cargo insurance not only involves the character of the goods themselves and the routes of trade but, like all other maritime ventures, is also vitally concerned with the carrying vessel. From the earliest days of overseas commerce, ships have been designed primarily as cargo carriers, and the story of the evolution of the modern steamer is largely the story of progress in designing ocean carriers that would cheaply and safely transport cargo. To this end various types of vessel have been designed, each type meeting in a special way some particular or general need in overseas commerce. Thus, there are single-, double-, and multiple-deck vessels, bulk carriers, tank vessels, refrigerator steamers, and many other types having special merits in connection with special trades. However, it is not always possible to find employment for vessels in the particular trade for which they are best adapted, and vessels may seek and find employment in trades to which they are not altogether suited. Herein lies the underwriter's chief problem with respect to the type of vessel. Perishable cargoes that can conveniently be carried in a double- or multiple-deck vessel, because this type provides safe storage without undue crushing, are sometimes of necessity laden in deep single-deck vessels, where the packages are subject to the severe crushing force of the cargo piled upon them, resulting, in the event of stress of weather, in heavy damage claims. Vessels used in heavy-cargo trades, such as the carrying of coal and ore, and not fitted for the transportation of perishable goods are sometimes used in such trade with resultant damage to the cargo.

Vessel Speed an Element in Cargo Insurance. The underwriter of cargo insurance is concerned not only with the vessel as a cargo carrier and its particular fitness for the carriage of the particular kind of goods under consideration, but also with the speed, size, and general structural condition of the vessel. As a rule, rates of premium in any particular class of business are predicated on vessels, known as *liners*, that have been specially designed and equipped for trade over the particular route in question. These vessels have considerable speed, are of a design suited to the needs of the particular trade and of a size proper for the safe navigation of the harbors to be visited on the route. Any departure from this standard presents a risk varying from the basis upon which the minimum rate has been predicated. A vessel of slower speed will involve a longer exposure to the hazards of the sea. One of different internal construction may expose the cargo to unforeseen perils, while a vessel larger in size than the ports of call will readily accommodate involves possible strandings or unusual lighterage risks.

Structural Design in Its Relation to Cargo. The structural design of a vessel has a material bearing upon the degree of hazard involved in an insurance of the cargo. In the event of a stranding, a double-bottom vessel is less apt to damage cargo. A vessel equipped with several watertight bulkheads is a better cargo risk than one without bulkheads, not only in the event of collision, but also in case the vessel gets on fire. A vessel equipped with modern fire-detection systems and fire-extinguishing equipment reduces the hazards of the voyage. Radar, loran, and other modern aids to safe navigation are all desirable equipment from the point of view of the underwriter. Steamers of the well-deck design have a tendency to damage cargoes through leakage, owing to the great weight of water that in rough seas may fall with crushing force in the well of the deck, sometimes forcing water through the hatches or through the openings in the surrounding deck erections. Furthermore, unless this type of vessel is designed quickly to discharge the water, the stability of the vessel may be seriously affected, especially if it is heavily loaded. A twin-screw steamer has manifest advantages over the single-screw type.

Natural Forces as Related to Cargo Insurance. Reference has already been made in some detail to the natural forces in and about the ocean and to the physical topography, not only of the ocean bed, but of the continental shores and of the harbors. Knowledge of these details must be applied practically in consideration of individual risks. The underwriter must carefully consider the route to be followed by the shipment for which insurance is desired. If the insurance offered relates to a voyage to or through the West Indies Islands, the underwriter will consider the time of the year, as the hurricane season brings increased perils on this route. So the approach of winter on the Great Lakes or on the St. Lawrence River will naturally call attention to the increased hazards of this period in Lake and St. Lawrence River trade. The ice floes of the North Atlantic in the spring and early summer will not be overlooked by the careful underwriter, nor will he forget the long nights involving increased perils in the Baltic trade in the winter months. The fact that a proposed voyage is through the inside passage to Alaska will recall to the underwriter's mind that this route is extrahazardous, and he will not overlook the fact that, at certain seasons of the year, fog makes navigation dangerous off the coast of Newfoundland and other similarly situated localities.

Optional Routes. The length of the route is also of importance to the cargo underwriters, the time, for instance, in going to Australia via the Panama Canal being less than when the Cape of Good Hope route is used. So the opening of new canals providing shorter routes may greatly affect the degree of hazard to which a risk will be exposed. However, a shorter route does not necessarily mean a safer route. For instance, some underwriters consider the trip from New York to Boston through the Cape Cod Canal a more dangerous route, owing to the currents in the Canal, than the longer route outside Cape Cod. The short route will ordinarily be used if it effects a saving in the cost of operating the carrying vessel, yet such decrease in the length of the voyage may materially increase the hazards from the underwriting point of view. The distance traveled is of relatively small importance in the consideration of underwriting problems.

Other Elements in Cargo Insurance. Valuation must be given proper consideration, as well as the amount of liability that the underwriter is willing to assume on the particular risk, which will be determined by the sum that he desires to retain and the amount that he knows, or has reason to expect, he can reinsure on satisfactory terms. The assured himself, whether principal or agent, and the general character and reputation of the various persons involved in the proposed venture will all be given their due weight in the consideration of such individual risk. To the experienced underwriter the consideration of all these questions and many others of perhaps equal importance becomes a matter of intuition or habit. A competent underwriter must have a large fund of information and be endowed with keenness of judgment.

Average Conditions. The conditions of average are of the most vital importance in cargo insurance. The policy form provides for payment of loss only if it amounts to 5 per cent, while in the memorandum clause further restrictions, relative to the percentage of loss for which the underwriter will respond, are added. The rate of premium depends largely on the degree of average that the underwriter accepts. Knowledge of the inherent qualities of each individual commodity is all-important. The memorandum clause does not attempt to enumerate all articles, and the restrictions on average therein set forth with respect to many commodities are unduly burdensome to the assured. To make commodities free of average unless general, or in other words to insure only against total losses and general-average claims, is to ignore completely the many partial losses, the direct result of the major sea casualties, *i.e.*, stranding, sinking, burning, and collision.

Free of Particular Average. It is but natural that, although the underwriter is unwilling to assume liability for ordinary partial losses due to the peculiar qualities of the particular article or to its form of package, he is content to bear partial losses that are the direct result of stranding, sinking, burning, or collision. Accordingly, the F.P.A. (free of particular average) clause was adopted. Basically it has two forms: one, the "F.P.A.E.C.," or free-of-particular-average-English-conditions clause; the other, the "F.P.A.A.C.," or free-of-particular-average-American-conditions clause. These two forms are somewhat different in their application.

American and English Average Clauses Contrasted. The American form of clause commonly used reads: "Free of particular average unless caused by stranding, sinking, burning, or collision with another vessel." The underwriter thus stipulates that he assumes no responsibility for partial loss unless such partial loss is proximately caused by one of the enumerated casualties. On the other hand, the English form of the clause in its simplest form reads: "Free of particular average unless the vessel or craft be stranded, sunk, burnt, or in collision." As in the American form, the underwriter stipulates that he shall be free from liability from partial loss in the ordinary case, but he agrees that the mere happening of one of the enumerated perils will nullify the average agreement, the policy then and thereafter being subject to the printed form with its specified average conditions. The underwriter under the F.P.A.E.C. clause assumes liability in accordance with the terms and conditions of the policy for any partial loss that may appear after the happening of one of the enumerated casualties, whether or not such partial loss is the result, directly or indirectly, of such casualty. The mere technical happening of the casualty has divested the underwriter of all the protection that the clause afforded.

Effect of the F.P.A.E.C. Clause. It is unfortunate that the "English-conditions clause" should have received the interpretation which the courts have given it, as it doubtless was originally intended that the meaning should be what the American clause clearly stipulates, namely, that the resultant partial loss must be the proximate result of the named casualty. The dominating position heretofore occupied by the English marine-insurance market has resulted in the English-conditions clause being generally used in the American market to the practical exclusion of the simpler and more logical American form. The English clause introduces an element of speculation into marine insurance as will be shown by the following illustration. A vessel containing a cargo of general merchandise insured on F.P.A.E.C. terms from New York to Sydney, Australia, in going out of the port of New York, strands on the channel bank, remains fast for a few minutes or a few hours, but with the rising tide floats free and, absolutely uninjured, proceeds on her journey. The cargo has not been disturbed or injured in any respect, yet because the vessel was stranded, the exception provided in the F.P.A.E.C. clause has been fulfilled and the goods are thereafter insured subject to the printed form of policy. Later in the voyage, through stress of weather, the decks open and water is admitted to the hold, damaging the cargo. Under the insurance on F.P.A.E.C. terms this loss, if amounting to the percentage required by the printed form, would be recoverable although the loss resulting from the leakage through the decks was not caused by the stranding. Under the American form the underwriter would not be liable for this loss.

F.P.A.E.C. Clause Illogical. A more pronounced illustration of the illogical working of the F.P.A.E.C. clause will appear from the following example. A vessel fully loaded with a cargo insured on F.P.A.E.C. terms meets with heavy weather during the course of her voyage, her seams open, considerable water is shipped, and the cargo is damaged approximately 90 per cent. The vessel, however, makes her port of destination, and the owners of the cargo face a heavy loss which, because of the F.P.A.E.C. conditions, cannot be recovered from the underwriters, none of the excepted casualties having occurred. However, when approaching her berth the vessel is run into by another vessel but does not suffer much damage through the collision. Nevertheless, the collision voids the average warranty, the cargo insurance automatically becomes subject to average, and the underwriters become liable for the particular average loss which had previously occurred through the leaking of the vessel.

Amended F.P.A.E.C. Forms. These two cases demonstrate that the use of the F.P.A.E.C. clause introduces an element of speculation into marine-insurance transactions. In order to avoid the consequences of the legal interpretation given to this clause, amendments have been made from time to time in its wording in order to lessen the possibility of claims being made that are not proximately caused by casualty and to provide for the payment of losses that, while fortuitous in their nature and not in any way caused by the inherent qualities of the articles themselves, would not be recoverable under the original F.P.A.E.C. form. In the 1946 revision of the Institute (London) Cargo Clauses (F.P.A.), the F.P.A. clause is expressed in the following words:

> Warranted free from Particular Average unless the vessel or craft be stranded, sunk, or burnt, but notwithstanding this warranty the underwriters are to pay the insured value of any package or packages which may be totally lost in loading, transhipment or discharge, also for any loss of or damage to the interests insured which may reasonably be attributed to fire, explosion, collision or contact of the vessel and/or craft and/or conveyance with any external substance (ice included) other than water, or to discharge of cargo at a port of distress, also to pay landing, warehousing, forwarding and special charges if incurred for which Underwriters would be liable under a policy covering Particular Average. This clause shall operate during the whole period covered by the Policy.

Stranding and Sinking. Frequently, cases have come into the courts, involving the interpretation of the words "stranded, sunk, or burnt" as used in the F.P.A. clause, to determine the degree of casualty necessary to nullify the free-of-average warranty. The decisions clearly indicate that to constitute a stranding there must be such a taking of the bottom as results in the complete stoppage of the movement of the vessel, and not merely "touch-and-go" where the vessel comes in contact with the bottom but does not actually lose her momentum, merely sliding off the obstruction and proceeding on her course. Few cases involving sinking have arisen, but question may be raised as to when a vessel is actually sunk. A vessel may be only partially submerged and yet be said to be sunk. For instance, a lumber-laden vessel may meet with disaster so that she commences to leak. The vessel will fill with water and the cargo will absorb much moisture but the buoyancy of the cargo, although wet, will keep the ship afloat. When the cargo is completely saturated and the vessel and cargo submerged as far as it is possible for them to submerge, the vessel and cargo may be said to be sunk. On the other hand, a vessel loaded with an under- and/or on-deck cargo of lumber might start to leak and fill with water, but the vessel, although submerged, would be prevented from sinking by reason of the buoyancy of the on-deck cargo. Such a vessel might readily be towed into a safe harbor and be salvaged without further damage to either vessel or cargo. It could not be said that such a vessel was sunk, as the saturation, which would have sunk the vessel and cargo as far as it would be physically possible to sink them, had not been completed before the vessel was brought into a position of safety.

Burning and Collision. Burning has also been a moot question, and it has been decided that, in order to have such a burning as will void the free-of-average warranty, there must be destruction of a portion of the ship. It may happen that a severe fire occurs in the cargo without doing any material damage to the ship itself, so that a strict construction of the word "burnt" would prevent the recovery of the loss on cargo. To avoid this possibility, the F.P.A. (1946) clause, quoted previously, provides that loss of or damage to the interest insured, reasonably attributable to fire, is recoverable. Collision is omitted in this form from the list of excepted casualties. Collisions often result in little or no damage to the ship or cargo, but as already pointed out, a harmless collision might, under the original F.P.A.E.C. form, admit claim for prior or subsequent damage in no way attributable to the collision. On the other hand, the omission of this casualty altogether might work injustice, in that a collision, while of little consequence to the ship itself, might, through the admission of water, result in serious damage to the cargo. Underwriters have therefore assumed liability for any loss or damage which may reasonably be attributed to collision or to contact of the vessel with any external substance (ice included) other than water, the exception in regard to water being made because a vessel, normally, is always in contact with water.

Other Casualties. Packages are often lost in loading, transshipment, or discharge, and this risk is covered notwithstanding the free-of-average warranty. Liability is also admitted for expenses that are incurred after the abandonment of the voyage, by the discharge of cargo at a port of distress, or other charges that result from the landing, warehousing, and forwarding of the cargo as the result of physical conditions that make it impossible for the vessel to fulfill her contract of carriage and yet have not resulted from any of the excepted casualties.

Duration of Risk. In determining the rate of premium to be charged in cargo insurance, it is important to consider to what extent the risk to be run is affected not only by geographical conditions but also by the length of time during which the commodity will be at the risk of the underwriter. This naturally leads to a further consideration of the warehouse-to-warehouse clause, which is one of the most generally used clauses in cargo underwriting.[1] This clause, while providing a broad form of protection, covers property only while out of the custody of the owners, during transit in the ordinary course from warehouse to warehouse. In the ordinary conditions of overseas commerce, this form of protection is usually sufficient for the assured. If ports become congested owing to shortage of steamers or because of strikes or other extraordinary conditions, the unusual delay to which shipments are subjected may raise the question of what "ordinary course of transit" means as used in the warehouse-to-warehouse clause. It seems clear that these words must be interpreted in the light of existing conditions, "ordinary course of transit" under strike conditions, for instance, having a totally different meaning from what it has under normal conditions. On the other hand, it cannot be presumed, if shipments are left on the wharf week after week while steamers sail for the port for which the goods are destined, that the goods are still in ordinary course of transit, despite the fact that the unusual delay occasioned is without the knowledge or consent of the owners of the goods. Because of the general use of the warehouse-to-warehouse clause, there has been added to the average clause quoted on page 238, the words "This clause shall operate during the whole period covered by the policy." Were this phrase not added, it might be assumed that the average clause applied only while the goods were on the overseas vessel. It is still better practice, however, to name the perils covered on shore as is done in the *shore-risks* clause on page 192.

Rate of Premium Based on Ordinary Transit. The underwriter, in fixing the rate of premium, is presumed to have made the charge adequate to cover usual delay under existing conditions but should not and will not be held to have provided protection if the usual delay is converted into unusual detention. Banks and shippers may require additional protection to provide for the contingency of unusual delay, and various clauses are devised extending the warehouse-to-warehouse clause to cover such a contingency. The great difficulty from the point of view of the underwriter is to establish a basis for

[1] See p. 160.

determining the premium to be charged, adequate to compensate him for the increased hazard assumed and yet not involving a system for calculating the time of detention so expensive in operation as to cost more than the additional premium charged. This difficulty has been solved in a manner satisfactory to merchant, banker, and underwriter by the use of the marine extension clause described on page 162.

Cancellation. Cargo risks are usually covered under open policies written without time limit or expiration date. Circumstances may arise where the assured or the underwriter desires to be released from his bargain. If this desire is mutual, no difficulty will arise, as both will consent to the termination of the contract. If, however, one party desires to continue the contract and the other to be released from it, there is no way of dissolving the agreement. Accordingly, it is customary to have a cancellation clause in any open policy unlimited as to time, providing that the contract may be canceled on 30 (or other stated number) days' written notice by either party to the other, such cancellation not to prejudice any pending risks. Similar clauses are usually found in policies written for a definite period.

Noncancelable Policies. In some rather infrequent cases underwriters have been persuaded to issue policies for a named period, say one year, without reserving the right to cancel the policy or to change the rates. Cargo underwriting is subject to so many outside influences that may seriously affect the hazards covered that an underwriter cannot foresee what may happen within a year. He may be burdened with an unprofitable contract from which he cannot extricate himself and under which he cannot obtain increased rate. Unfortunately, these agreements are, in practice, unilateral; that is, they bind the underwriter, but if the contract proves disadvantageous to the assured, he frequently refuses to fulfill his obligations, leaving the underwriter with two alternatives, either to modify or cancel the contract or to sue the assured for specific performance of his agreement. This type of contract should be discouraged, as more often than not it leads to unforeseen and undesirable results.

Cargo Clauses Are Numberless. The clauses used in connection with cargo insurance are numberless, referring as they do to every possible phase of cargo underwriting. A few, however, such as the warehouse-to-warehouse clause, the craft clause providing for lighterage risks from the shore to the vessel and from the vessel to the shore, and the deviation clause are common to most cargo insurances. The clauses customarily included in open cargo policies appear in the Institute cargo clauses in Appendix C, page 446. Other clauses have been devised primarily for special trades or for certain ocean routes. The most important of these many clauses will be considered in the following chapter in connection with the discussion of insurance on specific commodities.

CHAPTER 15

Specific Cargo Risks

Full-cargo Business. To enumerate and classify, from an underwriting standpoint, all the commodities that are the subject of cargo insurance would be a well-nigh endless task and one far beyond the scope of this book. It is possible, however, to indicate several broad headings under which commodities may be grouped and to give a brief description of the forms of insurance granted on some of the principal commodities in each group. Before doing this, however, it will be well to give some consideration to the peculiar hazards of full-cargo business. A full cargo may consist of any kind of goods, although it is more usual to find vessels so loaded with raw or bulk commodities.

A Seasonal Business—Congestion Hazard. As a rule, full-cargo business is seasonal and is confined at any given season to relatively few ports. For instance, in the movement of the United States cotton crop, the southern ports of the country are involved principally during the latter part of the year. The business centering in a few ports near the cotton-producing areas leads to congestion, and the wharves and streets in the neighborhood of the wharves become filled with cotton, inadequately protected from the elements and subject to conflagration hazard. Such congestion, while not peculiar to the cotton business, becomes more important in the movement of this crop, because it is customary for the marine underwriter to assume the interior fire and transit risks in the insurance of raw cotton. Similar congested conditions will be found in the movement of raw sugar, coffee, grain, hemp, and burlaps, but the congestion hazards in these trades are apt to result in losses largely due to hasty and careless handling which causes damage to the commodity itself. Thus, vessels may load in the rain causing, to a perishable cargo, damage for which an underwriter will have difficulty in denying liability if the insurance is subject to average. An underwriter is not liable for fresh-water damage unless he specially insures against this hazard, but it is not always possible to prove that damage to goods is due to fresh and not to sea water.

Overloading of Vessels. In these seasonal trades there is usually a scarcity of tonnage, with the inevitable result that there is a tendency to overload vessels unless careful inspection is maintained by underwriters. The question of loading, therefore, assumes great importance, and underwriters' boards have laid down rules in certain cases prescribing approved methods of stowage to which vessels must conform in order to obtain insurance. This is peculiarly true in the grain business. This commodity, because of its tendency to shift, becomes an extrahazardous risk unless proper stowage is obtained. In the case of lighter cargoes, where it is impossible to overload a vessel with the commodity itself, a condition of instability may result owing to the vessel's being top heavy. It is, therefore, usual to carry in the bottom of the holds of such vessels, ore, metal products, or other heavy materials in order to lower the center of gravity and thus increase the metacenter height. There is also the tendency to carry heavy deckloads of timber on such vessels. These deck cargoes may be poorly stowed or improperly secured, proving a menace to the under-deck cargo because part of the deckload may be lost, causing the vessel to get out of trim. Such cargoes greatly increase the fire hazard, owing to the difficulty of gaining access to the under-deck cargo.

Unfit Vessels Used to Carry Full Cargoes. The scarcity of tonnage in these seasonal trades also calls into service many vessels not fitted for the cargoes to be carried. In the raw-sugar trade from Cuba to the United States and in the export grain trade, vessels physically unfit for carrying these exceedingly perishable commodities are offered for charter. Such vessels, either because of their design or because of their age and physical condition, are not fit to withstand the hazards of the trade. The result is that often such vessels, encountering heavy weather, will leak, causing enormous damage to perishable cargoes. The effect of water on these perishable bulk cargoes, whether it obtains entrance because of the weakness of the ship or through a casualty, is very great.

These cargoes, consisting, as they usually do, of vegetable products, may, as in the case of sugar, rapidly dissolve or, as in the case of grain, swell and tend to burst the ship, thus causing further damage and perhaps the loss of the whole venture. Sometimes the tendency is to soften quickly, rot, and become unsalable as is the case with flax-seed, beans, and many of the vegetable fibers.

Fire Hazard. The fire hazard is of no little importance in the full-cargo business, especially in connection with commodities that are likely to heat. Proper ventilation is of the utmost importance in these trades. Soft coal, when carried on long voyages, may take fire unless the holds are cooled during the voyage. This can most easily be done by removing the hatches during fine weather. However, if the cargo is already on fire and smoldering, the admission of fresh air with the opening of the hatches will probably result in its bursting into flames. In the case of vegetable fibers, which ordinarily are carried long distances through the torrid zones, there is danger of fire from improperly cured fiber. The fire hazard is also serious in the case of cotton. If cotton is shipped wet, it may heat in the hold and spontaneous combustion may result, but more often cotton fires, which are very common on shipboard, are due to sparks lodging in the bales during loading caused, it may be, by stevedores smoking or by the hitting of the metal straps of the bales on the steel hatch coamings during stowage. There being much air in a cotton bale, the spark will live for many days, gradually eating its way into the bale and eventually causing the bale to take fire, perhaps after the vessel is far on her voyage. The carriage of petroleum products has grown to enormous proportions. A highly inflammable cargo under certain circumstances, nevertheless, because of the careful manner in which it is carried in specially designed tank steamers, it presents to the underwriter a desirable risk. The modern tanker is equipped with all possible safeguards during loading, transit, and discharge so that relatively few serious losses occur. Liquid gasoline in a fully loaded tanker is relatively safe, but the volatile fumes that develop as the tanker is unloaded present a serious hazard. A spark at this time can produce a tremendous explosion that often results in fatalities to the crew and in serious damage to the vessel. Bulk oil cargo is customarily insured under the very broad conditions of the bulk oil clauses.[1]

[1] See Lazard's "Marine Insurance Forms."

CLASSES OF CARGO

Cargo may be broadly divided into classes, each class containing those commodities which have a common origin. Thus may be grouped together the products of agriculture, of animals, of forests, of mines, or of manufacturers. It does not follow, however, that because two or more commodities fall into the same class, the risk on all is the same from an underwriting standpoint.

Products of Agriculture. The products of agriculture, both in bulk and in value, form one of the largest classes of cargo risks. This is true in large part because the raw commodity is grown principally in countries or in sections of a country not given to manufacturing. The raw product must be transported from the place of origin to the place of manufacture or consumption. This fact, coupled with the nature of the commodity itself, determines in large measure the conditions under which insurance protection is afforded.

Sweat Damage. Great progress has been made in controlling the precipitation of moisture in the holds of vessels. This precipitation is called sweat and most frequently occurs in transit from warm to cool areas and vice versa. It may also arise from the cargo itself if shipped in an improperly cured condition, as frequently happens in the case of raw skins. Many modern vessels have air-conditioning systems built into their holds, so that the danger of sweat damage is greatly reduced.

Skimmings Clause. Cocoa and coffee beans constitute a considerable proportion of the exports of some tropical regions. Both commodities are easily damaged and customarily are insured by underwriters on "with-particular-average" terms. Because of their transfer by water from a warm to a cool climate, insurance against sweat damage is frequently included. There is always a certain amount of moisture in the hold of a vessel, and if the cargo is not properly dunnaged and protected, sweat will reach it, causing damage which under extreme conditions may affect a considerable portion of the cargo. It is also usual to insure cocoa and coffee under the *skimmings clause.* In this clause the underwriter assumes liability for all partial loss through the bags being wet or stained by salt water, the coffee or cocoa affected being skimmed off and the damage assessed on the portion so segregated.

Raw Cotton. Raw cotton is grown in our Southern states; in

India, Africa, and Peru; and in limited quantities in some other parts of the world. The fiber is baled, but the condition of the bale varies in different countries. American cotton, when shipped in the standard 500-pound bale, is not sufficiently protected from the elements and from the soil and stain that inevitably accumulate during handling and transit. The result is that the cotton frequently arrives abroad damaged through these causes, and the consignees claim allowance for the damaged staple. Unfortunately, underwriters have assumed liability for this *country damage,* with the result that there has not been the same incentive to better bale protection and more careful handling that there would have been had the loss fallen on the shippers or consignees. Furthermore, in some European cities quite a thriving business has developed in the adjustment of country-damage claims and in the reconditioning of the bales, so that no great degree of pressure has been exerted on the shippers to provide a better package. It is true that a measure of progress has been made in the better compression of the cotton under the Webb system, but much remains to be done before a package is produced that can compare favorably with the Egyptian cotton bale. At present the cotton policy does not specify country damage as a peril but affords an all-risk cover under the following clause:

Against all risks of physical loss or damage from any external cause, irrespective of percentage, but excluding those risks excepted by the F. C. & S. and S. R. & C. C. clauses.

Schedule rating. The insurance of American-grown cotton is peculiar in that the insurance covers the ginned cotton from the time it is baled and weighed at the towns adjacent to the farms where the staple is grown. The insurance protection continues from this point until the cotton is delivered at the warehouse or mill of the consignee in Europe, Japan, India, or wherever the raw product is manufactured into cloth or other cotton products. The insured cotton is not in continuous transit. It is carried from places of purchase to concentration points where the bale is recompressed and reconditioned, and the cotton is sorted into the various grades and made into lots to fill the requirements of sales made by the owners. Schedule rating, so common in fire insurance and so unusual in marine insurance, finds its nearest approach in the rate tariffs in use in the raw-cotton trade. The various factors of fire risk in different locations; flood risk; transit risk by rail, by steamer, and by lighter; also country-damage risk and special-port risks are all factors in determining the rate charged.

Grain Cargoes. The insurance of grain cargoes involves one of the most interesting and most hazardous classes of risks in cargo underwriting. Grain being small in size and of smooth skin has a tendency to flow, and no little difficulty is experienced in stowing such cargoes so that the vessel will be stable when it sails and continue in that condition regardless of the weather encountered at sea. Various sets of rules have been formulated by government boards and by underwriters' boards, all having as their aim the fitting of vessels internally so that grain cargoes cannot shift. In general, these rules provide for shifting boards, temporary longitudinal bulkheads so fitted as to divide each hold into two smaller holds. The grain is fed into the holds and properly spread, boards are laid upon the grain, and on top of these are placed several tiers of grain in bags to prevent the movement of the cargo. In double-deck vessels, wing feeders are often required. These feeders are bins of considerable size which, with the rolling of the vessel and the movement of the cargo, feed down into the hold grain that will take the place of the shifted portion and restore the vessel to a condition of stability.

Standard clauses. Grain, being a very perishable commodity, is usually insured on free-of-average terms. When shipped in bags and thus in a measure protected, it may be insured subject to average. Grain insurance in the export trade is so important that the London and American Institutes, acting in conjunction with the London Corn Trade Association, have promulgated standard clauses under which export grain from the United States to the United Kingdom and to the Continent of Europe is insured. These clauses, with respect to average, provide a much broader protection than the customary free-of-particular-average-English-conditions clause affords.

Hard and Soft Grains. From the underwriting point of view, some grains are more hazardous than others. The harder cereals, such as wheat and rye, are much better risks than are corn and flaxseed, which, because of their softness, will rapidly spoil and become worthless in the event of damage. It is, in fact, exceedingly difficult to ship corn at certain seasons of the year without the cargo arriving at destination in a much deteriorated condition. While it is true that grain is insured on free-of-average terms, it is equally true that, if one of the excepted casualties occurs and the underwriter becomes liable for average, the loss may be serious because of the inherent qualities of the commodity. It also happens in the case of grains, such as flaxseed, for which there is ordinarily a limited market, that a comparatively slight damage due to a casualty may result in considerable loss owing to the lack of a market for this particular grain at the port of refuge. It is often not possible either to recondition grain at a port of refuge or carry the cargo forward to destination in its damaged condition, and a forced sale becomes necessary.

Vegetable Fibers. The fibrous commodities, of which hemp, sisal, and jute are the chief examples, are exceedingly perishable in their nature and are usually insured free of average. In the jute trade, special clauses have been promulgated by mutual agreement between the merchants and the underwriters. Fire is one of the chief hazards encountered in this trade and often occurs during unloading when care is not exercised to see that the stevedores do not smoke. When jute takes fire, the blaze is exceedingly difficult to extinguish, as the fire smolders and, even after it is apparently out, the jute will again burst into flame.

Raw Sugar. Raw sugar is a very perishable cargo, the principal cause of loss to this commodity being water. It is very soluble, and the admission of water to the hold will quickly result in serious damage. Sugar is usually insured subject to average, the minimum average payable depending in large measure on the length of risk. In the Cuban and Puerto Rican sugar trades, which are the most important in the American market, cargoes are insured subject to the *loss-in-weight* or the *loss-in-test* clause or both. Under the loss-in-weight clause the underwriter adjusts the loss on the basis of reduction in weight as shown by the invoice weights and the outturn weights, an allowance of 2 per cent being made for the absorption of moisture. In an adjustment under the loss-in-test clause, the percentage of damage suffered, as shown by comparing the sound and damaged values, is applied to the insured value of the damaged sugar, and the loss is thus determined.

Fruits and Vegetables. There are many other products of agriculture, such as fresh fruits and vegetables, that are a considerable item in marine insurance. These commodities are usually of so perishable a nature that they are insured free of particular average absolutely. However, when they are shipped in refrigerated compartments, it is usual to cover partial loss in the event of a breakdown of the refrigerating apparatus, provided such breakdown continues a certain number of days or hours. Underwriters will also cover the risk of the fruit's deteriorating owing to delay on the voyage, provided such delay causes the voyage to be prolonged beyond an agreed number of days. This period will depend on the length of the voyage and the speed of the steamer. Such insurance is provided under the *prolongation clause.* The transportation of apples from America to the United Kingdom is one phase of the fruit trade that involves enormous values. The carriage of bananas, pineapples, and other tropical fruits from the West Indies and Central America to United States ports is so important that lines of steamers especially designed for this trade are in constant operation between these ports. The fresh-fruit trade between South America and the United States is also important, bringing fruit from south of the equator to the United States during its winter season.

Products of Animals. The insurance of animal products occupies a large place in marine underwriting. With the discovery of improved methods for the curing and preserving of animal products, and with the perfecting of refrigerating machinery which permits the carriage of fresh and frozen meats for thousands of miles in perfect condition, a new and extensive field for marine underwriting came into being. Cured and pickled animal products are not an extrahazardous class of risk, as the commodity is usually well packed and not easily damaged and is accordingly insured on very favorable terms. Packing-house products, excluding fresh and frozen meats and the by-products of the packing plants, are usually insured subject to 3 per cent average on each package. In many cases the insurance is broadened to afford protection against practically all risks of transportation and navigation.

Some of the animal oils and greases that, under moderate heat, turn into oil are very hazardous if the risk of leakage is covered. The degree of risk in leakage insurance is dependent largely on the season of the year, the normal temperature of the route over which the cargo will pass, and the port of destination. The more heat to which these oils and greases are subjected, the more fluid they become and the greater the likelihood of leakage.

Refrigerated Goods. Fresh and frozen meats, when insured subject to average and subject to loss occasioned by the breakdown of the refrigerating apparatus, present a most hazardous risk. When it is considered that a commodity that will quickly spoil has to be carried a distance of 3,000 to 10,000 miles over routes which in many cases pass through the very hottest portions of the ocean, some conception will be gained of the hazards involved in this form of insurance. A number of years ago a fine refrigerator steamer, loaded with a valuable cargo of fresh and frozen meats, took fire while on the way from Australia to the United Kingdom and was compelled to enter Dakar, West Africa, a port very nearly on the equator. The fire was extinguished, but the refrigerating apparatus in one hold containing frozen mutton was so damaged that it was useless. The mutton in this hold quickly spoiled and had to be jettisoned, resulting in a very serious loss to the underwriters.

Dressed meats. Dressed meats are usually shipped either chilled or frozen. Chilled meat is kept at a temperature of 40 degrees or less, cool enough to prevent decomposition and yet not cold enough to freeze the meat. Frozen meat is frozen solid before shipment and is kept at a temperature of about 15 degrees. In the event of breakdown of the refrigerating plant, the spoilage of frozen meat is much more rapid than of chilled meat. Ordinarily, beef is shipped chilled, while mutton, poultry, rabbits, and the smaller pieces of meat are shipped frozen. The hazard of fresh- and frozen-meat insurance is further increased in many cases by the assumption of the risk from the moment the meat enters the cooling or freezing chambers of the packing plant, during transportation, and for a period not exceeding 60 days after arrival at destination. The risk prior to shipment on the ocean-going steamer is also limited to 60 days. This is the broadest form of cover granted in this trade, though there are many lesser forms of insurance in use. In fact, the London Institute of Marine Underwriters has promulgated at least 20 different clauses relating to the insurance of fresh and frozen meats. The insurance of these commodities is practically controlled by the London market, as the

United Kingdom and the Continental countries are more interested in this business than the United States, which is self-supporting in the matter of meat supplies.

Livestock. The shipment of livestock is of considerable importance in the insurance market. In this trade several kinds of insurance are afforded, ranging from that which assumes liability for only the absolute total loss of the vessel and her cargo, including the livestock insured, to insurance under full mortality conditions where the underwriter assumes liability for death of the animals, however caused, provided they were shipped in sound and healthy condition. Such insurance may terminate with the landing of the animals on shore, no liability being assumed for any animal walking ashore, regardless of its physical condition, or the risk may continue for a fixed period, say 5 days after the animals are landed. During this period, animals greatly affected by the sea voyage often die, and the underwriter assumes liability for this loss. The degree of hazard in the insurance of livestock is dependent largely on the nature and temperament of the animals. Sheep are more susceptible to pneumonia than are cattle, this disease often being the cause of death during transit. Horses, being more high-spirited than cattle, often become terrified in a storm, doing injury to themselves or to other animals. Mules, on the other hand, being phlegmatic in temperament and not readily susceptible to disease, are a comparatively safe risk in this very hazardous class.

Hides and Skins. The shipment of hides and skins is a substantial part of the trade in the products of animals and is very hazardous. Hides and skins are usually shipped in a partially finished state; that is, they are not processed to the point where they are ready for use in industry. Ordinarily, only two methods of treatment are used in preparing the raw material for shipment. The hides and skins may be cured and dried, tied into bales or bundles, and shipped, or they may be pickled and shipped in casks. Under either method, an extra-hazardous commodity is offered for insurance, for if the dried hides are wet, they will quickly rot, and the wet salted skins, if the brine is weakened, will rapidly deteriorate. In the event of a casualty the loss is usually large, and if the disaster happens far from a market or from a place where the commodity can be reconditioned, the danger of a total loss is great.

In the shipment of steer hides from South America, called *frigorificos*, indicating that the animals have been slaughtered in the big abattoirs and the skins properly prepared for shipment, a special method of stowage has been perfected. Instead of baling the skins they are salted down loosely in the hold of the vessel, each skin either being flat or rolled up. Unless the salting is very carefully done, considerable damage may result as a vessel on her voyage north has to pass through equatorial waters with great variations in temperature. Furthermore, unscrupulous shippers sometimes include hides from animals killed up-country or in city abattoirs that have not been properly processed. Such skins may deteriorate and, through contact, spread damage to frigorificos.

Furs are a hazardous cargo, but because of their value they are carefully packed and are less apt to sustain damage, the greatest risk probably being that of theft and pilferage. Notwithstanding the extra-hazardous nature of hide and skin shipments, insurance is offered on these commodities under the external-cause clause.[1] This form of insurance, or insurance against "all risks of transportation and navigation," affords ample opportunity for dispute in the adjustment of losses, as it is often difficult rightly to decide whether damage to these commodities is the result of an external cause or an internal condition due to imperfect curing or treatment of the skins.

Wool. One of the largest items among the products of animals is wool. This commodity is carefully baled and is carried long distances from Australia, New Zealand, and South America to the United States, as a rule suffering little damage unless serious disaster overtakes the carrying vessel. If the wool, in the event of such casualty, can be forwarded to a place where it can be reconditioned, the loss can be minimized, as the fiber does not deteriorate quickly. Two general classes of wool are shipped. The finer wools are used in the making of cloth; the coarser grades are used in the manufacture of carpets. Broad insuring conditions are granted on wool, and the insurance often attaches from the time the wool is sheared from the sheep. Sometimes the insurance also covers the risk while the wool is growing on the sheep.

Raw Silk. Before the development of synthetic fibers, raw silk, because of its high value, furnished a considerable volume of insurance.

[1] See p. 193.

Its great value, however, results in its being so well packed and so carefully handled in shipment that it is one of the best risks in the whole field of marine underwriting. Although very susceptible to injury, it is so packed that it cannot be damaged readily unless a serious casualty occurs. It is customarily shipped in well-prepared bales, or it may be imported in tin-lined cases and formerly was carried on the finest vessels operating from the silk ports. When this trade was at its height, Chinese and Japanese raw silks were transported across the Pacific Ocean by the fast passenger steamers then operating to West Coast ports of the United States and Canada, where special freight trains were in waiting to carry the cargoes overland at faster than passenger-train speed. This served the twofold purpose of reducing the time of transit and saving interest charges on the high values at risk. Little silk is imported at the present time.

Frozen Fruit, Vegetables, and Fish. A considerable business has developed in recent years in the shipment of quick-frozen fruits, vegetables, and fish. These commodities are processed at a very low temperature. During shipment this low temperature must be maintained or the commodities will quickly spoil.

Canned and Bottled Goods. Dairy Products. Canned and bottled goods, whether vegetable or animal products, should be insured free of average, partly because of the effect of moisture on the tin container and partly because of the expense of reconditioning the container, whether tin or glass, in the event of damage. Relabeling is usually necessary even if the damage is slight, resulting in expense oftentimes out of all proportion to the damage suffered. As a matter of practice, however, canned and bottled goods are insured on as favorable terms as packinghouse products. This condition is equally true of dairy products, particularly butter and cheese, which, because of their nature, should be insured on free-of-average conditions but are insured under full-average conditions and, in some instances, against all risks of transportation and navigation. Butter and cheese, when shipped in the warm summer months, should be stowed in cool air or refrigerated space.

Products of the Forest. Among the products of the forest, rubber and gum take a leading place. These commodities rank high as desirable subjects of insurance, being little susceptible to damage. The growth in volume of shipments of crude rubber from the tropical countries to the manufacturing centers of the world has been little short of marvelous. Improved methods of processing crude rubber have permitted its use in many lines of industry. Rubber is also imported in liquid form in tank steamers under the name of *latex*. Other gums also form a considerable part of the commerce of certain ports. The shipment of rosin and turpentine is of considerable importance in the trade of certain of the Southern ports of the United States.

Wood Cargoes. Insurance of the products of the forest in the form of logs, timber, and lumber usually covers on-deck cargoes. Ordinarily, these cargoes are light and buoyant, and in order to get the vessel in proper trim it is necessary to carry part of the cargo on deck. While rough logs and large timbers are not very susceptible to damage, sawed and finished lumber may considerably decrease in value through stain and through damage in handling. Although most of these products will float and therefore cannot readily be lost, the expense of handling the smaller pieces of finished lumber often makes salvage operations impracticable. The fact that these cargoes are carried on deck has a bearing on the risk as a whole, as the shifting or loss of a part or the whole of the deck cargo may result in the loss of the entire venture. The shipment of the roots and bark of forest trees is also an important part of overseas commerce, these commodities being extensively used in the arts, in medicine, and in industry.

Products of the Mines. The products of mines afford two extremes in the degree of risk that they offer to the underwriter. Metals, such as copper and tin in pigs, stand at the head of the list of commodities that offer little or no risk except that of total loss, while salt is about as poor a subject of insurance as the whole field affords. The nature of the commodity is the important factor, soluble minerals being bad risks, while the insoluble are in the very highest class. The demand for the precious and semiprecious metals in the arts and industries is very great. In the case of the baser metals such as tin, copper, and iron, which are produced in great abundance in certain countries but are scarcely to be found in others, an enormous overseas trade has developed. These commodities are usually insured free of particular average. However, in the event that a casualty occurs, unless it is a sinking to a depth where salvage operations are impracticable, the metals in pigs are practically uninjured, and the attendant loss is merely the salvage and reconditioning expenses. Under similar conditions the soluble minerals such as salt and nitrates would probably become a total loss.

Coal and Ore. Notwithstanding the tremendous increase in the use of oil as a fuel, coal is still an important and essential commodity in overseas trade. Being a rough dirty cargo, it is not shipped in the best vessels except where vessels are specially designed for this trade. For this reason the risk on coal is usually great. The commodity itself, however, is a satisfactory subject of insurance, especially the harder grades of coal. The softer coal, such as bituminous, English, and Indian coal, when shipped on long voyages in poorly ventilated ships, presents a dangerous fire hazard because of its tendency to heat. The shipment of bulk ores is in about the same class as coal. The greatest danger with all these heavy cargoes is the possibility of the vessel's being overloaded or improperly loaded, thus affecting its stability. It requires no little degree of skill to load these cargoes so that they will not shift and so that the vessel will not be unduly stiff.

Manufactured Products. The insurance of manufactured products affords the most diversified field in marine underwriting. Any individual consideration of these commodities is impracticable in this book, but the field embraces articles that present practically every problem with which marine underwriting is concerned. The business as a rule is general-cargo business; that is, vessels carrying manufactured goods will be loaded with many different products, including articles little susceptible to damage and those which are extremely perishable, together with commodities presenting all the intermediate degrees of hazard. Here the trite saying that the marine underwriter must know "everything about something," that is, his own business, and "something about everything" has its most complete illustration, in that the underwriter is called upon to decide under what conditions he will insure any given commodity, and upon the correctness of his judgment depends the success of his underwriting. Truly, in marine underwriting a "*little* knowledge is a dangerous thing."

Diversity of Risk. Mention may be made of a few manufactured articles merely to show the wide diversity of risk in this field. Cement has of late years become an important article of commerce. It is exceedingly hazardous owing to the fact that the addition of water turns the cement into stone, resulting in a total loss. Cases have occurred where cement, becoming wet in the hold of a vessel, has turned into stone, and the only way of removing the mass has been by dynamite. On the other hand, wheat flour, which, like cement, is a fine powder and is usually shipped in bags, is a very good insurance risk because of the fact, when wet, the flour near the bag forms a paste which protects the rest of the contents. The chief danger with flour is its tendency to spoil or to become grubby, risks which the marine underwriter endeavors to exclude. However, to meet competitive conditions, underwriters are sometimes compelled to insure against weevil damage. This is an exceedingly hazardous form of insurance and requires a careful inspection of freight cars and of steamers' holds to determine whether they are free from animal life. It is not unusual for underwriters to assume "all risks" on flour exported to the United Kingdom and to the northern ports of Europe. The bags in which much of the export flour is shipped are very susceptible to damage in handling, and a considerable part of underwriters' losses arises from shortage due to torn or broken packages.

Machinery. Machinery is an interesting subject of insurance because, in most cases, the breakage or loss of one small part of a machine will render useless the whole. Accordingly, underwriters have devised machinery clauses of various kinds, the underlying principle of all being that, in the event of loss, the underwriter assumes liability only for the part lost or broken and for the expense attending its replacement.

Burlap and Bags. Fire Hazard. Burlap and bags, great quantities of which are shipped, present peculiar hazards. Fire is one of the great hazards in this trade, while the damage caused by water staining the bales is also of considerable importance. The manufactures of petroleum, especially the volatile oils, constitute a serious fire hazard, and in the case of oils shipped in tins packed in wooden cases, the loss by leakage through the rusting of the tins is considerable, especially in the event of a serious disaster to the carrying vessel.

OTHER RISKS

Leakage and Breakage. While the policy in its original form does not assume liability for leakage unless caused by stranding or collision or for breakage, the exigencies of business require, in many cases, that leakage and breakage risks, however caused, be assumed by the underwriter. This is an extrahazardous form of insurance, and the successful underwriting of these risks depends, in large measure, on the formulation of clauses in which the burden of usual leakage or breakage losses is thrown on the assured. The underwriter becomes responsible for only those losses which, because of their degree, indicate that the commodity has been subjected to some unusual condition. The rate of premium for these forms of insurance depends in large measure on the article itself and the nature of its package. In the case of leakage, the heaviness of the oil or liquid and its tendency to thin and become more fluid under heat are significant. If the voyage is long, any leak in a package will probably result in a total loss of the contents, and under the pressure to which cargo is subjected in the hold of a vessel during the voyage, the probability of strain on the package is very great. Breakage, in even larger measure, is dependent on the commodity and its package. Small articles, well packed, will usually carry without breakage, and if breakage occurs, the loss will not be total but will probably involve only a few of the articles in the package. On the other hand, large single articles, such as statuary and plate glass, if broken at all, usually are a total loss, and it is almost impossible to name a rate within reason that is adequate to recoup an underwriter for losses sustained in insuring breakage on such articles. Such insurance is, as a rule, a matter of accommodation in connection with the general business of a merchant, and the underwriter does not expect that this particular portion of the business will pay for itself.

Common Carriers' Insurance. Steamship and other water-transportation companies, especially the coastwise, lake, and river lines, in order to attract business from the railroads, have offered rates of freight that include insurance or have offered to shippers their facilities in the procuring of insurance on cargo transported by their vessels. The carriers have arranged policies to cover these risks. These policies are written either in blanket form, the carrier paying a fixed annual premium, or in the open form under which reports of risks to which the policy is applicable are made. As a rule these policies differ little from those issued to merchants, but the valuation is sometimes based on "commodity values." Freight rates are charged in accordance with the class into which a commodity falls, and in the valuing of cargo by the carrier for insurance purposes the same principle is used, a value per ton of weight for each class being established and reports being made and premium charged on these values. In these policies the underwriter usually waives subrogation against the vessel with respect to the cargo insured, so that in the event of loss the underwriter has no recourse against the vessel for losses resulting from its negligence.

Carriers' Liability Policies. Marine-insurance policies are also issued to water-transportation companies to cover their liability, whether imposed by law or assumed by contract. A policy is issued to cover the liability of the carrier up to a named sum, say $500,000, whether this liability is assumed under a rate of freight that includes insurance or under an agreement with the shipper to insure his goods or is imposed by common or statute law. In this form of policy the coinsurance principle, so general in marine insurance, is not operative, the underwriter following the liability of the carrier up to the face amount of his policy. It is, however, usual, because of the large limits required by carriers, to place these liability policies on shares among a number of underwriting offices.

Common Carriers' Liability. In the insurance of cargo the liability of carriers[1] is an important element in determining the rate of premium to be charged. In general, land carriers, unless relieved by law, are liable for all damage suffered by property in their custody unless caused by inherent vice, improper packing, or an act of God or of the King's or the government's enemies. On the other hand, in order to encourage transportation by sea, the liability of carriers by water routes has been greatly modified by the enactment of statutes such as the Harter Act. While the underwriter, under his original form of policy, may assume responsibility for such losses notwithstanding the liability of the carrier, the assured agrees in the sue-and-labor clause to sue, labor, and travel in the defense, safeguard, and recovery of the property, so that he should file claim against the carrier to recover for the loss or damage suffered before calling on his underwriter to pay. In order that this duty and obligation may be more perfectly established it is usual to find, in cargo policies, clauses making the

[1] See Chap. 26.

policy void to the extent of any liability that a carrier may have under the common law or otherwise and also making the policy void if other insurance is provided by the carrier or other third person that would be valid if the policy held by the merchant had not been issued. Carriers, in many cases, have inserted in their bills of lading clauses to the effect that, in the event of their settling a claim on cargo, they shall have by assignment the benefit of any insurance on the property. Underwriters have in turn made their policies void if the assured accepts a bill of lading containing such a stipulation. In order to preserve his rights against carriers, the underwriter usually makes settlement of losses covered by the policy (but for which the carrier may be responsible), in the form of a loan, under a loan receipt calling for the repayment of the sum advanced only in the event of and to the extent of the insured's recovery from the carrier.[1]

Parcel-post and Registered-mail Insurance. The subject of cargo insurance is so vast that no effort has been made to treat it in detail, the foregoing discussion merely serving to indicate some of the problems confronting the underwriter in this branch. Under the heading of cargo insurance are usually included shipments made by parcel post, registered mail, or air mail, a somewhat troublesome form of insurance because ordinarily proper proofs of loss cannot be obtained. It is seldom known on what vessel a package is shipped, and the mere fact that it does not arrive at destination is usually the only proof of its loss. Whether nondelivery is due to a marine or transportation loss, a fire, or a theft cannot be established. Consequently an underwriter usually insures shipments by mail against all risks and charges a premium high enough to provide for all possible contingencies. Shipments by registered mail are more carefully watched than those by parcel post, and this method of transit is used in the shipment of securities and currency and other high-valued commodities of small bulk. Although insuring against "all risks," the underwriter on mail shipments does not assume liability for loss due to the malfeasance of an employee of the assured. Either this risk is specifically excluded, or the policy is so written that the underwriter's liability does not commence until the package is mailed and receipted for by the postal authorities.

[1] See p. 425.

Securities and Currency. In the shipment of securities and currency by registered mail, the underwriter may require that the contents be counted and the package sealed by a notary public, who, under his seal, gives a certificate of the contents of the package. The insurance of currency is more hazardous than the insurance of securities, because the latter can usually be replaced upon the giving of proper bonds, which are at the expense of the underwriter, whereas currency when lost cannot be reissued. The shipment of currency and bullion under bill of lading is also an important item of insurance, especially when it is necessary to ship gold from one country to another to equalize exchange rates by the settlement of international trade balances. Such shipments are insured against all transportation risks from bank to bank and, because of the extreme care and protection afforded, offer little except a total-loss, salvage, and general-average hazard to the underwriter.

CHAPTER 16

Hull Insurance

Classes of Hull Insurance. Hull insurance, the second of the three general divisions of marine insurance, may be subdivided into four broad groups, each characterized by the type of vessel insured, *viz.*, sail, auxiliary sail, steamer, and motor. These four classes may each be separated into insurance placed on trip risks and that placed on the annual or time basis. A trip insurance is one whose termini are mainly geographical, that is, a risk insured from one port to one or more other ports, with perhaps a continuation of the risk in the final port for a specified number of hours or days after safe arrival. An insurance on time, whether on the annual basis or for a shorter period, is limited entirely by the date of attachment and the date of termination, except in so far as the insurance may be made void by the breach of specific trading or other warranties. There is no limit in this country to the time for which a policy may be written, but in Great Britain the law provides a time limit of one year, and this period is by custom used in this country. In rare cases, a combination of the trip and time forms is found, wherein a vessel is insured for a named voyage, the total time at risk, however, to be definitely limited to a given number of days or months.

Single-vessel and Fleet Insurance. Hull insurance may again be considered as falling into two further groups, *viz.*, single-vessel and fleet insurance. Formerly, single-vessel risks were more common among sailing vessels than steamers. Usually, single individuals or groups of men jointly owned a sailing vessel, while steam tonnage was largely developed by companies that formed steamers into fleets and operated them over definite routes. In the case of steamer tonnage, it is not unusual to form a separate corporation to own each individual vessel, the corporation usually bearing the name of the vessel, as the "Greenways Steamship Corporation." Thus, even in large fleets, each vessel may be separately owned, although all the vessels in the fleet will be jointly operated by a corporation formed for this special purpose. The primary object in single-vessel ownership is to make each vessel a unit when any question of legal liability arises, so that any judgment obtained may be executed only against the guilty vessel and not against all the vessels, as might be the case if they were jointly owned. The managing corporation may charter all the vessels, or it may merely load them and manage their operation.

Single-vessel Risks. As a rule, single-vessel risks merit a higher rate of premium than vessels insured jointly as a fleet whether separately owned or not, since there is a spread of risk in the case of fleet insurance. A single-vessel risk is rated on its own merits. It stands or falls by itself. If the vessel is well built, in good condition, and owned by persons whose record as ship operators or owners is good, it will be favorably considered. If badly built and in poor condition, with the further handicap of poor ownership, either it will not be insured or, if insured by some venturesome underwriter, the policy will carry a high rate of premium.

Fleet Insurance. Fleet insurance presents a very different problem. As a rule, the formation of fleets is a gradual process. New vessels are added from time to time, with the result that in a fleet there are usually new vessels and old vessels, good vessels and those which are not so good. When vessels are considered as separate units, an underwriter is disposed to insure the newer and better vessels but hesitates to accept lines on the older and inferior vessels. In writing fleet insurance, however, he cannot as a rule pick and choose, but must write all or none. Accordingly, he accepts a percentage interest in the fleet, making a uniform rate for the whole or, as is often the case, dividing the fleet into groups in accordance with the merits of the respective vessels and fixing a rate for each group.

Moral Hazard. In all branches of marine insurance moral hazard is important, but it is particularly vital in hull insurance. The character of the owner and the experience and ability of the manager of a single vessel or of a fleet are primary considerations in the insurance of hulls. Bad ownership or incompetent management means many losses, some of which may present evidence of unfair dealing. No asset is so valuable to a shipowner as his reputation. A good record will procure insurance on vessels that, because of their age, for instance, would be otherwise uninsurable. On the other hand, a bad record in the owning and management of vessels that are in themselves good risks will make the procurement of insurance a difficult matter. Not only does bad management make difficult the procurement of insurance on the hull, but it also affects the placing of insurance on the cargo and freight. Ownership and management affect not only the occurrence of accidents to vessels through errors of judgment in navigation, owing to the employment of incompetent masters and crew, but also the physical upkeep of the vessel. A run-down vessel is a bad insurance risk and also a bad financial risk. A steamer with its delicate motive power cannot be neglected. A wooden sailing vessel cannot be neglected or its hull and rigging will deteriorate. Vessels need constant attention, and if, through mismanagement, an owner neglects the upkeep of his vessels, his loss record will soon reveal the fact, even if it is not otherwise discovered by the underwriters. High rates or no insurance at all will be the inevitable result.

Change of Ownership. Because the underwriter is so much concerned with moral hazard, it follows that he will wish to protect himself in the event of change of ownership of the vessel. This is done by the *change-of-ownership* clause which, in the Syndicate form,[1] immediately follows the naming of the assured and provides for termination of the policy in the event of change of ownership. Change of ownership might take place while the vessel is at sea on a voyage with cargo or in ballast. In that event the cancellation of the policy that would follow the transfer is suspended until arrival at final port of discharge if with cargo or at port of destination if in ballast. The clause provides for other contingencies so that no undue hardship will result. If the underwriters agree in writing to the change of ownership, then the clause does not operate. The Syndicate clause reads:

[1] In various places in this and the following chapters, for illustration, reference is made to the Syndicate form. This is the form used by the American Marine Hull Insurance Syndicate for the insurance of ocean-going vessels. The text of the form appears as Appendix F.

In the event of any change, voluntary or otherwise, in the ownership of the Vessel or if the Vessel be placed under new management or be chartered on a bareboat basis or requisitioned on that basis, then, unless the Underwriters agree thereto in writing, this Policy shall thereupon become cancelled from time of such change in ownership or management, charter or requisition; provided, however, that in the case of an involuntary temporary transfer by requisition or otherwise, without the prior execution of any written agreement by the Assured, such cancellation shall take place fifteen days after such transfer; and provided further that if the Vessel has cargo on board and has already sailed from her loading port, or is at sea in ballast, such cancellation shall be suspended until arrival at final port of discharge if with cargo or at port of destination if in ballast. This insurance shall not inure to the benefit of any such charterer or transferee of the Vessel, and if a loss payable hereunder should occur between such transfer and such cancellation the Underwriters shall be subrogated to all the rights of the Assured against the transferee, by reason of such transfer, in respect of all or part of such loss as is recoverable from the transferee and in the proportion which the respective amounts insured bear to the insured value. A pro rata daily return of net premium shall be made. The foregoing provisions with respect to cancellation in the event of change in ownership or management, charter or requisition shall apply even in the case of insurance "for account of whom it may concern."

Valuation. Determination of the valuation at which a vessel should be insured is not easy, owing to the various factors that affect the value. The amount should be fixed at the point where the owner will be fully reimbursed in event of total loss but will have no inducement to compass the destruction of his vessel in order to procure the insured value. The value of a vessel is sometimes thought of as the total present value of all the *net* freight that the vessel can earn during the ordinary period of such a vessel's usefulness plus its breakup value at the end of the period. This estimated value will vary from time to time as freight rates increase or decrease with the demand for tonnage. Other considerations, such as the increased cost of replacing a vessel at the time of renewing the insurance, her increased earning power during a period of high freights, or generally supply and demand, are determining factors in fixing the value of the vessel. During a period of one year the whole freight-rate and vessel situation may change, and a fair value at the inception of the policy based on the then-existing conditions may, before the policy expires, produce a situation that will tempt an unscrupulous owner to cast away his vessel.

Valuation Should Be Reasonable. To the underwriter who is issuing full-form insurance, that is, writing a policy covering particular-average losses as well as general-average and total loss, the valuation is vital, because his liability for partial loss is fixed by the percentage of the total value that he insures. If he does not insist on a reasonable value and prevent, by agreement, the placing of an undue proportion of the value against total-loss, general-average, and salvage charges, he will, in the event of partial loss, find that he is charged with an unreasonable amount as his share of the repair bills. In order to protect underwriters in this respect, it is usually warranted that only a stipulated percentage of the full value of the vessel may be placed under limited-form insurance. Reference has already been made to the custom of separating the total value into parts, one applying to the hull and its fittings and another to the machinery. In some cases, hull values are further divided into hull and cabin outfit, while the machinery value may be separated, in the case of refrigerated vessels, into propelling and refrigerating machinery. In the case of high-valued vessels there is sometimes insufficient insurance available in all the markets of the world to provide protection equal to the cost of the vessel. The device of determining the available insurance and making this amount the value of the vessel for insurance purposes has been adopted. This insurance is issued on a full form so that up to the total amount of the insurance the owner is covered against particular- and general-average losses and against total loss. The excess values in such cases may be assumed by the government, which usually has a financial interest in these large vessels. The insurance markets of the world are growing very fast, so that there are few vessels for which full commercial insurance is not available.

Dual-valuation Clauses. The *dual-valuation* clause provides for one value of the vessel with respect to the total- and/or constructive-total-loss claims and another, higher value with respect to all other losses covered by the policy. This clause in its customary form reads as follows:

(a) Insured value for total and/or constructive total loss purposes $............

(b) Insured value for purposes other than total and/or constructive total loss $............

In ascertaining whether the vessel is a Constructive Total Loss (a) shall be taken as the repaired value and nothing in respect of the damaged or break-up value of the vessel or wreck shall be taken into account.

In case of claim for total or constructive total loss (a) shall be taken to be the insured value and payment by the Underwriters of their proportions of that amount shall be for all purposes payment of a Total Loss.

Claims for unrepaired damage, even though otherwise recoverable hereunder, shall be disallowed hereunder to the extent that the allowance thereof would increase a particular average claim beyond the amount which would be recoverable hereunder for actual total loss; but this provision shall not affect or limit the liability of underwriters for sums which the assured has paid or is liable to pay by way of salvage, general average, sue and labor expenses or under the Collision Clause.

Warranted no Insurance on Disbursements or other total loss interests.

This form of clause serves a twofold purpose. First, the underwriter is assured that adequate insurance on full form will be taken by the owner so as to distribute properly the relatively high cost of repairs on a vessel that, because of age or inferior type, has a market value considerably less than the agreed value in the policy. Second, the protection afforded against total loss, the smaller of the dual values, is in relative agreement with the market value of the vessel, so that no improper inducement is offered the owner to cast away his vessel. Sometimes this form of clause is desired by the assured to enable him to place total-loss and excess-value insurance to a larger amount than would ordinarily be permitted under the usual hull clauses. This form of placing hull risks will be requested by hull owners only when a saving in premium results, the dual-valuation clause form of policy usually carrying a lower over-all rate of premium owing to the decreased liability for total losses. This latter use of the dual-valuation clause is naturally not encouraged by underwriters and will be granted only under exceptional circumstances.

The dual-valuation clause was in common use in the insurance of the war-built tonnage sold by the United States government after

World War II. Liberty and Victory ships particularly, which had been produced in very large numbers, were sold at a fraction of their replacement cost. In event of accident the cost of repairs would be very high, but if the vessel were a total loss, the owner would be fully reimbursed if he received his purchase price. Accordingly, the value for total-loss purposes under part (*a*) was approximately the purchase price, but for particular- and general-average claims under part (*b*) a much higher amount was used, which would enable the underwriter, without making the rate too high, to obtain a premium commensurate with the high cost of repairs.

Trading Warranties. The *trading warranties* are also of very great importance in the insurance of hulls. Vessels when built are usually designed for some specific service, such as lake trade, coastwise trade, or ocean service. If they are used out of these trades, weakness may develop, resulting in serious losses. Accordingly, when issuing policies, underwriters by express warranty definitely indicate the geographical limits within which the vessel may operate. These warranties range all the way from clauses limiting a vessel to service in a named port or along a limited strip of coast line to world-wide limits permitting trade on any of the seven seas. In policies insuring vessels operating on the Great Lakes and in certain other localities, a further trading warranty as to time is inserted, confining active operation to the open season of navigation.

Institute Warranties. The trading warranties in most general use are the Institute warranties (promulgated by the American Institute of Marine Underwriters) which permit practically world-wide trading. Vessels are, however, prohibited from entering certain areas such as Greenland waters and the Atlantic Coast of North America north of 43 degrees north latitude, except Halifax and two named bunkering ports. Likewise trading is prohibited on the Pacific Coast of North America north of 50 degrees north latitude, with the exception of Vancouver Island and Prince Rupert via Dixon Strait. Trading is not permitted to the Baltic Sea between November 1 and May 20, or to northern Russia or the Behring Sea or east Asian waters north of 46 degrees north latitude, except the port of Vladivostok. The clauses are rather long, but the exceptions relate to trade in the Arctic or Antarctic areas, where navigation is extremely hazardous, and provide that Indian coal and Polish coal shall not be carried on certain vessels during certain times of the year, since this type of coal is apt to heat during the voyage. By the payment of additional premium underwriters may be induced to waive certain of these warranties and permit navigation to these hazardous areas.

Loading Warranties. Loading warranties are not uncommon in hull policies. An old New York form used for sailing-vessel risks prohibits the vessel from loading more than her registered under-deck capacity with lead, marble, coal, or iron on any one passage and also warrants that the vessel will not use any of the Guano Islands or load lime under deck. These loading warranties are inserted because the cargo named is heavy and an undue quantity will imperil the safety of the vessel, because the commodity, as in the case of lime, is dangerous in its own nature, or because of serious navigation hazards, as at the Guano Islands.

Purpose of Warranties. Trading or loading warranties may be made in any form, but the object the underwriter has in mind in inserting them is to prevent the vessel proceeding, under the form of policy issued and at the rate charged, to other trades than that for which charge was made or for which the vessel is suited. The rate of premium depends in large measure on the trading warranties required. It is usually cheaper for the assured to restrict the trading warranties, obtaining a low basic rate, and then, if it becomes necessary to send the vessel out of these warranties, to obtain the underwriter's assent to such extended service by the payment of an additional premium.

Average Clauses. Average clauses in hull policies are usually either in the minimum-franchise form or in the deductible-average form. Insurance being an important item in the cost of operating a vessel, the assured seeks to obtain protection at the lowest possible cost. If his experience with respect to partial loss has been favorable, he may decide to assume small partial losses and thus obtain a reduced rate. It is therefore quite common to find in hull policies deductible-average clauses. The deductible franchise will vary from $500, as in the case of the Standard Lake Hull insurance form to several hundred thousand dollars, as in the case of some of the huge trans-Atlantic liners for which the procurement of full coverage is a difficult matter owing to the fact that their great value may exhaust the world's insurance market. Special inducement has to be offered to entice underwriters to write large lines, and the large deductible-average franchise is one of the baits offered.

Three Per Cent Average Clause. As a rule, the minimum-franchise form of average clause is used in hull policies, the franchise applying, in the case of steamers or motor vessels, to each valuation separately or to the whole value. The franchise is usually fixed at 3 or 5 per cent, but this percentage applied to a high value produces such a large sum as a minimum claim under the policy that the minimum amount in dollars is inserted, such as $4,850. In the Syndicate form both the percentage and the dollar amount are in the franchise clause, but the lesser amount that will permit a claim is used, as is indicated in the specimen adjustment on page 386.

Thirds off. The separate valuation clause contains the expression, "without deduction of thirds, new for old," which refers to one of the common principles of hull underwriting. This principle came into operation in the days of wooden ships and was based on the theory that in case of repairs to a vessel the new material supplied left the vessel in better condition than before the accident and that the underwriter should not, therefore, bear the whole burden of repair. That this theory was sound in the case of a vessel which had been in service for some time there can be no doubt, but in the case of new vessels meeting with disaster it is difficult to establish that the repaired vessel is a better one than it was before the disaster. Because it was impracticable to treat each case on its merits, an arbitrary percentage of deduction was adopted, and the *thirds-off* clause came into use. With the introduction of metal as a medium for the construction of vessels, it was still more difficult to prove that the new metal, inserted to replace the old, resulted in any improvement in the vessel, and the custom has grown of waiving this stipulation, or at least waiving it with respect to the steel or iron portions of the vessel.

Modified Thirds-off Clause. That the doctrine of the deduction of thirds is right in principle there can be no doubt, but that the arbitrary adoption of a fixed rate of deduction in all cases works a hardship on the assured is equally true. Many modifications of the thirds-off clause have been made, each intended to fix a scale of deductions that would be more equitable to the assured. In some of these clauses there is a sliding scale of deduction, the amount gradually increasing with the age of the vessel. This is especially true with respect to the yellow metaling on the hull of wooden vessels. The doctrine of *thirds off* is also applied in the settling of general-average losses with respect to damage suffered by the vessel. Here again, sliding scales of deductions have been adopted in order to arrive as nearly as possible at a fair basis for the settlement for all cases.

Machinery Claims. For many years after the introduction of steam engines as the motive power of vessels, it was doubtful whether the general words in the policy form reading "and all other like perils, losses, misfortunes, that have or shall come to the hurt, detriment or damage of the said vessel, or any part thereof" would include losses caused by the bursting of boilers or other losses occasioned through accident to the machinery of the vessel. To settle the point definitely, a test case with respect to the breakage of the air chamber of a pump operated by a donkey engine on the steamer *Inchmaree,* through the apparent negligence of the crew, was taken up to the House of Lords in England. After careful consideration of the facts in this case and of the conflicting decisions rendered in similar cases, they unanimously decided that such loss was not occasioned by a cause of the same nature as a peril of the sea and held that the underwriters were not liable. Following this decision, in order to protect shipowners against loss by casualties of this nature, the *Inchmaree clause* or *negligence clause* was introduced into hull policies. The clause as used in the Syndicate form follows:

This insurance also specially to cover (subject to the Average Warranty) loss of or damage to the subject matter insured directly caused by the following:

Accidents in loading, discharging or handling cargo, or in bunkering;

Accidents in going on or off, or while on drydocks, graving docks, ways, gridirons or pontoons;

Explosions on shipboard or elsewhere;

Breakdown of motor generators, or other electrical machinery and electrical connections thereto, bursting of boilers, breakage of shafts, or any latent defect in the machinery or hull, (excluding the cost and expense of replacing or repairing the defective part);

Contact with Aircraft or with any land conveyance;
Negligence of Master, Charterers other than an Assured, Mariners, Engineers or Pilots;
Provided such loss or damage has not resulted from want of due diligence by the Assured, the Owners or Managers of the Vessel, or any of them. Masters, Mates, Engineers, Pilots or Crew not to be considered as part owners within the meaning of this clause should they hold shares in the Vessel.

The *Inchmaree* clause appears in hull policies insuring vessels propelled by mechanical power and has the effect of adding new perils to those already enumerated in the printed policy. Up to 1928, the clause did not contain the words reading "Excluding, however, the cost and expense of replacing or repairing the defective part," and although the language seemed clear, there was considerable doubt as to the meaning of the clause, particularly with respect to that portion relating to latent defect. The framers of the original clause had no intention of including indemnity for the part containing the latent defect, but only for the damages resulting from the action of the imperfect part. Many adjustments were made, including the cost of replacing the defective part, and many underwriters, eager to appear liberal in their settlements, paid according to these adjustments. A number of law cases establish the principle that the clause does not provide reimbursement for the defective part.

Collision Liability. Incorporated in most hull policies is the *collision or running-down clause*, which, in reality, is a separate liability insurance. The perils clause in the policy takes care of physical losses sustained by the insured vessel through collisions. There may be, however, liability for the damage sustained by the vessel with which the insured vessel has collided or by its cargo or by the passengers or crew of this vessel. It is this liability which is covered by the collision or running-down clause. Under the law a vessel, if negligently colliding with another vessel, is liable for the resultant damage caused to the other vessel or its cargo and for loss of life or personal injury if occasioned by such negligence. This liability also extends to damage to piers, harbor walls, breakwaters, or other objects with which a vessel may negligently come into violent contact. There are various forms of collision clauses; the form in general use[1] affords protection against the liability for physical injury to another ship, its freight and cargo

[1] See Syndicate hull form, Appendix F.

and for demurrage due to its owner for the time he is deprived of the use of his vessel, but only to the extent of the amount insured under the policy. The underwriter, however, assumes no liability for injury to harbors, wharves, piers, stages, or other similar structures; for the removal of obstructions to navigation caused by the collision; or for loss of life or personal injury. The clause also excludes liability for loss of the cargo or the freight engagements of the insured vessel. The necessity of limiting liability to the proportion of the insured value that the underwriter assumes, not exceeding the face amount of the policy, is due to the fact that there is no limit to the liability of the vessel owner for losses due to negligence, all his property being subject to attachment unless he invokes the law and obtains a limitation of liability to the value of the offending vessel in her condition after the accident. This limitation will be granted by the admiralty courts if it can be established that the owner personally is free from contributory negligence. This is usually so in collision cases, the negligence being due to the master, mariners, or pilot. In the United States, the law permits a limitation of liability to the value of the offending vessel after the collision, to which is added the freight earned on the passage, unless there is loss of life or bodily injury, in which event the limitation may not be less than $60 per gross ton on seagoing vessels with respect to such claims. If the vessel is worth more than the claims against it, the owners will keep the vessel and pay the damages; if the claims exceed the value of the vessel, the owners will probably abandon the vessel to the claimants. In Great Britain the limitation of liability is fixed by law at £8 per gross ton in the event of property damage or at £7 per ton additional if there is loss of life or personal injury. These sums are fixed standards whether the ship is an old wooden sailing vessel or a new high-speed ocean greyhound and apply regardless of the real value of the vessel per ton.

Legal Expenses in Collision Cases. Under the collision clause underwriters agree to meet their respective proportions of the legal expenses in connection with the determination of the liability of the assured. Provision is also made for the settlement of losses, if it should be decided that both vessels are to blame for the collision, on the principle of cross liabilities in order to avoid a multiplicity of financial transactions. Owing to the fact that many vessels may be the property of a single owner and two of these vessels may come into collision, the clause provides that the fact of common ownership shall be disregarded and settlement made as if the vessels were separately owned. Provision is also made for adjustment of the liability under this clause by arbitration. The owners appoint one arbitrator, the underwriters a second, and these two arbitrators appoint a third before entering upon their conference, the decision of this arbitrator or of any two of the arbitrators to be binding on all concerned.

Club Insurance. The policy in its ordinary form does not afford protection against the liability of a vessel owner for damage to the cargo in his possession, due to negligence, or for injury to persons through acts of the owner or his agents. Neither does it provide protection against the liability, modified by exemption clauses, with which the owners are charged under the bill of lading. These liabilities being a serious matter for vessel owners, they have formed mutual protective associations which assume them, each owner entering his vessels in the association and paying a fixed rate per ton for the protection. The associations are sometimes called clubs and such insurance is commonly called club insurance. They have been established for many years in Great Britain. A mutual protective association of shipowners also operates in the United States, although much of the *protection-and-indemnity insurance*, as it is called, is written in the United States by marine-insurance companies.

Protection-and-indemnity Clause. The establishment of these clubs has a direct bearing on the ordinary form of marine insurance. It was formerly the custom for underwriters to assume under the collision clause only three-fourths of the collision liability and to assume none whatever for loss of life or personal injury; for damage to harbors, docks, piers; for damage to goods on board the vessel; or for any other liability imposed on the owner by law. This was done on the theory that leaving one-quarter of the collision liability with the owner would make him more diligent in seeing that his vessel was carefully navigated and that the other liabilities were not such risks as a marine underwriter should assume, because freeing the owners from these liabilities would result in less careful operation of vessels. The acceptance of these risks by the clubs, however, removed all the supposed advantages of leaving them with the owners, with the result that underwriters were willing to assume them. The three-quarters limitation is now usually omitted from the collision clause, and the other liabilities assumed by the clubs are sometimes insured by underwriters under protection-and-indemnity clauses. In many cases, however, these risks are, as a matter of economy, left with the clubs, this form of insurance being relatively inexpensive, although the members are subject to assessment. Some owners prefer to have all their liability covered under a single policy, and the protection-and-indemnity (P and I) clause will in such cases be inserted in the policy. This is the common practice in the insurance of river, harbor, and other small vessels. The usual practice with respect to ocean-going vessels is to insure the protection-and-indemnity risks separately, either in the clubs or with the marine-insurance companies.[1]

Cancellation and Lay-up Return Premiums. Reference has been made to the basic principle of marine underwriting that, the policy having attached, the premium is earned, regardless of the fact that through some unforeseen event, either transfer of ownership or loss of the vessel through a peril not insured against, the owner is divested of his property before the conclusion of the policy term, thus relieving the underwriter of a portion of his risk. Hull insurance being written as a rule for a period of a year, the strict enforcement of this rule in the case of sale of a vessel might work a hardship. Accordingly, it is customary to provide for the cancellation of the policy by mutual agreement, return of premium being made at a fixed rate for each uncommenced month. It also happens in many cases that vessels will be laid up for repairs or without employment for considerable periods. The rate charged is based on a vessel in navigation, whereas during the period of repair or nonemployment the vessel is in port exposed to a minimum of risk. Provision is therefore made for the payment of a return premium at a fixed rate for each consecutive period of 15 or 30 days the vessel may be laid up. A vessel is laid up only when it is out of commission and not engaged in the ordinary course of its employment. That is, a vessel cannot be considered as laid up when, because of the congested condition of a port, it remains in the harbor for a long period in order to discharge incoming cargo or to load outgoing shipments. Furthermore, the return is not allowed if the vessel is lying unemployed in a roadstead or in exposed and unprotected waters. Claims for lay-up returns are sometimes made under these

[1] For further discussion of protection-and-indemnity insurance, see p. 306.

circumstances, and careful scrutiny of them is always necessary. Lay-up claims should not be allowed when the lay-up is caused by repairs that are at the expense of the underwriters. Provision is made in many lay-up forms that no return premium shall be allowed if the vessel is under average, that is, if it is in a damaged condition. Lay-up indicates a voluntary act of the vessel owner by which he takes his vessel out of commission because of lack of demand for tonnage, the close of the navigation season, or overhauling. When a vessel is forced out of commission by casualty, it is not laid up, and the underwriter should not be called upon to pay a return of premium under the lay-up clause. The Syndicate form provides for various kinds of lay-up with varying return premiums, as follows:

In event of non-payment of premium thirty days after attachment this Policy may be cancelled by the Underwriters upon five days written notice being given the Assured. Such proportion of the premium, however, as shall have been earned up to the time of such cancellation shall be due and payable; but in the event of Total or Constructive Total Loss occurring prior to cancellation full annual premium shall be deemed earned.

To return { cents per cent. net for each uncommenced month if it be mutually agreed to cancel this Policy.

As follows for each consecutive 30 days the Vessel may be laid up in port, viz:—

	Without Cargo on Board	With Cargo on Board
1. Under repair	¢% net	¢% net
2. Not under repair	¢% net	¢% net

For the purpose of this clause a Vessel loading or discharging cargo shall be considered as "with cargo on board."

Provided always: (a) that in no case shall a return be allowed when the within named Vessel is lying in a roadstead or in exposed and unprotected waters.

(b) that in the event of a return for special trade, or any other reason, being recoverable, the above rates of return of premium shall be reduced accordingly. } and arrival

In the event of the Vessel being laid up in port for a period of 30 consecutive days, a part only of which attaches to this Policy, it is hereby agreed that the laying up period, in which either the commencing or ending date of this Policy falls, shall be deemed to run from the first day on which the Vessel is laid up and that on this basis Underwriters shall pay such proportion of the return due in respect of a full period of 30 days as the number of days attaching thereto bear to thirty.

Hull forms used in the insurance of Great Lakes vessels and yachts warrant that the vessel will be laid up during certain times of the year, winter, for instance, on the Great Lakes. The rates are predicated on this warranty, and no return of premium is made.

"And Arrival." The usual form of clause providing for lay-up and cancellation returns ends with the words "and arrival." The words appear to be meaningless, and it would seem that an expression covering the point intended could have been devised that would have been intelligible to the lay mind. Since the premium is earned when the policy attaches, destruction of the vessel before the expiration of the policy term will not give the assured the right to claim return premium for the unexpired time. The expression "and arrival" is a restatement of this principle. It means that, at the time of mutual cancellation or at the expiration of the policy term with respect to lay-up return-premium claims, the vessel must have been in existence and in good safety. Return premium will not be paid if the vessel has been lost or is missing. Lay-up returns are not claimable until after the expiration of the policy, and if the conditions of "and arrival" are fulfilled at the end of the policy term, the mere fact of the subsequent loss of the vessel will, of course, in no way affect the claim for lay-up return premium.

Extension into Port. A clause is usually found in hull policies providing that, if the vessel is at sea upon the expiration of the policy term, the policy may be extended at a prorata monthly premium until arrival in good safety at her port of destination or at the first port of call, provided request for such extension be made prior to the expiration of the policy. A similar privilege should always be granted for extending the policy to the port of destination if the vessel is in distress, at a port of refuge, or at a port of call, the underlying idea in each case being to relieve the assured from the burden of arranging new insurance when the vessel is at sea or when it is in a disabled or damaged condition.

General Average. Reference is frequently made in hull policies to general average, provision being made that these charges as well as salvage charges shall be payable in accordance with the York-Antwerp Rules if so provided in the contract of affreightment. It is also provided that, in cases where these rules do not apply, adjustment shall be made in accordance with the laws of the United States. The York-Antwerp Rules are considered in connection with the subject of general average.[1]

Total-loss-only Insurance. It is not unusual for owners, through desire or from necessity, to insure vessels on the *total-loss-only* form. This form is frequently used in the insurance of vessels that, because of their condition, cannot be written at favorable rates on full-cover form. In some cases this form of protection is broadened to include general-average and salvage charges in addition to total and constructive total losses. When the value of vessels is high, difficulty may be experienced in obtaining sufficient full-cover insurance, and the final lines are accordingly placed on the total-loss-only form. However, in order that the use of such insurance shall not be abused at the expense of the full-form underwriters, clauses have been devised limiting the percentage of the total amount which may be placed on this form. In some cases, owing to very high values, these warranties are waived, and a larger percentage of total-loss-only insurance is permitted.

Disbursements. Disbursements originally meant money that the master of a vessel spent during the voyage to pay charges incurred because of disaster or otherwise. The word is still used in this sense. However, it is customary today to think of disbursements, or, more properly, *disbursements insurance,* as part of the insurance placed by the hull owner on his vessel in an amount over and above the valuation to which he has agreed in the full-form policy. Formerly there was no limitation on the amount that could be insured on disbursements. It was not unusual for an owner, desirous of getting a good "lead"[2] on his risk, to offer an underwriter who would quote a

[1] See Chap. 25.

[2] When an underwriter who specializes in a class of business or who has a high reputation as a successful underwriter is willing to be the first one to sign for a share of a risk, he is said to "give a lead."

relatively low rate on a small amount of the full-form insurance a large line of disbursements insurance at a high rate. With this lead the owner might be able to place his full-form insurance at a relatively low cost. The underwriter granting the lead would be well paid, as his relatively small line of full-form insurance at the low rate, plus his larger line of disbursements at the relatively high rate, would average at a very attractive rate of premium. Disbursements insurance, being on an intangible interest, the value of the vessel having been agreed to in the hull policy, is placed with the proviso that the "policy is proof of interest" and/or "full interest admitted," commonly called *P.P.I.* and *F.I.A.* insurance. By the use of these words the underwriter is barred from alleging that no insurable interest existed.[1]

Port-risk Insurance. When vessels are laid up in port for long periods of time undergoing repairs or reconstruction or without employment, it is usual to place insurance on a port-risk-only form. Under this form of policy the assured often warrants that the vessel is laid up and out of commission and that it will be confined during the terms of the policy to the limits of the port described. Privilege is granted for the vessel to change docks or to go on dry dock in order to make repairs or alterations. The collision clause and the *Inchmaree* clause are usually incorporated, and it is sometimes agreed that average will be payable without reference to percentage; that is, the average clause does not require that any fixed franchise be attained to make a claim under the policy. As there are no navigation hazards in connection with port-risk insurance, except during docking and changing docks, the rate of premium is low. It is charged on a monthly basis or at an annual rate, usually subject to cancellation in accordance with the short-rate tables. These tables provide for a premium charge for the actual time at risk which is calculated, not as a prorata portion of the annual rate, but as a fixed percentage of the annual rate. The short rate is always higher than the prorata charge for the same period.

[1] In the disbursements section of the Syndicate policy on p. 286 the limitations now enforced for the use of such insurance are set forth in detail.

CHAPTER 17

Special Hull Forms

LARGE VESSELS

Special forms are widely used in hull insurance. They are not peculiar to any one company but have been formulated by underwriters' organizations and adopted by the individual companies in the issuance of their policies. The best talent in the underwriting field has lent its aid in the construction of these forms, and the primary idea underlying all has been to offer to the vessel owner the most complete protection consistent with conservative underwriting. As new situations develop, requiring a broadened form of protection, or underwriting experience suggests a more restricted form of policy, these forms are amended. Previously, the use of many different forms in hull underwriting had led to confusion and difficulty in making adjustments of loss. In cargo insurance, except with very large accounts, one underwriter will assume the whole risk, reducing his line if he considers it necessary by the procurement of reinsurance. In hull underwriting it has always been customary to have several underwriters on a single risk, hence the desirability of uniformity among the policies issued by the different underwriters.

Work of the Hull Associations. The former American Hull Underwriters' Association stood in the forefront in endeavoring to procure uniform standards of hull insurance and promulgated forms that are now in general use in this country. Working in close harmony with similar associations on the Pacific Coast and in Great Britain, forms were drawn up that were practically standard in all the underwriting markets of the world. Forms for steamer risks, port risks, and builder's risks were recommended by this organization. Similar associations, such as the Atlantic Inland Association, promulgated marine forms for the insurance of vessels navigating inland waterways. Associations of underwriters primarily interested in the insurance of sailing craft, such as the Provincial Schooner Association, issued forms especially adapted to that branch of underwriting, and forms especially designed for insurance of vessels on the Great Lakes are in common use.

Marine-insurance Syndicates. In 1921, at the request of the United States government, the American Marine Insurance Syndicates were formed. They were three in number, Syndicates A, B, and C. Syndicates B and C were underwriting organizations, while Syndicate A was a service association whose purpose was to inspect the hulls of vessels to determine whether they were kept in seaworthy condition. These Syndicates were formed as part of the program of the government for the rehabilitation of the American merchant marine. Their part in this program was to furnish an adequate marine-insurance facility for the protection of the merchant vessels sold by the government to private operators. Syndicate B provided insurance in American companies for the mortgaged interest in these vessels, while Syndicate C, composed of both domestic companies and alien companies licensed to do marine underwriting in the United States, provided an insurance facility for the insurance of the equity of the purchaser in the vessel and also for the insurance of iron or steel, mechanically propelled, ocean steamers flying the American flag. Syndicate A has been merged into a new organization, the United States Salvage Association, Inc., which provides for carrying on more extensively the work originally planned for Syndicate A. It has representatives at the important domestic and foreign ports competent to survey vessels and make reports thereon to the underwriters. The form of organization also contemplates doing salvage work, although this side of its activities has not been developed.

The Hull Syndicate. Owing to the cooperative efforts of the marine-insurance companies in the United States and the friendly attitude of the government, there had developed under the auspices of the Syndicates a substantial American hull-insurance market. It appeared wise to review the Articles of Incorporation. Syndicate B was no longer active; the hull market was Syndicate C. Accordingly, in 1943 a new syndicate, the American Marine Hull Insurance

Syndicate, came into existence and is now the American insurance market not only for American-owned ocean tonnage under the American flag or other flags but also for foreign-flag, foreign-owned ocean tonnage. In short, it has developed into an international market place for the insurance of ocean-going hulls.

Other syndicates under the same general management for the insurance of builder's risks, lake hulls, and tugboats were later organized and provide a facility sufficient to care for the insurance of such vessels. The membership in all syndicates is not the same, some companies underwriting independently in certain fields.

With the advent of the Syndicates, the need for the American Hull Underwriters' Association passed, and it was disbanded. The forms sponsored by this organization were adopted with minor changes by the Syndicates, which brought out the Syndicate forms for the insurance of hulls, disbursements, port risks, and builder's risks. The American Institute of Marine Underwriters now gives its approval to various forms of policies and endorsements to policies, for both hull and cargo insurance. These forms receive recognition both in the United States and abroad.

Basis of All Policies the Same. Although the forms of the various underwriters' organizations retain as their basis the old skeleton policy, particularly the clause enumerating the perils insured against, special clauses are incorporated dealing with conditions that are peculiar to hull insurance of the particular kind for which the form is used. In designing new forms there is always the danger of weakening the entire policy by the introduction of clauses ambiguous enough to permit of court interpretations foreign to the intention of the underwriters or that may undermine the whole basic fabric of the policy.

Rates of Premium. On application by owners or insurance brokers, organizations promulgate rates of premium for the insurance of vessels. None of these underwriters' organizations, except the Syndicates, are underwriting bodies, the rates indicated being merely suggestive and not binding on the members. The Syndicates, however, do underwriting through their elected manager under the advice and guidance of the underwriting committee chosen by the member companies. This committee consults with the manager as to the amount that the Syndicate should write on a submitted risk and the rate. This the manager quotes and, if the quotation is accepted, binds the risk, thus obligating each member company of the Syndicate to its agreed prorata share of the amount bound. A single policy showing the names of the member companies and the percentage assumed by each is then issued. The liability of the member companies is several and not joint. In other words, if a member should default, the other members are not legally obligated to make good his share of the policy.

The Making of the Rate. The cost of insurance is expressed in terms of rate per cent. The total-loss risk and the risk involved in insuring excess liabilities under disbursements policies are determined by experience figures showing the total losses and excess general-average and salvage charges paid over a period of years. The incidence of such losses is not the same over all routes. Furthermore, some fleets have much better records over a long period of time, with respect to total loss and major casualties, than do other fleets. Nevertheless the variation in the total-loss and excess-liabilities rates is confined within comparatively narrow limits. The real variation in rate is caused by the record of a vessel or a fleet with respect to particular-average losses. Some fleets have many casualties of a more or less serious nature, while with other fleets casualties are the exception. The underwriter must obtain sufficient premium to pay for losses, both total and partial. The premium must be sufficient to pay the acquisition cost, principally the broker's or agent's commission. It must provide for the company's expense of doing business (overhead) and leave a reasonable profit. (See statistics, pages 436, 437.)

The underwriter determines from his records the amount that he has paid in losses or has estimated he will have to pay on losses that have occurred but that have not been finally adjusted and subtracts any amounts paid for total losses. The resultant sum is divided by the gross tonnage of the vessel, and the loss cost per ton is thus determined. The amount that the owner wishes to insure under full form being known, the insured value per gross ton is determined by dividing this amount by the gross tonnage. Two like figures are now before the underwriter—the insured value per ton desired and the loss cost per ton. The first divided by the second will determine the rate of premium necessary to produce the necessary dollars to pay for losses other than total loss. To this rate is added the acquisition cost, the overhead cost, the allowance for normal profit, and the total-loss rate that already includes these extra items. The sum of these items is the rate for the full-form insurance.

In order to reduce his insurance costs or to persuade the underwriter to insure the risk, notwithstanding a bad loss record, the owner may offer to take a policy containing a deductible-franchise clause for, say, $10,000 each accident. If interested, the underwriter will then examine the loss record to determine how much of the previous claims would have been avoided if this deductible franchise had been in the previous policies. If the resultant figure induces him to consider insuring the risk, he will apply the foregoing method of determining the loss cost and quote a rate.

It must be realized that this explanation of hull rate making is an oversimplification of a difficult subject, but it may give the reader some idea of the many problems of rate making.

The Syndicate Form. As most of the hull insurance on ocean-going vessels is written in the American Marine Hull Insurance Syndicate, its form of policy, known as the "Syndicate form," is most commonly used. It is similar to the American Institute Time (Hulls) form used in general by the companies on ocean hull risks accepted outside the Syndicate. All policy forms, particularly those used for special purposes, are revised from time to time. Usually the changes are made for purposes of clarification after experience has indicated that the intent of a clause or clauses is not clear. At times changes are required to meet situations that arise from new court interpretations. The Syndicate and American Institute forms for ocean vessels have been examined recently and revised, largely to clarify certain clauses which experience indicated were not free of ambiguity. It is strongly urged that the student reading this chapter and the previous chapter take time to familiarize himself with the terms of the Syndicate form appearing in Appendix F, which includes the recent changes. As the Syndicate and ocean hull policy forms are in effect the same, the comments on some of the provisions of the Syndicate form which follow will apply equally to the Institute form.

In general, the Syndicate form follows the basic principles of marine underwriting discussed in the previous chapters but contains some special clauses. The format of the policy differs somewhat from the ordinary hull policy in order to provide for Syndicate underwriting. The usual arrangement of the clauses has been altered in part, so that the document can be more easily read. Following the name of the assured and before naming the payee of loss, the important change-of-ownership clause appears. Then come the time limits, the separate valuations, the rate of premium, and the provisions for the return of premium on cancellation of the policy or laying up of the vessel. The *adventure clause*, which, in the earlier hull forms, gave the vessel liberty to "proceed and sail to, touch and stay at any ports or places," etc., has been broadened to permit the vessel to do practically anything that a vessel could or would do, either in the ordinary course of the voyage or while in port or under repair.

Warranties. A series of warranties follows, the first being the trading warranties. To enable the assurers to be represented at surveys held to determine damage in the event of accident, and to provide that tenders may be received from bidders offering to repair the damage ascertained, a warranty provides that a penalty shall be applied if the owners fail to notify the underwriters of damage surveys or fail to take tenders *if so requested by the assurers.*

Disbursements Warranty. Insurance afforded by a policy on hull covering partial losses, total losses, and general-average and salvage charges is full-form insurance. The desirability of full-form underwriters restricting as far as possible the amount of insurance placed over and above the full-form insurance has been indicated. To ensure that this restriction shall be effective, hull policies generally contain a disbursements warranty. This warranty, although expressed in varying forms, has one primary purpose, namely, to require the assured to place under full-form insurance such a proportion of the total insurance desired that the excess amounts insured as disbursements, commissions or similar interests, freights, increased value, etc., shall not exceed a named percentage, usually 25 per cent of the full-form value. As many of these interests are intangible and not easily determinable, they are usually insured on P.P.I. (policy proof of interest) and F.I.A. (full interest admitted) conditions. The underwriter in granting insurance on these conditions agrees with the assured that the mere existence of the policy proves the interest and that between them, as far as the policy is concerned, the full interest of the assured to the extent of the amount of the policy is admitted. The disbursements warranty usually permits the assured to place over and above the agreed percentage additional amounts to cover actual freight interests at risk. It would be unfair for underwriters to try to prevent the insurance of a valid freight interest. However, provision is made that as the freight is earned the insurance on this interest is correspondingly reduced to a stated minimum. The explanation of the various freight interests will be left for a later chapter;[1] it will suffice for the present to state that freight is the money which the owner or operator receives either under charter or under bill of lading for the use of his vessel. A similar exception is made in the warranty in relation to premiums. These, too, being a valid insurable interest, underwriters could not, if they would, prevent their full insurance. This entire clause is aimed, not at the insurance of valid interests arising out of the ownership of vessel property, but at the practice of endeavoring to obtain cheap insurance by placing an undue portion of the value of a vessel under P.P.I. conditions at the comparatively low rate prevailing for this form of insurance. The lower the value in the full-form policy in relation to the true value of the vessel, the greater will be the percentage of loss in the event of a particular-average claim. Therefore, as the full-form value is lowered, the premium should be correspondingly increased, since the particular-average claims (not exceeding the insured value) will all fall on the full-form underwriters.

Syndicate Disbursements Warranty. In the revised Syndicate policy the disbursements warranty has been rewritten and appears in a new and greatly clarified form and reads as follows:

Additional insurances as follows are permitted:—

(a) DISBURSEMENTS, MANAGERS' COMMISSIONS, PROFITS OR EXCESS OR INCREASED VALUE OF HULL AND MACHINERY, AND/OR SIMILAR INTERESTS HOWEVER DESCRIBED, AND FREIGHT (INCLUDING CHARTERED FREIGHT OR ANTICIPATED FREIGHT) INSURED FOR TIME. A sum not exceeding in the aggregate 25% of the insured value of the Vessel.

(b) FREIGHT OR HIRE, UNDER CONTRACTS FOR VOYAGE. A sum not exceeding

[1] See Chap. 19.

the gross freight or hire for the current cargo passage and next succeeding cargo passage (such insurance to include, if required, a preliminary and an intermediate ballast passage) plus the charges of insurance. In the case of a voyage charter where payment is made on a time basis, the sum permitted for insurance shall be calculated on the estimated duration of the voyage, subject to the limitation of two cargo passages as laid down herein. Any sum insured under this Section shall be reduced as the freight or hire is earned by the gross amount so earned.

(c) ANTICIPATED FREIGHT IF THE VESSEL SAILS IN BALLAST AND NOT UNDER CHARTER. A sum not exceeding the anticipated gross freight on next cargo passage, such sum to be reasonably estimated on the basis of the current rate of freight at time of insurance, plus the charges of insurance. Provided, however, that no insurance shall be permitted under this Section if any insurance is effected under Section (b).

(d) TIME CHARTER HIRE OR CHARTER HIRE FOR SERIES OF VOYAGES. A sum not exceeding 50% of the gross hire which is to be earned under the charter in a period not exceeding 18 months. Any sum insured under this Section shall be reduced as the hire is earned under the charter by 50% of the gross amount so earned but where the charter is for a period exceeding 18 months the sum insured need not be reduced while it does not exceed 50% of the gross hire still to be earned under the charter. An insurance under this Section may begin on the signing of the charter.

(e) PREMIUMS. A sum not exceeding the actual premiums of all interests insured for a period not exceeding 12 months (excluding premiums insured under the foregoing Sections but including, if required, the premium or estimated calls on any Protection and Indemnity or War &c. Risk insurance) reducing pro rata monthly.

(f) RETURNS OF PREMIUM. A sum not exceeding the actual returns which are recoverable subject to "and arrival" under any policy of insurance.

(g) INSURANCE IRRESPECTIVE OF AMOUNT AGAINST:—Risks excluded by the F. C. & S. Clause, and risks enumerated in the American Institute War and Strikes Clauses and General Average and Salvage Disbursements.

Warranted that no insurance on any interests enumerated in the foregoing Sections (a) to (f), inclusive, in excess of the amounts permitted therein and no insurance subject to P.P.I., F.I.A. or other like term, on any interests whatever excepting those enumerated in Section (a), is or shall be effected to operate during the currency of this Policy by or for account of the Assured, Owners, Managers or Mortgagees. Provided always that a breach of this warranty shall not afford Underwriters any defense to a claim by a Mortgagee who has accepted this Policy without knowledge of such breach.

Section (a) refers to the intangible and largely indeterminable interests that in the ordinary disbursements clause are insured P.P.I., F.I.A. The insurance on these interests is limited in the aggregate to 25 per cent of the insured value in the full-form hull policy.

Sections (b) to (f) inclusive permit additional insurance over the 25 per cent restriction on various freight interests, on insurance premiums, and returns of insurance premiums that will accrue if the vessel is in existence at the expiration of the policy. However, these sections do not permit an unlimited amount of insurance on these interests but are subject to very definite restrictions as to voyages in sections (b) and (c), and as to length of time in section (d). Further provision is made for the automatic reduction of the amount of insurance in sections (b) and (d) as the freight is earned by the shipowner or charterer. In section (e) it is provided that the amount of premium insured shall be reduced pro rata monthly.

To provide against any possibility of misunderstanding, section (g) permits the insurance, irrespective of amount, of war risks, strike risks, and general-average and salvage disbursements.

The final paragraph of the warranty is a general warranty that the limitations set forth in sections (a) to (f) inclusive shall not be exceeded. It further provides that no insurance subject to P.P.I., F.I.A., or other like term shall be placed on interests other than those named in section (a). This requires that the interest described in sections (b) to (f) inclusive can only be insured under the conditions outlined in these various sections. There is a final provision that the insured interest of an innocent mortgagee shall not be affected by a breach of the disbursements warranty.

In many cases brokers desire the following warranty added to the disbursements warranty, which underwriters are willing to grant:

The warranty in this policy with respect to other insurance, commonly referred to as the "Disbursements Warranty" is modified in the following respects, namely, that any insurance which the Assured and/or their Managers are permitted to place on increased value of Hull or Machinery, freight, chartered freight, anticipated freight, earnings, hire, profits on time charter or charter for series of voyages may be placed on any one or more of the said interests interchangeably, so long as the total amount of insurance so placed does not exceed the amount permitted by the said warranty to be placed on all of such interests in the aggregate.

Breach of Certain Warranties Held Covered. In certain cases the assured is given opportunity to avoid the loss of his insurance through a breach of warranty, by giving notice to the underwriters in advance of the proposed breach or, in the event that breach happens without the previous knowledge of the owner, as soon as he is aware of such breach. These cases relate to description of cargo, trade, locality, and date of sailing.

Average Clauses. The usual form of 3 per cent average clause appears in this form of policy. One of the casualties enumerated in this clause is stranding, and in order to relieve underwriters of petty claims arising out of technical strandings, it is stipulated in a separate clause that grounding in the Panama Canal, the Suez Canal, the Manchester Ship Canal, or certain other enumerated waterways "shall not be deemed a stranding." The use of these channels at certain stages of the water may make grounding a natural occurrence, and the underwriter, by this stipulation, seeks to avoid claims for these inevitable happenings. Furthermore, it is provided in the average clauses that, in the event of stranding, the underwriters shall pay the expense of sighting the bottom, that is, dry-docking the vessel, if reasonably incurred, even if no damage is found. This provision places the underwriters in a strong position to insist on the examination of the vessel's bottom for possible injury, even if the owner prefers, owing to the delay involved, to defer such examination to a more convenient time. On the other hand, if the assured should dry-dock his vessel after a grounding in one of the excepted watercourses, the expense involved would not be at the charge of the underwriters because the casualty would not be a stranding within the meaning of the policy. It is also provided that in no event shall the underwriters be liable for claim for scraping or painting the bottom of the vessel. The average clause applies to each separate voyage, and the form relates in considerable detail what is meant by a voyage.

Contributory Values. Early in World War I when ship values began to increase by leaps and bounds, underwriters, in certain cases of general-average sacrifices and salvage expenditures, were held liable for these charges assessed against the vessel on her appraised value in the proportion that the amount insured by them bore to the insured value. Thus, instead of being held liable for their percentage of the portion of the assessment applicable to the policy value, they were held liable for the same percentage of the entire assessment. To avoid this difficulty, the following clause appears in the Syndicate policy form:

> When the contributory value of the Vessel is greater than the valuation herein the liability of these Underwriters for General Average contribution (except in respect to amount made good to the Vessel) or Salvage shall not exceed that proportion of the total contribution due from the Vessel that the amount insured hereunder bears to the contributory value; and if because of damage for which these Underwriters are liable as Particular Average the value of the Vessel has been reduced for the purpose of contribution, the amount of the Particular Average claim under this policy shall be deducted from the amount insured hereunder and these Underwriters shall be liable only for the proportion which such net amount bears to the contributory value.

This provision harmonizes with the British practice in similar cases set forth in Sec. 73 of the Marine Insurance Act.[1] A similar clause defines the policy liability with respect to expenditures for salvage, salvage charges, and expenses incurred under the sue-and-labor clause.

Lake Time Clauses. Insurance of steamers plying on the Great Lakes and waters tributary thereto is so different in many respects from insurance of vessels operating on the oceans that a special form, the Lake Time Clauses, has been promulgated by the underwriters. The Great Lakes Protective Association, an organization composed of vessel owners, has done much to improve conditions of management and operation on the Lakes. As tangible evidence of their belief in its efficiency, it carries 25 per cent of the value of the vessels entered in the Association in its insurance fund. Accidents resulting from faulty navigation have materially decreased under the influence of the Association. The Great Lakes are large bodies of water connected by narrow channels, and owing to the congestion in these connecting channels, accidents were of frequent occurrence until the Protective Association became powerful enough to control

[1] See Appendix I.

in a measure the navigation of these waters. Severe penalties for faulty navigation of member vessels have done much to remedy the former reckless striving of masters to reach lower Lake ports regardless of the danger they themselves incurred and the menace of their faulty navigation to other vessels. An organization of Canadian vessel owners is performing a similar service with respect to vessels under Canadian registry.

Restrictions as to Navigation. Perhaps the outstanding feature of the Lake form is the navigation restrictions. The Great Lakes are navigable for a portion of the year only, since conditions prior to April 16 and after November 30 ordinarily make navigation impossible or extrahazardous. These are the limits fixed for the operation of metal steamers, while wooden vessels are further restricted to sailings between May 1 and November 15, inclusive. The restrictive dates are sailing dates, vessels being permitted to proceed to destination even if some time elapses subsequent to November 15 or November 30, as the case may be. Geographically, navigation is limited to the Great Lakes and their tributaries, not below Kingston or Cape Vincent, Lake Ontario. These are the basic warranties upon which the rate of premium is calculated. Provision is made under certain conditions for extending the policy to insure steel steamers if navigating prior to the commencement or subsequent to the termination of the time warranties. An open season will sometimes permit early and late navigation. Under such favorable conditions, postseason navigation does not involve any undue hazard, as the government aids to navigation are not removed until about the middle of December. Notwithstanding these exceptional seasons, experience over a period of years proves conclusively that navigation beyond the warranty date is ordinarily extrahazardous, since freezing, stormy weather usually sets in on the Lakes about the first of December.

The additional premiums charged for postseason sailings are considerable, while the anteseason sailings are charged at double pro rata of the season rate, such navigation being permitted or being possible only in the case of an early spring. None of these extra sailings is covered unless special notice is given to the underwriters.

Winter Mooring Clause. Notwithstanding these time and trading warranties, Lake hull policies are ordinarily written for a period of one year, the vessels being laid up and out of commission during the closed season. The *winter-moorings* clause is incorporated in the policy, providing that winter mooring must be in places and under conditions satisfactory to the underwriters. A regular inspection of winter moorings is made by the underwriters with the result that conditions in this respect have greatly improved in recent years. Owing to the congestion in the handling of grain cargoes on the Lakes, it is customary for vessels at the lower Lake ports to retain their grain cargoes on the last trip down, discharging the grain from time to time during the winter as the congestion at the grain elevators is relieved. In like manner, grain is loaded on vessels moored at upper Lake ports during the winter and stored pending the opening of navigation, when the fully loaded vessel proceeds to her destination. This system of winter storage of grain aids greatly in the movement of the grain crop.

Deductible-average Clause. Instead of the average clause customary in the insurance of ocean vessels, a deductible-average clause with a deductible franchise of $500 is used in the Lake form. Adjustments are made on the basis of a 3 per cent average clause, but from the claim as adjusted on each accident $500 is deducted. In the event of total or constructive total loss no such deduction is made. It is further provided that the underwriters shall be liable, on account of any one accident, only for the excess over 3 per cent of the insured value with respect to all claims arising from damage by ice, except total or constructive total loss so caused. The collision clause also contains the $500 deductible franchise.

Lay-up Clause. As Lake vessels are permitted to navigate only during the open season, they must be laid up in port at all other times. The provision for lay-up returns therefore applies only to lay-ups occurring during the season of navigation, while the portion of the annual rate applying to the closed season represents merely a port-risk charge. In general the Lake form follows the wording of the Syndicate policy, being changed where necessary to meet the conditions peculiar to Lake navigation.

Wooden Sailing Vessels. Policies written to cover the hulls of wooden sailing vessels display few peculiarities, these policies ordinarily being written on forms that adhere very closely to the original basic form of policy. The average franchise is usually 5 per cent with provision made in some policies for a minimum claim for partial loss of $500. The thirds-off clause is usually incorporated with various modifications respecting anchors, chains, yellow metal or sheathing, and other metal parts of the vessel. There are very few of these vessels actively engaged in commercial service. The underwriting of wooden sailing vessels is done by only a limited portion of the insurance market. The amounts to be placed are relatively small, and the hazards are naturally greater than in the case of mechanically propelled metal vessels. In fact, the wooden-sailing-vessel business was in a decadent condition at the outbreak of World War I. The powered vessel had driven the few remaining wooden ships into the carrying of rough cargoes, such as coal and lumber in the coastwise trade. The demand for tonnage, however, caused a revival of the wooden sailing vessel, and during that war many ships of this type were built. Unfortunately, tempted by high freight rates, the owners of many of these vessels entered them in trade across the North Atlantic—a service for which they were poorly adapted—with the result that many fell a prey to marine perils while numerous others, because of their lack of speed and control, became victims of submarines. With the ending of World War I and the deflation of ship values, many sailing vessels disappeared under suspicious circumstances. In consequence of the great surplus of powered tonnage, the sailing vessel again fell into disuse, and no new tonnage of this character is being constructed for overseas service.

Marine Engines. Tremendous strides have been made in the development of engines for marine use. Vessels equipped with heavy oil engines are called *motor vessels* or *motors*. These engines must be distinguished from engines that develop their power from the explosion of volatile gases. The heavy oil engine, of which the diesel model is the common type, develops its power from self-ignition of low-grade oils under heavy compression. The advantages of this type lie in the use of low-grade oils which are readily obtainable; the saving of engine space, with a corresponding increase in cargo space; greater fueling range, since the oil bulks less than coal and is carried in the double-bottom tanks; and a reduction in engine-room personnel. The motor-engined vessel is insured on the same form and subject to the same conditions as steamers. The steam engine, usually of the turbine type, has been greatly improved, high-temperature and high-pressure boilers and engines having reduced the amount of space necessary for motive power. The advantages of the motor ship, in considerable measure, have thus been overcome by the steam-propelled, oil-fueled engines.

Although vessels equipped with oil engines or oil-fired boilers incur an extra expense for tank cleaning and testing when bottom-damage repairs are necessary, the economic advantages of oil fuel from the operator's point of view have to a great extent eliminated the coal-fired boiler.

New types of propulsion are in the experimental stage. Gas turbines may soon be practical for marine engines. Should atomic energy be harnessed for commercial use, a complete revolution in marine propulsion may occur.

CHAPTER 18

Special Hull Forms

SMALL CRAFT

Hull insurance is apt to be thought of only as the insurance of ocean-going steamers. On the contrary, a very considerable part of a hull underwriter's time is engaged in the insurance of small craft and of builder's risks. A large amount of premium is developed from the insurance of such vessels. As in the case of the insurance of Great Lakes vessels, the basic form of insurance policy is used and is adapted by special clauses to serve the particular purpose intended.

TYPES OF SMALL CRAFT

The expression *small craft* embraces a wide variety of vessels, each presenting a special underwriting problem. Such vessels may be very broadly grouped in the following classes, each of which will be considered individually:

1. Tugboats
2. Ocean barges
3. River and harbor vessels
4. Fishing vessels
5. Pleasure craft

Tugboats. The tugboat is a very special type of craft; it maneuvers in all sorts of waterways. It furnishes a power plant to vessels without power and to powered vessels whose engines are disabled or which are maneuvering in restricted waterways. A large merchant vessel seldom docks without the assistance of a tug. A vessel whose power has failed at sea is helpless until a tug or other vessel can take her in tow.

Tugs range in size from very small vessels to great, heavily powered vessels capable of meeting the hazards of any ocean. Oftentimes tugs tow dry docks and other structures halfway around the world. To keep attached to such a structure by hawsers and to keep it under control in calm and storm are among the most difficult tasks that any master has to perform. An ocean liner in docking may be aided by several tugs under the command of a supervising captain. He will probably be on the bridge with the vessel's captain and the harbor pilot, and for the time being the steamship and docking operation are under his control. On the Mississippi River a fleet of barges lashed together into a great floating island is maneuvered by a powerful tugboat pushing the tow through the narrow channels, under bridges, through locks, and around river bends that often seem impossible to negotiate. The value of large tugboats is frequently several hundred thousand dollars. And there are hundreds of smaller tugs that are engaged in the towing of carfloats, coal barges, and other vessels lacking power.

This outline presents a sketchy idea of the problem that confronts the tugboat underwriter. He not only assumes the responsibility for accident to the tug itself but also, in most cases, assumes the liability of the tugboat owner for negligence resulting in damage to his tow or to other property.

Syndicate Tug Form. A special Tug Syndicate has been organized for the sole purpose of insuring vessels of this type. A special policy is used which in general follows the Hull Syndicate form, but there are necessary modifications to fit it for its special purpose. There are two forms of this policy—one a limited form in which the liability risks are not covered, the purpose being to insure the tug itself; the other the full form which includes the negligence clause and the collision clause. This latter clause is quite different from the collision clause in the Syndicate hull policy in that it assumes liability for damage done to the tow by causing it to strand or damage resulting from causing the tow to come into collision with any other vessel or structure or otherwise. This imposes a very serious obligation on the underwriter. Most of the problems in tugboat underwriting arise from the liabilities imposed by this clause. Because of the nature of the business, losses of this kind are very frequent and lead to disputes and lawsuits which often remain unsettled for long periods of time. For this reason it is difficult to appraise the experience on tug underwriting, as there is often a doubt as to whether the tug will be held liable for negligence in any given case. The tug-form collision clause reads as follows:

And it is further agreed that if the Vessel hereby insured shall come into collision with any other Vessel, craft or structure, floating or otherwise (including her tow); or shall strand her tow or shall cause her tow to come into collision with any other vessel, craft, or structure, floating or otherwise, or shall cause any other loss or damage to her tow or to the freight thereof or to the property on board, and the Assured, as owner of the Vessel, in consequence thereof, or the surety for said Assured in consequence of his undertaking, shall become liable to pay and shall pay by way of damages to any other person or persons any sum or sums not exceeding in respect of any one such casualty the value of the Vessel hereby insured, we, the Underwriters, will pay the Assured such proportion of such sum or sums so paid as our subscriptions hereto bear to the value of the Vessel hereby insured. And in cases where the liability of the Vessel has been contested or proceedings have been taken to limit liability, with the consent in writing, of a majority (in amount), of the Underwriters on the hull and machinery, we will also pay a like proportion of the costs, which the Assured shall thereby incur or be compelled to pay; but when both Vessels are to blame, then, unless the liability of the owners of one or both of such Vessels becomes limited by law, claims under the collision clause shall be settled on the principle of cross liabilities, as if the owners of each Vessel had been compelled to pay to the owners of the other of such Vessels such one-half or other proportion of the latter's damage as may have been properly allowed in ascertaining the balance or sum payable by or to the Assured in consequence of such casualty. It is hereby further agreed that the principles involved in this clause shall apply to the case where two or more of the Vessels involved are the property, in part or in whole, of the same owners, all questions of responsibility and amount of liability as between such Vessels being left to the decision of a single arbitrator, if the parties can agree upon a single arbitrator, or failing such agreement, to the decision of arbitrators, one to be appointed by the managing owners of such Vessels, and one to be appointed by the majority (in amount) of hull and machinery Underwriters interested, the two arbitrators so chosen to choose a third arbitrator before entering upon the reference, and the decision of such single or of any two of such three arbitrators, appointed as above, to be final and binding. Provided always that this clause shall in no case extend to any sum which the Assured may become liable to pay, or shall pay for removal of obstructions under statutory powers, or for loss of life or personal injury.

Otherwise tug underwriting follows the principles used in the insurance of large vessels. The underwriter's judgment of the proper rate to charge naturally depends on the service in which the tug will be engaged and the experience developed in the previous insuring of the owner's vessel. It is difficult business to underwrite successfully, as the frequency of loss is high owing to the kind of navigation the tug is called upon to do.

Ocean Barges. Ocean barges are a very broad class under which many vessels fall. Merely to name some of the types will give an indication of the variety of problems that the underwriting of these vessels entails. The largest are the seagoing barges of steel and wood, a type rapidly disappearing from the commercial picture. Such vessels are strongly constructed to meet the hazards of ocean navigation. Many are reconstructed steamers or old sailing vessels. They are used only in the rough trades, such as the carrying of coal, ore, or lumber. They are subject in general to the same hazards as steamer tonnage in ocean trades. Restricted conditions of average are granted, and the rates are high. There are a few similar vessels in use on the Great Lakes.

River and Harbor Craft. *Barges.* River and harbor barges are of lighter construction and are in constant use in the harbors and on the rivers of the United States. They are used for the transfer of cargo from dock to dock within a harbor and may be of the open-deck type or may have houses on deck in which the cargo is stowed. Many of these barges are owned by railroads, and the cargo may be carried on the barge under the railroad bill of lading. Other harbor barges carry coal, and there are many tank barges used for the carriage of petroleum products. Other barges are constructed on the hopper principle with self-dumping equipment and are used by the sanitation departments of municipalities for the disposal of refuse at sea. The greatest growth in the use of nonpowered barges is on the Mississippi River and its tributaries. Millions of dollars have been spent in the development of these waterways. Hundreds of barges, mostly built of steel and usually of welded construction, navigate these waterways.

It is customary for them to proceed in groups, and the design of the barges varies so that they can be consolidated into great floats with a space at the rear into which the specially designed tug fits.

Carfloats and Ferryboats. In most harbors many carfloats operate. These vessels, with two or three car tracks on them, are usually square-ended and dock at specially constructed piers from which the cars can be backed on or to which they can be drawn off. These cars are usually moved by carfloat under the railroad bill of lading, and the railroad assumes its normal responsibility for the contents of the cars, notwithstanding the fact that the cars are water-borne. Many ferryboats are used to transfer passengers and vehicles across inland waterways.

Dredges. The insurance of dredges presents the underwriter with a unique problem. These very unwieldy vessels are heavily constructed for use in harbors and other sheltered places. They cost a great deal and to be profitably used must be transferred from port to port as dredging work offers. They are usually insured under a time policy restricting their use to inland waters. Frequently a special fire policy is issued, this risk being excluded from the marine policy. When they are to be moved from one port to another, the time policy is suspended and a trip-risk policy is issued. Usually it is required that preparation for the trip be made under the supervision of the underwriter's surveyor, who specifies not only how the towing shall be done but when. A favorable season of the year, a full-powered towing vessel, and temporary housing to avoid wave action are some of the necessary precautions to prevent disaster.

Miscellaneous. There are many water-borne structures, such as floating dry docks and landing barges, that never move. There are also special types of vessels, such as grain elevators, coal hoists, and derrick barges used for loading heavy cargo on vessels. Some of these vessels are self-propelled. All these types present special hull problems to the marine underwriter not only with respect to the insurance of the vessel itself but with respect to the owner's liability for negligence.

Fishing Vessels. *Auxiliaries.* More luster of the sea remains with the fishing fleets of the world than in any other marine field. Today, with the mechanization of fishing vessels, even that luster is fading. With the passing of the sailing ship much of the romance of the sea disappeared. Thousands of vessels, large and small, are engaged in the age-old business of fishing. Some of these depend for their power on sails, but many vessels so powered have an auxiliary engine. Most fishing vessels in the past were built of wood, but steel is coming into use, particularly in the trawlers and tuna vessels now being constructed. Some of these are of large size and powered with diesel engines.

Whaling Ships. In the early days of the United States whaling was a great industry. Sailing vessels specially designed for catching whales and rendering the oil went on long voyages lasting sometimes for several years. From these vessels, small boats propelled by oars hunted the whales, which were killed by a hand harpoon. The animal was brought alongside the big ship and cut into small pieces suitable for cooking in the rendering stoves. This type of whaling has ended, one or two old whaling vessels remaining at the dock as museums. In place of these vessels the modern steel, high-powered whaling factory catches the whale, drags the animal up an inclined port opening at the stern, and renders the oil, which is still a necessary commodity in the soap industry. Most of these vessels are foreign owned and are insured abroad under special conditions suitable for the particular service in which they are engaged. Each factory carries a group of killer boats, which are launched on the whaling grounds and kill the whales with the modern explosive harpoon. These small vessels are insured separately but in connection with the mother ship. Much of the hazard of whaling has thus been eliminated.

Pleasure Craft. *Sailing Vessels.* Under the general term *yacht insurance* is included the insurance of all types of pleasure craft, whether their motive power is sails or a mechanical device or a combination of both. A real yacht in the sporting sense is a vessel of various rigs depending solely on sails for its locomotion. It is a sport for the genuine amateur seaman, and whether the vessel is a large one, like those which race for the America's Cup, or a small catboat manned by a young boy, the sport has all the glamour and interest of the sea. A few large steam or diesel yachts are still in operation, but most of these were taken over by the government during World War II. Under present world conditions few people can maintain such vessels.

Power Boats. There has been a very great growth in what is called yachting but what should more correctly be called motorboating. With the congestion of motor cars on the highways, more and more people are turning to motorboating. Many companies produce motorboats on a mass-production basis. Formerly too little thought was given to the dangers inherent in a small vessel powered with a gas engine and having a galley serviced by a range fueled with bottled gas. Many explosions occurred, destroying the vessel and often killing or seriously injuring the persons on board. Yacht underwriters have in many cases been successful in persuading builders of motorboats to construct their vessels so that these hazards are eliminated to a very considerable degree. The Coast Guard is interested in promoting safe motorboating but does not wish to enforce stringent rules that would tend to destroy the freedom which the motorboat owner now enjoys. In cooperation with underwriters and builders they are endeavoring to have safe standards accepted. It must be remembered that many motorboats are operated by men with little mechanical ability and even less knowledge of the sea, of its traditions, and of its hazards.

Yacht Policy. Special forms of policy have been provided for the insurance of this rather specialized business, but it will not be possible to discuss them in detail. The broadest form consists of three sections as follows:

1. Hull insurance
2. *a.* Protection and indemnity insurance, covering liability for loss of life and personal injury and property damage
   b. Longshoremen's and Harbor Workers' Compensation insurance
3. Medical payments insurance

Section 1 covers the yacht or motorboat itself, both while navigating and during the out-of-season lay-up. The amount of insurance in this section should be the reasonable market value of the vessel. Section 2 is a cover similar to the protection-and-indemnity insurance which the owner of a commercial vessel places under a separate policy with the clubs or with a marine-insurance company. This section also covers workmen's compensation as required by the Federal Government Public Act 803 approved March 4, 1927. Limits are provided in the protection-and-indemnity section establishing the amount of liability covered in the event of a single person or more than one person being injured or killed in a single accident. Many owners buy very high limits in this personal-liability section. An amount is also inserted as the limit of liability for property damage. Section 3 provides, with stated limits, for medical, hospital, and other related expenses in the event of injury and reasonable funeral expenses in the event of death, without proof of legal liability. In short, the yacht policy offers to the owner of a yacht or a motorboat a form of insurance similar to that available to a motor-car owner. However, the policy is subject to marine law and interpretation.

The insurance of the hull presents certain unusual but interesting underwriting problems. The use of yachts is seasonal. In the North it is a late-spring, summer, and early-fall pastime; in the South and on the Pacific Coast yachts are used all the year. The policy provides time limits within which navigation is permitted. It provides that the yacht shall be used for pleasure only. The use of the boat for commercial purposes would greatly increase the probability of loss under the protection-and-indemnity section.

The policy insures property taken off the vessel and stored on shore to an amount not exceeding 20 per cent of the insured value. It contains a provision that loss of or damage to spars and/or sails while racing is not covered, but on payment of an additional premium such loss may be covered.

Yacht insurance is peculiarly susceptible to catastrophic loss, and in naming rates this factor is of first importance. During the navigating season, at night and often during the day, except on week ends, many harbors will be congested with yachts. A sudden squall or a severe storm may cause a yacht to drag from its moorings and damage not only itself but many other vessels. Many losses involving a number of yachts happen in this manner. Such storms may affect a long coast line with many yacht harbors. More serious are the hurricanes expected in the summer and fall in the South. Two such storms deviated from their usual path and came north, causing wholesale destruction to yachts and other property in the fall of 1938 and 1944. During the lay-up period many yachts are taken out of the water and stored in close proximity to one another in a yacht yard subject to a conflagration. The fire hazard is particularly serious in the early spring, when the owners commence to ready their yachts and are careless in the use of blowtorches, cigarettes, etc.

Finally, the owner of a yacht or motorboat has a peculiar affection for his vessel. The underwriter must recognize this psychological factor in dealing with him and his broker in placing the insurance and adjusting loss when it occurs.

BUILDER'S RISKS

Builder's-risk insurance, though based on the old form of marine policy, is so very different in the protection given that a special form of policy[1] has been designed to furnish the kind of insurance desired by builders. Up to the point where a new vessel is launched, there is no marine hazard. The protection afforded prior to that time is purely a shore cover, except in so far as materials designed for the vessel may be afloat on barges or other craft at the builder's yards or in transit to the shipyard. In the builder's-risk form of policy in present use, designed to overcome abuses that had entered into the writing of this class of insurance, the underwriter attaches his risk from the date the vessel's keel is laid. Premium is charged from that date on the total amount for which he would be liable should the vessel become a total loss after completion but before delivery.

Special Hazards Insured against. In addition to the perils set forth in the ordinary form of marine-insurance policy the underwriters on a builder's-risk policy also assume liabilty for the risks set forth in the following clause:

> This insurance is also to cover all risks, including fire, while under construction and/or fitting out, including materials in buildings, workshops, yards and docks of the assured, or on quays, pontoons, craft, etc., and all risks while in transit to and from the works and/or the vessel wherever she may be lying, also all risks of loss or damage through collapse of supports or ways from any cause whatever, and all risks of launching and breakage of the ways.

The foregoing clause outlines the protection afforded up to the point when the vessel takes the water. The underwriter further obligates

[1] See Appendix G, p. 463.

himself, in the case of failure to launch, to bear all subsequent ex
penses incurred in completing the launching. It occasionally happen
that, through some miscalculation in the construction of the ways o
through a mishap to them, caused frequently by their sinking due t
an insecure foundation, a vessel will fail to slide into the wate
causing serious damage not only to the ship itself but to the way
There is great danger that, in failure to launch, the whole structur
of the ship will be strained. The expense of completing the launchin
and repairing the ways and the ship is at the risk of the builder's-ris
underwriters.

Risks after Launching. The vessel having been successfull
launched, the underwriter continues on the risk and assumes liabilit
for all damage during the fitting out, the trial trips, and while th
vessel is proceeding to and returning from the trial course. The polic
contains the full four-fourths collision clause and, with respect to aver
age, agrees to pay all losses irrespective of percentage without th
deduction of thirds whether the average be particular or genera
Liberty is granted for the testing of the guns and torpedoes of a war
ship, but the underwriter assumes no liability for loss or damage to th
ship or machinery resulting from such test, unless the casualty result
in the total loss of the vessel. In the case of submarines, part of th
testing consists in the submersion and emersion of the vessel, and th
underwriter is liable for any mishap that may occur during this test
Submarines have at times successfully submerged but have failed t
emerge, causing considerable expense in raising the vessel.

Underwriter Guarantees Integrity of Material. The builder's-ris
form is so broad in the protection afforded that the underwriter i
reality guarantees the integrity of the materials entering into the con
struction of the vessel. If, on the trial trip, defects that necessitat
overhauling and additional expenses become manifest, claim for suc
loss is responded for by the underwriter. For instance, on the tria
trip, on account of the working of the engine, a flaw may develop i
the bedplate, necessitating stripping of the engine and placing a ne
bedplate. The actual cost of a new bedplate may in itself be small
but the expense involved in the installation of the new plate ma
result in a very heavy claim.

Special Clauses and Warranties. In the builder's-risk form of policy the underwriter also agrees to cover all damage to hull, machinery, apparel, or furniture caused by the settling of the stocks on which the vessel is being built or failure or breakage of shores, blocking, or staging or of hoisting or other gear, either before or after launching or while fitting out. The policy also contains a negligence clause and the protection-and-indemnity clause, not, however, covering liability for loss of life or personal injury. The collision clause is extended to cover risks ordinarily excluded by this clause, that is, responsibility for any sum that the assured may become liable to pay or shall pay for removal of obstructions under statutory powers or for injury to harbors, wharves, piers, stages, or similar structures. Owing to the very broad protection afforded by the builder's-risk form, underwriters find it prudent to insert warranties excluding certain perils. One of these warranties relieves the underwriters from claims arising directly or indirectly under workmen's compensation laws, employer's liability acts, or any other statutory or common law with respect to accidents to any person or persons whatsoever. The free-of-capture-and seizure clause and the strikers-and-locked-out-workmen clause[1] are also inserted. In order to offset the danger of earthquake shocks to vessels being built at yards on the Pacific Coast, a warranty is inserted freeing the underwriter from loss or damage caused by earthquakes. While the underwriter is liable for the repair of damages resulting during launching and trial trips, by warranty he declines to assume liability for any consequential damage or claims for loss through delay, however caused. Formerly, under builder's-risk policies it was customary to insure property while being conveyed from the place of manufacture to the vessel, as in the case of submarine engines built on the East Coast for installation in submarines being built on the West Coast, but by warranty this risk is now excluded from the policy. Several of these warranties may be waived by the payment of an additional premium.

In the event of loss or claim under this form of policy, the underwriter assumes liability for only his proportion of the loss, based on the relation which the amount insured by his policy bears to the completed contract price of the vessel.

Return Premiums. In the event that a vessel is completed prior to

[1] See p. 190.

the expiration of the policy term, provision is made for the payment of prorata return premium for the months not commenced upon. The underwriter, however, stipulates that such return premium shall not exceed a fixed portion of the total premium. Were an underwriter to receive only one-twelfth of the annual rate for a vessel completed in less than one month, the business would not, at the low rates prevailing, develop a sufficient fund of premium with which to pay losses.

MARINE PROTECTION-AND-INDEMNITY INSURANCE

At various points in the consideration of hull and cargo insurance reference has been made to protection-and-indemnity insurance, or "P and I insurance" as it is commonly called. While such insurance is not generally thought of when marine insurance is mentioned, it has such an important connection with hull and cargo underwriting that it will be profitable to consider briefly its salient features.

In the insurance law of the State of New York this type of insurance is described as follows:

> Marine protection and indemnity insurance, meaning insurance against, or against legal liability of the insured for loss, damage or expense arising out of, or incident to, the ownership, operation, chartering, maintenance, use, repair or construction of any vessel, craft or instrumentality in use in ocean or inland waterways, including liability of the insured for personal injury, illness or death or for loss of or damage to the property of another person.

The hull policy protects the owner or charterer of a vessel against loss to his vessel; the P and I policy covers his legal liability risks in the operation of his vessel. It is a very specialized business. In the United States two groups of stock companies and one mutual company provide a facility sufficient to meet the requirements of the merchant fleet. This is a comparatively recent development in this country, as prior to 1917 the P and I risks of United States shipowners were insured in the British market. There the business was largely with the clubs.[1] Just as other forms of marine insurance met the changing conditions that evolved as wooden vessels were supplanted by steel, as sail power gave way to mechanical power, so the protection afforded

[1] See p. 274.

by the P and I underwriter has kept pace with the ever-changing problems of ship operation in an expanding commercial world. Common-law liabilities have been modified by laws and rules defining and sometimes limiting the liabilities and the responsibilities of ship operators. The protection afforded under the P and I policy may be grouped into four very broad classes:

1. Liabilities with respect to persons
2. Liabilities with respect to cargo
3. Liabilities with respect to other property
4. Unusual expenses to comply with government regulations and fines and penalties incurred by violation of law

A brief description of each class may be helpful in understanding the variety of liabilities with which a ship operator may be faced.

Persons. To persons who have a right to be on board a vessel, the operator owes a duty to see that they do not come to harm through his negligence. This group includes passengers, ship visitors, the crew, and stevedores working on or about the ship. The operator is also liable for unusual expenses incurred in getting sick or injured seamen to shore. He is liable for *maintenance and cure* plus wages to the end of a voyage of seamen disabled by sickness or injury and for the care of such seamen left at foreign ports and the cost of getting them home when they have recovered.

Cargo. Much damage may be done to cargo if the ship is not properly prepared to receive it or if the cargo is improperly stowed or protected while in the custody of the vessel. If this damage is due to negligence on the part of the ship, the owner of the cargo has a right of action against the ship to recover his loss or damage. Such right is limited by the terms of the bill of lading and by laws modifying the liability of the shipowner, such as the Harter Act[1] and the Carriage of Goods by Sea Act.[2] This liability the P and I underwriter assumes under his policy. He assumes the owner's liability if the ship is found to be unseaworthy and the owner is held responsible for the resultant loss of or damage to cargo. He agrees to pay the share of

[1] See Appendix N, p. 507.
[2] See Appendix O, p. 509.

general-average uncollectible from the cargo, particularly if the vessel shall have been proved unseaworthy at the commencement of the voyage.

Other Property. The hull-insurance policy includes the collision clause under which the hull underwriter assumes responsibility for damage to other vessels by collision. This clause excepts, however, any liability for removal of obstructions under governmental direction, for injury to harbors, wharves, piers, stages, or other similar structures consequent on collision, or in respect of the cargo or engagement of the insured vessel (meaning freight interests), or for loss of life or personal injury. The P and I policy, subject to its terms and conditions, covers these excepted risks, except the "engagements of the insured vessel." These freight engagements the owner can insure under a freight policy. There are other causes of damage to property, liability for which the P and I underwriter assumes. A vessel proceeding through a restricted waterway at too great a speed creates a wash that may cause other vessels to break their moorings or to be forced against docks or driven ashore. Similarly, a vessel may be so negligently navigated as to crowd other vessels, causing collisions or stranding. A ship's tackle may fail, causing cargo to be dropped on barges or lighters lying alongside.

Government Regulations. A ship operator may be put to unusual expense by the enforcement of quarantine regulations. He may also have to pay fines or penalties for violation of federal, state, local, or foreign laws or ordinances by the owner, the master, or his agents. The P and I policy, subject to its terms and conditions, assumes liability for these unusual expenses.

In short, just as the hull underwriter and the cargo underwriter endeavor to assume losses resulting from the hazards to which hull and cargo are exposed, so in so far as practicable the P and I underwriter assumes the liabilities imposed by law or regulations upon the ship operator. Should the ship operator by special agreement or consent assume liabilities for which he is not legally responsible, such liabilities are not covered by the P and I policy.

The Policy. It is the almost invariable practice to issue a separate policy to the owner for his P and I protection. In the case of small craft, for instance, tugboats, certain P and I liabilities, other than loss of life and personal injury, may be included in the hull form. In the yacht policy even loss of life and personal injury may be included. However, yachts are subject to very different conditions of operation from the ordinary commercial vessel.

Rates. In general in the case of ocean-going vessels, the limits of liability for which the underwriter assumes responsibility are stated, but the premium is determined, not by a rate applied to this amount, but by a charge of so many cents or dollars per gross ton of the vessel. It is rather common practice for the owner or operator to assume all losses up to a stated amount. In such a case the P and I policy will contain a deductible-franchise clause relieving the underwriter of claims up to this amount, he paying only for such amount as the claim may exceed this sum. This scheme has two advantages. First, the owner can tell his captain and crew that any negligence or losses up to the stated amount come out of his pocket and thus try to induce them to exercise a high degree of care in the operation of the ship. Second, the underwriter is relieved of a multitude of small claims that are very expensive to adjust and that entail costs out of all proportion to the amounts involved.[1]

[1] For a lucid discussion of P and I insurance see Henry I. Bernard, "Protection and Indemnity Insurance," 2d printing, Lectures at Merchant Marine Academy, Kings Point, N. Y., Johnson & Higgins, New York, 1950. (Available on request to Johnson & Higgins.)

CHAPTER 19

Freight Insurance

Freight Insurance a Difficult Subject. Freight, the third great maritime interest, is of all the subjects of marine insurance the most difficult to comprehend. Why this should be so is somewhat hard to understand; nevertheless, the fact remains that more difficult and complicated questions arise in regard to freight than with respect to any other single marine-insurance interest. Perhaps a part of this difficulty arises through a confusion of terms, the word "freight," in this country at least, having a double meaning. As usually thought of by the lay mind, freight refers to goods, to the cargo of a vessel, or to the contents of a railroad car, and accordingly, the expression "freight" steamer or "freight" car is used, a meaning of the word that is quite foreign to the usage in Great Britain, where a freight car is referred to as a "goods truck." Unfortunately for the clear understanding of the subject of freight as used in shipping transactions and especially in marine insurance, there is this common and yet nontechnical meaning of the word.

Meaning of Freight in Marine Insurance. Freight, as used in marine insurance, has an entirely different meaning, having reference to the money paid to a vessel for the carriage of goods or to any common carrier for the transportation of property by rail, air, or water. The expression "freight rate" means the charge made by a carrier for the transportation of goods and merchandise, including animals. The expression "freight" is not used to mean the money received for the transportation of passengers, this being referred to as "passage money" in the case of water carriage over considerable distances and as "fare" in the case of short water trips or railroad or air transportation. Freight then, as used in transportation insurance, is an intangible interest, a financial benefit derived through the employment of vessels or transportation lines in the carriage of property. The fact that the interest is intangible, arising merely because of the existence of a contract that establishes a certain relation between the owner or the charterer of a vessel and the owner of property offered for transportation by that vessel, no doubt adds somewhat to the difficulty of understanding the subject. The forms of contract differ so widely, the duties and obligations of the two parties to the contracts are often so involved as to cause situations to arise that are complicated and difficult of explanation. The insurable interest in freight, depending on the terms of the contract of carriage and the terms of the contract of sale of the goods themselves, causes this subject to be wrapped up in all the mystery and complications that surround an intangible interest.

Vessels Built to Earn Freight. Merchant vessels are built for the primary purpose of earning freight and returning a profit to their owners. Their value lies solely in their ability to accomplish this end. It may be said that the value of a merchant vessel is the sum total of the freight which can be earned by its operation during the normal life of a ship, say 20 years, less the cost of earning this freight, plus the break-up value of the vessel as scrap at the end of its earning period. This theory has caused it to be argued that there is no insurable interest in the freight and that the insurance on the hull carries with it the insurance of the immediate and prospective earnings of the vessel. Practically, the value of a vessel is what it will bring in the market at any given time. This value will depend greatly on the demand for tonnage of the particular kind offered, the geographical position of the vessel with respect to prospective cargoes, the national flag of the vessel, her speed and fuel consumption, and many other considerations, all, however, having a direct bearing on the prospective net earning capacity of the vessel.

When Is Freight Earned? Under the original form of freight contract, the vessel is entitled to no compensation under a freight agreement unless and until it has fully and precisely fulfilled the contract of carriage, notwithstanding the fact that nonfulfillment of the contract has resulted through causes beyond the control of the owner or charterer of the ship or his agent, the captain of the vessel. Suppose a vessel owner were to contract to carry a parcel of goods from Liverpool to Shanghai for a named sum of money, and through causes beyond the control of the owner or captain, the vessel were compelled to enter the port of Hong Kong and there end the voyage and discharge and make delivery of the goods. Under the common law of England, the owner of the goods would be relieved from paying the freight stipulated in the contract, or any part thereof, because the owner of the vessel, the other party to the contract, had not fulfilled the terms of the agreement. In such a case the owner of the vessel has incurred almost all the expense necessary completely to fulfill his agreement, and these expenses of fuel, food, wages, etc., must be paid, notwithstanding the fact that he will receive nothing in return and will in addition lose his profit, that is, the net freight. This net freight is the only freight that can be considered in making up the value of the vessel itself, and were the theory that there is no insurable interest in freight put into actual practice, the owner would have no means of protecting himself against the loss of expenses incurred in the event of the freight not being earned. Of course, in the case just cited, if the vessel could not proceed beyond Hong Kong, the captain would endeavor to arrange for the forwarding of the cargo by other conveyances to Shanghai and thus earn the freight. The expense incurred in so forwarding the cargo might result in a loss to the vessel owner or charterer, recoverable under a policy on freight, provided the cause of the vessel entering Hong Kong in distress was a peril insured against.

Freight *Pro Rata Itineris Peracti.* The rule in most European countries other than Great Britain is less stringent than that outlined above. Freight *pro rata itineris peracti,* that is, an allowance of freight for the part of the contract performed, is granted to the vessel owner or charterer if the complete fulfillment of the contract is prevented by causes over which he has no control. In the United States, the British practice has been closely followed. Nothing short of exact compliance with the terms of the freight agreement is considered a fulfillment of the contract entitling the vessel owner to compensation. It does not follow, however, that an express agreement may not be made by the cargo owner to receive his cargo at a point short of destination upon payment to the vessel owner of an agreed amount of freight for the part of the voyage already completed. This is often done in order to obtain prompt possession of the property, since the vessel owner has the right to retain possession of the goods for a reasonable length of time if he considers that he will be able to forward them to destination and thus earn his freight. This right of the vessel owner to retain possession of the goods is a logical one, as otherwise the cargo owner, in the event of delay through marine peril or otherwise, could step in and demand possession of the property, thus preventing the vessel owner from earning his freight. If the cargo owner is unwilling to await the arrival of the vessel at destination or the forwarding by the vessel owner of the goods on some other conveyance, he may, by payment of full freight or by payment of prorata freight, if the amount of this can be determined amicably, usually obtain immediate possession of the property.

Prepaid and Guaranteed Freight. Again it must not be presumed, from this statement of the basic rule in regard to the earning of freight, that it is not possible for the vessel owner to make a freight contract by which he secures payment of the freight whether or not the voyage is fully performed. On the contrary, most freight contracts provide for prepaid freight or freight payable, vessel lost or not lost, otherwise known as guaranteed freight, that is, payment of the freight even if the goods are not delivered according to the terms of the contract, such nondelivery resulting from causes beyond the control of the vessel owner. If the freight is merely prepaid without any stipulation in the contract that the prepayment is to be retained whether the voyage is successfully completed or not, the prepaid freight must be returned if the voyage is not completed in accordance with the terms of the agreement of carriage. If the freight is prepaid absolutely or is guaranteed, which amounts to the same thing, the vessel owner has no freight at risk during the voyage, as he either has the freight in hand or has a contract under which the freight will be forthcoming whether or not the voyage is completed. The money paid or to be paid in such cases for the carriage of goods has thus lost its identity as freight, and while it may be insured by the cargo owner under the name of freight, it has in reality become part of the value of the goods and may rightly, if the cargo owner so elects, be included as part of such value, and be insured as goods.

Prepaid Freight Wrong in Principle. Contracts calling for the prepayment or the guaranteeing of freight are wrong in principle and become possible only when a situation exists in the tonnage market where the demand greatly exceeds the supply. In such event, the steamship owner or agent has the cargo owner at his mercy and can demand terms of payment that might not be tolerated in a competitive market. The owner of a vessel is, under the common law, obligated to deliver cargo received under a contract of carriage at the destination named and in the condition received, unless prevented by acts of God or of the King's enemies. While this basic law has been greatly modified by statute, in that vessel owners have been relieved of many of the obligations formerly imposed upon them, the law has not, in the absence of express agreement, relieved owners of the primary duty of fulfilling the contract of carriage to the letter. While the prepayment of freight in no wise relieves owners of the duty of exactly performing the contract, the fact that the freight money is in hand or guaranteed removes the chief incentive to the diligent prosecution of the voyage and makes the shipowner less likely in the event of disaster to use all possible efforts to carry the cargo forward to destination. Plausible excuses may be offered for not taking measures to forward cargo to destination, measures which, if the payment of the freight were dependent thereon, would seem the obvious course to pursue.

Underwriting Problems. The insurance of freight presents some very interesting underwriting problems owing to the fact that certain hazards may be at the risk of one party to the contract of carriage, while other hazards are at the risk of the other party. The relations established by charter parties and bills of lading as a rule determine the conditions with which freight insurance has to deal, and as the forms of these agreements are many, so the conditions involved in freight insurance are many. Were it possible in each case of freight insurance to scrutinize the terms of the freight agreement, much of the difficulty experienced in the insuring of freight would be eliminated.

Charter Parties. Under the charter party, the owner of a vessel hires it to a ship operator or to a merchant for a definite period of time or for a specific voyage, payment for the use of the vessel being stipulated in the agreement. The owner may turn the vessel over to the charterer, the latter agreeing to operate it, to insure it, and, at the end of the specified voyage or time, to return it to the owner in the same condition in which he received it. This is called a *bare-boat char-*

ter. A fixed price per day may be agreed upon for the use of the vessel, payment to be made monthly. It is usually stipulated that, if the vessel be lost or disabled so as to be unfit for service, the per-diem payment is to cease from the time the vessel is lost or during the period it is disabled. Under this state of facts, the vessel owner is not at all concerned in the success of the charterer in obtaining freight engagements for the vessel, except in so far as such inability may result in financial embarrassment of the charterer, but he is greatly concerned in the continued existence of the vessel in a navigable condition. This is not because loss or damage to the hull will affect him, this contingency by the terms of the agreement being at the risk of the charterer, but because the disabling of the vessel will cause payment of the charter money to cease. The owner of the vessel, therefore, has an insurable interest against loss through the occurrence of the perils that will cause the payments of the charter money called for by the terms of the contract to cease.

Charter Money. The forms of charter parties are various, calling for the chartering of the vessel under any one of a number of methods of operation and stipulating for the payment of the charter money in various ways. Charter money is the name by which freight is known when the payment is made for the use of an entire vessel or a part thereof under a charter-party form of agreement. Charter money may be paid by the day, month, or year, by the trip or round voyage, or it may be based on a unit of measure as so many dollars per ton or per bale. In any event, if the owner hires his vessel under charter party, this agreement fixes the respective liabilities of the two parties with regard to the vessel itself and its earnings, the freight or charter money. In many cases the owner will charter his vessel to a merchant who has goods to ship sufficient in quantity to furnish a full cargo for the ship. In such case, the sole duty of the cargo owner is to furnish the cargo, the vessel owner attending to the stowage and carriage of the goods and, in the absence of special agreement to the contrary, receiving his compensation at the stipulated rate on the right delivery of the cargo at the destination named.

Bill-of-lading Freight. Where a vessel is put on the berth to load general cargo for any merchant who may offer cargo for the intended port of destination, the second form of freight agreement, the bill of lading, comes into use. The bill of lading is a receipt for goods delivered to a vessel or a steamship company to be transported to the destination named therein, in accordance with the terms and conditions thereof, at the rate of freight stipulated. The sum total of all the bill-of-lading freight is the total gross earnings of the vessel for the contemplated trip and is at the risk of, and therefore insurable by, the owner or charterer, as the case may be, if the freight is not due from the cargo owners until the goods are delivered at destination. The owner or charterer of the vessel, however, has a lien on the goods and may retain possession of them until the freight is paid. Insurance placed on bill-of-lading freight is usually valued at freight list.

The bill of lading sets forth the terms of the contract of carriage but is only prima-facie evidence that the goods are on board. Before World War II, through bills of lading were issued covering the transportation of goods from point of origin, either at port or interior place to port or point of destination. Because of the difficulties arising out of a war economy, this form of "lading" was discontinued. Efforts are presently being made to restore the use of the through bill of lading, but so many difficulties arise, because of port and other regulations as an aftermath of the war, that the restoration of such documents is not feasible at the present time.

To prove whether or not the goods are actually on board the ship named in the bill of lading, the manifest must be examined. This document is made up by the purser of the ship from the master's or ship's receipts issued as the cargo is laden. The manifest lists the shipments one by one and may show in which hold each shipment is stowed. If not, the stowage plan will show the location of the shipment. These documents provide valuable information to underwriters in the event of casualty and are invaluable to the general-average adjuster in arranging the bonds and obtaining the deposits or underwriters' guarantees called for before cargo is released at destination. In many cases the bill of lading is issued without naming the vessel, or if the vessel is named, the goods may not be loaded on the named vessel. If the bill of lading is stamped "on board," it is presumed that the cargo is actually laden on the vessel named in the bill of lading. The shipment is "traced" by checking the manifest.

Delivery of Cargo in Specie. Under common law as amended by statute and under the ordinary form of bill of lading, while it is required that the owner or charterer deliver cargo at destination in order to earn freight, it is required only that such delivery be made *in specie.* The owner or charterer is deemed to have fulfilled his agreement if he delivers the same goods that he received, regardless of the fact that they may have been severely damaged through causes beyond his control. If, however, the goods are not delivered in the form in which they were received, the owner or charterer is in exactly the same position with respect to payment as if delivery had not been made. Thus, if cement is shipped, but through the entrance of water into the hold it arrives as stone, delivery cannot be made in specie, and the cargo owner will not be required to pay the freight. It is true, however, that, when goods are received in a damaged state caused by conditions for which the owner or charterer is not liable, the consignee may be compelled to pay full freight. The vessel has in all cases a lien on the cargo for the amount of freight thereon. There are, therefore, certain hazards in connection with freight that are at the risk of the cargo owner.

Collectible Freight or Freight Contingency. These hazards on freight that are at the risk of the cargo owner are insured as *collectible freight* or *freight contingency.* The risk assumed by the underwriter is comparatively small. If the goods are damaged during the course of the voyage, it does not necessarily follow that there will be a claim under the contingency-freight insurance, as the vessel may never arrive or on arrival the damaged goods may have changed in specie, thus relieving the cargo owner from any freight payment. If the goods are landed in specie, however, the freight is due. The cost of the goods is increased by the amount of freight so paid. It is on this basis that claim under such freight insurance is made. To the insured value of the goods is added the insured value of the freight contingency; the percentage of loss suffered by the goods as determined by a comparison of the sound and damaged market values of the property is applied to this combined insured value, and settlement made accordingly. Freight contingency or collectible freight is usually insured in the same policy as the goods themselves, the rate charged on the freight being, however, but a fraction, usually one-third, of the rate on the goods, in view of the few hazards to which this interest is exposed. The use of the words *collectible freight* in relation to the cargo owner should not be confused with the same expression when used to describe the interest of the vessel owner or charterer in bill-of-lading freight payable at destination. Owing to the double use of this expression it is preferable to refer to this bill-of-lading freight as *freight contingency* when considered from the point of view of the cargo owner.

Various Freight Interests in a Single Venture. It will thus be seen that many freight interests may be involved in a single venture. In the case of a vessel chartered on time and put on the berth by the charterer, the owner will have an insurable interest in the charter money if its payment is contingent on the continued existence of the vessel, the charterer will have an insurable interest in the bill-of-lading freight for the immediate voyage if not prepaid or guaranteed, while the cargo owner will have an insurable interest in the freight contingency. If the charterer has rechartered to another party who in turn puts the vessel on the berth, the original charterer may have an insurable interest in profits on charter, that is, the difference between the amount he will have to pay the owner and the amount to be paid to him by the party to whom he has rechartered the vessel. These cases present some of the more common and apparent freight interests.

Freight a Contingent Interest. Dead Freight. In principle, the insurance of freight differs not at all from the insurance of hull or cargo. The interest is intangible, being based merely on a contractual relation, but the perils to which the interest is exposed are precisely the same perils to which hull and cargo are exposed. The earning of the freight in most cases is dependent on the continued existence of the cargo and the successful prosecution of the voyage by the vessel.

It may happen that, after a merchant has engaged space in a vessel, the goods which he intended to ship are destroyed or he is for some other reason prevented from making the intended shipment. He may be able to substitute other goods, but if he cannot do this, and if the shipowner cannot obtain other cargo to fill the space, the merchant may have to pay for the space for which he contracted although the vessel sails with the space unused. The freight paid for unused space is *dead freight*. It may be that the shipowner can obtain cargo for the whole or part of the space engaged, but at a lower rate than the merchant was to pay. In this event the difference between the contract price and the freight received for the substituted cargo will have to be paid by the merchant. It is the shipowner's duty to use reasonable diligence to fill dead-cargo space and thus reduce the amount to be paid by the merchant. Dead freight is not an insurable interest, as the loss of the merchant is determined prior to the inception of the voyage, while the right of the shipowner to the dead freight is in no way contingent on the successful performance of the voyage.

When Does Insurable Interest Commence? The risks to which the interest of freight is exposed being the ordinary marine perils covered by a marine-insurance policy, the principal difficulty is to define precisely the insurable interest and the particular contingencies at the risk of the person desiring the insurance as shown by the contract of affreightment. To have an insurable interest in freight there must be a definite contract of employment for immediate or future execution. In the ordinary case of shipowners' freight, the payment of which is contingent on the successful execution of the freight agreement, the insurable interest commences when the ship is ready to receive the cargo or sails in ballast for the loading port. Thus, if a vessel under contract to carry a cargo of cement from Newport News to a River Plate port, for which it is to receive, say, $5,000 on the right delivery of the cargo at destination, sails from New York to Newport News in ballast, the owner has an insurable interest to the extent of $5,000 in the freight to be earned on the trip from Newport News to River Plate. If disaster overtakes the vessel between New York and Newport News, and the vessel is lost or so injured that the contemplated trip must be abandoned, there will be a total loss of the freight. If the cement is loaded, and the vessel proceeds on her journey but, through perils insured against, part of the cargo is so damaged that delivery of this part cannot be made, there will be a total loss of part of the freight, representing that portion of the freight applicable to the damaged cargo. Or, owing to stress of weather, a sacrifice of part of the cargo may be necessary for the safety of the entire venture, and a portion of the cement is jettisoned, thereby entailing the loss of the freight on this portion of the cargo. In this case, a general-average loss on freight will have occurred. If part of the cargo is damaged but is still in specie, the vessel owner will have no loss of freight, but there will be a particular-average claim on the freight under the policy covering freight contingency.

Future Freights. Future freights may be insured, provided there is a definite contract of affreightment. For instance, in the case cited in the preceding paragraph, the vessel owner might have a definite contract to carry a full cargo of wool from the River Plate to Boston, a lump-sum freight of $7,500 to be paid on right delivery of the wool at Boston. The owner can insure this freight on the trip from New York via Newport News to River Plate, because his interest in this return freight is not a speculative interest but a definite one arising out of a valid contract, the execution of which is dependent on the continued existence of the vessel. The mere knowledge or expectation on the part of the vessel owner that he would obtain a wool charter on arrival at the River Plate would not give him an insurable interest in the freight that he would earn if such a contract were made. If, however, while the vessel was on the way from Newport News to the River Plate such a contract should be consummated for the return trip, the insurable interest in the freight to be earned on the return trip would arise immediately. It is important, when insuring the freight to be earned on future trips, that the interest being insured be definitely described.

Anticipated Freight. In the case cited above, where the vessel sailed from Newport News without definite freight engagement after arrival at the River Plate, but with a reasonable expectation of obtaining a charter, the owner is not absolutely precluded from insuring his expectation. This is commonly done under the name of *anticipated freight,* the insurance obtained in the ordinary case being against total and constructive total loss only. There being no definite insurable interest that can be proved by the production of a contract of affreightment, such insurance is effected "policy proof of interest, full interest admitted." The policy is an honor document, payable by the underwriter on the production of proof of the loss of the vessel or of damage to the vessel making it impossible to commence the voyage. Such insurance is open to gross abuses and may in fact be used as a cloak for a mere gamble. For this reason, as already indicated in the discussion of hull insurance, most hull policies contain a warranty that the amount placed on P.P.I., F.I.A. form shall be limited to a fixed percentage of the insured value of the vessel.

On Board or Not on Board. The expression "on board or not on board" is frequently found in freight policies. The intent of this clause is not always clear, as it is evident that freight, being an intangible interest, cannot be on board the vessel. The goods, for the carriage of which the freight is to be paid, may or may not be on board in the case of chartered freight, as was indicated in the above-described case of the vessel sailing in ballast from New York to Newport News to load cement. The skeleton form of policy reads "beginning the adventure upon the said goods and merchandises from and immediately following the loading thereof on board the said vessel," etc., and while this phrase could not be held to refer to freight, it may be that "on board or not on board" is inserted to avoid the possible implication that the goods to which the freight relates must be on board before the risk will attach. The words are also used in connection with insurances on freight for a long round voyage, during which cargo will be loaded and discharged at way ports. The exact amount of freight at risk in such cases cannot be definitely determined, but if the vessel owner wishes a valued policy covering this freight rather than insurance on P.P.I. conditions, he will place the risk on board or not on board.

Chartered or as if Chartered. Coupled with this expression the words "chartered or as if chartered" will be found, or these latter words may be used alone. The meaning of this phrase is exceedingly doubtful, several decisions having been rendered on these words without shedding much light on their meaning. They would seem to be meaningless where the freight is actually under charter, but in cases where there is no definite charter, as where the owner employs his vessel for the carriage of his own property, this phrase could take on the meaning that the freight, while not actually chartered freight, was to be insured under as favorable conditions as would chartered freight. When the freight to be earned on a future voyage is insured during the present trip, and the contract for the future voyage is under agreement but has not been reduced to a formal charter, the combined expression "freight on board or not on board, chartered or as if chartered" would seem to provide specifically for both contingencies; *i.e.,* the fact that the goods to which the insured freight relates are not yet on board and that the formal charter has not yet been signed. The money that the owner of a vessel saves by carrying his own goods can be insured as freight in the same manner as freight to be earned for the carriage of the property of others.

Termination of Risk. A policy of insurance on freight continues to cover until the contract of affreightment is completed, broken up, or abandoned. It is not necessary, however, that the protection afforded be concurrent with the freight contract; it may cover only a portion of the intended voyage if such intention is clearly indicated in the policy. Freight may also be insured on time. That is, a policy may be written to cover the freight at risk on a vessel or a fleet of vessels for a definite period of time, say one year. The amount at risk at any one time is limited to a specific sum, and the freight is valued on some definite basis such as freight list or amount of charter. Under such a policy, in the event of loss the amount recoverable would be the proportion of the loss that the amount insured bears to the total amount of the freight list or of the charter. Declarations of insurance are made in the same manner as under an open cargo contract, premium being charged on the amounts as reported.

Amount Insured. The amount insured on freight should be limited to the gross amount at risk plus the cost of the insurance. No account is taken of the cost of earning the freight to be paid. Under a long-time charter the cost of operation may vary greatly, so that, if freight payments are made monthly, one month may show a considerable profit whereas a later month may result in an equal amount of loss. The amount at risk should be constant or, if insured for the whole amount of the charter, should be reduced proportionately month by month as the freight is earned. Again, a ship operator may charter a vessel for a lump-sum freight but, on putting the vessel on the berth, be able to obtain only a part cargo or, obtaining a full cargo, have a total freight list aggregating less than the amount paid or to be paid for the charter. Nevertheless, the bill-of-lading freight is the only freight he has at risk, the loss on the charter not being in any way involved in the successful prosecution of the voyage.

Duty Insurance. Import duty is another intangible subject of insurance which bears a striking resemblance, in the scope of the risk to which the interest is exposed, to collectible freight or freight contingency. In some countries there is an export duty which, like prepaid or guaranteed freight, becomes part of the value of the goods and may be insured as such. Import duties, however, are collected only on goods actually received into the country, whether such goods are in sound or damaged condition when received. Duty insurance is confined in large measure to imports into the United States which are taxable under the tariff. On such goods the government demands duty at the rate provided in the tariff and makes no allowance for depreciation due to damage unless a package is delivered empty or is so damaged as not to be worth the duty to be paid and is abandoned. In certain cases of loss, refund of duty is allowed, but such exceptions are rare. If a case of goods arrives in a damaged condition and full duty is paid, the loss on the goods is not only the depreciation on the invoice value but the same depreciation on the increased cost involved in the payment of the duty, the value of the article being judged in the American market on the basis of duty-paid commodities. Thus, in determining the percentage of loss the gross sound and damaged values are compared. This percentage is applied by the underwriter to the insured value. If the duty is insured, its insured value or the actual amount of duty paid will be added to the insured value of the goods and the percentage of loss applied to the combined amount. If, on the other hand, the duty is not insured, the percentage will apply only to the insured value of the goods, the loss on the duty paid being entirely at the risk of the assured. As in the case of freight contingency, there being no risk on duty until the goods arrive, the rate of premium charged on the amount of duty is low, usually one-third of the rate on the goods. In the case of both freight contingency and duty, after payment of the freight and/or the duty, the amount so paid becomes part of the value of the goods from the time of payment and is insured thereafter in the same manner as the goods to which the payments relate. This arrangement is important to the owner of the goods, since, under warehouse-to-warehouse policies, the goods remain at risk for some time after the charges have been paid. If the transit includes an interior rail or water haul, the goods may be exposed to serious transportation hazards.

Premium Due Even if Duty Not Paid. Merchants who are conscientious in reporting shipments applicable to open policies sometimes fail to report duties or collectible freight on shipments insured under such policies in cases where the vessel is lost at sea or where goods are destroyed before being laden on the vessel, on the theory that, while in such cases the underwriter may be liable for the loss on the goods, the question of duty or collectible freight is not involved. When a risk has once attached, the underwriter is entitled to all the premium for all the risks that would have been covered if the voyage had been fully completed. The right of the underwriter to premium on duty and collectible freight in the cases cited is therefore beyond question. In some cases underwriters agree to make adjustments, including the amount of duty paid, without requiring that separate reports of duty be made and separate premiums paid. Nevertheless, in such cases the assured actually pays premium for insuring the duty either by an increase of rate on the goods or by increasing the advance on the basic value, thus producing a larger amount against which the cargo rate is assessed.

Contingent Risks. Underwriters are sometimes asked to insure other types of contingent risks. A merchant may sell goods on f.o.b. or f.a.s. terms so that his legal liability for providing insurance ceases when the goods are water-borne (f.o.b.) or alongside the ship ready to be loaded (f.a.s.). However, if the draft for the goods has not been accepted or paid, and if he does not wish to depend on the credit of the consignee or lacks evidence that the consignee has insured the goods, he may insure the goods for his own account until the draft is paid. Underwriters usually charge less than the full-voyage rate for this contingent risk. Again, certain governments, for example, Argentina, require that all insurance, including insurance on exports and imports, must be placed with an insurance company chartered by that government. Such insurance probably would be written in the foreign currency of such government. The other party to the contract, whether shipper or consignee, might be unwilling to rely on this native insurance and for his own protection might again insure the goods with underwriters of his own choice. In such a case it is probable he would have to pay full rates for what is, in fact, double insurance, but he would not be subject to the rules with respect to double insurance.[1]

[1] See p. 203.

CHAPTER 20

War Insurance

The Problem. Two world wars and the continuing threat of further international conflict between major powers have made necessary a complete reappraisal of the problem of war insurance. It may be argued with considerable justification that modern bombs and the airplanes from which they can be dropped create a situation that makes impossible the assumption of the resultant losses by marine underwriters. Disregard of the heretofore accepted principles of international law adds to the problem of the war underwriter, as he has no knowledge of what any nation may do in armed conflict. From the time the German government in World War I sent its submarines into international waters, sinking unarmed merchant ships without warning, there has been a gradual deterioration of the respect in which international law and the rules of warfare have been held. Marine underwriters, who for hundreds of years have served merchants and shipowners in times of peace and of war, must consider whether the hazards of future warfare can be underwritten. To accept premium for assuming risks which, because of their severity, can lead only to the financial embarrassment of the companies cannot be justified. It must be remembered that prior to World War II underwriters assuming the risks of war on shore learned from the civil wars in Spain and China that modern war from the air produced catastrophic losses when whole areas of cities were destroyed. It became apparent that to insure war risks on shore was commercially impracticable.

War Insurance Vital. Overseas trade, which must be carried on whether peace or war prevails, cannot be conducted without some form of insurance protection. Until the risk becomes uninsurable commercially, it must be assumed that marine underwriters will continue to cover at least some of the hazards of war. While a state of international war exists, the insurance of war hazards occupies a dominant position in the world insurance markets. For many years prior to the outbreak of World War I there had been no serious conflict between major powers. On the contrary, intensive efforts had been made to prevent war by instituting a court for the adjudication of international disputes. Other efforts were made to establish codes for the conduct of war if it should come. Between the two world wars similar efforts were made. Attempts to outlaw the use of submarines, aircraft, and poison gas and other means of chemical warfare were made without success. World War II started with the unannounced invasion of Poland, and underwriters knew that little respect would be given to international law. Expediency was the rule in that war.

The Past No Certain Guide for the Future. Again we are passing through a period when most of the leading nations of the world are making a supreme effort to find some warless method of settling international disputes. Meanwhile, scientific inquiry continues, and new physical and chemical instruments of war are being perfected. The development of aircraft has made almost unbelievable strides since the close of World War II. Should a new war between first-class powers break out, it is almost certain that underwriters will face entirely new problems. It will be more profitable to consider the known past than to speculate on the probable war hazards of the unknown future. Present international effort is directed to the prevention of conflicts rather than to the formulation of rules for the conduct of wars. In the event of a future conflict involving maritime nations, the marine underwriter will approach the problem of insuring war hazards with an open mind ready to meet changing conditions as they arise. It will be best first to consider war insurance from a historical standpoint and then review the problems faced and solved in World War II and since then.

A Great War Thought to Be Impossible. Before 1914 the belief that wars of great magnitude were at an end was justified by the various efforts made during the latter part of the nineteenth century and the beginning of the twentieth to bring the nations of the world together with the object of establishing universal peace. Conferences of the nations were held at The Hague, but the result of these gatherings showed that not all nations were ready to submit their differences to an international court of arbitration. Efforts were therefore made to establish international rules of conduct, should war occur, that would safeguard noncombatants, protect peaceful commerce on the high seas, and, in connection with the destruction of belligerent commerce, at least save life. The Declaration of London was proposed, a code of laws for the conduct of naval warfare on the high seas embodying the well-established principles of international law and amplifying such principles to bring them more into conformity with the advanced ideas of humanity that the Hague Conferences had demonstrated reflected the desires of the larger part of the nations of the world. At the outbreak of World War I this declaration had been ratified by most of the powerful nations and had been accepted in principle by some that had not actually ratified it. Like all international agreements, unanimous consent was necessary, the will of the majority having no power over the minority. The Declaration of London was not, therefore, an enforceable international code. However, it laid down principles so well established by international law and usage and doctrines so in accord with the dictates of humanity that it was fair to assume that the spirit of the code would be observed in the conduct of maritime warfare.

Perils Judged by International Law. Underwriters in 1914 had little practical experience in the underwriting of war insurance. It was reasonable for them to assume that the hazards against which they would be called upon to furnish protection were those in connection with naval warfare conducted in accordance with this and other codes, such as the Declaration of Paris, and in accordance with the proposals offered for acceptance at the Hague Conferences. In general, it was assumed that the conduct of war on the high seas would follow international law and that underwriting based on that law would produce results satisfactory to both assured and underwriter. How far maritime warfare departed from these international rules is now well known, but underwriters fell into the common error of assuming that the war would be fought according to the laws governing civilized nations. Changes were made so quickly in the methods of warfare that underwriters were kept on the alert in order to make the conditions of their policies conform to the rapidly changing war conditions.

The Declaration of London. The Declaration of London had for its primary purpose the definition of that portion of international law relating to cases which would come before a prize court for adjudication. Study of it will give a fairly lucid idea of the principles upon which underwriters then felt they could rely in determining the hazards assumed when covering the risks of war.

Blockade in Time of War. The first subject treated in the Declaration was *blockade in time of war.* Immediately on the opening of hostilities in World War I, the Allied nations endeavored to enforce a blockade against the Teutonic powers. Under the earlier Declaration of Paris, certain rules were laid down for the conduct of a blockade, and these rules were incorporated in the new Declaration of London. It was held necessary that a blockade, in order to be binding, must be effective; that is, it must be sufficiently maintained actually to prevent access to the enemy coast line. The blockade would not be valid unless applied impartially to the ships of all neutral nations, but temporary raising of the blockade because of stress of weather would not invalidate it. The mere establishment of the blockade, however, would not make it effective unless it were properly proclaimed to the world, with specifications as to when it would begin, its geographical limits, and the period during which neutral vessels caught within the limits of the blockade might come out. Whether or not a neutral vessel might be captured for breach of blockade would depend on her knowledge, actual or presumptive, of the blockade, but it would be assumed that the vessel possessed such knowledge if she left a neutral port subsequent to the power to which such port belonged having received notification of the blockade. It was further ruled that the blockading forces must not bar access to neutral ports or coasts. Regardless of the question of ultimate destination of a vessel or of her cargo, it was stated that she could not be captured for breach of blockade if at the time she was on her way to a nonblockaded port. Under the Declaration, a vessel found guilty of breach of blockade was liable to condemnation. The cargo would be condemned unless it was proved that, at the time the goods were shipped, the shipper neither knew nor could have known of the intent to break the blockade.

Contraband of War. The second chapter of the Declaration of London dealt with contraband of war. The word *contraband* is derived from the original warnings served by belligerents on neutrals in early wars to the effect that certain trades were contrary to their ban or edict. Under the heading of contraband in the Declaration articles are grouped in three lists, the first of which could, without notice, be treated as absolute contraband. These articles are such as are directly used in the offensive or defensive operations of warfare. It was also provided that other articles exclusively used for war might be added to the list of absolute contraband by a declaration which must be proclaimed to all nations. The second list was composed of articles that, though capable of being used in war, were also useful for the purposes of peace. These, without notice, might be treated as conditional contraband. As in the case of absolute contraband, articles might be added to the list of conditional contraband if they were of the same character as the enumerated articles upon due notice being given to other nations. It was provided that the articles in the third list might not be declared contraband because these articles could not be presumed to be useful in war. In view of the devices of warfare developed in World War I, in the line of explosives, ammunition, and offensive weapons, some of the articles included in this last list, such as raw cotton used in the manufacture of gun cotton, silk used in airplane manufacture, rubber in the manufacture of shells and in the equipment of automobiles, created an anomalous situation.

Absolute Contraband. Absolute contraband was liable to capture if it could be shown that it was destined for territory belonging to or occupied by the enemy or the armed forces of the enemy, it being immaterial whether the carriage of such goods was direct or necessitated transshipment by land or water. The method of proof of such destination was carefully set forth in the Declaration. The articles contained in the list of conditional contraband were liable to capture only if it could be shown that they were destined for the use of the armed forces or of a governmental department of an enemy state, and provision was made for determining whether such goods were so destined. Conditional contraband was not liable to capture unless it was on board a vessel bound for territory belonging to or occupied by the enemy or was destined for the armed forces of the enemy and was not to be discharged at an intervening neutral port.

Carriage of Contraband Cause for Condemnation. A vessel carrying absolute or conditional contraband might be captured on the high seas and would be condemned if the contraband, reckoned by value, weight, volume, or freight, formed more than one-half the cargo. The contraband itself was liable to condemnation, and other goods belonging to the owner of the contraband and on board the same vessel were also liable to condemnation. If a vessel was encountered on the high seas while unaware of the outbreak of hostilities or of the declaration of contraband that applied to her cargo, the contraband could not be condemned except on payment of compensation. The same rule applied if the master, knowing of the outbreak of hostilities or of the declaration of contraband, had no opportunity of discharging the contraband. Where a vessel was stopped and contraband found, but not in sufficient proportion to condemn the ship, it was provided that she should be at liberty to proceed if the master was willing to hand over the contraband to the challenging ship. The captor was at liberty to destroy contraband received under these conditions.

Unneutral Service. The third chapter of the Declaration dealt with unneutral service, declaring that a vessel was subject to condemnation, first, if she was on a voyage undertaken with the special purpose of transporting individuals who were members of the armed forces of the enemy or for the purpose of transmitting intelligence to the enemy and, second, if the vessel knowingly transported a military detachment of the enemy or individuals who, in the course of the voyage, directly assisted the operations of the enemy. If the vessel was so used, cargo belonging to the owner of the vessel was also liable to condemnation. Furthermore, a neutral vessel would be condemned and would, in a general way, receive the same treatment as an enemy merchantman if she took part directly in hostilities, was under the orders or control of an agent of the enemy government, was exclusively in its employ, or was engaged exclusively in the transport of enemy troops or in the transmission of intelligence in the interest of the enemy.

Destruction of Neutral Prizes. Chapter four of the Declaration related to the destruction of neutral prizes. A neutral vessel that had been captured might not be destroyed by the captor, but must be taken into port for the determination of all questions concerning the validity of the capture. An exception was made in cases where the belligerent warship that had captured a vessel subject to condemnation would endanger herself or would involve in danger the enterprise in which she was engaged if she attempted to bring the captured vessel into port. Nevertheless, if conditions rendered excusable such destruction, all persons on board the captured vessel must be placed in safety and the ship's papers preserved in order that the validity of the capture might later be determined. The circumstances warranting the destruction of a neutral prize before the validity of capture was determined must be of an exceptional nature; otherwise the captor must pay compensation to the interested parties and the question whether the capture was valid would not be examined. If, on the other hand, the destruction was held to be justifiable but the capture invalid, the captor must pay compensation to the interested parties in lieu of restitution, which could not be made. The owner of the goods that were not subject to condemnation but that were destroyed with the vessel was entitled to compensation.

Transfer of Vessels. Convoy. Right of Search. Other chapters dealt with the transfer of enemy vessels to a neutral flag, the method of determining the enemy character of vessel and cargo, and ships sailing under convoy. It was provided that forcible resistance to the legitimate exercise of the right of stoppage, search, and capture involved in all cases the condemnation of the vessel. The cargo was treated as cargo on an enemy vessel, and goods owned by the master or owner were treated as enemy goods, If the capture of vessel or goods was not upheld by the prize court, or if the prize was released without judgment being given, the parties interested could claim compensation unless the capture itself were justified by the circumstances.

International Law Not Observed. The above-outlined principles were, in general, those by which underwriters felt that they would be governed in writing insurance against war perils. It was, however, early perceived that the rules observed in earlier wars and the rules proposed for the conduct of future wars would not be adhered to in this conflict, which quickly became worldwide and involved warfare with nations that had no respect for solemn treaty obligations and no reverence for international law. Accordingly, the Allied nations, while striving to adhere to the principles of the Declaration of London and of international law in general, were gradually forced to give a broad interpretation to those principles and in many cases to abrogate them. That such action did at times do violence to the rights of neutral nations cannot be doubted, but that such action was justified, considering the issues involved in the conflict, is now generally admitted.

Doctrine of Ultimate Destination. Preemption. Underwriters soon discovered that the blockade which was being enforced included neutral coasts and, because of the long coast line, could not really be effective. The doctrine of ultimate destination was revived and extended, when it was proved beyond doubt that the ports of certain neutral countries were being used merely as transshipment points on the route to the enemy. Furthermore, it was found that, owing to the secret methods used by the enemy to bring forward contraband, the search of vessels at sea was impracticable. This resulted finally in all vessels destined for neutral ports of countries adjacent to or in the vicinity of enemy territory being taken into Allied ports and there searched. This involved serious losses even when it was found that no contraband was on board. Furthermore, captured vessels were exposed to the dangers of navigation in belligerent waters protected by mine fields and other war devices. That the reason for making these captures was a justifiable one was amply demonstrated by the fact that manifests were found to be improperly drawn, describing packages as containing lawful commodities which in reality contained absolute contraband of war. Furthermore, the Allied governments exercised the right of preemption; that is, articles which were free from capture under international law but which it was clear would give aid or comfort to the enemy were taken by the Allied governments, and what they deemed just compensation was made to the owners. The lists of contraband articles changed so rapidly that it was almost impossible for underwriters to follow them.

Unforeseen Perils. On the other hand, the Teutonic allies, having no ports of their own into which they could bring prizes for adjudication, sank neutral vessels on the high seas in absolute violation of the rights of neutral nations. While the Allied nations endeavored to ease the burden of their search and blockade by making examination of vessels at the port of shipment, by granting licenses for forwarding goods, and by approval of shipments consigned in certain ways, as to the Netherlands Overseas Trust, the Teutonic allies carried on their illegal seizures and sinkings with increasing disrespect for the rights of neutrals and with disregard for the rights of enemy nonbelligerents and neutral citizens to safety of life and limb provided for under international law. Finally, with the issuance of a decree establishing a "barred zone" and the unrestricted destruction of vessels in the submarine campaign instituted by the German government, underwriters found themselves confronted with a situation without precedent.

Neutrality Warranties. In order to obviate some of the difficulties encountered in the insurance of war perils, clauses were devised from time to time varying the protection afforded. Neutrality clauses in various forms were drawn up under which it was warranted that, during the term of the insurance, the property insured was consigned to American or other neutral citizens, firms, or corporations and that the names and addresses of such consignees would be stated in the bill of lading. The property was also warranted for consumption in some specified neutral country. This warranty served to protect the underwriter from claim if deception was being practiced in regard to the neutrality of the shipment, breach of the warranty voiding the insurance.

Free-of-British-capture Clause. A clause further restricting the liability of underwriters in connection with the right of search and capture exercised by the Allied governments was, early in the war, inserted in many policies covering shipments to neutral countries. This warranty, which came to be the most used one in war insurance, read in its common form: "Warranted free from any claim arising from capture, seizure, arrest, restraints, preemption or detainments by the British government or their Allies." After the entrance of the United States into the war in 1917, it became customary to add "the United States government" to this clause. Other forms amplifying the meaning of this clause but having the same general purpose were used in connection with war insurance.

Trading with the Enemy. Early in the war, the Allies discovered that citizens of neutral countries, in violation of the principles of neutrality, were giving aid and comfort to the enemy in many ways. This led to "Trading with the Enemy Acts," under which enemies and what constitutes trading with the enemy were defined. Upon the entrance of the United States into the war, similar legislation was passed by Congress. Under the power of these Acts, lists were prepared containing the names of persons, firms, and corporations domiciled in neutral countries who were classed as enemies and subject to treatment as such by the Allied governments. Vessels owned by such enemies were posted as subject to treatment as enemy vessels. These names and vessels appeared in "proscribed" or "black" lists. It was not possible to keep informed of the many changes in such lists, and accordingly, clauses were drawn providing that the protection of the policy did not extend to any of the firms, corporations, or individuals coming within the ban of such Acts.

Licenses. Neutral governments, in order that they might be able to obtain supplies for their citizens, entered into arrangements with Allied governments by which goods consigned to certain governmental corporations and warranted for consumption in such countries would not be subject to capture, seizure, detention, or destruction. The most prominent of these corporations was the Netherlands Overseas Trust, to whose consignment vast quantities of stores entered Holland unmolested. A warranty of consignment to this Trust was inserted in many war-insurance policies, full war protection being afforded in such cases. For certain commodities licenses were granted by the Allied governments permitting the importation into neutral countries of definite quantities under restrictions set forth in the licenses. Full insurance against war perils was also granted on goods warranted shipped under such licenses.

Water-borne Clauses. It was in the light of this historical background that marine underwriters faced the unknown problems of World War II. Some new experience had been gained by the insurance of war perils on shore. In the civil wars in Spain and China losses incurred from bombing taxed the financial ability of the underwriters insuring the risks that produced them. Such shore risks thereafter were considered uninsurable commercially, and *water-borne clauses* were made part of war-risk policies. By their terms no war risks were covered on property on shore, and on property in transit war risks were covered only when the goods became water-borne on the ocean vessel. The water-borne clause used by marine underwriters does, however, subject to limitation of time, cover war risks on shore during transshipment.

Free-of-capture-and-seizure Clause. Because of the use of atom bombs during World War II and the development of weapons of war employing atomic fission or radioactive force since the close of that war, the free-of-capture clause has been reworded and in a marine cargo policy now reads:

Notwithstanding anything herein contained to the contrary, this insurance is warranted free from capture, seizure, arrest, restraint, detainment, confiscation, preemption, requisition or nationalization, and the consequences thereof or any attempt thereat, whether in time of peace or war and whether lawful or otherwise; also warranted free, whether in time of peace or war, from all loss or damage caused by any weapon of war employing atomic fission or radioactive force; also warranted free from all consequences of hostilities or warlike operations (whether there be a declaration of war or not) but this warranty shall not exclude collision, explosion or contact with any fixed or floating object (other than a mine or torpedo), stranding, heavy weather or fire unless caused directly (and independently of the nature of the voyage or service which the vessel concerned or, in the case of collision, any other vessel involved therein, is performing), by a hostile act by or against a belligerent power; and for the purpose of this warranty "power" includes any authority maintaining naval, military or air forces in association with a power.

Further warranted free from the consequences of civil war, revolution, rebellion, insurrection, or civil strife arising therefrom, or piracy.

The free-of-capture clause in the marine hull policy has been similarly changed.

Separate War Policy. Prior to 1938 it was the practice of underwriters, when requested to insure the risks of war, to delete the free-of-capture clause and thus restore the basic policy to its original form including war perils. In 1938 the underwriters decided that they would no longer follow this practice but would issue a separate war-risk policy citing precisely what war perils were covered and under what conditions they were insured. This new war-risk policy, whether for cargo or hull, is a complete contract. To avoid unnecessary detail by requiring the repetition of all the information that must be reported under the open marine policy, the open cargo war-risk policy (page 452) contains the following clause:

(No. 8) It is agreed that the report of shipments made under the policy against marine risks mentioned above shall be deemed to be reports under this policy also, and the assured agrees to pay premiums on all shipments insured under this policy at the war risk rates of this company as fixed from time to time.

It is advisable to insure both war and marine perils with the same underwriter so that no question may arise as to liability in the case of a missing vessel or where there may be doubt as to the real cause of loss. In the insurance of cargo this practice is customarily followed. In the case of hull insurance and of some cargoes, where the price was controlled by the government during World War II, this practice was not followed, as the United States government insured most hulls against war risks and absorbed the war risk on price-controlled commodities.

Perils Clause. The perils clause (1) in the Institute Cargo War Risk policy reads as follows:

> This insurance is only against the risks of capture, seizure, destruction or damage by men-of-war, piracy, takings at sea, arrests, restraints, detainments and other warlike operations and acts of kings, princes and peoples in prosecution of hostilities or in the application of sanctions under international agreements, whether before or after declaration of war and whether by a belligerent or otherwise, including factions engaged in civil war, revolution, rebellion or insurrection, or civil strife arising therefrom, and including the risks of aerial bombardment, floating or stationary mines and stray or derelict torpedoes and weapons of war employing atomic fission or radioactive force; but excluding claims for delay, deterioration and/or loss of market, and warranted not to abandon (on any ground other than physical damage to ship or cargo) until after condemnation of the property insured.

In Chap. 11 most of the perils named in this clause were considered, as they are perils named in the basic policy. In the free-of-capture clause new words appear, reading "also warranted free, whether in time of peace or war, from all loss or damage caused by any weapon employing atomic fission or radioactive force." In the perils clause, in addition to naming the usual war perils, the following words are added, "and weapons of war employing atomic fission or radioactive force." Much consideration has been given by underwriters to the grave question whether it is possible, commercially, to insure against the hazards of atomic fission or radioactive force. By these two clauses the marine underwriter states his present position with respect to this problem. First, as a peacetime problem, he is not willing to cover perils caused by a weapon of war employing these forces. He is content, under the marine policy, to cover these perils if they arise from the use of these forces in ways other than in connection with war weapons. In the war-risk policy he assumes these hazards arising from the use of such weapons. Whether, in the event of another war, the marine underwriters could continue to assume these hazards is very doubtful. From the experience at Hiroshima and Nagasaki and the later experimental explosions in the Pacific Ocean, it would seem that these forces produce catastrophic losses too great to be assumed commercially.

War and Marine Policies Not Coextensive. It does not follow because of clause 8 of the war-risk policy with respect to the reporting of shipments that the marine- and the war-insurance policies cover for the same period of time. Clause 4 of the Institute Cargo War Risk form makes the following limitations of time during which the war insurance is in force:

4. (a) The insurance against the risks enumerated in Clause 1, except the risks of floating or stationary mines and stray or derelict torpedoes, floating or submerged, referred to in (b) below, shall not attach to the interest hereby insured or to any part thereof

(i) prior to being on board an overseas Vessel (for the purpose of this Clause 4 an overseas Vessel shall be deemed to mean a Vessel carrying the interest from one port or place to another where such voyage involves a sea passage by that Vessel),

(ii) after being discharged overside from an overseas Vessel at the final port of discharge,

or

after expiry of 15 days counting from midnight of the day of arrival of the overseas Vessel at the final port of discharge, whichever shall first occur,

(iii) after expiry of 15 days from midnight of the day of arrival of the overseas Vessel at an intermediate port or place to discharge the interest for on-carriage from that or any other port or place by another overseas Vessel, but shall re-attach, as the interest is loaded on the on-carrying overseas Vessel. During the said period of 15 days the insurance remains in force whether the interest is awaiting transit or in transit between the overseas Vessels.

(b) The insurance against the risks of floating or stationary mines and stray or derelict torpedoes, floating or submerged, attaches as the interest hereby insured is first loaded on lighter, craft, or vessel after leaving the warehouse at point of shipment in transit for the destination declared hereunder, and ceases to attach as the interest is finally landed from the vessel, craft or lighter prior to delivery to warehouse at such destination. If the contract of affreightment is terminated at a port or place other than the destination named therein such port or place shall be deemed the final port of discharge for the purpose of this Clause. Shipments by air and/or mail, if covered by this Policy, are insured continuously from the time of leaving the sender's premises until delivered to the place of address.

It is a condition of this insurance that the Assured shall act with reasonable dispatch in all circumstances within their control. If anything contained in this Policy shall be inconsistent with this Clause 4 it shall to the extent of such inconsistency be null and void.

This keeps the war-risk cover in harmony with the water-borne theory.[1]

War and Marine Risks Separately Insured. While it is desirable that marine and war risks be covered in identical amounts by the same underwriter, it is not possible in all cases. Coverage by different underwriters often leads to considerable embarrassment where it is doubtful whether a loss to the insured subject is due to a marine or to a war peril. Where both war and marine insurance are covered in the same policy or with the same underwriters in separate policies, and the loss is a valid claim under either the war or the marine insurance, the only doubt being as to which policy was liable, the underwriter will settle the claim. Where, however, the war and marine insurance are placed with different underwriters, each may deny liability. Many such cases are carried to the courts, especially in connection with missing vessels, that is, vessels that sail but never arrive at their destination and from which no tidings are received indicating the cause of loss. In such cases, there formerly was a presumption that the loss was due to marine perils, but owing to the changed conditions of warfare and to the unrestricted use of submarines and airplanes, this presumption has in large measure disappeared, and individual losses are decided on their merits. Even where the full facts as to the cause of the loss are known, there may

[1] See pp. 325, 334.

be doubt whether the loss is a marine or war loss because of conflicting legal decisions. In some cases it may be doubtful whether the loss occurring is one covered by either a war or a marine policy.

Doubtful Losses. Such a case was that of the steamer *Canadia*, which in the early months of World War I was stopped off the Butte of Lewis by a British cruiser and boarded by an Admiralty officer. In order to facilitate examination of cargo, the steamer was ordered to Kirkwall. Against the advice of the master of the vessel, the Admiralty officer ordered the vessel to proceed over a dangerous course in the night, with the result that the vessel was run ashore and wrecked. The underwriters on the marine policies claimed that this was not a marine loss, the vessel being already captured and in charge of the Admiralty. The war underwriters claimed that the loss was due to a marine peril, notwithstanding the fact that an Admiralty officer was on board. Eminent counsel gave opinions pro and con, some even holding that the loss was not one contemplated by the coverage of either policy. The Court held the loss to be due to war perils.

In World War II the question of doubtful losses became a most serious one. The most outstanding case was that of the *Coxwold*. This vessel was in convoy on a voyage to Narvik, Norway. In a heavy rain squall and, as it developed, some miles off her course due to a tidal set, she ran ashore on the westerly side of the Isle of Skye, Scotland. She refloated without assistance, joined her convoy, and was later repaired. The British government, which had assumed the war risk, admitted that the vessel was engaged in a warlike operation but denied that the stranding was caused by this operation. The House of Lords held it to be a war loss.

The result of this decision was that British underwriters amended their marine policies so that similar casualties would be considered to be marine losses. American underwriters did not follow this practice because the United States government, through the War Shipping Administration, had assumed the risks of war on the merchant fleet and on certain cargo. The government wished to keep commodity prices down and so covered under its war-risk assumption certain losses due to wartime conditions. These included collision in convoy or resulting from vessels running without lights, stranding occasioned by removal of lights and other aids to navigation or due to navigation without the aid of a pilot. The American commercial insurance market broadened its war cover to conform to the government plan.

Thus the British and American war-risk policies differed. When war insurance was in one market and marine insurance in the other, the assured was in a most difficult position. A system was soon devised by which British underwriters, insuring war risks on a shipment insured against marine risks in the American market, covered the additional risks excluded by the free-of-capture-and-seizure clause in the American marine policy. While this situation existed, this procedure was called "marrying the clauses." Now the clauses in the two markets are similar.

Sanctions. Between the two world wars a new word entered marine insurance terminology. This word *sanctions* is difficult to define. It might be defined as "punitive measures to enforce observance of international obligations." The term was used in Roman law to signify a penalty visited upon a person who violated the law. On occasions in past history, so-called sanctions were applied by stronger states against weaker states. They sometimes took the form of withdrawing diplomatic officers, requiring a salute to the flag, enforcement of embargoes and pacific blockades, naval demonstrations, or reprisals of various kinds. In the Covenant of the League of Nations, Art. 16, it was provided that, if any member of the League should resort to war in disregard of its covenants, it should *ipso facto* be deemed to have committed an act of war against other members of the League. The other members undertook thereupon to subject the offending nation to the severance of all trade or financial relations, prohibition of all intercourse between their nationals and the nationals of the covenant-breaking state, and the prevention of all financial, commercial, or personal intercourse between the nationals of the covenant-breaking state and the nationals of any other state, whether a member of the League or not.

When Italy threatened to invade Ethiopia, efforts were made through the League of Nations to dissuade her. Failing this, it was urged that sanctions be applied to her by international agreement under Art. 16 of the Covenant. The use of sanctions is a warlike act to prevent hostilities. It has some of the same characteristics as an embargo or blockade, as it can be useful only if effective. The thought in the Italian case was that by withholding materials, such as oil and articles essential to the making of munitions or to the carrying out of warlike activities, Italy would not be capable of carrying out her warlike intentions. The scheme failed, as all nations would not agree to join in the sanctions. If the materials could be had from certain nations, the only effect of the sanctions would be to interfere with the normal commercial activities of the other nations willing to impose sanctions.

Frustration Clause. At the commencement of World War I there were many cargoes afloat in steamers, under Allied flags, destined for enemy ports. The captains of these vessels, upon receiving word of the threatened outbreak of war, usually made for their home ports. They could not thereafter legally sail for their port of destination, and the venture was accordingly terminated. The courts held that this amounted to a frustration of the venture caused by arrests, restraints, or detainments of kings, princes, or peoples—perils assumed in the policy when the free-of-capture-and-seizure clause is deleted. Following these decisions, underwriters added to their policies the frustration clause, which in its present form reads:

> Warranted free from any claim based upon loss of, or frustration of, the insured voyage or adventure caused by arrests, restraints or detainments.

and is now included in the war-risk policy.

New War Devices. Aside from breaches or modifications of international law, war perils differ little from war to war although the weapons used change greatly. The destruction of ships from within and from without is accomplished by new methods. Bombs placed in the cargo attached to clock devices set to cause explosion and destruction or to cause fire on the high seas, and bombs attached to the rudders of vessels and exploded by a mechanism wound up by the natural working of the rudder, are typical of the diabolical devices used in the destruction of vessels. The establishment of mine areas covering many square miles and extending into international waters, with the possibility that many of the mines will break loose and become floating traps for innocent vessels, and the removal of necessary aids to navigation, both produce conditions that make the navigation of vessels extremely hazardous.

Aircraft. The perils of war for which the underwriter assumes responsibility are not only on the seas and under the seas but also above the seas. Destruction by airplane or airship is one of the war perils included under the all-embracing term "men-of-war." The risk from this cause is a great hazard, particularly over ocean routes approaching the ports. Air raids are not confined to the ocean lanes but in many cases involve the destruction of ships in harbors. The risk of the underwriter is limited by the terms of the war-risk policy that contains the water-borne clause.

Submarines, Raiders, and Bombers. The three outstanding perils that the underwriter is called upon to assume and that are assumed without any restriction of liability by clause or otherwise are the destruction of vessels by submarines, by raiders, and by bombers. The activities of submarines compass the bulk of the destruction of commerce, but the operation of these sea wolves and of the bombers is in a measure limited geographically by the physical limitations of the craft themselves, whereas the activity of commerce raiders is world wide.

New and Unusual Hazards. In addition to the fact that the operation of submarines in the destruction of neutral vessels in a great many instances directly violates the rules of international law and the dictates of humanity, the use of this type of man-of-war produces new and unusual perils to navigation. The submarine, operating under water a part of the time, produces a menace to navigation similar in some respects to a submerged derelict, and not a few serious casualties have resulted through collisions with submerged submarines. Such casualties have occurred not alone in international waters but also in territorial waters. In harbors, vessels have collided with submerged submarines, and instances have been reported where a submarine, attempting to emerge directly beneath a vessel, caused serious damage to both craft. Vessels are compelled to navigate without showing lights and also encounter many unusual dangers in joining, sailing with, and parting from convoys.

The nature of the casualty, whether a war or a marine peril, in all these cases becomes a matter of dispute among underwriters with conflicting interests. The law reports are filled with interesting cases arising out of these unusual perils and situations.

Warranty of Proper Documents. Though not a question of war risk, a situation arose during World War II that created anxiety in the minds of marine underwriters. To enable ships to enter and leave ports without too much delay, they were required to carry certain prescribed documents to prove their nationality, etc. Without such documents a vessel might be held in port or prevented from entering a port. This might lead to the inability of the captain to refuel, to revictual, or in the event of damage to obtain necessary repairs and thus render the vessel unseaworthy. To avoid these difficulties, underwriters during the war included a warranty in their hull policies providing that the insurance was null and void if the vessel was not properly documented as set forth in considerable detail by the terms of the warranty.

Seizure. The cargo war policy also excludes loss or damage arising from certain acts of friendly governments. This exclusion reads:

> This insurance does not cover any loss or damage caused by or resulting from any of the following causes:
> (a) Commandeering, preemption, requisition or nationalization by the government (de facto or otherwise) of the country to or from which the goods are insured.
> (b) Seizure or destruction under quarantine or customs regulations.

It will be observed that the various items cited in part (*a*) are not necessarily warlike acts but may be the acts of civil or military authorities in furtherance of the economy of the country while engaged in or threatened by warlike activities. The actions cited in part (*b*) are normal activities of a government where a state of peace or war exists.

Cancellation Clauses. It is of the utmost importance to an underwriter that he provide for the cancellation of the war-risk cover on short notice, usually 48 hours, if conditions so change as to make the continuance of war-risk insurance inadvisable. Open cargo war-risk policies are usually permitted to run notwithstanding the rapidly changing conditions in an active war. On specific risks the underwriter is not bound by rates quoted if the vessel does not sail within the dates named. The rates charged on shipments applicable to open cargo war-risk policies are those in effect at the time of the attachment of the risk, usually either the date of sailing of the ocean vessel or the date of the ocean bill of lading. The fixing of war rates for sailings within a named period is sometimes made when the necessity of determining costs is imperative. Such arrangements are *forward bindings* and are granted by underwriters only under special conditions to which the assured must assent.

Hull war-risk insurance, in time of peace, is usually placed for a period of time, say 1, 2, or 3 months. The underwriter is unwilling to be bound irrevocably for such a period if war should threaten or commence. Hull war-risk insurance usually contains a prompt cancellation clause. The present American Institute war-risk hull clause contains the following automatic termination clauses, no special notice of cancellation being required:

A. In the event of outbreak of war between any of the four Great Powers (France, Great Britain and/or any of the British Commonwealth of Nations, the Union of Soviet Socialist Republics, the United States of America) this insurance will ipso facto terminate 48 hours from midnight G.M.T. of the day on which such outbreak of war occurs.

1. Nevertheless should the vessel:—

   (a) Be at sea when such outbreak of War occurs

   or

   (b) Being in a port when such outbreak of War occurs depart therefrom as a measure of safety in respect of an insured peril within 48 hours from midnight G.M.T. of the day on which such outbreak of War occurs,

this insurance shall be continued until midnight G.M.T. of the day on which the vessel is moored at the next port to which the vessel proceeds and 24 hours thereafter.

2. In no case shall this insurance extend beyond the natural expiry time of this policy except that if at such natural expiry time the vessel be at sea

   (a) without having departed from a port after such outbreak of War occurs

   or

   (b) after having departed within 48 hours from midnight G.M.T. of the day on which such outbreak of War occurs from the port in which she was when such outbreak of War occurred as a measure of safety in respect of an insured peril, this insurance shall be extended at a rate to be named by Underwriters until midnight G.M.T. of the day on which the vessel is moored at the next port to which she proceeds and 24 hours thereafter.

B. Notwithstanding any provisions in this policy or in any endorsements thereto to the contrary, this insurance will ipso facto terminate in the event the insured vessel is requisitioned, either for title or use, by the Government of the United States or of the country in which the vessel is owned or registered.

C. In the event of the termination of this insurance by reason of the outbreak of such a war or by the requisition of the insured vessel, pro rata net return of premium shall be payable to the Assured. Such return premium shall be paid on demand or as soon thereafter as practicable to do so. In no other event shall there be any return of premium.

Government War-risk Bureaus. During World War I many governments entered the field of war-risk underwriting. During that war hazards increased so rapidly and values involved in commercial sea ventures were so great that at times the marine-insurance market became demoralized. Rates fluctuated widely, and frequently the commercial market was inadequate to absorb the large values afloat on the extrahazardous routes. The various government war-risk-insurance schemes were welcomed by the underwriters, and their conduct was entrusted to some of the ablest underwriters in the various countries.

Between the two world wars in the United States the insurance bureau continued to function, but as a rule in harmony with the commercial market. In 1937, in an endeavor to prevent war, Congress passed the Neutrality Act. In part this provided that the insurance bureau of the Maritime Commission could not insure a vessel carrying contraband of war. World War II commenced, and it was not possible as a rule to tell whether a vessel was carrying or might carry contraband. The insurance bureau was thus rendered practically impotent, and the only market for war insurance was the commercial market. The Syndicate market was adequate for the insurance of hulls against both marine and war risks. The cargo market could cover any reasonable value against marine and war risks, since the cargo underwriters had established the American Cargo War Risk Reinsurance Exchange.

This condition continued until early in 1942 when Congress repealed the provision dealing with contraband, and the government insurance bureau was free to write war risks. From then on until the end of the war the government insured the war risks on the greater part of the American merchant marine that had been commandeered by the government. The marine risk was generally insured by the commercial underwriters.

It will be recalled that prices were controlled during World War II by the Office of Price Administration (OPA). As the hazards of war at sea increased during 1942 and thereafter, the prices on certain key commodities, like coffee and sugar, that moved over very hazardous routes could not be kept within the price ceilings if the premiums necessarily charged by the marine underwriters were added. The government insurance bureau absorbed the war losses on these commodities, charging a nominal rate for the insurance. This situation continued until these routes became less hazardous and the commercial premiums were low enough to permit their inclusion within the price ceilings, at which time the government ceased to insure these cargoes.

Strikes, Riots, and Civil Commotions. The risks of damage, theft, pilferage, breakage, or destruction by strikers, rioters, and participants in civil commotions (including vandalism, sabotage, and malicious mischief while goods are within the United States, its territories and possessions in the Western Hemisphere, Canada, and Newfoundland) have been insured as an additional coverage under marine policies issued in the United States subject to the special clauses approved by the American Institute which are quoted on page 191.

These risks, which to some extent are similar to the war perils, have been treated in the same manner with respect to the notice required for cancellation, the additional coverage being subject to cancellation by either party upon 48 hours written or telegraphic notice to the other party. In addition, the rates for insuring these risks are named as an addition to the marine rate, but as a matter of recent market practice, the additional premium for strikes and riots coverages has in most cases been included in the published war-risk rates.

CHAPTER 21

Reinsurance

The Problem. If an underwriter could build his own commercial world, it would be one in which he could construct a plan of operation under which he would write insurance in an amount no more and no less than he desired to undertake on any single risk. In some classes of insurance—that of hull insurance in the marine field—he can, to a degree, approach this ideal goal, for hull insurance as a rule is parceled out among many underwriters until the desired amount is obtained. In cargo insurance the custom is for one insurer to issue an open policy and up to its limit, which may be $2,000,000 on a single vessel, to cover all the cargo risks of a merchant. Underwriters can hope to have a successful result only if a *book of business* can be obtained that is spread over many risks in many places without excessive dollar exposures on any one ship or in any one place. How can such a result be attained and an underwriting business still be conducted in the customary manner of issuing policies that expose capital funds to much larger dollar risk than is desired by the underwriter? The answer to this ever-present problem is *reinsurance.*

Destruction of Large Values. The world has frequently been shocked by a great marine casualty, such as the destruction of a giant ocean greyhound, involving the loss of many lives and quickly causing the destruction of property valued at several millions of dollars. Or a short paragraph may be noted in the daily papers announcing that the steamer. . . . ., loaded with 20,000 bales of cotton, ran ashore on the coast of Ireland in a fog, that the crew were saved, but that the vessel and cargo would be a total loss. The loss is estimated at $1,500,000 for the vessel and $3,000,000 for the cargo—huge values, surely large enough to cause embarrassment to any but the strongest insurance company. The destruction of one of these great vessels, where no loss of life is involved, is quickly forgotten by the general public, but after the event has become but a memory to the lay mind, the underwriters are called upon to indemnify the owners of vessel and cargo for the losses suffered.

Reinsurance. The insurance on the vessel itself usually is widely distributed, but where there is a complete cargo of one commodity, as in the cotton case cited in the preceding paragraph, it often happens that the insurance on the whole cargo will be placed with one or two insurance companies. How can these companies stand the strain of a heavy loss of several million dollars in a single venture with the possibility, but not the probability considering the operation of averages, of suffering in a single year one or more similar losses? As losses should be paid out of income and not out of capital, how can such losses be absorbed without making inroads into capital and surplus? Reinsurance makes possible the issuance of policies for large amounts and, what is still more important, makes certain the payment of large losses if incurred. Reinsurance is the system by which one underwriter passes on to another underwriter the whole or part of the risks that he has insured for shipowner or merchant. The original insurance granted to shipowner or merchant is *direct insurance;* the insurance placed by the first underwriter with the second is *reinsurance.*

Distribution of Risks. When the S.S. *Titanic* struck an iceberg and sank in April, 1912, carrying with her scores of helpless human beings and cargo comparatively small in quantity but large in value, the marine-insurance world was stunned by the magnitude of the disaster, and more so considering that the vessel was on her maiden voyage and that the insurance on her had not been in force long enough to add any considerable sum to the income of the underwriters. But within a few weeks the owners of the vessel and cargo were reimbursed for the loss, and what had seemed a terrible financial blow had, after the first shock, caused but a ripple on marine-insurance waters. Into every corner of the marine-insurance world, in Europe, America, and the Far East, either through direct insurance or through reinsurance, the loss was felt and contribution to the indemnity was made.

Growth of Reinsurance. Reinsurance has greatly increased in volume in the last half century since the dawn of the new commercial era of big business. The values at risk in overseas commerce are enormous, and more and more frequently single enterprises engage the full capacity of a vessel. But large enterprises have become large in part by the elimination of unnecessary detail, and the managers of such enterprises have been unwilling to accept protection in small amounts widely distributed over the underwriting field. They have preferred and demanded concentration of protection in a few strong insurers, leaving the distribution of the heavy risk to the underwriters. This has, it is true, relieved the property owner of the detail involved in a multiplicity of policies but has thrown it in some measure upon the underwriter. However, by automatic reinsurance this detail is reduced to a minimum, and the dividing and distributing of risks continue until all the recognized underwriting capital in the markets of the world may be pledged directly or indirectly for the protection of these jumbo lines. Doubtless this has resulted in a degree of dissatisfaction among some of the smaller underwriters, who would prefer to have the prestige that large direct lines give rather than the more certain income obtained from a wide indirect distribution of smaller lines. While it is possible to give a wide direct distribution of the insurance on hulls in marine underwriting, such a method of transacting insurance would encounter difficulties in the placing of cargo insurance.

Necessity for Large Limits. These difficulties will be evident when one considers that in the importation of raw and manufactured products often the first advice of shipment to a merchant is a cable announcing that a steamer has left Singapore with $1,500,000 worth of crude rubber at his risk. Were it not possible for the assured to contract in advance under an open policy or policies for protection sufficiently large to take care of a shipment of this size, arrangements would be made to have the goods shipped insured, that is, on c.i.f. terms, the insurance being placed in foreign markets. It would be impracticable—if not impossible—for the merchant in this country to place such an amount in advance with scores of open-policy contracts ranging in amount from $5,000 to $200,000, the ordinary range of net capacity of the various companies. By *capacity* is meant the maximum amount which the underwriter has decided he is content to insure on any one steamer or in any one location under all policies that he may issue. This amount is determined by adding to the amount that he is willing to assume for his own account (his *retained line* or *net capacity*) the amount that he has arranged by contract to reinsure with other underwriters. An underwriter would not care to engage his maximum capacity for one shipper or when such a large cargo was an exception and the average shipment to the merchant did not exceed $250,000. Under the present system a few underwriters will jointly undertake the insurance of large maximum lines and, by reinsurance, obtain even on smaller declarations a fair run of business. On the other hand, when business eventuates quickly and a large amount of insurance is needed within a few days or sometimes a few hours, were it not possible to place large lines permitting the individual company to distribute the risk, modern business would encounter a handicap which would seriously interfere with the success of commercial undertakings where time is the controlling factor. There is ordinarily enough business to give every company sufficient direct insurance commensurate with its size, for even the largest insurer will not assume more than a limited number of open-policy accounts, that number being controlled largely by its reinsurance facilities, while many small accounts will be placed with the smaller but equally safe insurers. Safety should not be judged by the size of the insurer, but rather by the soundness of its underwriting methods. Most of the large insurers started on a small basis and by conservative methods have attained success.

Retained Lines. From time to time efforts have been made to enact laws that would limit the amount for which a marine underwriter could issue a policy. No success has attended these efforts. It is probable that from time to time such legislation will be proposed, and it is well to be forearmed against a seemingly beneficial form of aid to small insurers that would result adversely to all underwriting and put a serious handicap on business in general. In New York the legislature has recognized the peculiar conditions surrounding the placing of marine insurance and has removed all restrictions on the amount of liability that a marine company may assume, leaving the determination of retained lines to the individual judgment of each company. It is probably true that, except where through some inadvertence the procurement of reinsurance has been overlooked, marine underwriters will carry as a retained line much less than the prescribed limit of 10 per cent of the capital and surplus to which fire and other forms of insurance are limited by law.

Purpose of Reinsurance. Reinsurance then is the method by which liability is distributed over the entire underwriting market. It is a branch of insurance that directly concerns only underwriters, but the insuring public is indirectly interested, in that, by virtue of the system of interreinsurance, underwriters are enabled to spread their liability over vast numbers of risks with a moderate amount of liability on each risk, thus stabilizing the business. Reinsurance, ordinarily, is a matter of little interest to the public. When, however, it is considered that, through the process of reinsurance in time of war, enemies can obtain information in regard to the movement of ocean steamers and, in the fire reinsurance market, information as to the location of manufacturing plants in which government contracts are being executed, attention is directed to this vast and intricate system of distributing liability over the underwriting markets, not only of this country but of the entire world.

Reinsurance Not Different in Principle. Reinsurance in no wise differs in principle from any other form of insurance. The contractual relation is one between underwriter and underwriter instead of between merchant or shipowner and underwriter, but aside from this, the contract of reinsurance resembles *in toto* the ordinary mercantile contract of insurance. An underwriter obtains an insurable interest in each piece of property that he insures because he enters into a relation in which he is financially interested in the continued existence of such property. He will be financially hurt by its injury or destruction through the necessity of reimbursing the owner for the damage or loss incurred. There can, therefore, be no doubt that underwriters have an insurable interest in property that they insure. This being the case, there is no difference in principle between a contract of insurance and a contract of reinsurance. However, in practice, many conditions peculiar to reinsurance appear, and some consideration of them will aid in giving a better understanding of the subject.

Reinsurance Clause. Reinsurance may follow the precise terms and conditions of the original insurance, or the original underwriter may reinsure against only a part of the risks that he assumes direct. Thus, the original underwriter may insure property subject to average but not be able to find any other underwriter who is willing to reinsure on any but free-of-average terms. He may insure both war and marine but only desire to reinsure the marine risks. Various forms of reinsurance clauses are in use. The standard form prepared by the American Institute of Marine Underwriters to make a reinsurance contract subject to the original terms and conditions is as follows:

This reinsurance is subject to such risks (including war and strike risks covered by the original insurance and not declarable by the ceding company to the American Cargo War Risk Reinsurance Exchange), valuations and conditions, usual or unusual, as are or may be taken or granted by the reassured, including any alterations, amendments or extensions to which they may hereafter agree without notice to us, and to pay as may be paid by them, liable or not liable, and at the same time, all claims and losses; including sue and labor charges and other expenses (excepting expenses of their salaried employees) which may be incurred by the reassured or for which it may be liable.

The foregoing shall not be deemed to include any increase in the amount hereby reinsured or the limits of liability specified herein, or any renewal of policies written for a period of time, unless especially agreed to in writing hereon.

It is understood and agreed however that where the direct policy to the assured contains an Accumulation Clause, the reinsurers shall assume their proportion of any additional liability to which the reassured may be subject by reason of that clause, but in no event for more than double the amount for which they would be liable in the absence of such clause.

It is further understood and agreed that in the application of any net retention warranty or agreement, the reassured reserves the right to limit its own net loss in respect of any loss or series of losses arising out of one event involving business applicable to this reinsurance and/or other classes of business by means of excess of loss reinsurance and/or catastrophe reinsurance, and that such reinsurance is not to be considered as affecting the net retention of the reassured.

The *accumulation clause,* referred to in the third paragraph of the reinsurance clause, is a provision found in open cargo policies increasing the limit of liability to twice the normal amount if two or more cargoes at a transshipping port are loaded into the same vessel.

Reinsurer Bound by Acts of Reassured. The reinsurer, by this clause or by one of similar import, agrees to be bound by the underwriting judgment of the original underwriter as evidenced by the policies issued by him and to which the reinsurance contract in question relates, except in so far as exception to certain conditions may be embodied in the reinsurance policy. Furthermore, the reinsuring underwriter agrees to abide by the adjustment and mode of settlement arranged between the direct underwriter and his assured. When the amount of a loss is large, as in the cases cited in the opening of this chapter, and the reinsurance is placed locally, the financing of the payment of loss is a matter of considerable preparation. For instance, suppose X Insurance Company has suffered a loss of $1,500,000. Were it to pay this entirely out of its own funds it might require the liquidation of some of its securities, perhaps at a sacrifice, or their hypothecation as security for a loan. In practice, the settlement of such a loss calls for the outlay on the part of the original underwriter merely of an amount not exceeding his retained line. Several days before the claim is to be settled, notice is sent to the reinsuring underwriters stating that upon a certain day the loss is to be paid and requesting that payments covering their proportion of the loss be made to the original underwriter on or before that day. The underwriter draws his check for the entire amount of loss, depositing to his credit on the same day the checks of the reinsuring underwriters for their proportion of the payment, so that at the close of business on the day of payment the bank account of the original underwriter is depleted in an amount not greater than his retained line. This mode of settlement can be availed of only when the reinsuring underwriters are located in the same city as the original underwriter and are willing thus to assist him. They may, however, prefer not to reimburse him until he has made actual payment of loss. Where reinsurance is placed in other cities or in foreign markets, it is not always practicable to settle claims in this manner.

Limitation of Liability. Although it is true that under the law of New York, where a large proportion of the marine-insurance business of the United States is transacted, marine companies are unrestricted as to the amount of liability that they assume and retain, in practice underwriters have a definite limit on each class of business. However, with many contracts outstanding, there is no method by which an underwriter can control his initial liability on any one vessel. He does, to be sure, have a limit of liability under each contract that he issues, but in the processes of shipment many contracts may become operative in connection with shipments by a single vessel, with the result that the underwriter may have at risk by such vessel a liability greatly in excess of his normal retained line. Reinsurance against this contingency is usually taken out.

Definitions. Reinsurance contracts that provide for automatic attachment of the reinsurance protection are *treaties.* They are in two general forms. The first is mandatory, requiring that all risks described in the contract be reported. The second form gives the option to the original underwriter to report such risks as he wishes to reinsure, provided such desire is indicated on the original insurance before known loss has occurred. This second form of contract is called a *facultative* treaty.

In the reinsurance field the underwriter who places reinsurance is said *to cede* the reinsurance. The report of the reinsurance is called a *cession.* If the second underwriter reinsures part of what he has reinsured, he is said to *retrocede* and the amount so reinsured is known as a *retrocession.*

TYPES OF REINSURANCE CONTRACTS

In general, there are five forms of reinsurance contracts. These five forms are quota-share reinsurance, participating reinsurance, excess-of-line reinsurance, excess-of-loss reinsurance, and facultative or special reinsurance. Each form will be considered separately.

Quota-share Reinsurance. Under a quota-share contract one underwriter will cede to another underwriter an agreed percentage of every risk that he writes, subject to the original rates, terms, and conditions. For such reinsurance the original premium is to be paid, less an agreed percentage of discount. This discount covers (1) the brokerage paid by the ceding underwriter in acquiring the original risk, (2) the commission paid by the ceding underwriter to his agent with whom the broker placed the risk, (3) an overriding commission to compensate the ceding underwriter for his work in placing the original insurance on his records, and (4) a deduction to offset taxes and other known out-of-pocket expenses. Frequently such treaties will relate to cargo risks only or to hull risks only, or they may be limited to a named class of business or be general in their application. The risks written are listed in detail on large sheets called *bordereaux,* so that the reinsurer obtains a detailed description of every risk he reinsures. An underwriter may place shares of a treaty with several reinsuring underwriters and may, by multigraphing the bordereaux, at a single operation notify each reinsurer of the details of the various risks, figuring at the foot of his sheet the percentage of the whole ceded to each participant. Sometimes details are dispensed with, and only periodic reports of premiums and losses are made.

Participating Reinsurance. In the case of participating reinsurance, the underwriter agrees to give his reinsurers a definite proportion of all his business moving over specified routes of ocean travel or a definite share in a certain line of business moving over described routes of trade, or only a single account placed with the original underwriters may be involved, the reinsuring underwriters automatically covering under a prearranged contract a definite percentage of the insurance assumed by the original underwriter. Notwithstanding the protection afforded by such reinsurance, there is still the possibility that a line will remain greater than the normal line which the underwriter desires to retain. To provide against this contingency the underwriter contracts for excess-of-line reinsurance.

Excess-of-line Reinsurance. Under the excess-of-line form of contract geographical and time limits are definitely set forth, and a clause is inserted to the effect that the reinsurance is to attach at and from the first port within the geographical limits specified, at which the original underwriter has an excess under his various policies considered as whole, regardless of whether such policies cover direct lines received from the assured or reinsurance received from another underwriter. This excess will attach when the original underwriter has a retained line of any fixed amount, say $100,000, by any one steamer or at any one place as described in the contract and will cover such excess up to the limit of the excess contract on the commodities specified therein. It is usually provided that, in determining the amount covered by the excess reinsurance contract, the various interests of hull, freight, and cargo, including specie, profits, and any other interests, are to be taken into account. The original underwriter retains the insurance on all these interests as long as the net retained line does not exceed $100,000. In determining the retained line for the purpose of excess reinsurance, any share or special reinsurance is first deducted, and whatever remains at the risk of the original underwriter, after such deduction is made, is his retained line. The reinsurance contract may be taken out to cover only certain commodities such, for instance, as wool and hides under a policy covering from ports on the River Plate to Atlantic or Gulf ports of the United States. In such circumstances, if the retained line, considering all interests, exceeds $100,000, then there will be declared under the excess reinsurance contract only wool and hides until the retained line of the original underwriter is reduced to $100,000, the amount insured on wool and hides is exhausted, or the limit of the excess contract is reached.

Effect of Determination of Excess Amount. Once an excess has attached under an excess reinsurance policy, it continues to cover throughout the continuance of the risk as per original policy or policies, notwithstanding any discharge, transshipment, or division of interest, and any claim is settled pro rata. In other words, when an excess is determined, excess reinsurance becomes precisely of the same nature as share or participating reinsurance. For example, in the case of the wool and hides policy cited, if all the wool and hides were declared to the reinsurance underwriters, the reinsurer would assume the whole burden of the risk on wool and hides, provided the reinsurance was placed on original terms and conditions. If, on the other hand, the declaration gave a part of the wool and hides to the reinsuring underwriter, the retained line of the original underwriter consisting in whole or in part of wool and hides, the original and reinsuring underwriters would each be liable for their prorata proportion of any loss incurred on these commodities as in the case of share reinsurance. Excess reinsurance of this character differs from share reinsurance only in the method employed to determine the amount covered under the reinsurance contract.

Division of Interest. Division of interest frequently occurs through the transshipment of cargo. A steamer loads at a distant port a large quantity of goods on which an excess accrues. The vessel proceeds to a transshipping port, where she discharges her cargo which, instead of being reladen on a single steamer, is reladen on two steamers, on neither of which the original underwriter has an amount equal to his retained line under the excess policy. Notwithstanding this division of interest the relation between the original underwriter and his excess reassurers is not disturbed, the status of the risk having been fixed at the original point at which the excess attached, the reinsurance having assumed the nature of share reinsurance. The underwriters, original and reinsurer, continue through to destination by the transshipping steamers, each with his prorata share of the cargo on the original steamer subject to the accumulation clause referred to previously.

Complications at Transshipping Points. A complication may arise at a transshipping point if other cargo is laden on the transshipping steamers in such quantity that the unused portion of the net retained line of the original underwriter is exhausted and an excess amount results that the reinsuring underwriter can take without exceeding the limit of the reinsurance contract. Whether or not this new cargo can be brought into the reinsurance relation will depend upon the care that has been exercised in drawing up the reinsurance contract. A further complication will arise if cargo that originates at ports beyond the geographical limits of the reinsurance policy is loaded on the same transshipping steamer at the transshipping port and is at the risk of the original underwriter. It may further appear that a portion of this cargo originating outside the limits of the reinsurance policy in question already has reinsurance on it. The possibilities of complications arising in connection with the placing of excess reinsurance are endless, and no little degree of skill is required so to word these policies that the protection desired will really be afforded by the terms of the contract.

Prior Losses under Excess-of-line Contracts. It is customary to insert in excess-of-line reinsurance contracts a clause by which it is agreed that, in the event of any claim arising in craft or on shore prior to shipment or on board the vessel before completion of loading, the excess shall be ascertained by taking into account the whole of the interest shipped or intended to be shipped by the vessel declared, the loss to be settled pro rata. The effect of this clause is to render the reinsurance underwriter liable for his prorata share of the loss if the following facts can be definitely shown: first, that certain goods which have been damaged or destroyed before being laden on the vessel in question would, if not destroyed, have been loaded on such vessel in ordinary course of transportation and second, that, if they had been so loaded, their value, added to that of the goods which actually were loaded, would have produced an excess declarable under the contract. Goods loaded on a steamer may be damaged before the vessel has completed her loading and before cargo sufficient to determine that there will be a declaration under the reinsurance policy has been loaded at the risk of the original underwriter. In such case, there is usually little difficulty in determining what the total amount at the risk of the original underwriter would have been if the loading had been completed. The amount covered by the excess reinsurance policy can thus be established. If loss occurs to goods on board a lighter at or destined for the steamer or to goods on the wharf at which the steamer is loading, it is not difficult to determine whether the lost or damaged goods would have been loaded on board the steamer. But if the loss occurs on the railroad or on a connecting steamer, it becomes a matter of considerable difficulty to determine whether the goods would have connected with the steamer on which the excess would have accrued, and in cases where through bills of lading giving the name of the connecting steamer are not issued, the problem is increasingly difficult of solution.

Excess-of-loss Reinsurance. Under the form of excess reinsurance discussed up to the present point, it has been assumed that the original underwriter will know the exact amounts that are at his risk by any named steamer. On many routes, such as the coastwise routes of the United States, it is practically impossible for an underwriter to obtain tracings, that is, information as to the definite steamer by which the goods are forwarded, insurance being declared merely by naming transportation lines instead of steamers. An underwriter may unwittingly have at risk a liability greatly in excess of his normal line, yet his inability to obtain definite information precludes his obtaining excess-of-line reinsurance, which has as its basis the determination of retained lines. This difficulty is sometimes solved by an endorsement to an excess-of-line reinsurance contract providing that a fixed premium or a percentage of all the premium applying to these special routes or risks be paid. When a loss happens, full particulars of the affected shipment are declared and the loss is shared in the customary way. The underwriter may divide his accounts by placing share reinsurance, thus reducing his liability, but this still leaves the possibility of heavy liability being unwittingly assumed. To overcome this difficulty another form of excess reinsurance is obtained under which the measure of liability is not the amount at risk but the amount of loss incurred on any one vessel on any one passage during the period of the contract, usually one year.

Excess-of-loss reinsurance for business other than that of the character cited in the previous paragraph was, some years ago, rather frowned upon. A reinsurer always had in mind that the reinsurance might be used to aid the original underwriter in accepting inferior risks and passing most of the liability off to his reinsurers. His retained liability would be the loss only up to the excess-loss point. This point might be placed at a comparatively low figure, say $10,000. While this was a possibility, it did not work out that way, since the reinsurer, if claims were excessive, would refuse to continue the contract. These contracts were sometimes called *block covers.*

Work Saver. The detail involved in reporting under excess-of-line reinsurance covers is very great. Line cards listing all risks on each vessel must be kept if accurate declarations are to be made to the reinsurer. There is great delay in making final declarations to the original underwriter by assureds under open policies, and still longer time elapses before declarations are made to him of reinsurance under contracts that he has issued. The labor cost of keeping these records is considerable. To overcome these difficulties, excess-of-loss reinsurance, with its minimum of detail, has become an accepted system. The original underwriter exercises as much care in trying to produce a favorable underwriting experience for his reinsurer as he does in his original acceptance; otherwise he will lose his reinsurance, or its cost will be so increased as to absorb all the profit on his underwriting.

Rate Structure. One method of calculating premiums under these covers—and there are several modifications of this system—is to agree upon a provisional premium based upon experience, having in mind the excess losses that the reinsurer will be called upon to pay. The losses payable under the excess-of-loss cover are only those which happen or start to happen within the time limits of the cover, for instance, between midnight December 31, 1950, and midnight December 31, 1951. These covers are written as a rule for only one year subject to renewal. The provisional premium thus agreed is subject to adjustment when the loss experience for the year is determined, and it is usually agreed that the final premium the reinsurer will receive will be at least some percentage in excess of 100 per cent, say 150 per cent, of the losses incurred. The percentage in excess of 100 per cent is the *loading* and is intended to meet expenses and help to create surplus. It is almost always provided that the premium so determined is subject to minimum and maximum rates to be applied to all the premiums written by the original underwriter applicable to the class of risks reinsured, less share, participating, excess, or any other reinsurance premiums that he has paid (often for the purpose of protecting his excess-of-loss cover). This premium is the original underwriter's net premium for the purpose of determining the reinsurance premium applicable to the excess-of-loss cover. If the losses are nominal, the reinsurer receives the minimum rate, say 4 per cent of the original underwriter's net premium. If the losses are excessive, he receives premium equal to the losses incurred, plus the loading, up to the maximum rate, say 8 per cent of the net premium income of the original underwriter, and thus he may incur a very heavy loss, as the aggregate losses may be greatly in excess of the premium calculated at the maximum rate.

Excess-of-loss contracts are sometimes written on a noncancelable 5-year basis, the rate for the first year being determined on the basis of the loss cost of the previous 5 years, plus a loading, and the rate for each successive year being similarly determined, dropping the earliest year and adding the latest year. Such reinsurance contracts are *spread-loss covers.*

Catastrophe Reinsurance. An underwriter may be willing to face the possibility of suffering a loss of $100,000 but may feel that any loss greater than this amount would be out of all proportion to the average amount of liability that he purposes to carry. Accordingly, he contracts with other underwriters to assume liability under an excess-of-loss catastrophe cover for any loss occurring within certain geographical and time limits in excess of $100,000, up to an amount that he concludes would represent his greatest liability after deducting all other reinsurance. For such reinsurance a fixed annual premium is charged, based on such estimated figures as the original underwriter may be able to furnish. Such reinsurance is very speculative, the protection afforded, if the excess attachment point is high, being practically against total or constructive total loss only. Such reinsurance does at least ease the mind of the original underwriter in that he is reasonably certain, if he has procured sufficient excess reinsurance of this character, that he cannot suffer a loss greater than he is willing to bear.

Shore Reinsurance. Similar possibilities of excessive loss exist in connection with the interior risk which is involved in the transportation of goods and which is ordinarily insured in connection with the ocean risk. Shipments move over widely diverging routes to the great seaboard ports, resulting in the possibility of an underwriter's having excessive lines at railroad terminals or on steamship piers. A similar condition exists at ports of destination or at transshipping ports where, because of the arrival of two or more vessels at one time, congestion may result in an underwriter's unwittingly having heavy lines at risk in a single location. Since it is practically impossible to trace the lines at risk in such locations, underwriters contract for excess fire reinsurance based on the amount of loss that may be incurred. They will assume full liability for all loss not exceeding a fixed sum, say $50,000, while the reinsuring underwriters agree to reimburse the original underwriter for any losses in excess of this amount, but not exceeding a fixed limit. The possibility of loss under these excess contracts is not great, since they are not involved in minor losses, and the rate of premium charged is therefore comparatively low.

Coinsurance. Under the ordinary form of excess-of-line reinsurance, where the liability is predicated on the amount at risk, the reinsuring underwriter in effect becomes a coinsurer. His liability is measured by comparing the amount declared under the reinsurance policy with the total amount insured on such goods by the original underwriters. However, under excess reinsurance based on losses incurred, there is no question of coinsurance involved. This use of the word *coinsurance* should not be confused with its use when two or more underwriters, as original underwriters, share a merchant's business and thus become coinsurers.

Facultative or Special Reinsurance. While the discussion of reinsurance up to this point has concerned only open contracts, *facultative* or *special reinsurance* is constantly placed on individual risks, to which the same principles apply. Its complications are not likely to be so great as those which occur in the placing of open reinsurance contracts. It is placed on the participating or excess basis, either excess-of-line or excess-of-loss. Much facultative reinsurance is placed on hulls, the terms of the reinsurance frequently being more restricted than the original insurance. For instance, a great deal of hull reinsurance covers total-loss risks only.

Flat Reinsurance. The original underwriter may reinsure a definite amount under a facultative contract, say $50,000 on a certain risk, the amount not being subject to change if the retained line of the original underwriter is materially reduced or canceled in full. This is called *flat reinsurance.* Ordinarily, if the original line is never at risk, the underwriter with whom the flat reinsurance has been placed will consent to its cancellation. Sometimes flat reinsurance is placed without right of cancellation, in which event the original underwriter must pay the reinsurance premium notwithstanding the fact that he receives no original premium and that his reinsuring underwriter incurs no risk. There is a degree of justification for this attitude, in that the reinsuring underwriter, by accepting this flat reinsurance, may have engaged his entire capacity by the vessel in question. As notices of reduction of line or cancellation are usually received by the original underwriter after the vessel has sailed or when it is about to sail, the reinsuring underwriter is precluded from writing new insurance to replace that which it is sought to cancel and thereby loses business that otherwise might have been his. The word *flat* as used in connection with reinsurance means closed or determined, indicating that the transaction is a completed one and not subject to change.

OTHER FEATURES OF REINSURANCE

Reinsurance Syndicates. Frequently, after a long period of bitter competition for insurance between underwriters, with its usual attendant loss to them all, they will come together in the spirit of conciliation and agree one with the other to share a definite line of business in order to bring the rates to a level that will insure a profit on the business written. The profit results, not so much from the stabilization of rates, as from engineering efforts inaugurated to prevent or minimize loss. The original underwriter is free to charge any rate he wishes; only the reinsurance rate is fixed. To this end a syndicate or pool is formed in which each member agrees to reinsure with every other member of the agreement a predetermined proportion of all such business that he writes, definite rates of premium being arranged for the exchange of the reinsurance. This has a beneficial result, not only to the underwriting community but also to the insuring public. While competition undoubtedly produces lower rates and has a salutary effect, competition when carried to extreme lengths results in impaired security if the premium income is insufficient to pay for the losses incurred and capital and surplus are impaired. If underwriting can be put on a sound basis, by which the public pays to the underwriting community a premium sufficient to meet all the losses and the necessary expenses of the business and leave a fair margin of profit on the capital invested, a distinct benefit has been gained both by the insuring public and by the underwriters. This is the result of reinsurance syndicates properly conceived and efficiently conducted.

Reinsurance Subject to Original Conditions. In dealing with the original assured the underwriter is dealing with a specific risk. When he in turn reinsures his lines, he is usually reinsuring, not the risk of an individual assured, but the risks of a large number of original assureds, each one of whose policies involves a different set of conditions, and the reinsurance underwriter, especially of an excess reinsurance contract covering on cargo generally, is indirectly interested in all these differences. It is therefore desirable, where possible, that the reinsurance follow precisely the terms and conditions of the original insurance. The difference in terms between the original insurance and the reinsurance should not in the ordinary case extend beyond a difference in average conditions, much reinsurance being placed on F.P.A. terms regardless of the average conditions of the original insurance.

Reinsurance at Original Rates. If reinsurance is placed on original terms and conditions, it simplifies matters greatly to place the reinsurance at the original rates less a discount sufficient to offset the brokerage, taxes, and possibly other incidental expenses of the original underwriter. Participating reinsurance is usually so placed that the average conditions in the reinsurance policy follow precisely the original conditions. If the average conditions differ, some allowance should be made in the rate to compensate the original underwriter for the perils that remain at his risk. Excess-of-line reinsurance may be placed at original rates or may be arranged on a definite schedule of rates.

Partially Terminated Risks. Sometimes an underwriter's first knowledge that he is liable under open policies for more than his usual lines comes to him long after a vessel sails and perhaps even after it has been reported as passing a named point, say Gibraltar, on a voyage from Calcutta to New York. The underwriter desiring special reinsurance may obtain a favorable rate in such cases, since a considerable portion of the voyage has been accomplished.

Undesirable Risks. An underwriter is often obligated, either under an open policy or as a matter of accommodation to a good customer, to accept lines on a vessel that to him is most undesirable, because of size, age, nationality, trade, or other characteristic. He will then reinsure at the best rate obtainable, usually at more but sometimes at less than he receives, all or part of the undesired line. All underwriters do not view risks in the same way, and what seems a poor risk to one underwriter may appear to one less conservative to be a fairly desirable risk.

Reinsurance that is specially placed by an underwriter as a rule has to take its chances in the open market, and underwriters may incur a loss in placing such risks by having to pay a higher rate for the reinsurance than they received. Again, an underwriter may find other underwriters in the reinsurance market who, in an endeavor to obtain business, are willing to quote a rate which is less than that received on the original insurance. Whatever may be the state of the market, a prudent underwriter will obtain reinsurance in order that he may retain only a conservative line.

Arbitrage. Some reinsurance underwriters, unfortunately, will take advantage of a full market and charge a competitor, who must have accommodation, a rate greatly in excess of the market rate and greatly in excess of what experience has proved such a risk to be worth, knowing that they can under contract reinsurance or in some other reinsurance market again reinsure the whole or a part of the risk at a lower rate, thus making a profit. If the whole amount is reinsured by the second underwriter, the difference between the two rates will be clear profit, as he will incur no liability other than the guaranteeing of the reinsurance effected by him. The profit in this interchange of reinsurance is *arbitrage.*

Unterminated Risks. In some cases, through mismanagement or through a series of unfortunate losses, the capital of a company will become impaired, and being unable to raise additional funds to make good the impairment, the company will be obliged to retire from business. A number of unterminated risks will be outstanding at such time. In order not to delay the settlement of the affairs of the liquidating company and in order to protect the policyholders whose risks are still unterminated, the liquidating company will, if possible, reinsure its outstanding liability, usually referred to as its *insurance portfolio,* with other underwriters. It is primarily for this reason that written premiums are carried as a liability until earned. The laws of the various states require that premiums can be considered as an asset item only after the risk or a portion of a risk written for a period of time has terminated.[1] Because of this legal requirement the company in financial difficulty usually has enough money in hand to pay the premium for reinsuring its outstanding liability.

Overdue Vessels and Vessels in Disaster. Frequently, in case of vessels out of time, that is, vessels overdue at their ports of destination, in case of missing vessels, or in case of vessels that have met with disaster and whose fate is in doubt, underwriters will realize that they are carrying lines in amounts greater than they are prepared to lose and accordingly go into the reinsurance market to reinsure all or a part of their lines. The original underwriter is bound in all cases, and especially in cases of this nature, to make a full disclosure of the existing facts, the law respecting representation, misrepresentation, and concealment applying equally to direct insurance and reinsurance. Market rates in the case of overdue and missing vessels and vessels in disaster will rapidly soar, rates of 95 per cent being sometimes charged

[1] See p. 433.

where the situation of the vessel is known or presumed to be extremely perilous.

Foreign and Domestic Reinsurance. A very considerable part of the reinsurance of American companies is placed in the British market. This is and has been the great world reinsurance center. Before World War II much reinsurance was placed in Continental markets, and today Swiss companies do a large volume of reinsurance. The reinsurance market in the United States is steadily growing. Under multiple-power legislation, fire and marine companies can reinsure casualty companies and vice versa. This releases a large volume of insurance capital for reinsurance that was not permitted prior to the enactment of these new laws. A substantial part of reinsurance placed with American companies ultimately finds its way into foreign markets. It is reasonable to expect that in the future a smaller proportion of reinsurance will find its way into foreign markets.

Syndicate Reinsurance. It is customary in the operation of syndicates, such as the Hull Syndicate and the War Risk Reinsurance Exchange, for the subscribing companies to agree that they will not place reinsurance on their syndicate shares but will retain them net for their own account. Were this not done, each company wishing to reduce its commitment on high-valued hulls, for instance, would find itself competing with every other company for the limited reinsurance available. If any reinsurance is placed on such risks, it is done by the syndicate manager for account of all the subscribers, each paying his prorata share of the reinsurance premium.

Original Assured Indirectly Depends on Reinsurance. The insuring public should realize, when placing insurance with companies of moderate size that write large lines, that the company whose policy they hold probably is retaining but a small percentage of the liability assumed. Although in the event of a total loss the assured looks to the original company for the payment of loss, inasmuch as he bears no contractual relation to the reinsuring company, yet the security of his insurance rests indirectly on the stability of the reinsuring underwriters. It is therefore pertinent for an assured to make inquiry as to their soundness.

CHAPTER 22

Particular Average

CARGO

Losses the Foundation of Marine Insurance. Thus far, the consideration of marine insurance has been from the constructive side, which is primarily engaged in the accumulation and preservation of funds to provide indemnity for inevitable losses. While it is true that an undue proportion of losses will result in the destruction of marine-insurance companies, it is equally true that losses make the business possible. Underwriters do not invite losses; nevertheless they are welcomed in moderation as furnishing the very best reason for the origin and continuance of the business of insuring. When losses are reduced to a minimum, question arises whether it is not cheaper for an assured to carry his risk than to insure it. Fortunately for the insurance business, the assured who reasons thus, and who attempts to put his theory into practice, seldom succeeds and generally gains an entirely new point of view in regard to the hazards of marine transportation. Experience usually teaches merchants and shipowners a salutary lesson on the folly of endeavoring to insure without having a wide and varied distribution of risk. Until nature operating on the high seas changes its laws, losses will happen and the necessity for marine insurance will continue.

Conduct of Loss Affairs Important. The success or failure of an insurance company, while dependent in considerable measure on the judgment shown in underwriting, is in no less degree dependent on the conduct of its loss affairs. Undue liberality in the settlement of losses may result in impairment of capital, while unfair or parsimonious methods will surely be felt in injured reputation, which is only less fatal than impaired capital. A happy medium must be found where the assured will receive, as nearly as may be, full reimbursement for loss suffered, notwithstanding the fact that there may be, through no fault of his, some technical objection to the claim presented. An assured in paying premium expects to purchase, not a lawsuit, but insurance against possible loss. He does not profess to be an expert in the principles of insurance but relies on his underwriter or his broker to furnish the measure and kind of protection that his necessities require. Unfortunately, the assured in many cases is quite ignorant of the principles of insurance and objects to paying the price that would purchase the type of protection which would best serve his needs. In the event of loss he considers that the underwriter is unduly technical or even unjust when he refuses, for instance, to pay a particular-average claim under a policy issued on free-of-average terms and at a free-of-average rate.

Insurance Funds Must Be Conserved. Loss adjusters must be technical. Only by the closest scrutinizing of claims and by the most careful adjustments can marine insurance be kept on a paying basis. The results are so uncertain, the possibility of a series of heavy losses is always so imminent, the keen competition in the marine-insurance market makes the business so precarious that the greatest skill in underwriting and the most careful conservation of funds in the payment of losses and in the cost of operation are required in order that the balance may continue on the credit side of the books. Statistics aid materially in marine underwriting, but regardless of theories evolved from computations, unexpected losses will happen and must be paid. The assured in buying insurance receives a definite kind of protection and that alone, just as surely as, when he buys a ton of coal, he gets only coal and not, in addition, a quantity of kindling wood to ignite the coal. The business of loss adjusting is primarily that of measuring what the assured has bought and of delivering his purchase to him in the form of indemnity for loss, a task that at times requires the wisdom of a Solomon in view of the clauses that underwriters and brokers devise.

Loss Adjusting a Profession. Loss adjusting, while conducted in connection with and as a necessary part of marine underwriting, is a profession in itself and requires a kind of training different from that which develops a successful underwriter. It is true that underwriters as a rule understand the theory of loss adjusting and can and do adjust losses, but a too close adhesion to the caution and care needed in the adjustment of losses is apt to result in timidity in underwriting. Constant devotion to the adjustment of losses is apt to produce a state of mind where every risk written represents a possible loss rather than a possible safe arrival, an attitude of mind in an underwriter that can lead only to overconservatism in the selection of risks. Better underwriters are produced when the underwriter has a thorough knowledge of loss adjusting. The converse is equally true: a better loss adjuster results from a mind expert in the technique of loss adjusting with a theoretic knowledge of underwriting.

Specialization in Loss Adjusting. The field of average or loss adjusting is so broad that specialization has resulted. Some adjusters devote their time to losses on special interests, such as particular-average and total-loss cases. Others confine their work exclusively to general-average adjusting, which is a profession in itself and one requiring the highest degree of skill. General average is a much older method of maritime protection than is marine insurance. Its principles are founded on maritime law, and not on the law of marine insurance. General-average adjustments are never made in the offices of marine-insurance companies. These companies, however, retain on their staffs men skilled in the criticism of general-average adjustments who examine the statements as prepared by the adjusters to see whether the interests of all concerned in the case have been safeguarded.

Kinds of Loss. In general, losses may be divided into four broad classes: particular average, total loss of part of shipment, general average, and total or constructive total loss. Losses may be again considered with respect to cargo, hull, and freight. There are also the two broad fields of marine and war losses. Then there are liability claims that arise under the collision clause in hull policies and under protection-and-indemnity policies. Necessarily the limits of this book will prevent any exhaustive discussion of the subject of losses. An endeavor will be made to introduce the principal problems that loss adjusters meet in daily practice. With this introduction it is hoped that the legal textbooks can be read with greater understanding by the serious student.

Most Claims Are for Partial Loss. Particular-average or partial-loss claims are in number, and perhaps in financial loss suffered, the largest portion of marine losses. It is the cumulative effect of the vast number of particular-average claims presented to an underwriter that determines success or failure for his operations. General-average claims, though important and troublesome, are as a rule not sufficient in volume to have a material effect on the outcome of underwriting operations, the net loss after adjustment usually being a comparatively small percentage of the value at risk. Likewise, total losses, although they represent in many cases the loss of large values, fortunately are few in comparison with the total number of losses incurred in a given period. This fact is perhaps best shown by the low rates charged for marine risks as compared with the relatively high rates charged for war risks, since losses arising out of the latter class of perils usually result in total or constructive total losses. It may be said with considerable assurance that the field of particular average is where the real problem of marine insurance is found.

Particular Average Refers to a Special Interest. Phillips[1] defines particular average as "a loss borne wholly by the party upon whose property it takes place, and is so called in distinction from a general average for which diverse parties contribute." A particular average should be distinguished from the total loss of a part, which may occur when a shipment consists of various units, as when, out of a shipment of 50 bars of copper, 1 is lost during transshipment or, out of a lot of 50 bales of cotton, 1 is totally destroyed by fire. This is not a particular-average loss, but a total loss of an integral part of the entire shipment. Particular average is damage or loss suffered by a particular interest or by part of it which destroys less than the total value of the particular interest or the part of the particular interest involved. A particular average may attain such a percentage of the total value involved that the assured may, by exercising the right of abandonment, convert such particular average into a constructive total loss. This phase of the subject will be considered in a later chapter.[2] The adjustment of the total loss of part of a shipment is comparatively a simple matter. If the amount of insurance on that particular part is ascertained, the

[1] "A Treatise on the Law of Insurance," Sec. 1422.
[2] See p. 393.

underwriter's liability is fixed and determined, and he pays this sum plus whatever charges may accrue in the adjusting of the loss.

Particular Charges. Particular average must be distinguished from the particular charges incurred under the sanction and requirement of the sue-and-labor clause. These charges may be incurred in cases where there is no resultant damage to the property involved, the expenditures made having resulted in the prevention of damage. On the other hand, after the incurring of such charges, the vessel or cargo may become a total loss. Nevertheless, the underwriter remains liable for these charges, in such cases paying more than a total loss under his policy. Whether or not the property is damaged, these charges are not particular average but are special charges recoverable under the sue-and-labor clause and not under the perils clause. The franchise named in the policy does not apply to sue-and-labor charges. It must appear in support of a claim that the expenses incurred arose out of an endeavor to preserve the particular interest from a peril insured against under the policy.

Notice of Loss. The notice of loss or damage on an import shipment is usually conveyed to the company by the broker who has placed the policy. The assured presents the facts to the broker, and many times the claim ends right there, for it is the duty of the broker to advise his principal if a loss is not covered by the policy. This may be the case if the goods have been insured on F.P.A. terms and the damage is the result of sea-water damage, no casualty having occurred. Or the damage may not amount to the franchise required to permit a claim. The loss may be due to pilferage, breakage, leakage, or some other peril not covered by the policy. Sometimes a broker may have been remiss in not clearly explaining to his principal just what kind of insurance he had procured. True, the assured should have read his policy, but too often he relies implicitly on the broker and accepts his assurance of the extent of the coverage without confirming by the policy whether such assurance is true. This possibility is further evidence of the necessity of employing a professional, experienced broker in the placing of marine insurance. It is possible today to obtain in most cases the broadest form of policy, but the rate charged by the underwriter will be in harmony with the extent of the protection provided. In many cases the first notice the insurer receives of a loss on an export shipment is when the draft drawn on the company by its foreign settling agent is presented, the agent having already adjusted and paid the loss.

Proximate Cause. One of the first queries raised in the mind of the loss adjuster is, "What was the cause of the loss?" This again raises the age-old question of *proxima causa,* or proximate cause. Unless the proximate cause of the loss is a peril covered under the policy, there can be no valid claim. No other cause can be considered. What then is the doctrine of proximate cause? It has been considered in a previous chapter (page 175), but as it is so vital to the proper adjusting of claims, further consideration of the doctrine will be helpful. Frequently doubt does exist as to which of two perils—one insured against and the other expressly or impliedly excepted—operating simultaneously or in succession was the proximate and efficient cause of the loss. It must not be inferred that adjusters are unduly technical in the interpretation of policies, but when, for instance, two policies are outstanding, one covering marine perils and another covering war perils, each issued by a different insurance company, the determination of the cause of loss is obviously of the greatest importance. The principle is expressed in the legal phrase *causa proxima non remota spectatur,* which means that the real or proximate cause and not a remote cause is to be used in fixing the responsibility of the underwriter. It does not necessarily follow that the immediate cause of loss is the proximate cause. A vessel may be torpedoed, become unmanageable, and then strand and break up. Surely the final cause of loss is the stranding, but the real cause—the proximate cause—is the torpedoing. In the *Coxwold* case in World War II,[1] a very broad interpretation was given to the doctrine of proximate cause. Law books abound in cases—many of them war cases—where the question of proximate cause was referred to the courts for decision.

Losses Not Insured. In considering the fundamental principles of marine insurance it was pointed out that, while the policy is very broad in the coverage provided in the perils clause, a rule of reason is used in interpreting the policy. The final words in the perils clause read, "and all other perils, losses and misfortunes that have or shall

[1] See p. 339.

come to the hurt, detriment or damage of the said goods and merchandises, or any part thereof." This would seem to provide no avenue of escape for the underwriter. This was one of the parts of the insurance policy that early came before the courts for elucidation. As a result the doctrine of *ejusdem generis* was enunciated. By this doctrine it was held that the listing of perils one by one in the perils clause indicated that the underwriter, by the general words which followed, did not intend to do more than add, without naming them, other perils of the same general nature as those specifically enumerated. This doctrine has always been followed in the interpretation of the contract. Furthermore, if any express or implied warranty has been broken and not excused by the underwriter, the policy becomes void and no valid claim can be made for loss after the breach of warranty. The average conditions expressed in the policy and the terms of the memorandum clause must be examined to see if the claim meets the requirements of the franchise provisions.

In brief, the loss adjuster is bound to examine carefully the terms of the policy so as to make sure that a valid claim has been presented to him for adjustment and payment. This careful examination of the claim will necessarily involve a minute examination of the claim papers, invoice, bill of lading, etc., to determine by the terms of the sale that the property was at the legal risk of the assured and that the amount shown in the policy has been determined in accordance with the valuation clause in the policy. This may be a simple matter where the policy provides an insured value based on invoice plus 10 per cent. On the other hand, calculating the correct amount of insurance under some of the "highest market values during the voyage" clauses may require considerable inquiry to determine whether the amount declared for insurance conforms to the policy requirements.

Delay—Loss of Market. The marine-insurance policy is not a perfect contract of indemnity. It does not agree to place the assured in the same position he would have been in if the goods had arrived undamaged. The policy includes the following clause:

> Warranted free of claim for loss of market or for damage or deterioration arising from delay, whether such delay be caused by an insured peril or otherwise.

Because of market conditions a merchant may make an unexpected profit in a rapidly rising market or incur a serious financial loss in a rapidly falling market. As will be seen in the typical adjustment shown on page 377, the underwriter is not concerned with market fluctuations.

The Question of Franchise. Much of the work of underwriting resolves itself about the question of inserting clauses in the policy relating to particular average. The memorandum clause sets forth in considerable detail the percentage of damage that must be attained on various articles before claim may be made under the policy. Various other clauses are used in fixing the average franchises on particular commodities or in changing the franchises enumerated in the memorandum clause. These clauses come into play when a particular-average adjustment is to be made. The percentage of damage having been determined, reference is made to the policy to see what the franchise is. Unless the percentage of loss equals or exceeds the franchise, there is no liability under the policy. If the percentage of loss equals or exceeds the franchise, the loss is paid in full. On the other hand, with an average clause containing a deductible franchise, unless the percentage or amount of the loss exceeds the deductible franchise, there will be no liability under the policy. The only particular-average liability in such cases is the liability in excess of the deductible franchise, whether this franchise is expressed as a percentage or as a fixed sum.

Cause of Loss. The question of franchise, however, is not the only question raised by average clauses. There is the further consideration of the cause of loss. As pointed out previously, not every loss is covered by a policy of marine insurance, but only those which are the direct result of the perils enumerated or of others of the same nature. The broad protection granted by the policy is, in many cases, modified by the average clauses that limit recovery, for instance, to losses caused by stranding, sinking, burning, or collision. The cause of damage is ordinarily the first inquiry in loss cases, and if the loss is not occasioned by a peril insured against, no further action is taken. The cause of loss is not always easy to determine, as cargo that has been carried for long distances may be discharged in damaged condition without any apparent sea peril having intervened. In such cases test is usually made to determine whether the damage is the result of fresh or salt water, and if traces of salt appear, further search is made for possible leaks in the deck or shell of the vessel. Loss may be found to be due to fault on the part of the ship and therefore not be recoverable under the policy. Under present-day policies covering against "all risks of transportation and navigation" or covering losses "from any external cause," little question can arise whether the loss is the result of a peril insured against. Under such policy forms the underwriter must be on his guard to prevent claims being made for losses due to inherent vice or defect, improper manufacture or preparation of the insured articles, or delay.

Comparison of Gross Sound and Damaged Values. The adjustment of a particular average caused by damage is difficult and on goods arriving at destination in specie is determined by ascertaining the percentage of depreciation on the goods. This is done by comparing their gross sound value with their gross damaged value as fixed in the open market. When this percentage is found, it is applied to the insured amount under the policy, and settlement of loss is made accordingly. There is added to this sum whatever expenses may have been incurred in the settlement of the loss. In marine insurance, unlike ordinary fire insurance, the underwriter is merely a coinsurer of the property with the assured if the latter has not insured his property in full, and a particular average, no matter how small, will be adjusted by applying the percentage of depreciation to the amount insured on the damaged property. If the amount insured is less than the real value of the goods, the assured will assume the loss in proportion to the difference himself. A merchant importing goods will often discover when an adjustment of particular average is made that, through neglect to insure collectible freight and duty or through increase in the market, he has become a coinsurer with his underwriter for a considerable amount. If, on the other hand, the goods are insured for more than their real value the assured will recover more than the loss suffered. Here again marine insurance differs from fire insurance in that under a fire policy recovery under the standard form of policy is limited to the actual loss suffered.

Comparison of Gross Values Justified. In determining the percentage of loss suffered, the values taken for comparison are the gross values at destination; that is, the market values of the sound and damaged portions are compared. These values include freight, duty, and any charges incurred in order to place the particular goods in that particular market. Early in the development of marine-insurance law it was decided that the gross basis was the only fair way to adjust a particular-average claim. The market value is affected by the law of supply and demand and therefore fluctuates. Whether the market is high or low when the goods arrive, a comparison of the sound and damaged market values will remain constant. If the comparison was made on net values, that is, the market value of the goods, less the freight, duty, and other charges accruing, the percentage of damage would fluctuate, a falling market increasing and a rising market reducing the percentage. Let it be assumed that a shipment of 10 cases of cotton print goods, shipped from Liverpool for delivery at New York on c.i.f. terms, arrives damaged. The invoice value is $4,000, to which the usual 10 per cent is added, making $4,400. The charges accruing at New York, freight, duty, etc., amount to $1,000. The statement on page 377 will demonstrate that the amount of the claim, adjusted on the gross basis, will be the same whether the market has risen or fallen, whereas on the net basis the amount of the claim will be less on the rising market and more on the falling market. The gross basis is the only method that does not involve the underwriter in market fluctuations with which he is not, and should not be, concerned.

Freight and Duty. In applying the percentage of depreciation determined by the foregoing comparison, the question arises as to what is the insured value against which the determined percentage of depreciation is to be applied. If there are charges of freight and duty accruing at the port or place of destination, these charges will not be included in the insured value unless there is special provision in the policy providing for the insurance of such amounts. Since the determination of percentage of depreciation is made by a comparison of values after such charges have been paid, a careless assured may unwittingly become his own insurer for a considerable portion of the landed value of the goods. It is customary to insure the items of collectible freight and duty. In making the adjustment of particular average in such cases, the amount of these two items is added to the

GROSS BASIS

		Rising market		Falling market	
10 cases cotton print goods C.I.F.					
Invoice value	$4,000				
Plus 10 per cent	400				
Plus duty, freight and charges	1,000				
Insured value		$5,400		$5,400	
Insured subject to 5 per cent particular average; therefore amount necessary for claim is $270.					
Market value at New York		$6,000		$4,000	
Market value in damaged condition		3,000		2,000	
Depreciation		$3,000 or 50%		$2,000 or 50%	
Insured value $5,400. Claim is 50%			$2,700		$2,700
* Add adjusting charges incurred, such as auctioneer's commission, appraiser's fee, advertising, etc.			200		150
Total amount of particular average loss			$2,900		$2,850

* The auctioneer's commission and some other charges vary with the amount of proceeds.

NET BASIS

	Rising market		Falling market	
Market value at New York	$6,000		$4,000	
Less duty, freight, and charges	1,000		1,000	
Net value		$5,000		$3,000
Market value in damaged condition	$3,000		$2,000	
Less duty, freight, and charges	1,000		1,000	
Net value		$2,000		$1,000
Depreciation		60%		66⅔%
Insured value $5,400. Claim is		$3,240		$3,600
*Add adjusting charges incurred, such as auctioneer's commission, appraiser's fee, advertising, etc.		150		125
Total amount of particular average loss		$3,390		$3,725

* The auctioneer's commission and some other charges vary with the amount of proceeds.

amount insured on goods, and the percentage of depreciation is applied to this gross amount, so that the insured may receive full indemnity for the loss incurred.

Policy Value Controls. It must be borne in mind, however, that both the underwriter and the assured are bound by the valuation expressed in the policy, whether this value be high or low as compared with the true market value. Such a valuation may be called into question only in the event of an unwarrantably high value, where evidence indicates that the valuation was made with fraudulent intent.

Determining Depreciation by Appraisal. In the adjustment of particular average on goods, where the amounts and quantities involved are not large, it is customary to arrive at the percentage of loss by appraisal rather than by sale in the open market. If the assured and the underwriter's representative can come to an agreement on the percentage of loss, that percentage is applied to the insured value and the adjustment so made. If, however, the assured and the underwriter's representative cannot agree, it is customary to offer the goods at public auction. The expenses attending such sales are a charge against the underwriter, as in the illustration cited on page 377 showing these charges added to the loss in the adjustment.

Salvage Losses. If no question is raised as to the insured value, so that the question of coinsurance on the part of the assured does not enter into consideration, an underwriter, when goods are sent to auction, may pay for them as for a total loss and take an assignment of the damaged goods, receiving the proceeds of the auction sale as salvage against this total loss. In other cases, the assured receives the proceeds of the auction, and the underwriter pays the difference between the amount so received less the expenses incurred in the sale and the insured amount. When goods are sold at a port short of destination, adjustment is made either by the payment of a total loss, the underwriter taking the proceeds, or by the payment of the difference between the insured value and the proceeds. In all such cases the percentage of depreciation is not considered, and the loss is known as a *salvage loss.*

Certificate of Damage. Where goods arrive at a foreign port in a damaged condition, it is customary to call in the underwriter's representative, if there is one at the port, in order that he may make an appraisal of the damaged property. If the underwriter has no representative, a Board of Underwriters' representative or a Lloyd's agent or other competent appraiser will be appointed to make a survey and appraisal of the property. Where no experienced appraiser is available, two reputable merchants of the town, familiar with the class of goods under consideration, are often called upon to give their opinion of the percentage of damage sustained. A certificate setting forth the cause of the damage and the amount thereof is then issued by the appraisers, attached to the other papers in the case, and forwarded to the nearest point where the certificate or policy of insurance provides for payment of loss. If the appraiser called in cannot make an amicable adjustment of the loss, the damaged goods can always be sold in the open market and the loss suffered thus determined. This method of determining the extent of loss is in some cases disastrous to the underwriter, in that, through collusion, there is little competitive bidding at these sales.

Special Adjustment. Where different articles are insured under a policy and the separate values of these different articles are ascertainable, it is customary and proper to adjust particular average on each kind of goods separately, determining the percentage of damage suffered by each commodity and applying this percentage to the insured value of that particular commodity. In the case of goods that ordinarily are subject to leakage or loss or gain in weight, it is also customary and proper first to make allowance for such ordinary variation, adjusting the particular average on the remainder.

Special Cases. The underwriter by the *labels clause* guards against the assured's endeavoring to abandon canned or bottled goods where the labels have been damaged by an insured peril. As a rule the contents of the containers are unharmed and the liability is limited to the cost of new labels, wrappers, etc., and the cost of reconditioning to an amount not exceeding the insured value. This clause reads:

> In the case of damage affecting labels, capsules or wrappers, these assurers, if liable therefor under the terms of this policy, shall not be liable for more than an amount sufficient to pay the cost of new labels, capsules or wrappers, and the cost of reconditioning the goods, but in no event shall this company be liable for more than the insured value of the damaged merchandise.

In a similar manner, by the *machinery clause,* the underwriter guards against having a whole machine claimed for when the only damage is to a replaceable part. This clause reads:

> When the property insured under this policy includes a machine consisting when complete for sale or use of several parts, then in case of loss or damage covered by this insurance to any part of such machine, these Assurers shall be liable only for the proportion of the insured value of the part lost or damaged, or at the Assured's option, for the cost and expense, including labor and forwarding charges, of replacing or repairing the lost or damaged part; but in no event shall these Assurers be liable for more than the insured value of the complete machine.

Particular Average on Profits and Commissions. Partial losses on profits and commissions and other interests that are increments growing out of the transactions connected with the shipment of the goods are settled on the same basis as losses on the goods themselves. The only question in such cases is whether a profit or a commission was lost. The solution of this question is not always easy, for at the time of placing insurance on profits an actual profit may have existed, whereas at the time of the arrival of the goods market conditions may have so changed that the apparent profit has disappeared. If the goods had arrived in sound condition, the assured would have had no profit, and the question is raised whether the mere fact that the goods arrived in a damaged condition enables the assured to recover, under a profit insurance, a loss that actually was not suffered. Some underwriters take the position that, having accepted premium for the insurance of a profit which at the time did exist, they should respond in any event under such insurance if loss occurs. This position would seem to harmonize with the marine-insurance theory of reimbursing the assured for loss on the insured value even if this amount exceeds the true value.

Protest of Master. In order to establish a valid claim under a policy of marine insurance in its ordinary form, it is necessary to prove that a fortuitous accident has overtaken the vessel or that the damage suffered has resulted from causes beyond the control of the master or the owner of the cargo. The underwriter does not assume liability for all damage, irrespective of cause, but only for damage occurring through the fortuitous causes enumerated specifically in the policy and through other causes of like nature. He may therefore demand documentary evidence showing the occurrence of such peril or the existence of fortuitous circumstances which might readily have caused the damage. Such evidence ordinarily is furnished in one of two ways. Reference may be made either to the log book of the vessel showing that accident overtook it or that heavy weather or other fortuitous circumstances were encountered during the voyage. Preferably, however, the evidence is set forth in a document called the *master's protest.* In this document the master of the vessel, under oath, sets forth the events of the voyage, stating particularly the circumstances under which the damage suffered is alleged to have occurred or might have occurred and protesting against the master's or the vessel's being held responsible for such loss. This document serves a double purpose, in establishing the facts of the casualty and also in relieving the vessel prima facie from liability for the damage.

Proofs of Loss. In order to establish a valid claim for particular average on cargo, certain documents must be produced showing that the right to receive payment of loss on the property is vested in the claimant. The documents necessary so to establish the claim are the following:

1. The bill of lading for the goods must be produced. This is the ship's receipt showing that the goods in question were actually on board the vessel that has met with disaster or on which damage is alleged to have overtaken the goods. Owing to the fact that short shipments frequently occur after the bill of lading has been issued, it is always prudent to have the transportation company confirm that the goods were actually laden on the vessel named in the bill of lading.

2. The invoice, which shows the value of the goods and the accruing charges, must be produced. From this document the underwriter can determine whether the amount reported for insurance is the sum for which he assumes responsibility under the policy. The invoice also recites the terms of sale, thus showing whether the goods were at the risk of the assured during the voyage.

3. The insurance policy or the certificate of insurance, if one has been issued, must be produced. This document proves the insurance and also establishes to whom payment of loss is to be made.

Duplicate Documents. If an insurance certificate or special policy has been issued in duplicate, both documents should be surrendered. If this is not practicable, indemnity may be taken against the possibility that other claimants will appear with duplicate documents. This precaution is necessary, since these documents are negotiable merely by endorsement. If a survey and appraisal of the damaged property have been made, the certificate of the surveyor and appraiser will also accompany the loss documents.

Other Claim Documents. When the claim relates to loss due to theft or pilferage, the packer's list should be presented with the other documents. This list is prepared in the office of the shipper and shows what goods he alleges were placed in the packing case before it was closed for shipment. As the theft or pilferage might have occurred while the property was in the hands of the carrier, it is also customary to file claim for the loss against the carrier and to present a copy of the claim to the underwriter. Similar action should be taken by the assured in the event of other losses for which the carrier may be responsible, such as claims for oil damage, bad stowage, hook holes, breakage, sweat, or nondelivery.

CHAPTER 23

Particular Average

HULL AND FREIGHT

HULL

Particular average on hull and machinery presents many problems peculiar to this class of risk. Gradual and continuous depreciation is always taking place in the structure and fabric of a vessel. In the event that an accident occurs to the vessel, the question will often arise whether certain damage is the result of the casualty or of gradual deterioration known as *wear and tear.* Such loss, though undoubtedly a partial loss of the vessel, is not particular average.

In many cases it is necessary, in effecting repairs, to remove portions of the fabric of the ship, replacing the old with new material. Since the wear and tear can not always be separated from the casualty damage, the custom has grown, as already explained, of deducting thirds new for old to offset the replacement of wear-and-tear deterioration. It is important to understand how and where, in the adjustment of particular average on hull, credit is taken for this one-third or such modified fraction as may have been stipulated in the policy. The old material taken out of the vessel is of some value as scrap. This value is ordinarily determined by selling it. The question then arises whether credit for this old material should be taken in the adjustment before or after the deduction of one-third is made. It will be to the advantage of the assured if the credit is first taken and the thirds deducted from the remainder. However, this is not the method ordinarily followed, the prevailing rule being that the thirds are first deducted, credit then being taken for the value of the old material. The final result is the amount that the underwriters must pay, each in the proportion of insured value for which he is liable. This sound principle of adjusting has become rather academic, as the Syndicate hull form and other hull forms, because they are used principally in the insurance of metal vessels, contain the following clause:

> Average payable on each valuation separately or on the whole, without deduction of thirds, new for old, whether the average be particular or general.

The underwriter, nevertheless, is entitled to credit for the scrap value of old material.

Apportionment of Expenses. It is not at all unusual to find that, in cases where a vessel is sent to the repair yard to restore damage caused by perils insured against, the owners will take advantage of the opportunity to make repairs or alterations that are solely for the owners' account and in which the underwriters are not interested. Certain charges, as for dry-docking, are of mutual benefit to both underwriters and owners. In cases where the owners' work is essential to put the vessel in seaworthy condition, some fair apportionment of these expenses should be made. Where the repair work being done is solely for the underwriters' account, the necessary expenses incidental to the repairs are included in the adjustment and are paid by the underwriters.

Temporary Repairs. Temporary repairs are frequently made at a port of refuge, either because it is not practicable to effect permanent repairs or because an ultimate saving can be effected by making sufficient repairs to enable the vessel to proceed under a certificate of seaworthiness to a port where the permanent repairs can be readily and more cheaply made. In such cases the cost of the temporary repairs is borne by all interested in the venture as general average, it being assumed that such repairs have been reasonably and prudently made. Where, however, the owner desires temporary repairs made solely because of the delay involved in obtaining new parts or because of the difficulty of obtaining the use of a dry dock at the port where the vessel then is, there would seem to be no reason why the underwriters should be interested in the cost of the temporary repairs. The underwriters on hull are not interested primarily in the prompt repair of damage; their obligation is merely to make good to the assured damage suffered or to repair for his account such damage with reasonable diligence. If the owner, in order to obtain the use of his vessel quickly, desires to incur unusual expense to effect that end, these extraordinary expenses must be borne solely by him unless the ensuing delay would be unreasonable, when the cost of temporary repairs will be regarded as particular average.

This question of the reasonableness of the delay must be determined in each case by a consideration of all the pertinent facts with respect to costs and savings to be gained by prompt temporary repairs. While underwriters are interested in having repairs made promptly so that the damage will not increase, they also desire the repairs to be made economically. For this reason hull forms usually provide that tenders for repairs shall be taken from various repair yards, and in order to compensate the owner for the delay that this may entail, the forms also provide that an allowance shall be made to the assured, at the rate of 30 per cent per annum on the insured value, for the time actually lost in waiting for tenders that are accepted by or with the approval of the underwriters.

Valuation of Hulls. Attention has already been directed to the importance of inserting a fair valuation for vessels in policies covering particular average on hull and machinery. The necessity for this becomes apparent in the adjustment of particular-average claims. Being bound by the valuation expressed in the policy if made in good faith, whether this valuation be high or low, an underwriter becomes responsible for the percentage of particular average that the amount insured under his policy bears to the value of the vessel as stated therein, subject to the average franchise and other conditions of the policy. On a low-valued vessel he assumes a relatively greater proportion of loss than on a high-valued vessel. In the Syndicate and other hull forms the usual valuation clause provides for a franchise of 3 per cent (or unless amounting to $4,850) to be applied on each valuation separately or on the whole. This permits the assured to make a valid claim if the franchise is not attained on the combined valuations but is on either of the separate valuations; for instance,

Hull, tackle, etc., valued at $100,000	3% =	$3,000
Boilers, machinery, etc., valued at $50,000	3% =	1,500
		$4,500

Claim as adjusted on hull	$3,500
Claim as adjusted on boilers	1,200
	$4,700

If it were not for this clause, the claim on hull would be allowed, since it exceeds the 3 per cent requirement, but the claim on boilers would be rejected, since it does not equal the average requirement. The two items together equal $4,700, or more than the combined franchise requirement of $4,500, so the whole claim is allowed. In other words, the validity of the claim is determined by the franchise that requires the lesser amount of dollars, in this case the 3 per cent franchise. Therefore, on vessels of high value the 3 per cent is disregarded and $4,850 becomes the controlling franchise. This amount is a remnant of the old franchise of £1,000 that appears in British policies. When the pound sterling had an exchange value of $4.85 to the pound, the U.S. dollar equivalent of £1,000 was $4,850. This amount is still used in policies issued in the United States.

Cause of Damage to Hulls. As in the case of particular average on cargo, the cause of loss is a subject of pertinent inquiry in connection with claims on hull and machinery. In many instances the cause of loss is apparent, but in other cases, especially steamers or other mechanically propelled vessels, many and serious losses occur without apparently unusual conditions having been encountered during the voyage. Propeller blades will be lost, stern frames will be fractured, and accidents will overtake the machinery without any unusual strain being noticed. In such cases, it is often difficult to determine whether the damage is due to a latent defect or to the action of some external force. If the policy, as is usual, contains the Inchmaree clause, the question is of less importance, but even when this clause is used, many perplexing problems arise with respect to particular-average claims. The Inchmaree clause does not charge the underwriter with liability for the loss of the defective part.

It is agreed by the terms of the policy that grounding in certain connecting waterways, such as the Panama or Suez Canals, shall not be deemed to be a stranding. Vessels often rub the bottom in these relatively shallow waterways, and were it not for this clause, such touching of the bottom might be claimed to be a stranding that would effect a waiver of the application of the 3 per cent franchise. By reading the two clauses together the purpose of the clause will become apparent:

> Notwithstanding anything herein contained to the contrary, this policy is warranted free from particular average under 3 per cent., or unless amounting to $4,850, but nevertheless when the vessel shall have been stranded, sunk, on fire, or in collision with any other ship or vessel, underwriters shall pay the damage occasioned thereby, and the expense of sighting the bottom after stranding shall be paid, if reasonably incurred, even if no damage be found.
>
> Grounding in the Panama Canal, Suez Canal or in the Manchester Ship Canal or its connections, or in the River Mersey above Rock Ferry Slip, or in the River Plate (above a line drawn from the North Basin, Buenos Aires, to the mouth of the San Pedro River) or its tributaries, or in the Danube or Demerara Rivers or on the Yenikale Bar, shall not be deemed to be a stranding.

Hull policies are customarily written for a period of time, usually one year. At the expiration a vessel may be on a voyage. She may have been damaged, and repairs may not have been made. Again, question may arise as to what is a voyage and how the 3 per cent franchise is to apply if there is more than one accident on a voyage or on a series of voyages. There are sufficient possibilities to make the adjustment of the various losses a very difficult matter. To aid in a fair result to both owner and underwriter, the following clause is included in the Syndicate and other hull policies:

> The warranty and conditions as to Average under 3 per cent. or unless amounting to $4,850. to be applicable to each voyage as if separately insured, and a voyage shall commence at the Assured's election when the Vessel either begins to load cargo or sails in ballast to a loading port. Such voyage shall continue until the Vessel has made not more than three passages or not more than two passages with cargo (whichever first occurs) and extend further until the Vessel thereafter begins to load cargo or sails (whichever first occurs), but such extension shall not exceed 30 days in port. A passage shall be deemed to be from the commencement of loading at the first port or place of

loading until completion of discharge at the last port or place of discharge, or, if the Vessel sails in ballast, from the port or place of departure until arrival at the first port or place thereafter other than a port or place of refuge or a port or place for bunkering only. Each period in port of 30 days in excess of 30 days between passages shall itself constitute a passage for the purposes of this clause. When the Vessel sails in ballast to effect damage repairs such sailing or passage shall be considered part of the previous passage. In calculating whether the 3 per cent. or $4,850. is reached, Particular Average occurring outside the period covered by this Policy may be added to Particular Average occurring within such period, providing it occur on the same voyage as above defined, but only that portion of the claim arising within the period covered by this Policy shall be recoverable hereon. A voyage shall not be so fixed that it overlaps another voyage on which a claim is made on this or the preceding or succeeding Policy. Particular Average which would be excluded by the terms of this Policy shall not be included in determining whether the 3 per cent. or $4,850. is reached.

Sometimes a vessel suffers damage, but for some good reason repairs are not made. Before the expiration of the policy the vessel, owing to another casualty, becomes a total loss. During a policy term a vessel may have more than one accident, and the damage due to each accident may be repaired. The underwriter pays for all repairs. Until repaired, the vessel is worth its former value less the cost of repairs. Therefore, if the unrepaired ship is a total loss and the underwriter pays the insured value of the ship, he has by such payment paid the cost of the unrepaired damage. If the unrepaired vessel is a total loss under a subsequent policy with another underwriter, what happens? The owner, before placing the new insurance, should file a claim for unrepaired damage with the earlier underwriter. He also should, but usually does not, value his vessel with the new underwriter at an amount that allows for the deduction of the cost of the unrepaired damage. The Syndicate clause reads:

In no case shall underwriters be liable for unrepaired damage in addition to a subsequent total loss sustained during the period covered by this policy.

Documents Required. In submitting a particular-average claim on hull, the following documents should accompany the statement of claim:

1. Survey report
2. Approved repair bills
3. Captain's protest or copy of log entry
4. Insurance policy

FREIGHT

Partial Loss of Freight. Partial losses on freight present a more difficult problem, freight not being a tangible interest but one that is dependent on both the cargo and the ship. It follows that a partial loss of freight may result because of loss to ship or cargo or to both. Partial loss on this interest can be determined only by reference to the goods and the vessel. There are various ways in which a total loss of part, or a particular average, may arise on the interest of freight. Assume a policy on freight where the freight is at the risk of the ship and the amount insured under the policy is divisible into parts, as in the case of a policy covering a voyage consisting of two or more sections, each of which is severable and as to each of which the amount of freight applicable is determinable. If in this case the ship is lost after one or more sections of the voyage are completed, there will be a total loss of part of the freight equaling the amount of the unearned portion of the freight.

Collectible Freight. If the bill-of-lading freight is collectible at destination and, through perils insured against, part of the cargo is lost, or if a portion of the cargo because of damage cannot be delivered in specie and the vessel is thus prevented from earning the freight on this particular portion of the cargo, a total loss of part of the freight will result. Where, through the occurrence of perils insured against, the voyage is broken up by mutual consent short of the port or place of destination and freight *pro rata itineris peracti*[1] is paid, the difference between the amount so paid and the gross freight at risk is a particular average on freight.

Substitution of Vessel or Cargo. If, in the event that a vessel makes a port of refuge and is unable to prosecute the voyage, another vessel is obtainable to complete the voyage at less cost than the gross freight at risk, the vessel owner is obligated to make substitution. In such a case there is a particular average on freight equal to the cost of hiring

[1] See p. 312.

the new vessel. A freight loss of this character is a salvage loss. When the whole cargo is lost without loss of the vessel itself and another cargo, intended for the original destination, is taken at a lower freight rate at the same port, the loss, if any, on the freight is again a salvage loss and is the difference between the original freight and the new freight. This rule will hold good only in case the substituted cargo is to be carried to the same port as was the original cargo; otherwise there will be an abandonment of the voyage. The substitution of an entirely new voyage will result in total loss of freight on the original cargo.

Many times the substitution of another vessel at a port of refuge is arranged by the vessel owners under an agreement with cargo shippers whereby, in consideration of the vessel owners' waiving the second freight, the cargo shippers agree to contribute in general average to the vessel owners' detention expenses at the port of refuge until vessel repairs are completed. This substitution of one set of expenses for the other depends upon equity, and if it is unfair to either, it fails and thought must be given to whether vessel owners have the right to abandon the voyage or to hold the cargo. Under such circumstances the vessel owner does not lose freight but gives up freight to cover expenses that would not be recoverable if a separation of interests were effected by discharge of all cargo.

Freight Not Always Involved in Damage to Ship or Cargo. While the determination of a partial loss of freight is dependent on what happens to the ship or cargo, it does not follow that, because there is a particular average on vessel or cargo, there will necessarily be a particular average on freight. In fact, the reverse is often true. Many partial losses will be suffered by cargo when the freight will in no wise be affected, and the same is true in the case of particular average on hull. A partial loss on freight is more apt to result from total loss of a part of the cargo or from a partial or total loss of the vessel which results in the breaking up of the voyage.

Cargo delivered in a damaged condition but still in specie must pay full freight to the vessel, and consequently the vessel owner or charterer suffers no particular average on freight. The freight so paid, as in the case of prepaid or guaranteed freight, becomes part of the value of the goods and, if insured by the cargo owner in conjunction with the cargo, enters into the adjustment of the particular average on cargo. In the event of disaster the master should use every reasonable effort to carry cargo forward to destination in his own vessel or in a substituted vessel. If, through neglect, he fails to do this and a particular average on freight results, the underwriter on freight will not be liable for the loss.

CHAPTER 24

Total Losses—Collision Liabilities

TOTAL LOSSES

Definition. A *total loss* is defined by Phillips[1] as one wherein the subject of an insurance,

> . . . by the perils insured against, is destroyed or so injured as to be of trifling or no value to the assured for the purposes and uses for which it was intended, or is taken out of the possession or control of the assured, whereby he is deprived of it; or where the voyage or adventure for which the insurance is made is otherwise broken up by the perils insured against. In a total loss the assured is entitled to recover from the underwriter the whole amount insured by the policy on the subject so lost.

Constructive Total Loss. A *constructive* or *technical total loss* is one in which the property has not actually become a total loss but has been so injured that the part or remnant remaining is impossible of repair at a cost less than the value of the repaired subject or, if not badly injured, is in a position of such difficulty from the viewpoint of salvage that the cost of recovering it would equal or exceed its value when recovered. A technical total loss may result, however, by agreement or by implication of law when property is damaged beyond a fixed percentage of its value.

Adjustment May Be Simple. In many cases the adjustment of a total-loss claim is a simple matter, as where a vessel is in collision and sunk on the high seas, with no part of her value remaining and with no possibility of her recovery through salvage operations. While such cases are more or less frequent, a disaster overtaking the vessel will often present the question whether there is such a destruction as will warrant the assumption of total loss and settlement on that basis.

[1] A Treatise on the Law of Insurance," Secs. 1485, 1486.

Assured Must Endeavor to Preserve Property. It is the duty of an assured, by implication of law and by contract under the sue-and-labor clause, to use the utmost practical endeavor, in the event that casualty overtakes his property, to preserve it and to prevent loss to it. The measure of duty that is placed upon him is that action which a prudent uninsured owner would take under similar circumstances. The mere fact that the assured has an insurance policy under which he may obtain indemnity for his loss is no valid reason why he should not exercise the same care and diligence in preserving and recovering the property as would be the case were the loss to fall directly on him. This point of view is too often overlooked by the assured, with unfortunate consequences to the underwriter. It is primarily for this purpose that the sue-and-labor clause is inserted in policies, thus converting into an express obligation under the policy that which existed as a duty implied by law and requiring that the assured use due diligence in taking measures for saving and preserving the damaged property.

When Is a Thing Lost? The question whether a thing is lost arises in many cases. A vessel may strike a rock and, filling with water, sink but in such a position as to make operations for its raising and repair easy and comparatively inexpensive. In such case it cannot be said that the vessel is lost. Or a ship may be on fire and partially burnt. In order to extinguish the fire, the vessel may be flooded to such an extent that it settles on the bottom, but the cost of pumping out and floating the vessel and repairing the fire and water damage may represent but a small percentage of the total value saved. In such a case it cannot be said that the vessel is a total loss. The same rule applies to cargo. If, under similar circumstances, damage to goods will result in a total loss depends in large degree on whether or not the cargo is perishable. The casualty to a vessel slightly injured in collision, but sunk, may result in the total destruction of the cargo if it is susceptible to rapid disintegration by water, as in the case of sugar. On the other hand, a vessel so badly injured by collision or so badly ashore as to make salvage operations on the vessel impracticable may result in but little injury or expense in connection with a nonperishable cargo, such as pig copper.

When Does a Constructive Total Loss Occur? A vessel or its cargo may not be an actual total loss and yet be so badly damaged or in a position of such difficulty that the cost of repairing or the cost of extricating the vessel or the cargo from its position will be so great that a prudent uninsured owner would not undertake salvage operations on the damaged vessel or its cargo. In such a case he would conclude that the cost of extricating the vessel and cargo from their difficult position, of making the necessary repairs which would restore the vessel to her former condition, and of reconditioning the cargo to make it salable would exceed the value of the vessel or cargo when so restored. If this state of facts appears, it is proper for the assured to tender *abandonment* of the vessel or cargo to the underwriters and claim for a total loss. The decision to tender abandonment is reached by a consideration of the facts as they appear at that time. Subsequent events may prove that the situation was not so serious as it appeared and that the tender should not have been made. Nevertheless, if the tender of abandonment is made and accepted, the parties will be bound by the judgment reached and mutually accepted.

American and British Practices Differ. One of the greatest differences between marine-insurance practice in this country and in Great Britain is found in connection with constructive total loss. Under British practice, unless a vessel is so badly damaged that the cost of salvaging and repairing it would equal or exceed the value of the vessel when repaired, the insured value being assumed to be the repaired value, no claim may be made for a constructive total loss. On the other hand, the rule in the United States is more favorable to the assured and provides that, if a vessel is damaged to such an extent that the cost of salvage and of repair will exceed 50 per cent of the repaired value, the assured may claim as for a constructive total loss. The theory of constructive total loss applies both in Great Britain and in the United States, not only to hulls, but also to cargo or freight. In connection with the insurance of hulls, since the adoption of standard forms for use in both the British and American markets, the British custom has gained ground, and a clause providing for its application now appears in most hull forms used in America. The British theory seems the more logical as a basis for underwriting, the desire of underwriters being to discourage rather than to invite abandonment. The 50 per cent rule still applies in the United States to cargo losses when no substantial part of the goods arrives in specie at destination.

Abandonment. The subject of abandonment in connection with constructive total loss is one of great difficulty and presents many perplexing problems both to underwriters and to assured. The practice is an old one, and there is no definite set of rules governing the tender or acceptance of abandonment. In the case of an actual total loss, where there is no possibility of saving or of repairing the vessel, it is not necessary for an assured to abandon in order to claim a total loss. It is customary, however, for underwriters to take assignment of the property on payment of the total loss. Where there is an actual total loss, if the assured would exercise the right to claim from his underwriters, as for a constructive total loss, he must tender abandonment to his underwriters.

In this tender the assured must set forth the facts upon which he bases his allegation that the vessel is in such condition that a prudent uninsured owner would not deem it wise to undertake to save and repair it. If the interest insured is freight or cargo, a similar condition must be shown to exist. No special form of abandonment or any special form of acceptance by the underwriter is required. When abandonment is tendered and accepted, the underwriter pays the full insured value and takes the remnant of the property as it is, subject to whatever liens may exist against it. The mere acceptance of abandonment by the underwriter, however, does not make it incumbent upon him to accept the ownership of the wreck or remnant of the property, as such acceptance might put him in possession of property of less than no value, that is, property so burdened with liens as to be a liability rather than an asset or property in such a position as to be a menace to navigation, thus subjecting the underwriter to liability for damage sustained by other vessels coming into contact with the wreck.

Validity of Abandonment. The validity of an abandonment depends upon the facts existing when it is tendered. If, on the basis of those facts, the tender of abandonment is accepted, the relation of the assured and underwriter is definitely established. Subsequent improvement in the conditions surrounding the abandoned subject will not affect the validity of the abandonment; nevertheless, by mutual agreement the abandonment may be withdrawn, and the former relation existing between assured and underwriter reestablished. If the notice of abandonment as given to the underwriter sets forth facts that constitute a valid reason for acceptance of the tender but it is later proved that the facts were false and intended to deceive, the abandonment will not be effective, as it will be tainted with fraud and be void. Abandonment once made in good faith by the assured and accepted by the underwriter is irrevocable without the consent of the underwriter.

Tender Must Be Promptly Made. An assured must not unduly delay tendering abandonment to his underwriter. He must act with due diligence so that, if he is within his legal rights in making the abandonment and does not attempt to make any efforts to save the property, the underwriter will have the right to take possession of the property and do what he can to minimize the loss. While the assured is required to take measures for the preservation of the property and the underwriter is permitted to intervene in order to safeguard the property, such acts on the part of either assured or underwriter are not to be considered as a waiver or an acceptance of abandonment. Underwriters may always refuse to accept abandonment. As soon as a case appears hopeless, it is the usual practice for the owner to tender and the underwriter to refuse abandonment. The rights of both parties having thus been preserved, the assured should continue to seek means to recover the property under the requirements of the sue-and-labor clause until absolute proof of the constructive total loss of the property can be demonstrated.

Acceptance of Abandonment. It is not necessary for an underwriter to indicate his acceptance or declination of a tender of abandonment. However, delay in declining the tender, if unduly prolonged, might in some circumstances be considered as an acceptance. A tender may also be withdrawn at any time prior to acceptance. If the tender is accepted by the underwriter, it must be by persons whose measure of authority gives them the right to make such acceptance. It does not follow that, because a payment is made on account after tender of abandonment, the tender has been accepted. An acceptance of the tender is an implied admission of a right to abandon. It will also be observed that an abandonment tendered and accepted by a group of underwriters, as is frequently the case in hull insurance, does not make the underwriters liable as joint owners but merely as individual owners of shares in the salvage. If the underwriters upon the acceptance of abandonment do not wish to receive the salvage, they must give immediate notice to the assured of their disclaimer of such transfer.

Effect of Acceptance. The effect of acceptance of abandonment by the underwriter and of the transference to him of the wreck or salvage is to put the acts of persons in whose care the property may be at the risk of the underwriter. The assured himself becomes the trustee or agent of the underwriter, or if there are several underwriters, he becomes trustee or agent for them severally but not jointly. In the same manner, the agent of the assured (for instance, the master of the vessel in the case of a hull abandonment) becomes the agent of the underwriters. The underwriters, after acceptance, become to all intents and purposes the owners of the salvage, gaining all the benefits that such ownership carries with it and incurring all the burdens to the extent of their respective shares that such ownership implies.

Abandonment May Be Deferred by Mutual Consent. It is also proper for the assured and the underwriter, after an accident has occurred, by mutual consent to leave the question of abandonment in abeyance, the rights of neither to be affected by this arrangement. Whether or not the abandonment is finally made will depend upon the ultimate results of the disaster. The rule of abandonment works to the advantage of the assured to the extent that it is optional with him to abandon. An underwriter cannot compel an assured to abandon. In the case of the S.S. *Congress* during World War I when ship values were rising, the vessel was so badly damaged by fire as to permit a valid claim for constructive total loss, but owing to market conditions the value of the hull in its burned condition was more than the value of the vessel as stated in the policies of insurance. Had the assured tendered abandonment, and had the tender been accepted by the underwriters, they would have paid for total loss but would have obtained title to all the salvage remaining, which, in this particular case, was worth more than the insured value of the vessel. The assured being unwilling under the circumstances to abandon, an arrangement was made with the underwriters by which a partial loss of 95 per cent was paid and no abandonment made. The owners kept the remnant of their vessel, which they sold at a price exceeding the insured value of the whole. Repairs were made by the new owners, and the vessel then was worth considerably more than twice the original insured value.

Assignment Dates from Time of Loss. In an abandonment case, the assignment dates from the time of loss, and the only property transferred by such assignment is the property that existed at the time of the loss, subject to its encumbrances. The property received by an underwriter upon the acceptance of abandonment is called *salvage.* This word is also used to mean the amount of money that is awarded to a voluntary salvor or to one who, under contract, undertakes salvage operations.[1] The two meanings should not be confused.

Abandonment of Vessel Involves Freight. One peculiar feature of abandonment has been corrected by a clause inserted in most hull policies. An underwriter accepting the abandonment of a vessel becomes to all intents and purposes its owner and, as such, is entitled to any freight earnings that may accrue after the date of the accident if the vessel is repaired and enabled to proceed to her destination. The result is that the underwriter on the freight having an abandonment made to him at the same time and accepting abandonment has no salvage whatever, since the freight earned goes to the underwriter on the ship. This injustice has been corrected in most cases by inserting in policies on hull a clause reading:

> In the event of total or constructive total loss, no claim to be made by the underwriters for freight, whether notice of abandonment has been given or not.

No Abandonment if Loss Not Due to Insured Peril. No abandonment may be tendered under a policy containing a free-of-particular-average clause if none of the casualties enumerated in that clause has occurred. For instance, a cargo might be insured under the English free-of-particular-average terms (F.P.A.E.C.), and the vessel might not be stranded, sunk, burned, or in collision; yet, through the springing of a bottom plank in heavy weather or from other fortuitous causes, the cargo might be damaged 95 per cent. Under the American practice requiring but a moiety of damage to permit abandonment,

[1] See p. 430.

no abandonment could be made in this case because the loss was occasioned by a peril not excepted in the free-of-average clause. Mere delay in the forwarding of goods to their destination, caused by a peril insured against, will not give the right to abandon.

Total and Constructive Total Loss of Vessel. To have a valid claim for total loss on vessel, the vessel must be destroyed, lost, placed in a position where salvage is impossible, or reduced to a condition of irreparability. What constitutes irreparability is a question of fact and can be judged most accurately by the action that a prudent uninsured owner would take under the state of facts presented. The usual question is, "Will the cost of salvage and repairs exceed the repaired value?" As has already been indicated, it is an exceedingly hard matter to determine the real value of a vessel. In order to avoid this question, many hull policies provide that the insured value shall be taken as the repaired value. In determining whether there is a constructive total loss of vessel, there should be brought into consideration any temporary repairs and permanent repairs that may be necessary to restore the vessel to its former condition. To this sum is added the necessary expense that must be incurred in order to bring the vessel to the port of repair. If the casualty has resulted in general-average sacrifices or expenditures for which contribution will be received by the owners, deduction should be made of such expected recovery.

Total Loss of Cargo. In the case of cargo, a total loss will occur when the property is totally lost or destroyed, as in a case where a vessel is sunk to an extent precluding recovery of the cargo or where the cargo is completely destroyed by fire. It will often happen in case of fire that a cargo will not be touched by fire but its value will be completely destroyed by the smoke or by water or steam used to extinguish the fire. Goods may also be rendered worthless, not because of their destruction by perils insured against, but because the action of the peril has completely changed the nature or specie of the insured subject. It may also happen that a constructive total loss of cargo will result when the goods, though not excessively damaged, will cost so much to carry forward to destination that their value at destination will not equal the expenses necessary to place them there. This is frequently the case with bulky articles of small value, where the cost of handling and reconditioning is out of all proportion to the intrinsic value of the commodity.

Total Loss of Freight. Total loss of freight occurs when a ship and its cargo become a total loss, when there is an indefinite detention of the ship, or when other circumstances make it impracticable to forward the cargo and so earn the freight. In the case of a round-trip charter, if there is a total loss of the ship and cargo on the homeward passage and the freight is a lump sum for both outward and homeward passages, there will be a total loss of the entire freight. The same rule will apply to a constructive total loss of freight. If a vessel in ballast, proceeding under charter to a loading port, is lost, there will be a total loss of the entire freight on the proposed voyage. If goods under a collectible freight bill of lading arrive at port of destination in specie but in a worthless condition through perils insured against, there will be a total loss of freight which will be at the risk of the cargo and not the vessel owner and will be adjusted in connection with the settlement of loss on the cargo. A constructive total loss of cargo through war perils results in a constructive total loss of freight if the insurance on freight is against war risk.

War Losses. War losses fall into the same general classes as marine losses, but experience has proved that, owing to the nature of the peril, the majority of such losses are total. The method of adjustment is similar to that used in marine-loss adjusting. The problems that arise are very different, as was outlined in the discussion on war-risk underwriting.[1] Because of the continual variation in the decisions of the courts of the leading maritime nations, an adjuster cannot be so certain of his position as he is in the case of the adjustment of marine-insurance claims, where, in general, the law has remained unchanged over the centuries.

Missing Vessels. Vessels that sail and are never heard of again, "missing vessels," are among the most difficult war-loss problems. Prior to the outbreak of World War I it was a well-established and rarely disputed principle of marine-insurance law that a missing vessel was presumed to have been lost by a marine peril. This was a reasonable theory, in that naval operations were restricted and, unless the circumstances were unusual, definite particulars of the destruction of a merchant vessel by war peril would in due course be announced,

[1] See Chap. 20.

After belligerent governments began using mines, there was always the possibility that a missing vessel had been destroyed by a drifting mine. World War I witnessed the introduction of entirely new methods of naval warfare, in the sowing of mines at sea, in unrestricted and illegal submarine activities, and in illegal sinking of merchant vessels by raiders. Vessels on comparatively short trips, say of 3 or 4 days' duration, in coastal waters would sail but never again be spoken. To assume and to decide that such losses were the result of marine perils would be to take an attitude unjust to marine underwriters, especially if it could be established that the vessel was perfectly seaworthy when it sailed, and if, during the ordinary time in which the passage could be accomplished, there was no record of storm to which the loss of the vessel might be attributed. The courts held many such losses to be due to war perils. As the voyage lengthened, it became increasingly difficult to furnish satisfactory circumstantial evidence tending to establish the cause of loss of a missing vessel. The decisions rendered in the courts since the close of World War I determine that the former rule of marine loss in such cases is no longer applicable, and each case must be decided on its merits.

Presumption of Cause of Loss. In the normal case, where a vessel sails in a seaworthy condition and no evidence is forthcoming to indicate that it could have been lost by any peril other than those insured in the policy, it has always been assumed, after the lapse of a reasonable length of time without tidings from the vessel, that it has been lost through a peril of the sea. The length of time that must elapse before a vessel is presumed to be a total loss depends upon the circumstances of the particular case—the length of the voyage, the character of the voyage, the season of the year, and other factors of a similar nature. Under British practice, when a vessel has been missing for such a length of time that it can safely be presumed to be a total loss, it is posted at Lloyd's as missing. Ten days after such posting the loss payment becomes due, and claim may be made on the underwriters. In this country, the payment is usually due 30 days after the presumption arises that the vessel is lost. Formerly there seems to have been a custom that the presumption arose after the lapse of a year and a day, but this custom is now obsolete. When war conditions exist, in order not to hold up the settlement of claims on missing vessels, underwriters covering marine perils and those covering war-risk perils are usually disposed each to settle for 50 per cent of the loss without prejudice, permitting the question of liability to remain open until evidence is forthcoming to prove the cause of loss.

Documents Required. For a total loss claim on hull, the following documents are required:

1. Insurance policy
2. Affidavit of all the insurance on vessel in effect at time of casualty
3. Certificate of registry and enrollment (a governmental document showing the ownership of the vessel)
4. Captain's protest (see page 380)
5. If claim is for constructive total loss, evidence to prove vessel is a constructive total loss

If the claim is for total loss of cargo, the following documents are required:

1. Original and duplicate policies of insurance
2. Invoice
3. All negotiable bills of lading, endorsed
4. Statement from steamship company certifying that goods were on board at time of accident
5. Captain's protest

THIRD-PARTY LIABILITIES

An entirely different type of loss arises out of those very difficult claims under the collision or running-down clause incorporated in most hull policies.[1]

Collision Clause. In its original form the collision clause assumed only three-quarters of the owner's liability, as it was believed that safer navigation would result if one-quarter of the liability was at the risk of the owner. When the clubs began to insure this one-quarter, the hull underwriters, feeling that the advantage of the three-quarters

[1] Claims also arise under protection and indemnity covers, whether these are made part of the hull policy or are issued separately by protection-and-indemnity underwriters. Consideration of such claims is beyond the scope of this book.

clause was gone, offered a 100 per cent collision clause. This clause is limited in its application, being confined to damage resulting from forcible contact between two or more vessels and the legal expenses involved in the settlement of the respective liabilities. Such collisions may be grouped into three classes:

1. One vessel solely at fault
2. Both vessels at fault, either equally or in other proportions
3. Neither vessel at fault (in which case no liability results)

In a collision where one vessel is solely at fault, the adjustment of the liability is simple. If both vessels are at fault and the liability of neither has been limited by law, the adjustment becomes more complicated, for the collision clause provides that the claim may be settled on the principle of cross liabilities as if the owners or charterers of each vessel had been compelled to pay to the owners or charterers of the other of such vessels such one-half or other proportion of the latter's damage as may have been properly allowed in ascertaining the balance or sum payable by or to the assured or charterers in consequence of such collision. An adjustment following this theory would appear as follows:

United States Case. Ships *Ajax* and *Zero* are in collision. Both are to blame; therefore each is equally liable under United States law:

Ajax—damage to vessel....	$20,000	*Ajax*—liability.... 50% of $40,000	$20,000
Zero—damage to vessel....	40,000	*Zero*—liability.... 50% of $20,000	10,000
	$60,000	*Ajax* net liability..	$10,000

Sister-ship Clause. The collision clause also provides that, if both colliding vessels are of the same ownership, although the law would not permit them to claim on each other, nevertheless for the purpose of the insurance the liability shall be settled in the same manner as if the vessels were of different ownerships.

Thus the hull underwriter assumes not only the damage sustained by the insured ship due to the perils enumerated in the policy but also the damage done by that ship to other ships by negligent collision.

Both-to-blame Collision Clause. Under United States law, when both vessels are held to blame for a collision, each vessel is required to bear one-half of the total damages. By reason of bill-of-lading and statutory provisions, the shipowner is, in most instances, not liable for damage to cargo carried by his vessel if caused by collision. The owner of the cargo may recover such damage in full from the other negligent vessel, it being no defense to that vessel that the carrying vessel was also negligent. It has been held by the courts that neither bill-of-lading nor statutory provisions protecting the carrying shipowner from liability for the cargo damage affect the liabilities of the vessels as between themselves. Consequently in a both-to-blame case, the other ship may claim back from the carrying vessel one-half of the amount of its payment on account of its liability to the cargo, not as cargo damage but as an expense resulting from the collision. The collision clause in the shipowner's hull policy excludes any liability "in respect of cargo," and the shipowner's liability to reimburse the other shipowner for half of his payments to the cargo has been held to be such a liability. The net result of this would seem to make the P and I underwriters liable for this claim. In order to avoid this result, it has been usual for the vessel owner to include another clause in his bill of lading requiring the cargo owner to indemnify the vessel owner for this liability to the other vessel owner. The validity of this clause was presented to the courts for adjudication. The Supreme Court of the United States has recently held that the clause is invalid. Thus the liability for cargo loss or damage in a collision case remains at the charge of the colliding vessels. The carrier's liability to the other vessel for half the expense of paying the cargo claims will in turn probably be assumed by the P and I insurance. If the carriers do not change their bills of lading, cargo underwriters will probably continue to insert in the cargo policies the both-to-blame clause which reads:

> Where goods are shipped under a bill of lading containing the so-called "both-to-blame collision" clause, these assurers agree as to all losses covered by this insurance, to indemnify the assured for this policy's proportion of any amount (not exceeding the amount insured) which the assured may be legally bound to pay to the shipowners under such clause. In the event that such liability is asserted the assured agree to notify the assurers who shall have the right at their own cost and expense to defend the assured against such a claim.

CHAPTER 25

General Average

Definition. A short definition of *general average* might read "That which has been destroyed for all shall be replaced by the contributions of all." A general-average loss is one which is the result of a sacrifice voluntarily made, under fortuitous circumstances, of a portion of either ship or cargo or the voluntary incurrence of expense for the sole purpose of preserving the common interest from an impending danger. When a vessel becomes involved in a peril, and when, in order to save the common venture from that peril or to extricate it from its ultimate results, sacrifices are made or expenses are incurred by the master acting for the benefit of all concerned, these sacrifices and expenses must be borne by all the interests involved, whether ship, freight, or cargo. The values saved, as well as the values sacrificed, must contribute to this general average so that all the interests will be placed in the same relative position. The task of determining the sum that each interest shall pay or, in the event of an interest having been called upon to make a sacrifice, the amount that it shall receive is accomplished by general-average adjusters. The amount of detail involved in these cases depends in large measure on the number of interests involved and the number and nature of sacrifices and expenses incurred. The preparation of a general-average adjustment in the case of a vessel carrying bulk cargo owned by one interest is a simple matter. In the case of a large steamer, however, loaded with a miscellaneous cargo owned by hundreds of different shippers or consignees the stating of the general average is a task involving tremendous detail. The final average adjustment, as published and distributed to underwriters and shippers for their examination in such cases, sometimes occupies two or three volumes of 500 pages each.

It is felt by many that had marine insurance, as at present practiced, been devised 2,500 years ago, the need for general average would never have arisen. Marine insurance furnishes all the protection needed in the conduct of maritime ventures, and if a condition of affairs could be conceived where general average was proposed as a new theory to aid in the conduct of marine insurance, it would probably be dismissed as out of harmony with modern business methods. Antedating marine insurance, however, the practice of general average has become deeply rooted in the commercial law of all maritime nations.

Marine insurance was interested only indirectly in general average, and general average was not directly concerned with marine insurance. These two forms of maritime protection existed, each fulfilling its separate mission. Merchants who suffered loss in general-average sacrifices did not seek reimbursement under their insurance policies until they had received contribution from the other interests, after which they made claim upon their underwriters for the proportion of the loss not made good in general average. In fact, it is only within the last century and a half that the assured has made claim directly on the underwriter for losses suffered in general-average sacrifices. The underwriter now reimburses the assured for losses suffered, awaiting the stating of the general average in order to receive recoupment from the contributions made for the benefit of the owner of the lost or damaged property.

No Reasonable Substitute for General Average. Abandonment of the practice of general average has been advocated from time to time, one great object in modern business life being to use short cuts and to do away with unnecessary detail. Although it doubtless would be desirable to eliminate the inevitable detail and expense connected with the stating of general average, no practical plan has been formulated to accomplish this end. On the other hand, it cannot be ignored that the law of general average, in charging all interests with the cost of the sacrificed property, has had a salutary effect in preventing unnecessary destruction of property through jettison or otherwise in efforts to save vessels in positions of peril. If the ship had not been legally bound to contribute for jettisoned cargo, there is little doubt that much more cargo would have been destroyed in the past. No solution of the general-average problem will be satisfactory that merely eliminates the detail of the present system without preserving its beneficial features. Perhaps a closer union among the nations in the future will make possible international enactment on the subject. In the meantime general average is engrafted on marine insurance and is of such great importance that no consideration of marine insurance can be complete without at least an outline of the underlying principles of this branch of maritime law and practice.

The General-average Adjuster. The average adjuster takes complete charge of any case of general average. He is usually appointed by the owner of the vessel, since his is, as a rule, the largest single interest and because the vessel has a lien on the cargo for freight charges. When the vessel is released from the peril and arrives at the port of destination, the master is required to keep the interests together until security is given for the payment of such charges as may be assessed against each interest involved in the venture. Accordingly, a form of general-average bond[1] is prepared which recites the circumstances under which the general-average sacrifices were made and expenses incurred and wherein the signatories of the bond agree with the owners of the vessel and with one another to provide all necessary information. They also obligate themselves to pay the losses and expenses therein mentioned that may be shown to be a charge on the cargo of the vessel when the adjustment is completed. In addition to this bond, the adjusters may also demand security for the payment of the charges before they will release the goods. This security is given in one of two ways. If the goods are not insured, the owner is required to make a cash deposit sufficient to cover the estimated charges finally assessed against his particular interest. If the property is insured, the vessel owners are usually willing to accept the guarantee of the underwriters for such charges.[2]

Laws of General Average Not Uniform. There are no limits set with respect to the circumstances out of which a valid general average may arise. The laws of the various maritime countries differ from one another, and in our own country there is no uniformity among the customs of the various states. Efforts have been made to reconcile the differences and to produce an international code of general aver-

[1] See Appendix L.
[2] See Appendix M.

age, the York-Antwerp Rules being the nearest approach to such a code. Associations of average adjusters organized in this and other countries have adopted rules to aid in the adjustment of general average, but none of these efforts changes the law of general average as developed in the various countries. This code and these rules, when agreed to by the interested parties, merely furnish a basis for adjustment, but in so far as these rules do not cover the particular point involved, the law of the land where the voyage ends will govern unless otherwise provided in the freight contract.

Elements Necessary to Valid General Average. The elements necessary to make a valid claim for general average differ in the various countries, but the underlying principle is the same in all. In the United States it is established that the following circumstances must appear in order that the right to claim general-average contribution may arise:

1. The existence or the rapid approach of a peril common to all the interests—hull, freight, and cargo
2. A voluntary sacrifice reasonably made or an extraordinary expense justifiably incurred to avert the peril or to save the common interests from the effects of the peril
3. Preservation of a part of the venture
4. Freedom from fault on the part of those interested in the venture claiming contribution

The Peril and the Sacrifice. While the number of perils that give rise to general-average contribution has increased greatly since the original Rhodian theory of requiring contribution for jettison, the underlying principle governing the right to demand contribution has not changed. A peril must exist that it is to the advantage of every interest in the venture to avoid; that is, the peril must be of such a nature that there is impending danger of physical injury to the common interest. If a peril of this kind exists, voluntary sacrifices reasonably made in order to avert it or to free the venture from the probable effects of such danger must be paid for by a ratable contribution made by all concerned in the venture. These sacrifices may consist of the destruction or loss of part of the vessel or its cargo, as in the case of cutting away masts or spars or the jettison of goods to relieve the ship. Or they may be consequential damage resulting from efforts to save the venture, as when the engines of a steamer or the sails of a ship are subjected to abuses or uses of a different nature from those for which they were designed. Thus, if a steamer is stranded and, in an effort to float the vessel and thus save the entire venture, the engines are worked in an unusual manner and injured, such injury so incurred to the machinery is made good by all the interests. In the case of a vessel on fire, water or steam may be forced into the hold in an endeavor to extinguish the flame, doing damage to cargo not touched by the fire. The damage to such cargo, having been incurred voluntarily in an effort to benefit all concerned, would also be made good.

The Preservation of Part of the Venture. After these voluntary sacrifices have been made, the entire venture may become a total loss. In such a case the sacrifices made have accomplished no useful purpose, and the cargo voluntarily destroyed has merely met an earlier fate than that which was temporarily postponed by the sacrifices. Under the law of general average the saving of a part, at least, of the venture must result from the sacrifices made. At times, expenses are incurred by the master for the general benefit that, if reasonably and justifiably incurred, must be contributed for. After such expenses have been incurred or disbursements made for the general benefit, the venture may be completely lost. The purpose of general-average contributions is to work exact justice among the various interests exposed to the common peril, and it does not seem just that the subsequent loss of the venture should shift the burden of responding for general-average expenses incurred or disbursements made prior to such loss on to the master or the owner of the vessel. The master, during such a time of stress, is not only the agent of the owner of the vessel but is also the agent of each and every interest involved in the venture, and if he has acted within the bounds of such agency in incurring the expenses or in making the disbursements, each interest is bound for its ratable proportion of such expenses and disbursements based on the values existing at the time the expenses were incurred or the disbursements made. This requirement does not apply to sacrifices of parts of vessel or cargo for the reason indicated above.

It is possible in many cases for the master or agents to insure the amount of their expenses and disbursements against the risk of a subsequent loss of the vessel, but such insurance does not seem to be obligatory on the part of the master nor is the procurement of such insurance always possible. If the money disbursed is raised by the hypothecation of the ship or cargo under a bottomry or respondentia bond, the subsequent loss of the vessel will relieve the interests from the duty of contributing because the lender, in consideration of the high rate of interest received on his loan, assumes the risk of nonpayment through loss of the venture. In these days of rapid communication the raising of money by bottomry is discouraged and is practically unheard of.

What Is a Voluntary Sacrifice? While it is essential that the sacrifice made be a voluntary one, some latitude is given to the meaning of "voluntary." It may be that under circumstances of peril but a single course is open to the master, which he follows intuitively. If, however, in pursuing this natural course the vessel and cargo are subjected to hazards of an unusual nature and not in the ordinary contemplation of the parties, the sacrifice will nevertheless be considered as voluntary. Whether the loss or expense was reasonably incurred is also considered in the light of the circumstances existing at the time. Allowance is made for the fact that decisions must be quickly reached when a peril is impending. An action taken in the face of a rapidly approaching peril might involve unnecessary sacrifice when considered in the light of subsequent events; nevertheless if such action was justifiable under the circumstances, allowance will be made for the sacrifice incurred. However, contribution will not be allowed for sacrifices made if the claimant is willfully or negligently responsible for such sacrifices or if the peril, though feared, was not real. General average was instituted and has been continued in the maritime law for the purpose of working equity among persons some of whose interests, exposed to a common peril, have been sacrificed for the saving of the rest, and equity cannot be administered where the claimants do not come into the adjustment of the loss with clean hands.

The General-average Adjustment. General-average adjustments are made as a rule according to the law, customs, and usages of the port of destination unless otherwise agreed in the contract of affreightment, as in the case of bills of lading calling for adjustment in accordance with the York-Antwerp Rules. If the voyage is broken up at a port of refuge, it is customary to make the adjustment in accordance with the law and customs of that port unless otherwise agreed in the contract of affreightment. Where there is cargo destined for various ports and there is no agreement to the contrary, adjustment may be demanded with respect to the cargo destined for each port in accordance with the law and usages of that port. The adjustment is not made up until the arrival of the vessel or cargo at destination.

Contributory Values—*Hull.* Having obtained the signatures of the interested parties to the general-average bond and having obtained either underwriters' guarantees or cash deposits as security for the bond, the average adjuster proceeds with the compilation of the facts necessary to fix a proper apportionment of sacrifices made, of expenses incurred, and of moneys disbursed. Contribution being made on the net saved value plus the amount made good to the interest because of sacrifice made, the adjusters must fix a valuation for every interest concerned in the venture. As the valuation of a vessel may be considered from several angles, such as the cost of replacement, her freight-earning capacity, or her location with respect to possible freight engagements, the problem presented is one of considerable difficulty. The vessel is valued at the port at which the voyage terminates in her then-existing condition less the cost of any repairs made subsequent to the general-average act and prior to arrival and not allowed in the statement of the case. This value represents the amount saved to the owner by the general-average act. It is always a difficult matter to determine the real value of a vessel, and the fact that a ship when being valued for general-average purposes is usually in a damaged condition adds greatly to the difficulty of arriving at a fair valuation. Since the amount of payment to be made depends on the contributory value, the vessel owner will as a rule seek to have a low valuation made, whereas the cargo owners will naturally seek a full value for the vessel so that their contributions may be lower. It is customary for the adjusters to obtain the certificate of an expert as to the value of the vessel.

Freight. Freight contributes on the basis of bill-of-lading or chartered freight. If such freight is at the risk of the vessel owner, a deduction is made of the expense of earning the freight after the general-average act. Just as the vessel contributes on the net amount saved by the general-average act, so the freight should contribute on the net amount of freight saved. It is on this basis that freight contributes under the York-Antwerp Rules, and a similar basis of value for freight is used under the rules of practice of the Association of Average Adjusters of the United States. If the freight is prepaid and/or guaranteed, it is in reality part of the value of the cargo and is included in that value for purposes of contribution. The same difficult questions arise in regard to freight in a general-average adjustment as in the insuring of the interest itself, and a similar rule applies that he is liable for contribution in general average at whose risk the freight is.

Cargo. Cargo is valued for purposes of general-average contribution at its gross wholesale value at the port of destination in its then condition less charges accruing upon arrival, such as freight, duty, cartage, and other necessary expenses entering into the wholesale market at destination. These deductions do not include the cost of insurance or any other charges that have already entered into the cost of the goods. To the net value thus determined is added any amount made good in general average, and any special charges arising out of the casualty are deducted that are a lien on the particular item of cargo under valuation.

General-average Cases Often Complicated. The adjusters receive tenders for the repair of any damage received by the vessel, and a division is made of those damages resulting from general-average sacrifices and those resulting from ordinary marine perils. In general-average adjustments there is often a combination of general-average losses and disbursements, particular-average losses, and special charges incurred solely for the benefit of particular interests. This may be illustrated by the case of a vessel discovered on fire at sea. In order to extinguish the fire and save all the interests concerned, the hatches will be battened down, the ventilators closed, and either steam or water turned into the hold in an endeavor to extinguish the fire. If the efforts are successful, it will doubtless be found that only part of the cargo in that particular hold has been on fire and that packages not reached by the fire have nevertheless been badly damaged by the effect of the steam or the water used in the effort to extinguish the fire. In this particular case, the only items for which general-average contribution would be made are those portions of the vessel and cargo which have suffered by the water or the steam or through the efforts made to introduce the water or the steam and the extraordinary expenditures incurred in the general interest. The consequential loss or expenditures due to sacrifice for the general benefit must be made good in proportion to the values saved. The damage to the ship or cargo by the fire itself or any expense due solely thereto is not a general-average loss, but a particular-average loss, or a special charge, for which the affected interests alone are responsible.

Statement of Both General and Particular Average. The foregoing illustration will give an idea of the many and perplexing problems with which average adjusters are confronted. The average statement does not necessarily confine itself to the general-average loss. It may also state the particular-average losses when the same adjustment is to be used for claim under the insurance policies on the vessel. Furthermore, in the case of a severe fire many cargo interests may become unidentifiable, some which are fire damaged and some merely water damaged. It will be apparent that in a general-cargo steamer, where hundreds of interests are involved, the adjustment with respect to unidentifiable cargo is a matter requiring considerable care and skill. In the case of the vessel itself in the event of stranding, not voluntary, where the engines have been worked in an effort to extricate the vessel, and where the vessel has been subject to many unusual stresses, adjusters are confronted with a very difficult problem in determining what damage is the result of the stranding itself and at the risk of the vessel and what injuries should be contributed for as sacrifices made in the general interest. Sometimes during a single voyage two entirely separate general-average acts will be made. Because of jettison or delivery of cargo at intermediate ports reached during the interim between the two sacrifices, the interests involved in each case may not be the same or may be in different proportions, leading to complications requiring the use of all the analytical powers for which general-average adjusters are noted.

York-Antwerp Rules. In an effort to reconcile the differences in general-average practice in the various commercial nations and to provide a working code that would cover the ordinary general-average problem, the Association for the Reform and Codification of the Law of Nations held a meeting at York, England, in 1864 and another meeting in Antwerp in 1877. At the latter conference a code of rules for the stating of general average was adopted, the *York-Antwerp Rules.* Later, in 1890, the Association met at Liverpool, where the code was revised and the *York-Antwerp Rules, 1890,* were promulgated. This revised code was used until 1924, when the rules were again revised and extended at a meeting of the International Law Association held at Stockholm in September, 1924. The rules there adopted are the *York-Antwerp Rules, 1924.* These rules have been the basis of most general-average adjustments since that time. Exceptions to certain sections have been taken by different nations and the adjusters in those countries.

The desire for uniform practices continued to be the goal of maritime lawyers throughout the world. Various attempts at uniformity failed. In September, 1949, a meeting was held at Amsterdam of representatives from all the maritime law associations of the leading maritime nations of the world to discuss the law of general average. As a result the *York-Antwerp Rules, 1950,* were adopted, for submission to all nations. It is to be hoped that these rules will be universally accepted and thus aid materially in simplifying the practice of general-average adjusting.

Provisions for York-Antwerp Adjustments. It is customary to provide in bills of lading that adjustment of general average shall be made in accordance with the York-Antwerp Rules and to have provision made in insurance policies that general average may be so adjusted. The 1950 rules are so broad in their treatment of general average that most situations are provided for, but where the rules do not apply, or where no provision is made in the contract of carriage for the employment of the rules, the law applying at the port of destination determines the mode of adjustment. The changes from the 1924 version in the 1950 rules were made in an endeavor to reconcile conflicting views which arose in the interpretation and application of the 1924 rules. The new rules start with a Rule of Interpretation, making it clear that the 1950 rules are a general-average code. This rule also provides that "except as provided by the numbered rules, general average shall be adjusted according to the lettered rules." It is not within the province of this book to discuss the rules in detail. As some time may elapse before the 1950 rules are adopted by all maritime countries, in printing the rules[1] footnotes are included indicating the differences between the 1924 and the 1950 rules.

Lettered Rules. The seven lettered rules, A to G in the 1950 version, set forth the general principles which are to govern the general-average adjustment. A study of these rules in connection with the discussion in the earlier sections of this chapter should give the reader a picture of the very involved problems confronting the general-average adjuster as he takes the steps necessary to assemble the facts essential to the proper stating of the general average and making the final apportionment among the various interests.

Numbered Rules. The numbered rules, I to XIX, specify the various losses and expenses that are considered to be general-average sacrifices. The last three rules, XX, XXI, and XXII, govern the banking arrangements in connection with the adjustment. A commission of 2 per cent is allowed on certain disbursements. The cost of insuring these disbursements is also allowed as a general-average charge. Interest on expenditures, sacrifices, and allowances charged to general average is permitted at the rate of 5 per cent per annum. It is also provided that cash deposits paid to the adjusters as security for the final general assessment shall be treated as fiduciary funds and placed in a special bank account. Some of the many sacrifices that are named in the numbered rules are discussed in the following paragraphs.

Jettison of Cargo. Fire. The first sacrifice mentioned is *jettison*, the sacrifice that originally gave rise to general average. Rule I limits contribution for loss by jettison by stating that no jettison of cargo shall be made good as general average unless such cargo is carried in accordance with the recognized custom of the trade. The wording of this rule permits contribution even for the jettison of on-deck cargo if such cargo is customarily carried on deck on the affected voyage. If, in the ordinary case, cargo is jettisoned for the general safety, all consequential losses arising from such jettison are admitted in general average, whether such losses be to the vessel itself or to the other cargo

[1] See Appendix P.

through admission of water to the holds in uncovering the hatches to extract the cargo or from any other cause directly resulting from the sacrificial act. Thus in the case of extinguishing fire on shipboard, where damage results from measures taken to extinguish the fire or through the beaching or scuttling of a burning ship, allowance is made for such consequential damage. No allowance is made, however, for damage directly caused by the fire itself.

Cutting Away Wreck. Stranding. Where a vessel has been partially wrecked by a sea peril and portions of the spars remain, the cutting away of these remnants is not allowed for in general average under the York-Antwerp Rules. Under the law of the United States, however, allowance would be made for such parts cut away, if there would have been a reasonable chance, but for the continuance of the storm, of saving parts that, if saved, would have been of some value. Rule V of the York-Antwerp code provides that, when a vessel is voluntarily stranded under circumstances where, if such course were not adopted, it would inevitably be driven on shore or on rocks, no allowance shall be made for loss or damage to ship, cargo, or freight but that in all other cases of voluntary stranding for the common safety the consequential loss or damage shall be allowed as general average. The restriction in this rule with respect to voluntary stranding when a vessel would otherwise be inevitably driven on shore or on rocks is not in agreement with the law in the United States, where, to establish a case for contribution in general average, it is sufficient to show that the place of stranding was voluntarily selected by the master, rather than one forced on him by the elements. The fact that the vessel would apparently in any event have been lost does not destroy the right of the vessel to recover contribution from the cargo if it is saved because of the sacrifice of the vessel. The possibility always remains that through some unexpected circumstances the vessel, if not voluntarily stranded, might have been saved.

Injury to Engines or Sails. The York-Antwerp Rules provide that allowance is to be made for damage caused to the sails of a vessel or to the boilers or machinery of a steamer or other vessel propelled by mechanical power when such damage is the result of efforts made to float the stranded ship. To aid in floating a vessel which is ashore, it is usual to discharge her fuel, cargo, and stores into lighters in order to lighten her. The cost of extra handling, lighter hire, and reshipment of goods is admitted in general average. If a steamer, when leaving her port of departure, is adequately equipped with fuel for the prosecution of the proposed voyage but, because of perils encountered or other fortuitous conditions, so much is burned that she runs short of fuel, and if, in order to bring the entire venture safely to destination, the ship's stores or parts of the vessel or cargo are burned to produce power or the vessel has to make a port of refuge to obtain a supply of fuel, such extraordinary sacrifices and expenses are treated as general average. Unusual expenses incurred at a port of refuge for the common interest are general-average expenses, and the wages and maintenance of the crew, during the period of prolongation occasioned by putting into the port of refuge, are also allowed. When damage is suffered by cargo in the act of discharging, storing, reloading, and stowing because of the general-average act, such damage is allowed only when the cost of these measures, respectively, is admitted in general average.

Thirds Off. Separation of General and Particular Average. When repairing damage caused to vessels through general-average sacrifices, it was formerly the custom to deduct one-third from the cost of such repairs on the principle that new material was supplied for old. The injustice of this in the case of new vessels and in the case of metal vessels was so apparent that Rule XIII of the York-Antwerp code provides a definite scale for such deductions. When temporary repairs are made to a vessel, no deduction of thirds is made, since the temporary repairs are of no permanent benefit to the owner of the vessel.

Average adjusters must exercise the greatest care to allow in general average only such repairs to vessels as are the result of the general-average act, charging against the owner such repairs as are made necessary by injury suffered through marine perils.

Freight. If the freight is not prepaid or guaranteed and therefore is not a part of the value of the goods, it also is an interest involved in the general-average sacrifice. The amount made good to freight and the amount of and the value at which the freight is made a contributing interest are outlined in the rules. If the bill of lading does not provide for an adjustment in accordance with York-Antwerp Rules, the statement is drawn up in accordance with the law prevailing at port of destination unless there is some other custom in vogue. Thus, in the case of general-average sacrifices in connection with vessels from the United States bound for ports in the West Indies, it is usual to have the adjustment made in the United States, in accordance with the law of the port of departure.

Other Provisions. Rule XVI governs the amount to be made good for cargo lost or damaged by the sacrifice. Rule XVII sets out the formula by which the contributory values, or the values against which the general-average assessment shall be applied, are to be determined for hull, freight, and cargo. Rule XVIII gives the formula for the amount to be allowed as general average for damage or loss to the ship and her machinery and gear. Rule XIX deals with unusual situations where goods are loaded without the knowledge of the shipowner or are willfully misdescribed. Damage to such goods is not allowed as general average, but they must contribute if they are saved. The rules also provide for the revaluation of goods improperly valued.

Borderline Cases. It will be found that the laws of the various nations differ materially in certain respects from one another and from the York-Antwerp Rules. Enough, however, has been mentioned in the foregoing outline to indicate the many and difficult problems with which an average adjuster has to deal. Many cases will be on the border line, where it will be a matter of opinion whether the sacrifices made and the expenses incurred are in the nature of general average. The determination of these questions to the satisfaction of all parties interested requires the use of great skill and tact. Each underwriter who is interested in the venture and upon whom the liability for general-average contribution falls carefully scrutinizes the general-average adjustment when issued, to determine whether, in his opinion, the assessments and allowances made are just and in accordance with law or the rules of practice in view of the statement of the facts in the case as set forth at the beginning of the general-average statement. Sometimes years are taken in the final settlement of a case, during which time the expenses of the average adjusters steadily grow. Finally, however, the adjustment is completed, the settlements are made, and, in so far as it is humanly possible, exact justice is done to all the interests involved.

Documents Required. In general, the documents required by the adjusters, in order properly to state the case, are:

1. The manifest of cargo on board at time of casualty, showing freight pending
2. A copy of each form of bill of lading issued
3. Signed average bonds, deposit receipts, and guarantees of banks or underwriters taken as security for general-average assessments
4. Originals or certified copies of deck and engine-room log books for the voyage
5. The extended protest
6. Bills for extra expenses incurred at port of refuge, for repairs to ship, and for incidental expenses
7. Surveyor's report of damage to hull, machinery, and cargo
8. Statement of shipment and outturn of cargo by reason of the general-average sacrifice, including records as to its disposal, and of allowances agreed for its loss or damage
9. Statements of cargo values with account sales of cargo sold[1]
10. Certificate showing value of the vessel

The Statement. Many references have been made to the statement of general average. To give a better understanding of this statement, a simple general case is digested in the following pages. The facts are taken from an actual case, but the vessel's name and other items have been changed. The original statement consisted of almost 200 typed pages, 9½ inches wide by 14 inches long. There were 116 cargo interests involved and the ship itself. There was no freight at risk. The casualty, a fire in the cargo in No. 5 hold, occurred on May 15, 1946. The adjustment was issued on December 12, 1948. A condensation of the statement follows:

S.S. GREENWAYS

Voyage. Vessel sailed April 23, 1946, from Buenos Aires with a part general cargo. Called at Santos and loaded further cargo and sailed May 4 for

[1] See p. 503.

Boston and New York via Port of Spain for bunkers. May 15 smoke issuing from ventilators of No. 5 hold. Water was poured into hold. May 17 arrived at Port of Spain. Fire extinguished. June 9 arrived at Boston and unloaded Boston cargo. June 17 arrived New York and completed discharge.

Damage. Surveyors at Port of Spain recommended reloading of some damaged cargo removed to lighters in an effort to extinguish fire. Also dumped some damaged cargo certified as worthless. Vessel was also surveyed and certificate of seaworthiness granted. At New York other cargo found to be damaged. Vessel again surveyed. Damage not serious.

Log Books (Here follow six pages of extracts from log books).

Surveys and various certificates referring to surveys to vessel and certificate of value of vessel take eight pages.

Surveys on cargo occupy 42 pages.

Shipment and Outturn of Cargo. The statement goes into great detail with respect to the cargo damaged as a result of the fire and the efforts to extinguish it. Twenty of the 116 interests suffered damage. The number of packages shipped by each is shown. The outturn is shown in the following manner:

Interest No. 53: 135 bales lamb skins; 135 bales damaged by water used to extinguish fire, short or unidentified—dumped at Port of Spain

Interest No. 99: 165 bales greasy wool; 127 delivered sound, 37 wet, 1 burnt

Interest No. 28: 9,634 bags coffee; 9,566 delivered sound, 68 damaged by handling

Interest No. 50: 50 bales greasy wool; 23 delivered sound, 4 sold wet, 22 sold damaged by handling, 1 short or unidentified

Charges and Expenses. The following 56 pages set out in the greatest detail all the charges and expenses incurred at the various ports for surveyors, for port charges, for stevedoring, for lighter hire, for dumping cargo, for various kinds of labor and clerk hire, for taxi hire (from 48 cents to $3), for radio messages and cables, for towing, for insurance premiums on lightered cargo and on disbursements, and for the vessel owner's 2 per cent commission on disbursements, etc.

Allowances to cargo for loss and/or damage resulting from the efforts to extinguish the fire and the forced handling of cargo at Port of Spain are set out for each affected interest. This takes 14 pages. Interest No. 53 mentioned above, for instance, is allowed $34,604.80 as follows:

Interest No. 53 B/L No. 25 Buenos Aires to Boston
Shipper: Thomas Jones & Co.
Consignee: Wearever Wool Co.

There were shipped 135 bales wool lamb skins, all of which were wet, worthless and dumped at Port of Spain.

135 bales weighing 108,140 lb., net sound value....$34,604.80
Amount allowed in general average............$34,604.80

Each of the other damaged cargo interests is separately dealt with.

Allowances to vessel takes four pages.

Other Disbursements. To these cargo and vessel allowances are added the general-average disbursements, the interest on these disbursements and allowances at 6 per cent per annum, some special charges less credits, the general-average adjuster's fee and his commission of 2½ per cent for collecting and settling the general average, the latter a peculiarity of American practice.

All this work has been necessary to permit the preparation of a statement of the "Contributing Interests and Apportionment of General Average" which follows:

Vessel:		
Value in damaged condition.............	$425,000.00	
Add amount made good................	2,576.57	
	$427,576.57—pays	$30,092.32
Freight:		
None at risk		
Cargo:		
As detailed hereafter, including amounts made good..........	$2,222,017.23—pays	$156,382.89
	$2,649,593.80	$186,475.21

Equal to 7.0378792 per cent

Apportionment of General Average on Cargo: Thirty pages follow, detailing the debits and credits to each cargo interest. For instance, Interest No. 53, referred to above, shows:

Amount made good................................		$34,604.80
Contributory value................................		$34,604.80
Pays its proportion of general average................		$2,435.45
Receives amount made good.................	$34,604.80	
Interest on amount made good..............	5,003.38	39,608.18
Credit in general average...........................		$37,172.73

The final summary and balance sheet follows:

	Debit	*Credit*
Cargo	$129,193.14	$96,091.67
Owners of vessel		11,854.83
Other special credits		1,327.00
Average adjusters, fees		15,371.46
Average adjusters, collecting and settling commission		4,548.18
	$129,193.14	$129,193.14

General-average statements when completed, as in the foregoing illustration, are presented for acceptance to the interested underwriters and to owners who have no insurance. Attached is a bill detailing their individual interests and showing a net amount either due from them or to be received by them. Settlement of these net amounts is then made with the general-average adjusters, and the case is closed.

CHAPTER 26

Subrogation—Salvage

SUBROGATION

Open Items. The loss adjuster's task is not ended when he has settled the claims of his assured. Many of these settlements, though rightly paid to the assured, were losses caused in whole or in part by the negligent action or lack of action on the part of other persons or corporations. It is the duty of the assured to turn over to the underwriter, by assignment or otherwise, his rights against such other persons or corporations. Usually the other party is a transportation company of some kind—steamship, railroad, or motor-truck carrier or perhaps a warehouseman. Their responsibilities are known as third-party liabilities, which are in most cases very technical and legalistic rights of recovery, and only very superficial consideration can be given to them in this book. Hundreds of *open items,* referring to claims against third parties, are on the books of every insurance company insuring transportation risks. No well-managed company sets up any asset item in its statement for the expected recoveries, but whether or not the recovery is ultimately made may determine in considerable part the profit or loss on an underwriter's statement.

Subrogation. These rights of recovery accrue to the underwriter through the right of *subrogation.* While the underwriter may be liable under the policy of insurance for the loss incurred, it does not necessarily follow that he alone is responsible for the injury suffered. In many cases there arises, because of the accident causing the loss, a liability on the part of some third party to respond for the injury suffered by the assured through the loss or damage to his property. In a collision case one of the colliding vessels may be solely at fault and consequently liable for the damage caused, except in so far as such liability is limited by law, but this liability on the part of the colliding vessel does not exonerate the underwriters of the innocent vessel from their obligation to its owner under their policies of insurance. It would be unfair, however, for the underwriters to respond for the loss and for the assured to retain his right of action against the owners of the offending vessel. Accordingly, in order to preserve the equities, upon payment of loss by the underwriters they are by law vested with the benefits accruing from the right of action that has arisen in favor of the assured. Through this right of subrogation the underwriter, to the extent that he has indemnified the assured, is clothed with all the benefits arising from claims against third parties that have arisen out of the casualty, and the assured is obligated to lend his name and good offices in the collection of such claims. The expense of collection, legal and otherwise, will be assumed by the underwriters in proportion to the interest that they have in the claim. If the settlement under a policy covering the entire interest has been for a total loss and the property has been fully insured, the underwriter is entitled to the benefit of the right of action in full. If, on the other hand, the loss is but partial or the property is not fully insured, the underwriter will be subrogated only to the extent of the loss that he has paid. The right of subrogation arises at the moment of payment.

This right of subrogation must be distinguished from salvage, the interest in the subject matter itself which the underwriter obtains under an abandonment or by assignment. In the case of a particular average, the assured retains physical possession of the property; nevertheless, the underwriter, by virtue of the payment of partial loss, is subrogated to the rights of the assured against third parties because of the loss. In the case of a total or constructive total loss, assuming that the property has been fully insured, the underwriter obtains a full interest in the salvage and in addition, by this right of subrogation, is vested with a full interest in all claims arising out of the casualty up to the amount paid.

Underwriters' Liability. In the cargo policy most underwriters incorporate a clause under which the assured warrants that the underwriters shall be free of any liability for loss or damage to goods in possession of any bailee who may be liable for such loss or damage by law, under an insured bill of lading, or under a rate of freight that includes insurance or otherwise. It is further stipulated that the policy shall be void with respect to goods shipped under a bill of lading containing a provision that the carrier is to have the benefit of any insurance that may be placed on the goods.

Carriers Slow to Respond for Losses. A common carrier by land is held to a high degree of accountability, while a common carrier by water, although relieved of much of his legal liability under statute, is nevertheless still charged with considerable responsibility in connection with the safeguarding and protecting of property in his custody. Collections from common carriers are slow and in many cases uncertain, the carriers taking advantage of every possible technicality in order to avoid payment of losses due to their negligence. On the other hand, in order that modern business may continue uninterruptedly, merchants must be promptly reimbursed in the event that loss or damage overtakes their property. Thus, it has become the custom for underwriters to reimburse merchants for losses to their property caused by perils insured against but due to the negligence of the carriers, the merchants at the same time filing claim and endeavoring to recover from the carrier. In the event of recovery, the merchants reimburse the underwriters for the payment made.

Benefit-of-insurance Clause. In cases where this condition exists, the carriers, knowing that the merchant has been reimbursed for his loss, refuse to settle claims, taking the position that the merchant, having been reimbursed by his underwriter, has really suffered no injury. In order further to strengthen this position, clauses are inserted in bills of lading by which the carrier claims the full benefit of any insurance that may be effected upon, or on account of, said goods. The validity of these clauses is doubtful, but in order that the underwriters may not be embarrassed by the presence of such clauses in bills of lading, they insert in their policies a clause making the policy void with respect to merchandise shipped under bills of lading containing the stipulation that the carrier shall have the benefit of any insurance on the goods. This has the effect of annulling the advantage that the carrier hopes to get by his *benefit-of-insurance clause.* The courts have upheld the validity of this clause in insurance policies.

Loan Receipts. However, this clause in an insurance policy leaves the merchant without protection, so a further stipulation is made by which the underwriter agrees with the assured that, in the event of loss or damage covered by the policy, for which the carriers may be liable, the underwriter, in order to place the merchant in funds, will advance to him as a loan an amount approximating the loss suffered. This loan must be repaid if recovery is obtained from the carriers, except in so far as such recovery is insufficient under the terms of the policy to reimburse the merchant for his loss. A regular form of loan receipt is prepared in such cases, which is signed by the assured. The carriers have endeavored to establish legally that the loan receipt is but a subterfuge and that, owing to the fact that the merchant is really reimbursed by the underwriter for the loss that has occurred, the merchant is not injured by the nonpayment of the loss on the part of the carrier. This question was a disputed one for some time, but in a decision handed down by the Supreme Court of the United States the validity of the loan receipt was finally established in ocean-marine cases and the carrier is now held to strict accountability for damages in accordance with the liability imposed upon him by law.

Classes of Claims. These rights which underwriters obtain under subrogation may be grouped in four classes:

1. Rights against carriers by water and air
2. Rights against railroads and express companies
3. Rights against motor carriers
4. Rights against warehousemen

Carriers by Water. The ocean bill of lading is usually the contract of carriage that determines the respective obligations of the shipper and the carrier. In some cases the contract of carriage is a charter party. Under common law a carrier by land or sea was liable for the property entrusted to his care except for the acts of God and the King's enemies. Carriers by sea at an early date were relieved of many of their negligence liabilities by inserting clauses in bills of lading relieving them of their obligations. There was great conflict among the laws of the various maritime nations. The laws of some countries permitted these relief clauses; other countries forbade them. Many efforts to achieve uniformity were made unsuccessfully. In 1893 the

United States enacted the Harter Act, which provided that a shipowner was not liable for certain faults and could not escape liability for certain other faults. This Act applied to both inward and outward bills of lading and in practice has proved to be fair in operation to the parties to the bill of lading. For 30 years after the passage of the Act little progress was made toward international uniformity, which was so essential to fair competition among steamship carriers and so necessary to bankers and underwriters.

Hague Rules. In 1921, after having circulated draft rules to bring about regulation of foreign bills of lading, all the interests concerned were invited to send their representatives to The Hague in September. Out of these discussions a final form of suggested rules was unanimously agreed upon and became known as the Hague Rules, 1921. It was hoped that these rules would be voluntarily accepted and incorporated in bills of lading by reference, as general-average rules had been since 1860. This did not prove to be the case, for various groups of shippers objected. Efforts were then made to make the rules effective by legislation, but these efforts also failed.

Carriage of Goods by Sea Act. At long last on April 16, 1936, the Carriage of Goods by Sea Act, embodying the principles of the Hague Rules as amended, became law in the United States, and bills of lading issued in overseas commerce are subject to this Act. Similar Acts are now the law of the principal maritime nations, and uniformity has at last been achieved. The United States Act refers to foreign trade and in this field supersedes the Harter Act. The Harter Act still applies to domestic water shipments.

The advantage to the underwriter under this Act is that he now knows what the responsibility of the water carrier is. He knows that the carrier cannot force a shipper to accept a bill of lading which contracts the carrier out of his legal responsibility. The Act definitely fixes the dollar liability of the carrier for each package or unit of shipment. It provides a reasonable time—one year—in which to bring suit. It further provides that a benefit-of-insurance clause in the bill of lading is void, being deemed a clause relieving a carrier from liability. The Act does not apply to goods prior to loading or after discharge, during which periods the Harter Act governs. In the absence of restraining legislation, the ocean carrier is still free to contract himself out of his legal liabilities and the underwriter must still include the customary clauses restraining the assured from accepting such restricted bills of lading.

Carriage by Air. Cargo transportation by air is in its infancy, and it is not yet determined whether the responsibility of these carriers will follow the principles applying to land or water carriers or will develop along new lines. Different rules may apply to air transport over water and over land.

Rail and Express Carriers. No legislation similar to the Harter Act[1] or the Carriage of Goods by Sea Act has been passed for the benefit of railroads. They and the express companies are held to the common-law liability which relieves them of practically nothing except responsibility for the consequences of acts of God and acts of war. Marine underwriters, who now insure from warehouse to warehouse, suit their premium charge to this broad liability of the rail carrier. It becomes of the utmost importance, when an accident causes loss to goods under a rail bill of lading, to preserve all legal rights against the carrier. The assured under the sue-and-labor clause is morally obligated to preserve these rights. In addition some cargo policies now incorporate clauses which are so worded as legally to preserve these rights to the assured and the underwriter. One form of these clauses reads:

(A) Except as otherwise provided in (B) and (C) below, it is agreed that in the event the interest insured is covered by other insurance the loss shall be recoverable under the several policies in the order of the date of their attachment except that insurance attaching on the same date shall be deemed simultaneous and shall contribute pro rata.

(B) Warranted that any fire insurance granted herein shall be null and void to the extent of any fire insurance which the Assured or any carrier or other bailee has, at the time of the fire, and which would attach if this policy had not been issued.

(C) Warranted by the Assured free from liability for loss of or damage to goods in the possession of any carrier or other bailee who may be liable therefor. However, this Company agrees to pay to the Assured the difference between the amount which would be a claim under this policy if it did not contain this warranty and the amount recoverable by the Assured from such

[1] For the text of the Carriage of Goods by Sea Act, see Appendix O, and for the Harter Act, see Appendix N.

carrier or bailee, plus the costs and expenses of prosecuting the claim against such carrier or bailee. Pending collection from such carrier or bailee this Company agrees to advance as a loan such amount which would be a claim under this policy if it did not contain this warranty, repayable only to the extent of any net recovery from such carrier or bailee.

Notwithstanding the exemptions that carriers by water enjoy, they frequently assume, when in competition with railroads, liabilities equal to those of the rail carriers or offer a rate of freight that includes insurance.[1]

Motor Carriers. The very great increase in the amount of goods carried overland by motor trucks has presented another problem to the loss adjuster's recovery unit. For many years motor carriers gave receipts embodying such terms as they deemed proper, whether or not the shipper agreed. All rail carriers are common carriers; that is, they hold themselves in readiness to transport any shipper's goods. Some motor carriers are also common carriers. Many, however, are private carriers for hire, engaging their vehicles for the transport only of the property of named shippers. Since 1935, when the Motor Carriers Act became law, interstate trucking has been subject to its terms. As with any new legislation in a new field, countless questions arise as to the meaning and application of the law. The marine underwriter covering shipments to or from the warehouse in interstate commerce must base his rate on the risk presented, an important factor being the legal responsibility of the motor carrier. Some kinds of goods are subject to hijacking. Some routings require long-distance overnight hauls. Then there are the varying problems of intrastate hauling, subject to local laws. It is extremely difficult to appraise the risk in motor-truck hauling, as so much depends on the legal or assumed responsibility of the motor-truck carrier.

Warehousemen. During transit it is not unusual for goods to be temporarily warehoused. It is customary to continue to insure in warehouse imported goods while in their original import packages. It is also common practice to cover under a marine-insurance policy goods in warehouse prepared for and awaiting export shipment. The responsibility of the warehouseman, therefore, is important to the marine underwriter. Legally his responsibility is very limited. Unless

[1] See p. 258.

it can be proved that the warehouseman was negligent, no valid claim can be made against him. The test of his negligence is whether he used the same degree of care toward another's goods that a prudent man would use in caring for his own property. The prospect of recovering from a warehouseman is usually very slight, and the underwriter should charge full fire and other rates for property while temporarily stored in warehouse.

SALVAGE

There are two kinds of salvage. The first kind includes those values recovered from the sale or reconditioning of damaged property. The second kind is more properly called *marine salvage*. Salvage in the mind of the loss adjuster means the first kind. His file of open items always contains a number of cases where damaged goods are in the hands of auctioneers for sale or in the hands of processors for rehabilitation. In many cases the assured himself is willing to take over the damaged property and recondition it. This frequently happens in the case of damaged skins where the processor of the product will work the damaged goods through his plant before claim is made. Similarly, a manufacturer of rubber products is often willing to take the damaged crude rubber and process it. Damaged piece goods can often be refinished so as to reduce the loss materially. A cooperative assured frequently can reduce to a small amount what at first sight seems to be a heavy loss. Sometimes the assured, after processing, will withdraw the claim. When such cooperation is not possible, the adjuster will send the goods to a processing plant for treatment, paying the claim in full and taking the proceeds as salvage. When recoveries are made by way of salvage from carriers, the amount received, less expenses, is treated as a credit item in the underwriter's loss account.

Marine Salvage. Marine salvage is the saving of ships and their cargoes from the perils of the sea. The risks undertaken by a marine salvor vary from the operation of towing into port a small vessel disabled at sea to the very difficult operation of freeing a large ship grounded on a rocky coast, her hull punctured by the rocks. Marine salvage is a well-recognized profession, and throughout the maritime world salvage organizations of greater or less skill operate. Promptness is often the vital factor in determining whether a salvage operation will be successful. A vessel floundering helplessly at sea may sink, if not promptly taken in tow. A vessel badly ashore, if not quickly helped, may break up. Marine salvage may be grouped in the following classes: rescue tug work, off-shore salvage, harbor salvage, and cargo salvage.[1] Salvage facilities are also used for the removal of wrecks from waterways, but here as a rule little salvaged value results.

Underwriters Interested. Underwriters are vitally interested in marine salvage. When notified of a disaster at sea, the underwriter is immediately concerned as to whether salvage operations are possible. If it is a simple failure of engines or loss of propeller or rudder, arrangements will be made by the shipowner to send a suitable towing vessel to bring the vessel into port. The contract for such towage usually provides for a per-diem charge from the time the tug leaves for the rescue work until she returns with the disabled ship. Under such a contract, even if the operation is unsuccessful, the tug is paid for its use, and each underwriter will pay not only for a total loss under his policy but also for his prorata share of tug hire.

No Cure, No Pay. In difficult marine salvage work, where the probability of success or failure is hard to determine, the salvage organization usually enters into a *no-cure–no-pay* salvage agreement with the owner of the vessel who, as in the case of general average, acts for all the interests involved in the venture. Under this form of contract no price is fixed for the service, it being agreed that, if successful, the salvor will be reimbursed for his expenses and in addition will receive a "bonus" commensurate with the skill shown and the hazards encountered in the operation. If the venture fails, the salvor will receive nothing. No-cure–no-pay salvage is one of the most speculative of enterprises. The salvor incurs large costs in setting up an organization and keeping adequate ships, salvage men, and equipment always in readiness for immediate action. Consequently courts and arbitrators are reasonably generous in rewarding prompt, efficient, and successful salvage operations. The skilled salvage operator will not undertake a salvage case if he has no hope of a successful outcome. He

[1] See "Marine Salvage," a paper presented by Admiral William A. Sullivan, U.S.N., Retired, at the annual meeting of the Society of Naval Architects, Nov. 11, 1948.

may discontinue his efforts already commenced or enter into a fixed-price agreement with the shipowner if it appears to him that the outcome is hopeless.

Adjustment. Marine salvage is usually a disbursement in connection with a general-average case. In order to complete the general-average adjustment it is necessary to fix the award for marine salvage. This award is one of the items with which the general-average adjuster deals. At times problems arise as to a fair division of the salvage award between items solely for account of hull and cargo and those to which all interests must contribute in general average.

CHAPTER 27

Profit or Loss—Statistics

The policy has been issued; the premium determined and collected. Reinsurance has been placed when necessary and paid for. Losses have been reported and either paid or reserved against by setting up adequate liability items. Offsetting reinsurance has been collected on paid losses or asset items set up against the relative loss-liability items. Overhead expenses have been cared for, acquisition cost has been credited to the broker, and the state or federal authorities have been paid their respective taxes. At this point the question is, "Has the business been profitable or otherwise?" The purposes of insurance companies are, first, to provide the public with insurance protection and, second, to make a profit out of the operation. If the second purpose is not accomplished, the company will not be able to continue in order to achieve the first purpose. The insurance law provides that premium on policies written for a period of time, say 12 months, must be carried as a liability until it is earned by the gradual expiration of the policy month by month. The unexpired portion of the premium is shown as the *unearned-premium reserve* on statistical and accounting statements; the expired premium is shown as *earned premium.* The unexpired portion of the premium is carried as a liability item primarily to safeguard the policyholders in the event that a company gets into financial difficulties. In such case it is customary to reinsure the outstanding liability, and the unterminated-premium-reserve item provides the funds with which to buy this reinsurance.[1]

It is not within the province of this book to discuss the accounting procedures necessary for the efficient conduct of an insurance com-

[1] See p. 365.

pany. The marine-insurance operations of an insurance company are frequently conducted as a separate enterprise by managing agents,[1] but even when the work is conducted as part of the home-office administration, certain peculiar problems differentiate this business from the fire- and casualty-insurance sections of the company.

Freedom from Rating Laws. Fire- and casualty-insurance rates and conditions, in greater or lesser degree, are under the control of rating bureaus required by state insurance laws. Because of its international character no attempt has been made to control the rates charged for marine insurance. The marine-insurance underwriter must, if he is to succeed, be able to change immediately the rates he has been charging to meet competition of underwriters in the domestic or foreign market. The marine-insurance business is conducted in an atmosphere of free trade.

Marine Insurance Not an Exact Science. Marine underwriting is not scientific in the sense that life underwriting is. In this latter branch of insurance practice there have been worked out, in the mortality tables, predetermined and safe tables of the results that may be expected in the insurance of lives. The life underwriter is dealing with relatively stable conditions, perhaps the only undetermined factors in his problem being the possibility of unusually heavy mortality through war, pestilence, or some catacylsm affecting a large portion of the territory in which he operates. But these unusual conditions are so rare as to be almost negligible.

The marine underwriter is dealing with risks that are affected not only by the ordinary stable situations encountered every day but also by the rapidly changing conditions encountered on the seas. No chart or table can be devised that will show to a nicety how many days will be clear and how many stormy or that will measure the severity and direction of storms. He is dealing with problems over which the veil of the future is drawn, but he must rely on past experience and his judgment of changing conditions in order to arrive at conclusions of what probably will happen in the future. Furthermore, owing to the unusual physical hazards to which marine risks are subjected, the experience upon which the underwriter depends

[1] See p. 118.

must extend over a considerable period of time, 10 years perhaps being the shortest period from which to draw conclusions.

Preparation of Statistics. The marine managing agent or the marine department of an insurance company produces statistical records for the confidential use of the marine underwriter. Without such records, which are cumulated year after year, the marine underwriter would not know whether his operations had produced a profit or a loss or if the rates he was charging were adequate. The problem is so to tabulate the results of the company's business that, from the results shown over a considerable period of years, the underwriter can see what the past has revealed as a basis for forecasting the future.

To gain the advantages available through the use of modern tabulating machines, all the information on each insurance document, whether it be policy, loss draft, loss-estimate sheet, salvage-recovery sheet, or reinsurance report, is reduced to a predetermined code made up from the figures 0 to 9 and sometimes, in addition, the letters of the alphabet. Each document goes to coding clerks, who translate the sense of the document into the code. From this code other clerks, by use of punch machines, produce cards containing the information on the original document that is necessary for accounting and statistical purposes. The cards are then sorted into classes, and the printing-tabulating machines produce printed records of the statistical information desired.

Analysis. This statistical information is analyzed by the underwriter, or it may come to him in a form prepared by accountants who analyze the statistical figures and prepare from them a statement of the particular problem under review. It may have been the results of a particular hull owner in the operation of his fleet. Such an analysis, showing the aggregate results for a 5-year period but, for the purpose of economizing space, the casualties for only the last year, follows:

GREENWAYS STEAMSHIP COMPANY

Expiring Dec. 31, 1950—16 Vessels—Syndicate interest 37½ per cent
Present Conditions: Institute Trading Warranties

Type of Vessel		Gross tons	Valuation	Av. value gross ton
Passenger vessels				
3	8,481 × 3 ave.	25,443	$9,600,000	$377
Cargo C-1				
10	6,714 × 10 ave.	67,140	8,000,000	119
Cargo C-2				
3	8,204 × 3 ave.	24,612	3,600,000	146
16		117,195	$21,200,000	$181

Premium and Loss Summary

Year	Average value per ton	Earned premium	Paid and estimated losses	No. accidents	Loss ratio, per cent
1946	$186	$215,467	$25,099	3	12
1947	217	224,115	154,234	7	69
1948	108	35,511	23,780	2	67
1949	181	163,106	61,760	45	38
1950	181	134,586*	110,018	25	82
		$772,785	$374,891	82	49
			On 100% basis		54

* 84% of annual premium.

NOTE: See The making of the rate, p. 283.

GREENWAYS STEAMSHIP COMPANY
Gross-tonnage Basis (100%) Navigating

Year	*Premium income per gross ton*	*Lay-up returns per gross ton*	*Net earned premium per gross ton*	*Loss cost per gross ton*
1946	$4.50	$0.04	$4.46	$0.75
1947	4.30	0.10	4.20	2.84
1948	2.89	0.10	2.79	1.89
1949	3.91	.....	3.91	1.48
1950	3.65	.....	3.65	2.99
Average	$3.96	$0.04	$3.92	$2.13

Losses

Binder year 1950		*Damage*	*Paid*	*Estimated*
S.S. No. 1	2/21/50	Damage to gangway		$350
S.S. No. 2	1/30/50	Damage to gangway	$122.67	
	1/10/50	Struck submerged object		3,757
S.S. No. 3	1/22/50	Struck by barge	86.43	
	2/5/50	Stranded		6,750
	2/12/50	Struck by another vessel		7,125
	10/17/50	Struck submerged object		1,875
S.S. No. 4	1/14/50	Drifted ashore		750
	6/2/50	Collided with S.S. *Blank*	51.47	
S.S. No. 5	1/26/50	Struck by barge		675
	2/20/50	Struck by barge		225
	3/5/50	Collided with tanker		1,125
S.S. No. 6	2/24/50	Lost anchor and chain	3,554.21	
	8/1/50	Machinery damage		24,750
S.S. No. 7	2/8/50	Damage to boiler tubes		2,813
	3/6/50	Grounded		6,263
	9/27/50	Grounded		2,813
S.S. No. 8	5/17/50	Stranded		1,313
S.S. No. 9	3/10/50	Struck by derrick and tug		375
S.S. No. 10	3/3/50	Struck by tug		375
S.S. No. 11	5/27/50	Boiler damage		4,500
S.S. No. 12	7/27/50	Struck submerged object		2,813
S.S. No. 13	8/8/50	Collided with lighters		57
S.S. No. 5	9/4/50 9/6/50	Grounded Collided with tug }		37,500
Syndicate interest 37½ per cent			$3,814.78	$106,204
Total paid and estimated				$110,018.78

The foregoing tables show the statistics in a very abbreviated form. The statistics on the 62½ per cent placed outside the Syndicate are supplied by the broker on the fleet. This enables a computation to be made on the Syndicate share and also on the total line.

On the results indicated, the Syndicate manager offered to renew the line on expiring terms and conditions.

Deductions. The report, as in the case cited, shows only the gross underwriting result. It must be reduced by a percentage of the net premium income calculated to cover overhead charges for conducting the business, including items of salary, office rent, stationery, taxes, brokerage, and various other expenses essential to the conduct of a going concern. In this manner the final result of underwriting operations is arrived at. In the hull illustration no notice has been taken of the cost of reinsurance, although the Syndicate may have reinsured part of the fleet under review. The reason for this is that the underwriter seeks information as to the experience of the business that he writes compared with losses that he pays, after which is deducted the expense of doing business. The reinsurance that he procures does not alter this experience. It will increase his net profits if reinsurance recoveries exceed reinsurance premium payments; on the other hand, if reinsurance payments exceed the recoveries, the net profits of the business will be reduced. In determining experience, reinsurance is an item to be disregarded. Consideration of reinsurance figures over a long period of years will indicate if it has been profitable for the company to reinsure and may aid in drawing conclusions as to whether or not the company could prudently retain larger lines than has been the practice. As a matter of pure experience on the outcome of individual classes of business, however, these figures are of little importance. It would be entirely proper in the case of share reinsurance, where a company under treaty turns over to other underwriters a share of all or of a portion of its business, to consider in statistical figures only the net retention and the net loss paid, as the expense of doing business must be paid out of the net and not the gross premium. In such cases, the original company is acting merely as a distributor of the risk. The reinsurance, which may be disregarded, is special or excess reinsurance that the company may place from time to time to reduce its liability.

Statistics Must Be Accurate. It is true that the annual income-and-disbursements statement of the company will indicate whether operations have been profitable or otherwise, but this statement will not point out the strong or the weak points in the underwriting operations of the organization. The statistical tabulations alone can do this, and the value of the results thus produced will depend largely on the accuracy of the figures furnished and the ability, by analysis, to sift them thoroughly in order to learn the exact cause of an unprofitable outturn of any particular class of risk.

Competition. Statistical results enable the underwriter to determine his course of action with respect to the renewal of business. Hull insurance is written usually for one year. Perhaps three months before expiration the underwriter will ask for statistical information. This will be furnished not only for the current term but for a number of earlier years as shown in the foregoing example. If the results for several years have been profitable, the underwriter will wish to renew. Shall he renew on expiring terms or shall he reduce the rate? This will depend on at least two important factors. First, has his hull business generally been profitable? Second, even if it has not been profitable, what is the chance of a more favorable rate being quoted in another market? If a foreign market has been actively seeking business, is it apt to make unusual efforts to obtain the most profitable business? The underwriter must weigh these factors in quoting a rate.

Similarly in the case of a cargo, the underwriter will periodically review his experience on each account and on each class of business. If for a considerable period a profit has resulted, he may reduce his rate or broaden the insuring conditions. If, on the other hand, the results have been unfavorable, he may suggest to the broker of his assured that the rates should be raised or the insuring conditions limited. In many cases where the statistical information indicates a repetitive cause of loss that has made the business unprofitable, he will suggest measures that will tend to eliminate or lessen such losses. The marine underwriter is always interested in loss prevention and would prefer to improve his underwriting results by constructive action rather than obtain an increase in premium to offset a bad underwriting result.

Competition keeps rates fluctuating within narrow bounds, with the result that the margin of profit over a period of years in the marine-insurance business is not great. The business seems to run in cycles; after a long period of relative freedom from excessive losses a period will follow in which disaster follows on disaster with incredible rapidity, causing unusual and exceedingly costly results. The education of a marine underwriter never ends. Day by day he must be aware of the changing conditions that present new problems in overseas trade. His success or failure depends in large measure on his ability to understand these changing conditions as they affect his underwriting problems and to make correct decisions. Only long experience can develop this kind of ability.

A Selected List of Reference Books

ARNOULD, SIR JOSEPH: "Law of Marine Insurance and Average," 13th ed. by Lord Chorley of Kendal, London, Stevens & Sons, Ltd., Sweet & Maxwell, Ltd., 1950.

BERNARD, HENRY I.: "Protection and Indemnity Insurance," 2d printing, New York, Johnson & Higgins, 1950.

CARVER, THOMAS G.: "Law Relating to the Carriage of Goods by Sea," 8th ed. by J. S. Henderson and S. D. Cole, London, Stevens & Sons, Ltd., 1938. (Out of print: new edition in preparation.)

CHALMERS, SIR M. D.: "Marine Insurance Act, 1906," 4th ed. by J. G. Archibald, assisted by Charles Stevenson, London, T. Thornton Butterworth, Ltd., 1932.

CONGDON, ERNEST W.: "General Average," 2d ed., Reprint, New York, Edw. W. Sweetman, 1952.

CROSS, IRA B.: "Domestic and Foreign Exchange," New York, The Macmillan Company, 1923.

DOVER, VICTOR: "A Handbook to Marine Insurance," 4th ed., London, H. F. and G. Witherby, Ltd., 1936. (Out of print.)

ELDRIDGE, WILLIAM H.: "Marine Policies," 3d ed. by Harry Atkins, London, T. Thornton Butterworth, Ltd., 1938.

GOW, WILLIAM: "Marine Insurance," 5th ed. rev. by D. King-Page, London, Macmillan & Co., Ltd., 1931. (Out of print; reprint in preparation.)

GOW, WILLIAM: "Sea Insurance," London, Macmillan & Co., Ltd., 1914.

GREGORY, KELLER, and BISHOP: "Physical and Commercial Geography," Boston, Ginn & Company, 1912.

LAZARUS, GEORGE MAITLAND: "A Treatise on the Law Relating to Insurance of Freight," London, T. Thornton Butterworth, Ltd., 1915. (Out of print.)

LOWNDES, RICHARD: "Lowndes' and Rudolf's Law of General Average and the York-Antwerp Rules," 7th ed. by A. J. Hodgson and G. R. Rudolf, London, Stevens & Sons, Ltd., 1948.

MARTIN, FREDERICK: "History of Lloyd's and of Marine Insurance in Great Britain," London, Macmillan & Co., Ltd., 1876. (Out of print.)

OWEN, DOUGLAS: "Ocean Trade and Shipping," London, Cambridge University Press, 1914.

PARSONS, THEOPHILIS: "A Treatise on Maritime Law and General Average," 2 vols., Boston, Little, Brown & Company, 1859.

PHILLIPS, WILLARD: "A Treatise on the Law of Insurance," 2 vols., 5th ed., New York, Hurd & Houghton, 1867. (Out of print.)

SCRUTTON, SIR THOMAS E.: "The Contract of Affreightment as Expressed in Charter Parties and Bills of Lading," 15th ed. by Sir W. L. McNair and A. A. Mocatta, London, Sweet & Maxwell, Ltd., 1948.

TEMPLEMAN, FREDERICK: "Marine Insurance," 4th ed. by Frederick Templeman and C. T. Greenacre, London, Macdonald & Evans, 1934.

TRENERRY, C. F.: "The Origin and Early History of Insurance," London, P. S. King & Staples, Ltd., 1926.

TURNER, HAROLD A.: "The Principles of Marine Insurance," 2d ed., London, Stone & Cox, Ltd.

WALTON, THOMAS: "Know Your Own Ship," 25th ed., London, Charles Griffin & Co., Ltd., 1932.

WRIGHT, CHARLES, and FAYLE, C. E.: "A History of Lloyd's," London, Macmillan & Co., Ltd., 1928. (Out of print.)

Appendix A. Standard Application Form Used in Placing Special Risks on Cargo

CERTIFICATES REQUIRED
(Indicate by check)

Original
Duplicate
Triplicate

CARGO APPLICATION
SPECIAL RISK
Underwriters and Brokers Emergency Agreement Form

Provisional } (Indicate
Definite } by check)

(Space reserved for Company's use)

*Policy No.*____________

*Certificate No.*____________

Application for Insurance is hereby made by ____________ *as Brokers*

In name of ____________, *account of whom it may concern*

Loss, if any, payable to ____________ *or order*

For the amount stated below, on ____________

Valued at ____________

Per ____________

At and from ____________
(Meaning point where insurance begins)

____

To ____________
(Meaning point where insurance ends)

____

Subject to printed clauses on the back hereof (unless otherwise provided hereon) and other Special Conditions as follows:

____

____

____

____

____

____

*Amount under deck $*______ *Rate*______ *per cent.*

*Amount on deck $*______ *Rate*______ *per cent.*

*Brokerage*______ *per cent.*

(Space reserved for calculation of premium)

*New York*____________ *19* __

*Binding*____________ *for Company*

*Binding*____________ *for Applicant*

Per..................

(Front side)

Appendix A continued

1. Warranted free of capture, seizure, arrest, restraint, or detainment, and the consequences thereof or of any attempt thereat, (*piracy excepted*), and also from all consequences of hostilities or war-like operations, whether before or after declaration of war.

2. Warranted free of loss or damage caused by strikers, locked out workmen or persons taking part in labor disturbances or riots or civil commotions.

3. General Average and Salvage Charges payable according to Foreign Statement or per York-Antwerp Rules if in accordance with the contract of affreightment.

4. Held covered, at a premium to be arranged, in case of deviation or change of voyage or of any omission or error in the description of the interest, vessel or voyage.

5. Including (subject to the terms of the Policy) all risks covered by this Policy from shippers or Manufacturers' warehouse until on board the vessel, during transhipment if any, and from the vessel, whilst on quays, wharves or in sheds during the ordinary course of transit until safely deposited in consignees' or other warehouse at destination named in Policy, except that in respect to shipments to the River Plate, the risks under this insurance shall cease upon arrival at any Shed (transit or otherwise), Store, Custom House or Warehouse, or upon the expiry of ten (10) days, subsequent to landing, whichever may first occur.

6. Including risk of craft, raft and/or lighter to and from the vessel. Each craft, raft, and/or lighter to be deemed a separate insurance. The Assured are not to be prejudiced by any agreement exempting lightermen from liability.

7. Including all liberties as per contract of affreightment. The Assured are not to be prejudiced by the presence of the negligence clause and/or latent defect clause in the Bills of Lading and/or Charter Party. The seaworthiness of the vessel as between the Assured and the Assurers is hereby admitted.

8. Warranted not to cover the interest of any partnership, corporation, association or person, insurance for whose account would be contrary to the Trading with the Enemy Acts or other statutes or prohibitions of the United States and/or British Governments.

(*Reverse side of standard application form*)

Appendix B. Standard Form Used in Requesting Return Premium, Either Because of Cancellation or Reduction of Risk

U B E A

RETURN PREMIUMS

CANCELLATION--REDUCTIONS

....19.....

....Insurance Co............ ....(Agents)

Please cancel/reduce ....Date effective..

Insurance on...per..
(State interest insured) (give name vessel)

Assured..

Reason for cancellation/reduction ....

....

Basis upon which return premium to be made ....
(If "in accordance with policy conditions", so state otherwise clearly state basis upon which returns are to be made).

IDENTIFICATION OF ORIGINAL INSURANCE

(Give full identification of Risk. If "open" so state.)

Policy No.	From	To	Amount Insured
			$

.... Underwriter. .... Brokers.

CALCULATION OF RETURN PREMIUM

	Rate	Premium	Brokerage	Net Premium	
Original insurance $.	....	....	....	....	NET RETURN PREMIUM
Reduced to $.	....	....	....	....	
	RATE OF RETURN	Return Premium	Less B'kge.	Net Return Premium	
Amount cancelled $.	....	....	....		$........

Appendix C. American Institute Cargo Clauses

American Institute
(February 1949)

32 B-8

AMERICAN INSTITUTE CARGO CLAUSES

Warehouse to warehouse clause.

1. This insurance attaches from the time the goods leave the Warehouse and/or Store at the place named in the policy for the commencement of the transit and continues during the ordinary course of transit, including customary transhipment if any, until the goods are discharged overside from the overseas vessel at the final port. Thereafter the insurance continues whilst the goods are in transit and/or awaiting transit until delivered to final warehouse at the destination named in the policy or until the expiry of 15 days (or 30 days if the destination to which the goods are insured is outside the limits of the port) whichever shall first occur. The time limits referred to above to be reckoned from midnight of the day on which the discharge overside of the goods hereby insured from the overseas vessel is completed. Held covered at a premium to be arranged in the event of transhipment, if any, other than as above and/or in the event of delay in excess of the above time limits arising from circumstances beyond the control of the Assured.

It is necessary for the Assured to give prompt notice to these Assurers when they become aware of an event for which they are "held covered" under this policy and the right to such cover is dependent on compliance with this obligation.

Craft, &c., clause.

2. Including transit by craft and/or lighter to and from the vessel. Each craft and/or lighter to be deemed a separate insurance. The Assured are not to be prejudiced by any agreement exempting lightermen from liability.

Deviation clause.

3. This insurance shall not be vitiated by any unintentional error in description of vessel, voyage or interest, or by deviation, over-carriage, change of voyage, transhipment or any other interruption of the ordinary course of transit, from causes beyond the control of the Assured. It is agreed, however, that any such error, deviation or other occurrence mentioned above shall be reported to this Company as soon as known to the Assured, and additional premium paid if required.

F.P.A. clause.

4. Warranted free from Particular Average unless the vessel or craft be stranded, sunk, or burnt, but notwithstanding this warranty these Assurers are to pay any loss of or damage to the interest insured which may reasonably be attributed to fire, collision or contact of the vessel and/or craft and/or conveyance with any external substance (ice included) other than water, or to discharge of cargo at port of distress. **The foregoing warranty, however, shall not apply where broader terms of Average are provided for hereon or in the certificate or policy to which these clauses are attached.**

Warehousing & Forwarding Charges, Packages totally lost loading, etc.

5. Notwithstanding any average warranty contained herein, these Assurers agree to pay any landing, warehousing, forwarding and special charges for which this policy in the absence of such warranty would be liable. Also to pay the insured value of any package or packages which may be totally lost in loading, transhipment or discharge.

Labels clause.

6. In case of damage affecting labels, capsules or wrappers, these Assurers, if liable therefor under the terms of this policy, shall not be liable for more than an amount sufficient to pay the cost of new labels, capsules or wrappers, and the cost of reconditioning the goods, but in no event shall these Assurers be liable for more than the insured value of the damaged merchandise.

Machinery Clause

7. When the property insured under this policy includes a machine consisting when complete for sale or use of several parts, then in case of loss or damage covered by this insurance to any part of such machine, these Assurers shall be liable only for the proportion of the insured value of the part lost or damaged, or at the Assured's option, for the cost and expense, including labor and forwarding charges, of replacing or repairing the lost or damaged part; but in no event shall these Assurers be liable for more than the insured value of the complete machine.

G/A clause.

8. General Average and Salvage Charges payable according to United States laws and usage and/or as per Foreign Statement and/or as per York-Antwerp Rules (as prescribed in whole or in part) if in accordance with the Contract of Affreightment.

Explosion clause.

9. Including the risk of explosion, howsoever or wheresoever occurring during the currency of this insurance, unless excluded by the F. C. & S. Warranty or the S. R. & C. C. Warranty set forth herein.

Shore Clause

10. Where this insurance by its terms covers while on docks, wharves or elsewhere on shore, and/or during land transportation, it shall include the risks of collision, derailment, overturning or other accident to the conveyance, fire, lightning, sprinkler leakage, cyclones, hurricanes, earthquakes, floods (meaning the rising of navigable waters), and/or collapse or subsidence of docks or wharves, even though the insurance be otherwise F.P.A.

Bill of Lading &c., clause.

11. The Assured are not to be prejudiced by the presence of the negligence clause and/or latent defect clause in the Bills of Lading and/or Charter Party. The seaworthiness of the vessel as between the Assured and these Assurers is hereby admitted and the wrongful act or misconduct of the shipowner or his servants causing a loss is not to defeat the recovery by an innocent Assured if the loss in the absence of such wrongful act or misconduct would have been a loss recoverable on the policy. With leave to sail with or without pilots, and to tow and assist vessels or craft in all situations, and to be towed.

Inchmaree Clause

12. This insurance is also specially to cover any loss of or damage to the interest insured hereunder, through the bursting of boilers, breakage of shafts or through any latent defect in the machinery, hull or appurtenances, or from faults or errors in the navigation and/or management of the vessel by the master, mariners, mates, engineers or pilots.

Delay clause.

13. Warranted free of claim for loss of market or for loss, damage or deterioration arising from delay, whether caused by a peril insured against or otherwise, unless expressly assumed in writing hereon.

Both to Blame clause.

14. Where goods are shipped under a Bill of Lading containing the so-called "Both to Blame Collision" Clause, these Assurers agree as to all losses covered by this insurance, to indemnify the Assured for this policy's proportion of any amount (not exceeding the amount insured) which the Assured may be legally bound to pay to the shipowners under such clause. In the event that such liability is asserted the Assured agree to notify these Assurers who shall have the right at their own cost and expense to defend the Assured against such claim.

15. No recovery for a Constructive Total Loss shall be had hereunder unless the property insured is reasonably abandoned on account of its actual total loss appearing to be unavoidable, or because it cannot be preserved from actual total loss without an expenditure which would exceed its value when the expenditure had been incurred.

Constructive Total Loss Clause

16. Warranted that this insurance shall not inure, directly or indirectly, to the benefit of any carrier or bailee.

Carrier clause.

17. The following Warranties shall be paramount and shall not be modified or superseded by any other provision included herein or stamped or endorsed hereon unless such other provision refers specifically to the risks excluded by these Warranties and expressly assumes the said risks:—

(A) Notwithstanding anything herein contained to the contrary, this insurance is warranted free from capture, seizure, arrest, restraint, detainment, confiscation, preemption, requisition or nationalization, and the consequences thereof or any attempt thereat, whether in time of peace or war and whether lawful or otherwise; also warranted free, whether in time of peace or war, from all loss or damage caused by any weapon of war employing atomic fission or radioactive force; also warranted free from all consequences of hostilities or warlike operations (whether there be a declaration of war or not) but this warranty shall not exclude collision, explosion or contact with any fixed or floating object (other than a mine or torpedo), stranding, heavy weather or fire unless caused directly (and independently of the nature of the voyage or service which the vessel concerned or, in the case of a collision, any other vessel involved therein, is performing) by a hostile act by or against a belligerent power; and for the purpose of this warranty 'power' includes any authority maintaining naval, military or air forces in association with a power.

Further warranted free from the consequences of civil war, revolution, rebellion, insurrection, or civil strife arising therefrom, or piracy.

F. C. & S. Warranty.

(B) Warranted free of loss or damage caused by or resulting from strikes, lockouts, labor disturbances, riots, civil commotions or the acts of any person or persons taking part in any such occurrence or disorder.

S. R. & C. C. Warranty.

Special Terms and Conditions:—

Appendix D. Special Policy of Insurance Issued Under Open Policy

The Insurance Company

$.................................... No. |....................

New York,..

By this special policy of insurance

do make insurance and cause to be insured lost or not lost, for account of
at and from
to
in the sum of Dollars
on

Valued at sum insured. Shipped per

Loss, if any, payable to or order,
upon the surrender of this policy at the office of this Company in New York City, or at the office of its nearest settling agent, as per back hereof, computed at the current rate of exchange on the day of payment, and, on the payment being made, liability under this insurance shall be thereby discharged.

Marks and Numbers

Attention of the holder of this document is directed particularly to the SPECIAL NOTICE clause, as per back hereof, outlining the proper procedure in the event of the goods hereby insured arriving in a damaged condition.

The Revenue Laws of Great Britain require that this policy be stamped within ten days after receipt in the United Kingdom, otherwise loss cannot be collected there. Such stamps to be at the expense of the assured.

This Special Policy is subject to the following terms and conditions and also those printed on the reverse side hereof.

This insurance attaches from the time the goods leave the Warehouse and/or Store at the place named in the policy for the commencement of the transit and continues during the ordinary course of transit, including customary transhipment if any, until the goods are discharged overside from the overseas vessel at the final port. Thereafter the insurance continues whilst the goods are in transit and/or awaiting transit until delivered to final warehouse at the destination named in the policy or until the expiry of 15 days (or 30 days if the destination to which the goods are insured is outside the limits of the port) whichever shall first occur. The time limits referred to above to be reckoned from midnight of the day on which the discharge overside of the goods hereby insured from the overseas vessel is completed. Held covered at a premium to be arranged in the event of transhipment, if any, other than as above and/or in the event of delay in excess of the above time limits arising from circumstances beyond the control of the Assured.

d in original and duplicate, accomplished, the other to

Where goods are shipped under a Bill of Lading containing the so-called "Both to Blame Collision" Clause, this Company agrees as to all losses covered by this insurance, to indemnify the Assured for this policy's proportion of any amount (not exceeding the amount insured) which the Assured may be legally bound to pay to the shipowners under such clause. In the event that such liability is asserted the Assured agree to notify this Company who shall have the right at its own cost and expense to defend the Assured against such claim.

Warranted free from Particular Average unless the vessel or craft be stranded, sunk, or burnt, but notwithstanding this warranty this Company is to pay any loss of or damage to the interest insured which may reasonably be attributed to fire, collision or contact of the vessel and/or craft and/or conveyance with any external substance (ice included) other than water, or to discharge of cargo at port of distress. **The foregoing warranty, however, shall not apply where broader terms of Average are provided for herein or endorsed hereon.**

NOTE:—It is necessary for the Assured to give prompt notice to this Company when they become aware of an event for which they are "held covered" under this policy and the right to such cover is dependent on compliance with this obligation.

Where this insurance by its terms covers while on docks, wharves or elsewhere on shore, and/or during land transportation, it shall include the risks of collision, derailment, overturning or other accident to the conveyance, fire, lightning, sprinkler leakage, cyclones, hurricanes, earthquakes, floods (meaning the rising of navigable waters), and/or collapse or subsidence of docks or wharves, even though the insurance be otherwise F. P. A.

This Policy is issued, one of which being stand null and void

American Institute Clauses: This insurance, in addition to the foregoing, is also subject to the following American Institute Cargo Clauses (1949):

1. Craft, etc.
2. Deviation
3. General Average
4. Explosion
5. Bill of Lading, etc.
6. Inchmaree
7. Warehousing & Forwarding Charges
8. Constructive Total Loss

Warranted free of claim for loss of market or for loss, damage or deterioration arising from delay, whether caused by a peril insured against or otherwise, unless expressly assumed in writing herein.

The following Warranties shall be paramount and shall not be modified or superseded by any other provision included herein or stamped or endorsed hereon unless such other provision refers specifically to the risks excluded by these Warranties and expressly assumes the said risks:—

(A) F. C. & S. Notwithstanding anything herein contained to the contrary, this insurance is warranted free from capture, seizure, arrest, restraint, detainment, confiscation, preemption, requisition or nationalization, and the consequences thereof or any attempt thereat, whether in time of peace or war and whether lawful or otherwise; also warranted free, whether in time of peace or war, from all loss or damage caused by any weapon of war employing atomic fission or radioactive force; also warranted free from all consequences of hostilities or warlike operations (whether there be a declaration of war or not) but this warranty shall not exclude collision, explosion or contact with any fixed or floating object (other than a mine or torpedo), stranding, heavy weather or fire unless caused directly (and independently of the nature of the voyage or service which the vessel concerned or, in the case of a collision, any other vessel involved therein, is performing) by a hostile act by or against a belligerent power; and for the purpose of this warranty "power" includes any authority maintaining naval, military or air forces in association with a power.

Further warranted free from the consequences of civil war, revolution, rebellion, insurrection, or civil strife arising therefrom, or piracy.

(B) S. R. & C. C. Warranted free of loss or damage caused by or resulting from strikes, lockouts, labor disturbances, riots, civil commotions or the acts of any person or persons taking part in any such occurrence or disorder.

The following clauses shall have precedence of all others if in conflict therewith.

This policy is not transferable unless countersigned by a duly authorized representative of the Company.

Countersigned

....

In Witness Whereof, the President of the said Insurance Company hath hereunto subscribed his name, and caused the same to be attested by its Secretary, and this policy is made and accepted upon the above express conditions, the day and date first above written.

John Doe — Secretary

Richard Roe — President

ADDITIONAL TERMS AND CONDITIONS

Losses arising from breakage or leakage are excluded from this insurance unless caused by stranding or collision with another vessel, except when included in the average terms of this policy.

In case of damage affecting labels, capsules, or wrappers, this Company, if liable therefor under the terms of this policy, shall not be liable for more than an amount sufficient to pay the cost of new labels, capsules or wrappers, and the cost of conditioning the goods, but in no event shall this Company be liable for more than the insured value of the damaged merchandise.

When the property insured under this policy includes a machine consisting when complete for sale or use of several parts, then in case of loss or damage covered by this insurance to any part of such machine, this Company shall be liable only for the proportion of the insured value of the part lost or damaged, or at the Assured's option, for the cost and expense, including labor and forwarding charges, of replacing or repairing the lost or damaged part; but in no event shall this Company be liable for more than the insured value of the complete machine.

(A) Except as otherwise provided in (B) and (C) below, it is agreed that in the event the interest insured is covered by other insurance the loss shall be recoverable under the several policies in the order of the date of their attachment except that insurance attaching on the same date shall be deemed simultaneous and shall contribute pro rata.

(B) Warranted that any fire insurance granted herein shall be null and void to the extent of any fire insurance which the Assured or any carrier or other bailee has, at the time of the fire, and which would attach if this policy had not been issued.

(C) Warranted by the Assured free from liability for loss of or damage to goods in the possession of any carrier or other bailee who may be liable therefor. However, this Company agrees to pay to the Assured the difference between the amount which would be a claim under this policy if it did not contain this warranty and the amount recoverable by the Assured from such carrier or bailee, plus the costs and expenses of prosecuting the claim against such carrier or bailee. Pending collection from such carrier or bailee this Company agrees to advance as a loan such amount which would be a claim under this policy if it did not contain this warranty, repayable only to the extent of any net recovery from such carrier or bailee.

TOUCHING the adventures and perils which the said COMPANY is contented to bear, and takes upon itself in this voyage, they are of the seas, men-of-war, fires, enemies, pirates, rovers, assailing thieves, jettisons, letters of mart and countermart, reprisals, takings at sea, arrests, restraints, and detainments of all kings, princes or people, of what nation, condition or quality soever, barratry of the master and mariners, and all other perils, losses and misfortunes that have or shall come to the hurt, detriment or damage of the said goods and merchandises or any part thereof. AND in case of any loss or misfortune, it shall be lawful and necessary to and for the assured, their factors, servants and assigns, to sue, labor, and travel for, in and about the defense, safeguard and recovery of the said goods and merchandises, or any part thereof, without prejudice to this insurance; nor shall the acts of the insured or insurers, in recovering, saving and preserving the property insured, in case of disaster, be considered a waiver or an acceptance of an abandonment; to the charges whereof, the said Insurance Company will contribute according to the rate and quantity of the sum herein insured.

MEMORANDUM. It is also agreed, that bar, bundle, rod, hoop and sheet iron, wire of all kinds, tin plates, steel, madder, sumac, wickerware and willow (manufactured or otherwise), salt, grain of all kinds, tobacco, indian meal, fruits (whether preserved or otherwise), cheese, dry fish, hay, vegetables and roots, rags, hempen yarn, bags, cotton bagging, and other articles used for bags or bagging, pleasure carriages, household furniture, skins and hides, musical instruments, looking-glasses, and all other articles that are perishable in their own nature, are warranted by the assured free from average, unless general; hemp, tobacco stems, matting and cassia, except in boxes, free from average under twenty per cent., unless general; and sugar, flax, flax-seed and bread, are warranted by the assured free from average under seven per cent., unless general; and coffee in bags or bulk, pepper in bags or bulk, and rice, free from average under ten per cent., unless general.

Warranted by the insured free from damage or injury from dampness, change of flavor, or being spotted, discolored, musty or mouldy, except caused by actual contact of sea water with the articles damaged, occasioned by sea perils. In case of partial loss by sea damage to dry goods, cutlery or other hardware, the loss shall be ascertained by a separation and sale of the portion only of the contents of the packages so damaged, and not otherwise; and the same practice shall obtain as to all other merchandise as far as practicable. Not liable for leakage on molasses or other liquids unless occasioned by stranding or collision with another vessel.

If the voyage aforesaid shall have been begun and shall have terminated before the date of this policy, then there shall be no return of premium on account of such termination of the voyage.

THIS SPACE IS RESERVED FOR ENDORSEMENTS IN TRANSFER OF THIS DOCUMENT

SPECIAL NOTICE—IN CASE OF LOSS OR DAMAGE to the goods hereby insured, immediate application for survey, appraisal and authentication of proofs of loss should be made to the settling agent of the Company or to its correspondent, as the case may be, at the port of destination if there be one at such port, otherwise to the correspondent of The Board of Underwriters of New York, or, if there be none, to Lloyd's agent.

Any apparent loss or damage or irregularity in this shipment **SHOULD BE NOTED ON RECEIPT** given to the carriers and preliminary **CLAIM** should be **FILED** with them **IN WRITING IMMEDIATELY.** When survey is held to ascertain loss or damage the carrier should be given an opportunity of being represented and claim for actual loss **MUST BE FILED AGAINST THE CARRIER IN WRITING.**

Copies of notation on receipts and correspondence in connection with claim against carrier must form part of proof of loss under the Insurance Policy.

A full list of settling agents and correspondent of this Company appear below.

After a proper adjustment settlement of the loss may be made at the office of the nearest settling agent in the manner herein indicated.

This Company hereby agrees to a British Domicile for the purpose of any legal proceedings and will accept service of process in London at the office of

SETTLING AGENTS

ADELAIDE (So. Australia)
ALEXANDRIA (Egypt)
AMSTERDAM (Netherlands)
ANTWERP (Belgium)
BARCELONA (Spain)
BATAVIA (Java)
BOMBAY (India)
BREMEN (Germany)
BRISBANE (Australia)
BUENOS AIRES (Argentina)
CALCUTTA (India)
CAPE TOWN (So. Africa)
CARACAS (Venezuela)
COLOMBO (Ceylon)
COPENHAGEN (Denmark)
DAR-es-SALAAM (East Africa)
DURBAN (So. Africa)
EAST LONDON (So. Africa)
GENOA (Italy)
GLASGOW (Scotland)
HAMBURG (Germany)
HAVRE (France)
HONG KONG (China)
HONOLULU (Hawaii)
JOHANNESBURG (So. Africa)
KARACHI (India)
LISBON (Portugal)
LIVERPOOL (England)
LONDON (England)
For change, alteration or extension of this special policy required in Great Britain or European Countries apply to King William Street House, Arthur Street, London, E.C. 4.
LOURENCO MARQUES (Delagoa Bay) (E. Africa)
MADRAS (British India)
MANCHESTER (England)
MANILA (Philippine Islands)
MEDAN (Sumatra)
MELBOURNE (Australia)
MOMBASA (East Africa)
MONTEVIDEO (Uruguay)
PERTH (Australia)
PORT ELIZABETH (So. Africa)
PORT LOUIS (Mauritius)
PORT-OF-SPAIN (Trinidad)
RANGOON (Burma)
RIO de JANEIRO (Brazil)
ROTTERDAM (Netherlands)
SAMARANG (Java)
SAN FRANCISCO (California)
SANTOS (Brazil)
SAO PAULO (Brazil)
SHANGHAI (China)
SINGAPORE (Straits Settlements)
SOURABAYA (Java)
TIENTSIN (China)
TOKYO (Japan)
TRIESTE (Italy)
VALPARAISO (Chile)
YOKOHAMA (Japan)
ZANZIBAR (East Africa)

Appendix E. American Institute War Cargo Policy (March, 1951)

WAR RISK ONLY

Open Policy

Form No. 2-I

Policy No.............................

....19.......

THIS POLICY OF INSURANCE WITNESSETH, that in consideration of premiums as agreed to be paid, these Assurers do make insurance and cause

....to be insured, lost or not lost, for account of whom it may concern, against War Risks only, in accordance with the terms and conditions hereinafter set forth.

For not exceeding $................................. per any one Vessel.

This Policy shall cover only those shipments which are insured against marine risks under Policy No.................................of this Company, it being agreed that the description of such shipments, the valuations thereof, the voyage, the designation of the overseas vessel (which shall be construed to include aircraft if included under the marine policy) on which the goods are to be carried and the ports of loading and discharge, as reported under the said Policy against marine risks, shall be deemed incorporated herein. Notwithstanding the foregoing, this policy shall not cover purely domestic shipments by air between points in the Continental United States (excluding Alaska).

Any loss payable hereunder shall be payable in funds current in the United States, to the order of

....

thirty days after full proofs of loss and proofs of interest have been filed with these Assurers.

1. This insurance is only against the risks of capture, seizure, destruction or damage by men-of-war, piracy, takings at sea, arrests, restraints, detainments and other warlike operations and acts of kings, princes and peoples in prosecution of hostilities or in the application of sanctions under international agreements, whether before or after declaration of war and whether by a belligerent or otherwise, including factions engaged in civil war, revolution, rebellion or insurrection, or civil strife arising therefrom, and including the risks of aerial bombardment, floating or stationary mines and stray or derelict torpedoes and weapons of war employing atomic fission or radioactive force; but excluding claims for delay,

deterioration and/or loss of market, and warranted not to abandon (on any ground other than physical damage to ship or cargo) until after condemnation of the property insured.

2. Warranted free from any claim based upon loss of, or frustration of, the insured voyage or adventure caused by arrests, restraints or detainments.

3. This insurance does not cover any loss or damage caused by or resulting from any of the following causes:

   (a) Commandeering, preemption, requisition or nationalization by the government (de facto or otherwise) of the country to or from which the goods are insured.

   (b) Seizure or destruction under quarantine or customs regulations.

4. (a) The insurance against the risks enumerated in Clause 1, except the risks of floating or stationary mines and stray or derelict torpedoes, floating or submerged, referred to in (b) below, shall not attach to the interest hereby insured or to any part thereof

   (i) prior to being on board an overseas Vessel (For the purpose of this Clause 4 an overseas Vessel shall be deemed to mean a Vessel carrying the interest from one port or place to another where such voyage involves a sea passage by that Vessel),

   (ii) after being discharged overside from an overseas Vessel at the final port of discharge,

   or

   after the expiry of 15 days counting from midnight of the day of arrival of the overseas Vessel at the final port of discharge,

   whichever shall first occur,

   (iii) after expiry of 15 days from midnight of the day of arrival of the overseas Vessel at an intermediate port or place to discharge the interest for on-carriage from that or any other port or place by another overseas Vessel, but shall re-attach as the interest is loaded on the on-carrying overseas Vessel. During the said period of 15 days the insurance remains in force whether the interest is awaiting transit or in transit between the overseas Vessels.

   (b) The insurance against the risks of floating or stationary mines and stray or derelict torpedoes, floating or submerged, attaches as the interest hereby insured is first loaded on lighter, craft or vessel after leaving the warehouse at point of shipment in transit for the destination declared hereunder, and ceases to attach as the interest is finally landed from the vessel, craft or lighter prior to delivery to warehouse at such destination.

If the contract of affreightment is terminated at a port or place other than the destination named therein such port or place shall be deemed the final port of discharge for the purpose of this Clause.

Shipments by air and/or mail, if covered by this Policy, are insured continuously from the time of leaving the sender's premises until delivered to the place of address.

It is a condition of this insurance that the Assured shall act with reasonable dispatch in all circumstances within their control.

If anything contained in this Policy shall be inconsistent with this Clause 4 it shall to the extent of such inconsistency be null and void.

5. This insurance shall not be vitiated by deviation, over-carriage, change of voyage, or by any error or unintentional omission in the description of interest, Vessel or voyage, provided the same be communicated to this Company as soon as known to the Assured and an additional premium paid if required.

6. And in case of any loss or misfortune, it shall be lawful and necessary to and for the Assured, his or their factors, servants and assigns, to sue, labor and travel for, in and about the defense, safeguard and recovery of the said goods and merchandises, or any part thereof, without prejudice to this insurance; nor shall the acts of the Assured or Assurers, in recovering, saving and preserving the property insured, in case of disaster, be considered a waiver or an acceptance of an abandonment; and to the charges whereof, the said Assurers will contribute according to the rate and quantity of the sum hereby insured.

7. **General Average and Salvage Charges payable according to United States laws and usage and/or as per Foreign Statement and/or as per York-Antwerp Rules (as prescribed in whole or in part) if in accordance with the Contract of Affreightment.**

8. **It is agreed that the reports of shipments made under the Policy against marine risks mentioned above shall be deemed to be reports under this Policy also, and the Assured agrees to pay premiums on all shipments insured under this Policy at the war risk rates of this Company as fixed from time to time.**

9. **No claim shall be payable hereunder which arises from collision, contact with any fixed or floating object (other than a mine or torpedo), stranding, heavy weather or fire unless caused directly (and independently of the nature of the voyage or service which the Vessel concerned or, in the case of a collision, any other Vessel involved therein, is performing) by a hostile act by or against a belligerent power; and for the purpose of this paragraph "power" includes any authority maintaining naval, military or air forces in association with a power.**

10. It is agreed that this Policy is a separate and wholly independent contract and is not subject to any terms or conditions of the Policy against marine risks above mentioned (whether physically attached thereto or not) except as such terms or conditions shall have been expressly incorporated herein by reference.

11. This insurance may be cancelled by either party upon forty-eight hours written or telegraphic notice to the other party, but such cancellation shall not affect any shipment on which this insurance has attached under the terms of Clause 4 hereof prior to the effective date of such notice. Shipments on which this insurance has not so attached but for which, prior to the effective date of such notice, bills of lading have been issued and (in the case of exports) Certificates or Special Policies have been issued and negotiated, shall be covered from the time of loading on the overseas vessel, as provided in Clause 4, at the rates of this Company, provided that, prior to said effective date, such shipments were at the risk of the Assured and were covered under the said Policy against marine risks.

In the event of loss which may give rise to a claim under this Policy, prompt notice should be given to this Company.

Appendix F. Syndicate Hull Form (December, 1951)

Sum Insured $.................................... **Policy No.**

Premium $....................................

AMERICAN MARINE HULL INSURANCE SYNDICATE
BY THIS POLICY OF INSURANCE

The SUBSCRIBERS hereto, hereinafter referred to as the Underwriters, each severally, but not jointly, and not on the part of one for the other or any of the others, for their respective proportions as set forth herein, DO MAKE INSURANCE and cause to be insured, lost or not lost:

....

FOR ACCOUNT OF ....
but subject to the provisions of this Policy with respect to change of ownership.

In the event of any change, voluntary or otherwise, in the ownership of the Vessel or if the Vessel be placed under new management or be chartered on a bareboat basis or requisitioned on that basis, then, unless the Underwriters agree thereto in writing, this Policy shall thereupon become cancelled from time of such change in ownership or management, charter or requisition; provided, however, that in the case of an involuntary temporary transfer by requisition or otherwise, without the prior execution of any written agreement by the Assured, such cancellation shall take place fifteen days after such transfer; and provided further that if the Vessel has cargo on board and has already sailed from her loading port, or is at sea in ballast, such cancellation shall be suspended until arrival at final port of discharge if with cargo or at port of destination if in ballast. This insurance shall not inure to the benefit of any such charterer or transferee of the Vessel, and if a loss payable hereunder should occur between such transfer and such cancellation the Underwriters shall be subrogated to all the rights of the Assured against the transferee, by reason of such transfer, in respect of all or part of such loss as is recoverable from the transferee and in the proportion which the respective amounts insured bear to the insured value. A pro rata daily return of net premium shall be made. The foregoing provisions with respect to cancellation in the event of change in ownership or management, charter or requisition shall apply even in the case of insurance "for account of whom it may concern."

Loss, if any, (excepting claims required to be paid to others under the Collision

Clause), payable to ....

....

.... or order.

Sum Insured
Hereunder .... **Dollars,**

at and from the............day of......................19......., ...time

to the________________day of......................19____, ________________________________time.

Provided, however, should the Vessel at the expiration of this Policy be at sea, or in distress, or at a port of refuge or of call, she shall, provided previous notice be given to the Underwriters, be held covered at a pro rata monthly premium to her port of destination.

On the VESSEL called the ....

(or by whatsoever name or names the said Vessel is or shall be called).

The said Vessel, for so much as concerns the Assured, by agreement between the Assured and Underwriters in this Policy, is and shall be **valued at as follows:**

Hull, tackle, apparel, passenger fittings, equipment, stores, ordnance, munitions, boats and other furniture . . . . $..................

Boilers, machinery, refrigerating machinery and insulation, motor generators and other electrical machinery, and everything connected therewith $.................. $..................

Donkey boilers, winches, cranes, windlasses and steering gear shall be deemed to be a part of the hull and not of the machinery.

Held covered in case of any breach of warranty as to cargo, trade, locality or date of sailing, provided notice be given and any additional premium required be agreed immediately after receipt of advices of breach or proposed breach by Owners.

The Underwriters to be paid in consideration of this insurance the premium

as shown in the margin hereof, being at the rate of..................................per cent.

In event of non-payment of premium thirty days after attachment this Policy may be cancelled by the Underwriters upon five days written notice being given the Assured. Such proportion of the premium, however, as shall have been earned up to the time of such cancellation shall be due and payable; but in the event of Total or Constructive Total Loss occurring prior to cancellation full annual premium shall be deemed earned.

To return { cents per cent. net for each uncommenced month if it be mutually agreed to cancel this Policy.

As follows for each consecutive 30 days the Vessel may be laid up in port, viz:—

	Without Cargo on Board	With Cargo on Board
1. Under repair	¢% net	¢% net
2. Not under repair	¢% net	¢% net

For the purpose of this clause a Vessel loading or discharging cargo shall be considered as "with cargo on board."

Provided always: (a) that in no case shall a return be allowed when the within named Vessel is lying in a roadstead or in exposed and unprotected waters.

(b) that in the event of a return for special trade, or any other reason, being recoverable, the above rates of return of premium shall be reduced accordingly. } and arrival.

In the event of the Vessel being laid up in port for a period of 30 consecutive days, a part only of which attaches to this Policy, it is hereby agreed that the laying up period, in which either the commencing or ending date of this Policy falls, shall be deemed to run from the first day on which the Vessel is laid up and that on this basis Underwriters shall pay such proportion of the return due in respect of a full period of 30 days as the number of days attaching hereto bear to thirty.

Special Conditions and Warranties:— (The trading warranties are inserted in this space)

Additional insurances as follows are permitted:—

(a) **Disbursements, managers' commissions, profits or excess or increased value of hull and machinery, and/or similar interests however described, and freight (including chartered freight or anticipated freight) insured for time.** A sum not exceeding in the aggregate 25% of the insured value of the Vessel.

(b) **Freight or hire, under contracts for voyage.** A sum not exceeding the gross freight or hire for the current cargo passage and next succeeding cargo passage (such insurance to include, if required, a preliminary and an intermediate ballast passage) plus the charges of insurance. In the case of a voyage charter where payment is made on a time basis, the sum permitted for insurance shall be calculated on the estimated duration of the voyage, subject to the limitation of two cargo passages as laid down herein. Any sum insured under this Section shall be reduced as the freight or hire is earned by the gross amount so earned.

(c) **Anticipated freight if the vessel sails in ballast and not under charter.** A sum not exceeding the anticipated gross freight on next cargo passage, such sum to be reasonably estimated on the basis of the current rate of freight at time of insurance, plus the charges of insurance. Provided, however, that no insurance shall be permitted under this Section if any insurance is effected under Section (b).

(d) **Time charter hire or charter hire for series of voyages.** A sum not exceeding 50% of the gross hire which is to be earned under the charter in a period not exceeding 18 months. Any sum insured under this Section shall be reduced as the hire is earned under the charter by 50% of the gross amount so earned but where the charter is for a period exceeding 18 months the sum insured need not be reduced while it does not exceed 50% of the gross hire still to be earned under the charter. An insurance under this Section may begin on the signing of the charter.

(e) **Premiums.** A sum not exceeding the actual premiums of all interests insured for a period not exceeding 12 months (excluding premiums insured under the foregoing Sections but including, if required, the premium or estimated calls on any Protection and Indemnity or War &c. Risk insurance) reducing pro rata monthly.

(f) **Returns of premium.** A sum not exceeding the actual returns which are recoverable subject to and arrival under any policy of insurance.

(g) **Insurance irrespective of amount against:—**Risks excluded by the F. C. & S. Clause, and risks enumerated in the American Institute War and Strikes Clauses and General Average and Salvage Disbursements.

Warranted that no insurance on any interests enumerated in the foregoing Sections (a) to (f), inclusive, in excess of the amounts permitted therein and no insurance subject to P.P.I., F.I.A. or other like term, on any interests whatever excepting those enumerated in Section (a), is or shall be effected to operate during the currency of this Policy by or for account of the Assured, Owners, Managers or Mortgagees. Provided always that a breach of this warranty shall not afford Underwriters any defense to a claim by a Mortgagee who has accepted this Policy without knowledge of such breach.

Beginning the adventure upon the said Vessel, as above, and so shall continue and endure during the period aforesaid, as employment may offer, in port and at sea, in docks and graving docks, and on ways, gridirons and pontoons, at all times, in all places, and on all occasions, services and trades whatsoever and wheresoever, under steam, motor power or sail; with leave to sail or navigate with or without pilots, to go on trial trips and to assist and tow vessels or craft in distress, but if without the approval of Underwriters the Vessel be towed, except as is customary or when in need of assistance, or undertakes towage or salvage services under a pre-arranged contract made by Owners and/or Charterers, the Assured shall notify Underwriters immediately and pay an additional premium if required but no such premium shall be required for customary towage by the Vessel in connection with loading and discharging. With liberty to discharge, exchange and take on board goods, specie, passengers and stores, wherever the Vessel may call at or proceed to, and with liberty to carry goods, live cattle, &c., on deck or otherwise.

Touching the Adventures and Perils which we, the said Underwriters, are contented to bear and take upon us, they are of the Seas, Men-of-War, Fire, Lightning, Earthquake, Enemies, Pirates, Rovers, Assailing Thieves, Jettisons, Letters of Mart and Counter-Mart, Surprisals, Takings at Sea, Arrests, Restraints and Detainments of all Kings, Princes and Peoples, of what nation, condition or quality soever, Barratry of the Master and Mariners and of all other like Perils, Losses and Misfortunes that have or shall come to the Hurt, Detriment or Damage of the said Vessel, &c., or any part thereof; excepting, however, such of the foregoing Perils as may be excluded by provisions elsewhere in the Policy or by endorsement. And in case of any Loss or Misfortune, it shall be lawful and necessary for the Assured, their Factors, Servants and Assigns, to sue, labor and travel for, in, and about the Defense, Safeguard and Recovery of the said Vessel, &c., or any part thereof, without prejudice to this Insurance, to the Charges whereof the Underwriters will contribute their proportion as provided below. And it is expressly declared and agreed that no acts of the Underwriters or Assured in recovering, saving or preserving the property insured shall be considered as a waiver or acceptance of abandonment.

This insurance also specially to cover (subject to the Average Warranty) loss of or damage to the subject matter insured directly caused by the following:—

Accidents in loading, discharging or handling cargo, or in bunkering;
Accidents in going on or off, or while on drydocks, graving docks, ways, gridirons or pontoons;
Explosions on shipboard or elsewhere;
Breakdown of motor generators or other electrical machinery and electrical connections thereto, bursting of boilers, breakage of shafts, or any latent defect in the machinery or hull, (excluding the cost and expense of replacing or repairing the defective part);
Contact with Aircraft or with any land conveyance;
Negligence of Master, Charterers other than an Assured, Mariners, Engineers or Pilots;

Provided such loss or damage has not resulted from want of due diligence by the Assured, the Owners or Managers of the Vessel, or any of them. Masters, Mates, Engineers, Pilots or Crew not to be considered as part owners within the meaning of this clause should they hold shares in the Vessel.

In the event of accident whereby loss or damage may result in a claim under this Policy, notice shall be given in writing to the Underwriters, where practicable, prior to survey, so that they may appoint their own surveyor if they sc desire. The Underwriters shall be entitled to decide the port to which a damaged Vessel shall proceed for docking or repairing (the actual additional expense of the voyage arising from compliance with Underwriters' requirements being refunded to the Assured) and Underwriters shall also have a right of veto in connection with the place of repair or repairing firm proposed and whenever the extent of the damage is ascertainable the majority (in amount) of the Underwriters may take or may require to be taken tenders for the repair of such damage. In the event of failure to comply with the conditions of this clause 15 per cent. shall be deducted from the amount of the ascertained claim.

In cases where a tender is accepted with the approval of Underwriters, an allowance shall be made at the rate of 30 per cent. per annum on the insured value for each day or pro rata for part of a day from the time of the completion of the survey until the acceptance of the tender provided that it be accepted without delay after receipt of Underwriters' approval.

No allowance shall be made for any time during which the Vessel is loading or discharging cargo or bunkering.

Due credit shall be given against the allowance as above for any amount recovered:—

(a) in respect of fuel and stores and wages and maintenance of the Master, Officers and Crew or any member thereof allowed in General or Particular Average;

(b) from third parties in respect of damages for detention and/or loss of profit and/or running expenses; for the period covered by the tender allowance or any part thereof.

Notwithstanding anything herein contained to the contrary, this Policy is warranted free from Particular Average under 3 per cent., or unless amounting to $4,850., but nevertheless when the Vessel shall have been stranded, sunk, on fire, or in collision with any other Ship or Vessel, Underwriters shall pay the damage occasioned thereby, and the expense of sighting the bottom after stranding shall be paid, if reasonably incurred, even if no damage be found.

Grounding in the Panama Canal, Suez Canal or in the Manchester Ship Canal or its connections, or in the River Mersey above Rock Ferry Slip, or in the River Plate (above a line drawn from the North Basin, Buenos Aires, to the mouth of the San Pedro River) or its tributaries, or in the Danube or Demerara Rivers or on the Yenikale Bar, shall not be deemed to be a stranding.

Average payable on each valuation separately or on the whole, without deduction of thirds, new for old, whether the Average be Particular or General.

No claim shall in any case be allowed in respect of scraping or painting the Vessel's bottom.

The warranty and conditions as to Average under 3 per cent. or unless amounting to $4,850. to be applicable to each voyage as if separately insured, and a voyage shall commence at the Assured's election when the Vessel either begins to load cargo or sails in ballast to a loading port. Such voyage shall continue until the Vessel has made not more than three passages or not more than two passages with cargo (whichever first occurs) and extend further until the Vessel thereafter begins to load cargo or sails (whichever first occurs), but such extension shall not exceed 30 days in port. A passage shall be deemed to be from the commencement of loading at the first port or place of loading until completion of discharge at the last port or place of discharge, or, if the Vessel sails in ballast, from the port or place of departure until arrival at the first port or place thereafter other than a port or place of refuge or a port or place for bunkering only. Each period in port of 30 days in excess of 30 days between passages shall itself constitute a passage for the purposes of this clause. When the Vessel sails in ballast to effect damage repairs such sailing or passage shall be considered part of the previous passage. In calculating whether the 3 per cent. or $4,850. is reached, Particular Average occurring outside the period covered by this Policy may be added to Particular Average occurring within such period, providing it occur on the same voyage as above defined, but only that portion of the claim arising within the period covered by this Policy shall be recoverable hereon. A voyage shall not be so fixed that it overlaps another voyage on which a claim is made on this or the preceding or succeeding Policy. Particular Average which would be excluded by the terms of this Policy shall not be included in determining whether the 3 per cent. or $4,850. is reached.

No recovery for a Constructive Total Loss shall be had hereunder unless the expense of recovering and repairing the Vessel shall exceed the insured value.

In ascertaining whether the Vessel is a Constructive Total Loss the insured value shall be taken as the repaired value, and nothing in respect of the damaged or break-up value of the Vessel or wreck shall be taken into account.

In the event of Total or Constructive Total Loss, no claim to be made by the Underwriters for freight, whether notice of abandonment has been given or not.

In no case shall Underwriters be liable for unrepaired damage in addition to a subsequent Total Loss sustained during the period covered by this Policy.

General Average, Salvage and Special Charges payable as provided in the contract of affreightment, or failing such provision, or there be no contract of affreightment, payable in accordance with the Laws and Usages of the Port of New York. Provided always that when an adjustment according to the laws and usages of the port of destination is properly demanded by the owners of the cargo, General Average shall be paid in accordance with same.

And it is further agreed that in the event of salvage, towage or other assistance being rendered to the Vessel hereby insured by any Vessel belonging in part or in whole to the same Owners or Charterers, the value of such services (without regard to the common ownership or control of the Vessels) shall be ascertained by arbitration in the manner below provided for under the Collision Clause, and the amount so awarded so far as applicable to the interest hereby insured shall constitute a charge under this Policy.

When the contributory value of the Vessel is greater than the valuation herein the liability of these Underwriters for General Average contribution (except in respect to amount made good to the Vessel) or Salvage shall not exceed that proportion of the total contribution due from the Vessel that the amount insured hereunder bears to the contributory value; and if because of damage for which these Underwriters are liable as Particular Average the value of the Vessel has been reduced for the purpose of contribution, the amount of the Particular Average claim under this Policy shall be deducted from the amount insured hereunder and these Underwriters shall be liable only for the proportion which such net amount bears to the contributory value.

In the event of expenditure under the Sue and Labor Clause, this Policy shall pay the proportion of such expenses that the amount insured hereunder bears to the insured value of the Vessel, or that the amount insured hereunder, less loss and/or damage payable under this Policy, bears to the actual value of the salved property; whichever proportion shall be less.

If claim for total loss is admitted under this Policy and sue and labor expenses have been reasonably incurred in excess of any proceeds realized or value recovered, the amount payable under this Policy will be the proportion of such excess that the amount insured hereunder (without deduction for loss or damage) bears to the insured value or the sound value of the Vessel at the time of the accident, whichever value was greater.

And it is further agreed that if the Vessel hereby insured shall come into collision with any other Ship or Vessel and the Assured or the Charterers or the Surety in consequence of the insured Vessel being at fault shall become liable to pay and shall pay by way of damages to any other person or persons any sum or sums in respect of such collision, we, the Underwriters will pay the Assured, or the Charterers, or the Surety, whichever shall have paid, such proportion of such sum or sums so paid as our respective subscriptions hereto bear to the value of the Vessel hereby insured, provided always that our liability in respect to any one such collision shall not exceed our proportionate part of the value of the Vessel hereby insured. And in cases where the liability of the Vessel has been contested, or proceedings have been taken to limit liability, with the consent in writing of a majority (in amount) of Hull Underwriters, we will also pay a like proportion of the costs which the Assured or Charterers shall thereby incur, or be compelled to pay; but when both Vessels are to blame, then, unless the liability of the Owners or Charterers of one or both such Vessels becomes limited by law, claims under the Collision Clause shall be settled on the principle of Cross-Liabilities as if the Owners or Charterers of each Vessel had been compelled to pay to the Owners or Charterers of the other of such Vessels such one-half or other proportion of the latter's damages as may have been properly allowed in ascertaining the balance or sum payable by or to the Assured or Charterers in consequence of such collision; and it is further agreed that the principles involved in this clause shall apply to the case where both Vessels are the property, in part or in whole, of the same Owners or Charterers, all questions of responsibility and amount of liability as between the two Vessels being left to the decision of a single Arbitrator, if the parties can agree upon a single Arbitrator, or failing such agreement, to the decision of Arbitrators, one to be appointed by the Managing Owners or Charterers of both Vessels, and one to be appointed by the majority (in amount) of Hull Underwriters interested; the two Arbitrators chosen to choose a third Arbitrator before entering upon the reference, and the decision of such single, or of any two of such three Arbitrators, appointed as above, to be final and binding. Provided always that this clause shall in no case extend to any sum which the Assured, or the Charterers, or the Surety, may become liable to pay or shall pay for removal of obstructions under statutory powers, for injury to harbors, wharves, piers, stages, structures, or any other objects (excepting other Vessels and property thereon), consequent on such collision, or in respect of the cargo, baggage or engagements of the Insured Vessel, or for loss of life, or personal injury. And provided also that in the event of any claim under this clause being made by anyone other than the Owners of the Vessel hereby insured, he shall not be entitled to recover in respect of any liability to which the Owners of the Vessel as such would not be subject, nor to a greater extent than the Owners would be entitled in such event to recover.

Unless physically deleted by the Underwriters, the following warranty shall be paramount and shall supersede and nullify any contrary provision of the Policy:

F. C. & S. CLAUSE

Notwithstanding anything to the contrary contained in the Policy, this insurance is warranted free from any claim for loss, damage or expense caused by or resulting from capture, seizure, arrest, restraint or detainment, or the consequences thereof or of any attempt thereat, or any taking of the Vessel, by requisition or otherwise, whether in time of peace or war and whether lawful or otherwise; also from all consequences of hostilities or warlike operations (whether there be a declaration of war or not), but the foregoing shall not exclude collision, explosion or contact with any fixed or floating object (other than a mine or torpedo), stranding, heavy weather or fire unless caused directly (and independently of the nature of the voyage or service which the vessel concerned or, in the case of a collision, any other vessel involved therein, is performing) by a hostile act by or against a belligerent power, and for the purpose of this warranty "power" includes any authority maintaining naval, military or air forces in association with a power; also warranted free, whether in time of peace or war, from all loss, damage or expense caused by any weapon of war employing atomic fission or radioactive force.

Further warranted free from the consequences of civil war, revolution, rebellion, insurrection, or civil strife arising therefrom, or piracy.

If war risks are hereafter insured by endorsement on the Policy, such endorsement shall supersede the above warranty only to the extent that their terms are inconsistent and only while such war risk endorsement remains in force.

[There are inscribed in this space certain legal provisions relating to individual companies subscribing to the Policy.]

In Witness Whereof, the SUBSCRIBERS to AMERICAN MARINE HULL INSURANCE SYNDICATE, listed hereunder, have caused this Policy to be signed in their behalf severally, but not jointly, and not on the part of one for the other or any of the others, and for the proportion by them severally insured, by their duly authorized Attorney.

[The names of the various subscribing companies and the proportion of the total sum insured and accepted by each are inserted in this space.]

Total of Sum Insured $

Signed in New York, N.Y.,

this..............day of..19........

....

Attorney for the Individual Subscribers to

AMERICAN MARINE HULL INSURANCE SYNDICATE

Policy No.

Expires..**19**

Issued to

American Marine Hull Insurance Syndicate

Vessel

Broker

Appendix G. Syndicate Builder's Risk Form

BUILDER'S RISK—Form 50—Amended
(January 1939)
(F.C.&S. Nov. 1949)

13-A (Amended)

Amount Insured,

$..............................

Completed Contract Price

Rate.......... %

.... for account of themselves and/or any owner or owners of the vessel as interest may appear at the time of the happening of the loss. Loss, if any, payable in funds current in the United States to

.... or order

do make insurance and cause to be insured to the amount of ....

.... Dollars

for the period of time commencing .... at noon, New York time (which is warranted by the assured to be the date of laying of the keel) and ending ....

at noon, New York time, or until delivery at.. if delivered at an earlier date.

In the event of such delivery not being effected by..

this policy may be extended at .... monthly additional premium provided notice of the extension be given to this Company prior to ....

In no case shall this insurance extend beyond delivery of the vessel.

In the event of cancellation to return .... per cent. net for each uncommenced month cancelled, but such return shall not exceed in all ....

On Hull, Tackle, Apparel, Ordnance, Munitions, Artillery, Engines, Boilers, Machinery, Appurtenances, etc. (including plans, patterns, moulds, etc.) Boats and other Furniture and Fixtures and all material belonging and destined for ....

.... building at

....

as per clauses hereinbelow specified.

In the event of loss the underwriters shall not be liable for a greater proportion thereof than the amount of this insurance bears to the completed contract price.

This Company to be paid in consideration of this insurance.. Dollars

being at the rate of.................................per cent.

Premium,

$.................................

TOUCHING the Adventures and Perils which we, the said Underwriters, are contented to bear and take upon us, they are of the Seas, Men-of-War, Fire, Enemies, Pirates, Rovers, Thieves, Jettisons, Letters of Mart and Counter-Mart, Surprisals, Takings at Sea, Arrests, Restraints and Detainments of all Kings, Princes and Peoples, of what nation, condition or quality soever, Barratry of the Master and Mariners, and of all other like Perils, Losses and Misfortunes that have or shall come to the Hurt, Detriment or Damage of the said Vessel, &c., or any part thereof; excepting, however, such of the foregoing Perils as may be excluded by provisions elsewhere in the Policy or by endorsement. And in case of any loss or misfortune it shall be lawful for the Assured, their factors, servants and assigns, to sue, labor and travel for, in, and about the defense, safeguard and recovery of the said ship, &c., or any part thereof, without prejudice to this insurance; to the charges whereof the said insurance company will contribute according to the Rate and Quantity of the sum herein Assured. And it is expressly declared and agreed that no acts of the insurer or insured in recovering, saving or preserving the property insured shall be considered as a waiver or acceptance of abandonment. With leave to sail with or without pilots, to tow and be towed, and to assist vessels and/or craft in all situations and to any extent, and to go on trial trips. With liberty to discharge, exchange and take on board goods, specie, passengers, and stores, wherever the Vessel may call at or proceed to, and with liberty to carry goods, live cattle, &c., on deck or otherwise, but warranted free of any claim in respect of deck cargo. Including all risks of docking, undocking, changing docks, or moving in harbour and going on or off gridiron slipways, graving docks and/or pontoon or dry docks as often as may be done during the currency of this Policy.

CLAUSES FOR BUILDERS' RISK

This Insurance is also to cover all risks, including fire, while under construction and/or fitting out, including materials in Buildings, Workshops, yards and docks of the assured, or on quays, pontoons, craft, &c., and all risk while in transit to and from the works and/or the vessel wherever she may be lying, also all risks of loss or damage through collapse of supports or ways from any cause whatever, and all risks of launching and breakage of the ways.

This Insurance is also to cover all risks of trial trips, loaded or otherwise, as often as required, and all risks whilst proceeding to and returning from the trial course but warranted that all trials shall be carried out within a distance by water of 100 nautical miles of the place of construction or held covered at a rate to be arranged.

With leave to proceed to and from any wet or dry docks, harbours, ways, cradles, and pontoons during the currency of this policy

With leave to fire guns and torpedoes but no claim to attach hereto for loss or damage to same or to ship or machinery unless the accident results in the total loss of the Vessel

In case of failure of launch, underwriters to bear all subsequent expenses incurred in completing launch

Average payable irrespective of percentage, and without deduction of one-third, whether the Average be particular or general.

General Average and Salvage charges as per foreign custom, payable as per foreign statement, and/or per York-Antwerp rules, if required; and in the event of Salvage, towage, or other assistance being rendered to the Vessel hereby insured by any Vessel belonging in part or in whole to the same owners, it is hereby agreed that the value of such services (without regard to the common ownership of the Vessels) shall be ascertained by Arbitration in the manner hereinafter provided for under "Collision Clause," and the amount so awarded, so far as applicable to the interest hereby insured, shall constitute a charge under this policy

In the event of deviation to be held covered at an additional premium to be hereafter arranged

the underwriters on the hull and/or machinery (in amount), we will also pay a like proportion of the costs thereby incurred or paid; but when both Vessels are to blame, then, unless the liability of the owners of one or both of such Vessels becomes limited by law, claims under the Collision Clause shall be settled on the principle of CROSS LIABILITIES, as if the owners of such Vessels has been compelled to pay to the owners of the other of such Vessels such one-half or other proportion of the latter's damages as may have been properly allowed in ascertaining the balance or sum payable by or to the assured in consequence of such collision.

And it is further agreed that the principles involved in this clause shall apply to the case where both Vessels are the property, in part or in whole, of the same owners, all questions of responsibility and amount of liability as between the two Ships being left to the decision of a single Arbitrator, if the parties can agree upon a single Arbitrator, or failing such agreement, to the decision of Arbitrators, one to be appointed by the managing owners of both Vessels, and one to be appointed by the majority in amount of Underwriters interested in each Vessel; the two Arbitrators chosen to choose a third Arbitrator before entering upon the reference. The terms of the Arbitration Act of 1889 to apply to such reference, and the decision of such single, or of any two of such three Arbitrators, appointed as above, to be final and binding.

This clause shall also extend to any sum which the Assured may become liable to pay, or shall pay for removal of obstructions under statutory powers, or for injury to harbours, wharves, piers, stages, and similar structures.

PROTECTION AND INDEMNITY CLAUSE

It is further agreed that if the Assured shall by reason of his interest in the insured Ship become liable to pay and shall pay any sum or sums in respect of any reponsibility, claim, demand, damages, and/or expenses arising from or occasioned by any of the following matters or things during the currency of this policy, that is to say:—

Loss of or damage to any other ship or boat or goods, merchandise

Unless physically deleted by the Underwriters, the following warranty shall be paramount and shall

F. C. & S. CLAUSE

Notwithstanding anything to the contrary contained in the Policy, this insurance is warranted free restraint or detainment, or the consequences thereof or of any attempt thereat, or any taking d otherwise; also from all consequences of hostilities or warlike operations (whether there be a de any fixed or floating object (other than a mine or torpedo), stranding, heavy weather or fire concerned or, in the case of a collision, any other vessel involved therein, is performing) by a hostil any authority maintaining naval, military or air forces in association with a power; also warran war employing atomic fission or radioactive force.

Further warranted free from the consequences of civil war, revolution, rebellion, insurrection, or ci

If war risks are hereafter insured by endorsement on the Policy, such endorsement shall supersede risk endorsement remains in force.

To cover while building all damage to hull, machinery, apparel, or furniture, caused by settling of the stocks, or failure or breakage of shores, blocking or staging, or of hoisting or other gear, either before or after launching and while fitting out.

It is agreed that any changes of interest in the steamer hereby insured shall not affect the validity of this policy.

And it is expressly declared and agreed that no acts of the Insurer or Insured, in recovering, saving, or preserving the property insured shall be considered as a waiver or acceptance of abandonment.

This Insurance also specially to cover loss of or damage to the hull or machinery, through negligence of Master, Mariners, Engineers or pilots, or through explosions, bursting of boilers, breakage of shafts, or through any latent defect in the Machinery, or Hull, or from explosions or other causes, arising either on shore or otherwise, causing loss of or injury to the property hereby insured, provided such loss or damage has not resulted from want of due diligence by the Owners of the Ship or any of them, or by the Manager, and to cover all risks incidental to steam navigation, or in graving docks.

COLLISION CLAUSE

And it is further agreed that if the Ship hereby insured shall come into collision with any other Ship or Vessel, and the assured shall in consequence thereof become liable to pay, and shall pay by way of damages to any other person or persons any sum or sums not exceeding in respect of any one such collision the value of the Ship hereby Insured, we the assurers, will pay the assured such proportion of such sum or sums so paid as our subscription thereto bear to the completed contract price of the Ship hereby Insured. And in cases where the liability of the Ship has been contested, with the consent, in writing, of a majority of freight, or other things or interests, whatsoever on board such other ship or boat caused proximately or otherwise by the ship insured in so far as the same is not covered by the running down clause set out above.

Loss of or damage to any goods, merchandise, freight or other things or interests, whatsoever other than as aforesaid whether on board the said Steamship or not, which may arise from any cause whatever.

Loss of or damage to any harbour, dock (graving or otherwise), slipway, way, gridiron, pontoon, pier, quay, jetty, stage, buoy, telegraph cable, or other fixed or movable thing whatsoever, or to any goods or property in or on the same, howsoever caused.

Any attempted or actual raising, removal or destruction of the wreck of the insured ship or the cargo thereof, or any neglect or failure to raise, remove, or destroy the same.

Any sum or sums for which the Assured may become liable or incur from causes not hereinbefore specified, but which are or have heretofore been absolutely or conditionally recoverable from or undertaken by the Liverpool and London Steamship Protection Association, Limited, and/or North of England Protecting and Indemnity Association, but excluding loss of life and personal injury.

These assurers will pay the Assured such proportion of such sum or sums so paid, or, which may be required to indemnify the Assured for such loss, as their respective subscriptions bear to the completed contract price of the ship hereby insured, and where the liability of the Assured has been contested with the consent in writing of a majority (in amount) of the Underwriters on the ship hereby insured, those assurers will also pay a like proportion of the costs which the Assured shall thereby incur or be compelled to pay.

NOTWITHSTANDING THE FOREGOING, this Policy is:—

(A) Warranted free from any claim arising directly or indirectly under Workmens' Compensation or Employers Liability Acts and any other Statutory or Common Law liability in respect of accidents to any person or persons whomsoever.

(B) Warranted free of loss or damage caused by strikers, locked-out workmen or persons taking part in labour disturbances or riots or civil commotions.

(C) Warranted free of loss or damage caused by earthquake.

(D) Warranted free of any consequential damages or claims for loss through delay however caused.

(E) Warranted free from claim for loss or damage to engines, boilers and all other materials while in transport, except in the port at which the vessel is being built.

This policy shall not be vitiated by any unintentional error in description of interest or voyage, provided the same be communicated to Assurers as soon as known to the assured, and an additional premium paid if required.

The words "Owner" and "Assured" as used in this policy shall be interpreted to mean either "Builder" or "Owner" or both.

The terms and conditions of this form are to be regarded as substituted for those of the policy to which it is attached, the later being hereby waived.

Attached to Policy No. .... *of the* ....

Dated ....

Appendix H. Syndicate Disbursements Form

129-F

AMERICAN INSTITUTE
Time (Increased Value including Excess Liabilities)
December 1, 1951

Attached to Policy No...

for $... on..

This insurance covers only:—

(a) **TOTAL LOSS (ACTUAL OR CONSTRUCTIVE) OF THE VESSEL**

No recovery for a Constructive Total Loss shall be had hereunder unless the expense of recovering and repairing the Vessel shall exceed the insured value in policies on Hull and Machinery.

In ascertaining whether the Vessel is a constructive total loss the insured value in the policies on Hull and Machinery shall be taken as the repaired value, and nothing in respect of the damaged or break-up value of the Vessel or wreck shall be taken into account.

Provided that the policies on Hull and Machinery contain the above clauses with respect to the method of ascertaining whether the Vessel is a constructive total loss (or clauses having a similar effect) the settlement of a claim for total or constructive total loss under the policies on Hull and Machinery shall be accepted as proof of the total loss of the Vessel under this policy; and in the event of a claim for total loss or constructive total loss being settled under the policies on Hull and Machinery as a compromised total loss, the amount payable hereunder shall be the same percentage of the sum hereby insured as is paid on the sum insured under said policies.

Should the Vessel be a constructive total loss but the claim on the policies on Hull and Machinery be settled as a claim for partial loss, no payment shall be due under this Section (a).

(b) **GENERAL AVERAGE, SALVAGE AND SALVAGE CHARGES** not recoverable in full under the policies on Hull and Machinery by reason of the difference between the insured value of the Vessel as stated therein (or any reduced value arising from the deduction therefrom in process of adjustment of any claim which law or practice or the terms of the policies covering Hull and Machinery may have required) and the value of the Vessel adopted for the purpose of contribution to General Average, Salvage or Salvage Charges, the liability under this Policy being for such proportion of the amount not recoverable as the amount insured hereunder bears to the said difference or to the total sum insured against excess liabilities if it exceed such difference.

(c) **SUE AND LABOR CHARGES** not recoverable in full under the policies on Hull and Machinery by reason of the difference between the insured value of the Vessel as stated therein (or any reduced value arising from the deduction therefrom of any claim which the terms of the policies covering Hull and Machinery may have required) and the value of the Vessel adopted for the purpose of ascertaining the amount recoverable under the policies on Hull and Machinery, the liability under this Policy being for such proportion of the amount not recoverable as the amount insured hereunder bears to the said difference or to the total sum insured against excess liabilities if it exceed such difference.

: and shall supersede and nullify any contrary provision of the Policy:

is warranted free from any claim for loss, damage or expense caused by or resulting or of any attempt thereat, or any taking of the Vessel, by requisition or otherwise, all consequences of hostilities or warlike operations (whether there be a declaration ntact with any fixed or floating object (other than a mine or torpedo), stranding, of the voyage or service which the vessel concerned or, in the case of a collision, st a belligerent power, and for the purpose of this warranty "power" includes any also warranted free, whether in time of peace or war, from all loss, damage or force.

insurrection, or civil strife arising therefrom, or piracy.
shall supersede the above warranty only to the extent that their terms are inconsistent

Unless physically deleted by the Underwriters, the following warranty shall be paramour

F. C. & S. CLAUSE.

Notwithstanding anything to the contrary contained in the Policy, this insuranc
from capture, seizure, arrest, restraint or detainment, or the consequences therec
whether in time of peace or war and whether lawful or otherwise; also from
of war or not), but the foregoing shall not exclude collision, explosion or c
heavy weather or fire unless caused directly (and independently of the nature
any other vessel involved therein, is performing) by a hostile act by or again
authority maintaining naval, military or air forces in association with a power;
expense caused by any weapon of war employing atomic fission or radioactive

Further warranted free from the consequences of civil war, revolution, rebellion,

If war risks are hereafter insured by endorsement on the Policy, such endorsement
and only while such war risk endorsement remains in force.

(d) **COLLISION LIABILITY** (Including Costs) not recoverable in full under the Collision Clause in the policies on Hull and Machinery by reason of such liability exceeding the insured value of the Vessel as stated therein, in which case the amount recoverable under this Policy shall be such proportion of the difference so arising as the sum hereby insured bears to the total sum insured against excess liabilities.

Underwriters' liability under (a), (b), (c), and (d), separately, in respect of any one claim, shall not exceed the amount insured hereunder.

To return { cents per cent. net for each uncommenced month if it be mutually agreed to cancel this Policy.

As follows for each consecutive 30 days the Vessel may be laid up in port, viz:—

	Without Cargo on Board	With Cargo on Board
1. Under repair	¢% net	¢% net
2. Not under repair	¢% net	¢% net

For the purpose of this clause a Vessel loading or discharging cargo shall be considered as "with cargo on board".

Provided always: (a) that in no case shall a return be allowed when the within named Vessel is lying in a roadstead or in exposed and unprotected waters.

(b) that in the event of a return for special trade, or any other reason, being recoverable, the above rates of return of premium shall be reduced accordingly. } and arrival.

In the event of the Vessel being laid up in port for a period of 30 consecutive days, a part only of which attaches to this Policy, it is hereby agreed that the laying up period, in which either the commencing or ending date of this Policy falls, shall be deemed to run from the first day on which the Vessel is laid up and that on this basis Underwriters shall pay such proportion of the return due in respect of a full period of 30 days as the number of days attaching hereto bear to thirty.

The terms and conditions of the American Institute Time Hull Clauses current on the date of attachment of this insurance shall be deemed incorporated herein, in so far as they are not inconsistent with the provisions of this rider.

This slip is no part of the Policy, and is not to be attached thereto, but is to be considered as binding in honor on the Underwriters; the Assured, however, having permission to remove it from this Policy should they so desire.

Full interest admitted; the Policy being deemed sufficient proof of interest.

This insurance is without benefit of salvage.

Appendix I. Marine Insurance Act, 1906 [6 Edw. 7. Ch. 41]

Arrangements of Sections

Marine Insurance

Section

1. Marine insurance defined.
2. Mixed sea and land risks.
3. Marine adventure and maritime perils defined.

Insurable Interest

4. Avoidance of wagering or gaming contracts.
5. Insurable interest defined.
6. When interest must attach.
7. Defeasible or contingent interest.
8. Partial interest.
9. Re-insurance.
10. Bottomry.
11. Master's and seamen's wages.
12. Advance freight.
13. Charges of insurance.
14. Quantum of interest.
15. Assignment of interest.

Insurable Value

16. Measure of insurable value.

Disclosure and Representations

17. Insurance is uberrimae fidei.
18. Disclosure by assured.
19. Disclosure by agent effecting insurance.

Section
20. Representations pending negotiation of contract.
21. When contract is deemed to be concluded.

The Policy

22. Contract must be embodied in policy.
23. What policy must specify.
24. Signature of insurer.
25. Voyage and time policies.
26. Designation of subject-matter.
27. Valued policy.
28. Unvalued policy.
29. Floating policy by ship or ships.
30. Construction of terms in policy.
31. Premium to be arranged.

Double Insurance

32. Double insurance.

Warranties, &c.

33. Nature of warranty.
34. When breach of warranty excused.
35. Express warranties.
36. Warranty of neutrality.
37. No implied warranty of nationality.
38. Warranty of good safety.
39. Warranty of seaworthiness of ship.
40. No implied warranty that goods are seaworthy.
41. Warranty of legality.

The Voyage

42. Implied condition as to commencement of risk.
43. Alteration of port of departure.
44. Sailing for different destination.
45. Change of voyage.
46. Deviation.
47. Several ports of discharge.
48. Delay in voyage.
49. Excuses for deviation or delay.

Assignment of Policy

Section
50. When and how policy is assignable.
51. Assured who has no interest cannot assign.

The Premium

52. When premium payable.
53. Policy effected through broker.
54. Effect of receipt on policy.

Loss and Abandonment

55. Included and excluded losses.
56. Partial and total loss.
57. Actual total loss.
58. Missing ship.
59. Effect of transhipment, &c.
60. Constructive total loss defined.
61. Effect of constructive total loss.
62. Notice of abandonment.
63. Effect of abandonment.

Partial Losses (Including Salvage and General Average and Particular Charges)

64. Particular average loss.
65. Salvage charges.
66. General average loss.

Measure of Indemnity

67. Extent of liability of insurer for loss.
68. Total loss.
69. Partial loss of ship.
70. Partial loss of freight.
71. Partial loss of goods, merchandise, &c.
72. Apportionment of valuation.
73. General average contributions and salvage charges.
74. Liabilities to third parties.
75. General provisions as to measure of indemnity.
76. Particular average warranties.
77. Successive losses.
78. Suing and labouring clause.

Rights of Insurer on Payment

Section
79. Right of subrogation.
80. Right of contribution.
81. Effect of under insurance.

Return of Premium

82. Enforcement of return.
83. Return by agreement.
84. Return for failure of consideration.

Mutual Insurance

85. Modification of Act in case of mutual insurance.

Supplemental

86. Ratification by assured.
87. Implied obligations varied by agreement or usage.
88. Reasonable time, &c. a question of fact.
89. Slip as evidence.
90. Interpretation of terms.
91. Savings.
92. Repeals.
93. Commencement.
94. Short title.
SCHEDULES

A.D. 1906.

An Act to codify the Law relating to Marine Insurance.

[December 21, 1906.]

Be it enacted by the King's most Excellent Majesty, by and with the advice and consent of the Lords Spiritual and Temporal, and Commons, in this present Parliment assembled, and by the authority of the same, as follows:—

Marine Insurance

Marine Insurance Defined.

1. A contract of marine insurance is a contract whereby the insurer undertakes to indemnify the assured, in manner and to the extent thereby agreed, against marine losses, that is to say, the losses incident to marine adventure.

Mixed Sea and Land Risks.

2. (1) A contract of marine insurance may, by its express terms, or by usage of trade, be extended so as to protect the assured against losses on inland waters or on any land risk which may be incidental to any sea voyage.

(2) Where a ship in course of building, or the launch of a ship, or any adventure analogous to a marine adventure, is covered by a policy in the form of a marine policy, the provisions of this Act, in so far as applicable, shall apply thereto; but, except as by this section provided, nothing in this Act shall alter or affect any rule of law applicable to any contract of insurance other than a contract of marine insurance as by this Act defined.

Marine Adventure and Maritime Perils Defined.

3. (1) Subject to the provisions of this Act, every lawful marine adventure may be the subject of a contract of marine insurance.

(2) In particular there is a marine adventure where—

(*a*) Any ship goods or other movables are exposed to maritime perils. Such property is in this Act referred to as "insurable property;"

(*b*) The earning or acquisition of any freight, passage money, commission, profit, or other pecuniary benefit, or the security for any advances, loan, or disbursements, is endangered by the exposure of insurable property to maritime perils;

(*c*) Any liability to a third party may be incurred by the owner of, or other person interested in or responsible for, insurable property, by reason of maritime perils.

"Maritime perils" means the perils consequent on, or incidental to, the navigation of the sea, that is to say, perils of the seas, fire, war perils, pirates, rovers, thieves, captures, seizures, restraints and detainments of princes, and peoples, jettisons, barratry, and any other perils, either of the like kind or which may be designated by the policy.

Insurable Interest

Avoidance of Wagering or Gaming Contracts.

4. (1) Every contract of marine insurance by way of gaming or wagering is void.

(2) A contract of marine insurance is deemed to be a gaming or wagering contract—

(*a*) Where the assured has not an insurable interest as defined by this Act, and the contract is entered into with no expectation of acquiring such an interest; or (*b*) Where the policy is made "interest or no interest," or "without further proof of interest than the policy itself," or "without benefit of salvage to the insurer," or subject to any other like term:

Provided that, where there is no possibility of salvage, a policy may be effected without benefit of salvage to the insurer.

Insurable Interest Defined.

5. (1) Subject to the provisions of this Act, every person has an insurable interest who is interested in a marine adventure.

(2) In particular a person is interested in a marine adventure where he stands in any legal or equitable relation to the adventure or to any insurable property at risk therein, in consequence of which he may benefit by the safety or due arrival of insurable property, or may be prejudiced by its loss, or by damage thereto, or by the detention thereof, or may incur liability in respect thereof.

When Interest Must Attach.

6. (1) The assured must be interested in the subject-matter insured at the time of the loss though he need not be interested when the insurance is effected:

Provided that where the subject-matter is insured "lost or not lost," the assured may recover although he may not have acquired his interest until after the loss, unless at the time of effecting the contract of insurance the assured was aware of the loss, and the insurer was not.

(2) Where the assured has no interest at the time of the loss, he cannot acquire interest by any act or election after he is aware of the loss.

Defeasible or Contingent Interest.

7. (1) A defeasible interest is insurable, as also is a contingent interest.

(2) In particular, where the buyer of goods has insured them, he has an insurable interest, notwithstanding that he might, at his election, have rejected the goods, or have treated them as at the seller's risk, by reason of the latter's delay in making delivery or otherwise.

Partial Interest.

8. A partial interest of any nature is insurable.

Reinsurance.

9. (1) The insurer under a contract of marine insurance has an insurable interest in his risk, and may reinsure in respect of it.

(2) Unless the policy otherwise provides, the original assured has no right or interest in respect of such reinsurance.

Bottomry.

10. The lender of money on bottomry or respondentia has an insurable interest in respect of the loan.

Master's and Seamen's Wages.

11. The master or any member of the crew of a ship has an insurable interest in respect of his wages.

Advance Freight.

12. In the case of advance freight, the person advancing the freight has an insurable interest, in so far as such freight is not repayable in case of loss.

Charges of Insurance.

13. The assured has an insurable interest in the charges of any insurance which he may effect.

Quantum of Interest.

14. (1) Where the subject-matter insured is mortgaged, the mortgagor has an insurable interest in the full value thereof, and the mortgagee has an insurable interest in respect of any sum due or to become due under the mortgage.

(2) A mortgagee, consignee, or other person having an interest in the subject-matter insured may insure on behalf and for the benefit of other persons interested as well as for his own benefit.

(3) The owner of insurable property has an insurable interest in respect of the full value thereof, notwithstanding that some third person may have agreed, or be liable, to indemnify him in case of loss.

Assignment of Interest.

15. Where the assured assigns or otherwise parts with his interest in the subject-matter insured, he does not thereby transfer to the assignee his rights under the contract of insurance, unless there be an express or implied agreement with the assignee to that effect.

But the provisions of this section do not affect a transmission of interest by operation of law.

Insurable Value

Measure of Insurable Value.

16. Subject to any express provision or valuation in the policy, the insurable value of the subject-matter insured must be ascertained as follows:—

(1) In insurance on ship, the insurable value is the value, at the commencement of the risk, of the ship, including her outfit, provisions and stores for the officers and crew, money advanced for seamen's wages, and other disbursements (if any) incurred to make the ship fit for the voyage or adventure contemplated by the policy, plus the charges of insurance upon the whole:

The insurable value, in the case of a steamship, includes also the machinery, boilers, and coals and engine stores if owned by the assured, and, in the case of a ship engaged in a special trade, the ordinary fittings requisite for that trade:

(2) In insurance on freight, whether paid in advance or otherwise, the insurable value is the gross amount of the freight at the risk of the assured, plus the charges of insurance:

(3) In insurance on goods or merchandise, the insurable value is the prime cost of the property insured, plus the expenses of and incidental to shipping and the charges of insurance upon the whole:

(4) In insurance on any other subject-matter, the insurable value is the amount at the risk of the assured when the policy attaches, plus the charges of insurance.

Disclosure and Representations

Insurance is Uberrimae Fidei.

17. A contract of marine insurance is a contract based upon the utmost good faith, and, if the utmost good faith be not observed by either party, the contract may be avoided by the other party.

Disclosure by Assured.

18. (1) Subject to the provisions of this section, the assured must disclose to the insurer, before the contract is concluded, every material circumstance which is known to the assured, and the assured is deemed to know every circumstance which, in the ordinary course of business, ought to be known by him. If the assured fails to make such disclosure, the insurer may avoid the contract.

(2) Every circumstance is material which would influence the judgment of a prudent insurer in fixing the premium, or determining whether he will take the risk.

(3) In the absence of inquiry the following circumstances need not be disclosed, namely:—

(*a*) Any circumstance which diminishes the risk;

(*b*) Any circumstance which is known or presumed to be known to the insurer. The insurer is presumed to know matters of common notoriety or knowledge, and matters which an insurer in the ordinary course of his business, as such, ought to know;

(*c*) Any circumstance as to which information is waived by the insurer;

(*d*) Any circumstance which it is superfluous to disclose by reason of any express or implied warranty.

(4) Whether any particular circumstance, which is not disclosed, be material or not is, in each case, a question of fact.

(5) The term "circumstance" includes any communication made to, or information received by, the assured.

Disclosure by Agent Effecting Insurance.

19. Subject to the provisions of the preceding section as to circumstances which need not be disclosed, where an insurance is effected for the assured by an agent, the agent must disclose to the insurer—

(*a*) Every material circumstance which is known to himself, and an agent to insure is deemed to know every circumstance which in the ordinary course of business ought to be known by, or to have been communicated to, him; and

(*b*) Every material circumstance which the assured is bound to disclose, unless it come to his knowledge too late to communicate it to the agent.

Representations Pending Negotiations of Contract.

20. (1) Every material representation made by the assured or his agent to the insurer during the negotiations for the contract, and before the contract is concluded, must be true. If it be untrue the insurer may avoid the contract.

(2) A representation is material which would influence the judgment of a prudent insurer in fixing the premium, or determining whether he will take the risk.

(3) A representation may be either a representation as to a matter of fact, or as to a matter of expectation or belief.

(4) A representation as to a matter of fact is true, if it be substantially correct, that is to say, if the difference between what is represented and what is actually correct would not be considered material by a prudent insurer.

(5) A representation as to a matter of expectation or belief is true if it be made in good faith.

(6) A representation may be withdrawn or corrected before the contract is concluded.

(7) Whether a particular representation be material or not is, in each case, a question of fact.

When Contract is Deemed to be Concluded.

21. A contract of marine insurance is deemed to be concluded when the proposal of the assured is accepted by the insurer, whether the policy be then issued or not; and for the purpose of showing when the proposal was accepted, reference may be made to the slip or covering note or other customary memorandum of the contract, although it be unstamped.

The Policy

Contract Must be Embodied in Policy.

22. Subject to the provisions of any statute, a contract of marine insurance is inadmissible in evidence unless it is embodied in a marine policy in accordance with this Act. The policy may be executed and issued either at the time when the contract is concluded, or afterwards.

What Policy Must Specify.

23. A marine policy must specify—

(1) The name of the assured, or of some person who effects the insurance on his behalf:

(2) The subject-matter insured and the risk insured against:

(3) The voyage, or period of time, or both, as the case may be, covered by the insurance:

(4) The sum or sums insured:

(5) The name or names of the insurers.

Signature of Insurer.

24. (1) A marine policy must be signed by or on behalf of the insurer, provided that in the case of a corporation the corporate seal may be sufficient, but nothing in this section shall be construed as requiring the subscription of a corporation to be under seal.

(2) Where a policy is subscribed by or on behalf of two or more insurers, each subscription, unless the contrary be expressed, constitutes a distinct contract with the assured.

Voyage and Time Policies.

25. (1) Where the contract is to insure the subject-matter at and from, or from one place to another or others, the policy is called a "voyage policy," and where the contract is to insure the subject-matter for a definite period of time the policy is called a "time policy." A contract for both voyage and time may be included in the same policy.

(2) Subject to the provisions of section eleven of the Finance Act, 1901, a time policy which is made for any time exceeding twelve months is invalid.

Designation of Subject-matter.

26. (1) The subject-matter insured must be designated in a marine policy with reasonable certainty.

(2) The nature and extent of the interest of the assured in the subject-matter insured need not be specified in the policy.

(3) Where the policy designates the subject-matter insured in general terms, it shall be construed to apply to the interest intended by the assured to be covered.

(4) In the application of this section regard shall be had to any usage regulating the designation of the subject-matter insured.

Valued Policy.

27. (1) A policy may be either valued or unvalued.

(2) A valued policy is a policy which specifies the agreed value of the subject-matter insured.

(3) Subject to the provisions of this Act, and in the absence of fraud, the value fixed by the policy is, as between the insurer and assured, conclusive of the insurable value of the subject intended to be insured, whether the loss be total or partial.

(4) Unless the policy otherwise provides, the value fixed by the policy is not conclusive for the purpose of determining whether there has been a constructive total loss.

Unvalued Policy.

28. An unvalued policy is a policy which does not specify the value of the subject-matter insured, but, subject to the limit of the sum insured, leaves the insurable value to be subsequently ascertained, in the manner herein-before specified.

Floating Policy by Ship or Ships.

29. (1) A floating policy is a policy which describes the insurance in general terms, and leaves the name of the ship or ships and other particulars to be defined by subsequent declaration.

(2) The subsequent declaration or declarations may be made by indorsement on the policy, or in other customary manner.

(3) Unless the policy otherwise provides, the declarations must be made in the order of dispatch or shipment. They must, in the case of goods, comprise all consignments within the terms of the policy, and the value of the goods or other property must be honestly stated, but an omission or erroneous declaration may be rectified even after loss or arrival, provided the omission or declaration was made in good faith.

(4) Unless the policy otherwise provides, where a declaration of value is not made until after notice of loss or arrival, the policy must be treated as an unvalued policy as regards the subject-matter of that declaration.

Construction of Terms in Policy.

30. (1) A policy may be in the form in the First Schedule to this Act.

(2) Subject to the provisions of this Act, and unless the context of the policy otherwise requires, the terms and expressions mentioned in the First Schedule to this Act shall be construed as having the scope and meaning in that schedule assigned to them.

Premium to be Arranged.

31. (1) Where an insurance is effected at a premium to be arranged, and no arrangement is made, a reasonable premium is payable.

(2) Where an insurance is effected on the terms that an additional premium is to be arranged in a given event, and that event happens but no arrangement is made, then a reasonable additional premium is payable.

Double Insurance

Double Insurance.

32. (1) Where two or more policies are effected by or on behalf of the assured on the same adventure and interest or any part thereof, and the sums insured exceed the indemnity allowed by this Act, the assured is said to be over-insured by double insurance.

(2) Where the assured is over-insured by double insurance—

(*a*) The assured, unless the policy otherwise provides, may claim payment from the insurers in such order as he may think fit, provided that he is not entitled to receive any sum in excess of the indemnity allowed by this Act;

(*b*) Where the policy under which the assured claims is a valued policy, the assured must give credit as against the valuation for any sum received by him under any other policy without regard to the actual value of the subject-matter insured;

(*c*) Where the policy under which the assured claims is an unvalued policy he must give credit, as against the full insurable value, for any sum received by him under any other policy;

(*d*) Where the assured receives any sum in excess of the indemnity allowed by this Act, he is deemed to hold such sum in trust for the insurers, according to their right of contribution among themselves.

Warranties, &c.

Nature of Warranty.

33. (1) A warranty, in the following sections relating to warranties, means a promissory warranty, that is to say, a warranty by which the assured undertakes that some particular thing shall or shall not be done, or that some condition shall be fulfilled, or whereby he affirms or negatives the existence of a particular state of facts.

(2) A warranty may be express or implied.

(3) A warranty, as above defined, is a condition which must be exactly

complied with, whether it be material to the risk or not. If it be not so complied with, then subject to any express provision in the policy, the insurer is discharged from liability as from the date of the breach of warranty, but without prejudice to any liability incurred by him before that date.

When Breach of Warranty Excused.

34. (1) Non-compliance with a warranty is excused when, by reason of a change of circumstances, the warranty ceases to be applicable to the circumstances of the contract, or when compliance with the warranty is rendered unlawful by any subsequent law.

(2) Where a warranty is broken, the assured cannot avail himself of the defence that the breach has been remedied, and the warranty complied with, before loss.

(3) A breach of warranty may be waived by the insurer.

Express Warranties.

35. (1) An express warranty may be in any form of words from which the intention to warrant is to be inferred.

(2) An express warranty must be included in, or written upon, the policy, or must be contained in some document incorporated by reference into the policy.

(3) An express warranty does not exclude an implied warranty, unless it be inconsistent therewith.

Warranty of Neutrality.

36. (1) Where insurable property, whether ship or goods, is expressly warranted neutral, there is an implied condition that the property shall have a neutral character at the commencement of the risk, and that, so far as the assured can control the matter, its neutral character shall be preserved during the risk.

(2) Where a ship is expressly warranted "neutral" there is also an implied condition that, so far as the assured can control the matter, she shall be properly documented, that is to say, that she shall carry the necessary papers to establish her neutrality, and that she shall not falsify or suppress her papers, or use simulated papers. If any loss occurs through breach of this condition, the insurer may avoid the contract.

No Implied Warranty of Nationality.

37. There is no implied warranty as to the nationality of a ship, or that her nationality shall not be changed during the risk.

Warranty of Good Safety.

38. Where the subject-matter insured is warranted "well" or "in good safety" on a particular day, it is sufficient if it be safe at any time during that day.

Warranty of Seaworthiness of Ship.

39. (1) In a voyage policy there is an implied warranty that at the commencement of the voyage the ship shall be seaworthy for the purpose of the particular adventure insured.

(2) Where the policy attaches while the ship is in port, there is also an implied warranty that she shall, at the commencement of the risk, be reasonably fit to encounter the ordinary perils of the port.

(3) Where the policy relates to a voyage which is performed in different stages, during which the ship requires different kinds of or further preparation or equipment, there is an implied warranty that at the commencement of each stage the ship is seaworthy in respect of such preparation or equipment for the purposes of that stage.

(4) A ship is deemed to be seaworthy when she is reasonably fit in all respects to encounter the ordinary perils of the seas of the adventure insured.

(5) In a time policy there is no implied warranty that the ship shall be seaworthy at any stage of the adventure, but where, with the privity of the assured, the ship is sent to sea in an unseaworthy state, the insurer is not liable for any loss attributable to unseaworthiness.

No Implied Warranty that Goods are Seaworthy.

40. (1) In a policy on goods or other movables there is no implied warranty that the goods or movables are seaworthy.

(2) In a voyage policy on goods or other movables there is an implied warranty that at the commencement of the voyage the ship is not only seaworthy as a ship, but also that she is reasonably fit to carry the goods or other movables to the destination contemplated by the policy.

Warranty of Legality.

41. There is an implied warranty that the adventure insured is a lawful one, and that, so far as the assured can control the matter, the adventure shall be carried out in a lawful manner.

The Voyage

Implied Condition as to Commencement of Risk.

42. (1) Where the subject-matter is insured by a voyage policy "at and from" or "from" a particular place, it is not necessary that the ship should be at that place when the contract is concluded, but there is an implied condition that the adventure shall be commenced within a reasonable time, and that if the adventure be not so commenced the insurer may avoid the contract.

(2) The implied condition may be negatived by showing that the delay

was caused by circumstances known to the insurer before the contract was concluded, or by showing that he waived the condition.

Alteration of Port of Departure.

43. Where the place of departure is specified by the policy, and the ship instead of sailing from that place sails from any other place, the risk does not attach.

Sailing for Different Destination.

44. Where the destination is specified in the policy, and the ship, instead of sailing for that destination, sails for any other destination, the risk does not attach.

Change of Voyage.

45. (1) Where, after the commencement of the risk, the destination of the ship is voluntarily changed from the destination contemplated by the policy, there is said to be a change of voyage.

(2) Unless the policy otherwise provides, where there is a change of voyage, the insurer is discharged from liability as from the time of change, that is to say, as from the time when the determination to change it is manifested; and it is immaterial that the ship may not in fact have left the course of voyage contemplated by the policy when the loss occurs.

Deviation.

46. (1) Where a ship, without lawful excuse, deviates from the voyage contemplated by the policy, the insurer is discharged from liability as from the time of deviation, and it is immaterial that the ship may have regained her route before any loss occurs.

(2) There is a deviation from the voyage contemplated by the policy—

(*a*) Where the course of the voyage is specifically designated by the policy, and that course is departed from; or

(*b*) Where the course of the voyage is not specifically designated by the policy, but the usual and customary course is departed from.

(3) The intention to deviate is immaterial; there must be a deviation in fact to discharge the insurer from his liability under the contract.

Several Ports of Discharge.

47. (1) Where several ports of discharge are specified by the policy, the ship may proceed to all or any of them, but, in the absence of any usage or sufficient cause to the contrary, she must proceed to them, or such of them as she goes to, in the order designated by the policy. If she does not there is a deviation.

(2) Where the policy is to "ports of discharge," within a given area, which are not named, the ship must, in the absence of any usage or sufficient

cause to the contrary, proceed to them, or such of them as she goes to, in their geographical order. If she does not there is a deviation.

Delay in Voyage.

48. In the case of a voyage policy, the adventure insured must be prosecuted throughout its course with reasonable despatch, and, if without lawful excuse it is not so prosecuted, the insurer is discharged from liability as from the time when the delay became unreasonable.

Excuses for Deviation or Delay.

49. (1) Deviation or delay in prosecuting the voyage contemplated by the policy is excused—

(*a*) Where authorized by any special term in the policy; or

(*b*) Where caused by circumstances beyond the control of the master and his employer; or

(*c*) Where reasonably necessary in order to comply with an express or implied warranty; or

(*d*) Where reasonably necessary for the safety of the ship or subject-matter insured; or

(*e*) For the purpose of saving human life, or aiding a ship in distress where human life may be in danger; or

(*f*) Where reasonably necessary for the purpose of obtaining medical or surgical aid for any person on board the ship; or

(*g*) Where caused by the barratrous conduct of the master or crew, if barratry be one of the perils insured against.

(2) When the cause excusing the deviation or delay ceases to operate, the ship must resume her course, and prosecute her voyage, with reasonable despatch.

Assignment of Policy

When and How Policy is Assignable.

50. (1) A marine policy is assignable unless it contains terms expressly prohibiting assignment. It may be assigned either before or after loss.

(2) Where a marine policy has been assigned so as to pass the beneficial interest in such policy, the assignee of the policy is entitled to sue thereon in his own name; and the defendant is entitled to make any defence arising out of the contract which he would have been entitled to make if the action had been brought in the name of the person by or on behalf of whom the policy was effected.

(3) A marine policy may be assigned by indorsement thereon or in other customary manner.

Assured Who Has no Interest Cannot Assign.

51. Where the assured has parted with or lost his interest in the subject-matter insured, and has not, before or at the time of so doing, expressly or impliedly agreed to assign the policy, any subsequent assignment of the policy is inoperative;

Provided that nothing in this section affects the assignment of a policy after loss.

The Premium

When Premium Payable.

52. Unless otherwise agreed, the duty of the assured or his agent to pay the premium, and the duty of the insurer to issue the policy to the assured or his agent, are concurrent conditions, and the insurer is not bound to issue the policy until payment or tender of the premium.

Policy Effected Through Broker.

53. (1) Unless otherwise agreed, where a marine policy is effected on behalf of the assured by a broker, the broker is directly responsible to the insurer for the premium, and the insurer is directly responsible to the assured for the amount which may be payable in respect of losses, or in respect of returnable premium.

(2) Unless otherwise agreed, the broker has, as against the assured, a lien upon the policy for the amount of the premium and his charges in respect of effecting the policy; and, where he has dealt with the person who employs him as a principal, he has also a lien on the policy in respect of any balance on any insurance account which may be due to him from such person, unless when the debt was incurred he had reason to believe that such person was only an agent.

Effect of Receipt on Policy.

54. Where a marine policy effected on behalf of the assured by a broker acknowledges the receipt of the premium, such acknowledgment is, in the absence of fraud, conclusive as between the insurer and the assured, but not as between the insurer and broker.

Loss and Abandonment

Included and Excluded Losses.

55. (1) Subject to the provisions of this Act, and unless the policy otherwise provides, the insurer is liable for any loss proximately caused by a peril insured against, but, subject as aforesaid, he is not liable for any loss which is not proximately caused by a peril insured against.

(2) In particular,—

(*a*) The insurer is not liable for any loss attributable to the willful misconduct of the assured, but, unless the policy otherwise provides, he is liable for any loss proximately caused by a peril insured against, even though the loss would not have happened but for the misconduct or negligence of the master or crew;

(*b*) Unless the policy otherwise provides, the insurer on ship or goods is not liable for any loss proximately caused by delay, although the delay be caused by a peril insured against;

(*c*) Unless the policy otherwise provides, the insurer is not liable for ordinary wear and tear, ordinary leakage and breakage, inherent vice or nature of the subject-matter insured, or for any loss proximately caused by rats or vermin, or for any injury to machinery not proximately caused by maritime perils.

Partial and Total Loss.

56. (1) A loss may be either total or partial. Any loss other than a total loss, as hereinafter defined, is a partial loss.

(2) A total loss may be either an actual total loss, or a constructive total loss.

(3) Unless a different intention appears from the terms of the policy, an insurance against total loss includes a constructive, as well as an actual, total loss.

(4) Where the assured brings an action for a total loss and the evidence proves only a partial loss, he may, unless the policy otherwise provides, recover for a partial loss.

(5) Where goods reach their destination in specie, but by reason of obliteration of marks, or otherwise, they are incapable of identification, the loss, if any, is partial, and not total.

Actual Total Loss.

57. (1) Where the subject-matter insured is destroyed, or so damaged as to cease to be a thing of the kind insured, or where the assured is irretrievably deprived thereof, there is an actual total loss.

(2) In the case of an actual total loss no notice of abandonment need be given.

Missing Ship.

58. Where the ship concerned in the adventure is missing, and after the lapse of a reasonable time no news of her has been received, an actual total loss may be presumed.

Effect of Transhipment, &c.

59. Where, by a peril insured against, the voyage is interrupted at an intermediate port or place, under such circumstances as, apart from any special stipulation in the contract of affreightment, to justify the master in landing and re-shipping the goods or other movables, or in transhipping them, and sending them on to their destination, the liability of the insurer continues notwithstanding the landing or transhipment.

Constructive Total Loss Defined.

60. (1) Subject to any express provision in the policy, there is a constructive total loss where the subject-matter insured is reasonably abandoned on account of its actual total loss appearing to be unavoidable, or because it could not be preserved from actual total loss without an expenditure which would exceed its value when the expenditure had been incurred.

(2) In particular, there is a constructive total loss—

(i) Where the assured is deprived of the possession of his ship or goods by a peril insured against, and (*a*) it is unlikely that he can recover the ship or goods, as the case may be, or (*b*) the cost of recovering the ship or goods, as the case may be, would exceed their value when recovered; or

(ii) In the case of damage to a ship, where she is so damaged by a peril insured against that the cost of repairing the damage would exceed the value of the ship when repaired.

In estimating the cost of repairs, no deduction is to be made in respect of general average contributions to those repairs payable by other interests, but account is to be taken of the expense of future salvage operations and of any future general average contributions to which the ship would be liable if repaired; or

(iii) In the case of damage to goods, where the cost of repairing the damage and forwarding the goods to their destination would exceed their value on arrival.

Effect of Constructive Total Loss.

61. Where there is a constructive total loss the assured may either treat the loss as a partial loss, or abandon the subject-matter insured to the insurer and treat the loss as if it were an actual total loss.

Notice of Abandonment.

62. (1) Subject to the provisions of this section, where the assured elects to abandon the subject-matter insured to the insurer, he must give notice of abandonment. If he fails to do so the loss can only be treated as a partial loss.

(2) Notice of abandonment may be given in writing, or by word of mouth, or partly in writing and partly by word of mouth, and may be given in any terms which indicate the intention of the assured to abandon his insured interest in the subject-matter insured unconditionally to the insurer.

(3) Notice of abandonment must be given with reasonable diligence after the receipt of reliable information of the loss, but where the information is of a doubtful character the assured is entitled to a reasonable time to make inquiry.

(4) Where notice of abandonment is properly given, the rights of the assured are not prejudiced by the fact that the insurer refuses to accept the abandonment.

(5) The acceptance of an abandonment may be either express or implied from the conduct of the insurer. The mere silence of the insurer after notice is not an acceptance.

(6) Where notice of abandonment is accepted the abandonment is irrevocable. The acceptance of the notice conclusively admits liability for the loss and the sufficiency of the notice.

(7) Notice of abandonment is unnecessary where, at the time when the assured receives information of the loss, there would be no possibility of benefit to the insurer if notice were given to him.

(8) Notice of abandonment may be waived by the insurer.

(9) Where an insurer has re-insured his risk, no notice of abandonment need be given by him.

Effect of Abandonment.

63. (1) Where there is a valid abandonment the insurer is entitled to take over the interest of the assured in whatever may remain of the subject-matter insured, and all proprietary rights incidental thereto.

(2) Upon the abandonment of a ship, the insurer thereof is entitled to any freight in course of being earned, and which is earned by her subsequent to the casualty causing the loss, less the expenses of earning it incurred after the casualty; and, where the ship is carrying the owner's goods, the insurer is entitled to a reasonable remuneration for the carriage of them subsequent to the casualty causing the loss.

Partial Losses (including Salvage and General Average and Particular Charges)

Particular Average Loss.

64. (1) A particular average loss is a partial loss of the subject-matter insured, caused by a peril insured against, and which is not a general average loss.

(2) Expenses incurred by or on behalf of the assured for the safety or preservation of the subject matter insured, other than general average and salvage charges, are called particular charges. Particular charges are not included in particular average.

Salvage Charges.

65. (1) Subject to any express provision in the policy, salvage charges incurred in preventing a loss by perils insured against may be recovered as a loss by those perils.

(2) "Salvage charges" means the charges recoverable under maritime law by a salvor independently of contract. They do not include the expenses of services in the nature of salvage rendered by the assured or his agents, or any person employed for hire by them, for the purpose of averting a peril insured against. Such expenses, where properly incurred, may be recovered as particular charges or as a general average loss, according to the circumstances under which they were incurred.

General Average Loss.

66. (1) A general average loss is a loss caused by or directly consequential on a general average act. It includes a general average expenditure as well as a general average sacrifice.

(2) There is a general average act where any extraordinary sacrifice or expenditure is voluntarily and reasonably made or incurred in time of peril for the purpose of preserving the property imperilled in the common adventure.

(3) Where there is a general average loss, the party on whom it falls is entitled, subject to the conditions imposed by maritime law, to a rateable contribution from the other parties interested, and such contribution is called a general average contribution.

(4) Subject to any express provision in the policy, where the assured has incurred a general average expenditure, he may recover from the insurer in respect of the proportion of the loss which falls upon him; and, in the case of a general average sacrifice, he may recover from the insurer in respect of the whole loss without having enforced his right of contribution from the other parties liable to contribute.

(5) Subject to any express provision in the policy, where the assured has paid, or is liable to pay, a general average contribution in respect of the subject insured, he may recover therefor from the insurer.

(6) In the absence of express stipulation, the insurer is not liable for any general average loss or contribution where the loss was not incurred for the purpose of avoiding, or in connexion with the avoidance of, a peril insured against.

(7) Where ship, freight, and cargo, or any two of those interests, are owned by the same assured, the liability of the insurer in respect of general average losses or contributions is to be determined as if those subjects were owned by different persons.

Measure of Indemnity

Extent of Liability of Insurer for Loss.

67. (1) The sum which the assured can recover in respect of a loss on a policy by which he is insured, in the case of an unvalued policy to the full extent of the insurable value, or, in the case of a valued policy to the full extent of the value fixed by the policy, is called the measure of indemnity.

(2) Where there is a loss recoverable under the policy, the insurer, or each insurer if there be more than one, is liable for such proportion of the measure of indemnity as the amount of his subscription bears to the value fixed by the policy in the case of a valued policy, or to the insurable value in the case of an unvalued policy.

Total Loss.

68. Subject to the provisions of this Act and to any express provision in the policy, where there is a total loss of the subject-matter insured,—

(1) If the policy be a valued policy, the measure of indemnity is the sum fixed by the policy:

(2) If the policy be an unvalued policy, the measure of indemnity is the insurable value of the subject-matter insured.

Partial Loss of Ship.

69. Where a ship is damaged, but is not totally lost, the measure of indemnity, subject to any express provision in the policy, is as follows:—

(1) Where the ship has been repaired, the assured is entitled to the reasonable cost of the repairs, less the customary deductions, but not exceeding the sum insured in respect of any one casualty:

(2) Where the ship has been only partially repaired, the assured is entitled to the reasonable cost of such repairs, computed as above, and also to be indemnified for the reasonable depreciation, if any, arising from the unrepaired damage, provided that the aggregate amount shall not exceed the cost of repairing the whole damage, computed as above:

(3) Where the ship has not been repaired, and has not been sold in her damaged state during the risk, the assured is entitled to be indemnified for the reasonable depreciation arising from the unrepaired damage, but not exceeding the reasonable cost of repairing such damage, computed as above.

Partial Loss of Freight.

70. Subject to any express provision in the policy, where there is a partial loss of freight, the measure of indemnity is such proportion of the sum fixed by the policy in the case of a valued policy, or of the insurable value in the case of an unvalued policy, as the proportion of freight lost by the assured bears to the whole freight at the risk of the assured under the policy.

Partial Loss of Goods, Merchandise, &c.

71. Where there is a partial loss of goods, merchandise, or other movables, the measure of indemnity, subject to any express provision in the policy, is as follows:—

(1) Where part of the goods, merchandise or other movables insured by a valued policy is totally lost, the measure of indemnity is such proportion of the sum fixed by the policy as the insurable value of the part lost bears to the insurable value of the whole, ascertained as in the case of an unvalued policy:

(2) Where part of the goods, merchandise, or other movables insured by an unvalued policy is totally lost, the measure of indemnity is the insurable value of the part lost, ascertained as in case of total loss:

(3) Where the whole or any part of the goods or merchandise insured has been delivered damaged at its destination, the measure of indemnity is such proportion of the sum fixed by the policy in the case of a valued policy, or of the insurable value in the case of an unvalued policy, as the difference between the gross sound and damaged values at the place of arrival bears to the gross sound value:

(4) "Gross value" means the wholesale price or, if there be no such price, the estimated value, with, in either case, freight, landing charges, and duty paid beforehand; provided that, in the case of goods or merchandise customarily sold in bond, the bonded price is deemed to be the gross value. "Gross proceeds" means the actual price obtained at a sale where all charges on sale are paid by the sellers.

Apportionment of Valuation.

72. (1) Where different species of property are insured under a single valuation, the valuation must be apportioned over the different species in proportion to their respective insurable values, as in the case of an unvalued policy. The insured value of any part of a species is such proportion of the total insured value of the same as the insurable value of the part bears to the insurable value of the whole, ascertained in both cases as provided by this Act.

(2) Where a valuation has to be apportioned, and particulars of the prime cost of each separate species, quality, or description of goods cannot be ascertained, the division of the valuation may be made over the net arrived sound values of the different species, qualities, or descriptions of goods.

General Average Contributions and Salvage Charges.

73. (1) Subject to any express provision in the policy, where the assured has paid, or is liable for, any general average contribution, the measure of indemnity is the full amount of such contribution, if the subject-matter liable to contribution is insured for its full contributory value; but, if such subject-matter be not insured for its full contributory value, or if only part of it be insured, the indemnity payable by the insurer must be reduced in proportion to the under insurance, and where there has been a particular average loss which constitutes a deduction from the contributory value, and for which the insurer is liable, that amount must be deducted from the insured value in order to ascertain what the insurer is liable to contribute.

(2) Where the insurer is liable for salvage charges the extent of his liability must be determined on like principle.

Liabilities to Third Parties.

74. Where the assured has effected an insurance in express terms against any liability to a third party, the measure of indemnity, subject to any express provision in the policy, is the amount paid or payable by him to such third party in respect of such liability.

General Provisions as to Measure of Indemnity.

75. (1) Where there has been a loss in respect of any subject-matter not expressly provided for in the foregoing provisions of this Act, the measure of indemnity shall be ascertained, as nearly as may be, in accordance with those provisions, in so far as applicable to the particular case.

(2) Nothing in the provisions of this Act relating to the measure of indemnity shall affect the rules relating to double insurance, or prohibit the insurer from disproving interest wholly or in part, or from showing that at the time of the loss the whole or any part of the subject-matter insured was not at risk under the policy.

Particular Average Warranties.

76. (1) Where the subject-matter insured is warranted free from particular average, the assured cannot recover for a loss of part, other than a loss incurred by a general average sacrifice, unless the contract contained in the policy be apportionable; but, if the contract be apportionable, the assured may recover for a total loss of any apportionable part.

(2) Where the subject-matter insured is warranted free from particular average, either wholly or under a certain percentage, the insurer is nevertheless liable for salvage charges, and for particular charges and other expenses properly incurred pursuant to the provisions of the suing and labouring clause in order to avert a loss insured against.

(3) Unless the policy otherwise provides, where the subject-matter in-

sured is warranted free from particular average under a specified percentage, a general average loss cannot be added to a particular average loss to make up the specified percentage.

(4) For the purpose of ascertaining whether the specified percentage has been reached, regard shall be had only to the actual loss suffered by the subject-matter insured. Particular charges and the expenses of and incidental to ascertaining and proving the loss must be excluded.

Successive Losses.

77. (1) Unless the policy otherwise provides, and subject to the provisions of this Act, the insurer is liable for successive losses, even though the total amount of such losses may exceed the sum insured.

(2) Where, under the same policy, a partial loss, which has not been repaired or otherwise made good, is followed by a total loss, the assured can only recover in respect of the total loss:

Provided that nothing in this section shall affect the liability of the insurer under the suing and labouring clause.

Suing and Labouring Clause.

78. (1) Where the policy contains a suing and labouring clause, the engagement thereby entered into is deemed to be supplementary to the contract of insurance, and the assured may recover from the insurer any expenses properly incurred pursuant to the clause, notwithstanding that the insurer may have paid for a total loss, or that the subject-matter may have been warranted free from particular average, either wholly or under a certain percentage.

(2) General average losses and contributions and salvage charges, as defined by this Act, are not recoverable under the suing and labouring clause.

(3) Expenses incurred for the purpose of averting or diminishing any loss not covered by the policy are not recoverable under the suing and labouring clause.

(4) It is the duty of the assured and his agents, in all cases, to take such measures as may be reasonable for the purpose of averting or minimizing a loss.

Rights of Insurer on Payment

Right of Subrogation.

79. (1) Where the insurer pays for a total loss, either of the whole, or in the case of goods of any apportionable part, of the subject-matter insured, he thereupon becomes entitled to take over the interest of the assured in whatever may remain of the subject-matter so paid for, and he is thereby subrogated to all the rights and remedies of the assured in and in respect of that subject-matter as from the time of the casualty causing the loss.

(2) Subject to the foregoing provisions, where the insurer pays for a partial loss, he acquires no title to the subject-matter insured, or such part of it as may remain, but he is thereupon subrogated to all rights and remedies of the assured in and in respect of the subject-matter insured as from the time of the casualty causing the loss, in so far as the assured has been indemnified, according to this Act, by such payment for the loss.

Right of Contribution.

80. (1) Where the assured is over-insured by double insurance, each insurer is bound, as between himself and the other insurers, to contribute rateably to the loss in proportion to the amount for which he is liable under his contract.

(2) If any insurer pays more than his proportion of the loss, he is entitled to maintain an action for contribution against the other insurers, and is entitled to the like remedies as a surety who has paid more than his proportion of the debt.

Effect of Under Insurance.

81. Where the assured is insured for an amount less than the insurable value or, in the case of a valued policy, for an amount less than the policy valuation, he is deemed to be his own insurer in respect of the uninsured balance.

Return of Premium

Enforcement of Return.

82. Where the premium, or a proportionate part thereof is, by this Act declared to be returnable,—

(*a*) If already paid, it may be recovered by the assured from the insurer; and

(*b*) If unpaid, it may be retained by the assured or his agent.

Return by Agreement.

83. Where the policy contains a stipulation for the return of the premium, or a proportionate part thereof, on the happening of a certain event, and that event happens, the premium, or, as the case may be, the proportionate part thereof, is thereupon returnable to the assured.

Return for Failure of Consideration.

84. (1) Where the consideration for the payment of the premium totally fails, and there has been no fraud or illegality on the part of the assured or his agents, the premium is thereupon returnable to the assured.

(2) Where the consideration for the payment of the premium is apportionable and there is a total failure of any apportionable part of the consideration, a proportionate part of the premium is, under the like conditions, thereupon returnable to the assured.

(3) In particular—

(*a*) Where the policy is void, or is avoided by the insurer as from the commencement of the risk, the premium is returnable, provided that there has been no fraud or illegality on the part of the assured; but if the risk is not apportionable, and has once attached, the premium is not returnable:

(*b*) Where the subject-matter insured, or part thereof, has never been imperilled, the premium, or, as the case may be, a proportionate part thereof, is returnable:

Provided that where the subject-matter has been insured "lost or not lost" and has arrived in safety at the time when the contract is concluded, the premium is not returnable unless, at such time, the insurer knew of the safe arrival;

(*c*) Where the assured has no insurable interest throughout the currency of the risk, the premium is returnable, provided that this rule does not apply to a policy effected by way of gaming or wagering;

(*d*) Where the assured has a defeasible interest which is terminated during the currency of the risk, the premium is not returnable;

(*e*) Where the assured has over-insured under an unvalued policy, a proportionate part of the premium is returnable;

(*f*) Subject to the foregoing provisions, where the assured has over-insured by double insurance, a proportionate part of the several premiums is returnable:

Provided that, if the policies are effected at different times, and any earlier policy has at any time borne the entire risk, or if a claim has been paid on the policy in respect of the full sum insured thereby, no premium is returnable in respect of that policy, and when the double insurance is effected knowingly by the assured no premium is returnable.

Mutual Insurance

Modification of Act in Case of Mutual Insurance.

85. (1) Where two or more persons mutually agree to insure each other against marine losses there is said to be a mutual insurance.

(2) The provisions of this Act relating to the premium do not apply to mutual insurance, but a guarantee, or such other arrangement as may be agreed upon, may be substituted for the premium.

(3) The provisions of this Act, in so far as they may be modified by the agreement of the parties, may in the case of mutual insurance be modified

by the terms of the policies issued by the association, or by the rules and regulations of the association.

(4) Subject to the exceptions mentioned in this section, the provisions of this Act apply to a mutual insurance.

Supplemental

Ratification by Assured.

86. Where a contract of marine insurance is in good faith effected by one person on behalf of another, the person on whose behalf it is effected may ratify the contract even after he is aware of a loss.

Implied Obligations Varied by Agreement or Usage.

87. (1) Where any right, duty, or liability would arise under a contract of marine insurance by implication of law, it may be negatived or varied by express agreement, or by usage, if the usage be such as to bind both parties to the contract.

(2) The provisions of this section extend to any right, duty, or liability declared by this Act which may be lawfully modified by agreement.

Reasonable Time, &c. a Question of Fact.

88. Where by this Act any reference is made to reasonable time, reasonable premium, or reasonable diligence, the question what is reasonable is a question of fact.

Slip as Evidence.

89. Where there is a duly stamped policy, reference may be made, as heretofore, to the slip or covering note, in any legal proceeding.

Interpretation of Terms.

90. In this Act, unless the context or subject-matter otherwise requires,—

"Action" includes counter-claim and set off:

"Freight" includes the profit derivable by a shipowner from the employment of his ship to carry his own goods or movables, as well as freight payable by a third party, but does not include passage money:

"Movables" means any movable tangible property, other than the ship, and includes money, valuable securities, and other documents:

"Policy" means a marine policy.

Savings.

91. (1) Nothing in this Act, or in any repeal effected thereby, shall affect—

(*a*) The provisions of the Stamp Act, 1891, or any enactment for the time being in force relating to the revenue;

(*b*) The provisions of the Companies Act, 1862, or any enactment amending or substituted for the same;

(*c*) The provisions of any statute not expressly repealed by this Act.

(2) The rules of the common law including the law merchant, save in so far as they are inconsistent with the express provisions of this Act, shall continue to apply to contracts of marine insurance.

Repeals.

92. The enactments mentioned in the Second Schedule to this Act are hereby repealed to the extent specified in that schedule.

Commencement.

93. This Act shall come into operation on the first day of January one thousand nine hundred and seven.

Short Title.

94. This Act may be cited as the Marine Insurance Act, 1906.

SCHEDULES

FIRST SCHEDULE

Form of Policy

Be it known that as well in own name as for and in the name and names of all and every other person or persons to whom the same doth, may, or shall appertain, in part or in all doth make assurance and cause and them, and every of them, to be insured lost or not lost, at and from

Upon any kind of goods and merchandises, and also upon the body, tackle, apparel, ordnance, munition, artillery, boat, and other furniture, of and in the good ship or vessel called the whereof is master under God, for this present voyage, or whosoever else shall go for master in the said ship, or by whatsoever other name or names the said ship, or the master thereof, is or shall be named or called; beginning the adventure upon the said goods and merchandises from the loading thereof aboard the said ship,

upon the said ship, &c.

and so shall continue and endure, during her abode there, upon the said ship, &c. And further, until the said ship, with all her ordnance, tackle, apparel, &c., and goods and merchandises whatsoever shall be arrived at

upon the said ship, &c., until she hath moored at anchor twenty-four hours in good safety; and upon the goods and merchandises, until the same be there discharged and safely landed. And it shall be lawful for the said ship, &c., in this voyage, to proceed and sail to and touch and stay at any ports or places whatsoever

without prejudice to this insurance. The said ship, &c., goods and merchandises, &c., for so much as concerns the assured by agreement between the assured and assurers in this policy, are and shall be valued at

Touching the adventures and perils which we the assurers are contented to bear and do take upon us in this voyage: they are of the seas, men of war, fire, enemies, pirates, rovers, thieves, jettisons, letters of mart and countermart, surprisals, takings at sea, arrests, restraints, and detainments of all kings, princes, and people, of what nation, condition, or quality soever, barratry of the master and mariners, and of all other perils, losses, and misfortunes, that have or shall come to the hurt, detriment, or damage of the said goods and merchandises, and ship, &c., or any part thereof. And in case of any loss or misfortune it shall be lawful to the assured, their factors, servants and assigns, to sue, labour, and travel for, in and about the defence, safeguards, and recovery of the said goods and merchandises, and ship, &c., or any part thereof, without prejudice to this insurance; to the charges whereof we, the assurers, will contribute each one according to the rate and quantity of his sum herein assured. And it is especially declared and agreed that no acts of the insurer or insured in recovering, saving, or preserving the property insured shall be considered as a waiver, or acceptance of abandonment. And it is agreed by us, the insurers, that this writing or policy of assurance shall be of as much force and effect as the surest writing or policy of assurance heretofore made in Lombard Street, or in the Royal Exchange, or elsewhere in London. And so we, the assurers, are contented, and do hereby promise and bind ourselves, each one for his own part, our heirs, executors, and goods to the assured, their executors, administrators, and assigns, for the true performance of the premises, confessing ourselves paid the consideration due unto us for this assurance by the assured, at and after the rate of

IN WITNESS whereof we, the assurers, have subscribed our names and sums assured in London.

N.B.—Corn, fish, salt, fruit, flour, and seed are warranted free from average, unless general, or the ship be stranded—sugar, tobacco, hemp, flax, hides and skins are warranted free from average, under five pounds percent, and all other goods, also the ship and freight, are warranted free from average, under three pounds percent unless general, or the ship be stranded.

Rules for Construction of Policy

The following are the rules referred to by this Act for the construction of a policy in the above or other like form, where the context does not otherwise require:—

Lost or not Lost.

1. Where the subject-matter is insured "lost or not lost," and the loss has occurred before the contract is concluded, the risk attaches unless, at such time the assured was aware of the loss, and the insurer was not.

From.

2. Where the subject-matter is insured "from" a particular place, the risk does not attach until the ship starts on the voyage insured.

At and From. [Ship.]

3. (*a*) Where a ship is insured "at and from" a particular place, and she is at that place in good safety when the contract is concluded, the risk attaches immediately.

(*b*) If she be not at that place when the contract is concluded the risk attaches as soon as she arrives there in good safety, and, unless the policy otherwise provides, it is immaterial that she is covered by another policy for a specified time after arrival.

[Freight.]

(*c*) Where chartered freight is insured "at and from" a particular place, and the ship is at that place in good safety when the contract is concluded the risk attaches immediately. If she be not there when the contract is concluded, the risk attaches as soon as she arrives there in good safety.

(*d*) Where freight, other than chartered freight, is payable without special conditions and is insured "at and from" a particular place, the risk attaches pro rata as the goods or merchandise are shipped; provided that if there be cargo in readiness which belongs to the shipowner, or which some other person has contracted with him to ship, the risk attaches as soon as the ship is ready to receive such cargo.

From the Loading Thereof.

4. Where goods or other movables are insured "from the loading thereof," the risk does not attach until such goods or movables are actually on

board, and the insurer is not liable for them while in transit from the shore to the ship.

Safely Landed.

5. Where the risk on goods or other movables continues until they are "safely landed," they must be landed in the customary manner and within a reasonable time after arrival at the port of discharge, and if they are not so landed the risk ceases.

Touch and Stay.

6. In the absence of any further license or usage, the liberty to touch and stay "at any port or place whatsoever" does not authorise the ship to depart from the course of her voyage from the port of departure to the port of destination.

Perils of the Seas.

7. The term "perils of the seas" refers only to fortuitous accidents or casualties of the seas. It does not include the ordinary action of the winds and waves.

Pirates.

8. The term "pirates" includes passengers who mutiny and rioters who attack the ship from the shore.

Thieves.

9. The term "thieves" does not cover clandestine theft or a theft committed by any one of the ship's company, whether crew or passengers.

Restraint of Princes.

10. The term "arrests, &c., of kings, princes, and people" refers to political or executive acts, and does not include a loss caused by riot or by ordinary judicial process.

Barratry.

11. The term "barratry" includes every wrongful act willfully committed by the master or crew to the prejudice of the owner, or, as the case may be the charterer.

All Other Perils.

12. The term "all other perils" includes only perils similar in kind to the perils specifically mentioned in the policy.

Average unless General.

13. The term "average unless general" means a partial loss of the subject-matter insured other than a general average loss, and does not include "particular charges."

Stranded.

14. Where the ship has stranded, the insurer is liable for the excepted losses, although the loss is not attributable to the stranding, provided that

when the stranding takes place the risk has attached and, if the policy be on goods, that the damaged goods are on board.

Ship.

15. The term "ship" includes the hull, materials and outfit, stores and provisions for the officers and crew, and, in the case of vessels engaged in a special trade, the ordinary fittings requisite for the trade, and also, in the case of a steamship, the machinery, boilers, and coals and engine stores, if owned by the assured.

Freight.

16. The term "freight" includes the profit derivable by a shipowner from the employment of his ship to carry his own goods or movables, as well as freight payable by a third party, but does not include passage money.

Goods.

17. The term "goods" means goods in the nature of merchandise, and does not include personal effects or provisions and stores for use on board.

In the absence of any usage to the contrary, deck cargo and living animals must be insured specifically, and not under the general denomination of goods.

SECOND SCHEDULE

Enactments Repealed

Session and chapter	Title or short title	Extent of repeal
19 Geo. 2. c. 37.	An Act to regulate insurance on ships belonging to the subjects of Great Britain, and on merchandises or effects laden thereon.	The whole Act.
28 Geo. 3. c. 56.	An Act to repeal an Act made in the twenty-fifth year of the reign of his present Majesty, intituled "An Act for regulating Insurances on Ships, and on goods, merchandises, or effects," and for substituting other provisions for the like purpose in lieu thereof.	The whole Act so far as it relates to marine insurance.
31 & 32 Vict. c. 86.	The Policies of Marine Assurance Act, 1868.	The whole Act.

Appendix J. Marine Insurance (Gambling Policies)

A Bill to Prohibit Gambling on Loss by Maritime Perils (1909)

Be it enacted by the King's most Excellent Majesty, by and with the advice and consent of the Lords Spiritual and Temporal, and Commons, in this present Parliament assembled, and by the authority of the same, as follows:—

1. *Prohibition of Gambling on Loss by Maritime Perils.*—(1) If
   (a) Any person effects a contract of marine insurance without having any bona fide interest, direct or indirect, either in the safe arrival of the ship in relation to which the contract is made or in the safety or preservation of the subject-matter insured, or a bona fide expectation of such an interest; or
   (b) Any person in the employment of the owner of a ship, not being a part owner of the ship, effects a contract of marine insurance in relation to the ship, and the contract is made "interest or no interest," or "without further proof of interest than the policy itself," or "without benefit of salvage to the insurer," or subject to any other like term,

   the contract shall be deemed to be a contract by way of gambling on loss by maritime perils, and the person effecting it shall be guilty of an offence, and shall be liable, on summary conviction, to imprisonment, with or without hard labour, for a term not exceeding six months, or to a fine not exceeding one hundred pounds, and in either case to forfeit any money he may receive under the contract.

   (2) Any broker through whom, and any insurer with whom, any such contract is effected shall be guilty of an offence and liable on summary conviction to the like penalties if he acted knowing that the contract was by way of gambling on loss by maritime perils within the meaning of this Act.

   (3) Proceedings under this Act, shall not be instituted without the consent of the Attorney-General.

   (4) Proceedings shall not be instituted under this Act against a person (other than a person in the employment of the owner of the ship in relation to which the contract was made) alleged to have effected a contract by way of gambling on loss by maritime perils

until an opportunity has been afforded him of showing that the contract was not such a contract as aforesaid, and any information given by that person for that purpose shall not be admissible in evidence against him in any prosecution under this Act.

(5) If proceedings under this Act are taken against any person (other than a person in the employment of the owner of the ship in relation to which the contract was made) for effecting such a contract, and the contract was made "interest or no interest" or "without further proof of interest than the policy itself," or "without benefit of salvage to the insurer" or subject to any other like term, the contract shall be deemed to be a contract by way of gambling on loss by maritime perils unless the contrary is proved.

(6) Any person aggrieved by an order or decision of a court of summary jurisdiction under this Act, may appeal to quarter sessions.

(7) For the purposes of this Act the expression "Owner" includes charterer.

(8) Subsections (3) and (6) of this section shall not apply to Scotland.

2. *Short Title.*—This Act may be cited as the Marine Insurance (Gambling Policies) Act, 1909, and the Marine Insurance Act, 1906, and this Act may be cited together as the Marine Insurance Acts, 1906 and 1909.

Appendix K. Statement of Value Used in General Average

Interest No.________

B/L________

S/S "   "

Statement of Value, of goods discharged from the above vessel which arrived

at   on

having sailed from   on

GROSS WHOLESALE MARKET VALUE in the port of discharge, of the following goods, in the condition in which they were landed (regardless of when, or how the goods were sold, or even if they have not been sold).

Note: This value must include freight, duty, and landing charges paid.
If some of the goods were landed in damaged condition, their value (in damaged condition) should be shown separately.

MARKS AND NUMBERS	NUMBER OF PACKAGES AND DESCRIPTION OF GOODS	WEIGHT OR QUANTITY	GROSS WHOLESALE MARKET VALUE ON	
			@	AMOUNT
Invoice value, or insured value is NOT the value required here. (Those values are to be inserted below as indicated)				
				$

Deduct: Cash Discount (if any),   % $

CHARGES (to be deducted):

- **Freight,** as per B/L (if not prepaid or guaranteed) . . $______
- **Import Duty paid, net** . . . . ______
- **Landing Charges:** Cartage (if any) . . . . ______
  - Labor (if any) . . . . ______
  - ______ . . . . ______
- **Brokerage** (if any) paid . . . . ______
- ______ . . . . ______
- ______ . . . . ______ **(Total Deduct)** ______

INVOICE VALUE of the above goods is________   Net Cash Value $________

________Company insured them for________

IT IS CERTIFIED that the above is a correct statement of the Net Cash Value of the Goods described above, and is furnished for General Average purposes.

Dated________

Address________   *Signature________

*** To be signed only by an authorized person.**

Appendix L. Average Agreement

AVERAGE AGREEMENT

AGREEMENT made as of the day of , 19

between

owners of the

parties of the first part, and the several parties, subscribers hereto, parties of the second part, WITNESSETH:

WHEREAS, it is alleged that said vessel, laden with cargo, sailed from

on or about , 19 , for

and that in the prosecution of her voyage

and

WHEREAS, by reason of occurrences on the voyage, certain losses and expenses were, and other losses and expenses may be, incurred, which may constitute a charge by way of general average, or otherwise, upon said vessel, her earnings and her cargo, or which may apply to and be due from specific interests:

NOW THEREFORE we, the subscribers, being or representing owners, shippers or consignees of such of the cargo of said vessel as is severally described and set opposite our respective signatures hereto, in consideration of the premises and of the delivery of such cargo as may be saved, do hereby, for ourselves and our principals and executors and administrators, severally and respectively, but not jointly, nor one for the other, covenant and agree to and with the owners of said vessel for themselves and for all interests concerned in the venture aforesaid, and one with the other, that so much of the losses and expenses aforesaid as upon an adjustment of the same to be stated by

Average Adjusters, according to the provisions of the contract of affreightment and to the laws and usages applicable, may be shown by the statement to be a charge upon said cargo, or to be due from us, shall be paid by us respectively according to our ratable proportion thereof, to the owners of said vessel or

in and for settlement in accordance with said statement.

Should the value of the services rendered to said cargo be determined by settlement or arbitration, we do hereby severally covenant and agree to pay each our ratable proportion of any sum thus fixed; and in the event of suit being brought to recover for such services, we do hereby severally covenant and agree to give bond for our respective interests in the same manner as if the salvors had required such bond direct from us before surrendering the cargo, and to pay and satisfy fully our ratable proportion of any final judgment rendered therein, and when the amount of the salvage services has been determined we authorize the payment of the proportion of same applying to the cargo described below from the deposit collected in respect to said cargo.

We do hereby severally authorize and direct our respective insurers and all other persons and corporations, who or which guarantee the payment of any general average and/or salvage and/or special charges and/or any amounts that may become due from us under this agreement, to pay for and in our behalf unto the owners of said vessel or
for the purposes aforesaid, the amounts shown by said statement to be due from us respectively.

We do hereby severally promise and agree to furnish promptly, on request of said adjusters, all such information and documents as they may require to prepare said statement, and in the event of inability or failure to do so in respect to any shipment or shipments, said adjusters are authorized to prepare said statement on such information as they can by reasonable diligence obtain, and such statement shall be binding as respects the information so acted upon; but if, thereafter, proper information and documents are furnished the adjusters and request is made that such statement be amended, it shall be amended, provided the party making the request pays the expenses of preparing and collecting under the amendment, but the vessel owners, adjusters and trustees shall be under no responsibility in respect of any payment or distribution to or settlement with any other interest which may have been previously made under the original statement.

This agreement may be executed in several parts, which shall constitute one agreement, by the parties of the second part, and upon such execution and the release of said cargo by the parties of the first part, shall have full force and effect.

IN WITNESS WHEREOF, we have executed these presents in the City of as of the day and year first above written.

(This document must be signed by a member of the firm or an officer of the Company, or person having power-of-attorney, and if signed by an officer or attorney it must be so designated hereon.)

....

....

B/L No.	No. of Pkgs.	GOODS	MARKS AND NOS.	AMT. OF INVOICE	NAME OF UNDERWRITER

Appendix M. General Average Guarantee

FORM OF UNDERWRITERS GUARANTEE FOR THE PAYMENT OF

GENERAL AVERAGE, SALVAGE AND SPECIAL CHARGES

New York,.................................19.......

Messrs.

In consideration of the delivery
from the SS
of the following goods or such part of same
as may be landed. viz:-

Shipped by
Consigned to
without the requirements of a deposit, we hereby
guarantee the payment of all Proper General
Average, Salvage and/or Special Charges for which
said goods are liable.

....

L1788 1M 8-47

Appendix N. The Harter Act

ACT OF CONGRESS, APPROVED FEBRUARY 13, 1893

An Act relating to navigation of vessels, bills of lading, and to certain obligations, duties, and rights in connection with the carriage of property.

Be it enacted by the Senate and House of Representatives of the United States of America in Congress assembled,

Section 1. That it shall not be lawful for the manager, agent, master or owner of any vessel transporting merchandise or property from or between ports of the United States and foreign ports to insert in any bill of lading or shipping document any clause, covenant, or agreement whereby it, he, or they shall be relieved from liability for loss or damage arising from negligence, fault, or failure in proper loading, stowage, custody, care, or proper delivery of any and all lawful merchandise or property committed to its or their charge. Any and all words or clauses of such import inserted in bills of lading or shipping receipts shall be null and void and of no effect.

Section 2. That it shall not be lawful for any vessel transporting merchandise or property from or between ports of the United States of America and foreign ports, her owner, master, agent or manager to insert in any bill of lading or shipping document any covenant or agreement whereby the obligations of the owner or owners of said vessel to exercise due diligence, properly equip, man, provision, and outfit said vessel, and to make said vessel seaworthy and capable of performing her intended voyage, or whereby the obligations of the master, officers, agents, or servants to carefully handle and stow her cargo and to care for and properly deliver same, shall in any wise be lessened, weakened, or avoided.

Section 3. That if the owner of any vessel transporting merchandise or property to or from any port in the United States of America shall exercise due diligence to make the said vessel in all respects seaworthy and properly manned, equipped, and supplied, neither the vessel, or owners, agents, or charterers shall become or be held responsible for damage or loss resulting from faults or errors in navigation or in the management of said vessel, nor shall the vessel, her owner or owners, charterers, agent, or master, be held liable for losses arising from dangers of the sea or other navigable waters, acts of God, or public enemies, or the inherent defect, quality, or vice of the thing carried, or from insufficiency of package, or seizure under legal process, or for loss resulting from any act or omission of the shipper or owner of the goods, his agent or representative, or from saving or attempting to save life or property at sea, or from any deviation in rendering such service.

Section 4. That it shall be the duty of the owner or owners, master, or agent of any vessel transporting merchandise or property from or between ports of the United States and foreign ports to issue to shippers of any lawful merchandise a bill of lading, or shipping document, stating, among other things, the marks necessary for identification, number of packages, or quantity, stating whether it be carrier's or shipper's weight, and apparent order or condition of such merchandise or property delivered to and received by the owner, master, or agent of the vessel for transportation, and such document shall be prima facie evidence of the receipt of the merchandise therein described.

Section 5. That for a violation of any of the provisions of this Act the agent, owner, or master of the vessel guilty of such violation, and who refuses to issue on demand the bill of lading herein provided for, shall be liable to a fine not exceeding two thousand dollars. The amount of the fine and costs for such violation shall be a lien upon the vessel, whose agent, owner, or master is guilty of such violation, and such vessel may be libeled therefor in any district court of the United States, within whose jurisdiction the vessel may be found. One-half of such penalty shall go to the party injured by such violation and the remainder to the Government of the United States.

Section 6. That this Act shall not be held to modify or repeal sections forty-two hundred and eighty-one, forty-two hundred and eighty-two, and forty-two hundred and eighty-three of the Revised Statutes of the United States, or any other statute defining the liability of vessels, their owners, or representatives.

Section 7. Sections one and four of this act shall not apply to the transportation of live animals.

Section 8. That this Act shall take effect from and after the first day of July, eighteen hundred and ninety-three.

Appendix O. U.S. Carriage of Goods by Sea Act (April 16, 1936, Effective July 15, 1936)

Public. No. 521, 74th Congress (S. 1152)
49 U.S. Statutes at Large, 1207–1213
Title 46, U.S. Code, 1300–1315

AN ACT RELATING TO THE CARRIAGE OF GOODS BY SEA

Be it enacted by the Senate and House of Representatives of the United States of America in Congress assembled,

SCOPE—OCEAN BILLS OF LADING—FOREIGN TRADE—INWARD & OUTWARD
U.S. Code, Title 46, Sect. 1300. 49 Stat. 1207

That every bill of lading or similar document of title which is evidence of a contract for the carriage of goods by sea to or from ports of the United States, in foreign trade, shall have effect subject to the provisions of this Act.

TITLE I
(The Hague Rules)
Terms Defined
U.S. Code, Title 46, Sect. 1301. 49 Stat. 1208

SECTION 1. When used in this Act—

CARRIER

(a) The term "carrier" includes the owner or the charterer who enters into a contract of carriage with a shipper.

CONTRACT OF CARRIAGE UNDER B/L—WHEN B/L ISSUED UNDER CHARTER PARTY

(b) The term "contract of carriage" applies only to contracts of carriage covered by a bill of lading or any similar document of title, insofar as such document relates to the carriage of goods by sea, including any bill of lading or any similar document as aforesaid issued under or pursuant to a charter party from the moment at which such bill of lading or similar document of title regulates the relations between a carrier and a holder of the same.

GOODS—LIVE ANIMALS—DECK CARGO

(c) The term "goods" includes goods, wares, merchandise, and articles of every kind whatsoever, except

Live animals and

Cargo which by the contract of carriage is stated as being carried on deck and is so carried.

SHIP

(d) The term "ship" means any vessel used for the carriage of goods by sea.

CARRIAGE OF GOODS, FROM LOADING UNTIL DISCHARGE

(e) The term "carriage of goods" covers the period from the time when the goods are loaded on to the time when they are discharged from the ship.

CARRIER'S DUTY AND RIGHTS

U.S. Code, Title 46, Sect. 1302. 49 Stat. 1208

RISKS—SEC. 2. Subject to the provisions of section 6, under every contract of carriage of goods by sea, the carrier in relation to the loading, handling, stowage, carriage, custody, care, and discharge of such goods, shall be subject to the responsibilities and liabilities and entitled to the rights and immunities hereinafter set forth.

RESPONSIBILITIES AND LIABILITIES—SEC. 3

U.S. Code, Title 46, Sect. 1303. 49 Stat. 1208
Due Diligence before Beginning Voyage

(1) The carrier shall be bound, before and at the beginning of the voyage, to exercise due diligence to—

(a) Make the ship seaworthy;
(b) Properly man, equip, and supply the ship;
(c) Make the holds, refrigerating and cooling chambers, and all other parts of the ship in which goods are carried, fit and safe for their reception, carriage, and preservation.

CARRIER'S DUTY TO CARGO

(2) The carrier shall properly and carefully load, handle, stow, carry, keep, care for, and discharge the goods carried.

BILL OF LADING TO ISSUE—ESSENTIAL STATEMENTS

(3) After receiving the goods into his charge the carrier, or the master or agent of the carrier, shall, on demand of the shipper, issue to the shipper a bill of lading showing among other things—

IDENTIFICATION MARKS

(a) The leading marks necessary for identification of the goods as the same are furnished in writing by the shipper before the loading of such goods starts, provided such marks are stamped or otherwise shown clearly upon the goods if uncovered, or on the cases or coverings in which such goods are contained, in such a manner as should ordinarily remain legible until the end of the voyage.

NUMBER OR WEIGHT OF PACKAGES, ETC.

(b) Either the number of packages or pieces, or the quantity or weight, as the case may be, as furnished in writing by the shipper.

ORDER & CONDITION OF GOODS—INACCURATE OR UNCHECKED INFORMATION

(c) The apparent order and condition of the goods: PROVIDED, That no carrier, master, or agent of the carrier, shall be bound to state or show in the bill of lading any marks, number, quantity, or weight which he has reasonable ground for suspecting not accurately to represent the goods actually received, or which he has had no reasonable means of checking.

B/L PRIMA FACIE EVIDENCE OF RECEIPT OF GOODS—POMERENE ACT NOT AFFECTED

(4) Such a bill of lading shall be prima facie evidence of the receipt by the carrier of the goods as therein described in accordance with paragraphs (3) (a), (b), and (c) of this section: PROVIDED, That nothing in this Act shall be construed as repealing or limiting the application of any part of the Act, as amended, entitled "an Act relating to bills of lading in interstate and foreign commerce," approved August 29, 1916 (U.S.C., Title 49, secs. 81–124, 39 Stat. 638), commonly known as the "Pomerene Bills of Lading Act."

ACCURACY OF MARKS, ETC.—GUARANTEED BY SHIPPER; INDEMNITY FOR ERROR

(5) The shipper shall be deemed to have guaranteed to the carrier the accuracy at the time of shipment of the marks, number, quantity, and weight, as furnished by him; and the shipper shall indemnify the carrier against all

loss, damages, and expenses arising or resulting from inaccuracies in such particulars. The right of the carrier to such indemnity shall in no way limit his responsibility and liability under the contract of carriage to any person other than the shipper.

NOTICE OF LOSS OR DAMAGE—VISIBLE DAMAGE

(6) Unless notice of loss or damage and the general nature of such loss or damage be given in writing to the carrier or his agent at the port of discharge before or at the time of the removal of the goods into the custody of the person entitled to delivery thereof under the contract of carriage, such removal shall be prima facie evidence of the delivery by the carrier of the goods as described in the bill of lading.

NOTICE OF LOSS OR DAMAGE—CONCEALED DAMAGE

If the loss or damage is not apparent, the notice must be given within three days of the delivery.

NOTICE ENDORSED ON RECEIPT

Said notice of loss or damage may be endorsed upon the receipt for the goods given by the person taking delivery thereof.

NOTICE NOT REQUIRED IF JOINT INSPECTION HAD

The notice in writing need not be given if the state of the goods has at the time of their receipt been the subject of joint survey or inspection.

TIME FOR SUIT, ONE YEAR

In any event, the carrier and the ship shall be discharged from all liability in respect of loss or damage unless suit is brought within one year after delivery of the goods or the date when the goods should have been delivered:

EFFECT OF FAILURE TO GIVE NOTICE

PROVIDED, That if a notice of loss or damage, either apparent or concealed, is not given as provided for in this section, that fact shall not affect or prejudice the right of the shipper to bring suit within one year after the delivery of the goods or the date when the goods should have been delivered.

MUTUAL RIGHTS OF INSPECTION AND TALLY, IN CASE OF LOSS

In the case of any actual or apprehended loss or damage the carrier and the receiver shall give all reasonable facilities to each other for inspecting and tallying the goods.

"SHIPPED" BILL OF LADING

(7) After the goods are loaded the bill of lading to be issued by the carrier, master, or agent of the carrier to the shipper shall, if the shipper so demands, be a "shipped" bill of lading: PROVIDED, That if the shipper shall have previously taken up any document of title to such goods, he shall surrender the same as against the issue of the "shipped" bill of lading, but at the option of the carrier such document of title may be noted at the port of shipment by the carrier, master, or agent with the name or names of the ship or ships upon which the goods have been shipped and the date or dates of shipment, and when so noted the same shall for the purpose of this section be deemed to constitute a "shipped" bill of lading.

NEGLIGENCE CLAUSES OTHER THAN PROVIDED IN ACT, NULL & VOID

(8) Any clause, covenant, or agreement in a contract of carriage relieving the carrier or the ship from liability for loss or damage to or in connection with the goods, arising from negligence, fault, or failure in the duties and obligations provided in this section, or lessening such liability otherwise than as provided in this Act, shall be null and void and of no effect.

BENEFIT OF INSURANCE CLAUSES, NULL AND VOID

A benefit of insurance in favor of the carrier, or similar clause, shall be deemed to be a clause relieving the carrier from liability.

RIGHTS AND IMMUNITIES—SEC. 4

U.S. Code, Title 46, Sec. 1304. 49 Stat. 1210

Immunities—Unseaworthiness without Want of Due Diligence—Burden of Proof

(1) Neither the carrier nor the ship shall be liable for loss or damage arising or resulting from unseaworthiness unless caused by want of due diligence on the part of the carrier to make the ship seaworthy, and to secure that the ship is properly manned, equipped, and supplied, and to make the holds, refrigerating and cool chambers, and all other parts of the ship in which goods are carried fit and safe for their reception, carriage, and preservation in accordance with the provisions of paragraph (1) of section 3. Whenever loss or damage has resulted from unseaworthiness, the burden of proving the exercise of due diligence shall be on the carrier or other persons claiming exemption under this section.

EXEMPTIONS FROM LIABILITY FROM DESIGNATED CAUSES

(2) Neither the carrier nor the ship shall be responsible for loss or damage arising or resulting from—

(a) Act, neglect, or default of the master, mariner, pilot, or the servants of the carrier in the navigation or in the management of the ship;
(b) Fire, unless caused by the actual fault or privity of the carrier;
(c) Perils, dangers, and accidents of the sea or other navigable waters;
(d) Act of God;
(e) Act of war;
(f) Act of public enemies;
(g) Arrest or restraint of princes, rulers, or people, or seizure under legal process;
(h) Quarantine restrictions;
(i) Act or omission of the shipper or owner of the goods, his agent or representative;
(j) Strikes or lockouts or stoppage or restraint of labor from whatever cause, whether partial or general: PROVIDED, That nothing herein contained shall be construed to relieve a carrier from responsibility for the carrier's own acts;
(k) Riots and civil commotions;
(l) Saving or attempting to save life or property at sea;
(m) Wastage in bulk or weight or any other loss or damage arising from inherent defect, quality, or vice of the goods;
(n) Insufficiency of packing;
(o) Insufficiency or inadequacy of marks;
(p) Latent defects not discoverable by due diligence; and

OTHER CAUSES, NOT THE FAULT OF CARRIER; BURDEN OF PROOF

(q) Any other cause arising without the actual fault and privity of the carrier and without the fault or neglect of the agents or servants of the carrier, but the burden of proof shall be on the person claiming the benefit of this exception to show that neither the actual fault or privity of the carrier nor the fault or neglect of the agents or servants of the carrier contributed to the loss or damage.

SHIPPER NOT RESPONSIBLE FOR DAMAGE TO CARRIER, ETC. WITHOUT FAULT

(3) The shipper shall not be responsible for loss or damage sustained by the carrier or the ship arising or resulting from any cause without the act, fault, or neglect of the shipper, his agents, or his servants.

DEVIATIONS

(4) Any deviation in saving or attempting to save life or property at sea, or any reasonable deviation shall not be deemed to be an infringement or breach of this Act or the contract of carriage, and the carrier shall not be liable for any loss or damage resulting therefrom: PROVIDED, however, That if the deviation is for the purpose of loading or unloading cargo or passengers it shall, prima facie, be regarded as unreasonable.

VALUATION OF CARGO—DECLARATION OF EXCESS VALUE

(5) Neither the carrier nor the ship shall in any event be or become liable for any loss or damage to or in connection with the transportation of goods in an amount exceeding $500 per package lawful money of the United States, or in case of goods not shipped in packages, per customary freight unit, or the equivalent of that sum in other currency, unless the nature and value of such goods have been declared by the shipper before shipment and inserted in the bill of lading.

DECLARATION OF VALUE NOT CONCLUSIVE

This declaration, if embodied in the bill of lading, shall be prima facie evidence, but shall not be conclusive on the carrier.

INCREASED MAXIMUM VALUE CLAUSES AUTHORIZED

By agreement between the carrier, master, or agent of the carrier, and the shipper, another maximum amount than that mentioned in this paragraph may be fixed: PROVIDED, That such maximum shall not be less than the figure above named.

CARRIER'S LIABILITY NOT TO EXCEED ACTUAL DAMAGE

In no event shall the carrier be liable for more than the amount of damage actually sustained.

EFFECT OF MISSTATEMENTS AS TO NATURE OR VALUE OF GOODS

Neither the carrier nor the ship shall be responsible in any event for loss or damage to or in connection with the transportation of the goods if the nature or value thereof has been knowingly and fraudulently misstated by the shipper in the bill of lading.

INFLAMMABLE, EXPLOSIVE, DANGEROUS CARGO—CHARACTER CONCEALED—TREATMENT, DISPOSITION, ETC.

(6) Goods of an inflammable, explosive, or dangerous nature to the shipment whereof the carrier, master, or agent of the carrier, has not consented

with knowledge of their nature and character, may at any time before discharge be landed at any place or destroyed or rendered innocuous by the carrier without compensation, and the shipper of such goods shall be liable for all damages and expenses directly or indirectly arising out of or resulting from such shipment.

INFLAMMABLE, ETC., CARGO—CHARACTER NOT CONCEALED—TREATMENT, DISPOSITION, ETC.

If any such goods shipped with such knowledge and consent shall become a danger to the ship or cargo, they may in like manner be landed at any place or destroyed or rendered innocuous by the carrier without liability on the part of the carrier except to general average, if any.

SURRENDER OF RIGHTS AND IMMUNITIES AND INCREASE OF RESPONSIBILITIES AND LIABILITIES—SEC. 5

U.S. Code, Title 46, Sec. 1305. 49 Stat. 1211

Surrender of Rights—Acceptance of Increased Liabilities Authorized

A carrier shall be at liberty to surrender in whole or in part all or any of his rights and immunities or to increase any of his responsibilities and liabilities under this Act, provided such surrender or increase shall be embodied in the bill of lading issued to the shipper.

ACT NOT APPLICABLE TO CHARTER PARTIES—BUT B/L ISSUED UNDER CHARTER PARTY SHALL COMPLY WITH ACT

The provisions of this Act shall not be applicable to charter parties, but if bills of lading are issued in the case of a ship under a charter party they shall comply with the terms of this Act.

GENERAL AVERAGE CLAUSES AUTHORIZED

Nothing in this Act shall be held to prevent the insertion in a bill of lading of any lawful provision regarding general average.

SPECIAL CONDITIONS—SEC. 6

U.S. Code, Title 46, Sec. 1306. 49 Stat. 1211

Cargo of Unusual Character May Be Carried on Special Terms upon Non-Negotiable Receipts

Notwithstanding the provisions of the preceding sections, a carrier, master or agent of the carrier, and a shipper shall, in regard to any particular goods be at liberty to enter into any agreement in any terms as to the responsibility and liability of the carrier for such goods, and as to the rights and immunities of the carrier in respect of such goods, or his obligation as to seaworthiness (so far as the stipulation regarding seaworthiness is not contrary to public policy), or the care or diligence of his servants or agents in regard to the loading, handling, stowage, carriage, custody, care, and discharge of the goods carried by sea: PROVIDED, That in this case no bill of lading has been or shall be issued and that the terms agreed shall be embodied in a receipt which shall be a non-negotiable document and shall be marked as such.

Any agreement so entered into shall have full legal effect: PROVIDED, That this section shall not apply to ordinary commercial shipments made in the ordinary course of trade but only to other shipments where the character or condition of the property to be carried or the circumstances, terms, and conditions under which the carriage is to be performed are such as reasonably to justify a special agreement.

LIABILITY FOR GOODS PRIOR TO LOADING OR AFTER DISCHARGING FROM SHIP

U.S. Code, Title 46, Sec. 1307. 49 Stat. 1212

SEC. 7. Nothing contained in this Act shall prevent a carrier or a shipper from entering into any agreement, stipulation, condition, reservation, or exemption as to the responsibility and liability of the carrier or the ship for the loss or damage to or in connection with the custody and care and handling of goods prior to the loading on and subsequent to the discharge from the ship on which the goods are carried by sea.

SHIPPING ACT, 1916—LIMITATION OF LIABILITY STATUTES

U.S. Code, Title 46, Sec. 1308. 49 Stat. 1212

SEC. 8. The provisions of this Act shall not affect the rights and obligations of the carrier under the provisions of the Shipping Act, 1916, 39 Stat. 728, 46 U.S. Code 801, or under the provisions of sections 4281 to 4289, inclusive, of the Revised Statutes of the United States; 46 U.S. Code 181–189, or of any amendments thereto; or under the provisions of any other enactment for the time being in force relating to the limitation of the liability of the owners of seagoing vessels.

TITLE II

(Additional Provisions)

DISCRIMINATION BETWEEN COMPETING SHIPPERS NOT PERMITTED

U.S. Code, Title 46, Sec. 1309. 49 Stat. 1212

SECTION 9. Nothing contained in this Act shall be construed as permitting a common carrier by water to discriminate between competing shippers similarly placed in time and circumstances, either (a) with respect to their right to demand and receive bills of lading subject to the provisions of this Act; or (b) when issuing such bills of lading, either in the surrender of any of the carrier's rights and immunities or in the increase of any of the carrier's responsibilities and liabilities pursuant to section 5, title I, of this Act; or (c) in any other way prohibited by the Shipping Act, 1916, 39 Stat. 728, 46 U.S. Code 801, as amended.

THROUGH OCEAN BILLS OF LADING ISSUED BY RAILROAD CARRIERS UNDER INTERSTATE COMMERCE ACT, SUBJECT TO THIS ACT

U.S. Code, Title 49, Sec. 25, 49 Stat. 1212

SEC. 10. Section 25 of the Interstate Commerce Act (41 Stat. 498, 49 U.S. Code 25) is hereby amended by adding the following proviso at the end of paragraph 4 thereof: "PROVIDED, HOWEVER, That insofar as any bill of lading authorized hereunder relates to the carriage of goods by sea, such bill of lading shall be subject to the provisions of the Carriage of Goods by Sea Act."

BULK CARGO—WEIGHTS ASCERTAINED BY THIRD PARTIES

U.S. Code, Title 46, Sec. 1310. 49 Stat. 1212

SEC. 11. Where under the customs of any trade the weight of any bulk cargo inserted in the bill of lading is a weight ascertained or accepted by a third party other than the carrier or the shipper, and the fact that the weight is so ascertained or accepted is stated in the bill of lading, then, notwithstanding anything in this Act, the bill of lading shall not be deemed to be prima facie evidence against the carrier of the receipt of goods of the weight so inserted in the bill of lading, and the accuracy thereof at the time of shipment shall not be deemed to have been guaranteed by the shipper.

HARTER ACT AND ANY OTHER LAW REMAIN APPLICABLE BEFORE LOADING AND AFTER DISCHARGING CARGO

U.S. Code, Title 46, Sect. 1311. 49 Stat. 1212

SEC. 12. Nothing in this Act shall be construed as superseding any part of the Act entitled "An Act relating to navigation of vessels, bills of lading, and to certain obligations, duties, and rights in connection with the carriage of property," approved February 13, 1893, 27 Stat, 445, 46 U.S. Code 190–198, or of any other law which would be applicable in the absence of this Act, insofar as they relate to the duties, responsibilities, and liabilities of the ship or carrier prior to the time when the goods are loaded on or after the time they are discharged from the ship.

SCOPE OF ACT

U.S. Code, Title 46, Sect. 1312. 49 Stat. 1212

SEC. 13. This Act shall apply to all contracts for carriage of goods by sea to or from ports of the United States in foreign trade.

TERMS DEFINED—UNITED STATES

As used in this Act the term "United States" includes its districts, territories, and possessions:

ACTION BY PHILIPPINE LEGISLATURE MAY EXCLUDE APPLICATION

PROVIDED, HOWEVER, That the Philippine Legislature may by law exclude its application to transportation to or from ports of the Philippine Islands.

TERMS DEFINED—FOREIGN TRADE

The term "foreign trade" means the transportation of goods between the ports of the United States and ports of foreign countries.

DOMESTIC, COASTWISE, ETC. TRADE—APPLICATION OF ACT TO B/L BY AGREEMENT

Nothing in this Act shall be held to apply to contracts for carriage of goods by sea between any port of the United States or its possessions, and any other port of the United States or its possessions: PROVIDED, HOWEVER, That any bill of lading or similar document of title which is evidence of a contract for the carriage of goods by sea between such ports, containing an express statement that it shall be subject to the provisions of this Act, shall be subjected hereto as fully as if subject hereto by the express provisions of this Act:

CLAUSE PARAMOUNT—EVERY OUTWARD FOREIGN B/L SHALL STATE THAT IT HAS EFFECT SUBJECT TO THIS ACT

PROVIDED FURTHER, That every bill of lading or similar document of title which is evidence of a contract for the carriage of goods by sea from ports of the United States, in foreign trade, shall contain a statement that it shall have effect subject to the provisions of this Act.

SUSPENSION OF TITLE I BY PRESIDENTIAL PROCLAMATION

U.S. Code, Title 46, Sect. 1313. 49 Stat. 1213

SEC. 14. Upon the certification of the Secretary of Commerce that the foreign commerce of the United States in its competition with that of foreign nations is prejudiced by the provisions, or any of them, of title I of this Act, or by the laws of any foreign country or countries relating to the carriage of goods by sea, the President of the United States may, from time to time, by proclamation, suspend any or all provisions of title I of this Act for such periods of time or indefinitely as may be designated in the proclamation.

RESCISSION OF PROCLAMATION

The President may at any time rescind such suspension of title I hereof, and any provisions thereof which may have been suspended shall thereby be reinstated and again apply to contracts thereafter made for the carriage of goods by sea.

EFFECTIVE DATE OF SUSPENSION OR RESCISSION

Any proclamation of suspension or rescission of any such suspension shall take effect on a date named therein, which date shall be not less than ten days from the issue of the proclamation.

APPLICABLE LAWS DURING SUSPENSION

Any contract for the carriage of goods by sea, subject to the provisions of this Act, effective during any period when title I hereof, or any part thereof, is suspended, shall be subject to all provisions of law now or hereafter applicable to that part of title I which may thus have been suspended.

EFFECTIVE DATE

U.S. Code, Title 46, Sec. 1314. 49 Stat. 1213

SEC. 15. This Act shall take effect ninety days after the date of its approval; but nothing in this Act shall apply during a period not to exceed one year following its approval to any contract for the carriage of goods by sea, made before the date on which this Act is approved, nor to any bill of lading or similar document of title issued, whether before or after such date of approval in pursuance of any such contract as aforesaid.

SHORT TITLE

U.S. Code, Title 46, Sec. 1315. 49 Stat. 1213

SEC. 16. This Act may be cited as the "Carriage of Goods by Sea Act." Approved by the President, April 16, 1936.

Appendix P. York-Antwerp Rules 1950

WITH FOOTNOTES SHOWING CHANGES FROM RULES OF 1924
SUPPLIED BY THE EDITORS OF AMERICAN MARITIME CASES

RULE OF INTERPRETATION

In the adjustment of general average the following lettered and numbered Rules shall apply to the exclusion of any Law and Practice inconsistent therewith.

Except as provided by the numbered Rules, general average shall be adjusted according to the lettered Rules.[1]

[LETTERED RULES].

RULE A. There is a general average act when, and only when, any extraordinary sacrifice or expenditure is intentionally and reasonably made or incurred for the common safety for the purpose of preserving from peril the property involved in a common maritime adventure.

RULE B. General average sacrifices and expenses shall be borne by the different contributing interests on the basis hereinafter provided.

RULE C. Only such losses, damages or expenses which are the direct consequence of the general average act shall be allowed as general average.

Loss or damage sustained by the ship or cargo through delay, whether on the voyage or subsequently, such as demurrage, and any indirect loss whatsoever, such as loss of market, shall not be admitted as general average.[2]

RULE D. Rights to contribution in general average shall not be affected, though the event which gave rise to the sacrifice or expenditure may

[1] The caption "Rule of Interpretation" and both introductory sentences are new, and may be contrasted with 1890 Rule 18, which was abandoned in 1924.

The second introductory sentence embodies the English MAKIS clause, 1929. The purpose of the sentence is to obviate the effect and reasoning of an English decision concerning a vessel named *Makis*, wherein the court decided that the Numbered Rules will be construed to give effect to, and not to contradict, the Lettered Rules. The British underwriters and shipowners desire the opposite view; this desire is expressed in the second sentence. See Lowndes and Rudolf on *General Average*, 7th ed. p. 344.

[2] The second sentence is recast. The general sense remains the same.

have been due to the fault of one of the parties to the adventure; but this shall not prejudice any remedies which may be open against that party for such fault.[1]

RULE E. The onus of proof is upon the party claiming in general average to show that the loss or expense claimed is properly allowable as general average.

RULE F. Any extra expense incurred in place of another expense which would have been allowable as general average shall be deemed to be general average and so allowed[2] without regard to the saving, if

[1] In Lowndes and Rudolf, *op. cit.*, at p. 357, the following passage occurs: "A good deal of discussion took place after the 1924 Rules were published as to the efficacy of Rule D in cases where the Harter Act would apply. The view was held, in the United States particularly, that the use of Rule D by itself would not effect the same result in the United States Courts as the Jason clause. Seeing that the latter was specially drafted to march with the Harter Act, to the extent even of using the same phraseology as far as possible, this view seemed justified. . . . There is nothing really antagonistic between Rule D and the Jason clause in its old, or its revised form, and in the case of shipments to which the Harter Act applies, in connection with which litigation may ensue in the Courts of the United States, there would seem to be no reason why both the 1924 Rules and the Jason clause should not appear in the bill of lading. . . ."

Lowndes and Rudolf's reference to the 1924 Rules would include Rule D.

As the Jason clause has not been written into the 1950 Rules, *it must still be added to every bill of lading* to which the Harter Act might in some respect apply and which might result in litigation in the United States Courts. The present scope of the Harter Act is discussed in Knauth, "Ocean Bills of Lading," 3d ed., 1947, at p. 126–127 and 132–138; that statement differs in some respects from the scope stated in Lowndes and Rudolf at p. 358.

The current text of the Jason clause is as follows:

"In the event of accident, danger, damage, or disaster, before or after commencement of the voyage resulting from any cause whatsoever, whether due to negligence or not, for which, or for the consequence of which, the Carrier is not responsible, by statute, contract, or otherwise, the goods, the shipper and the consignee, jointly and severally, shall contribute with the Carrier in general average to the payment of any sacrifices, losses, or expenses of a general average nature that may be made or incurred, and shall pay salvage and special charges incurred in respect of the goods. If a salving ship is owned or operated by the Carrier, salvage shall be paid for as fully and in the same manner as if such salving ship or ships belonged to strangers."

[2] The following words are new:
"without regard to the saving, if any, to other interests."

any, to other interests, but only up to the amount of the general average expense avoided.

RULE G. General average shall be adjusted as regards both loss and contribution upon the basis of values at the time and place when and where the adventure ends.

This rule shall not affect the determination of the place at which the average statement is to be made up.

[NUMBERED RULES]

RULE I. *Jettison of Cargo.*

No jettison of cargo shall be made good as general average, unless such cargo is carried in accordance with the recognised custom of the trade.

RULE II. *Damage by Jettison and Sacrifice for the Common Safety.*

Damage done to a ship and cargo, or either of them, by or in consequence of a sacrifice made for the common safety, and by water which goes down a ship's hatches opened or other opening made for the purpose of making a jettison for the common safety, shall be made good as general average.

RULE III. *Extinguishing Fire on Shipboard.*

Damage done to a ship and cargo, or either of them, by water or otherwise, including damage by beaching or scuttling a burning ship, in extinguishing a fire on board the ship, shall be made good as general average; except that no compensation shall be made for damage to such portions of the ship and bulk of cargo, or to such separate packages of cargo, as have been on fire.

RULE IV. *Cutting away Wreck.*

Loss or damage caused by cutting away the wreck or remains of spars or other things which have previously been carried away by sea-peril, shall not be made good as general average.

RULE V. *Voluntary Stranding.*

When a ship is intentionally run on shore, and the circumstances are such that if that course were not adopted she would inevitably drive on shore or on rocks, no loss or damage caused to the ship, cargo and freight or any of them by such intentional running on shore shall be made good as general average, but loss or damage incurred in refloating such a ship shall be allowed as general average.

[1] In all other cases where a ship is intentionally run on shore for the common safety, the consequent loss or damage shall be allowed as general average.

RULE VI. *Carrying Press of Sail—Damage to or Loss of Sails.*

Damage to or loss of sails and spars, or either of them, caused by forcing a ship off the ground or by driving her higher up the ground, for the common safety, shall be made good as general average; but where a ship is afloat, no loss or damage caused to the ship, cargo and freight, or any of them, by carrying a press of sail, shall be made good as general average.

RULE VII. *Damage to Machinery and Boilers.*[2]

Damage caused to machinery and boilers of a ship which is ashore and in a position of peril, in endeavoring to refloat, shall be allowed in general average when shown to have arisen from an actual intention to float the ship for the common safety at the risk of such damage; but where a ship is afloat no loss or damage caused by working the machinery and boilers, including loss or damage due to compounding of engines or such measures, shall in any circumstances be made good as general average.[3]

RULE VIII. *Expenses Lightening a Ship when Ashore, and Consequent Damage.*

When a ship is ashore and cargo and ship's fuel and stores or any of them are discharged as a general average act, the extra cost of lightening, lighter hire and reshipping (if incurred), and the loss or damage sustained thereby, shall be admitted as general average.

RULE IX. *Ship's Materials and Stores Burnt for Fuel.*

Ship's materials and stores, or any of them, necessarily burnt for fuel for the common safety at a time of peril, shall be admitted as general average, when and only when an ample supply of fuel had been provided; but the estimated quantity of fuel that would have been consumed, calculated at the price current at the ship's last port of departure at the date of her leaving, shall be credited to the general average.

[1] The introductory word "But" has been deleted.

[2] The caption formerly read:
"Damage to Engines in Refloating a Ship."

[3] The following words are added:
"including loss or damage due to compounding of engines or such measures."
And these words are also added:
"in any circumstances."

RULE X. *Expenses at Port of Refuge, etc.*

(a). When a ship shall have entered a port or place of refuge, or shall have returned to her port or place of loading in consequence of accident, sacrifice or other extraordinary circumstances, which render that necessary for the common safety, the expenses of entering such port or place shall be admitted as general average; and when she shall have sailed thence with her original cargo, or a part of it, the corresponding expenses of leaving such port or place consequent upon such entry or return shall likewise be admitted as general average.

[1] When a ship is at any port or place of refuge and is necessarily removed to another port or place because repairs cannot be carried out in the first port or place, the provisions of this Rule shall be applied to the second port or place as if it were a port or place of refuge. The provisions of Rule XI shall be applied to the prolongation of the voyage occasioned by such removal.

(b). The cost of handling on board or discharging cargo, fuel or stores whether at a port or place of loading, call or refuge, shall be admitted as general average when the handling or discharge was necessary for the common safety or to enable damage to the ship caused by sacrifice or accident to be repaired, if the repairs were necessary for the safe prosecution of the voyage.

(c). Whenever the cost of handling or discharging cargo, fuel or stores is admissible as general average, the cost of reloading and stowing such cargo, fuel or stores on board the ship, together with all storage charges (including[2] insurance, if reasonably[3] incurred) on such cargo, fuel or stores, shall likewise be so admitted. But when the ship is condemned or does not proceed on her original voyage, no storage expenses incurred after the date of the ship's condemnation or of the abandonment of the voyage shall be admitted as general average. In the event of the condemnation of the ship or the abandonment of the voyage before completion of discharge of cargo, storage expenses, as above, shall be admitted as general average up to the date of completion of discharge.

(d). If a ship under average be in a port or place at which it is practicable to repair her, so as to enable her to carry on the whole cargo, and if, in order to save expense,[4] either she is towed thence to some other port or

[1] The entire second paragraph of Rule X (a) is new.
[2] The word "fire" has been deleted.
[3] The word "reasonably" is new.
[4] The word "expenses" has been changed to "expense."

place of repair or to her destination, or the cargo or a portion of it is transshipped by another ship, or otherwise forwarded, then the extra cost of such towage, transshipment and forwarding, or any of them (up to the amount of the extra expense saved) shall be payable by the several parties to the adventure in proportion to the extraordinary expense saved.

RULE XI. *Wages and Maintenance of Crew and Other Expenses bearing up for and in a Port of Refuge, etc.*[1]

(a). Wages and maintenance of master, officers and crew reasonably incurred and fuel and stores consumed during the prolongation of the voyage occasioned by a ship entering a port or place of refuge or returning to her port or place of loading shall be admitted as general average when the expenses of entering such port or place are allowable in general average in accordance with Rule X(a).[2]

(b). When a ship shall have entered or been detained in any port or place in consequence of accident, sacrifice or other extraordinary circumstances which render that necessary for the common safety, or to enable damage to the ship caused by sacrifice or accident to be repaired, if the repairs were necessary for the safe prosecution of the voyage, the wages and maintenance of the master, officers and crew reasonably incurred during the extra period of detention in such port or place until the ship shall or should have been made ready to proceed upon her voyage, shall be admitted in general average. When the ship is condemned or does not proceed on her original voyage, the extra period of detention shall be deemed not to extend beyond the date of the ship's condemnation or of the abandonment of the voyage or, if discharge of cargo is not then completed, beyond the date of completion of discharge.[3]

Fuel and stores consumed during the extra period of detention shall be admitted as general average, except such fuel and stores as are consumed in effecting repairs not allowable in general average.[4]

Port charges incurred during the extra period of detention shall likewise be admitted as general average except such charges as are incurred solely by reason of repairs not allowable in general average.[5]

[1] The words "and other Expenses bearing up for and" have been added.

[2] Rule XI (a) was formerly part of Rule XX (1924).

[3] The text of former Rule XI has been recast as Rule XI (b) with substantially the same meaning.

[4] This paragraph was formerly part of Rule XX (1924).

[5] This paragraph is new.

(c). For the purpose of this and the other Rules wages shall include all payments made to or for the benefit of the master, officers and crew, whether such payments be imposed by law upon the shipowners or be made under the terms or articles of employment.[1]

(d). When overtime is paid to the master, officers or crew for maintenance of the ship or repairs, the cost of which is not allowable in general average, such overtime shall be allowed in general average only up to the saving in expense which would have been incurred and admitted as general average, had such overtime not been incurred.[2]

RULE XII. *Damage to Cargo in Discharging, etc.*

Damage or loss of cargo, fuel or stores caused in the act of handling, discharging, storing, reloading and stowing shall be made good as general average, when and only when the cost of those measures respectively is admitted as general average.

RULE XIII. *Deductions from Cost of Repairs.*

In adjusting claims for general average, repairs to be allowed in general average shall be subject to deductions in respect of "new for old" according to the following rules,[3] where old material or parts are replaced by new.

The deductions to be regulated by the age of the ship from date of original register to the date of accident, except for provisions and stores, insulation, life- and similar boats, gyro compass equipment, wireless, direction finding, echo sounding and similar apparatus, machinery and boilers for which the deductions shall be regulated by the age of the particular parts to which they apply.

No deduction to be made in respect of provisions, stores and gear which have not been in use.[4]

The deductions shall be made from the cost of new material or parts, including labour and establishment charges, but excluding cost of opening up.[4]

Drydock and slipway dues and costs of shifting the ship shall be allowed in full.[4]

No cleaning and painting of bottom to be allowed, if the bottom has not been painted within six months previous to the date of the accident.[4]

[1] Rule XI (c) is new. See former Rule XX.

[2] Rule XI (d) is new. See former Rule XX.

[3] The word "viz" has been deleted and these words have been added: "according to the following rules, where old material or parts are replaced by new."

[4] This paragraph is new.

A.—*Up to 1 year old.*

All repairs to be allowed in full, except scaling and cleaning and painting or coating of bottom, from which one-third is to be deducted.[1]

B.—*Between 1 and 3 years old.*

Deduction off scaling, cleaning and painting bottom as above under Clause A.[2]

One-third to be deducted off sails, rigging, ropes, sheets and hawsers (other than wire and chain), awnings, covers, provisions and stores and painting.[2]

One-sixth to be deducted off woodwork of hull, including hold ceiling, wooden masts, spars and boats, furniture, upholstery, crockery, metal- and glass-ware, wire rigging, wire ropes and wire hawsers, gyro compass equipment, wireless, direction finding, echo sounding and similar apparatus, chain cables and chains, insulation, auxiliary machinery, steering gear and connections, winches and cranes and connections and electrical machinery and connections other than electric propelling machinery; other repairs to be allowed in full.[2]

Metal sheathing for wooden or composite ships shall be dealt with by allowing in full the cost of a weight equal to the gross weight of metal sheathing stripped off, minus the proceeds of the old metal. Nails, felt and labour metalling are subject to a deduction of one-third.[2]

C.—*Between 3 and 6 years.*

Deductions as above under Clause B except that one-third be deducted off wood work of hull including ceiling, wooden masts, spars and boats, furniture, upholstery, and one-sixth be deducted off iron work of masts and spars and all machinery (inclusive of boilers and their mountings).[3]

D.—*Between 6 and 10 years.*

Deductions as above under Clause C, except that one-third be deducted off all rigging, ropes, sheets, and hawsers, iron work of masts and spars, gyro compass equipment, wireless, direction finding, echo sounding and similar

[1] These words are added:
"scaling and cleaning and"

[2] These provisions have been wholly recast.

[3] The word "insulation" has been deleted.

These words have been added:
"wood work of hull including hold ceiling, wooden masts, spars and boats, furniture, upholstery."

apparatus, insulation, auxiliary machinery, steering gear, winches, cranes and connections and all other machinery (inclusive of boilers and their mountings).[1]

E.—*Between 10 and 15 years.*

One-third to be deducted off all renewals, except iron work of hull and cementing and chain cables, from which one-sixth to be deducted, and anchors, which are allowed in full.[2]

F.—*Over 15 years.*

One-third to be deducted off all renewals, except chain cables, from which one-sixth to be deducted, and anchors, which are allowed in full.[3]

RULE XIV. *Temporary repairs.*

Where temporary repairs are effected to a ship at a port of loading, call or refuge, for the common safety, or of damage caused by general average sacrifice, the cost of such repairs shall be admitted as general average.

[4] Where temporary repairs of accidental damage are effected merely to enable the adventure to be completed, the cost of such repairs shall be admitted as general average without regard to the saving, if any, to other interests, but only up to the saving in expense which would have been incurred and allowed in general average if such repairs had not been effected there.

No deductions "new for old" shall be made from the cost of temporary repairs allowable as general average.

[1] The following words have been omitted:
"donkey engines, steam . . . renewal of."
The following words have been added:
"gyro compass equipment, wireless, direction finding, echo sounding and similar apparatus, insulation, auxiliary machinery."

[2] Slight change in the last 7 words. No change in meaning. The words "repairs and" are deleted.

[3] The words "repairs and" are deleted. The remaining words are rearranged without change of sense.
Former Rule XIII-G and all the other paragraphs of Rule XIII (9 in number) are deleted.

[4] The first word "But" is deleted.
Between the words "general average . . . only up to," the following words are new:
"without regard to the saving, if any, to other interests, but"

RULE XV. *Loss of Freight.*

Loss of freight arising from damage to or loss of cargo shall be made good as general average, either when caused by a general average act, or when the damage to or loss of cargo is so made good.

Deduction shall be made from the amount of gross freight lost, of the charges which the owner thereof would have incurred to earn such freight, but has, in consequence of the sacrifice, not incurred.

RULE XVI. *Amount to be made good for Cargo Lost or Damaged by Sacrifice.*

The amount to be made good as general average for damage to or loss of goods sacrificed shall be the loss which the owner of the goods has sustained thereby, based on the market values[1] at the last day of discharge of the vessel or at the termination of the adventure where this ends at a place other than the original destination.

Where goods so damaged are sold and the amount of the damage has not been otherwise agreed, the loss to be made good in general average shall be[2] the difference between the net proceeds of sale and the net sound value at the last day of discharge of the vessel or at the termination of the adventure where this ends at a place other than the original destination.

RULE XVII. *Contributory Values.*

The contribution to a general average shall be made upon the actual net values of the property at the termination of the adventure, to which values shall be added the amount made good as general average for property sacrificed, if not already included, deduction being made from the shipowner's freight and passage money at risk, of such charges and crew's wages as would have been incurred in earning the freight had the ship and cargo

[1] These words are deleted:
"date of the arrival of the vessel."
These words are substituted:
"last day of discharge of the vessel."

[2] These words are deleted:
"calculated by applying to the sound value on the date of arrival of the vessel the percentage of loss resulting from a comparison of the proceeds with the sound value on the date of sale."
These words are substituted:
"the difference between the net proceeds of sale and the net sound value at the last day of discharge of the vessel or at the termination," etc.

been totally lost at the date of the general average act and have not been allowed as general average; deduction being also made from the value of the property of all charges incurred in respect thereof subsequently to the general average act, except such charges as are allowed in general average.

Passengers' luggage and personal effects not shipped under bill of lading shall not contribute in general average.

RULE XVIII. *Damage to Ship.*

The amount to be allowed as general average for damage or loss to the ship, her machinery and/or gear when repaired or replaced shall be the actual reasonable cost of repairing or replacing such damage or loss, subject to deduction in accordance with Rule XIII. When not repaired, the reasonable depreciation shall be allowed, not exceeding the estimated cost of repairs.[1]

Where there is an actual or constructive total loss of the ship the amount to be allowed as general average for damage or loss to the ship caused by a general average act shall be the estimated sound value of the ship after deducting therefrom the estimated cost of repairing damage which is not general average and the proceeds of sale, if any.

RULE XIX. *Undeclared or Wrongfully Declared Cargo.*

Damage or loss caused to goods loaded without the knowledge of the shipowner or his agent or to goods wilfully misdescribed at time of shipment shall not be allowed as general average, but such goods shall remain liable to contribute, if saved.

Damage or loss caused to goods which have been wrongfully declared on shipment at a value which is lower than their real value shall be contributed for at the declared value, but such goods shall contribute upon their actual value.

RULE XX.[2] *Provision of Funds.*

A commission of 2 per cent. on general average disbursements, other than the wages and maintenance of master, officers and crew and fuel stores not replaced during the voyage, shall be allowed in general average, but when the funds are not provided by any of the contributing interests, the necessary cost of obtaining the funds required by means of a bottomry bond or other-

[1] A minor change in arrangement of words does not affect the meaning.

[2] Former Rule XX is deleted. Its content is now found in Rule XI.
New Rule XX is former Rule XXI.

wise, or the loss sustained by owners of goods sold for the purpose, shall be allowed in general average.[1]

The cost of insuring money advanced to pay for general average disbursements shall also be allowed in general average.

RULE XXI.[2] *Interest on Losses made in general average.*

Interest shall be allowed on expenditure, sacrifices and allowances charged to general average[3] at the rate of 5 per cent, *per annum,* until the date of the general average statement, due allowance being made for any interim reimbursement from the contributory interests or from the general average deposit fund.

RULE XXII.[4] *Treatment of Cash Deposits.*

Where cash deposits have been collected in respect of cargo's liability for general average, salvage or special charges, such deposits shall be paid without any delay[5] into a special account[6] in the joint names of[7] a representative nominated on behalf of the shipowner and a representative nominated on behalf of the depositors in a bank to be approved by both. The sum so deposited, together with accrued interest, if any, shall be held as security for payment to the parties entitled thereto of the general average, salvage or special charges payable by cargo in respect to which the deposits have been collected. Payments on account or refunds of deposits may be made if certified to in writing by the average adjuster. Such deposits and payments or refunds shall be without prejudice to the ultimate liability of the parties.

[1] These words are new:
"other than the wages and maintenance of master, officers and crew and fuel and stores not replaced during the voyage."

[2] Formerly Rule XXII.

[3] The following words have been deleted:
"at the legal rate per annum prevailing at the final port of destination at which the adventure ends, or where there is no recognized legal rate."

[4] Formerly Rule XXIII.

[5] The following words are deleted:
"earning interest if possible."

[6] The words "without delay" are new.

[7] The references to trustees and a trust are deleted, and a joint account is provided for. Other changes in wording are minor.

Index

A

Abandonment, 207, 370, 394–395, 424
  acceptance of, 396
    effect of, 397
  may be deferred, 397
  none if loss not due to insured peril, 398
  optional with assured, 397
  promptness of tender of, 396
  purpose of clause, 207
  special form not necessary, 395
  underwriter liable for expense in, 208
  validity of, 395
  of vessel involves freight, 398
  of voyage terminates insurance, 167
Absolute contraband, 329
Accident, unavoidable, 178
Accumulation clause, 352
Additional insurance, 172
Adjusters, general-average, 95, 405, 407
Adjustment of loss, 200
  by appraisal, 378
  basis for, net-value, 377
    salvage, 378, 390
    sound-value, 375
  documents required, for cargo, 381
    for hull, 388
  on freight, 389
  general-average, 405, 407
  of marine salvage, 432
  separate valuations, hulls, 385, 386
  total loss, 392
  war losses, 400
Adventure clause (hulls), 285
Age of discovery, 7
Agent, insurable interest of, 136, 235
  insurance in name of, 141
Agent, managing, 110, 118
  misrepresentation by, 224
Aids to navigation, 34
Air-conditioning systems, 246
Airplanes, 161, 186, 192, 428
  in war risk, 326, 342
All-risks policies, 193
  on flour shipments, 257
  on furs, 253
  losses under, 375
  on mail shipments, 260
American Bureau of Shipping, 76, 98
  The American Record, 100
    page of, 101
  history of, 100
  load lines assigned by, for U.S. Coast Guard, 76
American Cargo War Risk Reinsurance Exchange, 30, 345, 366
American Hull Underwriters' Association, 280, 282
American Institute of Marine Underwriters, 29, 102, 268, 282
  clauses, cargo, 446
    hull, 284
  war cargo policy, 452
American Marine Hull Insurance Syndicate, description of, 103, 281–282
  hull policy form, 455
  origin of, 28, 281
American Record, The, 100, 101
"And arrival," meaning of, 277
Anticipated freight, 286, 320
Antitrust laws, 28
Application (insurance), 128
  and control of policy, 132
  standard form of, 443–444
Apportionment of expenses, particular average on hull, 384

Appraisal of loss, 378, 382
Appraisers' stores, risks in, 161
Arbitrage, 364
Arrests, 188
Assailing thieves, 87, 184–185
Assignment, of policies, 148
  of property under abandonment, 398, 424
Assured, 141, 235
Assurer, 141
"As their respective interests may appear," use of expression, 148
"At and from," 154, 164
Atlantic Inland Association, 280
Atom bombs, 335–336
Atomic age, 31
Atomic power, 69, 294
Attachment of policy, 158–159
  on cargo risks, 159, 164
  on freight risks, 319
  on hull risks, 158, 166
  warehouse-to-warehouse, 160
Attestation clause, 209
Auxiliary vessels, 66, 262, 299
Average adjusters, 95
  definition of, 2, 93
Average clauses, 201, 235
  in builder's-risk form, 304
  in hull policies, 269, 289, 386–388
  in Lake hull form, 292
  in loss adjusting, 374, 386
  purpose of, 202
  and reduction of cost of insurance, 202
  three per cent clause, 270
Averages, use of, in fixing rates, 96

B

Bacterial action, 122
Bad stowage, 29, 91, 123, 193
Balance of trade, 63
  settlement of, 63–64, 261
Ballast, vessels in, 84
Ballast tanks, purpose of, 84
Bare backs (rubber), 229
Bare-boat charter, 54–55, 314
Barges, 295, 298
Barratry, 177, 183
Bars, effect of, on harbor development, 43
Barter as earliest form of trade, 48–49
Battleships, 186
Benefit-of-insurance clauses, 425, 427
Bibliography, 441–442
Bill, of exchange, 51
    collection of, 61
    definition of, 50
    origin of, 49–50
    specimen of, 60
    trading in, 62
  of lading, 51, 91, 373, 426
    adjustment under York-Antwerp Rules, 414, 417, 419
    clause relieving of liability for seaworthiness, 218
    clean, 57
    definition of, 51, 55–56
    determination of liability of carrier by, 56, 404
    insurance of freight, 315
    insured, 258, 424
    on-board, 316
    on-deck, 156
    proof, of interest, 200, 314
      of loss of cargo, 381
    through, 316
    uniform, 57
Binders, 129
Black lists in war, 334
Blanket policies, 140, 150
  advantages of, 151
Block covers, 359
Blockade, deviation permitted, 208
  in time of war, 328
    violation of, as barratry, 183
Board of Underwriters of New York, 29, 102
Bombs, 187, 341–342
Bonded warehouses, 124
  risks in, 161
Bonds in general average, 407, 410, 419
Book policies, 150
Bordereaux, 355
Both-to-blame collision clause, 403
Bottomry, 2

Bottomry bonds, as early form of indemnity, 2
forms distinguished, 3
Grecian Exchange for placing of, 4
laws to regulate, 5–6
lender, insurable interest of, 137, 410
Breach of warranty (hulls), held covered, 289
with respect to innocent parties, 287
Breakage, 90–91, 382
insurance against, 257
Breakwaters to control wave force, 37
Brokers, 110, 128, 371
as aid in progressive underwriting, 113
commissions of, 116
duty of, twofold, 114
early use of, 13, 111
in Great Britain, 119
and guarantee of premiums, 116
misrepresentation by, 224
services of, in losses, 115–116, 371
as specialists in insurance, 112
as underwriters, 117
Bruges as important port, 7
Builder's risks, 280, 303
broad policy form, 303–304
after launching, 304
special clauses and warranties, 304
Syndicate form, 463
Bulk-cargo carriers, 70, 256
Bulk cargoes, coal and ore, 256
insurance of, 160, 229, 245, 256
measurement of, 107
oil, 245
shifted, 80
stowage of, 103
Bullion insurance, 157, 261
Buoyancy, 74
center of, 78, 80
forces of, 79
reserve, 75
Burlaps and bags insurance, 243, 257
Burning, 239

C

Calms, 33
effect of, on sailing vessels, 41
Cancellation of contracts, 129–130, 192, 275
by breach of contract, 167
of cargo risks, 241
clause on, 192, 241
of hull risks, 275
noncancelable policies, 241
of strikes, riots risks, 346
of war risks, 192, 343
Canned and bottled goods insurance, 254
Capacity, dead-weight, 74–75, 81
Carbon dioxide systems, 181
Carfloats, 299
Cargo battens, 70
Cargo vessels, 69
tramps, 54
Cargoes, 65, 88, 307
attachment of policy, 159, 164
bulk (*see* Bulk cargoes)
crushing of, 90
effect on, of design of vessel, 233
of length of risk, 239
of natural forces on vessel, 234
of routes of vessels, 234
of speed of vessel, 233
of type of vessel, 232–234
excepted risks, 213
general and full, 88, 228, 243–245
heating of, 193
insurance of, 157, 227
particular average on, 367
pressure of, 90–91
refrigerated, 90, 92, 157, 250–251
risks after discharge of, 159, 165
separation of damaged goods, 213
shifted, 80, 90
susceptibility of, to damage, 211
under- and on-deck, 228
Carriage of Goods by Sea Act, 57, 123, 136, 177, 307, 427
text of, 509
Carriers, classes of, 426
common, 54
and insurable interest, 136
insurance of, 258, 424
liability of, 89, 91, 423–424
liability clauses of, 206
liability policies of, unvalued, 170, 259

Carriers, losses, 193
responsibility of, 122, 185, 259, 423, 426
Carthaginians, 4, 49
Casting away, 179, 266–267
Catastrophe losses, reinsurance of, 360
war, 325, 337
on yachts, 302
Cause of loss, 374
Cement insurance, 256
Center, of buoyancy, 78, 80
of gravity, 78–80, 244
Certificate, of damage, 201, 232
by appraisal, 378
of enrollment, 200
(*See also* Special policy)
Chafing risks, 123, 193
Charter money insurance, 315
Charter party, 54, 314
forms of, 55
as proof of interest, 200, 314
Chartered or as if chartered in freight insurance, 321
Charterer, insurable interest of, 136
Charts, 34, 103
Civil War, effect of, on marine insurance, 23
Class of vessel, signification of, 98
Classification societies, 98, 223
books and codes, 100, 125, 129
discrimination by, 26, 100
load lines assigned by, 76
rival organizations, 99
sample page, 101
work of, 98, 106
Climate, effect of oceans on, 34
Clipper ships, 22–23
Club insurance, 274, 402
Coal hoists, 299
Coal insurance, 245, 256
Cocoa insurance, 246
Coffee insurance, 246
Coinsurance, 204–205, 375, 378
in general average, 93
in reinsurance, 361
Collapse of docks in shore clause, 193
Collectible freight, 317
loss on, 375, 389
Collision, 90, 178, 239
on builder's risks, 304–305
Collision, legal expenses in cases of, 273
liability adjustment, 403
liability insurance, 272–273, 402
limitation of, 273
liability losses, 402
in time of war, 342
Commerce, definition of, 47
growth of, 33
in Middle Ages, 5
Commercial codes (*see* Law codes)
Commercial documents, 51, 161
Commercial goodwill, 87
Commercial standards, 87
Commission merchant, insurable interest of, 136
Commissions, 136, 140, 157
particular-average, 380
Common carriers (*see* Carriers)
Competition, 22, 29–31, 96, 439
effect of, on rates, 96, 197, 439
with foreign companies, 26
Composite vessels, 65
construction of, 67
Concealed damage, 124
Concealment, 223
in reinsurance, 365
and voiding of policy, 154
Concrete vessels, 65*n*.
Conditional contraband, 329
Congestion hazard, 243
Consignee, has insurable interest, 135
Construction of policies, 130–133
Constructive total loss, 94, 369, 393, 395, 399
definition of, 392
difference between American and British practices in, 394
Consular invoice, 54
Contingent risks, 324
Contraband, absolute and conditional, 329
of war, 206, 328, 345
Contract of marine insurance, elements of, 125
imperfect contract of indemnity, 121
rules for construction of, 130
early, to be enrolled, 9, 12
to be in writing, 9

Contract of sale, 50
and relation of buyer and seller, 53
Contracts of marine insurance, as effected by mail, 133
avoidance of, 224
cancellation and modification of, 129
Contributory values in general average, 289, 411–412
Convoy ships, 331
"Cornering the market" prohibited by law, 146–147
Corporate underwriting, 125, 141
capital invested in, 27
companies first organized, 14, 19
failures, 22
foreign competition, 26
monopoly in, 14
efforts to break, 17–18
mutual companies, 24
in United States, 21, 125, 141
Cost and freight (c. & f.) sales, 51
description of, 52
Cost, insurance, and freight (c.i.f.) sales, 51, 204, 349
description of, 53
Cost sales, definition of, 51
Cotton insurance, 246–247
Countersignature of policy, 133
Country damage, 247
Coxwold case, 339, 372
Craft clause, 159, 241
Cross liabilities, 273, 403
Crusades, effect of, on early trade, 5, 48
Crushing of cargo, 90
Currency insurance, 260–261
Currents, ocean, 32
effects of, on climate, 40
on harbor development, 40
on ocean routes, 35
on shipping, 39
and ocean streams, 33, 40
Customhouse, risks in, 161
Customs and usages, in commercial transactions, 53, 131
and adaptation of marine insurance to, 229–230
in marine insurance, 2, 8, 19–20, 130, 225
Cutting away wreck in general average, 416
Cyclones, 193

D

Dairy products insurance, 254
Darkness, effect of, on marine insurance, 42, 234
Dead freight, 318
Dead-weight capacity, 74–75, 81
Deckloads (*see* On-deck cargoes)
Declaration, of London, 327–328, 331
of Paris, 327
Deductible-average clauses, 201
on Great Lakes form, 292
in hull insurance, 284
Definition of marine insurance, in general, 121
in New York State, 137
Delay, 122, 373
not cause of loss, 375
and right to abandon, 399
in transit, 122, 161, 176
and voiding of contract, 220
Delivery in specie, 52, 316, 390
(*See also* Freight)
Demand for goods, 48
Demurrage, 273
Derailment, 193
Derrick barges, 299
Destroyers, 186
Detainments, 188
Deterioration, 122
Deviation, 162
clause on, 162, 169, 242
doctrine of "no deviation," 167–168, 208
in event of blockade, 208
occurrence of, 168
Diesel-type engine, 65, 293
fire hazard on vessels with, 181
in fishing trade, 66, 300
in yachts, 300
Difference in conditions, insurance covering, 205
Disbursements insurance, 140, 278
disbursements warranty, 285
policy form, 466
purpose of, 285

Disbursements insurance, Syndicate clause, 286–288
Displacement, 73, 79, 106
Displacement curve, 73
Distributing marine losses, 1
Doctrine, of *ejusdem generis,* 189, 373
 of proximate cause, 175
  (*See also* Proximate cause)
 of ultimate destination, 332
Documents, in commercial transactions, 51
 duplicate, use of, in losses, 382
 in loss adjusting, cargo, 381, 402
  general-average, 419
  hull, 388, 402
 negotiation of, 58, 148–149
 as symbols of ownership, 59
 transfer of, 59
Doldrums, effect of, on ocean navigation, 36
Double insurance, 203
 contingent insurance not, 324
 in Great Britain, 204
 unusual, 204
Downhill to Europe, 37
Draft (*see* Bill of exchange)
Dredges, 299
Dressed meats insurance, 251
Dual-valuation clauses, 266
Due course of transit, 124, 161
 premium based on, 240
Duration of risk, effect of, on rate of premium, 240
Duties, in general average, 412
 insurance of, 322–323
 particular average on, 375–376
 payment of, 53, 161

E

Earthquakes, as cause of tidal waves, 39
 excluded from builder's-risk policy, 305
 hazard of, 90
Economic Cooperation Administration (ECA), effect of, on marine insurance, 30
Eddies, tidal, 39
Ejusdem generis, doctrine of, 189, 373
Electric-drive engines, 72
Enemies, 187
Engines, 72, 293
 damage to, in general average, 416
 turbine, 65, 72, 294
 turbogas, 69, 294
Errors of judgment, effect of, on insurance, 177
Ex-dock sales, 165
Excess reinsurance, excess-of-line, 355–357
 excess-of-loss, 358–359
Explosion clause, 190
Express companies, liability of, 428
Express warranties, 218, 222
 loading, 269
 pertaining to material conditions, 222
 trading, 268
Extension into port on hull policies, 277
External-cause clause, 193
 in insurance of furs, 253
 losses under, 375
Extrinsic evidence in construction of policies, 132

F

Factor (commission merchant), insurable interest of, 136
Factors in marine underwriting, 98
Facultative reinsurance, 354, 362
Falling markets, effect of, on insurance, 232
Federal Maritime Commission, 102
Ferryboats, 299
Fire protection, 68, 180–181, 233
Fires at sea, 90, 180
 full cargoes, 245
 general average, 415
 serious hazard of, 245, 257
Fishing vessels, 295, 299
Flat reinsurance, 362
Fleet insurance, 262–263
 attachment of, 166
Floods as shore-risk peril, 90, 193
Flour insurance, 257

Fog, cold, to control fires, 182
effect of, on marine insurance, 41, 176, 234
"For account of," purpose of phrase, 144
Fore-and-aft rigged ships, 66
Fortuitous losses, 121, 189
Franchise, meaning of, 201
question of, in losses, 374
Fraud, 176, 224, 226
in bottomry, 6
in falling markets, 232
in letters of indemnity, 58
losses due to, 176
prevention of, by Lloyd's agents, 18
rules for, 7
unethical practices, 146
in United States, 22
in valuation, 170, 378
and voiding of policy, 154, 224
Free-alongside (f.a.s.) and free-on-board (f.o.b.) sales, description of, 51, 324
Free-of-British-capture clause, 333
Free-of-capture clause, 189, 335
in builder's-risk policy, 305
Free-of-particular-average (F.P.A.) clauses, 203, 205, 213, 235, 371, 398
F.P.A.A.C. (free-of-particular-average-American-conditions) and F.P.A.E.C. (free-of-particular-average - English - conditions), 236
F.P.A.E.C. clause, amended, 237
effect of, 236–237
nullifying of warranty, 238
Freeboard, 75, 107
Freezing of liquids, 90
Freight, 28, 65
amount insured, 322
anticipated, 320
attachment of risk, 319
bill of lading, 315
on board or not on board, 321
chartered or as if chartered, 321
collectible, 317
as contingent interest, 318
dead, 318
delivery in specie, 52, 316, 395
Freight, future, 320
in general average, 417
guaranteed, 313
insurance of, 140, 157, 227
involvement of, by abandonment of vessel, 398
meaning of, 310
net, 312
particular average on, 376, 389
prepaid and guaranteed, 313
pro rata itineris peracti, 312, 389
termination of risk on, 322
when earned, 311
Freight contingency, 317, 322–323
loss on, 390
Freight list, 200, 316
Fresh-water damage, 193
Frigorificos (hides) insurance, 253
Frozen goods, 157, 251, 254
Fruits insurance, 249
Frustration clause, 341
Fuel oil, 70
damage due to, 91, 193
Full cargoes, 228, 243–245
Full form hull insurance, 266, 278
Full interest admitted (F.I.A.), in disbursements insurance, 285
in freight insurance, 320
in hull insurance, 279
Full market, 146
Furs insurance, 253
Future freights, 320

G

Gambling policies, 127
British Act, 20
Lloyd's organized to stop, 15
Gas engines in yachts, 301
General average, 369–370, 405
contributory values, 93, 290, 411–412
definition of, 2, 94, 405
as early form of insurance 2, 94
elements necessary for, 408
guarantee, 116, 407, 419, 506
jettison, 182
justification for, 406
laws on, nonuniformity of, 407
in memorandum clause, 209
no reasonable substitute for, 406

General average, part must be saved in, 409
reasons for, 95
reference to, in cargo policy, 213
in hull policy, 278
sample statement, 419–422
statement of value, 503
valuation, 93
and voluntary sacrifice, 410
General-average adjusters, 95, 405, 407
General-average adjustment, 410
General-average bond, 116, 407, 419, 504–505
General order stores, risks in, 161
Genoese, 5
Good faith, 108, 125, 127, 154, 223
Government insurance, 345
Government price control, effect of, on war risks, 336, 346
Grain elevators, 299
Grain insurance, 248–249
on Great Lakes, 292
Great Lakes Protective Association, 290
Gregorios case, 179
Gridiron (load line), 75–77
Gross tonnage, 106
Guaranteed freight, 313
Guidon de la Mer, 8
Gum insurance, 254

H

Hague Conferences on arbitration, 327
Hague Rules, 57, 123, 427
text of, 509
Hanseatic League, 5–7, 9, 11
in Steelyard, 9
Harbors, 37, 42, 234
types of, 43–46
Harter Act, 177, 259, 307, 427
text of, 507
Hazards, 87, 89–90
Heating of cargo, 193
Heavy-oil engine, 293
Hemp insurance, 243, 249
Hides and skins insurance, 252
Highest-market-value clauses, 171, 373
Hook-hole damage, 123, 193, 382
Hull, 65, 262
attachment of risk, 158, 166
builder's risk, 303
cancellation of policy, 130
dual-valuation clause, 266
insurance of, 140, 157, 227, 262
Lake vessels, 290
particular average on, 383, 386
premium rates, 282–284
single vessels and fleets, 262–263
small craft, 295
special forms for, 280
Syndicate forms, 284
valuations, 173, 265, 385
wooden vessels, 292
yachts (pleasure craft), 300
Hull associations, 280
Hull voyage, definition of, 387
Hurricanes, as marine hazard, 36, 90, 193, 234
power of, 38

I

Ice, effect of, on marine insurance, 41–42, 106, 234
on ocean routes, 37
Icebergs as serious marine peril, 42
Illicit or prohibited trade, 206
Implied warranties, 125, 215
breach of, excusing of, 221
of legal conduct of voyage, 215
may be made express warranty, 218, 221
of no deviation, 221
other, 221
of prompt attachment, 220
of seaworthiness, 215
waiver of, 215, 218
Improper handling, 29
Inchmaree clause, on builder's risks, 305
on cargo risks, 180
on hull risks, 271–272, 386
Increased values, 171–172
Individual underwriters, 13, 16, 111, 125
at Lloyd's, 13
in United States, 20, 141

Inherent vice, 122, 176, 219
carrier not liable for, 259
in particular average, 375
Inland marine insurance, 137–138
Inquiries, 129
Institute trading warranties, 268
Insurable interest, 126
definite description of, 145
existence of, 146
extent of, 134
in freight risks, 319
necessity for actual, 134
persons having, 135–137
in reinsurance, 351
Insurance, 6
additional, 172
Chamber of, in Bruges, 7
commercial transactions made possible through, 86
early forms of, 2
effect of, 96
first use of word, 6
government, 345
marine (*see* Marine insurance)
origin of, 1
and restoration of property, 214
subject matter of, 155
(*See also* specific types of insurance)
Insurance certificate (*see* Special policy)
Insurance companies, first organization of, 14, 16
new, in England, 19
in United States, 21
Insurance Exchange in Greece, 3
Insurance law, British Marine Insurance Act, 20
first decisions, 19
first English statute, 12
in New York State, 137
in United States, 27
(*See also* Law codes and rules)
Insurance policy, first English, 9
Lloyd's, 16
proof of loss, cargo, 381
hull, 388
provision for adjustment under York-Antwerp Rules, 414
Insurance textbooks, *Guidon de la Mer,* 8
Internal-combustion engines, 72
International law, observation of, 331
war perils judged by, 327
Invoice, 50
consular, 54
definition of, 51
proof of loss, 381
terms of sale in, 51, 373
Iron in shipbuilding, 23, 67
Isherwood system, 70

J

Jettison, 2, 90, 182, 406, 408, 415
early example of, 1
Jute insurance, 249

K

"Kings, princes, or people" in perils clause, 189

L

Labels clause, 379
Labor risks, 190, 346
"Laden or to be laden," meaning of, 157, 159
Lake time clauses, 290
Lake vessels, 67, 71
Large limits and reinsurance, 349
Latent defect (*see* Inchmaree clause)
Launching risks in builder's-risk form, 303
Law, of inertia, 79
of insurance (*see* Insurance law)
of place in construction of policies, 133
Law codes and rules, Barcelona, 7
first English, 12, 19–20
"Laws of Wisby," 5
Lombards, 10–11
Recessi (Lübeck), 5
Rhodian, 2, 408
in United States, 27
Lawful goods, 155
Lay-up return premiums, 275–277
Lay-up warranties on Lakes, 292

Lead for sounding, 34
Leads in placing risks, 278
League of Nations, 340
Leakage losses, 90, 176, 250
  on animal oils, 250
  insurance of leakage risks, 257
  risk of, excepted in policy, 214
  on tank cargoes, 245
Legal conduct, 92
  implied warranty of, 215
Legal expenses in collision cases, 273
Legality of contract, 125–127
Letters, of credit, 62
  of indemnity, against clean bill of lading, 57
    for outstanding documents, 382
  of mart and countermart, 187
Liabilities, cross, 273, 403
Liability, of carriers, 89, 426
    insurance of, 151
  limitation of, in collision cases, 272–273
    in reinsurance, 353
  of warehousemen, 89
Liability policies, 140
  unvalued, of carriers, 151–152
Licenses, export and import, 54
  government permits, 64, 92
Lighterage risks, 90, 159–160, 241
Lighthouses, 34
Lightning, 90, 178
Limitation of liability (*see* Liability)
Line cards 359
Liners, 54, 69
Livestock insurance, 156, 252
Lloyd's, London, brokers at, 111
  Grecian Exchange similar to, 4
  organization of, 15
  posting of missing vessels at, 401
  records of, 104
  reorganization of, 17
  system of commercal intelligence, 17
  underwriting at, 126
Lloyd's agents, 18, 379
Lloyd's Classification Society, 98
Lloyd's coffee house, 13
Lloyd's List, control by Lloyd's, London, 15
  publication of, 13
Lloyd's News, 13
Lloyd's Register of Shipping, 98–99
Load lines, 75, 91, 217
  gridiron, Lake vessels, 77
    ocean vessels, 76
  legislation on, 75–77
  modification of, during war, 78
Loading of vessels, 81, 91, 105
Loading warranties, 269
Loan receipts, 260, 425, 429
Local agents, 119
Log of vessel, 200, 419–420
Lombard Street, 11
Lombards, 6–7, 9–12
Longitudinal framing, 70
Longshoremen's and Harbor Workers' Compensation Insurance, 301
Loran, 34, 233
Lord Mansfield, father of insurance law, 20
Loss of market, 373
Loss adjusting, 368–369
  general-average, 369, 410
  in reinsurance, 353
Loss cost per ton, 283, 436–437
Loss orders, 149
Losses, 94, 367, 374, 433
  adjustment of, 200, 367
  catastrophe (*see* Catastrophe losses)
  cause of, 374
  definition of situation involving, 393
  doubtful, 339
  due to fraud, 176
  fortuitous, 121, 189
  general-average, 369
  not covered by policy, 176, 372
  not insured, 372
  particular-average, 367, 369, 413, 417
  payable in foreign countries, 9, 149
  payment under loan receipt, 260
  preventable, 88
  proof and payment of, 200, 381
  salvage, 378, 390
  separation of damaged goods, 214
  services of broker in 115–116, 120
  total loss, 369, 392
    of part, 369
  war, 400

"Lost or not lost," in freight insurance, 313
  meaning and use of words, 153, 209
Lumber cargoes insurance, 255

M

Machinery, claims on, 271, 385–386
  damage to, as peril of sea, 90
  insurance of, as cargo, 257
    as hull, 266
Machinery clause, 257, 380
Mail insurance, 260
Malicious mischief in strikes, riots clause, 191, 346
Managing agents, 110, 118
Manifest, 58, 316, 419
Marine engine, 68
  in general average, 416
  types of, 72, 293
Marine extension clauses, 162, 241
Marine hazards, 35
Marine insurance, adaptation of, to trade customs, 229
  cooperation with United States government, 29
  definition of, 121, 137–138
  effect of, 96
  in England, 9
  first law statute on, 12, 19, 20
  foreign competition in, 26
  growth of, 15, 27
  inland, 137–138
  mutual companies, 24
  necessity of, to overseas trade, 50
  new factors in, 31
  not exact science, 434
  origin of, 1, 6, 50
  in United States, 20–23, 26–29
  well established in fifteenth century, 8
Marine Insurance Act, 1906, of Great Britain, 20, 178
    attachment of risk, 159
    brokers in Great Britain, 119
    contributory values, 290
    double insurance, 204–205
    form of policy, 141
    kings, princes, or people, 189
    text of, 468
Marine Insurance Gambling Policies Act, 1909, history of, 20
  text of, 501
Marine protection and indemnity insurance (*see* Protection and indemnity insurance)
Marine salvage, 430
  "no-cure-no-pay" agreement," 431
  (*See also* Salvage)
Mariner's compass, 7
Maritime interest, on bottomry or respondentia bonds, 3
  rate of, fixed in Rome, 4
Market-value clauses, 171
"Marrying" of war clauses, 340
Master of vessel, 104, 157, 264
  master's receipt, 200, 316
Measurement of ships, 106
  cargo capacity, 107
Medical-payments insurance on yachts, 301
Memorandum clause, 209, 235
  purpose of, 211–214, 373–374
Men-of-war, 186
Mercantile customs (*see* Customs and usages)
Merchant marine, decline of, 23, 26
  organization of Syndicates, 281
  revival of, 28
  in United States, 22
Metacenter, 80
  in vessels in ballast, 84
Metacenter height, control of, 81, 244
Metal vessels, 65
  construction of, 67–68
Metals and minerals insurance, 255
Mines, 187, 338, 341
Misrepresentation, 223, 365
Missing vessels, 8
  cause of loss, 401
  reinsurance of, 365
  in time of war, 338, 400–401
Monopoly of corporate underwriting, 14–17
  repeal of, 18
Monsoons as marine hazard, 36
Moral hazard, 108, 117, 230
  effect of valued policies, 170

Moral hazard, in ownership of vessels, 104, 263
Mortgagee, effect of wrongdoing by assured on, 179, 288
insurable interest of, 135
as payee of loss 148
Motor trucks, liabilities of, 423, 429
risks, 161, 192
Motor vessels, 262, 293
(*See also* Yachts)
Mutual marine insurance companies, 24–25

N

Nationalistic insurance schemes, 31
Nationality, 103
Natural decay, loss due to, 176
Natural law, 33
Navigation, 32
aids to, 34
Negligence, 122, 177, 196, 425
Negligence clause (*see* Inchmaree clause)
Negotiaton of documents, 58, 148–149
Net freight, 265, 312
Net tonnage, 106
Net-value adjustment, 377
Netherlands Overseas Trust, 332, 334
Neutrality Act (1937), 345
"No-cure–no-pay" in marine salvage, 431
"No deviation" doctrine, 167–168, 208
Noncancelable policies, 241
in reinsurance, 360
Nondelivery losses, 382
Nondelivery risks, 185
Notice of loss, 371

O

Ocean barges, 295, 298
Ocean currents (*see* Currents)
Ocean distances, 35
Ocean navigation, 33
Oceans, effect of, on climate, 34
Office of Price Administration (OPA) control of war rates, 346
Oil, damage from, 123, 382
use of, to control waves, 38
Oil cargoes, insurance of, 245, 257
Omnibus clause, 189
"On board or not on board," 321
On-deck cargoes, 90, 155, 228
in general average, 415
in lumber trade, 255
unsafe deckloads, 8, 244
Open policies, 58, 133, 140
attachment of risk, 154, 158
cancellation clause, 130
explanation of, 149
not "catchall," 144
reinsurance of, 350
special policies under, 148
tailor-made, 150
Order documents, bill of lading, 56
to destroy negotiability, 149
draft or bill of exchange, 60
special policy, 58, 148
Ordinary transit (*see* Due course of transit)
Ore insurance, 256
Overinsurance (*see* Double insurance)
Overloading of vessels, 8, 78, 244
Overseas trade, British, 10
in United States, 22–23, 27
Ownership of vessels, 104
change of, 264
insurable interest of owner, 135
in time of war, 331

P

Packer's list, proof of contents, 382
Packing of goods, 29, 47, 87, 107
control of, by physical environment, 229
improper, 258
Parcel-post insurance, 260
Partial loss, particular and general average distinguished, 2
Participating reinsurance, 355
Particular average, 367, 370, 383, 412
adjustment of, by appraisal, 378
salvage, 378, 424
sound-value, 375–378
combined with general average, 413
definition of, 2, 94, 370

Particular average, on duty, 376
on freight, 389–391
on hull, 383, 386
unrepaired damage, 388
on profits and commissions, 380
retention of property by assured, 424
Particular charges, 371, 412
Payee of loss, 148
Payment of loss in foreign countries, 9, 149
Pegged currencies, 171
Perils of and on sea, 176–178
Perils clause, 174–175, 371
Permanent covers in Great Britain, 152
Phoenicians, 4
Physical forces, effect of, on marine insurance, 32–33, 35
Pilferage, 29, 87, 90, 123, 184, 253, 382
Pirates, 184, 186
as war peril, 186
Pleasure craft (*see* Yachts)
Plimsoll mark, 78, 217
Policy (marine-insurance), 121, 139, 433
assignment of, 148
book, 150
countersignature of, 133
form of, British, 496
necessity for basic, 227, 282
specimen cargo, 142–143
standard, adoption of, in Great Britain, 16, 141
none in United States, 140
modern, broadness of, 124
rules for construction of, 130, 498
signature of, 209
special, 58–59, 140
types of, 139
in United States, 140
war-cargo, 452
Policy proof of interest (P.P.I), in disbursements insurance, 285
in freight insurance, 320–321
in hull insurance, 279
Pool reinsurance, 362–363
Port of refuge, sale of goods at, 231
Port-risk insurance, 279
Posting at Lloyd's, missing vessels, 401
Postseason navigation on Great Lakes, 291
Power boats (*see* Yachts)
Preemption, 332
Premium charge, 121, 126, 197, 282, 433
based on ordinary transit, 240
clause in policy, 197
on duty insurance, 323
earned when risk attaches, 198, 323
effect of competition on, 439
P and I insurance, 309
payment not guaranteed by broker, 116
quotations by Syndicates, 282
rates in Great Britain, 198
on risk insured after arrival, 209
uniform rate desirable, 211
valid consideration, 126
war risks, 345
Prepaid freight, principle of, 313
Pressure of cargo, 90–91
Printed, written, and stamped words, relative importance of, 131
Prior loss under excess reinsurance, 357
Prior-loss clause, 154, 173
Privateers, 187
Processes of trade, 47
Products, of agriculture, 230, 246
of animals, 246, 250
of forest, 230, 246, 254
of manufacturers, 246, 256
of mines, 230, 246, 255
Profits, 140, 157, 171–172
particular average on, 380
Prolongation of transit, 122
clause on, 250
Prompt attachment of risk, and delay, 220
implied warranty of, 220
Proof of interest and loss, 199, 200, 381, 388
Protection and indemnity insurance (P and I), 274, 306
on builder's risks, 305
on damage, to cargo, 307
to other property, 308
definition of, 306

Protection and indemnity insurance (P and I), form of policy, 308
government regulations on, 308
on injury to persons, 307
liability policy, 306
rates for, 309
on yachts, 301
Protest of master, 200, 380, 389, 402, 419
Provincial Schooner Association, 281
Proximate cause, 122, 175, 179, 190, 201, 236–237, 372
explanation of doctrine, 175

Q

Quota-share reinsurance, 354

R

Races (tidal), 39
Racial characteristics, effect of, on insurance, 230
Radar, 34, 233
Radio, 3
as aid to navigation, 34
effect of, on sue-and-labor clause, 196
Raiders, 342
Railroads, liabilities of, 423, 428
Rating laws and marine insurance, 434
Rats on shipboard, 178
Reciprocating engine, 72
Reefs, effect of, on harbor development, 43
Refrigerated cargo, 90, 92, 157, 250–251
Register of insurance, in England, 12
in France, 9
Registered-mail insurance, 260
Reinstatment clause in blanket policies, 151
Reinsurance, 30, 280, 347, 433
claim of original assured on, 366
definition of, 348, 354
excess-of-line, 355–357
excess-of-loss, 358–359
Reinsurance, facultative, 354, 362
flat, 362
foreign and domestic, 366
growth of, 348
insurable interest of underwriter, 137, 351
loss adjusting in, 353
noncancelable policies in, 360
of open policies, 350
of overdue vessels, 365
of partially terminated risks, 364
participating, 355
principles and purpose of, 351
quota-share, 354
representation in, 365
special, 362
in statistical records, 438
subject to, acts of reassured, 353
original conditions and rates, 363
syndicates or pools, 362–363, 366
types of contracts, 354
of undesirable risks, 364
of unterminated risks, 365
Reinsurance clause, 351
Repair yard, builder's-risk form, 280, 303
insurable interest of contractor, 136
Representation, 223
disclosures in, 224–225
effect of, 224
implications in, 225
in reinsurance, 365
Reprisals, 188
Respondentia bond, 3
insurable interest of lender, 137, 410
Restraints, 188
Restriction of navigation limits, on Great Lakes, 291
on yachts, 302
Retained line, meaning of, 350
not limited by law, 353
Return premium, 198
in basic policy form, 210
builder's-risk, 305
in Great Britain, 120
lay-up, 275–277
for overinsurance, 204
standard form for claiming, 445
Right of search in war, 331

Risk after discharge from vessel, 165
duration of, and rate of premium, 240
River and harbor craft, 72, 295, 298
"Roaring forties," effect of, on ocean navigation, 36
Romans, 4
Rosin insurance, 255
Rovers, 184, 186
Royal Exchange, 11, 15
Rubber insurance, 229, 254
Rules for construction of contracts, 130
in Great Britain, 498
Running-down clause (*see* Collision)

S

Sabotage in strikes, riots clause, 191, 346
Safety at sea, 75, 91
Sailing vessels, 66, 262
difficulties of construction, 66–67
in general average, 416
insurance of, 292
Sales at port of refuge, 231
ex-dock, 165
types of, 50–54
Salt insurance, 255
Salvage, definition of, 398, 424, 430
(*See also* Marine salvage)
Salvage associations, 103, 281
Salvage loss, 378, 390
Sanctions, 340
Schedule rating in insurance of cotton, 247
Scrip certificates, 24
redemption of, 24
Sea codes (*see* Law codes)
Sea train, special type, 71
Sea-water damage, 90, 178
Seaquakes as cause of waves, 39
Seaworthiness, implied warranty of, 157, 177, 215
at inception of risk, 217
no fixed standard of, 216
not applicable to time hull risks, 217
proof of breach, 219
tests of, 216
Seaworthiness, of vessel, not cargo, 219
waiver of warranty, 218
Securities insurance, 157, 260–261
Seizure by friendly government, 343
Self-insurance, 97, 367
Self-trimming vessels, 70–71
Separate valuations, in adjustment of particular average, 385–386
in hull policies, 173, 266, 384
Share reinsurance, 355
Shifted cargoes, 80, 90
Shifting boards, 105, 248
Shipbuilding, 65, 98
Shipments, tracing of, 316
Shippers, responsibility of, 87, 90
Shipping documents, 47, 51
Shoals, effect of, on harbor development, 43
Shore risks, 159, 165, 192
clause on, 192
reinsurance of, 361
and war risks, 325, 337
Short-rate table, 279
Sideboard in insurance office, 16
Silk insurance, 253
Single-vessel risks, 262–263
attachment of, 166
Sinking, 90, 178, 238
Sister-ship clause, 403
Skimmings clause, 246
Small craft, 295
Smoke-detection systems, 181
Sonic depth finders, 34
Sound-value adjustments, 375–376
specimen of, 377
Spanish-American War, effect of, on marine insurance, 26
Special charges, 371
Special policy, definition of, 51
evidence of insurance, 133
issued under open policies, 58
proof of loss, 381
reason for, 59
for single risk, 140
transferring payment of loss, 148
wording of form, 448
Special reinsurance, 362
Specie insurance, 157
Spontaneous combustion, 176, 245

Spread-loss cover, 360
Square-rigged ships, 66
Stability of vessels, 72, 78
Stamp Act in Great Britain, 152
Standard form of policy, adopted by Lloyd's, London, 16
in Great Britain, 141, 496
none in United States, 140
Statement of value, form for, 503
in general average, 419
Statistics, 368, 433, 435
adjustment of deductions, 438
specimen of hull, 436–437
Steamship routes, 37
Steamships, 262, 294
earliest types of, 23
liabilities as carriers, 423
special designs for, 71
Steel vessels, modern, 68
steel supersedes iron, 67–68
Steelyard, 9
Stevedoring, 81, 185
improper, 193
minimizing of strains, 82
smoking during loading, 245, 249
Stiff vessels, 80, 256
Stipulations, 222
Storms (periodic), 36, 106
effect of, on insurance, 176
Stowage of cargoes, bad, 29, 91, 123, 193
loading problems, 81
and losses 382
Stranding, 90, 178, 238
general average, 416
necessary conditions in, 289, 386
Stresses and strains 81–85
Strikes, riots, and civil commotions, 346
in builder's-risk policy, 305
clause on, 190
Subject matter of insurance, 155
Submarines, 186, 342
Subrogation, 172, 193, 423
distinguished from abandonment, 207
Sue-and-labor clause, 195–196, 259, 371, 393
applies to specific property, 196
Sue-and-labor clause, enforcement of rights by assured, 196, 428
waiver clause, 195
Sugar insurance, 243, 249, 393
Supercargo, 195
Surprisals as war peril in British policy, 188
Surveyors, 102, 382, 389, 419–420
Surveys of vessels, periodical, 99
Sweat damage, 193, 246, 382
Symbols, of ownership, 59
of value, 49
Syndicate, American Marine Hull Insurance, description of, 103, 281–282
hull forms, 264, 284
origin of, 28, 281
reinsurance by, 366
text, of builder's-risk form, 463
of disbursements form, 466
of hull form, 455
Syndicates, cargo reinsurance by, 362, 366

T

Taint damage, 193, 213
Takings at sea, 188
Tank cargoes, 245
Technical total loss (*see* Constructive total loss)
Technical words, use of, in policies, 131
Telephone, ship-to-shore, 34
Temporary repairs, 384
Tender of abandonment, 395–396
Tender vessels, 80
Tenders for repairs, 285, 385
Termini of policies, 154, 262
attachment of risk, 158–159, 166
by breach of contract, 167
freight risk, 319, 322
risks after discharge, 165
termination of risk, until safely landed, 159
Terms, of cost and freight sales, 52
of cost, insurance, and freight sales, 53
of cost sales, f.o.b. and f.a.s., 51
as shown by invoice, 50–51

Theft, 29, 87, 90, 123, 184, 253, 382
Thieves, 87, 184–185
Third-party interests, 179
Third-party liabilities, 402, 423
Thirds off, 270
  in general average, 417
  in particular average, 383
  on wooden sailing vessels, 293
Tidal eddies and tidal waves caused by seaquakes, 39
Tides, 35
  effect of, on harbor development, 40
    on shipping, 39
Tonnage of vessels, 106
Torpedoes, 187
Total loss, 94, 369–370, 392, 399
  assignment of property, 398, 424
  of cargo, 399
  definition of, 392
  of freight, 400
  of part, 94, 369–370
  on salvage basis, 378
  of vessel, 399
  in war, 400
"Total-loss-only" forms in hull insurance, 278
  (*See also* Disbursements)
"Touch-and-go," 238
Tracing of shipments, 316
Trade, balance of, 63
  illicit or prohibited, 206
  processes of, 47
  types of, 49
Trade customs, 229–230
Trade routes, 229–230
  effect of natural conditions on, 32–33
  opening of new, 48
Trade winds, effect of, on ocean navigation, 36
Trading with the enemy, 183, 333
Trading warranties, 262, 268, 285
  on Great Lakes, 291
Tramps, 54
Transfer, of documents by endorsement, 59, 148
  of interest, 148
    in hull insurance, 285
    to neutral flag, 331
Transit floater policies, 140, 151
  unvalued, 152
Transit interruptions, 92
Transportation insurance, 124
Transshipments, 88
Trawlers, 300
Treaty of Paris, 187
Treaty reinsurance, 354
Trial trips under builder's-risk form, 304
Trim, of lumber vessels, 255
  of vessel, 85
  vessel out of, 244
Trustee for creditors, insurable interest of, 136
Tugboats, 295–298
  collision clause, 297
  Syndicate tug form, 296
Tuna vessels, 300
Turbine engines, 65, 72, 294
Turbogas engines, 69, 294
Turpentine insurance, 255
Types of vessels, 65
  effect of, on cargo insurance, 232–234
Typhoons as marine hazard, 36

U

Ultimate destination, doctrine of, 332
Unavoidable accident, 178
Under-deck loading of goods, 155
Underinsurance, 205
Underwriter, agents of, appraisal of damage by, 378–379
    certification to cause and extent of damage by, 201, 232, 378
    for underwriting, 118–119
  meaning of word, 13
  (*See also* Individual underwriters)
Underwriters, organizations of, 102, 231
  supervision of loading by, 244
Underwriting (marine), factors influencing, 98
  problems of, 86
Unearned premium reserve, 365, 433
Unethical practices (*see* Fraud)
United States government attitude toward marine insurance, 29–30

United States Salvage Association, 103
  purpose of, 281
Unneutral service, destruction of prizes, 330
Unrepaired damage on hulls, 388
Unseaworthiness, 178
  (*See also* Seaworthiness)
Usage (*see* Customs and usages)

V

Valuations, 92, 170, 235
  additional insurance, 172, 286
  agreed-value clauses, 92, 123
  basis of, 171
  in builder's risks, 303
  cannot be opened, 378
  commodity, 258
  contributory, 289, 411–412
  determination of, 170
  dual-valuation clauses, 266–268
  duty insurance, 322–323
  in freight policies, 322
  of hulls, 171, 173, 265, 385
  marine policies valued, 170
    justification of, 170, 205
  market-value clauses, 171
  necessity for reasonable, 266
  separate valuation clause, 266
Vandalism in strikes, riots clause, 191, 346
Vegetable fibers insurance, 245, 249
Vegetables insurance, 249
Venetians, 5
Vessel owner, responsibility of, 91
Vessels, auxiliary, 66, 262, 299
  in ballast, 84
  cargo, 54, 69
  class of, signification of, 98
  composite, 65, 67
  concrete, 65*n*
  floating of, 72
  Lake, 67, 71
  log of, 200, 419–420
  masters of, 104, 157, 264
  metal, 65, 67–68
  missing (*see* Missing vessels)
  overloading of, 8, 78, 244
  ownership of (*see* Ownership of vessels)
Vessels, periodical surveys of, 99
  righting of, after rolling, 78
  sailing (*see* Sailing vessels)
  seaworthiness of, 219
  self-trimming, 70–71
  single-deck, 88
  stability of, 72, 78
  stiff, 80, 256
  tender, 80
  tonnage of, 106
  total loss of, 399
  trim of, 85, 244, 255
  tuna, 300
  types of, 65
    effect of, on cargo insurance, 232–234
  unseaworthiness of, 178
Vice propre losses, 122, 176, 219
  carrier not liable for, 259
Voluntary sacrifice in general average, 410

W

Wager policies, 8, 20
Waiver of warranty of seaworthiness, 218
Waiver clause in sue-and-labor clause, 195
War bureaus, 345
War insurance, 325, 370
  Institute policy form, 452
  separate policy issued, 335, 452
  on shore, 325, 334
  war-exclusion clause, 189
  war and marine policies not coextensive, 337
  war perils, 184, 186, 336, 342
War losses, 400
War Shipping Administration, 339
Warehouse-to-warehouse cover, 124, 159–162, 241
  risk on duty, 323
Warehousemen, liabilities of, 423, 429
Warranties, breach of, 289
  disbursements, 285
  express, 222
  of good safety, 154
  in hull policies, 269, 285

Warranties, implied, 215
  lay-up, on Great Lakes, 291
  neutrality, 333
  of proper documents, 343
Washing overboard as distinguished from jettison, 182
Water-borne clauses in war, 334, 338
Water routes, 32
Waves, 32, 178
  control of, by breakwaters, 37
    by oil, 38
  effect of, on harbors, 38–39, 42
  force of, 37
  tidal, 39
Wear-and-tear damage, 176, 383
Weevil-damage insurance, 257
Welding, failures of, 68
Well-deck steamers, 233
Westerlies (winds), 36
Whaling ships, 300
"Whom it may concern" not all-inclusive, 147
Why vessels float, 72
Why vessels right after rolling, 78
Winds, 32–33, 35
  effect of, on harbors, 42
    on insurance, 176
    on trade routes, 36
  as marine hazard, 36, 90
Wing feeders, 105, 248
Winter-mooring clause on Great Lakes, 291
Winter storage of grain, 292
"Without benefit of salvage," meaning of, 172
Wood cargoes insurance, 255
Wooden ships, 65
  difficulties in construction of, 66–67
  insurance of, 292
Wool insurance, 253
World wars, effect of, on marine insurance, 27, 30, 325

Y

Yachts, 295, 300
  policy for, 301
  power boats, 300
  sailing-type, 300
  steam and diesel, 300
York-Antwerp Rules, 408, 412–413
  lettered, 415
  numbered, 415
  referred to in hull policies, 278
  text of 1950, 521

Warranties, implied, 213
Waste (or Great Lakes), 281
[illegible], 132
of cargo, [illegible] discharging, 213
Washing overboard as distinguished from jettison, 138
Water [illegible] in war, 234, 238
Water routes, 32
Waves, 42, 179
control of, by breakwaters, 37
[illegible], 28
[illegible], on harbors, 38, 39, 42
force of, 37
tidal, 29
Wear and tear damage, 176, 381
Weevil damage insurance, 217
Welding, failures of, 60
Welded steamers, 13
Westerlies (winds), 36
Whaling ships, 300
"When it may concern" not exclusive, 132
Why vessels float, 72
Why vessels right after rolling, 73
Winds, 32–36
effect of, on harbors, 41
on insurance, 175
on trade routes, 36
as nuclear forces, 36, 90
Wing [illegible], 246
Wintermooring clause on Great Lakes, 281
Winter seasons of grain, 269
"Without benefit of salvage," meaning of, 272
Wood carriers, insurance, 229
Wooden ships, 13
difficulties in construction of, 67
insurance of, 292
Wool insurance, 233
World wars, effect of, on marine insurance, 27, 29, 223

Y

Yachts, 295, 300
policy for, 301
power boats, 301
sailing, 301
steam and diesel, 300
York-Antwerp Rules, 398, 411, 413
[illegible], 413
numbered, 413
[illegible] to [illegible], 278
text of 1950, 521